D0927837

Genesis A
A New Edition

Genesis A
A New Edition

A. N. Doane

The University of Wisconsin Press

Published 1978

The University of Wisconsin Press
Box 1379
Madison, Wisconsin 53701

The University of Wisconsin Press, Ltd
70 Great Russell Street, London

First printing
Printed in the United States of America

For LC CIP information see the colophon

ISBN 0-299-07430-7

For

Henry, Peter and Molly

Contents

Preface   ix

Abbreviations   xiii

Introduction

    I   The Manuscript   3

   II   Language and Date   25

  III   The Poem   38

   IV   Bibliography   97

Genesis A: Text   109

Commentary   225

Glossary   329

    Proper Names   413

Preface

A new edition of *Genesis A* needs little apology.
This important work is the longest Old English poem except for *Beowulf*, and by many is considered one of the
most ancient. Yet it has never received the editorial
attention its significance justifies. It is one of the
few remaining Old English poems which has not appeared
in a separate edition with full apparatus. Nor has its
text been set within the relevant contexts of heroic
poetry and early medieval Genesis exegesis. The only
separate edition is the slight and unsatisfactory school-
text of Ferdinand Holthausen (1914), an edition having
only the sketchiest aids to the reader and a text marred
by innumerable arbitrary emendations and regularizations.
For nearly a half century, the standard text has been
G. P. Krapp's in Volume I of the Anglo-Saxon Poetic Records (1931). Unfortunately, the plan of that series
precluded any apparatus other than a description of
the manuscript (incompletely carried out by Krapp in
Volume I and continued in Volume II, *The Vercelli Book*)
and a recording of editorial variants. Some textual
difficulties are helpfully discussed, but Krapp often
seems to have had in mind editors rather than readers
when he compiled his very brief notes. The text is very
accurately transcribed, but presented in a format which
is frequently ambiguous. Krapp allowed emendations rather freely, but not to the same extent as Holthausen.
The magnitude of editing the whole corpus of Old English poetry necessarily meant Krapp could take only a
passing interest in *Genesis A*, so there is virtually
no comment on the content or background of the poem.
In spite of these remarks, I must record my enormous
debt to Krapp's exceedingly faithful and clear editorial work. One frequently disagrees with his decisions,
but he is almost never plainly wrong, and one seldom
needs to go beyond what he says concerning the older
editions. More recently, *Genesis A* was edited by David
M. Wells as an unpublished doctoral dissertation (University of North Carolina, 1969). Wells includes a
useful translation that clears up several syntactical
points. The very brief apparatus advances the state of
the text only slightly beyond Krapp's, and adds only
slightly to our knowledge of the background of the poem.

ix

I am glad to acknowledge my use of this edition, which
I have tried to use as sparingly as possible. Individual points of reference are noted in the Commentary.

In scale, this new edition is modeled on Wrenn's
edition of *Beowulf* (1953; rev. ed., 1958). Like Wrenn,
I have attempted to maintain a balance between literary
and historical matters on the one hand, and linguistic
comment on the other. Ideally, I aim at a similarly wide,
though much smaller audience. As I worked, I tried to
keep in mind as prime user the graduate student approach-
ing this poem seriously for the first time. I have
therefore included an abundance of relevant and practical material, even when it is already well-known. Naturally, I hope that some aspects of this edition will
prove of interest and utility to advanced students of
early English as well.

One of my main concerns has been to present *Genesis
A* not just as a poem, but as a successful biblical poem.
Therefore, the Introduction concentrates largely on its
"biblical" style, that is, the way its style emerges
from the interaction of the traditional poetic and the
Vulgate text. The line-by-line Commentary, for the same
reason, is in great measure devoted to the biblical
content of the poem, drawing attention to the parallels
and contrasts to traditional exegetical material on
Genesis. I am aware of many omissions and faults in
this department, but hope that this work will at least
draw attention to certain features and attract more
comment, particularly on the relation of *Genesis A* to
the liturgy, an area that can be greatly developed. To
facilitate the comparison of source and product, I have
given a parallel text of the Vulgate, keyed to the text
of the poem.

My editing principles have been more conservative
than those of previous editors of *Genesis A*. Since the
poem exists in a single late copy, as is the case with
nearly all Old English poems, an editor can only determine what the forms of the manuscript are, and attempt
to interpret what they meant to their copyist. Emendations ought to be allowed only where there is a reasonable
certainty that the copyist did not understand what he
wrote or that he miswrote. In such a situation, all
changes which deviate from a purely diplomatic transcript
are more or less subjective, and all substantive changes
tend to enter the text on a more or less ad hoc basis.
Therefore, even in cases where the text obviously seems
to be disturbed, I have made every attempt to construe
the text as it stands, perhaps erring too far in this
direction, as such conservative decisions eventually

themselves become "bold". For the most part I have
relegated possible and probable emendations to the
Commentary and only introduce into the text such
changes as are minimally necessary to achieve clarity
and continuity of meaning in confused passages. I
have regarded every emendation as, strictly speaking,
a logical absurdity, and practically speaking, a small
defeat, an abandonment of the text, necessary sometimes
for providing sense without restoring it. For with only
the one text to go by, we can have no sense of the
earlier stages of a suspected corruption except by
guesswork and imagination, and can therefore supply
only what we already know or can imagine, which can
never certainly be the same as the unknown that is
sought. "Obvious" scribal errors, those which any
informed reader may easily spot and correct, and which
we may reasonably presume the scribe himself, if he
had noted them, would have corrected without reference
to his exemplar, may fall outside this category, but
in practice, the line between scribal slips and substantive errors is so thin as to be in most cases invisible. For this reason, I tend to leave bad enough
alone, on the theory that obvious difficulties left
in the text will call attention to themselves, and
may even spur some annoyed scholar to find a better
solution more readily than bad readings emended out
of the way. In more than one place the resultant
readings are not offered as final or satisfactory,
least of all to myself (see e.g., 135, 1405).

On the positive side, the retention and construing of difficult passages previously emended has
improved the sense of the poem in not a few places
(e.g., 1664, 1693, 1912, 2642), and after what I hope
was due weight being given to the arguments for these
traditional emendations, I have in many cases disgarded them, while of course retaining many others.
As a general rule, I allow emendations only where
both meter and grammar are faulty, or where the syntactical confusion is inherently clashing, so that
one element must be changed to allow another to remain. Wherever some kind of sense can be attained,
I have refrained from emending, least of all merely
to make "improvements" in meter, sense or spelling
in difficult passages which can otherwise be construed.

During many years work on this edition I have
accumulated many debts. Notwithstanding my fore-
going remarks, the greatest debt, which I humbly
acknowledge, is to all the critics and editors who
have gone before me with this poem, and established

the form and meaning of its text. On a more personal
level, I am thankful to all those who, in person and
in correspondence, have shown interest in this edition.
Among those who have helped me more than I can appro-
priately thank are, first, Fr. L. K. Shook, of the
Pontifical Institute in Toronto, who directed my dissertation on *Genesis A* and who convinced me that a new
edition was both necessary and possible; my colleages
at Madison, especially Professors Frederic G. Cassidy,
John McGalliard, Richard N. Ringler, Donald W. Rowe
and Jerome Taylor, who read and commented on this edition at various stages of its development; my first
and best teacher of Old English, Professor Alain Renoir,
of the University of California, Berkeley and my friend,
Professor Ronald E. Buckalew of the Pennsylvania State
University who also kindly read and commented on parts
of the work. At the earliest stages of my work on
Old English biblical poetry, I was constantly helped
and heartened more than I can say by my friends and
former colleagues, Dr. Ian Jamieson and Mr. Harold
W. Orsman of Victoria University of Wellington and
Dr. Lee Ramsey. Improvements to the edition were
suggested by Dr. Derek Brewer of Emmanuel College,
Cambridge. My acknowledgements are due to D. G.
Vaisey, Keeper of Western Manuscripts, Bodleian Library, Oxford, for permission to use the Junius 11
manuscript on various occasions and to publish the
edition made from it, and to the staff of that splendid
establishment who were always so helpful, particularly
Dr. Albinia de la Mare. Finally, my special thanks to
Martha G. Blalock for her extensive assistance with the
Glossary and proofreading.
    A grant from the University of Wisconsin Graduate
School made it possible for me to consult the manuscript in the Summer of 1972, and part of the work
was completed while I was a Fellow of the American
Council of Learned Societies in 1973-74.

Madison, Wisconsin   A. N. Doane
April, 1978

Abbreviations

ASPR	G. P. Krapp and E. V. K. Dobbie, *The Anglo-Saxon Poetic Records*, 6 vols. (New York, 1931-53)
Bliss	Alan J. Bliss, *The Metre of Beowulf* (Oxford, 1958)
Braasch	Theodor Braasch, *Vollständiges Worterbuch zur sog. Caedmonschen Genesis*, Anglistische Forschungen 76 (Heidelberg, 1933)
Brodeur Studies	Stanley B. Greenfield, ed., *Studies in Old English Literature in Honor of Arthur Gilchrist Brodeur* (Eugene, Ore., 1963)
Brunner	Karl Brunner, *Altenglische Grammatik nach der angelsächsischen Grammatik von Eduard Sievers* (3rd. ed., Tübingen, 1965)
B-T, B-T Supp.	Joseph Bosworth and T. Northcote Toller, *An Anglo-Saxon Dictionary* (Oxford, 1898); Toller, *An Anglo-Saxon Dictionary, Supplement* (Oxford, 1921)
Campbell	Alistair Campbell, *Old English Grammar* (Oxford, 1959)
CCSL	Corpus Christianorum, Series Latina
Charles	R. H. Charles, ed., *The Apocrypha and Pseudepigrapha of the Old Testament in English*, 2 vols. (Oxford, 1913)
Clark-Hall	John R. Clark Hall, *A Concise Anglo-Saxon Dictionary*, with a supplement by Herbert D. Merritt (4th ed., Cambridge, 1969)
EEMF	Early English Manuscripts in Facsimile
EETS	Early English Text Society
F-T	Hjalmar Falk and Alf Torp, *Wortschatz der Germanischen Sprachenheit* (Göttingen, 1909)
Ginzberg	Louis Ginzberg, *The Legends of the Jews*, tr. Henrietta Szold and Boaz Cohen, 7 vols. (Philadelphia, 1909-38)
G-K, Sprch.	C. W. M. Grein, *Sprachschatz der angelsächsischen Dichter*, rev. F. Holthausen and J. J. Köhler (Heidelberg, 1912) [the original editions (Sprch.) formed Vols. 3 & 4 of Grein's *Bibliothek der angelsächsischen Poesie*]

Hept.	S. J. Crawford, ed., *The Old English Version of the Heptateuch, Aelfric's Treatise on the Old and New Testament and his Preface to Genesis,* EETS o.s. 160 (1922)
Holthausen, *Etym. Wörtb.*	Ferdinand Holthausen, *Altenglisches Etymologisches Wörterbuch* (Heidelberg, 1934)
JJJ.	E. A. Kock, *Jubilee Jaunts and Jottings* (see Bibliography, section I)
Lye-Manning	Edward Lye, *Dictionarium Saxonico et Gothicolatinum,* ed. Owen Manning (London, 1772)
LXX	The Septuagint (Greek) version of the Old Testament
Millward	Celia M. Millward, *Imperative Constructions in Old English* (The Hague, 1971)
NM	*Neuphilologische Mitteilungen*
OED	*Oxford English Dictionary*
PG.	Patrologia Graeca
PL.	Patrologia Latina
PPP.	E. A. Kock, *Plain Points and Puzzles* (see Bibliography, section I)
Q-W	Randolph Quirk and C. L. Wrenn, *An Old English Grammar* (New York, n.d.)
Sprch.	see G-K
V.L.	Vetus Latina (Old Latin versions of Genesis, see Bibliography, section G.a.)
Vulg.	Jerome's Vulgate translation of the Bible (see Bibliography, section G.a.)
ZfdA	*Zeitschrift für deutsches Altertum*

Abbreviations of Titles of Poems

AN	*Andreas*	GB	*Genesis B*
AZ	*Azarias*	GN	*Genesis A*
BW	*Beowulf*	GU	*Guthlac*
CH	*Christ*	HL	*Heliand*, ed. E. Sievers
CS	*Christ and Satan*		(see Bibliography, D)
DN	*Daniel*	HY	Caedmon's *Hymn*
DR	*Dream of the Rood*	JL	*Juliana*
EL	*Elene*	JU	*Judith*
EX	*Exodus*	PP	*Paris Psalter*
FA	*Fates of the Apostles*	PX	*Phoenix*

Introduction

I. The Manuscript[1]

A. General Description

   Genesis A is preserved in a unique copy, Junius
11 in the Bodleian Library, Oxford. It is the most
sumptuous and interesting of the four codices preserving large amounts of Old English poetry.[2] It is a
great illustrated book, prepared with special care
and expense. Its dimensions are 324mm. high by about
180mm. wide. It consists of 116 parchment leaves, pa-
ginated i-ii, 1-229 (+1).[3] PP. 1-142 contain *Genesis*,
the interpolated *Genesis B* occupying PP. 13-40[4]; PP.
143-229 contain the poems known as *Exodus*, *Daniel* and
Christ and Satan. A single hand has written the texts
of *Genesis*, *Exodus* and *Daniel*, following a uniform
lay-out, most pages being ruled for 26 lines, a few
for 25, with spaces left blank for illustrations and
large capitals throughout, although the zoomorphic
capitals and the illustrations have not been completed beyond P. 96. *Christ and Satan* is written by
three other scribes according to a different lay-out
and may not have been part of the original plan for

[1]   The manuscript has been described frequently. Fundamental is the introduction of Sir Israel Gollancz,
*The Cædmon Manuscript of Anglo-Saxon Biblical Poetry,
Junius XI in the Bodleian Library* (Oxford, 1927),
henceforth referred to as *Cædmon MS* (the correct designation of the MS is "Junius 11"). Also important
are: the introduction of George Philip Krapp, *The Junius Manuscript*, Anglo-Saxon Poetic Records I (New York,
1931); B. J. Timmer, ed., *The Later Genesis* (Oxford,
1948, rev. ed., 1954), 1-3, 10-15; F. H. Stoddard,
"The Caedmon Poems in MS. Junius XI," *Anglia* 10 (1888),
157-67.
[2]   The other poetical codices are: The Vercelli Book,
The Exeter Book, The "Nowell Codex" ("Beowulf Manuscript," Cotton Vitellius A.xv.), edited and described in The Anglo-Saxon poetic Records, Volumes II,
III, IV, respectively. In this edition all citations
of Old English poetry, except *Genesis A*, refer to
the ASPR editions, unless otherwise noted.
[3]   Throughout this edition pages of Junius 11 will be
indicated by capital P. and page number.
[4]   Lines 235-851 of *Genesis*, for the text see ASPR I.
A brief description and further references are given
in the Commentary, 234-852.

the book.[5] At the end of *Christ and Satan* is written
"FINIT LIBER II: AMEN" in majuscule capitals; it may
be presumed that whoever wrote this was thinking that
the part of the book by the first scribe formed "Liber I" but there is no such inscription at the end of
Daniel. Within the manuscript there are no titles,
the only division between the poems being the same as
for sections, a large capital and a blank line or two,
except that new poems always begin at the top of the
page. The separation into distinct poems is made purely
on circumstantial evidence, difference of subject matter, differences of style and language, etc.[6] At the
top of P. 1, the first page of *Genesis A*, a sixteenth
century hand has written "Genesis in lingua Saxania,"
while on the facing frontispiece a medieval cataloger
has noted "Genesis in anglico."[7] The first three poems
are divided into sections and numbered by the scribe,
starting with **vii** and running sporadically up to **lv**.
Genesis occupies sections [i] through **xli**.

On the whole, the manuscript is in excellent condition. The parchment and ink in many places give
an impression of being brand-new, while in no place
is material damaged beyond recovery due simply to
the physical condition of the page. However, a
number of pages have been cut out or otherwise lost,
leaving many gaps in the text which arose with this
manuscript.

B. The Gatherings

The manuscript consists of seventeen gatherings,
the normal gathering being in eight, i.e., eight folios, or sixteen pages. PP. 1-142, *Genesis*, coincide with the first eleven gatherings, four complete,
the rest being imperfect, one (the second) being very
fragmentary. No folios have been lost since Junius
numbered the pages (ca. 1651). The collation of the

[5] See Merrel D. Clubb, ed., *Christ and Satan, an
Old English Poem* (New Haven, 1925), ix-xvii.
[6] Earlier editors printed the contents of the manuscript continuously as if it contained one text.
The present division and titles stem from Grein's
edition in the *Bibliothek der angelsächsischen Poesie*
(1857).
[7] On the history of the manuscript in the middle ages
and early modern times, see Timmer, *Later Genesis*, 5-8.

Genesis part of the manuscript is as follows:[8]

> I five, a bifolium followed by three singletons;
> II two, two singletons separately rebound; III[8],
> 6 and 7 lost after P. 22; IV-VI[8]; VII[8] + 1 leaf
> after 7 (PP. 87-88); VIII[8], 3 lost after P. 94;
> IX[8], 3 lost after P. 108, 5 lost after P. 110;
> X[8], 1 lost after P. 116, 5 lost after P. 122;
> XI[8], 4 lost after P. 134.

For the most part, missing pages cause little difficulty as to the scope and nature of the text-losses
since single pages have been cut out cleanly without
disturbing the gatherings, and the Vulgate provides
at least a clue to their probable content (see the
textual notes to 2044, 2381, 2418, 2512, 2599, 2806).
The second gathering is more difficult and must be
discussed in some detail.
Between the first and second gatherings (i.e., between PP. 8-9, lines 167-68 of *Genesis A*) a gap and
a general weakening of the binding suggest that an
entire gathering was removed at some time before the
manuscript was rebound in the fifteenth century. The
rebinding did not effectually repair this damage.
The supposition that a whole gathering is missing here
is reinforced by the presence at this place of two
disjunct leaves (numbered PP. 9-12) which are best
explained as the remains of such a lost gathering.
The two leaves have been joined together by a parchment slip (about 1.5" by 12") containing fragments
of Latin prayers written in a hand of the late thir-
teenth or early fourteenth centuries.[9] Since the
writing runs under the bound leaves, it is clear
that it is earlier than the incorporation of the
slip into the binding. The slip, with the two
loose leaves, is loosely sewn to gathering III,
but does not form an integral part of it. The
most likely sequence is that two leaves from an
excised gathering were preserved loose in the
book for a long time (as is suggested by the uniformly diminished size of these two leaves) and

---

[8]   The collation follows N. R. Ker's format (*A Catalogue of Manuscripts containing Anglo-Saxon* [Oxford,
1957], 407-08). Ker mistakenly collates Gathering
VIII "VIII[6] + 1 leaf after 4 (pp. 99-100)."
[9]   This dating is according to Miss de la Mare of the
Bodleian staff (May, 1974). The writing on the slip
is usually identified as of the fifteenth century.

were refastened to the rest of the book as an
emergency measure, using the parchment slip, before the general rebinding of the fifteenth century.
In the rebinding, gatherings II (the two loose
leaves) and III, still loosely joined together,
were individually resewn into the new binding.[10]
Diagram (1) shows the present disposition of the
second gathering:

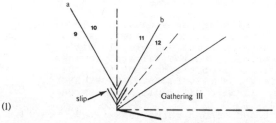

(1)

The projecting tags of folios *a* and *b* nest together
as shown. Presumably on the basis of this configuration, Stoddard, Gollancz and Timmer reconstruct
the gathering so that *a* and *b* are folios 4 and 6 of
the complete original gathering.[11] But at the top
of the spine the tag of *b* is folded under *a* and rests
against P. 11, making it clear that the present configuration is not necessarily the same as the original one. From the shapes of the tags of the two
folios it is also clear that they never formed one
sheet. Because of the obvious gaps in the text
between PP. 8 and 9 on the one hand and between PP.
12 and 13 on the other, it is certain that neither
of the extant folios could have formed the outer
leaves of the gathering. The two extant leaves are
scored on opposite sides, showing that *a* is from the
left side of the gathering (considering it opened
at the middle sheet) and *b* from the right, that is,
they are in the right order as presently bound.
Presuming that this was once a normal gathering in
eight, and scored normally, all in one operation,
the relative heaviness of the scoring on the two

[10] Timmer, *Later Genesis*, 3, takes the handwriting on
the slip to be of the fifteenth century, but if it is
a century or more earlier, then the temporary repair
could have taken place rather earlier than the general
rebinding.
[11] Stoddard, *Anglia* 10, 159-60; Gollancz, *Cædmon MS*,
cix; Timmer, *Later Genesis*, 13-14.

sheets is important. The scoring of *a* is finer
and probably closer to the top sheet than that
of *b*. Hence, however *a* is placed, *b* must be
further inside the gathering. Three reconstructions
are possible if *a* is in fact closer to the top sheet
than *b* :

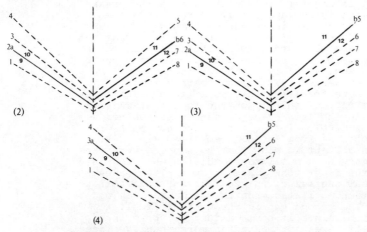

(2)   (3)

(4)

If we place *a* as the second folio, then *b* may be
either fifth or sixth. If we place *a* as third, then
b must be fifth. But the state of the scoring suggests that neither leaf is as far into the gathering
as figures (3) and (4) show. Therefore, purely
on the physical evidence, (2) is the most likely
reconstruction, but (2) posits a gap of three leaves
after P. 10, which is difficult to reconcile with
the textual evidence. Purely on the basis of the
amount of text most likely missing, (4) is the
best reconstruction. [12]

[12] The reconstruction making *a* the fourth and *b* the
sixth folios is only possible if *a* was rescored apart
from the general scoring of the sheets of the gathering. Timmer is altogether too positive about this being the arrangement of the gathering, which he offers
as "proof" of his hypothesis that *Genesis B* was only
interpolated into *Genesis A* at the time the Junius 11
manuscript itself was prepared. He says the gathering
was written on as normally, but then the scribe was
directed to include the text of *Genesis B*. In order
to harmonize it with *Genesis A*, therefore, he had to

C. Missing Material

    Whatever arrangement is adopted as best for
the second folio, it seems certain that there are
three gaps in it, affecting the text of *Genesis A*
visibly in two places (after lines 168 and 234) and
invisibly in one (after line 205, where the break
in the sense is not apparent). A reconstruction
of the material missing because of these gaps is
complicated in the first place by the fact that some
illustrations were probably on these leaves, though
it is impossible to say how many or how much space
they occupied, secondly by the fact that the *Genesis A* poet was conflating and rearranging his
material more freely at this point than was his usual practice, and thirdly by the fact that *Genesis
B* begins in the third gap, we cannot say where, so
that it is doubly difficult to judge how much or
what is missing from either poem after line 234.
It should be kept in mind that both poems were perhaps already in a mutilated condition when the interpolation first took place in an earlier manuscript (but see below, pp. 20-22), and that both were
only further mutilated when the gathering was disturbed. The second gap is the most difficult to
account for, since it could amount to up to three
leaves (six pages, or space for more than 200 lines
of verse if no illustration-space was on the lost
pages) or two or one (140, 70 lines of verse respectively). There is no gap in the sense after line
205; if there indeed had been several pages of verse
after 205 originally, then the poet was rearranging

---

cut leaves out of the second gathering which conse-
quently fell apart (see *Later Genesis*, 14-15). This
assumes three things, none of them necessary in themselves or confirmed by the evidence of the MS: (1)
that the text of Junius 11 was copied out after the
book had been bound, rather than when it was still in
loose gatherings, (2) that Gathering II was disturbed
at the time of writing, not later, and therefore, (3)
the two leaves that survive of Gathering II were preserved loose in the book for 400 years, until the rebinding in the fifteenth century. On *a priori* grounds
(1) and (3) are most improbable. The only fact, and
that not easy to interpret, is that the important
loss of the Fall of Man from *Genesis A*, the beginning
of *Genesis B* and the fragmentary Gathering II all coincide. That fact does not make all three features
necessarily of simultaneous occurrence.

and expanding his material very freely at this point
and the contents cannot be recovered with any assur-
ance. Otherwise there must have been an unusual
amount of illustration. One indication of the amount
of material actually missing is the sectioning. At
line 135 (P. 8, first gathering) section [iii] (un-
numbered in the MS) begins, and at line 246 (P. 14,
third gathering) section vi, so that large parts of
three sections are lost. The sections in the earlier
parts of *Genesis A* average about 70 lines of verse,
and in *Genesis B* over 100, so that even by a conservative estimate at least 100 lines have been lost
from the second gathering as a whole.[13] This does
not seem a large enough number of lines to accommodate all the *possible* missing material that may be
postulated.
    The following list attempts to set out the sim-
plest possible disposition of material missing
from the second gathering:

     First Lacuna, after line 168 (one or two leaves):
        (a) Genesis 1.11-1.25, The Third through
           Sixth Days up to the creation of Adam
        (b) Genesis 2.7, Creation of Adam
        (c) ?Genesis 2.8-9, 2.15, Establishment of
           Paradise
        (d) ?Genesis 2.16-17 Prohibition against the
           Fruit of the Tree of Knowledge

     Second Lacuna, after line 205 (one, two or
       three leaves):
        (e) ?Genesis 2.19-20, Naming of the Animals
           [perhaps omitted altogether by the poet
           at line 172, where 2.18 and 2.21 are
           run together]
        (f) ? Genesis 2.23-25, Marriage of Adam and
           Eve
        (c) ?Genesis 2.16-17
        (g) ?Genesis 1.29-30, God giving Authority
           to Adam over all Living Things
        (h) Genesis 2.2-3, The Sabbath

---

[13] From the beginning of section iii (line 135) to
the beginning of section vi (*Genesis B*, line 245)
there are 111 lines. Counting sections iii and iv
as 70 lines and v as 100 we get 240, leaving 130
missing lines.

Third Lacuna, after line 234 (one or two leaves):
  ?*Genesis B* begins with ?repetition of Creation of Adam and Eve, ?Description of Paradise
(d²) Beginning of Prohibition [text opens
    at 235 with the end of the Prohibition]

Depending on the relative sizes posited for the
first and second gaps, the narrative units (c) and
(d) could go in either. (c) would make good sense
after the creation of Adam and Eve. (d) could go
after their creation except for the difficulty that
it was traditionally held that since Eve was created
after God gave the Prohibition to Adam, she had not
heard it, except indirectly, thus establishing the
important point that her obedience was due to Adam.
It would be uncharacteristic of the *Genesis A* poet
to break such an important orthodox pattern, although,
as its opening shows, *Genesis B*, equally characteristically, does break it.
    The important point that must be noted is that
the only material absolutely and certainly lost from
Genesis A in the third gap is Genesis 3.1-7, the
Fall of Man, the only verses of Genesis which *Genesis
B* is concerned with. It is a very reasonable presumption that it is the previous loss of this material
from *Genesis A* which was the occasion for the interpolation of *Genesis B* in the first place (see below
p. 22).
    In gathering seven both sides of an extra folio
(PP. 87 and 88) contain full-page illustrations by
the second artist (see below, p. 17). The tag of this
added leaf projects between PP. 74 and 75.
    Five single leaves have been cut out from ga-
therings eight through eleven. The loss of text is
easily ascertained by the correspondences with the
biblical text. After P. 94 one leaf has been cut
out, but no material appears to be missing and we
must assume that the leaf contained illustrations,
or blanks for them. The leaves cut out after PP.
116, 122, 134 contained very little text, presumably
the excisions being for the sake of the fair parchment. The excised leaf after P. 108 contained a
complete episode, 18.1-11, Abraham entertaining the
three angels; so did the leaf after P. 110, corresponding to Genesis 18.22-33, Abraham pleading for
the lives of the just in Sodom. I am inclined to
believe that both these leaves were cut out by some
early scholar as examples of Anglo-Saxon, especially
as the later passage would have had the Old English

for 50, 45, 30, 20 and 10. The excisions mentioned
in this paragraph have left knife-marks which correspond perfectly to the projecting tags of the excised
leaves, suggesting that they were cut out after the
fifteenth-century rebinding (otherwise these correspondences would have been disturbed) and before Junius numbered the pages about 1651.

D. The Text and Writing

     The evidence of the manuscript indicates that
the scribe was following an exemplar which contained
the same texts in the same order, including *Genesis B*,
but perhaps not *Christ and Satan*. Blank spaces are
left for illustration and large capitals after P. 96,
suggesting that a plan was before the scribe as he
wrote. The exemplar may have been illustrated, or
the scribe may have been extrapolating illustrations
from some other book into his unillustrated exemplar
(see below pp. 20-24). In the earlier pages there are
signs that the scribe and illustrator are leapfrogging
each other; at least that seems the only possible explanation for the mistaken placing of the capital B
on P. 18 and the consequent missectioning forced on
the scribe.[14] The artist who drew the series of great
zoomorphic capitals on PP. 1-73 may have preceded the
scribe, because the beginning lines of each section
of the text conform to the outlines of the capitals,
suggesting that the scribe wrote around capitals that

[14] The last word of section **vi** is *gelæston* (*Genesis B*
321b), and after it the scribe made his usual mark
for ending a section, ∴ ; evidently, the illustrator had already made the zoomorphic B (of *Brand*, 325a)
at the top of the next page (P. 18), forcing the
scribe to continue the text from 321 to 325 and to
begin section **vii** at Brand, although that entails beginning a section in mid-sentence. The bottom of P.
17 is occupied by an illustration, coming right up
to the last unwritten feint. The states of P. 17 and
P. 18 suggest that illustrator and scribe were working
in turn, that the capital *B* was drawn before the text
on P. 18 was written and that the picture of P. 17 was
drawn in the space after the text was written, but
since P. 17 and P. 18 are opposite sides of the same
leaf, it is difficult to see exactly what process was
going on (see Gollancz, *Cædmon MS*, xxx-xxxi).

were already there.[15]   If the capitals were written
first, a similarly laid out and capitalized exemplar
is clearly implied. But against this is the fact that
the plain capitals of the pages after P. 73, presumably drawn by the scribe himself as he wrote the text,
also have conforming lineation. This could imply
either that the scribe copied throughout an element
of design that was before him, and when he found out
that the initialler was no longer working on this
book, went back and filled in the capitals himself,
or that some details of the design were being introduced by the scribe himself. It should be noted that
the spaces for capitals which are left blank in
Exodus (P. 146 [H], P. 148 [H], P. 149 [O]) also have
conforming lineation. The most conclusive evidence
for a preexisting exemplar already containing the
first three Junius poems (even if it was not illustrated[16]) is the section numbering. Although the
numbering is not completely or consecutively carried
out, the earlier sections being very sporadically
numbered, yet when the numbers begin to appear regularly in the later sections they are correctly
numbered, counting from the beginning of the book.
This would have only come about if a correctly numbered ancestor containing *Genesis* (including *Genesis B*),
Exodus and *Daniel* stood behind Junius 11.[17]
     "Liber I", containing *Genesis*, *Exodus* and *Daniel*,
is written in a single insular minuscule hand typical

[15] This is the interpretation that Gollancz, *Cædmon
MS*, xix, puts on the evidence.
[16] The first illustrator depicts the ark as a dragon
ship, the second as a box. The latter is similar to
the depiction of the ark in the "Cotton" Genesis
tradition, and suggests that the second illustrator
followed a different model than the first; perhaps when
the second illustrator began, the exemplar of Junius
11 was no longer available. The whole question is
complex: see below, pp. 20-24. For the ark-tradition
see George Henderson, "Late Antique Influences in some
English Medieval Illustrations of Genesis," *Journal of
the Warburg and Courtauld Institutes* 25 (1962), 172-98,
esp. 186-87.
[17] This conclusion conflicts with those of Timmer, Raw,
and Ohlgren (see below); the only alternative to seeing
a complete exemplar behind Junius 11 is to assume that
the scribe more than once counted back over the unnum-
bered sections without at the time writing the section
numbers in.

in its forms of the late tenth century. The handwriting is distinctive, clear and regular, but not particularly elegant. The distinctive early forms are the three-stroke *a*, characteristic of the late tenth century,[18] the short ascenders and descenders in general,[19] the open loop of the *p*;[20] the early form *e* with a large top loop becomes less frequent as the scribe progresses and is doubtless from his exemplar. There are a few carolingian minuscule hooked *a*'s in *Genesis B*, probably going back ultimately to a continental copy of the Old Saxon version of that poem. On the other hand, the straight-sided undotted *y* is of the eleventh-century type. The handwriting of the three scribes of Liber II has a distinctively later, eleventh-century, cast. On the basis of the "early" forms Keller dated the hand of the scribe of "Liber I" as "the last decades of the tenth century,"[21] Ker as late tenth or early eleventh.[22] As will be noted below, these conclusions do not jibe with the dates given for the illustrations by Wormald (second quarter of the eleventh century). It is perhaps best to think of the "Liber I" scribe's hand as old-fashioned and to prefer the later date. The subject of the date of the manuscript will be returned to in the next section.

    Sprinkled through the text with no great frequency or regularity are a number of small majuscule capitals of eclectic type. They are used regularly for the first word or words of a new section. They are also used irregularly to mark what appear to be paragraphs, and most often correspond to what may be marked as a new sentence. A few times they are used in the middle of sentences, frequently in *Ac* or *Ic* (or other pronoun). I suspect that the small capitals that appear in this manuscript are just the irregular remnants of a much more systematic use of small capitals in an ancestor. Occasionally it is not clear that a capital is intended, since many of them are just the small letters written bigger.[23]

[18] Wolfgang Keller, *Angelsächsische Palaeographie*, Teil I, *Palaestra* 43, i (Berlin, 1906), 39.
[19] *Ibid.*, citing Thompson, Pal. Soc. Fac. II, 14.
[20] Ker, *Catalogue*, 408.
[21] *Op. cit.*, 39.
[22] *Catalogue*, 408.
[23] In this edition, an attempt has been made to show large and small capitals, where these are clearly intended by the scribe, even though they seldom agree with modern coventions of paragraphing or punctuation.

On the whole, the text is written carefully,
the scribe making frequent erasures and corrections
from his exemplar as he proceeds. Many of his obvious miswritings have been overlooked, however. In
addition, there are a number of corrections by other
hands, consisting of added letters, letters deleted
by subscribed dots or by alteration of one letter to
another. The majority of the corrections are by one
hand. There are many other occasional corrections
added by diverse hands. The majority of the non-
scribal corrections are of obvious slips that anyone
could have seen and corrected without reference to
an exemplar. One correction (*his* added in 781, apparently an Old Saxon usage) implies reference to an
exemplar. Much of the main corrector's work is not
merely the alteration of obvious errors, but part of
a deliberate plan of orthographical reform.[24] Traditional poetic anglianisms, e.g., *alwalda*, 246, *tene*,
248, *befælled*, 371, are corrected to regular 1W-S *eal-
walda, tyne, befylled*. Earlier forms are corrected
to later, e.g., *getrimede*, 248, *him*, 250, *niotan*, 401,
become *getrymede, heom, neotan*. In *Genesis B*, where
nearly all these normalizations occur, Old Saxon *her-
ran*, 263, *wende, hebban*, 259, *heofne*, 339, 350, *men*,
451, are altered to Old English *hearran, awende, a-
hebban, heofnon, menn*. These purely orthographical
corrections are mainly limited to the earlier parts
of *Genesis B* and the work of the erratic first scribe
of *Christ and Satan* (PP. 213-15); while it is not
absolutely certain that both sets of corrections are
by the same hand, the probability is that they are,
and that it was the unusual orthography of these
two "intruders" into the series *Genesis, Exodus,
Daniel* which attracted the attention of the "main"
corrector in the first place.[25]

As was customary in Old English manuscripts of
poetry, the scribe wrote the verse out in full manuscript lines, to the edge of the right margin, like
prose. However, he indicated the verse and half-ver-
ses by a system of points, raised above the line. In
Junius 11 the verse-pointing is more complete and more
consistently and correctly carried out than in any
other poetical manuscript. The scribe was extremely
careful to preserve these points from his exemplar,

[24] These corrections may represent preparations for
Junius 11 to be recopied, rather than corrections of
what the Junius scribes wrote.
[25] See Krapp, *Junius Manuscript*, xiii.

and his lozenge-shaped points can usually be distinguished from those added by other hands. Unsure,
irregular and mistaken pointing occurs frequently
only at those places which on other grounds may be
considered corrupt (and frequently provides evidence
that the corruption is of long standing and puzzling
to the scribe). In *Genesis B* the pointing is not
so accurate as in *A*, due probably to the unusually
long lines prevalent in the Old Saxon poem. There,
many points have been added by scribe or correctors
to break the lines into shorter units, suggesting
that the scribe understood the points as clause mar-
kers rather than as strictly metrical regulators.

Because the metrical points occur at the end
of nearly every half-line, they coincide with places
where sentence punctuation is called for, but they
appear to have the function of grammatical punctuation only incidentally. The scribe regularly uses
only the point, but at the end of sections he often
puts a point and line ($\cdot \smile$) or three points ($\therefore$),
though many sections end only with the usual point
or no mark at all. Other hands have added various
points, semi-colons, tags, hyphens and dashes in
haphazard fashion, generally in ways that make sense
as punctuation.

The scribe uses only a few standard abbreviations, always consistent and clear. The note 7 for
and (*ond*) is used, with a couple of exceptions, and
it appears frequently for the prefix *and-* (*7swarode*).
þ is regular for *pæt*. Final nasals are occasionally
indicated by a superscribed line (i.e., -*a* = -*um*),
this sign usually only occurring at or near the end
of manuscript lines to achieve justification. Medial
nasals are very infrequently so indicated (e.g.,
frõne = *fromne*, 1961). Unusual is *ʒ-* for *ge-*. The
strictly Latin abbreviation p is used to write *percoba* (Noe's wife, 1548 and probably from a gloss).
Numbers are as frequently written as Roman numerals
as they are spelled out.

Accents have been added over about 3,100 words
in the whole manuscript.[26] Many are faint, some have

<hr>

[26] The frequencies in the following paragraph, and
most of the examples, have been taken from G. C.
Thornley, "The Accents and Points of MS. Junius 11,"
Transactions of the Philological Society (1954), 178-205.
See also D. G. Scragg, "Accent Marks in the Old English
Vercelli Book," *Neuphilologische Mitteilungen* 72 (1971),
699-710.

been erased, others have doubtless faded without
trace. A good many visible in the manuscript do not
show up in the facsimile. A few, no doubt, are by
the scribe, but the majority seem added by other
hands and attribution to one source or the other
seems on the whole impossible. The accents are of
a variety of forms, length, thickness and darkness.
No particular system appears to govern their placement. Most are on grammatically long vowels, but
about 750 are on short vowels. For instance, *ac* is
accented 82 time and *is* 22. Some probably served
to mark stress, as aids to a lector, but not many
can be explained this way. Thornley thinks they
may be related to the notation of Gregorian chant.[27]
The accents are relatively frequent and regular over
proper names, corresponding in most cases to the
Septuagint stressing of the names, e.g., *cananéa*
(1772, etc. = χαναναιοι), *égypta* (1845, etc. =
αἴγυρτος), *ismaél* (2299 = ισμαήλ), etc.[28] These learned accentuations do not correspond to the probable
stress of the words as they would have been understood in the classical period of Old English versification, where stress of foreign names was on the
first syllable, regarded as long.[29] Sometimes the
normal Old English stress has influenced the placing
of accents (*áda* 1077 = αδά), or both the normal and
"learned" stresses are marked (*ádám(e)*, 882, *ágár*, 2800).
Some double accents occur, perhaps to indicate dieresis, *ááron*, 1710, etc., *isáác*, 2329, etc.[30]

E. The Illustrations

        In a textual edition a full scale discussion
of the illustrations would be out of place, but since
they have an important bearing on the questions of

[27] *Art. cit.*, 183-203.
[28] *Ibid.*, 179-81. Thornley gives a complete list of
all the accented names and their corresponding Greek
stress.
[29] See Commentary, 1962, and Campbell §§549 ff.
[30] Thornley gives further examples, 180-81. Because
of their diverse shapes, darkness, grades of legibility,
various origins, etc., and also because of their uncertain purpose, it has seemed more misleading than
helpful to include them in the edited text. Krapp
gives a list of those visible in the facsimile in
The Vercelli Book, ASPR II (New York, 1932), liii-lxxx.

the date, provenance and compilation of the manuscript, they must be discussed in some detail.[31]
    Illustrations were planned for the whole of
"Liber I," but in fact only 48 were ever completed,
running through P. 96, after which the spaces are
still blank. Three illustrators worked on the book,
the first doing the pictures through P. 68, the second those from P. 73 to P. 84 and PP. 87-88 (an added
folio containing only the two full-page illustrations).
The third illustrator is responsible for a single
unfinished picture, quite different in style and scale
from the others, on P. 96. These pictures illustrate
the texts of *Genesis A* and *B*. Whether the illustrators were following an illustrated Old English exemplar, or some other, and to what extent they were being original, is a difficult question, which will be
taken up below. Some of the earlier pictures have
titles or descriptions in Old English and Latin by a
hand different than the scribe's or illustrator's.[32]
The work of the first two illustrators is in the so-
called "Winchester style," a designation which can
apply to work not only from Winchester, but to nearly
any of the late tenth, or early eleventh centuries
done in reformed Benedictine houses of the south and
fenlands.[33] Although improving slightly as it goes
along, the work of the first illustrator is generally
rather crude and unsure by the best standards of
"Winchester" work. The second illustrator is a much
better draftsman and executor. The great decorated
zoomorphic capitals, with which the sections of the
poems begin, probably were done by the first illustrator, although one cannot be sure of this. They
continue through P. 73, and isolated ones occur on P.

---

[31] For the illustrations themselves, the facsimile must
be consulted as well as Gollancz' valuable description
and interpretation of them (*Caedmon MS,* xxxiii-xlvii).
Rather poor quality, out-of-context reproductions of the
Junius illustrations are included as an appendix
to Charles W. Kennedy, *The Caedmon Poems, translated
into English Prose* (London, 1916).
[32] For the titles to the pictures see Krapp, *Junius
Manuscript,* xvi-xvii. A. J. Bliss, "Some Unnoticed
Lines of Old English Verse," *Notes and Queries* 216 (1971),
404,   points out that five of the inscriptions make
good OE. verse (see note 49, below).
[33] Francis Wormald, "Decorated Initials in English MSS.
from A.D. 900 to 1100," *Archaeologia* 91 (1945), 133.

79 and P. 143 (the beginning of *Exodus*).[34] The re-
mainder of the great capitals are plain, and presumably by the scribe himself. It should be pointed
out that whoever did them the zoomorphic capitals
are in a different style than the illustrations, as
if the artist were following a pattern book, or carefully copying capitals he found already in his exemplar, while treating the pictures more freely.[35]
In the capitals there are, for example, different conventions for eyes and wings than in the illustrations
and the designs are generally firmer and more serene.
The acanthus of the capitals is firm, solid and rounded, while in the pictures it is nervous and pointed.
      Wormald, on the basis of a wide comparison of
"Winchester" drawing, and on the alleged Scandinavian
tendencies in the style of the Junius drawings (inter-
lace and grotesques), dates the work of the first two
illustrators in the second quarter of the eleventh
century.[36] It will be noted that this date does not
agree with the date arrived at by paleographical evidence, which places the book at the end of the tenth
century (see above, p. 13). Probably the best explanation of the discrepancy is that the handwriting is
old-fashioned or provincial, since it would tend to
preserve an archaic style more easily than the drawings. On this basis, Wormald's date of 1025 for the
pictures is to be preferred as the date for the writing as well.
      M. R. James noticed an entry in a catalogue of
Prior Eastry: an "English book" formerly belonging
to Christ Church, Canterbury, listed as "Genesis

---

[34] The circumstantial evidence points to the first il-
ustrator who stops on P. 68. The decorated capitals of
P. 71, P. 73, and especially, P. 79, are rather
plainer and weaker than the others and may be by another hand. The capital Ð on P. 75 is an odd one,
plain, but with a little scroll on the cross-stroke,
as if the resolve to give up decorated capitals were
only slowly fading.
[35] Compare the very similar isolated zoomorphic capital on f. 49 r. of the Vercelli Book (facsimile ed.
Massimiliano Foerster [Max Förster], *Il Codice Ver-
cellese* . . . [Rome, 1913]) and those in the *Heliand*
MS (Cotton Caligula A.vii), R. Priebsch, *The Heliand
Manuscript, Cotton Caligula A. vii in the British
Museum: A Study* (Oxford, 1925), plts. iv and v.
[36] Francis Wormald, *English Drawings of the Tenth
and Eleventh Centuries* (London, 1952), 41.

Anglice depicta."[37] But as Gollancz pointed out, and
the editors of Cotton Claudius B. iv believe,[38] it
just as well or better applies to the great prose
Hexateuch ("The Ælfric Hexateuch") which in fact be-
longed to St. Augustine's, Canterbury. As was mentioned already, P. ii bears a fourteenth-century cat-
aloguer's title "Genesis in anglico," recalling the
Prior Eastry entry, but the Claudius incipit
is even closer.[39] Although there is little conclusive
evidence, Wormald and Ker agree in accepting the
Christ Church provenance as fairly likely.[40]

On P. 2 there is a small medallion portrait by
the first illustrator, labeled *Aelfwine*. Gollancz
tried to identify this "Aelfwine" with the Aelfwine
who became abbot of Newminster, Winchester in 1035.[41]
Apart from its being a common name, the objection to
the identification has been recently brought up that
the figure in the portrait has neither tonsure nor
ecclesiastical dress, and hence cannot be Abbot Aelfwine.[42] One might add that his dates seem too late for
him to be patron to an early eleventh-century manuscript.[43]

[37] *The Ancient Libraries of Canterbury and Dover*
(Cambridge, 1903), 509.
[38] C. R. Dodwell and Peter Clemoes, *The Old English
Illustrated Hexateuch, B.M. Cotton Claudius B.iv*,
EEMF 18 (Copenhagen, London and Baltimore, 1974),
15; see Gollancz, *Caedmon Manuscript*, xxxvii.
[39] The incipit of Claudius B.iv is "Genesis anglic[e],"
whereas Junius 11 has "Genesis in anglico" written
on the frontispiece.
[40] Wormald, *English Drawings*, 76; Ker, *Catalogue*, xliii.
[41] *Caedmon MS*, xxxvii.
[42] Barbara Raw, "The Probable Derivation of most of
the Illustrations in Junius 11 from an Illustrated Old
Saxon *Genesis*," *Anglo-Saxon England* 5, ed. Peter Clemoes (Cambridge, 1976), 135.
[43] There are several incidental pictures in the manuscript, a lion on P. 31, a binding design on P. 225,
a small building, with the ink washed off on P. 128
(noticed by D. M. Wells, "A Critical Edition of. . .
Genesis A . . .", upub. doc. diss., University of North
Carolina, 1969, p. xii); several new drypoints, considered by their discoverer to be preliminary sketches
by the illustrators, have turned up: see T. H. Ohlgren,
"Five New Drawings in the *MS Junius 11*: Their Iconography and Thematic Significance," *Speculum*, 47 (1972),
227-233.

        Recent work on the illustrations has opened se-
veral new questions on the compilation of the manuscript, while emphasizing the complexity of the problems involved. Gollancz naturally assumed that scribe
and illustrators were cooperating in an integrated
effort.   Thus, for example, he interpreted the
words *healf trymt*, "half page" on P. 98 and P. 100 as
instructions that a half-page space be left for illustration, and indeed these pages are followed by
half-blank pages. He takes this apparent cooperation
as betokening efforts to introduce pictures into a manuscript following an unillustrated exemplar. George
Henderson, however, marshals massive evidence that
indicates that the opposite was the case, that the
scribe and illustrators were mostly at odds. In the
first place, the pictures are generally not very
well aligned with the text they are supposed to be
illustrating.[44] Secondly, the disposition of spaces
left for illustration are erratically dispersed (e.g.,
the elaborately developed Wars of Abraham have no
spaces for illustration though they cover seven pages, while the relatively uninteresting material corresponding to Genesis 4-5, the lineage of Adam, is
generously illustrated.)[45] Henderson draws no hard and
fast conclusions, but suggests that spaces are being
disposed by a scribe following an old and imperfect
illustrated Genesis, leaving no blanks where the model is missing leaves. At any rate, the lack of relation between text and pictures on the one hand, and
the inconsistencies in the scribe's disposition of
space and the illustrator's uses of it, suggests that
there was less than the full cooperation that such a
fancy undertaking implies.
        Barbara Raw's important article[46] also notes

[44] "The Programme of Illustrations in Bodleian MS XI,"
in *Studies in Memory of David Talbot Rice*, ed. Giles
Robertson and George Henderson (Edinburgh, 1975), 113-45.
For example, the large space left on P. 81 directly
following the Tower of Babel episode is not used for
the tower, but for two small genre scenes, and the
picture of the Tower itself is crammed into the half-
page space overleaf, where the text is dealing with
Loth and Abraham (*ibid.*, 130).
[45] *Ibid.*, 134-35.
[46] See note 42, above. This article presents the significant conclusions of her unpublished London M.A.
thesis, "The Story of the Fall of Man and the Angels
in the MS Junius 11 and the Relation of the Manuscript
Illuminations to the Text" (1953).

the fact of the misalignment of pictures and text
and comes to a very definite conclusion. Not only
are the pictures separated from their text, sometimes by as much as several pages, but, she notes,
they often do not agree in their content with what
the poet describes. This is especially notable
in the pictures of Enoch (PP. 60 and 61, Enoch
standing on a dragon, listening to an angel, ascen-
ding into Heaven, not one of which is explicitly
mentioned in *Genesis A*), and the pictures of the
Rebellion and Fall of the Angels on PP. 2 and 3,
which though placed with the brief Fall of the Angels
described at *Genesis A* 47ff., agree better with the
account of the Fall in *Genesis B*. Raw notes that
the pictures fall into three distinct groups, distinguished by their format: (1) an isolated trio
of pictures showing God creating (PP. 6 and 7) perhaps following an (ivory) triptych; (2) the series
of pictures showing enthroned patriarchs, births and
deaths framed by arches and arcades (PP. 53-9, 62-3),
representing the descendants of Adam (Genesis 4 and
5); and (3) the major group, comprising the rest of
the pictures: the Fall of the Angels, Adam and Eve,
Cain and Abel, Enoch, Noah and Abraham. What unites
the last group is affinity with motifs in Carolingian-
Ottonian painting which are in one way or another connected with Tours, which strongly suggests a single
Carolingian model for the third group of pictures.[47]
Moreover, the Enoch material fits pretty exactly the
Cain-Enoch episode of the Old Saxon *Genesis*, the original of *Genesis B*,[48] while the first depiction of
the Fall of the Angels (P. 3) has two near-quotations
of *Genesis B* inscribed on it.[49] The striking conclusion she draws from all this is that the main group
of Junius pictures stems from a set of illustrations
accompanying the Old Saxon *Genesis*, which came over
to England in a more complete form than we now have
it, in the illustrated ancestor of the Junius 11 illustrations.

[47] Raw summarizes the evidence on p. 146 of her article.
[48] That is, Fragment II, lines 130b-150, where the
narrative goes directly from Cain to Enoch and his
battle with Antichrist without genealogical detail.
For the text, see Otto Behaghel, ed., *Heliand und
Genesis*, rev. Walther Mitzka (8th ed., Halle, 1965).
[49] Viz.: "hu s[e] engyl ongon ofermod wesan" (cf.
GB 293, "þæt his engyl ongan ofermede wesan"), and
"her se hælend gesce[op] helle heom to wite" (cf.
GB 318-20).

Thomas H. Ohlgren, in a nearly simultaneously
published article, comes to the same conclusion by
a slightly different route.[50] He also considers the
illustrations on PP. 2-3 crucial, but sees their icon-
ographical filiation with the widespread tradition
of Spanish Beatus-Apocalypse illustrations.[51] He supposes that the likeliest way of transmission of their
images to England was by way of Fleury, citing as
intermediary the sculptured capitals in the ambulatory
of the Benedictine abbey of Saint-Benoit-sur-Loire.[52]
Like Raw, he concludes that the original of the Junius
11 illustrations was a complete, illustrated copy of
the Old Saxon *Genesis*.

The implications of this doubly-confirmed new
idea are immediately obvious. First of all, it
suggests that the reason that *Genesis B* was interpolated into *A* was not esthetic, as nearly everybody
assumes,[53] but practical. The compiler of Junius 11,
or, as I believe, of its exemplar, had on the one
hand a body of Old English texts (our *Genesis A,
Exodus* and *Daniel*), badly marred because the crucial
episode of the Fall of Man was missing. On the other
hand he had a complete, illustrated Old Saxon *Genesis*
(already translated into English Saxon?). He therefore took only what was lacking in his primary material, the illustrations and the Fall of Man (including, because inextricably bound up with it, the
Fall of the Angels) and disgarded the rest. If Raw
and Ohlgren are right, the Junius illustrations imply
that the Old Saxon *Genesis* was once complete from
the Fall of the Angels, and included the creation of
Adam and Eve and ran up to at least the earlier portions of the history of Abraham (or at least to Noe's
ark, see n. 16 above). When it came to England, the
Old Saxon *Genesis* was not a fragment, or at least it
was a much longer fragment than it is now. Why then
was the text of *Genesis A* preferred? Two reasons suggest themselves. First, as an ancient English poem,
probably an old possession of the house where the

---

[50] "Some New Light on the Old English *Caedmonian
Genesis*," *Studies in Iconography* 1 (1975), 38-75.
Ohlgren's conclusions are not quite independent of
Raw's, since he relies heavily on her unpublished
thesis; see note 46, above.
[51] For details, see *ibid.*, 41-44.
[52] *Ibid.*, 50.
[53] E.g., C. L. Wrenn, *A Study of Old English Literature* (London, 1967), 99; Priebsch, *Heliand MS*, 47.

exemplar of Junius 11 was compiled, it was regarded
as precious and inspired, while the outlander, whatever its interest or value, was a novelty. *Genesis
A* may even have been a famous text, with the status
of a standard classic. Secondly, *Genesis A* is a continuous text, and as a presentation of the Bible, much
more useful and reliable than the episodic and ten-
dentious Old Saxon *Genesis*.

In positing Fleury as the source of much of the
iconography of the Junius 11 illustrations and its
supposed Old Saxon original, Ohlgren comes to the
conclusion that the likeliest provenance for our manuscript is Newminster, Winchester, a house which had
been reformed and remonasticized in 963.[54] Fleury was
instrumental in the tenth-century Benedictine revival
in England and hence more likely to have contact with
a reformed house than with Christ Church, Canterbury,
not reformed until Archbishop Aelfric (995-1005). But
Ohlgren takes no account of St. Augustine's, Canterbury, which was probably always monastic.[55] In fact,
as Ohlgren himself mentions, both Canterbury and Winchester had close ties with Fleury.[56] His other reason for preferring the Newminster provenance is that
Junius 11 shows no resemblance to the illustrated
Hexateuch, Cotton Claudius B.iv, a known St. Augustine's production. But directly counter to this is
the fact that the Junius resembles known Newminster
manuscripts even less (viz., Cotton Titus D. xxvi
and xxvii).[57] While the differences between Junius 11
and Claudius B. iv are extreme, there are also
striking similarities: the peculiar motif in both of
the ark as a great pyramidical dragon-ship (Junius
PP. 66, 68, Claudius ff. 14rv, 15rv), for one. More
importantly, the genealogical series of pictures in
both manuscripts are of the same type (compare Junius
PP. 53-59, 62-63 to Claudius 10v, 11rv, 12r).[58] Similar are the drapery of the female figures and their

---

[54] Ohlgren, "New Light," 63-64.
[55] Dom David Knowles, *The Monastic Order in England,
A History of its Development from the Times of St
Dunstan to the Fourth Lateran Council, 940-1216* (2d
ed., Cambridge, 1966), 34-35.
[56] "New Light," 63.
[57] Raw, "Probable Derivation," 135. See Wormald,
English Drawings, pl. 16 (b).
[58] The pictures of Claudius B.iv are reproduced in
Clemoes and Dodwell, *The Old English Hexateuch* (see
note 38, above).

postures of grief, the wrapped corpses, the enthrone-
ments; the Junius arcading is lacking in the small
framed Claudius pictures, but appears to similar
effect in Claudius 27v-28r. It is these scenes which
the Junius illustrator had to work out for himself
since they could not have appeared in a series of
illustrations accompanying the Old Saxon *Genesis*,
which skips over Genesis 4 and 5, and it is precisely
at this point where Junius and Claudius most closely
correspond. When the model failed him, it appears
likely that the Junius illustrator turned to a tradition of genealogy illustration current in Canterbury. [59]

[59]   Dodwell (*ibid.*, 66), thinks the Claudius illustrator notably free of extraneous influences and rejects
a suggestion by Henderson ("Late Antique Influences,"
172-98) that his depiction of corpses follows some
Byzantine model.

Postscript

    Since this book went to press, a new edition of
Exodus by Peter J. Lucas has appeared (London, 1977),
in which the editor "with some confidence" assigns
the writing of MS Junius 11 to Malmesbury about 1000.
His reasons are (1) the "identity" of the second Junius
artist with that of the Virtues and Vices illustrations
in the "Corpus Prudentius" (MS CCC 23), a book recently
assigned to Malmesbury; (2) the similarity of aspects
of the Junius iconography with that of certain sculptured medallions in the south porch of Malmesbury Abbey (ca. 1170-80); (3) the identification of the Junius
"Aelfwine" portrait medallion with Abbot Aelfwine of
Malmesbury (ca. 1043/4-1045/6). Only (1) seems a
really strong point against the traditional assignment
of Junius 11 to Canterbury, but I have not yet had
the chance to assess Lucas' evidence carefully. The
relevant bibliography is: Lucas, *ed. cit.*, 2-4; O. Pächt
and J.J.G. Alexander, *Illuminated Manuscripts in the
Bodleian Oxford*, III (London, 1973), 5; E. Temple,
Anglo-Saxon Manuscripts 900-1066 (London, 1976), no.
58, 76-78; K.J. Galbraith, "The Iconography of the Biblical Scenes at Malmesbury Abbey," *Journal of the
British Achaeological Association* 28 (1965), 39-56.
Lucas' detailed and original discussion of Junius 11
should be consulted by the user of this book.

                                    A.N.D.

II. Language and Date

A. Language

Like Melchisedech, *Genesis A* is without father, without mother, without genealogy. The confident standards which once placed the poem in a Northumbrian home in the late seventh or early eighth centuries have been hopelessly eroded. The loss of confidence in linguistic evidence in just the last quarter-century is shown by a comparison of the linguistic apparatuses of Timmer's edition of *Genesis B* (1948) and Irving's of *Exodus* (1953) with that of Ferrell's *Daniel* (1974); the latter offers only a few notes on the most outstanding forms "made as a tentative guide to the reader,"[1] while the earlier editions, though cautious about the older linguistic criteria, are able to come to rather elaborate and confident conclusions about the composition and homes of their poems. The circumstance which separates Timmer and Irving from Ferrell is Kenneth Sisam's landmark study, "Dialect Origins of the Earlier Old English Verse."[2] He shows convincingly that it is impossible to say with confidence what "preserved layers" can be discerned in any poetic text extant in a single manuscript. The evidence of the bulk of the poetry points to a standardized "mixed" poetic dialect which reflects no single area's dialect (and the dialect boundaries were doubtless more fluid than the scanty monuments can indicate) and no actual spoken language of any area or time:

> As we go farther back in time, the grammarian's conception of poetry, classified according to the local dialects spoken by its makers, becomes less useful and creates many difficulties. More attention should be given to the probability that there was a body of verse, anonymous and independent of local interest, which was the common stock of the entertainment or instruction of the English peoples. A poem, wherever composed, might win its way into the common stock. The native metre, based primarily on the alliteration of stressed syllables, carried well

---

[1] Ferrell, *Daniel*, p. 13. For details of these editions see the Bibliography, Section D.
[2] In *Studies in the History of Old English Literature* (Oxford, 1953), 119-39.

because in this essential the usage of seventh-
century Northumbria and tenth-century Wessex was
the same; but any local dialect forms that affected the verse-structure were a handicap to cir-
culation. A poet might prefer to take his
models from the common stock rather than from
the less-known work of his own district.   In
this way poems could be produced that do not
belong to any local dialect, but to a general
Old English poetic dialect, artificial, archaic,
and perhaps mixed in its vocabulary, conservative in inflexions that affect the verse-
structure, and indifferent to non-structural
irregularities, which were perhaps tolerated
as part of the colouring of the language of
verse.[3]

Genesis A, like nearly all other Old English
poetry, presents a variety of forms, within a matrix
that is essentially West-Saxon. Traditionally, some
of the forms which diverge from the West-Saxon norm
(as established by Ælfric and other late writers who
were consciously composing in a strict language) may
be interpreted as non-West-Saxon, others as early,
or very late West-Saxon. The assumption is that the
variety of forms has, at least to some extent, been
accidentally accumulated as the result of repeated
copyings at different times and places, each copying
leaving some traces of a language different from that
of the original author and scribe. In a late manuscript such as Junius 11, the accumulation has been
going on so long, that it is no longer possible to
separate all the strands or reconstruct the processes
that went to make up the language of the poem as we
now have it. Most irregular forms are sporadic, and
their significance is by no means easy to determine.[4]
On the other hand, certain non-standard features are
numerous enough that, although they are sporadic and
in a sense accidental, they do appear to make some
sort of pattern. Almost any non-standard form, except for those few which occur in patterns of frequency,
is possibly a mistake, or a non-significant vagary
of the scribe. Every explanation must be regarded
cautiously. All that can be done is the listing of
the outstanding non-standard forms, with comment. A
little interpretation will be appended.

---

[3] Sisam, *Studies*, 138
[4] See Ferrell's excellent summing-up of the problem,
Daniel, pp. 10-13.

Analysis of Forms[5]

    a. The interchange of *ie, i, y* (both long and
short) may be taken as a characteristic of late-West-
Saxon and has presumably entered the poem in the
course of tenth-century copying. Examples are
very frequent in *Genesis A* (Campbell, §§ 39, 315-18).

ie > y > i   *hīre* 2798 beside *hȳre* 1750 &c; *līfe* 1916
            beside *lȳfaδ* 2520; *cīgde* 1807 beside *cȳgde*
            2910 &c; *cirm* 2549 beside *cyrm* 2409; *gistas*
            2474, *gistum* 2494 beside *gystas* 2487,
            giestum 2442, *scippend* 137 beside *scyppend*
            65, 206 &c.

  y > i   *cining* 2, 24, 50, 107 beside usual *cyning*;
            drihten, only GN form; *brittade* 1181 be-
            side *bryttedon* 1602 &c; *mine* 869 (for *myne*);
            hige beside *hyge* about equally; *pinceδ*
            2478, 2896.

  i > y   *gerysne* 169, 1565, *gerysnu* 2247 beside
            gerisne 2478, *gerisno* 2434; *clypte* 1569
            (from *clippan*); *pyss*-forms are very spor-
            adic against *piss*-forms (5x, 23x).

    ie   is the eW-S spelling of lW-S *y* arising
            from mutation and palatal diphthongiza-
            tion. *ie* appears frequently in GN: e.g.,
            īowe 1541, *īewde* 1785 beside *ȳwan*; *-scīene*
            1827, 2737; *andgiettacen* 1539; *ansīen* 1261;
            -strīenan 966, 1118 beside *strȳnan*; *gield*
            101, 1109, *gieldan* 1978 beside *gyld, gyl-*
            dan; *gielp-* 96 beside *gylp* 2410; *gīen(a)*
            beside Angl. *gēn(a)* (Campbell, § 185);

[5] That the language of GN is West-Saxon need not be
proved, but for an excellent demonstration of the West-
Saxon matrix of GB by a comparison with Aelfric's prose,
see Timmer, *Later Genesis*, pp. 19-21. In the following
discussion the terms of convenience are West-Saxon,
early and late (W-S, eW-S, lW-S), Anglian (Angl.), including Mercian and Northumbrian, Kentish (Kt.). The
dialectal names refer to certain documents which do not
necessarily come from the same areas as the name of
the dialect implies (e.g., Vespasian Psalter, the chief
example of Mercian, was written at Canterbury). On
the documents constituting dialect evidence, see Campbell, §§ 5, 6, 256. On the paucity and ambiguity of
the evidence for all but W-S see Sisam, "Dialect Origins," 120-21, 135 et passim.

giest- 2448, *giestum* 2442 beside *gyst,*
gist; *gīet(a)* beside *gȳt(a)*; *īecte* 1122,
2378 beside *īcte* 1190; *-ciest* 1317; *nīed-*
929, 1977 beside *-nȳd* 2030; *nīehstan* 1400;
stīep 60; *tīedrað* 1512. (This feature
distinguishes GN from EX, which shows only
one doubtful *ie*-form, *onnīed* 149, and from
DN, which shows only *prēanīed* 213.)

   b. Other forms of West-Saxon type:

lāgon 2076, pret. pl. of *licgan* str. vb. 5: restora-
         tion of *ā* before back vowel (Campbell § 162).
cucu 1297 beside *cwic* (Angl. & poet.); *wucan* 1465,
         1477, 2770; *wuduwan* 2010 beside *wydewan*
         2133, combinative back-umlaut of *i* (but
         always *sweotol*, &c), probably W-S, or non-
         Angl.: the mixture of forms is common in
         poetry (Campbell, § 218).
glæd-stede 2843 appears beside glēd-styde 1810 "place
         of fire," "altar." If the former is not
         merely "happy place", it represents a
         development **glōd- > *glōēd- > glēd- > glæd-.*
         "Occasionally the graph *æ* is used to repre-
         sent the mutation of *ō*," (Campbell, § 198).
         Sievers called *glæd-* here "hypersaxon" (see
         Menner, *Anglia* 70, 292, n.1). Similar
         must be *æðele* 63 = *ēðele* < *ōēðele*.
hȳdig   usual form in GN (except *ofer-hygdig* 66, po-
         etic?): W-S compensatory lengthening fol-
         lowing loss of *g* (Campbell, § 243). If
         pine 2482 = *pīgne* "food," it belongs here
         (see Commentary).
hrēaw 1447 acc. sg. beside *hrǣs* 1985 gen. sg.: lW-S
         approximation of *-æ(u)-* to *-ea-* with re-
         introduction of *w* (Campbell, § 273).
weor- > *wur-* , e.g., *wurðan* 1102, 2207, *gewurðan* 1691,
         wurðiað 1758, *gewurðod* 2107, 2137, *wurð-*
         licor 2094 beside *(ge)weorðan, weorðade,*
         &c (Campbell, § 321); by inverted spelling,
         if a noun, is *gewyrc* 1309, **-weorc > *-wurc*
         > -wyrc.
sylf &c (13x) beside *self* &c (32x), *(ge)syllan* (5x)
         beside *(ge)sellan* (6x) (Campbell § 325).
ecg-wale 2089 dat. sg. (for *-wæle*): lW-S extention of
         -a- of pl. to sing.? (see Brunner, § 240,
         anm. 2), but sporadic extension of this
         sort is common to all dialects (Campbell, §
         161); *wræce* 2586 beside *wrace* 71: the fai-
         lure here of *-a-* to extend to all cases
         may be eW-S (Campbell, § 589 (1)).

io spellings. These could be Anglian survivals or
penetrations, but most likely survivals
of an earlier W-S recension. This graph
tends to disappear in lW-S (see Campbell,
§ 296):
līodende 182, str. vb. 2 (< Gmc. *-ēu-*)
līod-geard 229 (*i*-mutation of *ēo*, Campbell,
§ 202)
scīo 1103, *tīode* 173 (by contraction).
hlioðo 1439 beside *hleoðo, hlið* (back-umlaut)
wrȳon 1572 (= *wrēon*), *fyore* 1184 (= *feore*)
probably belong here (cf. GB 581 *un-*
trȳowða) as eW-S, but the spellings may
show Kentish influence (*e* and *y* equivalent graphs in Kt., Campbell §§ 288, 298).
(There are 4 spellings *io*, one *yo* in GB,
none in EX or DN).

nīor 2091 is probably late Kentish for W-S
nēar (Campbell, § 235 (2)).

c.   Forms of non-West-Saxon type:

wērlogan 36 beside *wǣrloga(n)* (4x): Gmc. *ǣ* > *ē*   (Campbell, § 128); so *gedǣde* 2894 < Angl. *-dēde*
(sporadic in poetry, for W-S *gedyde*; see
Campbell, § 768).
waldend, &c.: retraction of *-æ-* to *-a-* before *l* + consonant is, in respect of certain words,
the most consistent nW-S feature of GN,
but this feature is common in poetic language, and in respect of a few words, in
southern scribal practice.[6] (Campbell, § 143)
aldor(-) always in GN except *ealdor* 2504,
ealdorgedāl 1959, *ealdordōm* 1197
alwalda 2827, *al(l)wihta* 193, 1290, beside
eallwihta 113, 978, *ealltela* 1905, the
simplex is always *eall*
waldend always, *nalles* (6x), *nales* (2x,
graphic simplification, Campbell, § 66)
hals-fæst 2240 beside *heals-mægeð* 2156

gegærwan 2856 (W-S *gegyrwan*), retraction
of *-æ-* to *-a-* before *r* > *æ* by *i*-mutation.

---

[6]   See E. G. Stanley, "Spellings of the *Waldend* group,"
in *Studies in Language, Literature and Culture of the
Middle Ages and Later*, ed. E. B. Atwood and A. A. Hill
(Austin, 1969), 38-69.

seolf (3x): breaking of *e* before *lf*, nW-S (Campbell, § 146).

fere dat. sg. 1544 beside *fære*: second fronting of *æ*
　　　　　to *e*, found chiefly in the Vespasian Psalter,
　　　　　rare elsewhere (Campbell, § 164); apparently
　　　　　belonging here is *-getel* 2756 beside *-getæl*
　　　　　1420, but difficult because the second front--
　　　　　ing normally fails before *l*, the only exam-
　　　　　ple being the doubtful *hel* "concealed" VP
　　　　　39,11 (Campbell, § 165). A confusion rela-
　　　　　ted to this sound may be at 1358, where
　　　　　the scribe wrote *-pæl*, then he or another
　　　　　corrected to *-pel*.
sceolde 2117, pret. s., "he protected" (i.e., *scylde*)
　　　　　is difficult. Perhaps the MS-form repre-
　　　　　sents nW-S **scelde* reformed with a W-S
　　　　　palatal glide diphthong on the model of
　　　　　sculan / sceolde (cf. *geomor* = *Gomer* 1610, see
　　　　　Commentary), or perhaps represents W-S false
　　　　　substitution of *eo* for *ie* (Campbell, § 202
　　　　　and f.n. 1 on p. 81).
ea > e by *i*-mutation (W-S *ea > ie > y*): of *ea* by
　　　　　breaking before *r*, *wergðo* 1755; of *ēa* < Gmc.
　　　　　au, *lēge* 44 beside *līge*, *gesēne* 2807 (W-S
　　　　　gesīene), *tēmað* imperative 196 beside *tȳmdon*
　　　　　1242. These are spellings of Anglian type,
　　　　　frequently in poetry and sometimes in W-S
　　　　　texts (Campbell, § 200). *i*-mutation of
　　　　　ea fails in *befealdest* 1010 but is of W-S type
　　　　　(= Angl. **befaldest*, unmutated and retracted).
dēore 951, 2745 beside *dȳre*, no *i*-mutation of *ēo < īo*
　　　　　is nW-S (Campbell, § 201 (1)), but *dēore*
　　　　　is frequent in poetry.
deoreð 1984, &c. Back-mutation is general in W-S be-
　　　　　fore labials and liquids but sporadic in
　　　　　GN, e.g., *weorold* 1963 only, otherwise
　　　　　always *woruld* (with combinative back-um-
　　　　　laut); *werod (-ed)* always. Back-umlaut
　　　　　of *e* before other consonants is nW-S but
　　　　　common in poetry; GN shows *freoðo* 1838,
　　　　　1347 &c. beside *friðo* 57, *fryðo* 1513,
　　　　　freðo 1487; *hlioðo* 1439, *hleoðo* 1459,
　　　　　hleoðu 1803; *meotodes* 189, otherwise al-
　　　　　ways *metod* (this isolated example might
　　　　　better be considered Kt. rather than Angl.)
　　　　　(Campbell, § 210). The non-poetic *esol*
　　　　　2867 lacks back-umlaut.
a > æ > ea by second fronting and back-mutation is
　　　　　Mercian (Vespasian Psalter) but a common
　　　　　poetic feature, e.g. in GN, *cearum* 2795,

(g)eador 2559, *ealo-* 2410, *eafora* usually, beside W-S *afera* 2054 (Campbell, § 207).

hēhsta 51 by smoothing is a general Anglian characteristic (cf. W-S *hīehsta, hīesta*), Campbell, §§ 222-233, but lW-S smoothing of *ea > e* occurs sporadically (Campbell, § 312). GN shows *nēh* 2051 beside *nēah, -tēna* 1397 beside *tȳno, tīena* (< **tehin-* ?, the form is difficult, see Brunner, § 129, anm. 6), *werg* 906, 1250 (poetic?), *wexað* imperative 196 beside *weaxað* 1532, *wī-bedd* (< *wīoχ-*) 1791, 1806, 1882 beside *wēo-bedd* 2842, *twīh* 2255 (W-S *-twēoh*).

eo / ea   Confusion of these sounds is a feature of North., but in GN only very doubtful evidence appears. *behēowan* [MS -heopan] for *-heawan*, with rounded second element? (cf. Campbell, § 278 (a)), but the MS-form could also represent lW-S assimilation of the diphthong to *-w-* (Campbell, § 274), or merely an erroneous series of scribal corrections (**-heaw-*, miswritten as *-heap-* corrected to *-hoop-* ?). *hige-trēawa* 2369 for *-trēowa*, unrounded second element (cf. Campbell, § 278 (b)) but the change is not regular in North. before *w* (Campbell, § 279). *feallan* 2038 is taken as *fēollan* pret. pl. (unrounded second element) by Krapp, but in this edition as pres. subj. pl. (see Commentary 2037-38).

ēd 1405 (= *ead?*) is very likely corrupt (see Commentary), but may be explained as a late monophthongization (Campbell, § 329 (2)).

gescaft 131 beside *gesceaft* "creation." The development may be prim OE. **-scæft > *-sceaft* (by influence of palatal)> **-scæft* (monophthongization)> *-scaft* and hence may be considered a very early example of the Middle English form of the word.[7]

d.   Vowels of unstressed syllables

-ade   pret. of wk. vb. II, the ending which prevails in Kentish and Anglian but is sporadic

---

[7]   See S. R. T. O. d'Ardenne, Þe *Liflade ant te Passiun of Seinte Iuliene*, EETS 248 (1961), p. 183.

in eW-S and poetry (Campbell § 757): e.g.,
miclade 1243, *nȳttade* 1598, *reordade* 1253,
segnade 1365, *þingade* 1009, *weorðade* 1886,
wīsade 2446, *wrīðade* 1702, &c.

hȳrde 2696 is probably to be explained as syncopated
late form of ds. *hīrede* "family" (Campbell §§ 392-93, cf. § 372).

Leveling of final vowels occurs sporadically but frequently: *roderas* gen. sg. 98, 148; *freo-*
licu (= *-e,* so ed.) 184; *pǣre* gen. pl.
1522; *lande* gen. pl. 1795; *wegan* 2097 =
wegen past. part.? (see Commentary); *drehta*
2251 = *drehte* (so ed.); so also the weakening or loss of final unstressed nasals is
frequent: e.g., pret. pls. in *-an* 1974,
1801, 1697, 1061, 1064, 1233, 1975, 940,
87, 2038? etc.; *gombon* = *gomban* 1978, *sū-*
ðon = *sūðan* 1975, *feorren* = *feorran* 1836;
swefyl 2417 beside *swefl* 2543, *mægyn* 52
for *mæg(e)n.* According to Kemp Malone this
leveling, common in all four poetic manuscripts, reflects real pronunciation and is
an early manifestation of M.E. leveling.[8]
However, if Malone's lists are anywhere
near complete, leveling occurs in GN proportionately less frequently than in any
other Junius 11 poem.

e. Consonants

Unvoicing of final consonants occurs sporadically:
genearwot 2604 beside *genearwad* 921;
ādǣlte 218 (corrector has altered to
ādǣlede); MS *gesetet* 100 is by a corrector (note GB 459, *metot* = *metod*)
(cf. Campbell, § 450); perhaps *prȳdig*
1986 for *prȳðig* represents medial unvoicing (cf. *sedes* 1133 for *sethes*)
but probably miswriting of *d* for *ð.*
teoche 1688 beside *teohhe* 959: eW-S spelling of the
consonant group (Campbell, § 63).
hucse 2339 beside *husce* 2384: metathesis of [sk]
(unpalatalized) to [ks] is lW-S (Camp-
bell, § 440).

---

[8] "When did Middle English Begin?" *Curme Volume of
Linguistic Studies*, Language Monographs 7 (Baltimore,
1930), 110-17.

frið-gedāl 1142, *stīð-frihþ* 107 beside *stīð-ferhð*,
　　　　etc.: metathesis of *r* before *h(þ)*
　　　　(Campbell 459 (3)). *frið* is poetic
　　　　and lW-S, *ferhþ* > *fyrhþ* > **firþ* > *friþ*
　　　　(Campbell, § 477 (6) & f.n. 7).
wǣrfæsne 1011 for *wǣrfæstne*: loss of *t* between *s* and
　　　　another consonant is lW-S (Campbell, §
　　　　477 (2)).
brember 2929, *ambrafel* 1962 (Vulg. "Amrafel"): in-
　　　　trusion of *b* is perhaps W-S (Campbell, §
　　　　478 (1)).
emne 1943 beside *efne* (4x); *mamres* 2152 (< **mammres* ?
　　　　< **mambres* < Vulg. *Mambre*): lW-S assim-
　　　　ilation? (see Campbell, § 484).

　　f.　Accidence

hlēo dat. sg. (m.-wa) 102 (also AN 567) uninflected
　　　　(usually *hleōwe*) (Campbell, § 584 (1)(b)).
suno acc sg. 1615 beside *sunu*: late? (Brunner, § 271
　　　　anm. 1).
sunu gen. pl. 1606 beside *suna*, resembles the usual
　　　　Rushworth[1] form (Mercian) (Brunner, § 271
　　　　anm. 2).
blǣdæ 1474 acc. sg. (f.-ō), *hlǣdræ* 1675 acc. pl. (f.-
　　　　jō) may be explained as survivals of ear-
　　　　lier Anglian inflections (Campbell, § 587)
　　　　or merely as spellings influenced by the
　　　　stem-vowels.
fremu acc. sg. 1843, *fǣhðu* gen. sg. 1378, lW-S exten-
　　　　sion of *-u* of nom. to other cases of sg.
　　　　(Campbell, § 571).
tūddor dat. sg. 914, 1613 beside *tūdre* (6x) appears to
　　　　be from archaic IE -es/-os stem (Campbell,
　　　　§ 635)
wæl 2161: uninflected locative? (Campbell, § 571).
fǣgerro 1812, *sigoro* 1270, *egipto* 1866, gens. pl. in
　　　　-o are probably to be considered "late
　　　　OE." rather than lW-S (Campbell, § 377).
wǣrlogona gen. pl. (masc. wk.) 2411: *-ona* is a rel-
　　　　atively rare eW-S form (Brunner, § 216,
　　　　anm. 3).
pæne for *pone* 221, 2645 is a peculiar lW-S form (Camp-
　　　　bell, § 380) but both occurrences are emen-
　　　　dations of *pære*.
gehwǣre dat. f. 1374 is late (Brunner, § 341, anm. 4).
　　　　The substitution of *gehwām* improves the
　　　　meter (see Commentary).
twā f. for *twēgen* m.? at 2210 (see Commentary); *tū* n.
　　　　for pl. masc. or m.f. at 2780 probably can-
　　　　not be considered irregular.

Subj. pl. in -*e* occurs several times (see Commentary,
          1587a). Loss of -*n* < *-*in* is eW-S (Camp-
          bell, § 472).

     g. Vocabulary

     GN contains a number of words that do not occur
in WS prose, but which may be considered part of the
poetic vocabulary and therefore are not dialectally
significant, e.g. *bēacen, bepeccan, (e)aldor* (in the
phrase *tō . . . aldre* "forever"), *hlēoðor, morðor,
nympe, penden* (glossed *"þa hwile"* at GB 245).[9] As
specifically Anglian vocabulary may be noted *feoð* "he
hates" (**fēogan*) (Campbell, § 761 (5)); *fetigean* as
wk. II is Anglian, poetic and occasional W-S, the
usual W-S form is *feccan* I. W-S vocabulary may be seen
in the numerous verbs with *on-* prefixes (Campbell,
§ 76), in the replacement of all *lybban* forms with
lifian (1W-S, Campbell, § 762). Anglian usage may
perhaps be seen in *mid* with acc. (3x) vs. 80x with
dat. or instr., also *in* with dat. (3x), with acc. (1x),
as opposed to W-S *on*.
     In general, the vocabulary of GN does not dis-
tinguish it from the bulk of OE. poetry.[10]

     h. Conclusion

     The great mixture of forms, within a West-Saxon
matrix, is merely the language of verse, and does not
help to date or place the poem. *Genesis A* shows no
especially early forms, while the late forms are consistent with the date of the manuscript. The Anglian
forms are poetic, not geographic and, considering
the length of the poem, are only a sprinkling in a
language otherwise very consistent.
     There are, however, a number of early West-Saxon
forms, particularly the spellings *ie* and *io*. These
separate *Genesis* from *Exodus* and *Daniel*. The latter
poems show only one *ie* spelling each (*onnied* EX 139,
preanied DN 213). I can find no *io* spellings in
either. On the other hand, *Genesis B* shows numerous
ie and *io* spellings, suggesting that *A* and *B* under-
went common revision which excluded *Exodus* and *Daniel*.[11]

---

[9] See Irving, *Exodus*, pp. 22-23.
[10] But see R. J. Menner, "The Date and Dialect of
Genesis A," *Anglia* 70 (1951), 285-94.
[11] Sisam, "The Exeter Book," in *Studies*, 103 (see n.
2, above), points out that only the forms *com(on)*
appear in GN and GB, EX and DN show *cwom(on)*.

Neither of the latter two poems appear to have gone
through an early West-Saxon stage of transmission.[12]

Sievers[13] divided *Genesis* into three parts: *Genesis I*, 1-234, *Genesis II = Genesis B*, *Genesis III*,
852-2936. He posited distinct origins for the three
parts. Menner, discussing this thesis, did not attempt
to decide on the unity of I and III.[14] Yet it must be
admitted that there is a distinct difference in the
language of I and III. I will briefly summarize.
First, there is a higher proportion of Anglian (poetic?)
words in I: *werlogan* 36, *lege* 44, *temað* 196, *hehsta*
51, *wexað* 196. Second, of the five *io* spellings in
Genesis A, three are in I (lines 173, 182, 229). Third,
numerous forms, not in themselves dialectally significant, appear in I and not in III: e.g., all *cining*
spellings, *meotodes* 189 (III has *metod-*), *-ponce* 93
(III has *-panc-*), *naman* (III has *noman*), gen. sg. in
-as 98, 148, *peostrum* 127, 144 (III has *pystr-*), *cymð*
6 (III always *cymeð*), *-hygdig* 66 (III *hydig*). Fourth,
numerous forms in I agree with II (*Genesis B*) against
III: e.g., *naman* 128, 140, GB 343, gen. sg. *-as* 98, 148,
GB 485 *dreamas*, *mægyn* 52 and GB 269 (but cf. *swefyl* in
III, 2417), and particularly the proportion of *io*
spellings in I (3x), II (5x in 617 lines), III (2x).

While diverse origin of I and III cannot be ruled
out, it is not the only or the most likely explanation.[15]
Though rather fragmentary, and by the nature of the material composed more freely than III, I does not on
grounds of style or treatment of the source differ
enough from III to justify a theory of diverse origin.
The differences between I and III are essentially a
greater poetic element and a greater share of early
West-Saxon features in I. Timmer showed the prominent
early West-Saxon strain in *Genesis B*.[16] The reasonable presumption is that the translation from Old Saxon
to West-Saxon was made in Alfredian times and copied
few enough times that these early West-Saxon forms
have not been smoothed out. I tend to believe that
the differences between I and III arose when the
interpolation of *Genesis B* took place, about the same
time as the translation was made, and that I bears

---

[12] My conclusion and Menner's, "Date and Dialect," 292,
f.n. 3.
[13] "Caedmon und Genesis," in *Britannica, Max Förster
zum 60. Geburtstage* (Leipzig, 1929), 72 ff.
[14] "Date and Dialect," 286, f.n. 2.
[15] For these theories see Introduction, pp. 39-40, below.
[16] *Later Genesis*, pp. 21-24.

the signs of an incomplete revision made at that time,
which brought the earlier poem into early West-Saxon
forms.[17] Presumably the revision of III was not as thor-
ough, or was by a different person, while *Exodus* and *Daniel* may not at that time have formed part of this group.

B.   Date

There is nothing which puts a precise date on
the original composition of *Genesis A*. From the time
of Junius, the first editor, it has been put early.
The *terminus ad quem* is the date of the Manuscript
itself, ca. 1000-25. No one has ever placed it so
late. The *terminus a quo* is much hazier, perhaps the
generation before 680, the date of the death of
Abbess Hild, Caedmon's patroness, will do. If it
is true that *Genesis A* was partially revised at the
time of the translation of *Genesis B*, then the later
terminus can be placed ca. 900. But to date the poem
ca.650-ca.900 is merely to say it is an Old English
poem. Several attempts to place it late, in the late
ninth or tenth centuries, have not been successful.[18]
Only a relative date can be given to *Genesis A*.
In style, vocabulary and meter it closely resembles
Beowulf, Exodus and *Daniel* and differs from the poems
known to be late. Menner, using vocabulary as a

[17] Just as Junius 11 shows signs of partial normali-
zing revision, see Introduction, p. 9, above. The date
for the composition of GB has been placed early in the
tenth century, as the eW-S forms suggest, and also in
the late tenth by Priebsch, Gerould (see Timmer, *Later
Genesis,* p. 43) and Ohlgren, "Some New Light on the
Old English *Caedmonian Genesis*," *Studies in Iconography* 1 (1975), 61-62.
[18] Siever's late ninth-century Saxon provenance was dis-
proved by Menner, "Date and Dialect;" more recently
Dietrich Hofmann, "Untersuchungen zu der altenglischen Gedichten *Genesis* und *Exodus*," *Anglia* 75 (1957),
1-34, on the basis of a few very questionable "parallels" between GN and Old Norse poetic diction, said
GN and EX were composed late, and in the Danelaw.
This fragile argument was easily broken by Edward
B. Irving, "On the Dating of the Old English Poems
Genesis and *Exodus*," *Anglia* 77 (1959), 1-11. In spite
of the title of his article, Irving does not argue
for a particular date for GN, only against Hofmann's
late date.

criterion of date, placed *Genesis A* early, and with
Beowulf.[19] His argument for "early" does not convince
but his establishment of the extensive common vocabulary of the two poems places them together. Klaeber
showed the relationship of the syntax of the two poems
and particularly their common relationship to certain features of the Vulgate, which implies the priority
of *Genesis A*.[20] Any dating of *Genesis A* must be on
a sliding scale, but *Genesis A* and *Beowulf* must slide
together. Any date in the eighth century seems reasonable, and there are no reasons against the old assignment of the poem to Bede's Northumbria, though a
Mercian or south-western home is also possible.[21]

[19] "Date and Dialect," 286-89.
[20] "Die ältere Genesis und der Beowulf," *Englische
Studien* 42 (1910), 321-38, see below, pp. 94 ff.
[21] On the traditional dating of GN and BW see Klaeber,
Beowulf and the Fight at Finnsburg (3rd ed., Boston,
1950), pp. cvii-cx.

III. The Poem

A. Literary Treatments of *Genesis A*[1]

The proper study of *Genesis A* only became possible after Eduard Sievers had made the fundamental
discovery that lines 235-851 were an interpolation
of a West-Saxonized version of an Old Saxon poem,
quite distinct in origin from the rest.[2] Sievers was
not concerned with *Genesis A* as such, but assumed
its unity of origin and its literary inferiority to
B. After this discovery the first scholarly examin-
ations of *Genesis A* focussed on the question of sources. Adolf Ebert[3] surveyed the poem and came to the
conclusion that it was an intelligent adaptation of
the Vulgate into culturally familiar terms by one
poet who knew the Bible well. The only evidence of
influences upon the "additional material" in the
poem are a few parallels with Christian Latin poetry.
A few years later Erwin Hönncher took up the same
question more systematically.[4] A section-by-section
analysis showed outside influence only on the opening
"hexameral" part (lines 1-111), predominantly that
of Gregory the Great on the Fall of the Angels. Hönncher rejected Ebert's hypothesis that the poet used
Avitus or any other Latin-Christian poetry. Hönncher
defended the poem against Sievers' judgement of artis-
tic inferiority, noting the poet's tendency to get
away from "dry paraphrase" at every opportunity.[5] In
the Abrahamic parts of the poem especially, the poet

---

[1] For an excellent brief description of *Genesis A*
see Geoffrey Shepherd, "Scriptural Poetry," in *Con-
tinuations and Beginnings*, ed. E. G. Stanley (London,
1966), 1-36, esp. 24-30; a brief review of modern
criticism of *Genesis A* is given by Stanley B. Greenfield, *A Critical History of Old English Literature*
(New York, 1968), Ch. VIII, esp. pp. 147-50.
[2] Sievers' discovery is based on an analysis of the
text of 235-851 printed with parallel passages from
the *Heliand*, in *Der Heliand und die angelsächsische
Genesis* (Halle, 1875).
[3] "Zur angelsächsischen Genesis," *Anglia* 5 (1882),
124-33.
[4] "Über die Quellen der angelsächsische Genesis,"
Anglia 8 (1885), 41-84.
[5] *Ibid.*, 56.

only treats the "heroic" aspects of the story, creating what might be called an *Abrahamslied*.[6] Ebert and
Hönncher take for granted the unity of authorship of
all but *Genesis B*; this question was taken up directly
by Heinze[7] and Graz[8], who confirm the unity on linguistic and metrical grounds.

When the accretion theory of composition of old
Germanic poems was in vogue, *Genesis A* naturally became a target of this approach.[9] Hugo Balg attempted
to prove that the Caedmonian poems *Genesis*, *Exodus* and
Daniel were the work of at least seven poets.[10] Hans
Jovy, on the basis of very selective verbal parallels
and their distribution, believed that the genealogies
were by a later redactor who welded together an originally episodic poem.[11] The most elaborate and precise
attempt to define the question of authorship and unity
was among the last work of the great Sievers.[12] Contra-
dicting his own previously held view of the unity of *A*,
he published in 1929 a new dissection based on his
Schallanalyse, the technique of linguistic analysis
that attempted to go beyond the MS forms to distinguish the personal "voices" of the original poets
themselves. Sievers thought he discerned in the
earlier part of the poem before *Genesis B*, the work
of two poets, a Kentishman and a Northumbrian (the
latter being Caedmon himself) and in the later parts
no fewer than eight distinct ninth-century Saxon
poets, the whole being a cooperative monastic labor
similar to the OHG *Tatian* and the Weiner *Genesis*.
The poem achieved its present relative uniformity
through the work of an Alfredian redactor who worked
over the previously existing poems, adding comment,

---

[6] Hönncher, "Quellen," 66.
[7] Alfred Heinze, *Zur altenglischen Genesis* (Berlin,
1889).
[8] Friedrich Graz, *Die Metrik der sog. Cædmonschen
Dichtungen mid Berücksichtigung der Verfasserfrage*
(Weimar, 1894).
[9] A succinct account of *Liedertheorie* is given by
Fr. Klaeber, ed., *Beowulf and the Fight at Finnsburg*
(3d ed., Boston, 1950), cii-cvii.
[10] *Der Dichter Caedmon und seine Werke* (Bonn, 1882).
[11] "Untersuchungen zur altenglischen Genesis-dichtung,"
Bonner Beiträge 5 (1900), 1-32. Although his contri-
bution to the *Verfasserfrage* appears worthless, Jovy's
article contains valuable textual notes.
[12] "Caedmon und Genesis," in *Britannica, Max Förster
zum 60. Geburtstage* (Leipzig, 1929), 57-84.

improving details of translation of the Vulgate and
in general manifesting certain "antiquarian" inter-
ests.[13]

Apart from questions of sources and authorship,
criticism of *Genesis A* has habitually fastened on the
relationship—we can almost say on the relative proportions—of "Christian" to "Germanic" in the poem,
with opinions ranging from those who see it as
a rather uninteresting example of faithful "Cloister-
work" of a relatively well-educated man carrying out
a serious educational purpose,[14] to those who see
him as a deliberate or unconscious "transformer" of
the Bible into Germanic and heroic terms.[15] In a
brief but sensitive treatment along the latter lines,
J. M. Evans notes the essential difference between
Genesis A and other Old English biblical poetry on
the one hand and Latin biblical poetry on the other.[16]
The English poetry has an heroic substratum which
transforms the poetry at every level. The result of
the combination of heroic style and scriptural story
was two-fold: old words such as *dom*, *wyrd*, *lof*, etc.
acquired new resonance as Latin technical meanings
became attracted to them, and yet the subtler aspects
of Christian teaching were generally coarsened and
simplified.[17] F. L. Utley, while making useful con-
tributions to the understanding of the poet's debt
to a tradition of exegesis, emphasizes the folkloris-
tic elements, as, for example, God's "signing" of
the Ark *agenum spedum*, 1365 f., translated "he blessed
the ark with his own luck," and explained as a manifestation of the pre-Christian concept of *mana* or

---

[13] See Robert J. Menner, "The Date and Dialect of
Genesis A 852-2936," *Anglia* 70 (1951), 285-94, who
summarizes "Caedmon und Genesis" and effectively ex-
plodes its arguments.
[14] E.g., Henry Bradley, "The 'Cædmonian' Genesis,"
*Essays and Studies by Members of the English Associa-
tion* 6 (1920), 7-29.
[15] E.g., Arthur S. Skemp, "The Transformation of Scriptural Story, Motive and Conception in Anglo-Saxon
Poetry," *Modern Philology* 4 (1907), 423-70; so crude
as to be hardly worth mentioning is C. C. Ferrell, *Teutonic Antiquities in the Anglo-Saxon Genesis* (Halle,
1893).
[16] *Paradise Lost and the Genesis Tradition* (Oxford,
1968), 145-48.
[17] For an example of what Evans considers such a "coars-
ening," see Commentary, 86b-91.

spirit-power.[18] Very recently, Bennett Brockman has
reasserted the essentially heroic cast of *Genesis A*
in an examination of the Cain and Abel episode.[19] He
finds the poet chiefly interested in the situation
of Cain as an heroic exile figure, subject to certain
death because of his unprotected status. Brockmann
acknowledges that in places the poet may have intended to show something of the traditional exegetical framework that invested the episode in learned
commentaries, but essentially the appeal is always
to the familiar social situation, the biblical story
made over into a contemporary legal situation.[20]
        The poem has been specifically examined in the
light of the oral-formulaic theory several times.
George Clark considered the type-scene of "The Traveler Recognizing his Goal" and showed how traditional ways of handling the theme provided the poet
with materials for the expansion of the simple Vulgate account of Abraham's journey to Sodom (2399-
2406a) and his approach to Egypt (1816b-22a) into
something more elaborately fitting for the style of
poetry.[21] Robert P. Creed gathered parallel phrases
from other poems and on this basis demonstrated the
formulaic basis of the Sacrifice of Isaac episode.[22]
He compares the same story in *Exodus* 397-446 and finds
the *Genesis A* version much more sophisticated in its

[18] Francis Lee Utley, "The Flood Narrative in the Junius Manuscript and in Baltic Literature," in *Studies in
Old English Literature in Honor of Arthur Gilchrist
Brodeur*, ed. Stanley B. Greenfield (Eugene, Ore.,
1963), 213.
[19] " 'Heroic' and 'Christian' in *Genesis A*: The Evidence
of the Cain and Abel Episode," *Modern Language Quarterly*
35 (1974), 115-128.
[20] My own reaction to this episode is that the poet
makes remarkably little of the opportunity to develop
the exile theme offered by the text; see Commentary
1038b-1039.
[21] "The Traveler Recognizes his Goal: A Theme in
Anglo-Saxon Poetry," *JEGP* 64 (1965) 645-59. Clark
notes that the assignment of the Sacrifice of Isaac
to the morning-time is formulaic (GN 2875b-77a), in
contrast to the Vulgate, which mentions no time and
Juvencus, who places the event at the Christologically
significant *noon* (Clark, pp. 650-52).
[22] "The Art of the Singer: Three Old English Tellings
of the Offering of Isaac," in *Old English Poetry: Fifteen Essays* (Providence, 1967), 69-92.

awareness of exegetical implication and narratively
effective in its use of formulas; the poet uses his
traditional formulaic technique to extract the max-
imum drama from the episode. In fact, while much
of the poem is relatively flat, the Isaac episode is
its high point, an achieved effect of climax, and it
is this, rather than any exegetical rationale, which
gives us the sense that the poem does not break off
at this point, but finishes.

It will be obvious to the reader that the critical fortunes of *Genesis A* have closely followed the
main lines of the criticism of Old English literature
in general over the last century. The poem's individual form, features and subject matter have been
of less concern than those general attributes which
it shares with most other, especially earlier, Old
English poetry. The specifically biblical form and
content of the poem have in most of these studies
been considered only incidentally. Therefore, the
most important study of this poem has been that work
which has attempted to address itself to the essential facts of this poem, separating it from all
others and placing it in an appropriate intellectual
setting. That work is Bernard F. Huppé's lengthy
analysis in his ground-breaking book, *Doctrine and
Poetry*.[23] Huppé's basic contention is that the poem
is steeped in the exegetical techniques and presup-
positions of allegorical biblical commentary in the
"Augustinian" tradition. It is not a matter of small
points of detail here and there, or of "borrowings",
but forms the deepest layer of the poet's thought,
and is the very bones of the poem.[24] Since Huppé
wrote, no critic of *Genesis A* has been able to ig-
nore the influence of traditional exegesis. Yet
while many of its detailed points are fine, and its
general approach unqualifiedly right, Huppé's book

[23] *Doctrine and Poetry: Augustine's Influence on Old
English Poetry* (New York, 1959). Chapter V, 131-216,
is an analysis of *Genesis A*.
[24] Occasional points of agreement between the poem and
traditional exegesis had been noted before, e.g.,
Samuel Moore, "The Old English 'Genesis,' lines 1145
and 1446-48," *Modern Language Review* 6 (1911), 199-202
[on apocryphal Seth legends and Noe's raven]; Oliver
F. Emerson, "Legends of Cain, especially in Old and
Middle English," *PMLA* 21 (1906), 831-929; S. J. Crawford, "The Caedmon Poems," *Anglia* 49 (1929), 279-84
[on the sources of the hexameral opening].

is flawed by a flat assumption of ideational unity
that becomes the basis of analysis, without any
clear sense that unity must arise out of the text of
the poem. The assumption is clearly stated though
put as a question: "In the light of Augustinian
theory of literature may the poem *Genesis* be shown
to have a unifying theme which unites all parts of
the poem and to which the interpolated portion [*Genesis B*] is also appropriate?"[25] The last phrase reveals the reverse logic of much of the argument.
Huppé finds that the opening theme of praise, imitated from the Preface to the Canon of the Mass, is
the unifying factor throughout the poem, along with
the idea of the growth of the Two Cities, an idea
consciously developed to bring out the theme of those
who praise and those who fail to praise God. *Genesis
A* is not merely an English poetic version of Genesis
for a rude audience, but a programmatic poem intended
to bring out the hidden spiritual meanings inherent
in the text.[26] In itself the assumption is promising,
but too easily and simply carried forward as a basis
for all critical operations by Huppé, leading to conclusions that often do not arise out of the text or
even go against it.[27] Perhaps in 1959 an assumption
of unity seemed a necessary critical starting-point.
Nevertheless, it is supererogatory to criticize Huppé
at this point. The flaws of his book are obvious,
his influence undeniable: anyone now who writes on
the Old English scriptural poetry at once criticizes
his method and pays homage to his idea.

Recent work that has been most valuable has
placed *Genesis A* squarely in a biblical tradition,
taken account of its traditional poetic method, and
dealt in some depth with individual features and
episodes. For the poem is not made out of a single
overriding idea, but consists of many small details

[25] *Doctrine and Poetry*, p. 133.
[26] "*Genesis A* has a theme wrested out of the very
structure of Genesis, out of the patristic understanding of the basic prophetic meaning of the first book
of the Bible. In this sense, *Genesis A* stands at the
beginning of the great medieval literature that, with
the symbolic meaning of the Bible always at the center
of consciousness, was to extend the imagination beyond
the structural limitations of biblical commentary in
such works of culmination as the *Divine Comedy* and
Piers Plowman" (*Ibid.*, p. 209).
[27] For an example, see my note 42, below.

brought together by the needs of the source-text and
the knowledge and interest of the poet. I will mention three recent approaches which have borne fruit.
Fred C. Robinson has shown the rich associations the
biblical names held for the poet and the intricate
nature of his learning as he turns the Latin onomas-
ticon into Old English verse.[28] Milton McC. Gatch has
shown by an art-historical approach to Noah's raven
the richness and depth of one tradition on which the
poem drew.[29] Roberta Frank[30] has examined the deliberate etymological word-play ("paronomasia") and
demonstrates how at a number of places the idea of
God as *weard* concatenates with God as *word*, so that,
e.g., the opening is much more richly suggestive than
the literal translation could suggest:

> Us is riht micel   ðæt we rodera *weard*
>   *wereda* wuldorcining,   *wordum* herigen...

This particular group of morphologically similar forms
(*w-r-d*) shows up in clusters at several critical
places, leading to the conclusion, "The biblical
exegete states [his] doctrine directly; the Old English poet prefers to suggest it through artful and
subtle sound congruences."[31] It may be said that her
conclusion mirrors in small the technique of the
poet at all levels.

B. Biblical Poetry

The problem which *Genesis A* presents, a sacred
subject rendered into what was recently "pagan" verse
form, goes to the very core of Christian poetry. From
its beginnings with Juvencus (third century) to its
culmination with Milton, the chief impulse of Chris-

---

[28] "The Significance of Names in Old English Literature," *Anglia* 86 (1968), 14-58 (see Commentary, 1144b-45).
[29] "Noah's Raven in Genesis A and the Illustrated
Old English Hexateuch," *Gesta* 14.2 (1975), 3-15.
Gatch shows that the poet knew the tradition of the
raven perching on dead corpses instead of returning
to the ark, but because the poet does not mention them
explicitly, will not allow that he knew the various
moral applications given to the raven (see Commentary,
1438b-1448, 1447) and even goes so far as to return
to something like the old emendation of *se feond(e)*.
[30] "Some Uses of Paronomasia in Old English Scriptural
Verse," *Speculum* 47 (1972), 207-226.
[31] *Ibid.*, 212-13.

tian poetry was "Virgilian" in form and scope, secular in language and biblico-liturgical in content. The
classical forms and rules existed in a highly developed state and were ready for exploitation when Christian rhetoric reached the stage where verse expression became necessary. Classical technique provided
ready-made means for molding sacred subject matter.
Recurrent poetic Gospels and Creations were not
comparable to the sterile reduplication of classical
subject-matter in late epic, for the myth of Calvary
did not exist on the same level and was not judged
by the same standards as the myth of Troy. Christian
poetry was propagandistic, ever-new by its message,
spreading the good news throughout the books of the
world. It replaced the worldly lies of the old poets
with the most urgent truth, while taking on the prestige of classical poetry and the official functions
of imperial panegyric. Classical pagan poetry was
an adumbration of true poetry, providing only the outer
form. To rehabilitate Virgil as a Christian *poeta
vates* was the natural charge of Christian poets; re-
shaping the language of the author of the Forth Eclogue
proved a relatively easy task. The cento was the obvious means. In a sense, all biblical poetry grows
out of cento. Proba sings that by redirecting and
rearranging Virgil's language she will show how the
poet has already sung of the deeds of Christ. At
this moment, as Max Wehrli says, "the heathen *poeta
vates*, the poet as seer or veiled theologue, as
in the 'allegories' of Homer, becomes a Christian
singer, and it is now the Holy Ghost who is called
upon as the inspirer of wisdom poetry."[32]

Genesis is not only the subject, but the model
for sacred poetry. The spirit which informed everything "in the beginning" informs song. The creation
the Christian poet so often sings of is his pattern
for poetry. Creation as book, and Bible as world
provide a new life-giving goal to poetry: the biblical poem is an exalted part of God's scheme of creation and salvation, an adjunct to the Bible, and a
means of discovery of God's plan. A purely philological concept: "Scripture into poetry" is thus com-
plemented by its mystical corollary: "poetry into
Scripture." Even as he reforms biblical matter into

---

[32] "Sacra Poesis: Bibelepik als europäische Tradition,"
in *Die Wissenschaft von deutscher Sprache and Dichtung
. . . Festschrift für Friedrich Maurer* ed. S. Guten-
brunner et al. (Stuttgart, 1963), 268.

correct modes of classical verse, the poet is being
informed by biblical pattern and biblical wisdom—
by the spirit—and is informing his poem by it. It
is not the skill of the poet, but the excellence of
the matter which gives worth to poetry.

This concept is widened, deepened and explicated
in monastic culture. Reforming the Bible into verse
becomes a systematized discipline. As Latin becomes
more remote from the spoken language the utility of
composing Latin biblical verses subtly changes. Now,
as well as prophecy, the cultivation of scriptural
poetry can be understood as "teacher" to the misdirec-
ted and "snare" to the lazy. The functional aspect
of scriptural poetry is emphasized even more when the
vernacular languages come into play in England and
Germany, giving rise to a sacred poetic using the
techniques of the old secular, heroic song, on the
analogy of the rise of biblical poetry in Latin. At
the same time, poetry into Scripture becomes a moti-
vating force in the monastic life of the spirit, of
which the inspired career of Caedmon is not an isolated
case, but the most famous and typical example.[33] The
lesson to be drawn from Bede's story of Caedmon is
that poetry is an angelic, sacred gift. Poetic composition is typologically linked to creation and conversion, for the poetic act is simultaneously discovery of self, world and God.

The monastic act of composition is of the same
order as the monastic act of reading. Both are based
on the Bible, meditative, concerned with spiritual
association and recovery.[34] They are alike in uniting
philology and mystery.[34] The art of grammar is intellectual, human, rulebound and includes the category
"Scripture into poetry." But the understanding of
which philology is a means is an inspired inner activity, *concordia cordis*, the multiplying of meanings
through biblical reminiscence, spiritual nourishment
from sacred words. The difference between inspired
reading and inspired composition is only in the direction of the flow of words.

The two sides of the poetic act, literal and

---

[33] Geoffrey Shepherd, "The Prophetic Caedmon," *Review
of English Studies* n.s. 5 (1954), 113-22 gives other
instances of the inspired monastic singer in English
and Irish tradition.
[34] See Jean Leclerq, *The Love of Learning and the Desire for God: A Study of Monastic Culture*, tr. Cath-
arine Misrahi (New York, 1961), 99-100.

spiritual, are graphically portrayed in the so-called
Prefaces to the Old Saxon *Heliand*.[35]   The prose "Praefatio" says that Louis the Pious comissioned "a certain man of Saxon race, who among them was held to
be no mean poet, to try to translate the Old and New
Testaments into German poetry, so that the sacred
text might be revealed not only to the learned, but
also to the unlearned." This account implies the
faithful, dutiful, literal side of vernacular poetic
activity, carried out as a practical educational and
missionary task. This same prose text contains,
either as amplification or by interpolation, a brief
account of the inspired poet who in a dream is told
to sing and who receives the power to obey from above.
This story, obviously derived from Bede's miracle
of Caedmon, demonstrates the strength, coherence and
wide dispersion of the Caedmonian tradition of the
inspired vernacular poet. The "Praefatio" shows us
the professional courtly poet of the old tradition,
whose technique can produce verses at the command of
a royal patron, transformed into the divine poet, who
sings because of a typologically parallel new command
enlivening his technique.

[35] The German scholar Flacius Illyricus in his *Cata-
logus Testium Veritatis* (Strasburg-in-Alsace and Basel,
1562), 93-94, printed from an unknown source two Latin
pieces, one in prose, the "Praefatio in librum anti-
quum lingua Saxonica conscriptum," the other in verse,
"Versus de poeta interpreti huius codicis," purporting
to explain the origin of some vernacular biblical poetry, which Flacius did not print or identify further.
The pieces are now generally associated with the Old
Saxon *Heliand*: the authenticity and early date of at
least the prose piece is not generally doubted. For
a full discussion and translation of these texts, see
Francis P. Magoun, Jr., "The *Praefatio* and *Versus* Associated with some Old Saxon Biblical Poems," in *Medieval Studies in Honor of J. D. M. Ford*, ed. U. T.
Holmes, Jr., and J. Denomy (Cambridge, Mass., 1948),
107-36; skepticism about the genuineness of these pieces has recently been revived by Theodore Anderson,
"The Caedmon Fiction in the *Heliand* Preface," *PMLA* 89
(1974), 278-84. The Caedmon story itself, too famous
to recount here, is found in Bede's *Ecclesiastical
History of the English Peoples*, ed. Bertram Colgrave
and R. A. B. Mynors (Oxford, 1969), 414-21 (iv. 24);
for discussion, see C. L. Wrenn, "The Poetry of Caedmon," *Proceedings of the British Academy* 32 (1946),
277-95.

Biblical poetry is rich in contradictions. The
clash of logic and structure, of outer technique and
inner inspiration, of text and formula, these are
inherent in the genre and must not be smoothed over.
Philology as inspiration; letter as spirit; the old
song as the new; the literal mode of epic as the
vehicle of multi-leveled allegorical modes of Scripture; the entertainments in the tongues of heathens
as the glorifications of the life of Christ—for a
monastic audience the contemplation of such oppositions
presented not perplexities but fruitful analogies to
their own conversion, and to the Word made flesh.
Bede, a poet in both Latin and English, revels in
the contradictions apparent in the activity of the
Christian *vates*. The Bible itself has taught him
poetry, but the pagans have taught him its specific
forms: "elegiaco metro composuimus, et imitari morem
sacrae scripturae." His elegiacs, under heavy pressure from liturgical content, are "converted" to
their sacred function quite self-consciously:

Alma Deus Trinitas, quae saecula cuncta gubernas,
    Adnue iam coeptis, alma Deus Trinitas.
Bella Maro resonet; nos pacis dona canamus,
    Munera nos Christi, bella Maro resonet.
Carmina casta mihi, fedae non raptus Helenae;
    Luxus erit lubricis, carmina casta mihi.
Dona superna loquar, miserae non proelia Troiae;
    Terra quibus gaudet, dona superna loquar. [36]

The Bible gave men the gift of poetry and
showed them all its possibilities. Imitation of epic,
founded on spiritual reading and meditation, is
merely fulfilling a divine plan laid down at Creation.
Men make poetry in the languages and modes they know,
but the spirit is the same; God is the God of all
languages and it is only piety which determines the
rank of any human utterance. With such a spirit Otfrid sends forth his versified life of Christ: "It
is . . . fitting that in whatever manner, either in
corrupt or perfect art, the human race should praise
the Author of all things, Who gave them the plectrum
of the tongue to sound among themselves the word of
His Praise; Who seeks in us not the adulation of po-
lished words but a devout mood of meditation and the
accumulation of works by pious toil, not empty lip-
service." [37]

[36] Bede, *Eccel. Hist.*, iv. 20 (ed. cit., 396-98).
[37] Otfrid, *Ad Liutbertum*, tr. F. P. Magoun, Jr.,
PMLA 58 (1943), 888.

C. *Genesis A* and the Biblical Tradition

In Old English a great part of the extant poetry may be termed "biblical," in Old Saxon all. Its quality ranges from the arid literalism of *The Paris Psalter* to the splendors of *The Dream of the Rood*. Nevertheless, it may be divided into two broad categories, according to its response to Scripture. In the one group are those poems which take their narrative form and meaning from a biblical text which is closely followed and which have as their aim a paraphrase, or analogical imitation of the text. *Genesis A, Daniel* and the *Heliand* are examples of this type having epic form, while many others, such as the Exeter *Lord's Prayer*, have more modest form and scope. In the other group are those poems which use a biblical text or episode as the formal means for presenting a specific doctrine of the Church which does not explicitly appear in the original text. For example, *Judith* follows a text which in the original is a narrative compendium of Old Testament liturgy and law meant for the hellenized Jews of the diaspora. Its outlook is rigidly Pharisaical. But the Old English poem ignores this aspect of the original and reforms the narrative so that a specific Christian doctrine of fortitude and temperance emerges— the heroine of the Hebrews becomes a Christian saint. *Genesis B* is also of this second type, the story of the Fall providing the occasion for an intensive examination of the nature of the will and the process of sinning.[38]

In both types of poem a three-fold process is taking place, in varying proportions: a text is being followed or imitated, however freely; an exegetical attitude towards that text is being defined, however modestly or unconsciously; and a system of traditional formulaic equivalents is being utilized as the technical means for giving form and expression to the words, concepts and actions thought to be intrinsic to the original. The better of these poets are attempting to create verbal structures which will elicit by familiar means (formulaic poetry) spiritual or doctrinal responses deemed similar to those which the sacred texts are supposed to elicit from trained audiences.

[38] For a survey of O.E. scriptural poetry, see Geoffrey Shepherd, *Scriptural Poetry* (cited, note 1, above).

While in some ways *Genesis A* is a relatively
simple poem, yet it has behind it and informing it
a vast complex of traditional doctrinal and exegetical ideas. Like the text it follows, it is constructed
linearly, but at every point takes account of, or at
least reflects the doctrines and topics that had attached themselves to the text of Genesis. Its procedure is not to divide Scripture into episodes which
are then treated freely as narrative (the method of
most German and Middle English biblical poems) or to
unify the material by foregrounding certain themes or
narrative elements (as does *Genesis B*), but to deal
philologically with each word, phrase and sentence of
the text as it appears: selecting, admitting, omitting
and changing material on a spontaneous, continuing *ad
hoc* basis, seamlessly weaving into the translation itself such explanatory material as was required to
make the literal meaning of the text clear, sound and
complete according to the canons of Genesis-exegesis
that prevailed in the West between Augustine and An-
selm.

To the biblical scholar or poet of the patristic or early medieval periods, traditionally derived
and communally accepted increments of apocryphal,
historical and interpretive material had come to be
considered part of the literal text itself, e.g., the
killing of Cain by Lamech, the interpretation of the
"sons of God" as the descendants of Seth, the fate of
Enoch, etc. Furthermore, the spiritual meaning of
the text, the complex and gradually-growing, ever-
shifting mass of "pious meditations or religious
teaching for which the text is used merely as a convenient starting-point,"[39] was the immediate object
of biblical understanding. Yet to the practical
observer, the untrained eye, the spiritual meanings
were outside of, or in medieval terms, hidden within
the literal text, showing themselves only to those
educated in the traditions and techiques of biblical
exegesis. Therefore, while the poet of *Genesis A*
is primarily interested in establishing the literal
sense according to the broad medieval understanding
of that term, he sees it as his task to bring to that
text, to interpolate into it, such traditional narrative and explanatory material as was thought necessary to complete and clarify the literal meaning of
the text, and to handle all of his material in such

---

[39] Beryl Smalley, *The Study of the Bible in the Middle Ages* (2d ed., Oxford, 1952), 2.

a way as to suggest or allow the main outlines of
extra-literal interpretations that were universally
felt to be the soul of divine reading. Such additions
were not inventions of the poet, nor were they merely
adjuncts of his naturally expansive and explanatory
poetic style, but derived from a long-standing tradition of Genesis exegesis.

    In representing and interpreting a literal text,
the poet was bound by his point of view to follow it no
matter how far that literal text might take him, which
from our point of view is often well outside the
strict letter of the text. As his task also included
suggesting the essential established non-literal sig-
nifications of the literal meaning, he was led even
further from the letter, lest slavishness reduce
poetry to an empty husk of words. When, for example,
the biblically-trained reader (and the technique of
biblical allegory is equally a technique of reading as
of writing) considered the words: "Coepitque Noe vir
agricola exercere terram, et plantavit vineam" (9.20),
the "bare text" which we see was for him suffused with
rich but disciplined suggestions. Claudius of Turin
reads this place and remembers the words of Christ in
the garden, "Pater mi, si possibile est, transeat a
me calix iste" (Matt. 26.39) and thinks of the Passion.[40] Bede, too, remembers the Passion as he reads
of Noah, but the words concord with other places for
him, and the resonances transform the events: Noah's
planting figures the Lord's establishment of the
Synagogue among the Jews—"vineam ex Egypto transtu-
listi" (Ps. 79.9)—and the parable of the vineyard
(Matt. 21) charges the Old Testament passage with prophetic insight.[41] To merely see a man planting out
vines, to believe in Moses as a reporter and not in
Christ as the inspirer, not to read *in Christo*, is
to see blindly. The poet's job is to open the passage
not only to the event, but to the true events behind
it. When he represents this place, his technique is
not to impose a discursive spiritual interpretation
upon it, but to allow for the fact that there inevitably is one in the mind of the reader or hearer; he
leaves suggestive interstices of meaning, which may be
filled with innumerable associations as the passage

[40] *Commentariorum in Genesim,* PL. 50, 935B [attributed
to Eucherius of Lyon].
[41] *In Genesin*, ed. Ch. W. Jones, CCSL 118A (Turnhout,
1967), 136.

is recited or read, so that hearing of Noah is thinking
of Christ:
```
        ÐA Noe ongan    niwan stefne
        mid hleomagum    ham staðelian
        and to eorðan him    ætes tilian,
        won and worhte,    wingeard sette,
        seow sæda fela,    sohte georne
        þa him wlitebeorhte    wæstmas brohte,
        geartorhte gife,    grene folde.
                                  (1555-61)
```
These *gife*, glorious and bearing fruit, legitimately
open up to all that the reader sees, so long as they
bear Christian fruit in the mind. In a similar way,
when Adam and Eve hide themselves from God's approach,
the wording suggests their impending judgement, and
the final judgement (860-63). Unfortunately, this
technique of reading and composing seems like a kind
of day-dreaming to the modern mind, repugnant to any
well-disciplined literary instincts. It is this
difference in reading technique which, more than any
other single factor, makes it difficult to approach
and understand Old English biblical poetry on its own
terms.[42]

[42] The mistake to which common-sense is most prone
is the minimization or elimination altogether of
spiritual content once felt behind a literal text.
However, as moderns, lacking a real feeling for the
mode of thought of biblical poetry, we cannot approach
these texts unaided by outside documents to supply
spritual content. Free association by "spiritualizing" critics tends to lead to gross departures from
the text and serves little critical function. The
examples afforded by Huppé in *Doctrine and Poetry* are
egregious. E.g., pp. 183 f., in taking a spiritual approach
to the Tower of Babel episode, he interprets GN 1649-
51, which expands the biblical statement "They fared
from the east" to include possessions, to mean that
the poet intentionally is emphasizing "the attention
of the evil ones to worldly goods, which is the implicit cause for their 'retreat from the light.'" He
cites for this view Chrysostom, calling that the "standard" interpretation. But there is no evidence that
the poet knew much about Eastern exegetical topics.
Rather, the migration with possessions is a well-established formulaic theme in the poem, extrapolated
from other biblical occurrences (see Intro., pp. 81-
83). What is more, in this search for developed
exegesis in the poem, Huppé has overlooked the obvious

Yet for all this, it must be emphasized that
while the spiritual meaning was all-important in this
type of poetry, at least Old Testament poetry, the
specific approach of *Genesis A* is predominantly literal, though in the broad sense outlined above. Those
biblical poems which by their style and form of address suggest the most "popular" audience and the
most openly didactic purpose (e.g., *Genesis B, Judith*
--their lateness is probably a factor) are also the
ones which appear the most complex and explicit doctrinally. It was a scholarly, special task to understand the literal text. While it was fundamental
that a basic grasp of the literal meaning must
underlie any allegorical understanding,[43] it was
not often thought fitting that the whole literal
sense should be made directly available to the uninitiated. The teacher ruminated and digested
the unpalatable perplexities of the text and com-
municated only the nourishment, the spiritual part.
The characteristic sermon technique was to pass as
quickly as possible from the text to its interpretation. Augustine had taught that not all of Genesis could be taken in its literal sense, that some
things lead to blasphemy or illicit behavior if
taken in their simple sense by the uninitiated be-
liever. In these cases the faith was revealed only
through figures and mysteries which needed to be
explained.[44] The poet takes the prudent course,
steering clear of extreme difficulties by means of
omission or broad re-interpretations. In places
profound mysteries beyond human comprehension con-
descend to human sense by being clothed in familiar
spatial and temporal concepts[45] just as the Lord

---

element that is there--foregrounded precisely because
it is the one element not part of the formulaic theme
being used--the pride of the builders (cf. GN 1617b-
77a). The Latin commentators constantly repeated this
topic: the followers of Nimrod were "giants" of pride,
the pride which lead to the confusion of tongues (cf.
Isidore, *Quaestiones de Veteri et Nouo Testamento*, PL.
83, 237-38).
[43] "Prius historiae fundamenta ponenda sunt, ut aptius
allegoriae culmen priori structurae superponatur"
(Alcuin, *Interrogationes et responsiones in Genesin,*
PL. 100, 559A).
[44] *De Genesi contra Manichaeos*, PL. 34, 223.
[45] Augustine, *De Genesi ad litteram imperfectus liber*,
PL. 34, 233.

appeared to Abraham in the form of three men. The
poet must make each place in his poem speak to the
spiritual well-being of his audience. He never for-
gets that Genesis is the most profound and "philo-
sophical," as well as the most diverse, of the historical books of the Old Testament.

     To make a literal text that deals with the ac-
tual words of Scripture and yet suggests its inner
meanings is to aim high. Augustine recognized that
"the true goal of the exegete is to understand the
whole narration of Scriptures in a literal and not
a figurative sense, even though this may remain a
goal not everywhere attainable. . . ."[46] If much of
Genesis A seems exegetical in intent, that is simply
a result of the poet's inevitable mental apparatus.
Explanations which seems so obscurely related to the
text or outside it altogether were part of his task
of making the textual meaning clear to the intended
audience, according to its knowledge, preparation,
needs and expectations, not evidence of any especially
"spiritual" approach. What sets the poet apart is
his ability to see Genesis *as a text*, as a fixed form
of words which must be reproduced as entirely as possible (*Daniel* does not conceive of the text as a whole
and the *Exodus*-poet cannot be said to be dealing with
the words of his source at all). Only a few learned
men ever achieved the level of seeing the Bible this
way. The poet's object is to change the mysterious
text into the only formal discourse available in the
vernacular, dealing with the text as such, giving
it to an audience which could never have achieved it
in other ways. That he sees through the eyes of his
own age is the least remarkable element of this per-
formance. That the extra-literal element is so inob-
trusive is evidence of the intensity of his contemplation and the discipline of his art. No other
extant Old English biblical poem can match it in this
respect, for all others succumb to fatuous literal-
ness, hardly more than a poetic gloss (*Paris Psalter*),
select (*Daniel, Genesis B, Judith*), or give way to
expressive complexity that baffles all sense of the
literal text (*Exodus*). In comparison with these,
Genesis A gives the impression of classical restraint
and clarity of purpose.

     In one sense *Genesis A* is, as a once often-ap-
plied term of abuse had it, a *blosse Paraphrasis*; but

---

[46] Charles S. Singleton, *Dante Studies 2: Journey to
Beatrice* (Cambridge, Mass., 1958), 174.

this term can only be understood properly if we accord "paraphrase" the dignity and beauty it connoted
in the early Middle Ages, when applied to a reworking
of Scripture. In the world of the poet, paraphrase
was the highest peak which scholarship and poetry
working together could attain. Milton reserves it
for the cardinal Book VII of *Paradise Lost. Genesis
A* is the result of the interaction of the text with
a vast body of pre-existing material; the way it is
worked into a unified narrative reflects the living
attitude toward Genesis of the learned thought of the
post-patristic era. It is impossible to speak of
"sources" in any narrow sense. The Vulgate text is
the only antecedent that can be traced with any as-
surance, and its direct working can be demonstrated
in nearly every line of the poem. Nevertheless,
Genesis A is made up out of a mass of traditional
notions held in a state of mental suspension by a
certain learned poet and precipitated into form by
the process of composition. The poet would have
understood that ultimately his material came from
many books, but he certainly did not have to refer
to books in particular instances in order to include
points of information or exegesis.[47] He had only one
book open before him as he worked. His problem was
not one of gathering information—it was no doubt
rooted in his mind—but expressing familiar Latin
words and ideas in a medium alien to them. His "learning" was an inevitable adjunct to the text as he understood it, not part of a conscious program of display
or complication, or poetic re-formation of his Vulgate source.

The poet's area of original activity is bounded
by his material and his technique. Any transformation of the original that takes place as a result
of his art is at the level of stylistic detail, and
even this is largely beyond the poet's area of individual innovation. As far as one can tell from the
poem itself, the poet intended that the larger matters

---

[47] See Commentary 227b; contrast what may be interpreted as the deliberately scholarly method of Cynewulf
(clad in heroic garb): *Ic pysne sang / siðgeomor fand
// on seocum sefan, / samnode wide . . .* (FA 1-2). On
the nature of "sources" and "influence" in early medieval biblical scholarship, see M. L. W. Laistner,
"Some Early Medieval Commentaries on the Old Testament," in *The Intellectual Heritage of the Early Middle Ages*, ed. Chester G. Starr (Ithaca, 1957), 181-83.

of form, structure, meaning, those issues that interest modern criticism the most, are outside the
discussion for the most part, or may be discussed only
in relation to the Vulgate, its set meanings and its
ultimate sources. The content is transmitted by
an intermediate text which is already of well-deter-
mined meaning now reproduced in a new medium having
its own dynamics. The poet is presiding, modulating,
guaranteeing the authenticity of the message, but
is not an originator. In any biblical poem, by a
universal convention, God, not the poet, is the author. Any understanding of *Genesis A* as poetry is
therefore dependent on an understanding of the poet's
concept of the Bible and Genesis and biblical wisdom.
We cannot read *Genesis A* merely in its own right—
to do it justice we must read it as "Genesis," a
measured, analogical response to the holy text as it
was traditionally understood. The only means of understanding it today is by comparing the poem, section
by section, with the corresponding biblical text and
accompanying biblical wisdom, accumulated from Paul
and the fathers and generations of monastic commentators. To facilitate such a comparison, the Vulgate
text and representative selections of the accumulated
commentary tradition have been presented as part of
this edition. It is this material which helps us
to open out the poem, to understand its "digressions,"
"variations" and "expansions," which on their face
are of the nature of Old English heroic poetry, but
which in content conform to the requirements of scriptural knowledge. Such passages are adduced for comparison, not as "sources": no one can know exactly
what the reading of our poet was, or even what books
were available at given times in given centers in
Anglo-Saxon England. That the poet was learned in
the conventional biblical lore of his time, that he
used books not merely as formulaic symbols, but as
the tools of his craft, I do not doubt. What books
he heard read or read for himself beyond the Vulgate
Genesis, no one can say. In a few cases there is no
doubt that the poet had read or heard a specific
patristic topic, e.g., the raven of Noah, but we can
never tell the exact form he knew it in, or the exact
work or works behind his knowledge of the topic.
Passages are given as general background to a point,
to demonstrate in relation to specific places in
Genesis what the available ideas were within the
specific time brackets appropriate to this poem
(in any case, little change in the content of the
Genesis tradition can be detected between the se-

venth and the eleventh centuries), and to show in
specific places the similarity of the themes and
thoughts of the poem to the exegetical thought of
the early Middle Ages.

    The tradition of scriptural knowledge in the
early Middle Ages is remarkable chiefly for its
steadiness and for its progressive standardization
and diminution. Virtually everything significant
that was to be discovered or said before the thir-
teenth century existed in some form in patristic
writings. After this, scholarship is concerned with
preserving and passing on what has been found. Isidore's exegetical works represent a considerable,
though faithful and well-proportioned, reduction of
Augustine's exegesis, and Alcuin marks yet a further
stage of curtailment and categorization. Biblical
exploration and speculation gave way to encyclopedic
and instructional writing. Bede alone is a fresh
mind in the Augustinian tradition. In terms of content, we may consider *Genesis A* fully within the
Western historical-allegorical tradition established
by Augustine, bracketed in time by the Genesis-exegesis of Bede and Aelfric. In content the early
medieval Genesis tradition does not differ from Augustine's exegesis, but a difference in method and
emphasis is apparent during and after the Carolingian period.[48]

    For the purposes of illustrating traditional
content in *Genesis A* works both earlier and perhaps
later than the poem are useful, so long as they are
in the Latin, Augustinian, tradition.[49] We can trace

[48] E.g., a new emphasis on the mechanics of the literal narrative, a practical concern for teaching,
widespread adoption of the *quaestio* form, development
of elaborate divisions into allegorical levels; see
Evans, *Paradise Lost and the Genesis Tradition*, 154
and Smalley, *Bible in the Middle Ages*, 37-46.
[49] For commentaries referred to in this edition, see
the Bibliography: besides the standard reference works
cited, a fairly complete annotated list of Greek and
Latin Genesis commentaries is given in F. E. Robbins,
The Hexaemeral Literature (Chicago, 1912), 93-104.
See also the bibliography of Evans, and supplementing
it, Michael Benskin and Brian Murdoch, "The Literary
Tradition of Genesis," *Neuphilologische Mitteilungen*
76 (1975), 389-403. Occasional reference to Greek
fathers has been unavoidable, but I have used these
only where it appears that the comment in question has
passed into the Latin tradition. A surprising fea-

most of the additions to the literal text to ideas
that had long been commonplaces in the West,
illustrated by hexameral writings of Ambrose, Augustine, Jerome, or from the standard selections from
these authors to be found in the compilations of Isidore, Alcuin, Hrabanus, Remigius of Auxerre, Angelomus and Aelfric. The poet works eclectically within
the bounds established by this traditional data.
There is little evidence that our poet borrowed directly from Christian Latin poetry. His method is
entirely alien to it, though not his impulse or his
inspiration, for his response is to a poetic technique
having its own conventions, traditions and demands,
completely outside the classical tradition. The poem
is so faithful to the literal sense, so little concerned with decoration as such that nothing seems further removed from the self-conscious gorgeousness of
Avitus or Dracontius, or, at the other extreme, from
the epigrammatic inclusiveness of Cyprianus Gallus.

-----

ture of *Genesis A* is the considerable amount of material that can be traced only to Jewish sources, not
appearing in the Latin tradition until Carolingian
times or later. Many of these items are discussed by
Aaron Mirsky, "On the Sources of the Anglo-Saxon *Genesis* and *Exodus*," *English Studies* 48 (1967), 385-97,
who, however, thinks that these poets knew Talmudic
and midrashic material directly. There is no evidence
for the presence of Jews in Anglo-Saxon England, nor
can Hebrew studies be said to have flourished there.
One must assume that much of this material came from
ephemeral or lost Latin compilations from the contin-
ent, where there was regular contact with Jews and
Jewish scholarship. There was also a widespread cir-
culation of Latin versions, now lost, of apocryphal
literature, in Anglo-Irish circles; see D. N. Dumville,
"Biblical Apocrypha and the Early Irish, A Preliminary
Investigation," *Proceedings of the Royal Irish Academy*
73.C (1973), 299-338. Some of the similarities *Genesis
A* has to haggadic tradition may be coincidence, independent resolutions of purely narrative problems.
Of course, much originally Jewish comment was en-
shrined in the standard commentaries, e.g., the
Raven feeding on corpses instead of returning to
the Ark.

D. *Genesis A* and the Vulgate

The biblical text behind *Genesis A* appears to
be a Vulgate of a fairly pure Roman or Gregorian
type, predominantly Jeromian, with some admixture
of Old Latin elements, though so few early manuscripts
of Genesis are available that the exact type of Latin text the poet followed probably cannot be established.[50] But *Genesis A* is close enough to its original and clear enough as a translation that at
several points specific Vulgate and Old Latin ([V]e-
tus [L]atina) influences can be differentiated, indicating the precision and textual awareness with
which the poet worked as he followed a mixed text of
Genesis.[51]

A few examples, from many more or less clear,
will suggest the general situation. Vulgate readings
can be seen behind: GN 853 *ofer midne dæg* (Vulg. 3.8,
"post meridiem," V.L., "ad vesperam"); the exile imagery
of GN 1018 ff. (Vulg. 4.12, "vagus et profugus," V.L.,
"gemens et tremens"); GN 2020 f. *abraham* [acc.] *secan
...pam ebriscan* (Vulg. 14.13, "Abram Hebraeo," V.L.,
"Abram transfluviali"); GN 1248 *bearn godes* (Vulg.
6.2, "filii dei," V.L., "angeli dei"); GN 1962 *ambrafel* (Vulg. 14.1 "Amraphel," V.L., "Amarfal"); GN
2027, 2152 *aner* (Vulg. "Aner," V.L., "Aunan"); GN

[50] ". . . insofar as the *Codex Amiatinus* [a complete
Bible written in Northumbria in the seventh century
following a south-Italian model and one of the most
important witnesses to Jerome's text] . . . typifies
the type of text circulating in northern England,
that text was . . . of very heterogeneous provenance"
(Raphael Loewe, "The Medieval History of the Latin
Vulgate," in *The Cambridge History of the Bible 2:
The West from the Fathers to the Reformation*, ed. G. W.
Lampe [Cambridge, 1969], 130).
[51] In this edition, Old Latin readings (V.L.) are
taken, without discrimination as to their origin,
from the reconstruction of B. Fischer, *Vetus Latina:
Die Reste der altlateinischen Bibel* . . . (Freiburg,
1951). By "Vulgate" is meant the text printed in
*Biblia Sacra iuxta latinam vulgatam versionem ad
codicum fidem:* Vol. I, Genesis, ed. H. Quentin by Papal Commission (Rome, 1926). The "Old Latin" are those
multifarious versions of relatively unfixed readings
which circulated before and after Jerome made his
translations, and which generally follow the Septuagint (LXX) Greek version of the Old Testament.

2839 *bersabea* [gen. pl.] (Vulg., "Bersabee," V.L. "Pu-
teus Iuramenti"); GN 1962 *orlahomar* (Vulg. 14.17,
"Chodorlahomor," V.L., "Codorlamor").

The following readings of *Genesis A* seem to be
following, or influenced by, Old Latin elements in
the poet's exemplar: GN 1799,1876, 1930 *bethlem* (V.L.,
"Bethel," var. "Bethlem," "Betleem," Vulg., "Bethel");
GN 1628 *nebroðes* [MS *nebreðer*] (V.L., "Nebroth,"
Vulg., "Nemrod" [cf. *Solomon & Saturn* 214 *Nebrondes*]);
GN 1736, &c, *carran* (V.L. "Charra(n)," Vulg., "Haran");
GN *sarra, sarre, sarrai* [nom.], *sarran* [gen., dat.],
sarrai [dat.], *sarran* [acc.], V.L., "Sarra," Vulg.
"Sarai," "Sara."[52] GN 200-13 seems to reflect a mixed
reading of 1.28, Vulg., "animantibus" (= *lifigende* 203),
V.L., "pecorum" (= *feoh* 201)—the whole passage reflects
the greater concreteness of the V.L. but not the
wording. GN 972 *oðer his to eorðan elnes tilode*
resembles V.L. 4.2, "Cain autem operatur terram
(Vulg., "et Cain agricola"). GN 1285 ff. *Noe wæs
god, nergende leof*, &c, cf. V.L. 6.9, "Noe homo
iustus et perfectus erat in generatione sua et placuit deó"(Vulg., "cum Deo ambulavit"). The rooms
in the ark, called "mansiunculas" in Vulg (6.14) are
called *reste* at GN 1304, perhaps following V.L. "nidos." GN 1436 ff., *þa fandode forðweard scipes /
hwæðer sincende sæflod þa gyt / wære*, &c agrees with
the syntax of V.L. 8.7, "et emisit corvum ut videret
utrum cessasset aqua..." (Vulg., "dimisit corvum...").
Similarly, GN 1456, *no hweðere reste fand*, agrees with
V.L. 8.9, "non inveniens columba requiem pedibus
suis..." (Vulg., "non invenisset ubi requiesceret pes
eius..."); GN 1730 *ofer caldea folc*, V.L. 11.31 et
passim, "de regione Chaldaeorum..." (Vulg., "de Ur
Chaldeorum"); GN 2382 ff. *þa þæt wif ahloh...husce
belegde / on sefan swiðe*, V.L. 18.12, "risit autem
Sarra in semetipsa" (Vulg. "quae risit occulte");
GN 2459 f., *þæt mid þam hæleðum hæman wolden / un-
scomlice...*, V.L. 19.5, "educ illos ad nos ut coitum
faciamus cum eis" (Vulg. "ut cognoscamus eos"); GN
2855, *hrincg þæs hean landes*, V.L. 22.2, "in terram
altam" (var., "terram excelsam") (Vulg., "in terram
visionis").

[52] *Sarra* is not a stable form in the V.L., but pre-
dominates in the "African" tradition (i.e., Augustine
and Cyprian), used both before and after Genesis 17.15.
Perhaps the double *r* in *Genesis A "sarra"* and *"carran"*
is orthographic indication of lengthening of the stress
syllable (cf. Campbell §558).

A careful comparison of the text of *Genesis A*
with that of the Vulgate (in this edition the two texts
are given parallel) reveals that the poet has systematically, virtually phrase by phrase, reproduced in
traditional poetry the essential meaning of the Latin
Genesis which he had before him as he worked. The
paraphrase is nearly complete and continuous up to
Genesis 22.13. It is apparent that at almost every
point the details of the Vulgate diction and syntax
are influencing the style as well as the matter. At
times a sentence is rendered almost as literally as
it would be in a prose translation, but this appears
not to be the main object. Much material is added
and omitted, but these additions and omissions seem
to be the product of a continuous and spontaneous
effort to clarify and expand according to the needs
of audience and verse technique. Changes from the
original text are so evenly distributed, and their
occurrences explainable by factors so consistent, so
obviously arising from local difficulties, that they
can hardly be said to be either the product of later
interference or part of a conscious program of rein-
terpreting the biblical text in the manner of, say,
Exodus.[53] Very probably the poem developed and changed
during its long transit from the first written version to the Junius Manuscript, but apart from a few
obvious interpolations and corruptions, nothing definite can be shown; we have to take the poem as the
product of the last shaping hand, and to this last
hand we must give the title *Genesis A*-poet. Overall,
as comparison with the Vulgate shows, the poem appears
to be remarkably free from corruptions.[54]

[53] It seems to me that such unity as the poem has is
not the result so much of conscious art as of an age-old
unity of interpretation, where everything is read *in
Christo*, and of a unity of technique, which automatically brings all material into a similar narrative and
stylistic configuration. The ancient commentaries and
capitula recognize the heterogeneous nature of Genesis
and its oneness only in its prophetical, typological
function.
[54] For losses in the poem due to damage to the manuscript, see Introduction, pp. 8-11. In many cases the
disturbed pointing and hazy syntax suggest corruption
which has been smoothed over scribally, so that the
text nearly always makes some kind of sense. A number of lines have only one hemistich, with no break
in sense. There is no way of telling if these are
instances of corruption and loss or the result of im-

In this orderly presentation of the original
such displacement of material as occurs comes
about as a response to specific critical problems
cropping up in the original text. To cite the most
obvious instance, the creation of woman, twice-told
in Genesis, occurs only once in *Genesis A*. In the
poem, Eve is created in the succession of the Works
of the Days, where the material of 1.27 belongs, but
following the more circumstantial details of 2.18-22
(cf. lines 169 ff.). In general, rearrangements seem
to be merely for the purpose of clarifying confusing
points, eliminating repetition, or for making explicit
what the poet takes to be the proper meaning of the
text, where the original is laconic or unclear. For
example, lines 1628b-48 rearrange the matter of the
original in this order: 10.8, 10.9, 10.10, 11.2, 11.1,
10.20, 10.21, 10.25. This serves to bring together
Babylon, its ruler Nimrod and the Tower of Babel so
as to suggest the common topic, "Nimrod ruler of Babylon and Confusion." The collocation of Nimrod and
the confusion of tongues economically suggests that
Nimrod was the tower builder and that it was Nimrod's
pride in doing so which caused God's anger towards
men, the traditional explanation of 11.1-9, but not
stated in the text of Genesis. At the same time, the
opposite life of Heber and his descendants is con-
trasted with the inhabitants of "Babylon" more explicitly than in the original. The poet probably
took all of this section, verses 10.8 through 11.9,
as one unit of narrative, as the traditional exegesis
tends to do. He rearranged within the unit to make
the received meaning clear in his narrative as it
was clear to him when he read the original text. In
other words, such rearrangements do not disturb the
concept of a simple, linear narrative presentation:
they are carried out with the simplest expository aims
in view.

E. Omissions

Throughout his version of Genesis, the poet
omits verses and parts of verses. Altogether, nearly
150 verses of the original are entirely omitted and

---

perfect composition, possibly a feature of this poet's
style. For discussion of possible corruptions, see
Commentary, 221-24a, 869, 906b-907, 1400-01, 1490-93,
1546-49, 1705a, 1767-68, 1774b-76a, 2210a, 2628-32a,
2720-2721a.

about 350 rendered in one way or another, although
even of these a good number have had material in them
omitted or altered. Close scrutiny of these omissions
shows that although the poet has undertaken to render
the whole text as he finds it, various local exigencies have compelled him to leave out numerous verses
and verse-parts, often in order to be more faithful
to the meaning as he understands it.

Few if any episodes are ignored altogether.
Omissions are spread fairly evenly through the whole
poem. Overall, the ratio of omitted whole biblical
verses to those represented is two to five. In most
chapters the actual ratio of omissions is considerably
lower, and in any given chapter the omissions are
pretty evenly distributed. Chapters 12, 19, 20 and
22 are witnesses to the methodical approach of the
poet. Because these chapters consist almost entirely
of useable, non-duplicated narrative material almost
everything is represented. It is not because of their
interest as narrative that these chapters are so fully
rendered, for much of this material is pedestrian, not
noticed, proportionately, even in most commentaries.
The poet's main principle of selection seems to be
that material must be new, and must not retard the
advance of the narrative by repetition or obscurity;
if material is difficult but important, it must be
clarified so that it serves to explain the central
meaning of the episode in which it appears. The very
high ratio of omissions in certain chapters can best
be explained by this principle. For instance, Chapter 10 (5 verses omitted for every 2 translated) and
Chapter 11 (2:1) are mainly genealogical and these
genealogies have been greatly abridged—though not
omitted—while the first genealogy, in Chapter 5 (1:4)
is very fully represented. Chapter 15 (2:1) has been
truncated by the omission of the long description of
the sacrifice, perhaps because it implied a moral
allegory too complex and difficult to render adequately.
The numerous omissions in Chapters 7 and 8 are dictated almost entirely by the fact that those chapters
are full of duplicated material due to the double
source of the original.

Experience must have told the poet that a good
portion of Genesis was intractable when brought into
confrontation with his poetic system—not so much
the larger elements of the original, but innumerable
details of expression within verses, sentences,
phrases—the formulas of expression that Jerome
used to represent *his* original. Link-passages, epithets, standardized expressions of emotion, rela-

tionship, perception, etc., tend to be eliminated or
replaced on purely stylistic grounds. Partly this is
the result of the sheer inconvenience of reproducing
merely stylistic features in another language, partly
the result of the fact that the traditional poetic
had its own formulaic basis and means for saying or
accomplishing the same things.

Omissions more deliberate on the poet's part
and affecting larger areas of text are those which
are made on grounds of content alone. These may be
analyzed into fairly objective categories, and on
the whole the reasons for them are not hard to find.
Least surprising are the numerous omissions of
strictly Jewish ceremonial or tribalistic detail,
matters of least interest to a Christian, monastic,
Anglo-Saxon audience, at least on a literal level.
The poet is not rigorous about this—the reference
to the prohibition of blood (Genesis 9.4, cf. GN
1518-20) is not only retained, but expanded along
levitical lines. More typical is his treatment of
circumcision, which is spiritualized as the *sign* of
the covenant leading to salvation (the commentators
identified it with Baptism); hence, the literal details of 17.11 disappear (cf. GN 2312 ff.). The
long ritualistic digression about Abraham's litiga-
tion with Abimelech over the well at Bersabee (21.
25-32) drops out, except for the place-name itself.
The feast at the ablactation of Isaac (21.8) goes.
The long, detailed description of the sacrifice
(15.8-17), narratively and doctrinally obscure,
goes out, 15.7 and 15.18 thereby coming together,
following the example set by Augustine.[55] The insti-
tution of marriage under the Old Law (2.23-24) is
replaced by a description of Eve's beauty (185-91)
(the marriage of Adam and Eve may once have been in
a part now lost, see above, p. 9).

A few omissions probably are expurgations of
morally ambiguous material, dangerous to the unlearned.
Thus, 20.12-13, which plainly says that Sara is Abraham's sister and then rationalizes a lie, is rendered only very obscurely (1704-07, 2713-16). Sara's
lie in the face of God (18.15) was no doubt a bad example and is omitted. Noah's drunkenness and careless
self-exposure is considerably covered up, following
the patristic admonition; though he uses the word
limnacod (1566a), the poet does not really trans-

[55] *De ciuitate Dei*, xvi, 24, ed. B. Dombart and A.
Kalb, CCSL 48 (Turnhout, 1955), 526.

late 9.22. The bold anthropomorphism associated
with Noah's sacrifice (8.21-22) is supressed. Perhaps the poet has deliberately avoided mention of
Adam and Eve's nudity before the Fall (2.25) because
of the difficulty of presenting unashamed nakedness.

Very many difficult proper names, especially
those in genealogical passages, are jettisoned. To
judge by some of those that are used, they must have
cost some trouble (cf. 1960 *orlahomar* for "Chodorlahomor"), and are subject to a lot of scribal corruption (e.g., 224, MS *hebeleac* for "(H)evilath," 1628
MS *ne breðer* for "Nebroðes"). Hence the name of
Abraham's steward (15.2) is gone, as is the massive
explosion of unmanageable and meaningless names in
15.19-21, the sons of Iaphet and Gomer, unnecessary
place-names, geographical details (e.g., of the king-
doms of Nemrod only the significant "Babylon" is
mentioned), and so on. Similarly, etymological interpretations of proper names are often ignored,
though the poet shows some interest in this area
(see 1485-87a and Commentary); thus, e.g., the naming
of Eve (3.20), "the mother of all living," is passed
over. The way the poet handles the interpretation
of *Segor* = "Parva" is typical of his method. Genesis
19.20 is not explicit about what the name means,
though Jerome is.[56] Just the details that bring this
meaning out are used: *Ic wat hea burh her ane neah, /
lytle ceastre* (2519 f.).

It is surprising how much of the numerical detail is carried over from the original, especially
considering how difficult it must have been to render
metrically and formulaically. Of course, many numbers
drop out, some are rounded off, or obliquely expressed,
but the impression is never of misapprehension or
vagueness, nor of oral or imperfect transmission.
Most of the omitted numbers occur in the Noah episode,
where the days and months are reckoned several times.
The poet obviously considers this material important
and reduces it in such a way that the numerical detail still comes through. The treatment of 7.11 demonstrates his careful planning. The statement of
7.11 is made in the poem, but utilizing the simpler
numerical material of 7.6, achieving clarification
and abridgement in a way authorized by the Bible
itself:

[56] *Liber interpretationis hebraicorum nominum*, ed.
P. de Lagarde, CCSL 72 (Turnhout, 1959), 72.

7.11 Anno sescentesimo vitae Noe, mense secundo,
     septimodecimo die mensis, rupti sunt omnes
     fontes abyssi magnae. . . .
7.13 In articulo diei illius ingressus est Noe,
     et Sem, et Cham, et Iafeth. . . .
7.6 [Eratque sescentorum annorum quando diluvii
     aquae inundaverunt super terram.]

                    noe hæfde,
        sunu lameches,   syxhund wintra
        þa he mid bearnum   under bord gestah....
               ...drihten sende
        regn from roderum....   (1367-69, 1371-72)

There seems to be an operative principle that
the poem shall not repeat material that appears more
than once in the original unless there is some special reason. The Vulgate is a text of many repetitions, partly the result of the collocation of different redactions of the same story, partly stylistic.
Generally, the poet presents such duplicated matter
once only. In the course of making so many omissions
he inevitably creates a new narrative texture, tighter
and more linear, less stable and objective. The
results of this type of reworking are particuarly
obvious in the Flood story, which is a web of duplicated material arising from the complicated blending
of two sources by a later redactor.[57] The historical
reasons for these duplications would of course not
have been evident to the poet; he treats them as
matters of style, reproducing the essential matter
and bringing the narrative into accord with the
practices of Old English poetic narrative, which
uses its own sort of variation and duplication of
material.

For an example of how the poet handles this
most important type of omission, compare lines 196-
205 with Genesis 1.28-30. Here the principle of
eliminating duplication yields a reproduction of all
the essentials of 1.28 and a rejection of 1.29-30,
though they may have influenced the wording. Verse
29 is an amplification of the meaning of the whole
passage, introducing nothing new, and repeating
similar syntactical patterns of 1.28 and 1.30. Syntactically, stylistically and semantically, verse
30 is a substantial repetition of 28, as well as em-
ploying a Vulgate formula of ending which the poet

[57] See J. Skinner, *A Critical and Exegetical Commentary on Genesis* (2d ed., Edinburgh, 1930), 147-50.

consistently ignores. The poet tarries over the
meanings of 1.28, repeating some of its central ideas
and developing them thematically, but always the wording is rigorously influenced by the Vulgate. The
actual process of formulaic composition, which tends
towards expansion and exploitation of material to the
full, virtually pre-empts any other source of repetition.

    Other sources of omissions which should be
briefly mentioned are omissions of material which
has become redundant because of other omissions or
alterations the poet has made (e.g., 2.5 "et homo
non erat qui operaretur terram" must go because by
this point, GN 210 ff., man has already been created
according to 1.27); omissions of some details because
of expansion of others ("prius autem quam irent cubitum" [19.4] is replaced with an elaborate description of night falling over the Sodomites [2450-53]);
conflation of two or more passages of similar style
or content so that the distinct elements of each
are evident in an entirely new structure (e.g., 7.6
and 7.11, cf. GN 1367-75).

    The poet's consistency in the matter of omis-
sions is illustrated by the very interesting series
of omissions in Chapter 17, where the desire to
avoid repetition begins to endanger the balance,
tone, even the central point of the whole episode.
Each omission is sensible in itself, but results in
taking the passage out of the narrative realm. The
poet sees the point of God's appearance to Abraham
as being His promise to him, a motif that has already appeared, and which is therefore not repeated
with any emphasis. As similar elements of the promise, 17.2 and 17.10 are brought together (GN 2306-
12). Practically everything else from 17.3 to 17.10
disappears. The reason for the long omission in this
important passage is that the reinforcement of the
central point is treated merely as repetition. Gone
is "Cecidit Abram pronus in faciem" (17.3), the lead-
up to God's mighty utterance in 17.4, because the
promise itself is now gone. 17.5 is obviously redundant as "Abraham" is the only name which has appeared
throughout *Genesis A*. 17.6-9 are repetitions of 17.2,
simply reinforcing the establishment of the Covenant.
From a narrowly technical standpoint, the poet has
been consistent and logical, but his method has mutilated the narrative. But lest we think that this
is evidence of his ignorance, we must note that what
the poet has in fact done, by a new distribution of
the balance of the passage (2306-37), is to reinterpret

the original so that not the promise but the circumcision now occupies the limelight. This is the same
shift of emphasis that takes place in medieval commentaries on this chapter, where the establishment of
the Jewish covenant is played down and the allegorical
interpretation of circumcision as Baptism is pre-emi-
nent.[58]

        The omissions in *Genesis A*, far from suggesting
careless or naive work, evidence a skilled craftsman,
responsive to the needs of his traditional poetic medium, but also highly aware of his responsibilities to
an outside text and its attendant "learned" traditions. The nature of the omissions reveals that this
reworking of Genesis could not have been carried out
by any man not completely familiar with the text and
the traditions behind it. No ignorant or unlettered
scop could have accomplished the complex adaptation
these omissions imply by hearing verses read to him,
in the manner described by Bede of Caedmon. No one
but an expert could have chosen verses so consistently,
which to render, which to omit, which to alter,
which to conflate, and have treated them so harmon-
iously, according to the various conflicting demands
which his task imposed upon him.

F. Additions

        There are nearly 300 isolable additions of
content in *Genesis A* which extend over more than
half a line. They go beyond the necessary changes
implicit in any translation, especially when the
donor text is laconic and the receptor dilative.
Many of these additions consist of variation, and
the elaboration of detail suggested by the original.
But many are also substantial additions that are
meant to clarify or supplement the text. Others go
beyond the stage of translation altogether and are
there to supply exegetical comment on Genesis. Additions of this sort have already been noticed, and
individual cases are discussed with appropriate
detail in the Commentary.

        Ebert classified the additions of *Genesis A* as
explanations of biblical statements, motivations for
biblical actions or expanded descriptions of charac-

[58] See Pseudo-Bede, *In Pentateuchum commentarii*, PL.
91, 236-37.

ter, landscape and objects.[59] Such additions are suf-
ficiently obvious to the reader aware of the Vulgate
and do not need to be described in detail. Some of
these additions become little episodes in themselves,
crafted according to the spirit and the needs of
the poetic system. The two most spectacular additions
illustrate the two main tendencies of the elaboration
in the poem: on the one hand, the non-biblical opening (1-111) serves to introduce most of the standard
hexameral topics which were universally thought of as
part of the literal sense though not appearing in
the text of Genesis.[60] On the other hand, the long
expansions and additions in the translation of
14.1-16 (GN 1960-2101), the "war of the kings," are
the result of the natural pressure of the verse medium itself. A contrast should be noted between the
treatment of this section before line 1982, where the
expansions are solidly based on the text, however
much that is changed, and after line 1982, where the
expansion is entirely "free," responding only to the
demands of the poetic tradition, developing the theme
of battle. While the content of the Vulgate does
not authorize such expansion, it does not forbid it
either, and the poet is uniquely free to respond to
the tendencies of his medium.

There are several "homiletic" intrusions,
pure comment of a pious nature intended to relate
the events of the narrative to the moral life of the
audience. These usually have narrative form, and
blend fairly inobtrusively into the biblical events.
Such are 952-964, on God's mercy to the fallen human race; 987-1001 on the "tree of sin" growing out
of Cain's crime; 1937b-1959, an elaborate comment,
with liturgical overtones, on the obedience and rewards of Abraham and Loth; 2562b-2575, a bookish comment on Loth's wife (see Commentary); 2736-41, on the
obedience of Abraham. 1717b-1718, *for ðon hie* [Abra-
ham and Loth] *wide nu / dugeðum demað drihta bearnum*,
is obscure, but seems to reflect a liturgical, mystical intention (see Commentary). Comments of this sort
are common in Old English biblical poetry, and their
familiar presence may have made it easier for some-
one to interpolate *Genesis B* into the poem, which itself has a considerable amount of this type of material, and which may have been regarded, above everything

[59] "Zur angelsächsischen Genesis," *Anglia* 5 (1882),
124-27.
[60] See Commentary, notes to the first 111 lines.

else, as an extended homiletic comment on the Fall of
Man, appropriate in the context of a vernacular Genesis story in the literal mode.

G. The Style of *Genesis A*

Germanic alliterative poetry had been developing
for hundreds of years before *Genesis A* was composed
and had evolved its own highly elaborate techniques
and vocabulary. It had developed in a certain pre-
Christian cultural environment to meet certain limited
cultural demands. While working within this fully-
fledged poetic-linguistic system, the poet of *Genesis
A* was deriving his statements, content and meaning
from sources external to his verse tradition and developing them according to demands entirely alien
to it. In spite of this, his verse technique was
continuously working according to its own inescapable
internal logic. Thereby arose a confrontation of
styles, a gap between source and product. This
confrontation of styles is one of the principal
esthetic facts of the Old English biblical poems in
general, and of *Genesis A* in particular.
The influence of the Latin text being followed
has the tendency to pull the linguistic organization
of the poem out of plumb, as it were, to attract it
away from the familiar patterns which it would assume if free to develop under the pressure of only
the forces inherent in the verse tradition itself.
At the same time, the poet must have been aware of
the deficiencies of his style for rendering a text
expressed in a style so alien to his own. New means
and new norms had to be found to expand and justify
his own traditional style. Not only convenience but
choice dictated that the text being imitated, itself
a text of the highest authority, beauty and prestige,
should supply the source for stylistic enrichment.
Certainly nothing in the native rhetoric could match
the syntactical resources which the Vulgate offered,
nor could anything compete with the status of the sacred text, the imitation of which was an ideal, all
other stylistic considerations aside. It is the Vulgate which provides a model for syntactic and lexical
innovation, and it is the interaction of linguistic
habits from the native poetic and conscious imitation
of a new stylistic force which underlies the stylistic
tensions marking *Genesis A*.
A fixed text replaces the traditional freely
developed story of the old heroic tradition, and ela-

boration, the soul of poetic technique, is curtailed
by the need to present a steady flow of incident as
dictated by the text, which must be represented with
an acceptable degree of accuracy and doctrinal sound-
ness. Therefore the development of the poem is linear, "sequential," following the words of the text,
rather than "complemental."[61] The concentration is on
the word and what the word means, and how it acts in
a dynamic stylistic situation. The concern is not
with the tensions of an imaginary dramatic action or
the development of a traditional character, but with
the tensions between what the text requires to be
said and the various expressions available from the
traditional poetic for saying it. In the old poetry
the story is *in* the technique. In *Genesis A* it is
extrinsic to it. The poetic itself exercises its pull
and tends to concentrate little spaces of speech-mat-
ter around character and incident, so that we have
the curious phenomenon of intensive but ephemeral
treatment of heroic figures who have no function, or
actions which seem to begin and come to nothing:

> longe siððan
> geared gumum   gold brittade.
> se eorl wæs æðcle,   æfæst hæleð
> and se frumgar   his freomagum leof.
>   (1180-83)
> Abraham maðelode.   hæfde on an gehogod
> þæt he gedæde swa   hine drihten het...
>   (2893-94)

The second passage introduces a speech only two lines
long.

Elaboration of this type, which is an automatic
outgrowth of technique, and out of which formulaic

---

[61] "The setting out of the material is not in *Beowulf* an evolution, following one main line or con-
necting thread. Instead, the subject is disposed
as a circumscribed field in which the themes are
drawn out by a centre of attraction—in this case
the character of the good warrior . . . . the
structure of the poem is not sequential, but complemental; at the outset certain parts of a situation
are displayed, and these are given coherence and significance by progressive addition of its other
parts" (Joan Blomfield, "The Style and Structure of
Beowulf," *Review of English Studies* 14 [1938],
396 and 399).

poems are made, can only be applied haltingly in a
poem inhibited by a text, and only to minor characters and incidents. The definitive nature of the
text means elaborations must be carefully controlled
(in contrast to Cynewulf's sources, which are richly
suggestive to him, but do not have a sacred status
and may therefore be surpassed). In the case of important figures the possibility of free elaboration
was pre-empted to a high degree by an already established tradition of elaboration through exegesis.
Thus, for example, the figure of Melchisedech (14.
18-20), who might have offered opportunity for development of the stock figure of the "wise old king,"
was already the subject of symbolic elaboration in
both Testaments and in the Fathers, leaving the poet
room for only the briefest, blankest of introductions
by way of elaboration (2100b-03a, see Commentary).
The main characters, Adam, Noah, Loth, Abraham, offer
even less opportunity, since their traditional "biblical" meanings do not easily coincide with types
from the old heroic tradition. The only real opportunities for pure elaboration were in some of the "bad"
characters, such as the Sodomites, the northern kings
(Chapter 14) and Pharaoh, though even here common
sense is not always safe against the surprises of
traditional exegetical developments.[62] And even as
the biblical style presents persons and events sparingly, it does so with a subtle, pregnant blankness,
which is not the way of the old poetry.[63]
        It is not surprising, then, that *Genesis A* is

[62] For instance, the attitude to Loth and his daugh-
ters understandably fluctuates, see Bede, *In Gen.*,
CCSL 118A, 227 et passim; Ps.-Bede, *In Pent. Comm.*,
PL. 91, 240D; Hrabanus Maurus, *Allegoriae in universam
Sacram Scripturam*, PL. 112, 1001A, s.v. *mons*. On
Abimelech, see Commentary 2641b-2642.

[63] Cf. Erich Auerbach's famous comparison of the
styles of Homer and the Elohist: on the one hand "externalized uniformly illuminated phenomena, at a
definite time and in a definite place, connected together without lacunae in a perpetual foreground," on
the other, "the externalization of only so much of the
phenomena as is necessary for the purpose of the
narrative, all else left in obscurity . . . the whole
permeated with the most unrelieved suspense and directed towards a single goal. . . " (*Mimesis: the Rep-
resentation of Reality in Western Literature*, tr.
Ralph Mannheim [Princeton, 1953], 11-12).

not the highest peak of Old English poetry, for it has
had to forego much of what makes heroic poetry what
it is   in order to satisfy by a kind of compromise
the two demanding traditions out of which it is made.
Yet *Genesis A* is a considerable success both as Bible
and as poem because it has achieved a vernacular rep-
resentation of the true Genesis, and also is a brilliant sustained response to the original text; intractable as the material often seems, the poet always gives it in verses perfectly autochthonous in
form, in meaning true to the spirit of the original,
not distorting or debasing the scale and spirit of
the model, and not enfeebling the old poetic by mere
literalism.   Indeed, *Genesis A* appears to open new
paths for native poetry.

H. Formulas—Demands and Limitations

It is beyond argument that *Genesis A* is composed of formulas, which were, for the most part,
from the common stock of traditional Old English
verses, or were new ones formed on patterns established in the common stock.   I therefore do not
intend to "prove" that *Genesis A* is formulaic, or
to define, once again, what formulas are: to most
who read this the issue will be familiar.[64] The object of the present discussion is simply to suggest
the problems which the poet faced when he approached
the task of translating a set text with the tools
of traditional formulaic verse technique.

The formulas in *Genesis A* are of various layers
according to their antiquity.   While no one formula
may be dated or identified as of a certain period or
source of origin, it is fairly certain that those
formulas which show some kinship with similar poetic
formulas in other Germanic languages are the oldest.[65]
We can see this kinship exhibiting itself in otherwise
unrelated poems of differing times and areas, as, for
example, in a recurrent creation/chaos theme using
similar formulas and collocations:

[64] Creed shows, by means of parallels from other OE.
poetry, the formulaic or stereotyped nature of the
phrasing and diction of the Sacrifice of Isaac episode; see note 22 above.
[65] See F. P. Magoun, Jr., "A Note on Old West-Germanic
Poetic Unity," *Modern Philology* 43 (1945), 77-82.

Dat gafregin ih mit firahim   firiuuizzo meista,
dat ero ni uuas noh ufhimil,
noh paum noh heinig   noh pereg ni uuas,
ni [sterro] noh heinig   noh sunna ni scein,
noh mano ni liuhta,   noh der mareo seo.[66]

. . . vasa sandr ná sær,   né svalar unnir;
jörð fansk æva   né upphiminn;
gap vas Ginnunga,   en gras hvergi.[67]

                        . . . nimeð
. . . se swearta lig,   sæs mid hyra fiscum,
eorþan mid hire beorgum,   ond upheofon
torhtne mid his tunglum.
                  . . . Grornað gesargad
eal middangeard   on þa mæran tid.[68]

We can distinguish many formulas which came down
whole from pre-Christian sources, or at least appear
to go back to some earlier common-meeting point: e.g.,
gomban gieldan (GN 1978), *gambra* . . . *gelden* (HL
355, cf. BW 11); *in undor edoras* (GN 2447, 2489), *undar ederos* (HL 4943); *wordum and dædum* (GN 2352),
uuordon endi dadean (HL 1990); *him wæs þearf micel*
(GN 2054), *uuas im tharf mikil* (HL 2376); *þa him
wæs are þearf* (GN 1591), *uuas im buotons tharf* (HL
2298), etc.[69] We can see others, particularly those
displayed in Caedmon's *Hymn*, which are Christian, but
formed on old patterns and current in *Genesis A*. Thus,
heofonrices weard (*Hymn* 1b, GN 1363, etc.) is no
doubt a re-formation of some old phrase such as *gum-
rices weard* (actually occurring, DN 176), *ece drihten*
(*Hymn* 4a, 8a, GN 7, etc.) of some such phrase as
*leofne drihten, and so on.[70] The examples of Chris-

---

[66] *Wessobrunner Gebet*, ed. W. Braune, *Althochdeutsches
Lesebuch* (4th ed., Halle, 1897), 78.
[67] *Völuspá*, ed. F. Jónsson, *Sæmundr-Edda* (2d ed.,
Reykjavik, 1926), 1-2.
[68] *Christ* 964-68, 970-71; cf. GN 79-100, 103-105a,
116b-117a (= Genesis 1.2).
[69] *Heliand*, ed. E. Sievers (Halle, 1878).
[70] The examples follow those of H. Marquardt, "Zur
Entstehung des *Beowulf*," *Anglia* 64 (1940), 153. For
further discussions of the relationship of OE. and
O.S. formulaics, see Robert L. Kellogg, "The South
Germanic Oral Tradition," in *Franciplegius: Medieval
and Linguistic Studies in Honor of F. P. Magoun, Jr.*,
ed. J. B. Bessinger and R. P. Creed (New York, 1965),
66-74; Michael J. Capek, "A Note on Formula Development in Old Saxon," *Modern Philology* 68 (1970), 357-63.

tian formulas available from Caedmon's *Hymn* are of
course only a tiny sampling of those which must have
existed at an early time and were not recorded.[71] It
is certain that they were in a constant state of
flux and subject to continual re-formation and redis-
covery as part of a living oral tradition. Further,
the poetic vocabulary of Christian *scopas* was under
intense and constant pressure by liturgical and biblical terminology for some time before *Genesis A* was
composed. It must have contained a vast hoard of expressions conformable with both existing Latin terms
and formulaic patterns handed down from the native
poetic tradition.[72]

    More importantly, we can see the formulaic basis,
extending back into inherited tradtion, of the simpler syntactical patterns of *Genesis A*. For example,

                lig eall fornam
     þæt he grenes fond   goldburgum in . . .
                    (GN 2550-51)

corresponds to Genesis 19.25 ". . . et subvertit civitates has, et omnem circa regionem, universos habitatores urbium. . . ." It also corresponds to the
syntactic pattern

             dat inan wic furnam[73]

consisting of a second half-line ending with the
pret. *fornam* in stress-position, e.g. EX 289b *suð-
wind fornam*, DW 488b *þe þa deað fornam*, 557b *heapo-
ræs fornam*, 695b *wældeað fornam*, etc., AN 994b
ealle swylt fornam, EL 131b *sume wig fornam*, etc.,
HL 2218b *thena the err doð fornam*.

    Another example:

             dat in dem sciltim stont[74]

The formula consists of a second half-line B-type
(mostly 3B1) with particles running up to a disyl-
labic substantive followed by the stressed pret. sing.

---

[71] Here is the complete "Caedmonian" testimony to
Genesis A: HY 1b: GN 1363, 1484, 1744, 2073; HY 2a:
GN 189; HY 2b: GN 93, 1524, 2341, 2647; HY 4a & 8a:
GN 7, 1885; HY 5a: GN 112; HY 5b: GN 993, 1135, 1284,
1554, 2472; HY 7a: GN 986, 1554, 136, 1206, 1378; HY
7b: GN 2758, 2896; HY 8b: GN 469, 623; HY 9b: GN 5,
116, 150, 173, 852, 901, 1359, 1427.

[72] For the influence of Latin terminology on OE. poetic expression, see J. W. Rankin, "A Study of the
Kennings in Anglo-Saxon Poetry," *JEGP* 8 (1909), 357-
433; 9 (1910), 49-84.

[73] *Hildebrandslied*, 43b, from Braune, *Lesebuch*, 76-77.

[74] *Ibid.* 64b.

stod. It is a traditional expression indicating manner of or relation to existence. It is not the com-
monest, or the prose way of expressing such concepts,
nor is it the same formula if the verb is out of
stress-position (e.g. GU 215a *stod seo dygle stow*).
Examples of this formula are: DN 556b *þæt ær fæste
stod*, CS 718b *þæt he on botme stod,* 723b *þæt he on
grunde stod*, BW 145b *oð þæt idel stod*, 1913b *on lande
stod*, AN 254b *se ðe on greote stod*, 738b *þæt he on
foldan stod*, DR 38b *hwæðre ic fæste stod*, HL 4906b
than ik undar iuuuomu folke stod, 3908b *he on middien
stod*, 4240b *huand he an themu uuihe stod*. *Genesis A*
uses this formula to approximate the Vulgate several
times: 214b *hwæðre wæstmum stod* (2.5 "omnem que her-
bam regionis priusquam germinaret"), 1701b *on sennar
stod* (derived from 11.2 "campum in terra Sennaar" but
corresponding to the place and meaning of 11.9). Of
particular interest is

                              hergas wurdon
          feower on fleame,   folccyningas,
          leode ræswan.   him on laste stod
          hihtlic heorðwerod. . . .   (2073-76)
This is part of the extraordinarily expanded paraphrase of 14.14, where the Old English formula in
question renders "et persecutus est eos." Obviously,
this formula is a clumsy equivalent, using a verb of
existence to render a verb of motion. But in many
such cases the poet has rendered the sense of the
text by using an expression that came readily to hand:
he was not at liberty to invent new expressions that
did not correspond to those already in the inherited
pattern, *just* to make word-for-word equivalents.[75]
     The stiffness which the formulaic patterns im-
pose on the translation can be seen in the use of the
formulaic system based on the verb *gewitan*, "to depart." It occurs very frequently in West-Germanic
poetry (52x in GN, 28x in BW, 65x in HL, once in *Hildebrandslied*, 18a *forn her ostar geuueit*). These formulas occur so frequently because of the commonness of
the expressed idea, of course, but also because they
are extremely flexible, and hence technically useful.
The base word, *gewitan*, is capable of appearing in
all parts of the line and in various tenses and
moods. The optional dependent infinitive helps fill
the line and provides the possibility of modifying
the sense of the formula. Most importantly, it

---

[75] See A. N. Doane, "'The Green Street of Paradise,'
A Note on Lexis and Meaning in Old English Poetry,"
Neuphilologische Mitteilungen 74 (1973), 456-65.

automatically provides a syntactical situation which
allows for further development and can suggest a
following half-line by limiting possibilities when
the dependent infinitive must be accommodated. But
however useful, such a system has the disadvantage,
or distorting effect, of imposing a durative function
where the Latin seldom requires it, analysing the
action of the verb into two stages, the first syntactically functional but only nominally meaningful.
It easily tends to become mere filler. Sometimes it
achieves happy equivalents, especially for the colorless *ingredior / egredior*:

GN 1746	gewit þu nu feran and þine fare lædan
12.1	egredere de terra tua et de cognatione tua

GN 1345	gewit þu nu mid hiwum on þæt hof gangan
7.1	ingredere tu . . . in arcam

GN 1049b	him þa cain gewat [gongan]
4.16	egressusque Cain

GN 1767	him þa abraham gewat æhte lædan
12.4-5	egressus est itaque Abram. . . . Tulit-
	que. . . substantiam

But such apparent semantic equivalence fades when the
great variety and dynamism exhibited by the Latin
verbs are compared to the static Old English formulas
that render them: "venit. . . portans" (*gewat fleogan*
1471b), "vade" (*gewit . . . feran* 2850), "tulit . . .
et eduxit" (*gewat . . . feran* 1730), "pertransivit"
(*feran gewat* 1779a), "ascendit" (*gewat . . . gangan*
2593b), "reversa est" (*gewat secan* 1460), "fugam iniit"
(*fleon gewat* 2264b), "descendit" (*gewat . . . secan*
1817), and so on. The poet no doubt deserves credit
for conforming his limited expressions to the multiple,
plastic, precise lexicon of the Vulgate as well as he
does. There is no such variety or flexibility available to him simply because the *gewitan*-system can adequately express any syntactical situation in which the
idea of departure is explicit or implicit, and few new
formulas are developed because few are needed. Single
occurrences of need do not breed new expressions. This
is the principle of formulaic economy in action, where
a poet tends to be limited to those well-tried expressions which have proved useful in countless repetitions
of a given idea.[76] Little conscious seeking for new

---

[76] William Whallon, "The Diction of *Beowulf*," *PMLA* 76

combinations takes place, nor is exact verbal equivalence the normal aim. Even in the infinitive element,
which allows a finer adjustment of the meaning to the
original, there is not as much freedom evident as one
might expect. The actual infinitives used are traditional and semantically inexact; a few preponderate
(e.g., *lædan, feran, gangan, secan, seon, nerian,
fleon*) while many others occur only once or twice.
Any semantic lack tends to be made up by the use of
supplementary substantives, in conformity with the
needs of the substantive dominated verse-system (e.g.,
GN 2005b-06a *gewat seo wæpna laf / fæsten secan* for
14.10 "et qui remanserant, fugerunt ad montem").

While this formula-system is used transparently,
without concern for the gap between the verbal detail
of the original and the translation, there is a tendency, if the formulas lead too far from the intent of
the original, to bring the meaning back into line with
additional correcting matter. Thus, "et ecce unus qui
evaserat nuntiavit Abram . . ." (14.13), where an
idea of speaking is uppermost, becomes *him þa secg
hraðe / gewat siðian* (2018), where the incidental idea
of motion is stressed. Having gotten so far, the poet
must clarify this motion and the subordinate "evaserat"
becomes the theme of the sentence:

> him þa secg hraðe   gewat siðian,
> *an gara laf,   se ða guðe genæs*
> abraham secan.   (2018-20)

The formula has postponed the main statement for two-
and-a-half lines, which is only brought back in the
next sentence:

> se þæt orlegweorc
> þam ebriscan   eorle gecyðde . . . (2020-21).

The advantage of such a procedure is that it automatically leads to the poetic elaboration of the text.
The poet lopes from one broad idea to the next, foregrounding and elaborating subordinate grammatical material, so that it all subsists on the same "epic"
level.

The traditional formulas evolved because of the

(1961), 309-19, has shown that the "formulaic economy"
of *Beowulf*, while great compared to that of "literary"
poetry, is not so developed as that of Homeric poetry,
where there tends to be *one* formula only for a given
idea in a given metrical situation. The instances I
have given show that in *Genesis A* there are several
expressions for the idea of "departing" that are func-
tionally and semantically identical and interchangeable
in a variety of semantical and metrical situations.

need to say given things at some length, in differing
syntactical situations. The need to say something was
always more immediately pressing than the exact im-
port of what was said. If not quite precise, a statement could be adjusted by further elaboration, and
indeed, the imprecision of the available means both
limited the expectations and critical capabilities of
the audience, and gave opportunity for carrying on
the poem by requiring explanation (as imprecision in
the language of ordinary speech both limits expression and necessitates explanatory elaboration). It
is one of the most essential and useful features of
formulaic poetry, though far from the laconic and
precise style of the original.

Such an elaborate and varied way of making
statements often produces meaning, in the unexamined,
uncompared utterance, that seems more meaningful than
its function really intends or permits. A famous
example is the expression applying to Hrethel's
death in *Beowulf*: *Godes leoht geceas* (2469b). This
is not as significant or pietistic as it sounds; it
means no more than "he died" and may be compared to
a similar circumlocution concerning Scyld's death
(BW 26 f., cf. GN 1175 ff.). Yet it produces a semantic "excess" as a by-product of technique. Even
in the case of poets who are no longer strictly "oral"
in their method (and I do not mean to imply here that
I believe *Beowulf* is *oral*-formulaic, though at some
point its predecessors were), or even those composing
from a text, the technique, and to a large extent,
the poetic habits of mind, are formed by the traditional training of poets, rather than by a "learned"
environment or improved resources.

In *Genesis A*, because we have an external text
which shows exactly what these formulaic expressions
mean, we have a valuable control which often shows
clearly how the simpler statements get elaborated, yet
mean no more than the original. The Vulgate formula
for dying is "et mortuus est." It so happens that the
Genesis A-poet also has a formula for the same idea,
pa he forp gewat [*seon*] (GN 1068b, 1178b, 1192b, 1742b,
etc.). Although the Old English expression is metaphorical, while the Vulgate expression is not, they
are alike in being short, fixed and colorless. We saw
how the former arose. Its very frequency and
stability suggests that it has no "excess of meaning."
But for the sake of variation, another formulaic system is frequently employed which makes more elaborate
but essentially no more meaningful statements of the
same idea:

                          ealra hæfde
         twelfe and nigonhund   þa seo tid gewearð
         þæt he friðgedal   fremman sceolde.
         him æfter heold   þa he of worulde gewat
         enos yrfe   siððan eorðe swealh
         sædberendes   sethes lice.   (1140-45)

5.7   Et facti sunt omnes dies Seth nongentorum
         duodecim annorum et mortuus est. Vixit
         vero Enos . . . .

         adam on eorðan   ealra hæfde
         nigenhund wintra
         and þrittig eac   þa he þas woruld
         þurh gastgedal   ofgyfan sceolde. (1124-27)

5.4   Et factum est omne tempus quod vixit Adam,
         anni nongenti trigenta, et mortuus est.

                      swealt þa he hæfde,
         frod fyrnwita   fif and nigonhund.   (1153-54)

5.11 Factique sunt omnes dies Enos nongentorum
         quinque annorum et mortuus est.

Similar expressions are used of the posterity of Cain,
though in the Vulgate the formula "et mortuus est"
does not appear at this point:

         Siððan mathusal   magum dælde,
         bearn æfter bearne   broðrum sinum,
         æðelinga gestreon   oð þæt aldorgedal
         frod fyrndagum   fremman sceolde,
         lif oflætan.   (1069-73)
4.18 . . . et Mathusahel genuit Lamech.

Obviously, the poet's object is not the particular
meanings of *friðgedal, gastgedal, aldorgedal,* nor
does he intend a comparison between them. If he
meant anything beyond the simple concept "he died,"
which is in the text he is following, he would surely
have distinguished the quality of the deaths of the
offspring of Cain from those of the blessed Sethites.
But Seth's death is called *wælrest* (1643), which, if
taken at its full semantic value, has violent conno-
tations utterly inappropriate to the situation. Neither is the poet concerned to reproduce accurately the
words of the Vulgate, nor to preserve the stability
and symmetry which mark its style. Rather, we have

here an amplification of the bare text, a purely stylistic transformation. To be sure, in the process of
repeating so often variations upon so simple a theme,
the resources are strained to the limit, for the symmetry of the original manifests itself by the more or
less equal weight given to each death and by formulaic
stereotyping in the unusual repetition of the *-gedal-*
formula which has a "literary" effect foreign to the
best oral poetry. But the poet's intention and method
are formed by his instinct that the sound and texture
of his treatment are more important than the exact
details of meaning.[77]

      Not all the poet's formulas are inherited. Like
any good formulaic poet he added something to the tradition that came to him. The text demands and suggests
many new concepts and expressions to which the poet
had to respond with at least some new resources, and
the text gives us the means of spotting some of these
innovations. There are many layers and systems
of formulas which have arisen because of the need
for particular responses to the text which, when
once formulaically established, prove useful beyond
immediate demands of context. The idea of *migration*
is a frequently repeated pattern of the original. The
earlier biblical occurrences of this idea include the
taking of family and possessions. Thus, 11.31, the
first such passage, reads: "Tulit itaque Thare Abram
filium suum, et Loth filium Aran filium filii sui et
Sarai nurum suam, uxorem Abram filii sui, et eduxit
eos de Ur Chaldaeorum ut irent in terram Chanaan. . ."
and *Genesis A* responds:

[77] This is clearly shown by a careful comparison of
Genesis A 192-98a and 1504b-05, 1510b-17; these two
groups represent similar formulaic passages in the Vulgate, 1.28 and 7.1 respectively. There is too much
thematic and formulaic consistency for a poet who is
consciously looking for different ways of expressing
the same Vulgate statement *while comparing texts*, and
yet there is too much variation if a conscious attempt is being made to reproduce the similarity of
the two Vulgate passages. Rather than pedantic cross-
referencing, what we seem to have here is genuine
spontaneous formulaic composition—the poet responding
to the text in front of him in both cases. The similarities are due to the formulaic constants in the
OE. formulaic stock, the differences to the essential
differences in the two contexts.

       gewat him þa mid cnosle   ofer caldea folc
       feran mid feorme,   fæder abrahames,
       snotor mid gesibbum.   secean wolde
       cananea land.   (1730-33)

A few lines later, God's speech, "Egredere de terra
tua, et de cognatione tua, et de domo patris tui..."
(12.1), becomes

       gewit þu nu feran   and þine fare lædan,
       ceapas to cnosle.   carram ofgif,
       fæder eðelstol.   (1746-48)

The idea of taking possessions is in the Old English,
but not in the Latin. In the next occurrence, the idea
of taking possession *is* in the Latin and *Genesis A* has

       Him þa abraham gewat   æhte lædan
       of egipta   eðelmearce,
       gumcystum god,   golde and seolfre, etc.
             (1767-69, cf. 12.4-5)

In 12.14, the idea of possessions is not expressed,
but it appears in the Old English:

       Þa com ellenrof   eorl siðian,
       abraham mid æhtum   on egypte. . . . (1844-45)

Thus, the poet has by now established a definite formulaic way of dealing with "migration," based on earlier
biblical occurrences. Once the pattern has been established, it functions with a logic of its own, whatever
the details of the original:

       GEwat him þa mid bryde   broðor arones
       under abimelech   æhte lædan
       mid his hiwum. (2621-23 = 20.1; cf. 1873-77 = 13.1)

Because on many occasions when Abraham completes a migration, he tends, according to the text, to set up
an altar (so GN 1791 *wibed worhte* = "aedificavit. . .
altare," similarly GN 1806, 1882), when he completes
his final migration in the poem he sets up an altar,
although an altar is not mentioned in Genesis at
this point (21.33 = GN 2840-43).

    The development of formulaic expressions and
themes under the influence of the text of Genesis can
be seen everywhere in the poem. It is one of the
main principles of traditional poetry that it must
absorb and transform new material when it interacts
with outside influences. If it does not it dies; the
Paris Psalter is formulaic poetry in its death throes,
unable to change or absorb. Such interaction is an
organic process and, although this process of
composition is in a sense very special to this type
of scriptural poetry, it is probably not much different in kind from the interaction of old and new elements that takes place in any oral poem except that
because of the text which causes many unfamiliar

things to be said, and many of them repeated, there
are more opportunities for devising new formulas and
themes than is usually the case in secular formulaic
poetry. The processes behind *Genesis A*'s composition,
then, are not really alien to oral-formulaic poetry;
the essential difference is that so many things are
originating from one poet in the course of one composition, and relatively few of them are developed
beyond this one composition and passed on to be re-
fined by other poets. Faithfulness to the text is the
source of originality here, and yet the novelty draws
the expressions away from the life-giving traditions
which feed this kind of poetry at the roots, preven-
ting *Genesis A* from achieving that highly-wrought perfection which marks the best, and thoroughly traditional, Anglo-Saxon poetry.

I. The Style of *Genesis A*: Diction

The diction of *Genesis A* stems from the traditional poetic diction of oral alliterative poetry.
In its main features it is similar to that of most
other Old English poetry and need not be broadly
discussed here.[78] The main interest of the diction
of this poem is that it uses the traditional diction
as a response to the lexis of a specific Latin text.
The influence of the Vulgate words has its effect
upon the traditional poetic lexis, pulling it towards
the Latin semantically. Formally, the diction of
Genesis A follows the decorums of traditional poetic
usage, but semantically it is not free, and not quite
normal. In the traditional poetry there was little
stimulus towards, because little need for, a precise
diction. Individual poems developed words freely, the
general meanings of words sharpened by their association with other words in particular contexts, by the
repetition of terms for one object, person or action,
and by the free combination of words to create new
concepts. Basically, the traditional poetry was
not committed to an exactly conceived meaning, but
developed meanings out of the dynamic interactions of
words in context.
But a poetic translator was not free to expand

---

[78] For general discussions of OE. poetic diction, see
Stanley B. Greenfield, *A Critical History of Old
English Literature,* 69-79; Arthur G. Brodeur, *The
Art of Beowulf* (Berkeley and Los Angeles, 1960), 1-70.

and qualify his diction in the usual way. The text
he followed was finite, fixed, and forced him to precision, yet the demands of his art forced him to
vary and multiply his lexis, to find not one precise
word for each Vulgate word (as the O.E. prose Genesis
tends to do), but to find many equivalents, so as to
fashion the Vulgate style into the multilexis of poetic style. The Vulgate lexis shows lexical economy
and semantic repletion, that is, in the Vulgate the
terms *arca*, *terra*, *angelus*, *caelum*, etc. are formally
constant, whatever semantic shades they might have
in different occurrences. The opposite is true in
Genesis A: there a given Vulgate form is represented
by many different O.E. forms, but this lexical variety
does not accommodate a similar variety of meanings
in different contexts. For example, the Vulgate occurrences of "terra" are met by *Genesis A* with a ple-
thora of forms: *eorðe*, *folde*, *land*, *woruld*, *woruldrice*, *middangeard*, etc., occurring in about the same
proportionate frequency as the same words do in *Beowulf*. On the other hand, the lexis of *Genesis A* is
pulled out of alignment by the probable existence of
"right" gloss-words for particular Vulgate words.
For example, the usual word for *civitas* in the established diction of poetry and late West Saxon prose
is *burh*. But the Vespasian Psalter gloss, along with
other O.E. psalter glosses, invariably shows *cester*,
which must have been felt as the proper "biblical"
word.[79] Comparing the words in *Genesis A* which translate an occurrence of *civitas* with the occurrence in
Genesis A of words meaning *city* not directly corres-

[79] The tradition of gloss words in the OE. psalter is
remarkably constant from the ninth through the eleventh centuries. In citing the Vespasian Psalter glosses of the ninth century I do not mean to imply that
there is any direct connection between Vespasian and
Genesis A. My point is merely that the tradition was
widespread and must have been somewhat earlier than
Vespasian itself, that for common biblical texts such
as Genesis and the Psalter there was probably a well-
fixed tradition of written and oral glosses even before continuous written glosses became common. The
text of Vespasian is Sherman M. Kuhn, *The Vespasian
Psalter* (Ann Arbor, 1965); for a discussion of the
Psalter gloss tradition in Anglo-Saxon England, see
Minnie Cate Morrell, *A Manual of Old English Biblical
Materials* (Knoxville, 1965), 45-153, with extensive
further references; for Vespasian, see *ibid.*, 49-81.

ponding to a Vulgate occurrence of *civitas* and the
frequencies of the corresponding words in *Beowulf*, we
find the following pattern:

	GN = *civitas*	GN (free)	BW
burh	12x	3x	6x
ceaster	6x	2x	—[80]
fæsten	3x	1x	3x
Overall Totals[81]	27x	9x	13x

While *burh* appears as the normal poetic word in
nearly half of all occurrences, in *Genesis A* the
apparent gloss-word for *civitas*, that is, *ceaster*,
shows up at a ratio of 1:4, while it does not appear as a simplex in *Beowulf* at all.

The lexical "repletion" of *Genesis A* is the
result of the need to decorate and vary the diction
by a poet sensitive to the requirements of his style.[82]
The treatment of "arca" will show this concretely.
Genesis A uses *earc* most commonly, and this appears
to be the common gloss-word. *Earc* occurs 7x translating *arca* directly, 4x "freely." In addition,
however, the following equivalents occur, the lexical variety having no other discernible function
than to vary the style (frequencies after words refer to direct translations of *arca* and free occurrences, respectively): *scip* (2x, 3x), *merehus* (1x, 1x),
geofonhus (—, 1x), *fær* (2x, 3x), *wudufæsten* (1x, —),
pellfæst (—, 1x), *hrof* (1x, —), *lide* (1x, 1x), *hof*
(1x, 3x), *bord* (1x, 1x), *nægledbord* (—, 2x), *mereciest* (—, 1x), *holmærn* (1x, —), *hus* (—, 1x), *wæg-*

---

[80] *Beowulf* has *ceasterbuend* (1x).
[81] Including occurrences of all other words meaning
civitas besides *burh, ceaster, fæsten*.
[82] Contrast the *Paris Psalter*, which follows the
gloss tradition word for word as much as the exigencies of poetic composition will allow, admitting
frequent "unpoetic" words, such as *onsceoniendlice,
mildheortness*, etc., while unnaturally restricting
the poetic lexis to a relatively few items, frequently
repeated as mere filler. See the remarks of Kenneth
and Celia Sisam, "The Psalm Texts," in *The Paris Psalter: MS. Bibliotheque Nationale Fonds Latin 8824*,
EEMF 8, ed. Bertram Colgrave (Copenhagen, 1958), 17.

bord (—, 1x), *enge* (subs.) (—, 1x), *wægþel* (1x, 2x),
cofa (1x, —). At first sight this varied lexis suggests varied meanings, but a scrutiny shows that the
poet has cleverly limited his meanings, often by different combinations of the same elements, to two: the
ark as a chest to live in, the ark as ship. The first
idea is biblical, the second common-sense and common
tradition. [83] With such diction, there is no semantic
fluidity, none of the dazzle so prominent a feature
of the diction of *Beowulf*. Overall, the poet manages
to reproduce the effect of the steadiness and precision of meaning of the Vulgate, while reaching for the
lexical variety, if not spontaneity, of the old poetic
diction. The result seems rather flat, but it is probably an achieved effect. The poet's problem, given
his medium, was more likely a tendency towards over-
elaboration, and he is everywhere consciously reining
himself in.
     The poet is apparently more concerned with the
narrative function and ideational clarity of his diction than with the simple "poetic" production of
words. Mere formal equivalents are seldom accepted.
When Vulgate diction gives a problem of meaning, a
literal translation is avoided, often replaced by a
more meaningful or decorous substitute from the poetic stock: in no place does the poem appear to ex-
ceed the bounds of normal O.E. poetic diction. At
times the poet flattens, generalizes or re-forms exact and striking Vulgate words, but he also steers
clear of the exaggerated diction and implied metaphor of Cynewulfian poetry. He is not interested
in the poetic terms for their own sake (except perhaps in the battle sections), but in producing a so-
ber copy of the original.
     Thus, for example, "vernaculos suos" (14.14), trans-

---

[83] The situation is similar in the Noah excursus of
Exodus (lines 362-76), where the names for the ark
are *maðmhord* (368) and *scip* (375). Perhaps by coincidence, but probably reflecting different exemplars
at some stage of Junius 11's descent, the first illustrator presents the ark as a great three-storied
dragon-ship (P. 66, P. 68), while the second illustrator shows a palette-shaped box, perhaps, since it
appears to be studded with nails, influenced by the
text of the poem (P. 73; cf. *nægledbord* 1418, 1433);
see Introduction, I The Manuscript (p. 12, n. 16).

lated in the prose Genesis[84] *inbrydling*, becomes *his heorðwerod*, GN 2039. "Circumceditur (17.10 et passim), literally translated in *Hept.* by *emsnidan* (= *ymb-*), is replaced by *sigores tacn* at GN 2313, etc. (influenced by "in signum foederis" 17.11, cf. Commentary 2312-14a). "Dure accepit hoc" (21.11) becomes a poetic formula, *weorc on mode* (GN 2792; cf. BW 1418, JL 72), while *Hept.* is explanatory, *undernam hefiglice ðas word.* "A filo subtegminis usque ad corrigam caligae" (14.23) is familiarized to *sceat ne scilling*, GN 2144, while *Hept.* limps in with *ænne ðwang.* "Levo manum meam" (14.22) is explained by *ic pe gehate*, GN 2139.[85] Where the Vulgate has "dixit" (4.10) when God pronounces the judgement of Cain, *Genesis A* has *pingade* (1009b), exactly interpreting the tone of the original. "Fratres" in 13.8 means "uncle and nephew" and is translated *gemagas*, GN 1904.

Flatness is especially evident in the compounds, and exact prose meanings, as well as nominal poetic fitness, govern their use. Compounding was the most important poetic device available to Old English poets. In the parts of the poem "freely" developed, the compounds are as frequent and exuberant as any in the corpus; the following are some examples from the many compounds unique to *Genesis A* occurring in "free" passages (that is, not directly translating Vulgate words): *æsctir* 2069, "glory in war," *æscpracu* 2154, "spear-strength, battle," *cwealmprea* 2509, "deadly terror," *deoreðsceaft* 1984, "dart," *ecgwal* [-*wæl*] 2089, "sword-slaughter," *guðflan* 2063, "war-arrow," *guðspell* 2097, "news of war," *heahprea* 2547, "extreme terror," *orlegceap* 1994, "battle bargain" (see Commentary), *wigcyrm* 1990, "battle noise." These compounds are, however many, nevertheless uncharacteristic of the poem as a whole, and occur frequently only in the "free" portions. In lines 2046-80, translating only thirteen words of the Vulgate (14.15), there are nineteen compounds, while lines 2291-2396, heavily involved with the translation of most of eleven verses

---

[84] *The Old English Version of the Heptateuch*, ed. S. J. Crawford, EETS o.s. 160 (1922). Mention of this work (*Hept.*, prose Genesis), always implies a reference to the verse and chapter numbers, which correspond to those of the Vulgate.

[85] Apparently, an explanation of this verse was generally felt to be necessary; cf. Ps.-Bede, *In Pent. comm.*, PL. 91, 234B: "Quoque dicit, 'levo manus meam,' genus jurandi est."

of the Vulgate, contains only nine compounds (one,
wæpnedcynn, a prose word, repeated); the first passage has eight unique compounds, the second only
three.

      Overall, *Genesis A* is not so rich in compounds
as *Beowulf*, neither in respect of originality nor
frequency. There are 1070 distinct compound-words[86]
in *Beowulf* according to Klaeber, approximately 668 of
which are unique to that poem. There are in *Genesis
A* about 500 distinct compound-words and only 234 are
unique. There seems to be a higher proportion of
common prose-compounds in *Genesis A* than in *Beowulf*.
As might be expected, the vast majority of compounds
in *Genesis A* are unremarkable in themselves and make
no striking effects as poetry in their contexts. For
example, Cain is called *ordbana* 1097, "the first
murderer"—contrast Grendel, BW 2079, *muðbona* "one
who kills with his mouth." Yet morphologically the
two are identical, and *ordbana,* in another instance,
could well be "heroic."[87] Similarly prosaic in its
use, though striking as a lexical item is GN 2496,
gistmægen, "a force made up of visitors," which refers simply to the protecting angels who visited Loth
in Sodom.

      Compounds figure very little in the actual
translation of the text. Often they are used as
verse fillers, following up a key word as variation
once the poet has safely anchored the meaning with a
simplex: *ongyn þe* scip *wyrcan* / merehus *micel* (GN
1302b-1303a) for "Fac tibi arcam . . . ." *Wærfæst*
is used eleven times in *Genesis A* (five times in all
other poetry combined), applying to Abraham, to Loth,
to these two together, to God at the Flood time, to
Thare, to Abel, to God's will, and so on. In each
of these cases it is a simple attributive, filling a
line, alliterating, carrying out certain stylistic
functions, but not so much contributing to the meaning
as simply not offending *against* it. This is so often
the case with the "poetic" diction in this poem. There
are over 1200 individual occurrences of compounds in
Genesis A, yet of these, only about fifty are directly
representing a Latin word, while fewer than twenty
represent in any way a double concept that is corres-
pondingly in the Latin.

[86] By "distinct compound" is meant a compound word
having two meaningful stressed elements.
[87] Brodeur, *Art of Beowulf*, 255, would take *ordbana* as
"one who kills with the point of a spear."

The relative infrequency with which compounds directly represent a Vulgate word; the accuracy and plainness with which compounds do represent Vulgate words when they are called upon; the preference for simplexes to translate particular Vulgate words and the use of compounds chiefly as variations; the tendency for the O.E. poetic lexis to be pulled towards the biblical lexis; the frequency with which the poet re-forms Vulgate diction to obtain clarity in his version; the startling exuberance of those passages not directly translating the Bible; these features of the diction suggest that the poet was working through his poetic medium to produce a biblical style compatible with poetry, not merely paraphrasing the Bible in ready-made phrases. It is evidence of a conscious attempt to reform the poetic style itself.

J. The Style of *Genesis A*: Syntax

The basic problem of the poet-translator was to adapt pre-existing syntactical resources from the native formulaic tradition to the more diverse and complex patterns demanded or suggested by the Vulgate. One example will suggest the difficulty he faced. A common device of rhetorical elaboration in Old English poetry is to state the positive and negative aspects in an apparently adversative construction using *ne . . . ac*.[88] The simple use of this construction, and its likely antiquity, are shown by *Finnesburh* 3-5:

> Ne ðis ne dagað eastan,   ne her draca ne fleogeð,
> ne her ðisse healle   hornas ne byrnað;
> ac her forþ berað,   fugelas singað . . . .

The device occurs frequently in *Genesis A* in those places where the poet is not dealing with the words of the Vulgate, as in this example from the hexameral opening:

> heo on wrace syððan
> seomodon swearte,   siðe ne þorfton
> lude hlihhan   ac heo helltregum
> werige wunodon   and wean cuðon. . . . (71-74)

The *ne . . . ac* construction is a rhetorical device which provides expansionary and repetitive material,

----

[88] The *ne . . . ac* construction is examined in detail by Randolph Quirk, *The Concessive Relation in Old English Poetry* (New Haven, 1954), 48-58.

often of low semantical effect, as for example, *Genesis A* 1394-97, occurring between passages of more
exact translation.[89] Formally, the construction is
simply the negative/positive pattern, its importance
from the point of view of formulaic composition being
this very simplicity and consistency, though its functions vary considerably, from adversative, to concessive,[90] to what is in fact merely a way of adorn-
ing a positive statement. It was available to the
poet as part of his poetic system and could be adapted to situations which arose from the Latin text. For
example, he adapts it to a negative/negative configuration of the Vulgate:

>   Abraham, Abraham . . . *non* extendas manum tuam
>   super puerum, *neque* facias illi quidquam . . .
>   (22.11-12)
>   Abraham leofa,   *ne* sleah þin agen bearn
>   *ac* þu cwicne abregd   cniht of ade . . .
>   (2914-15)

The adversative configuration is used to translate and
bring out implied adversatives in the original:

>   ne sceolon unc betweonan   teonan weaxan,
>   wroht wriðian—   ne þæt wille god—
>   // Ac wit synt gemagas   (1902-04)
>
>   Ne, quaeso, sit iurgium inter me et te . . .
>   // fratres enim sumus.   (13.8)

And inverted:

>   ne þearft þu þe wiht ondrædan,
>   þenden þu mine lare læstest   // ac ic þe lif-
>   igende her
>   wið weana gehwam   wreo and scylde
>   folmum minum   ne þearft þu forht wesan (2169-72)
>
>   Noli timere, Abram, // ego protector tuus sum ...
>   (15.1)

At times the simple negative of the Vulgate is aug-

---

[89] E. B. Irving, Jr., *A Reading of Beowulf* (New Haven,
1968), 4, has characterized the construction (in *Beowulf*) as "a form of statement in terms of extremes,
where the poetic energy may originate in the violent
oscillations of sense from one extreme to another."
[90] Quirk, *Concessive Relation*, 52.

mented with the useful adversative system, which provides material for safe expansion:

>   abrecan ne meahton
> reðemode   reced æfter gistum,
> swa hie fundedon,   ac þær frome wæron
> godes spellbodan.   (2493-96)

> . . . ita ut ostium invenire non possent. (19.11)

Adaptations of the adversative configuration itself
occur:

> Næfre gerefan   rædað þine
> eafora yrfe   *ac* þin agen bearn
> frætwa healdeð . . . .   (2188-90)

> *Non* erit hic heres tuus, *sed* qui egredietur
> de utero tuo . . . .   (15.4)

The important point is that the poet is always trying to align the traditional rhetorical patterns to
those presented by the Vulgate, and even when he is
not able to do this exactly, he still augments or
changes in such a way that the meaning of the original
is reinforced rather than weakened. When a pattern
from the poetic tradition is available it is used
again and again; new inventions are not looked for
even though at times the syntactical patterns of the
original may have little similarity to the traditional
Old English ones immediately available.

Although the syntax of the Vulgate is being
expressed in terms of traditional poetic resources,
the elaborate development of particular syntactical
situations in the Old English text is a direct reflex of the poet's consciousness of a text which he
is encountering sentence by sentence. *Genesis A* consists of a series of equivalents which seem to be
constructed on a pragmatic basis according to the
traditional techniques of the native system and with
more or less success in each individual instance.
Much of the poem happens to be literal, word-for-word
translation, although the achievement of such does
not seem to be the prime objective. What is domin-
ant is the preservation of a nominal syntactical
equivalence. Even when sentences have been completely
recast, they still often follow the syntax of the
Vulgate:

>   ic þe wære nu,
> mago ebrea,   mine selle . . . (2204-05)

In illo die pepigit Dominus foedus cum Abram ...
                              (15.18)
On the authority of the following "dicens," 15.18 is
made part of God's speech which is begun at 15.7 (although that verse and the intervening matter is mostly
omitted) and third person becomes first. But the syntactical parallel is completely maintained:

In illo die pepigit Dominum foedus cum Abram

     nu   selle   ic mine wære   þe

     Yet there are countless instances where the
syntax presented by the Vulgate comes into direct
confrontation with the stylistic norms of Old English
poetry. Through these conflicts the poetic style of
Genesis A is whetted and matured. The resources
available to the poet seem to expand and flex, responding to the more supple Latin medium. As the
poem grows out of the intense pressures set up by
two widely different sets of demands, a rich blend
of style results. Often the details of syntax and
meaning may appear to differ greatly at the same time
that it is obvious that the syntactical structure of
the Old English situation is beholden to the Vulgate.
Differences that occur are the result of the relative
intractability of the poetic syntactical system, which
is bound to a great degree by prescribed rhetorical
and metrical patterns. One example may be given from
countless available of how the shape of the Vulgate
contains but does not entirely control the shape and
detail of the Old English syntax:

     [1]   ego Dominus
     [2]   qui eduxi te de Ur Chaldeorum
     [3]   ut darem tibi terram istam
     [4]   et possideres eam   (15.7)

     [1]   Ic eom se waldend / [2] se þe for wintra fela
           of caldea   ceastre alædde
           feowera sumne, / [3] gehet þe folcstede
           wide [4] to gewealde.   (2201-04)

The solid underlining indicates syntactical equivalence, broken underlining notional equivalence, where
some lexical adjustments have been made. But even as
close as [1] and [2] are, necessities of verse have
exerted their influence and slight changes have crept
in that change the emphasis and cast of the statement:
an article is inserted in 2201a to make up an a1-type;

for wintra fela and *feowera sumne* are formulaic intrusions to fill the line and provide alliteration
(note how they cooperate with the meaning: there *were*
four refugees from Ur [cf. 11.31], and no doubt many
years passed from the time of Thare's conversion until the entry into Chanaan). "Ur" is replaced by
ceastre in the same grammatical situation (oblique
case with dependent genitive); while *ceastre* is brought
in to provide the headstave, it at the same time generalizes the statement, giving it a universal applica-
tion. Rather than translating the syntax of the
Vulgate, [3] and [4] interpret it: [3] has a characteristic parallel structure, *alædde/gehet*, rather
than the purpose clause with *gehet,* for the *ut*-clause.
The inflected infinitive and the *pæt*-clause were
available, of course, but parallelism appears to be
preferred because closer to poetic style than further syntactic development would be.[91] Having avoided
the purpose-clause, the poet must do something else
with [4], since it also depends on *ut*. He substi-
tutes the convenient formula of low semantic value,
wide to gewealde, adverb plus prepositional phrase,
which with *folcstede gehet*, expresses the point
clearly enough, "promised [it] . . . for a dominion." [92]
   However often and to whatever degree a particular passage is forced by the exigencies of Old
English poetics to deviate from the Vulgate in pattern
or meaning, it is still nearly always clear that it
is formed in the first place on the Vulgate pattern.
There are many passages which in length and internal
complexity go far beyond the one-and-a-half lines that
Malone posited as the "plurilinear unit" of the developed middle period of Old English poetic style.[93] The
syntax of long passages of continuous response is elaborated in a way determined partly by outside linguistic factors and not merely by internal demands. Pre-

[91] Cf. *Hept.*, "ic ðe þis land forgeafe to agenne."
[92] Note the lexical congruity between the usual sense
of *folcstede (gewealdan)*, "to have control of the
battlefield," "win victory" (cf. *Brunanburh* 41, JU
319, *Riddle* 5.11, BW 1463) and its use here: "to have
a place for (your) own people to live in," where its
usual semantic sense is moribund, but its heroic lexical function is alive. By such details translation
becomes poetry.
[93] Kemp Malone, "Plurilineal Units in Old English
Poetry," *Review of English Studies* 19 (1943), 201-04.

sumably, if poets had never decided to imitate Latin
texts, these elaborated structures would have never
come about. Klaeber[94] noted the similarity in structure of *Genesis A* 2816 ff. and *Beowulf* 1180 ff., a
similarity which evinces an interesting development
of the traditional Germanic verse style. The source
for the *Genesis A* passage is 21.23:

> [1]   Iura ergo per Dominum
> [2]   ne noceas mihi
> [3]   et posteris meis, stirpique meae
> [4]   sed juxta misericordiam
> [5]   quam feci tibi
> [6]   facies mihi
> [7]   et terrae in qua versatus es advena.

                    [1] ic þe <u>bidde</u> nu,
    wine ebrea,   wordum minum
    [cf. 2,4,5] <u>þæt</u> þu tilmodig   treowa selle,
    wæra þina   [cf. 2,6] <u>þæt</u> þu wille me
    wesan fæle freond   fremena to leane
    [5]<u>þara</u> þe ic to duguðum   ðe gedon hæbbe,
    [7]<u>siððan</u> ðu feasceaft   feorran come
    on þas werþeode   wræccan laste.
    [4]<u>Gyld</u> me mid hyldo,   [5] þæt ic þe hneaw ne wæs
    landes and lissa.   [4] wes þissum leodum nu
    [3] and mægburge   minre arfæst.
    gif þe alwalda,   ure drihten,
    scirian wille   se ðe gesceapu healdeð . . . .
                    (2816-28)

The expansion takes place on the pattern of the
þæt-clause which naturally follows "bidde," translating "jura"; "bidde" acts as a headword for the
whole passage. The impulse for a continuous succession of subordinate clauses may spring from the structure of the Latin passage. The *Genesis*-passage proceeds by a series of repetitions of the basic pattern set up by "bidde"/"þæt"; there is a parallel repetition of the head-word in the form of the imperatives, "þu selle," "þu wille," "gyld," "wes," all
followed by dependent clauses repeating the initial
pattern. At the same time, characteristic things are
happening, changing the structure from the original:
instead of "quam," a genitive clause is translating
[5], "þara þe," and the neatness of [5,6] is broken

[94] Fr. Klaeber, "Die ältere Genesis und der Beowulf,"
Englische Studien 42 (1910), 321-38; cf. Marquardt,
Anglia 64, 152-58.

up. Eventually, the meaning of the Vulgate is revealed as the clausal repetitions unwind. The elaboration is a development out of genuine Old English
resources in that it is building up parallel structures,
but rather than mere one-verse epithets, or self-
contained syntactic structures within the half-line,
as in Caedmon's *Hymn* and *Finnesburh*, the parallels are
lengthy inter-dependent clauses which spring from the
Vulgate structure, yet possess a life and movement of
their own. The same is true in the passage from *Beowulf* which Klaeber cites in comparison with this one.[95]
That sentence is also developed in large parallel clausal structures, of a kind it is difficult to imagine
being possible before Latin-English poems like *Genesis
A* had made stylistic possibilities explicit, and integrated them into an enlarged stock of poetic resources:

Ic minne <u>can</u>

glædne Hroþulf,	<u>þæt</u> he þa geogoðe wile
arum healdan,	<u>gyf</u> þu ær þonne he,
wine Scildinga,	worold oflætest;
<u>wene</u> ic <u>þæt</u> he mid gode	gyldan wille
uncran eaferan,	<u>gif</u> he þæt eal gemon,
hwæt wit to willan	ond to worðmyndum
umborwesendum ær	arna gefremedon.

(*Beowulf* 1180-87)

It is remarkable, everything considered, that
we can compare the styles of *Beowulf* and *Genesis A* at
all, that the biblical paraphrase should have this independent life. The poet is not aiming for a bare
translation, but is trying to realize the full potentialities of the native tradition. It is the Vulgate itself which provides the hints of syntactical
possibilities inherent in the poet's medium, and it
is the Vulgate which is determining, in a general
way, what direction the development of the verse
style will take, not only in *Genesis A*, but in a
whole tradition of verse to follow.[96] New stylistic
resources became the poet's, whether or not he was
aware of them, as he compared, consciously or unconsciously, his traditional means to the varieties

---

[95] Klaeber, "Genesis und Beowulf," 331.
[96] No doubt, *Genesis A* and *Daniel* were not the only
verse paraphrases ever written in OE. Any poet facing
the task would have had analogous problems and responses. If the Vulgate had not affected poetic style so
crucially, we can imagine it taking different directions;
cf. skaldic verse and the OE. verse *Solomon and Saturn*.

of biblical syntax. The interaction of poetry and
Scripture meant in this case a fuller poetry than had
been possible in the simple tradition before Latin
texts became objects of poetry. Making poetry had
always meant theme-elaboration. To elaborate themes
and still to represent the original, the available
structures had to be enlarged: the model for enlarge-
ment was the thing being imitated. The interaction
of meaning, structure, repetition, versification bred
more complex units of syntax. In theory, it was not
impossible to simplify native verse-structure to render the literal text. The *Paris Psalter* does in fact
proceed in this way. But the cost of such a reductive
approach was enormous: outlandish and impoverished
diction, uncharacteristic, repetitive syntax, repres-
sion of elaboration and variation. This feeble method
emasculates the alliterative tradition while infla-
ting the original. Both poetry and Bible are lost.
Such a method would not suggest itself to any poet
working in a living and significant tradition of
formulaic poetry.

The *Genesis A* poet, responsible to his art,
takes the bold course. Rather than being cowed by the
differences of the two mediums, he turns them to advantage. He lets his syntax grow into a flexible,
responsive instrument. He turns the redundancy and
expansion natural to his technique to the purposes of
translation, always making the "excess" meaning bear
on the received interpretations of biblical explanation. The decorums of his style, which if badly hand-
led could mislead the audience, become the means whereby the original may be more clearly understood. When
we consider the compositional imperatives of his craft,
the pressures to say new things in strange, diverse
syntactical patterns, and the necessity of keeping
within the bounds of sound doctrine and exegesis while
conveying the essential meaning of each biblical statement, we can appreciate how narrow the poet's field
of choice really was, and given the difficulty of the
terms of his undertaking, how well he fulfilled his task.

IV. Bibliography

A. The Manuscript

Gollancz, Sir Israel, *The Caedmon Manuscript of Anglo-Saxon Biblical Poetry, Junius XI in the Bodleian Library* (Oxford, 1927) [facsimile].
Bliss, A. J., "Some Unnoticed Lines of Old English Verse," *Notes and Queries* 216 (1971), 404 [on five titles to the illustrations].
Stoddard, F. H., "The Caedmon Poems in MS. Junius XI," *Anglia* 10 (1888), 157-67.
Thornley, G. C., "The Accents and Points of MS. Junius XI," *Transactions of the Philological Society* (1954), 178-205.

   [*Valuable discussions of the Manuscript will be found in* Krapp *and* Wells, *section C, below, and in* Timmer, *section D, below*]

B. The Illustrations

Henderson, George, "Late Antique Influences in some English Medieval Illustrations of Genesis," *Journal of the Warburg and Courtauld Institutes* 25 (1962), 172-98; "The Programme of Illustrations in Bodleian MS XI," *Studies in Memory of David Talbot Rice*, ed. Giles Robertson and George Henderson (Edinburgh, 1975), 113-45.
Ohlgren, Thomas H., "Five New Drawings in the MS Junius 11: their Iconography and Thematic Significance," *Speculum* 47 (1972), 227-33; "Some New Light on the Old English *Caedmonian Genesis*," *Studies in Iconography* 1 (1975), 38-75.
Raw, Barbara, "The Probable Derivation of most of the Illustrations in Junius 11 from an Illustrated Old Saxon *Genesis*," *Anglo-Saxon England* 5, ed. Peter Clemoes (Cambridge, 1976), 133-48.
Wormald, Francis, "Decorated Initials in English MSS. from A.D. 900 to 1100," *Archaeologia* 91 (1945), 107-36; *English Drawings of the Tenth and Eleventh Centuries* (London, 1952).

C.   Editions of *Genesis A* [in chronological order]

   a.   Full Editions

Junius, Franciscus, *Caedmonis monachi paraphrasis
      poetica Genesios ac praecipuarum sacrae pa-
      ginae historiarum, abhinc annos M.LXX. Anglo-
      Saxonice conscripta & nunc primum edita* . . . .
      (Amsterdam, 1655).
Thorpe, Benjamin, *Caedmon's Metrical Paraphrase of
      Parts of the Holy Scriptures in Anglo-Saxon*
      (London, 1832).
Bouterwek, Karl W., *Caedmon's des Angelsächsen
      biblische Dichtungen* (Elberfield, 1849-51,
      Gütersloh, 1854; repr. 1968).
Grein, Christian W. M., *Bibliothek der angelsäch-
      sischen Poesie*, Vol. 1 (Göttingen, 1857).
Wülker, Richard P., *Bibliothek der angelsächsischen
      Poesie*, Vol. 2 (Leipzig, 1894) [revision of
      Grein, more conservative text].
Holthausen, Ferdinand, *Die altere Genesis mit Ein-
      leitung, Anmerkungen, Glossar und der lat-
      einischen Quelle* (Heidelberg, 1914).
Krapp, George Philip, *The Junius Manuscript*, The
      Anglo-Saxon Poetic Records, Vol. 1 (New York,
      1931).
Wells, David M., "A Critical Edition of the Old
      English *Genesis A* with a Translation," unpub.
      doc. diss., University of North Carolina, 1969.

   b.   Partial Editions [minor editions of no inde-
        pendent interest are not listed]

Ettmüller, Ludwig, *Engla and Seaxna Scôpas and Bô-
      ceras* (Quedlinburg and Leipzig, 1850) [lines
      852-964].
Greverus, J. P. E., *Caedmon's Schöpfung und Abfall
      der bösen Engel aus dem Angelsächsischen über-
      setzt nebst Anmerkungen* (Oldenburg, 1852)
      [lines 852-964]
Zupitza, Julius, *Altenglisches Übungsbuch* (Vienna,
      1874) [lines 2846-2936].
Kluge, Friedrich, *Angelsächsisches Lesebuch* (Halle,
      1888) [lines 1-234].
Bright, James W., *An Anglo-Saxon Reader* (New York,
      1891) [lines 2846-2936].
Klaeber, Fr., *The Later Genesis and Other Old English
      and Old Saxon Texts Relating to the Fall of
      Man* (Heidelberg, 1913) [lines 852-964].

Cassidy, Frederic G. and Richard N. Ringler, *Bright's
    Old English Grammar and Reader, Third Edition*
    (New York, 1971) [lines 2846-2936].
Marckwardt, Albert H. and James L. Rosier, *Old English
    Language and Literature* (New York, 1972) [lines
    1285-1496; 1960-2095].

D.   Editions of Other Primary Sources Cited

Krapp, George Philip and Elliott Van Kirk Dobbie, *The
    Anglo-Saxon Poetic Records*, Vols. 2-6 (New
    York, 1932-53) [Vol. 1 is *The Junius Manuscript*,
    see section C, above]

  Genesis B:
Timmer, B. J., *The Later Genesis* (Oxford, 1948).
Vickrey, J. F., Jr., "Genesis B: A New Analysis and
    Edition," unpub. doc. diss., University of
    Indiana, 1960.

  Exodus:
Irving, E. B., Jr., *The Old English Exodus* (New
    Haven, 1953, repr. 1970) [notes, corrections
    and additions publ. in *Anglia* 90 (1972), 289-334].

  Daniel:
Farrell, R. T., *Daniel and Azarias* (London, 1974).

  Christ and Satan:
Clubb, Merrel D., *Christ and Satan, An Old English
    Poem* (New Haven, 1925).

  Beowulf:
Klaeber, Fr., *Beowulf and the Fight at Finnsburg*
    (3rd ed., Boston, 1950).
Wrenn, C. L., *Beowulf with the Finnesburg Fragment*
    (rev. ed., London, 1958).

  Other Old English Poetry:
Chambers, R. W., *Widsith: A Study in Old English
    Heroic Legend* (1912, repr. New York, 1965).
Gradon, P. O. E., *Cynewulf's Elene* (London, 1958).

  Heliand and the O.S. Genesis
Behaghel, Otto, *Heliand und Genesis*, rev. Walther
    Mitzka (8th ed., Halle, 1965).
Sievers, Eduard, *Heliand* (Halle, 1878).

Other:
Braune, Wilhelm, *Althochdeutsches Lesebuch* (4th
    ed., Halle, 1897)
Jónsson, Finnur, *Sæmundr-Edda* (2d ed., Reykjavík,
    1926).

E. Translations of *Genesis A* [Translations are
    included in the editions of Bouterwek,
    Thorpe and Wells, in section C, above. Par-
    tial translations are not listed here.]

Kennedy, Charles W., *The Caedmon Poems, translated
    into English Prose* (London, 1916, repr. 1965).
Mason, Lawrence, *Genesis A, translated from the
    Old English* (New York, 1915).

F. Glossary

Braasch, Theodor, *Vollständiges Wörterbuch zur sog.
    Caedmonschen Genesis*, Anglistische Forschungen
    76 (Heidelberg, 1933).

G. Genesis and its Commentaries

  a. Texts

*Biblia Sacra iuxta latinam vulgatam versionem ad
    codicum fidem; Volume I* Genesis, ed. H. Quen-
    tin (Rome, 1926) [critical edition of the Vulgate].
*Vetus Latina: Die Reste der altlateinischen Bibel
    nach Petrus Sabatier neu gesammelt und herausge-
    geben von der Erzabtei Beuron: 2* Genesis, ed.
    B. Fischer (Freiburg, 1951).

  b. Commentaries

    [*The standard bibliography of patristic material
    (up to Bede) is* Eligius Dekkers and Aemilius Gaar,
    Clauis Patrum Latinorum, Sacris Eruditi 3 (2d ed.,
    Bruges, 1961); *the standard catalogue of medieval
    commentaries is* Friedrich Stegmüller, *Repertorium
    Biblicum Medii Aevi,* 7 vols. to date (Madrid, 1940
    [1950]-1961). *Some bibliographical and historical
    guidance will be found in* Frank Egleston Robbins,
    *The Hexaemeral Literature: A Study of the Greek
    and Latin Commentaries on Genesis* (Chicago, 1912),
    93-104. *See also* Evans, section I, *below, supple-*

mented by Michael Benskin and Brian Murdoch,
"The Literary Tradition of Genesis," *Neuphilologische Mitteilungen* 76 (1975), 389-403.]

Ælfric, "Ælfric's Version of Alcuini Interrogationes
    Sigeuulfi in Genesis," ed. G. E. MacLean,
    Anglia 7 (1884), 1-59; *Exameron Anglice*, ed.
    S. J. Crawford, Bibliothek der angelsächsischen
    Prosa 10 (Hamburg, 1921, repr. 1968); *The Old
    English Version of the Heptateuch, Aelfric's
    Treatise on the Old and New Testament and his
    Preface to Genesis*, ed. S. J. Crawford, EETS
    o.s. 160 (1922, repr. 1969).
Alcuin, *Interrogationes et responsiones in Genesin*,
    PL. 100.
Ambrose, *Exameron, De paradiso, De Cain et Abel, De
    Noe [et arca], De Abraham, De Isaac vel anima*,
    PL. 14.
"Ambrosiaster", *Quaestiones Veteris et Noui Testamenti*
    PL. 35.
Angelomus of Luxeuil, *Commentarius in Genesin*, PL. 115.
Augustine, *De ciuitate Dei*, ed. B. Dombart and A. Kalb,
    CCSL 47-48 (Turnhout, 1955); *Confessiones*, PL.
    32; *Contra Faustum Manichaeum*, PL. 42; *Enchiri-
    dion ad Laurentium*, PL. 40; *De Genesi ad litte-
    ram libri xii*, PL. 34; *De Genesi ad litteram
    imperfectus liber*, PL. 34; *De Genesi contra Man-
    ichaeos*, PL. 34; *Quaestionum in Heptateuchum
    libri vii*, ed. I. Fraipont, CCSL 33 (Turnhout,
    1958); *Sermones de Vetere Testamento*, ed. C.
    Lambot, CCSL 41 (Turnhout, 1961).
Bede, *In Genesim*, ed. Ch. W. Jones, CCSL 118A (Turn-
    hout, 1967) [see also Ch. W. Jones, "Some Intro-
    ductory Remarks on Bede's Commentary on *Genesis*,"
    Sacris Erudiri 19 (1972), 115-98].
[Claudius of Turin], *Commentariorum in Genesim*, PL.
    50 [attributed to Hilary of Arles].
[Cyprianus Gallus?], *In Genesim ad Leonam Papam*, PL. 50
    [attributed to Hilary of Arles]; *Heptateuchos*,
    PL. 2, 1097 (1155); 19, 345 [attributed to Ju-
    vencus].
Eustathius, *In Hexaemeron S. Basilii latina metaphra-
    sis*, PL. 53.
Glossa Ordinaria, PL. 113.
Hrabanus Maurus, *Commentariorum in Genesim*, PL. 107.
Isidore of Seville, *Etymologiarum*, ed. W. M. Lindsay,
    2 vols. (Oxford, 1911); *Quaestiones de Veteri
    et Nouo Testamento*, PL. 83.
Jerome, *Liber interpretationis hebraicorum nominum*,
    ed. P. de Lagarde, CCSL 72 (Turnhout, 1959);

Liber quaestionum hebraicarum in Genesim, ed.
    ibid.
Liber de ordine creaturarum, PL. 83 [attributed to Isi-
    dore of Seville].
Petrus Comestor, *Historia scholastica*, PL. 198.
[Ps.-Bede], *In Pentateuchum commentarii*, PL. 91;
    *Quaestionum super Genesim, ex dictis patrum,
    dialogus*, PL. 93; *De sex dierum creatione*,
    PL. 93.
Remigius of Auxerre, *Commentarius in Genesim*, PL. 131.

Cassuto, Umberto, *A Commentary on the Book of Genesis*,
    tr. Israel Abraham, 2 vols. (Jerusalem, 1961).
Rad, Gerhard von, *Genesis: A Commentary*, tr. John H.
    Marks (London, 1961).
Skinner, J., *A Critical and Exegetical Commentary on
    Genesis* (2d ed., Edinburgh, 1930).

H.   Studies of *Genesis A* [the list is selective before
     ca. 1930; for older work see the bibliography
     in Krapp, *The Junius Manuscript*]

Balg, Hugo, *Der Dichter Caedmon und seiner Werke* (Bonn,
    1882)
Bammesberger, Alfred, "Zu altenglisch *berofan* in *Gen-
    esis* 2078b," *Die Sprache* 19 (1973), 205-07.
Bradley, Henry, "The 'Caedmonian' Genesis," *Essays and
    Studies by Members of the English Association* 6
    (1920), 7-29.
Brockman, Bennett A. "'Heroic' and 'Christian' in
    Genesis A: The Evidence of the Cain and Abel
    Episode," *Modern Language Quarterly* 35 (1974),
    115-28.
Crawford, S. J., "The Caedmon Poems," *Anglia* 49 (1929),
    279-84.
Creed, Robert B., "The Art of the Singer: Three Old
    English Tellings of the Offering of Isaac," *Old
    English Poetry: Fifteen Essays*, ed., *idem* (Pro-
    vidence, 1967), 69-92; "*Genesis* 1316," *Modern
    Language Notes* 73 (1958), 321-25.
Ebert, Adolf, "Zur angelsächsischen Genesis," *Anglia* 5
    (1882), 124-33.
Ferrell, C. C., *Teutonic Antiquities in the Anglo-Saxon
    Genesis* (Halle, 1893).
Gatch, Milton McC., "Noah's Raven in Genesis A and the
    Illustrated Old English Hexateuch," *Gesta* 14.2
    (1975), 3-15.

Graz, Friedrich, "Beiträge zur Textkritik der soge-
    nannten Caedmonschen Genesis," *Festschrift zum
    70. Geburtstage Oskar Schade* (Königsberg, 1896),
    67-77.
Heinze, Alfred, *Zur altenglischen Genesis* (Berlin, 1889).
Hofmann, Dietrich, "Untersuchungen zu der altenglischen
    Gedichten *Genesis* und *Exodus*," *Anglia* 75 (1957),
    1-34.
Holthausen, Ferdinand, "Studien zur altenglischen
    Dichtung," *Anglia* 46 (1922) 52-62 [additions and
    corrections to his edition of *Genesis A*].
Hönncher, Erwin, "Über die Quellen der angelsäch-
    sische Genesis," *Anglia* 8 (1885), 41-84.
Huppé, Bernard F., *Doctrine and Poetry: Augustine's
    Influence on Old English Poetry* (New York,
    1959) [Chapter V is on *Genesis A*].
Irving, Edward B. "On the Dating of the Old English
    Poems *Genesis* and *Exodus*," *Anglia* 77 (1959), 1-11.
Jovy, Hans, "Untersuchungen zur altenglischen Genesis-
    dichtung," *Bonner Beiträge* 5 (1900), 1-32.
Klaeber, Fr., "Altengl. Genesis 1491 f.," *Archiv für das
    Studium der neueren Sprachen und Literaturen* 158
    (1941), 123-24; "Die ältere Genesis und der Beowulf,"
    Englische Studien 42 (1910), 321-38.
Menner, Robert J., "The Date and Dialect of *Genesis A,
    852-2936*," *Anglia* 70 (1951), 285-94.
Michel, Laurence, "*Genesis A* and the 'Praefatio', *Mo-
    dern Language Notes* 62 (1947), 545-50.
Mirsky, Aaron, "On the Sources of the Anglo-Saxon
    Genesis and *Exodus*," *English Studies* 48 (1967),
    385-97.
Moore, Samuel, "The Old English 'Genesis', lines 1145
    and 1446-48," *Modern Language Review* 6 (1911),
    199-202.
Robinson, Fred C., "The Old English Genesis, lines
    1136-37," *Archiv für das Studium der neueren
    Sprachen und Literaturen* 204 (1968), 267-68.
Rosier, James L., "God on the Warpath: *Genesis A*
    2112," *Archiv für das Studium der neueren
    Sprachen und Literaturen* 202 (1965-66), 269-71;
    "*Hrincg* in *Genesis A*," *Anglia* 88 (1970), 334-36.
Sievers, Eduard, "Caedmon und Genesis," *Britannica:
    Max Förster zum 60. Geburtstage* (Leipzig, 1929),
    57-84.
Utley, Francis Lee, "The Flood Narrative in the Junius
    Manuscript and in Baltic Literature, *Studies in
    Old English Literature in Honor of Arthur Gil-
    christ Brodeur*, ed. Stanley B. Greenfield
    (Eugene, Ore., 1963), 207-26.

I.   Works which include discussion of *Genesis A*

Bradley, Henry, "Some Emendations in Old English
      Texts," *Modern Language Review* 11 (1916), 212-15.
Brook, G. L., "The Relation between the Textual and
      the Linguistic Study of Old English," *The
      Anglo-Saxons,* ed. Peter Clemoes (London, 1959),
      280-91.
Clark, George, "The Traveler Recognizes his Goal:
      A Theme in Anglo-Saxon Poetry," *JEGP* 64 (1965),
      645-59.
Cosijn, Peter, J., "Anglosaxonica," *Paul und Braune's
      Beiträge* 19 (1894), 441-61 [textual notes];
      "Anglosaxonica II," *ibid.* 20 (1895), 98-116
      [textual notes].
Dietrich, Franz, "Zu Cädmon," *Zeitschrift für deut-
      sches altertum* 10 (1856), 210-67 [textual notes].
Dustoor, P. E., "Legends of Lucifer in Early English
      and in Milton," *Anglia* 54 (1930), 213-68.
Emerson, Oliver F., "Legends of Cain, especially in
      Old and Middle English," *PMLA* 21 (1906), 831-929.
Evans, J. M., *Paradise Lost and the Genesis Tradtion*
      (Oxford, 1968).
Frank, Roberta, "Some Uses of Paronomasia in Old Eng-
      lish Scriptural Verse," *Speculum* 47 (1972),
      207-26.
Graz, Friedrich, *Die Metrik der sog. caedmonschen
      Dichtungen und Berücksichtigung der Verfasser-
      frage* (Weimar, 1894).
Greenfield, Stanley B., *A Critical History of Old Eng-
      lish Literature* (New York, 1968).
Grein, Christian W. M., "Zur Textkritik der angelsäch-
      sischen Dichter," *Germania* 10 (1865) 416-29
      [textual notes].
Hill, Thomas D., "Some Remarks on the Site of Lucifer's
      Throne," *Anglia* 87 (1969), 303-11.
Holthausen, Ferdinand, "Zu altenglischen Denkmälern,"
      Englische Studien 51 (1917), 180-88 [textual notes];
      "Beiträge zur Erklärung und Textkritik alteng-
      lischen Dichter," *Indogermanische Forschungen*
      4 (1894), 379-88 [textual notes].
Hulbert, J. R., "On the Text of the Junius Manuscript,"
      JEGP 37 (1938), 533-36.
Kock, Ernst A., "Interpretations and Emendations of
      Early English Texts," V *Anglia* 43 (1919) 298-312;
      VII *Anglia* 44 (1920) 245-60; IX, X *Anglia* 46
      (1922), 63-96, 173-90; *Jubilee Jaunts and Jottings:
      250 Contributions to the Interpretation and Pro-*

        sody of Old West Teutonic Alliterative Poetry,
        Lunds Universitets Årsskrift, N.F., Avd 1, Bd.
        14, Nr. 26 (1918); *Plain Points and Puzzles:
        60 Notes on Old English Poetry, ibid.*, N.F.,
        Avd. 1, Bd. 17, Nr. 7 (1922).
Larés, M.-M., "Échos d'un rite hiérosolymitain dans
        un manuscrit du haut Moyen Age anglais," *Re-
        vue de l'histoire des religions*, 165 (1964),
        13-47 [relation of Junius 11 to Eastern liturgies
        of Easter Week].
Malone, Kemp, "When did Middle English Begin?" *Curme
        Volume of Linguistic Studies*, ed. Werner Leopold
        and A. J. Friedrich Zieglschmid, Language Mono-
        graphs 7 (Baltimore, 1930), 110-17.
Morrell, Minnie Cate, *A Manual of Old English Biblical
        Materials* (Knoxville, 1965).
Rieger, Max, "Die alt- und angelsächsische Verskunst,"
        Zeitschrift für deutsche Philologie 7 (1876), 1-64
        [textual and metrical notes].
Robinson, Fred C., "The Significance of Names in Old
        English Literature," *Anglia* 86 (1968), 14-58.
Salmon, Paul, "The Site of Lucifer's Throne," *Anglia*
        81 (1963), 118-23.
Schmitz, Theodor, "Die Sechstakter in der altenglischen
        Dichtung," *Anglia* 33, 1-76 [hypermetric lines in
        GN, 28-32].
Shepherd, Geoffrey, "The Prophetic Caedmon," *Review of
        English Studies* n.s. 5 (1954), 113-22; "Scrip-
        tural Poetry," *Continuations and Beginnings:
        Studies in Old English Literature*, ed. E. G.
        Stanley (London, 1966), 1-36.
Sievers, Eduard, "Zu Codex Junius XI," *Paul und Braune's
        Beiträge* 10 (1885), 195-99 [textual notes]; *Der
        Heliand und die angelsächsische Genesis* (Halle,
        1875) [discovery of *Genesis B*].
Sisam, Kenneth, *Studies in the History of Old English
        Literature* (Oxford, 1958).
Skemp, Arthur S., "The Transformation of Scriptural
        Story, Motive and Conception in Anglo-Saxon
        Poetry," *Modern Philology* 4 (1907), 423-70.
Wehrli, Max, "Sacra Poesis: Bibelepik als europäische
        Tradition," *Die Wissenschaft von deutscher Sprache
        und Dichtung: Methoden, Probleme, Aufgabe; Fest-
        schrift für Friedrich Maurer zum 65. Geburtstage
        am 5 Januar 1963*, ed. S. Gutenbrunner, et al.
        (Stuttgart, 1963), 262-83.
Wrenn, C. L., "The Poetry of Caedmon," *Proceedings of
        the British Academy* 32 (1946), 277-95; *A Study of
        Old English Literature* (London, 1967).

J.   Other Works, Cited in the Commentary of this
     Edition

Bloomfield, Leonard, "Old English Plural Subjunctives
     in *-E*," *JEGP* 29 (1930), 100-13.
Callaway, Morgan, *The Consecutive Subjunctive in Old
     English* (Boston and London, 1933).
Clemoes, Peter, "Cynewulf's Image of the Ascension,"
     *England Before the Conquest: Studies in Pri-
     mary Sources Presented to Dorothy Whitelock,*
     ed. Peter Clemoes and Kathleen Hughes (Cambridge,
     1971), 293-304.
Dodwell, C. R. and Peter Clemoes, *The Old English
     Illustrated Hexateuch, B.M. Cotton Claudius
     B.iv,* Early English Manuscripts in Facsimile 18
     (Copenhagen, London and Baltimore, 1974).
Förster, Max, "Beiträge zur altenglischen Wortkunde
     aus ungedruckten Volkskundlichen Texten," *Eng-
     lische Studien* 39 (1908), 321-55.
Gueranger, P. L. P., *The Liturgical Year,* tr. L. Shep-
     herd, 15 vols. (4th ed., Worcester, 1895-1903).
Grimm, Jakob L. K., *Andreas und Elene* (Cassel, 1840).
Gordon, E. V., *An Introduction to Old Norse*, rev. A.
     R. Taylor (2d ed., Oxford, 1962).
Kemble, John M., *The Dialogue of Salomon and Saturnus,
     with an historical introduction* (London, 1848).
Klaeber, Fr., "Notes on Old English Prose Texts,"
     Modern Language Notes 18 (1903), 241-47.
Marquardt, Hertha, *Die altenglischen Kenningar, ein
     Beitrag zur Stilkunde altgermanischer Dichtung*
     (Halle, 1938).
Parsch, Pius, *The Breviary Explained*, tr. William Nay-
     den and Carl Hoegerl (St. Louis, 1952).
Pope, John C., *The Rhythm of Beowulf: An Interpreta-
     tion of the Normal and Hypermetrical Verse
     Forms in Old English Poetry* (rev. ed., New
     Haven and London, 1966).
Shipley, George, *The Genitive Case in Anglo-Saxon
     Poetry* (Baltimore, 1903).
Vermes, Geza, *Scripture and Tradition in Judaism:
     Haggadic Studies,* Studia Post-Biblica 4 (Leiden,
     1964).
Woolf, Rosemary, *The English Mystery Plays* (London, 1972).
Wright, J., *Old English Grammar* (Oxford, 1925).

Genesis A

NOTE ON THE TEXT

*The text is based on two collations of the Manuscript, Junius 11
in the Bodleian Library, Oxford, and constant reference to Gollancz' facsimile,* The Caedmon Manuscript of Anglo-Saxon Biblical Poetry, Junius XI
in the Bodleian Library *(Oxford, 1927). My aim has been to report the
manuscript forms with a minimum of emendation and typographical intrusion.
The lay-out and punctuation attempt to follow the MS as much as is possible
in the rigidities of type, while arranging the lines and punctuating as
seemed necessary for the convenience of the modern reader. Sections and
capitals (large and small) are given as in the MS, without emendation. All
punctuation is editorial, and is limited to marking sentences and setting
off parallelisms, except where special difficulties call for more pointing.
The pointing in the MS is unusually complete and correct and is carefully
followed: all divergences from the MS pointing are noted in the textual
notes. Pointing is indicated by the usual means of line division and mid-
line caesural spaces.*

*Readings in the text which differ from the scribe's in any way are
indicated by italics and explained in the textual notes. Alterations, corrections and emendations appearing in the MS are noted, and those few which
are adopted in this edition are also in italics. A notice of a MS alteration or erasure without attribution implies that it is by the scribe. In
each case of MS alteration what appears to be the scribe's final choice is
adopted, unless manifestly in error. Modern emendations which are adopted
in this edition are attributed to their originator in the textual notes
(e.g., a note, "Grein and edd." means that the particular reading adopted
in the text was first given by Grein in his edition and followed by all
subsequent editors (see the chronological list of editions in the Bibliography, Section C).*

Abbreviations of þæt, and, *and final nasals are silently resolved (see Introduction I D, p. 15). Roman numerals are spelled out
and noticed. Accents are not reported (see Introduction, pp. 15-16).
Other marks and features, such as added punctuation, incidental glosses, doodles, etc., are noticed only where they appear to have a bearing
on the text. Added metrical points are regularly noticed.*

*The Vulgate Genesis, parallel to the text of the poem, is that of
H. Quentin,* Biblia Sacra iuxta Latinam Vulgatam Versionem ad Codicum Fidem;
Librum Genesis ex interpretatione Sancti Hieronymi, *etc. (Papal Commission,
Rome, 1926). Verses of the Vulgate are given approximately opposite the
lines of the poem to which they correspond. Whole verses omitted from
the poem are usually not given, unless they are essential for understanding
the context. Square brackets indicate parts of verses omitted from the
poem. Round brackets indicate material affecting* Genesis A, *but not directly translated or paraphrased. V.L. stands for the Old Latin (Vetus
Latina) version, ed. B. Fischer,* Genesis: Vetus Latina: Die Reste der altlateinischen Bibel, nach Petrus Sabatier neu gesammelt und herausgegeben
von der Erzabtei Beuron *(Freiburg, 1951).*

U S IS RIHT MICEL   ÐÆT we rodera weard, [P. 1]
wereda wuldorcining, wordum herigen,
modum lufien. he is mægna sped,
heafod ealra heahgesceafta,

5   frea ælmihtig. næs him fruma æfre,
or geworden ne nu ende cymþ
ecean drihtnes ac he bið a rice
ofer heofenstolas heagum þrymmum.
soðfæst and swiðfeorm sweglbosmas heold

10   þa wæron gesette wide and side
þurh geweald godes wuldres bearnum,
gasta weardum. hæfdon gleam and dream
and heora ordfruman engla þreatas,
beorhte blisse. wæs heora blæd micel.

15   þegnas þrymfæste þeoden heredon,
sægdon lustum lof, heora liffrean
demdon: drihtenes dugeþum wæron
swiðe gesælige. synna ne cuþon,
firena fremman ac hie on friðe lifdon

20   ece mid heora aldor. elles ne ongunnon
ræran on roderum nymþe riht and soþ
ær ðon engla weard for oferhygde
dæl on gedwilde. noldan dreogan leng
heora selfra ræd ac hie of siblufan

25   godes ahwurfon. hæfdon gielp micel
þæt hie wið drihtne dælan meahton
wuldorfæstan wic werodes þrymme,
sid and swegltorht. him þær sar gelamp,
æfst and oferhygd and þæs engles mod

30   þe þone unræd ongan ærest fremman,
wefan and weccean. þa he worde cwæð,
niþes ofþyrsted, þæt he on norðdæle
ham and heahsetl heofena rices

1 *No point afer* MICEL; ÐÆT *spelled out.* 4 *No point after*
ealra. 9 *Point after* soðfæst; swiðfeorm: *Bouterwek & edd.—*
-ferom: MS. 12 gleam and, m 7 *on erasures.* 14 beorhte, h
added above the line by another hand. 17–18a *Pointed* demdon
drihtenes dugeþum · wæron swiðe gesælige · 22 wearð: *Zupitza*
and Holthausen— weard: *MS.*

         agan wolde.   þa wearð yrre god
35   and þam werode wrað   þe he ær wurðode
         wlite and wuldre.   sceop þam werlogan
         wræclicne ham   weorce to leane,
         helleheafas,   hearde niðas.
         heht þæt witehus   wræcna bidan,
40   deop, dreama leas   drihten ure,
         gasta weardas,   þa he hit geare wiste,
         synnihte beseald,   susle geinnod,
         geondfolen fyre   and færcyle,
    rece and reade lege.   heht þa geond þæt rædlease hof
45 weaxan witebrogan.   hæfdon hie wrohtgeteme
    grimme wið god gesomnod.   him þæs grim lean becom.
         cwædon þæt heo rice,   reðemode,
         agan woldan   and swa eaðe meahtan.
         him seo wen geleah   siððan waldend his,   [P. 4]
50   heofona heahcining,   honda arærde
         hehste wið þam herge.   ne mihton hygelease,
         mæne wið metode,   mægyn bryttigan
         Ac him se mæra   mod getwæfde,
         bælc forbigde.   þa he gebolgen wearð,
55   besloh synsceaþan   sigore and gewealde,
         dome and dugeðe   and dreame benam
         his feond, friðo   and gefean ealle,
         torhte tire,   and his torn gewræc
         on gesacum swiðe   selfes mihtum
60   strengum stiepe.   hæfde styrne mod
         gegremed grymme,   grap on wraðe
         faum folmum   and him on fæðm gebræc
         yr' on mode.   æðele bescyrede
         his wiðerbrecan   wuldorgestealdum.
65   Sceop þa and scyrede   scyppend ure
         oferhidig cyn   engla of heofnum,
         wærleas werod.   waldend sende
         laðwendne here   on langne sið,
         geomre gastas.   wæs him gylp forod,
70   beot forborsten   and forbiged þrym,
         wlite gewemmed.   heo on wrace syððan
         seomodon swearte,   siðe ne þorfton

36 *No point after* -logan. **38** -heafas, -as *crowded and joined
by several unusual strokes so that the word appears at a
glance to be* heaftas. **47** rice, r *altered from* m; *no point
after* -mode. **48** *No point after* woldan. **50** *No point after*
-cining. **52** bryttigan, *Krapp & Holthausen report* bryttigin,
but the scribe has written bryttian *and then squeezed the g
over the a so that the descender of the a appears to be i.*
53 *No point after* mæra. **69** gylp, l *over erasure.*

       hlude hlihhan   ac heo helltregum
       werige wunodon   and wean cuðon,
75   sar and sorge,   susl þrowedon
       þystrum beþeahte,   þearl æfterlean
       þæs þe heo ongunnon   wið gode winnan.
       þa wæs soð swa ær   sibb on heofnum,
       fægre freoþoþeawas   frea eallum leof,
80   þeoden his þegnum.   þrymmas weoxon
       duguða mid drihtne   dreamhæbbendra.

[ii]   **W**ÆRON þa gesome   þa þe swegl buan,   [P. 5]
       wuldres eðel.   wroht wæs asprungen,
       oht mid englum   and orlegnið
85   siððan herewosan   heofon ofgæfon,
       leohte belorene.   him on laste setl
       wuldorspedum welig   wide stodan
       gifum growende   on godes rice,
       beorht and geblædfæst,   buendra leas,
90   siððan wræcstowe   werige gastas
       under hearmlocan   heane geforan.
       þa þeahtode   þeoden ure
       modgeþonce   hu he þa mæran gesceaft,
       eðelstaðolas,   eft gesette,
95   swegltorhtan seld   selran werode
       þa hie gielpsceaþan   ofgifen hæfdon
       heah on heofenum.   forþam halig god
       under roderas feng   ricum mihtum
       wolde þæt him eorðe   and uproder
100   and sidwæter   geseted wurde,
       woruldgesceafte   on wraðra gield
       þara þe, forhealdene,   of hleo sende.
       Ne wæs her þa giet   nymþe heolstersceado
       wiht geworden   ac þes wida grund
105   stod deop and dim,   drihtne fremde,
       idel and unnyt.   on þone eagum wlat
       stiðfrihþ cining   and þa stowe beheold,
       dreama lease,   geseah deorc gesweorc

---

75 sar and, *the final stroke of* r *curved up and touching the* ꝸ *but the ligature has been erased.* **79** *No point after* -þeawas. **82** *No point after* buan. **93** *Point after* gesceaft *added.* **94** *Point after* -staðolas *added.* **99** þæt, *spelled out; point after* eorðe *added.* **100** *Point after* -wæter *added;* geseted: *Junius & most edd.—* gesetet: *MS, final* t *altered from another letter by a corrector.* **101** *Point after* -gesceafte *added.* **102** *No point after* forhealdene. **103b** *is relatively indistinct, because written over erasures in a different, browner ink.* **104** *Point after* grund *added.*

1.1   In principio creavit Deus caelum et terram

1.2   terra autem erat inanis et vacua

           et tenebrae super faciem abyssi

           et spiritus Dei ferebatur super aquas *cf. 103-06a*
1.3   dixitque Deus fiat lux
           et facta est lux

1.4   [et vidit Deus lucem quod esset bona]   *cf. 131b-33a*

      et divisit
           lucem ac tenebras   *cf. 140-41a*
1.5   appellavitque
           lucem
           diem

           (. . . factumque est vespere et mane dies unus. . .)

           et tenebras noctem

```
           semian sinnihte,    sweart under roderum,
110        wonn and weste   oð þæt þeos woruldgesceaft
           þurh word gewearð   wuldorcyninges.
           her ærest gesceop   ece drihten,
           helm eallwihta,   heofon and eorðan,
           rodor arærde /    and þis rume land              [P. 6]
115        gestaþelode   strangum mihtum,
           frea ælmihtig.    folde wæs þa gyta
           græsungrene.    garsecg þeahte
           sweart synnihte   side and wide,
           wonne wægas.    þa wæs wuldortorht
120        heofonweardes gast    ofer holm boren
           miclum spedum.    metod engla heht,
           lifes brytta,   leoht forð cuman
           ofer rumne grund.    raþe wæs gefylled
           heahcininges hæs.    him wæs halig leoht
125        ofer westenne    swa se wyrhta bebead.
           þa gesundrode    sigora waldend
           ofer lagoflode   leoht wið þeostrum,
           sceade wið sciman.    sceop þa bam naman
           lifes brytta.    leoht wæs ærest
130        þurh drihtnes word    dæg genemned,
           wlitebeorhte gescaft.    wel licode
           frean æt frymðe   forþbæro tid,
           dæg æresta.    geseah deorc sceado
           sweart swiðrian    geond sidne grund.


[iii]      þA SEO tid gewat     ofer tiber sceacan    [P. 8]
            middangeardes.    metod æfter sceaf
            scirum sciman,    scippend ure,
           æfen ærest.    him arn on last,
           þrang þystre genip    þam þe se þeoden self
140        sceop nihte naman.    nergend ure
           hie gesundrode.    siððan æfre
           drugon and dydon    drihtnes willan,
           ece ofer eorðan.    ða com oðer dæg,
           leoht æfter þeostrum.    heht þa lifes weard
145        on mereflode    middum weorðan
           hyhtlic heofontimber.    holmas dælde
           waldend ure    and geworhte þa
```

112 *Point after* gesceop *added.*   114 *Point after* arærde *added.*
115 *Points after* gestaþelode & mihtum *added.*   116 gyta, *a has
been erased but is clearly visible.*   119 wægas *(so Junius and
most edd.; Thorpe* wegas*) written* wẹgas.   122 *Point after* brytta
added.   126 *Point after* gesundrode *added.*   133 *Points after*
æresta & sceado *added.*   134 *Point after* swiðrian *added.*   135
No point after gewat.   141 *No point after* gesundrode.   145
No point after -flode.

1.6   (Dixit quoque Deus)
      fiat firmamentum in medio aquarum . . . / 1.7 et fecit
            Deus firmamentum / divisitque

            aquas quae erant sub firmamento [ab his quae erant
            super firmamentum]

1.9   (Dixit vero Deus)
      congregentur aquae quae sub caelo sunt in locum unum

            et appareat arida / (factumque est ita)

1.10 et vocavit Deus aridam terram
            congregationesque aquarum [appellavit maria]

2.18 [dixit quoque Dominus Deus]
      non est bonum esse hominem solum

      faciamus ei adiutorem similem sui

2.21 inmisit ergo Dominus Deus soporem in Adam

      cumque obdormisset tulit unam de costis eius
            et replevit carnem pro ea / 2.22 et aedificavit
            Dominus Deus costam quam tulerat de Adam in
            mulierem . . .

```
            roderas fæsten.     þæt se rica ahof
            up from eorðan      þurh his agen word,
150         frea ælmihtig.      flod wæs adæled
            under heahrodore    halgum mihtum,
            wæter of wætrum     þam þe wuniað gyt
            under fæstenne      folca hrofes.
            þa com ofer foldan  fus siðian
155   mære mergen þridda.     næron metode ða gyta
      widlond ne wegas nytte    ac stod bewrigen fæste
      folde mid flode.    frea engla heht
            þurh his word wesan     wæter gemæne
            þa nu under roderum     heora ryne healdað,
160         stowe gestefnde.    ða stod hraðe
            holm under heofonum     swa se halga bebead,
            sid ætsomne     ða gesundrod wæs
            lago wið lande.     geseah þa lifes weard
            drige stowe,    dugoða hyrde,
165         wide æteowde    þa se wuldorcyning
            eorðan nemde.    gesette yðum heora
            onrihtne ryne,    rumum flode
            and gefetero[de]    .  .  .
      [iv]            .  .  .  .  .  .  .  .
            ne þuhte þa gerysne    rodora wearde        [P. 9]
170         þæt adam leng    ana wære
            neorxnawonges    niwre gesceafte
            hyrde and healdend.    forþon him heahcyning,
            frea ælmihtig    fullum tiode
            wif, aweahte    and þa wraðe sealde,
175         lifes leohtfruma,    leofum rince.
            he þæt andweorc    of adames
            lice aleoðode    and him listum ateah
            rib of sidan.    he wæs reste fæst
            and softe swæf,    sar ne wiste,
180         earfoða dæl    ne þær ænig com
            blod of benne    ac him brego engla
            of lice ateah    liodende ban,
            wer unwundod.    of þam worhte god
            freolice fæmnan,    feorh in gedyde,
```

150 flod: *Junius & edd.*— fold: *MS.*   155 metode, *final* e *added above the line by scribe;* gyta, a *imperfectly erased and with it the point.* 156 *Point after* -lond. 165 *No point after* -cyning. 168 gefetero . . ., *last letters on P. 8. One or more leaves are missing between P. 8 and P. 9.* 169 rodora, a *altered from* u. 170 adam, *scribe wrote* adame *but* e *has been erased; no point after* leng. 171 *No point after* -wonges. 176 andweorc, and- *spelled out; point after* adames *added.* 179 *Point after* swæf *added.* 184 freolice: *Grein,* Spr. *I, 345 & edd.*— freolicu: *MS;* gedyde, ge- *added above the line by a different hand in light brown ink.*

(*cf.* 2.7. . . . et inspiravit in faciem eius spiraculum
        vitae) / 1.27...(ad imaginem Dei creavit illum)

                    masculum et feminam creavit eos
1.28   benedixitque illis Deus et ait / crescite et multipli-
            camini et replete terram

                    et subicite eam
        et dominamini piscibus maris
                et volatilibus caeli
        et universis
                animantibus quae moventur super terram

1.31   viditque Deus cuncta quae fecit . . .

(2.1   Igitur perfecti sunt caeli et terra et omnis ornatus
            eorum)

 2.6   sed fons ascendebat e terra inrigans universam super-
            ficiem terrae.
 2.5   et omne virgultum agri antequam oreretur in terra
        omnemque herbam regionis priusquam germinaret
        non enim pluerat Dominus Deus super terram
        et homo non erat qui operaretur terram
2.10   et fluvius egrediebatur de loco voluptatis ad inrigan-
            dum paradisum
        qui inde dividitur in quattuor capita *cf. 219b & 2.8*

185   ece saula.   heo wæron englum geli*c*e.
        þa wæs adames bryd   [P. 10]
        gaste gegearwod.   hie on geogoðe bu
        wlitebeorht wæron   on woruld cenned
        meotodes mihtum.   man ne cuðon
190   don *ne* dreogan   ac him drihtnes wæs
        bam on breostum   byrnende lufu.
        þa gebletsode   bliðheort cyning,
        metod alwihta   monna cynnes
        ða forman twa,   fæder and moder,
195   wif and wæpned.   he þa worde cwæð:
        "temað nu and wexað,   tudre fyllað
        eorðan ælgrene   incre cynne,
        sunum and dohtrum.   Inc sceal sealt wæter
        wunian on gewealde   and eall worulde gesceaft.
200   brucað blæddaga   and brimhlæste
        and heofonfugla.   Inc is halig feoh
        and wilde deor   on geweald geseald
        and lifigende   ða ðe land tredað,
        feorheaceno cynn   ða ðe flod wecceð
205   geond hronrade.   Inc hyrað eall."

        .   .   .   .
        þa sceawode   scyppend ure   [P. 11]
        his weorca wlite   and his wæstma blæd
        niwra gesceafta.   neorxnawang stod
        god and gastlic,   gifena gefylled
210   fremum forðweardum.   fægere leohte   [P. 12]
        þæt liðe land   lago yrnende,
        wylleburne.   nalles wolcnu ða giet
        ofer rumne grund   regnas bæron,
        wann mid winde   hwæðre wæstmum stod
215   folde gefrætwod.   heoldon forðryne
        eastreamas heora   æðele feower
        of þam niwan   neorxnawonge.
        þa wæron adælte   drihtnes mihtum
        ealle of anum   þa he þas eorðan gesceop
220   wætre wlitebeorhtum   and on woruld sende.

185 saula, *final -a clumsily altered to long* e *by a different hand;* gelice, *scribe wrote* glic, *corrector added final -e in different ink over the point and added a new point.* 190 don ne dreogan, *scribe wrote* don 7 dreogan; *corrector cancelled* 7 *and wrote* ne *above.* 197 *No point after* -grene. 205 eall, *last word on P. 10; one or more leaves missing between P. 10 and P. 11.* 207 blæd, b *altered from* þ. 208 neorxnawang, *Krapp reports* -wong; *a/o is ambiguous;* Wells *considers that* wang *appears to have been altered from* stod *by scribe.* 215 *No point after* gefrætwod. 218 adælte, *corrector has altered* t *to* e *and added* d *above the line (i.e.,* adælede). 220 wætre, e *altered from* i *by scribe.*

2.11   nomen uni Phison
    ipse est qui circuit
        omnem terram Evilath (*var.* Euilat, Ephilat,
        Heuilath)
    ubi nascitur aurum / 2.12 et aurum terrae illius
        optimum est ibique invenitur bdellium et lapis
        onychinus
2.13   et nomen fluvio secundo Geon ipse est
        qui circuit omnem terram Aethiopiae
2.14   nomen vero fluminis tertii Tigris
    ipse vadit contra Assyrios
    fluvius autem quartus ipse est Eufrates.

3.8   [et cum audissent vocem Domini Dei] deambulantis in
        paradiso ad auram post meridiem

    abscondit se Adam et uxor eius a facie Domini Dei
    in medio ligni paradisi

3.9   vocavitque Dominus Deus Adam
        et dixit ei ubi es
3.10   qui ait
        vocem tuam audivi in paradiso et timui eo quod
        nudus essem et abscondi me

þæne hatað ylde,   eorðbuende,
fison folcweras   sæ foldan dæl
brade bebugeð   beorhtum streamum,
hebeleat, utan.   on þære eðyltyrf
225 niððas findað   nean and feorran
gold and gymcynn,   gumþeoda bearn,
ða selestan   þæs þe us secgað bec.
þonne seo æftre   ethiopia
land and liodgeard   beligeð uton
230 ginne rice   þære is geon noma.
þridda is tigris.   seo wið þeodscipe,
ea inflede,   assirie belið.
Swilce is seo feorðe   þa nu geond folc monig
weras eufraten   wide nemnað.

. . . . . .

þa com feran   frea ælmihtig   [P. 40, line 8]
ofer midne dæg,   mære þeoden,
on neorxnawang   neode sine.
855 wolde neosian   nergend usser,
bilwit fæder,   hwæt his bearn dyde.
wiste forworhte   þa he ær wlite sealde.
gewitan him þa gangan   geomermode
under beamsceade,   blæde bereafod.
860 hyddon hie on heolstre   þa hie halig word
drihtnes gehyrdon   and ondredon him
þa sona ongann   swegles aldor
weard ahsian   woruldgesceafta.
het him recene to   rice þeoden
865 his sunu gangan.   him þa sylfa oncwæð,
hean hleoðrade   hrægles þearfa:
"Ic wreo me her   wæda leasne,
liffrea min,   leafum þecce.
scyldfull mine,   sceaðen, is me sare

221 þæne: *suggested by Cosijn,* Beiträge *19, 446—* þære: *MS.*
223 bebugeð, u *seems to have been altered to* i. 224 hebeleat:
Grein— hebeleac: *MS.* 227 *No point after* selestan. 228 *No
point after* ethiopia. 229 *Point after* land; liodgeard, *a
corrector has altered* i *to long* e. 232 assirie, *corrector
has "tailed" the* e (= assiriæ?) *and added point.* 234 nemnað,
*last word on P. 12; several leaves are missing between P. 12
and P. 13. On the top of P. 13 the interpolated* Genesis B *begins (lines 235-851), running to line 8 of P. 40: line 8
reads:* hu hie on þam leohte forð libban sceolden · þa com /
feran, *etc.; there is nothing in the MS to indicate the end
of* Genesis B. 852 *No point after* feran. 855 *No point after*
neosian. 863 *No point after* ahsian. 866 hean, *the form of
the final letter is between* n *and* r, *though* n *is no doubt intended. Junius prints* hean *in text,* hear *in Errata, all
others* hean. 867 *No point after* her.

3.11   cui dixit
           quis enim indicavit tibi quod nudus esses

       nisi quod ex ligno
           de quo tibi praeceperam ne comederes comedisti
3.12   dixitque Adam
           mulier quam dedisti sociam mihi
           dedit mihi de ligno et comedi

3.13   et dixit Dominus Deus ad mulierem
           quare hoc fecisti

       quae respondit
           serpens decepit me

       et comedi
3.14   et ait Dominus Deus ad serpentem

870   frecne on ferhðe,   ne dear nu forðgan
           for ðe andweardne.   ic eom eall eall nacod."

[xv]   HIM ða ædre god   andswarede: [P. 42]
         "saga me þæt, sunu min,   for hwon secest ðu
         sceade sceomiende?   þu sceonde æt me
875   furðum anfenge,   ac gefean eallum
           for hwon wast þu wean   and wrihst sceome,
           gesyhst sorge   and þin sylf þecest,
           lic mid leafum,   sagast lifceare
           hean hygegeomor   þæt þe sie hrægles þearf
880   nymþe ðu æppel   ænne byrgde
           of ðam wudubeame   þe ic þe wordum forbead?"
           him þa adam eft   andswarode:
           "me ða blæda on hand   bryd gesealde,
           freolucu fæmne,   freadrihten min
885   ðe ic þe on teonan geþah.   nu ic þæs tacen wege,
           sweotol on me selfum.   wat ic sorga ðy ma."
           Ða ðæs euan frægn   ælmihtig god:
           "hwæt druge þu, dohtor,   dugeþa genohra
           niwra gesceafta   neorxnawanges
890   growendra gifa   þa þu gitsiende
           on beam gripe,   blæda name
           on treowes telgum   and me on teonan
           æte þa untreme?   adame sealdest
           wæstme þa inc wæron   wordum minum
895   fæste forbodene."   him þa freolecu mæg,
           ides æwiscmod,   andswarode:
           "Me nædre beswac   and me neodlice
           to forsceape scyhte   and to scyldfrece,
           fah wyrm þurh fægir word   oð þæt ic fracoðlice
900   feondræs gefremede,   fæhðe geworhte
           and þa reafode   swa hit riht ne wæs
           beam on bearwe   and þa blæda æt."
           þa nædran sceop   nergend usser,
           frea ælmihtig,   fagum wyrme

871 andweardne, and- *spelled out.*   872 *No point after* god.
876 þu, þ *is crowded in, u corrected from* t *by scribe.*   880
Point after æppel *added;* byrgde, *a different hand has added*
-st *(high* s*) above the point.*   883 ða, *scribe wrote* ðe, *made
an attempt to alter* e *to* a *and then added* a *above.*   885b ic,
added above the line by scribe.   888   dohtor, r *is 2-shaped
and crowded in at end of MS line.*   894 *Point after* wæstme,
no point after wæron.   896 andswarode, and- *spelled out.*   899
Point after fah, *added?*

(3.14) (quia fecisti hoc maledictus es) [inter omnia
           animantia et bestias terrae] / super pectus tuum
           gradieris et terram comedes

           cunctis diebus vitae tuae
   3.15 inimicitias ponam inter te et mulierem
         et semen tuum et semen illius ipsa conteret caput tuum
         et tu insidiaberis calcaneo eius

   3.16 mulieri quoque dixit
         [multiplicabo aerumnas tuas et conceptus tuos]

         in dolore paries filios et sub viri potestate eris
             et ipse dominabitur tui

   3.17 ad Adam vero dixit

         [quia audisti vocem uxoris tuae]

             et comedisti de ligno ex quo praeceperam tibi
             ne comederes / maledicta terra in opere tuo
         in laboribus comedes eam
             cunctis diebus vitae tuae / 3.19 in sudore vultus
             tui vesceris pane
         donec revertaris in terram de qua sumptus es
         [quia pulvis es et in pulverem reverteris]

   3.21 fecit quoque Dominus Deus Adam et uxori eius tunicas
             pellicias / et induit eos

905   wide siðas   and þa worde cwæð:
       "þu scealt wideferhð,   werg, þinum breostum
       bearme, / tredan   brade eorðan,   [P. 43]
       faran feðeleas   þenden þe feorh wunað,
       gast on innan.   þu scealt greot etan
910   þine lifdagas   swa þu laðlice
       wrohte onstealdest   þe þæt wif feoð,
       hatað under heofnum   and þin heafod tredeð
       fah mid fotum sinum.   þu scealt fiersna sætan
       tohtan niwre.   tuddor bið gemæne
915   incrum orlegnið   a þenden standeð
       woruld under wolcnum.   nu þu wast and canst,
       lað leodsceaða,   hu þu lifian scealt."

                       xvi.

       Ð A to euan   god yrringa spræc:
           "wend þe from wynne.   þu scealt wæpnedmen
920   wesan on gewealde   mid weres egsan
       hearde genearwad,   hean þrowian
       þinra dæda gedwild,   deaðes bidan
       and þurh wop and heaf   on woruld cennan
       þurh sar micel   sunu and dohtor."
925   Abead eac adame   ece drihten,
       lifes leohtfruma,   lað ærende:
       "þu scealt oðerne   eðel secean,
       wynleasran wic,   and on wræc hweorfan
       nacod niedwædla   neorxnawanges,
930   dugeðum bedæled.   þe is gedal witod
       lices and sawle.   hwæt, þu laðlice
       wrohte onstealdest.   forþon þu winnan scealt
       and on eorðan þe   þine andlifne
       selfa geræcan,   wegan swatighleor
935   þinne hlaf etan   þenden þu her leofast
       oð þæt þe to heortan   hearde gripeð
       adl unliðe   þe þu on æple ær
       selfa forswulge.   forþon þu sweltan scealt."
       Hwæt, we nu gehyrað   hwær us hearmstafas   [P. 45]
940   wraðe onwocan   and woruldyrmðo.
       hie þa wuldres weard   wædum gyrede,
       scyppend usser,   het heora sceome þeccan

---

906 werg, g *larger than usual and on erasure (of i?); point
added after* þinum, *no point after* breostum.   **907** bearme: *Etmüller & Kock (JJJ., 29)—* bearm: *MS.*   **908** feorh, r *added
above the line.*   **914** *No point after* niwre, *point after* tuddor.
917 hu: *Krapp—* nu: *MS (all edd. up to Krapp report* hu).   **918**
No point after euan.   **927** oðerne, ð *over small hole, no point
after this word.*   **933** andlifne, and- *spelled out.*

3.23 emisit eum Dominus Deus de paradiso voluptatis
        (ut operaretur terram de qua sumptus est)
3.24 eiecitque Adam / et collocavit ante paradisum
        voluptatis / cherubin
        et flammeum gladium atque versatilem

      ad custodiendam viam ligni vitae

4.1   Adam vero cognovit Havam uxorem suam
        quae concepit et peperit Cain [dicens
        possedi hominem] (per Dominum) / 4.2 rursusque
          peperit fratrem eius Abel

      fuit autem Abel pastor ovium et Cain agricola

4.3   factum est autem post multos dies
        ut offerret Cain de fructibus terrae munera Domino
4.4   Abel quoque obtulit de primogenitis gregis sui et de
        adipibus eorum / et respexit Dominus ad Abel et
        ad munera eius / 4.5 ad Cain vero et ad munera
        eius non respexit / iratusque est Cain vehementer
        et concidit vultus eius

4.8   [dixitque Cain ad Abel fratrem suum egrediamur foras
        cumque essent in agro] / consurrexit Cain adversus
          Abel fratrem suum et interfecit eum

   frea frumhrægle. het hie from hweorfan
   neorxnawange on nearore lif.
945 him on laste beleac liðsa and wynna
   hihtfulne ham halig engel
   be frean hæse fyrene sweorde.
   ne mæg þær inwitfull ænig geferan
   womscyldig mon ac se weard hafað
950 miht and strengðo. se þæt mære lif,
   dugeðum deore, drihtne healdeð.
   No hwæðre ælmihtig ealra wolde   [P. 46]
   adame and euan arna ofteon,
   fæder æt frymðe þeah þe he him from swice
955 Ac he him to frofre let hwæðere forð wesan
   hyrstedne hrof halgum tunglum
   and him grundwelan ginne sealde.
   het þam sinhiwum sæs and eorðan
   tuddorteondra teohha gehwilcre
960 to woruldnytte wæstmas fedan.
   Gesæton þa æfter synne sorgfulre land,
   eard and eðyl, unspedigran
   fremena gehwilcre þonne se frumstol wæs
   þe hie æfter dæde of adrifen wurdon.
965 Ongunnon hie þa be godes hæsc
   bearn astrienan swa him metod bebead.
   Adames and euan aforan wæron
   freolicu twa frumbearn cenned,
   cain and abel. us cyðað bec
970 hu þa dædfruman dugeþa stryndon,
   welan and wiste, willgebroðor.
   oðer his to eorðan elnes tilode.   [P. 47]
   se wæs ærboren. oðer æhte heold
   fæder on fultum oð þæt forð gewat
975 dægrimes worn. hie þa drihtne lac
   begen brohton. brego engla beseah
   on abeles gield eagum sinum.
   cyning eallwihta caines ne wolde
   tiber sceawian. þæt wæs torn were
980 hefig æt heortan. hygewælm *a*steah
   beorne on breostum, blatende nið,
   yrre for æfstum. he þa unræden
   folmum gefremede, freomæg ofsloh,
   broðor sinne and his blod ageat,
985 cain abeles. cwealmdreore swealh

959 gehwilcre: *edd.*— gehilcre: *MS.* **965** *No point after* þa.
968 *No point after* twa. **969** *Point after* cain. **972** *No point*
after eorðan. **980** hygewælm asteah: *Wülker & edd.*— hyge wæl/
mos teah *(wæl at end of MS line): MS.*

4.9   et ait Dominus ad Cain
          ubi est Abel frater tuus
      qui respondit

          nescio
          num custos fratris mei sum

4.10 dixitque ad eum
          quid fecisti

      vox sanguinis fratris tui clamat ad me de terra

4.11 nunc igitur maledictus eris super terram
      quae aperuit os suum et suscepit sanguinem fratris tui
          de manu tua / 4.12 cum operatus fueris eam
          non dabit tibi fructus suos
      vagus et profugus eris super terram

4.13 dixitque Cain ad Dominum

      maior est iniquitas mea quam ut veniam merear

þæs middangeard,   monnes swate,
æfter wælswenge.   wea wæs aræred,
tregena tuddor.   of ðam twige siððan
ludon laðwende   leng swa swiðor
990   reðe wæstme.   ræhton wide
geond werþeoda   wrohtes telgan.
hrinon hearmtanas   hearde and sare
drihta bearnum.   doð gieta swa.
Of þam brad blado   bealwa gehwilces
995   sprytan ongunnon.   we þæt spell magon,   [P. 48]
wælgrimme wyrd,   wope cwiðan
nales holunge   Ac us hearde sceod
freolecu fæmne   þurh forman gylt
þe wið metod æfre   men gefremeden,
1000   eorðbuende   siððan adam wearð
of godes muðe   gaste eacen.

xvii.

Ð A worde frægn   wuldres aldor
cain hwær abel   eorðan wære.
Him ða se cystleasa   cwealmes wyrhta
1005   ædre æfter þon   andswarode:
"ne can ic abeles   or ne fore,
hleomæges sið.   ne ic hyrde wæs
broðer mines."   him þa brego engla,
godspedig gast,   gean þingade:
1010   "hwæt befealdest þu   folmum þinum
wraðum on wælbedd   wærfæsne rinc,
broðor þinne,   and his blod to me
cleopað and cigeð?   þu þæs cwealmes scealt
wite winnan   and on wræc hweorfan,
1015   awyrged to widan aldre.   ne seleð þe wæstmas eorðe
wlitige to woruldnytte   ac heo wældreore swealh
halge of handum þinum.   forþon heo þe hroðra oftihð,
glæmes grene folde.   þu scealt geomor hweorfan,
arleas of earde þinum   swa þu abele wurde
1020   to feorhbanan.   forþon þu flema scealt
widlast wrecan,   winemagum lað."
Him þa cain   andswarode:
"Ne þearf ic ænigre   are wenan
on woruldrice   ac ic forworht hæbbe,
1025   heofona heahcyning,   hyldo þine,

987 aræred, *the second r over an erasure, and misshapen, but
apparently by scribe.* 1000 *No point after* wearð. 1003 *No
point after* abel. 1005 *No point after* þon; andswarode, *and-
spelled out, first* d *partly crossed as if for an* ð. 1022 *No
point after* cain.

4.14 ecce eicis me hodie a facie terrae
      et a facie tua abscondar / et ero vagus et profugus
          in terra / omnis igitur qui invenerit me

          occidet me

4.15 dixitque ei Dominus
      nequaquam ita fiet

      sed omnis qui occiderit Cain
          septuplum punietur

      posuitque Dominus Cain signum
          ut non eum interficeret
          omnis qui invenisset eum

4.16 egressusque Cain
          a facie Domini
          habitavit
          in terra profugus ad orientalem plagam Eden
4.17 cognovit autem Cain uxorem suam
      quae concepit et peperit
      Enoch

      et aedificavit civitatem
          [vocavitque nomen eius ex nomine filii sui Enoch]

4.18 porro Enoch genuit

          Irad

      et Irad genuit Maviahel

<pre>
          lufan and freode.   forþon ic / lastas sceal   [P. 49]
          wean on wenum   wide lecgan.
          hwonne me gemitte   manscyldigne
          se me feor oððe neah   fæhðe gemonige
1030   broðorcwealmes.   ic his blod ageat,
          dreor on eorðan.   þu to dæge þissum
          ademest me fram duguðe   and adrifest from
          earde minum.   me to aldorbanan
          weorðeð wraðra sum.   ic awyrged sceal,
1035   þeoden, of gesyhðe   þinre hweorfan."
          Him þa selfa oncwæð   sigora drihten: [P. 50]
          "ne þearft ðu þe ondrædan   deaðes brogan,
          feorhcwealm nu giet   þeah þu from scyle
          freomagum feor   fah gewitan.
1040   gif monna hwelc   mundum sinum
          aldre beneoteð   hine on cymeð
          æfter þære synne   seofonfeald wracu,
          wite æfter weorce."   hine waldend on,
          tirfæst metod,   tacen sette,
1045   freoðobeacen, frea   þy læs hine feonda hwilc
          mid guðþræce   gretan dorste
          feorran oððe nean.   heht þa from hweorfan
          meder and magum   manscyldigne,
          cnosle sinum.   him þa cain gewat
1050   gongan geomormod   gode of gesyhðe,
          wineleas wrecca   and him þa wic geceas
          eastlandum on,   eðelstowe
          fædergeardum feor   þær him freolecu mæg,
          ides æfter æðelum   eaforan fedde.
1055   Se æresta wæs   enos haten,   [P. 52]
          frumbearn caines,   siððan ongon
          mid þam cneomagum   ceastre timbran.
          þæt wæs under wolcnum   weallfæstenna
          ærest ealra   þara þe æðelingas,
1060   sweordberende,   settan heton.
          þanon his eaforan   ærest wocan,
          bearn from bryde,   on þam burhstede.
          Se yldesta wæs   iared haten,
          sunu enoses.   siððan wocan
1065   þa þæs cynnes   cneowrim icton,
          mægburg caines.   malalehel wæs
          æfter iarede   yrfes hyrde
          fæder on laste   oð þæt he forð gewat.
</pre>

1027 *No point after* wenum.   1028 *No point after* gemitte.
1036 Him, *capital* H *much larger than normal, as if indicating
a sub-section; no point after* oncwæð.   1052 *No point after* on.
1059 *The mid-line point is after* þara.   1062 burhstede, -stede
*is the only word on the last line of P. 50; the letters are of
normal size, but spaced out over half a line.*   1063 *No point
after* wæs.

       et Maviahel genuit Mathusahel

       et Mathusahel genuit Lamech

4.19   qui accepit uxores duas

       nomen uni Ada et nomen alteri Sella *(4.20, Iabel, omitted)*
4.21   et nomen [fratris eius (i.e., Iabel)] Iubal
            ipse fuit pater canentium cithara et organo

4.22   Sella quoque genuit Tubalcain
            qui fuit malleator et faber in cuncta opera

       aeris et ferri . . .

4.23   dixitque Lamech uxoribus suis

            Adae et Sellae
       (audite vocem meam uxores Lamech
       auscultate sermonem meum
       quoniam occidi virum in vulnus meum
       et adulescentulum in livorem meum)

4.24   septuplum ultio dabitur de Cain

       (de Lamech vero septuagies septies)

4.25   cognovit quoque adhuc Adam uxorem suam
       et peperit filium
       vocavitque nomen eius Seth

```
           Siððan mathusal    magum dælde,
1070       bearn æfter bearne    broðrum sinum,
           æðelinga gestreon    oð þæt aldorgedal
           frod fyrndagum    fremman sceolde,
           lif oflætan.    lameh onfeng
           æfter fæder dæge    fletgestealdum,
1075       botlgestreonum.    him bryda twa,
           idesa on eðle,    eaforan feddon,
           ada and sella.    þara anum wæs
           iabal noma.    se þurh gleawne geþanc
           herbuendra    hearpan ærest
1080       handum sinum    hlyn awehte,
           swinsigende sweg,    sunu lamehes.
```

xviii.

```
       SWYLCE on ðære mægðe    maga wæs haten
        on þa ilcan tid    tubalcain.
        se þurh snytro sped    smiðcræftega wæs
1085   and þurh modes gemynd    monna ærest,
       sunu lamehes,    sulhgeweorces
       fruma wæs ofer foldan    siððan folca bearn
       æres cuðon    and isernes,
       burhsittende,    brucan wide.
1090   þa his wifum twæm    wordum sægde
       lameh seolfa,    leofum gebeddum,
       adan and sellan,    unarlic spel:
       "ic on morðor ofsloh    minra sumne
       hyldemaga,    honda gewemde
1095   on caines    cwealme mine,
       fylde mid folmum    fæder enoses,
       ordbanan abeles,    eorðan sealde
       wældreor weres,    wat gearwe
       þæt þam lichryre    on last cymeð
1100   soðcyninges    seofonfeald wracu
       micel æfter mane.    min sceal swiðor          [P. 55]
       mid grimme gryre    golden wurðan
       fyll and feorhcwealm    þonne ic forð scio."
       þa wearð adame    on abeles gyld
1105   eafora on eðle    oþer feded,
       soðfæst sunu.    þam wæs seth noma.
       se wæs eadig    and his yldrum ðah
       freolic to frofre    fæder and meder,
```

1069 mathusal, h *written above the line by scribe.* **1079** *No point after* ærest. **1088** æres: *Thorpe & edd.* — ærest: *MS; no point after* isernes. **1090** *No point after* twæm. **1093** sumne: *Grein & edd.* — sune: *MS.* **1095** *No point after* caines. **1100** *No point after* -cyninges. **1104** *No point after* adame. **1107** *Point after* his.

(4.25)   dicens
        posuit mihi Deus semen aliud pro Abel

              quem occidit Cain

    5.3   vixit autem Adam

              centum triginta annis / et genuit . . .
        vocavitque nomen eius Seth *(cf. 1106)*
    5.4   et facti sunt dies Adam postquam genuit Seth
              octingenti anni / genuitque filios et filias
    5.5   et factûm est omne tempus quod vixit Adam
              anni nongenti
              triginta
              et mortuus est

    5.6   vixit quoque Seth centum quinque annos

              et genuit Enos /(cf. 4.26 sed et Seth natus est
              filius quem vocavit Enos
              iste coepit invocare nomen Domini)

    5.7   vixitque Seth postquam genuit Enos octingentis septem
              annis / genuitque filios et filias
    5.8   et facti sunt omnes dies Seth
              nongentorum duodecim annorum
              et mortuus est

    5.9   vixit vero Enos nonaginta annis

```
                adames and euan,    wæs abeles gield
1110            on woruldrice.     þa word acwæð
                ord moncynnes:    "me ece sealde
                sunu selfa,    sigora waldend,
                lifes aldor    on leofes stæl
                þæs þe cain ofsloh    and me cearsorge
1115            mid þys magotimbre    of mode asceaf
                þeoden usser.    him þæs þanc sie."
                Adam hæfde    þa he eft ongan
                him to eðulstæfe    oðres strienan
                bearnes be bryde,    beorn ellenrof,
1120            prittig and hundteontig   þisses lifes
                wintra on worulde.    us gewritu secgað
                þæt her eahtahund    iecte siððan
                mægðum and mæcgum    mægburg sine.
                adam on eorðan    ealra hæfde
1125            nigenhund wintra
                and prittig eac    þa he þas woruld
                þurh gastgedal    ofgyfan sceolde.
                him on laste seth    leof weardode,              [P. 56]
                eafora æfter yldrum,    eþelstol heold,
1130            and wif begeat.    wintra hæfde
                fif and hundteontig    þa heo furðum ongan
                his mægburge    men geicean
                sunum and dohtrum.    sedes eafora
                se yldesta wæs    enos haten.
1135            se nemde god    niðþa bearna
                ærest ealra    siððan adam stop
                on grene græs,    gaste geweorðad.
                Seth wæs gesælig.    siððan strynde
                seofon winter her    suna and dohtra
1140            ond eahtahund.    ealra hæfde
                twelf and nigonhund    þa seo tid gewearð
                þæt he friðgedal    fremman sceolde.
                him æfter heold    þa he of worulde gewat       [P. 57]
                enos yrfe    siððan eorðe swealh
1145            sædberendes    sethes lice.
                he wæs leof gode    and lifde her
                wintra hundnigontig    ær he be wife her
```

1118 eðulstæfe: *Grein & Wülker (Holthausen & edd.*, eðel-)—
edulf stæfe: *MS.*   **1120** þrittig and hundteontig: *Thorpe &
edd. (reading xxx and c; Wells spells out the numerals when-
ever they occur abbreviated)*—   xxx · wc *("wyn" for* 7*): MS.*
1124 *Point after* hæfde *added?*   **1126** þrittig— xxx: *MS.*   **1127**
No point after gastgedal.   **1130** *No point after* hæfde.   **1136**
ærest, æ *altered from* u.   **1138** Seth, *small, very faint* d
written above et *(cf. 1133b); no point after* strynde.   **1140**
ond, *spelled out; no point after* -hund.   **1141** twelf—
xii · : *MS.*

          et genuit Cainan
5.10   post cuius ortum vixit octingentis quindecim annis

          et genuit filios et filias / 5.11 factique sunt
             omnes dies Enos nongentorum quinque annorum
             et mortuus est

5.12   vixit quoque Cainan septuaginta annis

          et genuit Malalehel

5.13   et vixit Cainan postquam genuit Malalehel
             octingentos quadraginta annos / genuitque
             filios et filias
5.14   et facti sunt omnes dies Cainan nongenti decem anni
             et mortuus est

5.15   vixit autem Malalehel
             sexaginta quinque annos

          et genuit Iared

5.16   et vixit Malalehel postquam genuit Iared . . .
          (et genuit filios et filias)
5.17   et facti sunt omnes dies Malalehel
             octigenti nonaginta quinque anni et mortuus est

5.18   vixitque Iared centum sexaginta duobus annis

þur*h* gebedscipe bearn astrynde.
him þa cenned wearð cainan ærest
1150 eafora on eðle. siððan eahtahund
and fiftyno on friðo drihtnes
gleawferhð hæleð geogoðe strynde,
suna and dohtra. swealt þa he hæfde,
frod fyrnwita *fif* and nigonhund.
1155 þære cneorisse wæs cain*an* siððan
æfter enose aldordema,
weard and wisa. wintra hæfde
efne hundseofontig ær him sunu woce.
þa wearð on eðle eafora feded, [P. 58]
1160 mago cain*an*es, malalehel wæs haten.
siððan eahtahund æðelinga rim
and feowertigum eac feorum geicte.
enoses sunu ealra nigonhund
wintra hæfde þa he woruld ofgeaf
1165 and tyne eac þa his tiddæge
under rodera rum rim wæs gefylled.

.viiii.

[xviiii] **H**IM on laste heold land and yrfe
malalehel siððan misscra worn.
se frumgara fif and sixtig
1170 wintra hæfde þa hc be wife ongann
bearna strynan. him bryd sunu,
meowle to monnum brohte. Se maga wæs
on his mægðe, minc gefræge,
guma on geogoðe iared haten.
1175 lifde siððan and lissa breac
malalehel lange / mondreama her, [P. 59]
woruldgestreona, wintra hæfde
fif and hundnigontig þa he forð gewat
and eahtahund. eaforan læfde
1180 land and leodweard. longe siððan
geared gumum gold brittade.
se eorl wæs æðele, æfæst hæleð
and se frumgar his freomagum leof.
fif and hundteontig on fyore lifde
1185 wintra gebidenra on woruldrice

1148 þurh: *edd.—* þur: *MS.* 1154 fyrnwita, a *altered from* e;
*the old point is hence written over and a new point added by
scribe;* -wita *was reported as* -witet *by all edd. before Krapp;*
fif— v· : *MS.* 1155 cainan, *two letters erased after* cain-,
almost certainly -an; *edd. (except Wülker) print* cainan. **1160**
cainanes: *Thorpe & edd. (except Wülker)—* caines: *MS.* 1172 *No
point after* wæs. 1177 *No point after* hæfde. 1179 *No point
after* -hund.

```
              et genuit Enoch
  5.19   et vixit Iared postquam
              genuit Enoch
              octingentos annos / et genuit filios et filias
  5.20   et facti sunt omnes dies Iared
              nongenti sexaginta duo anni et mortuus est




(5.21   porro Enoch vixit sexaginta quinque annis et genuit
              Mathusalam)
  5.22   et ambulavit Enoch cum Deo
              postquam genuit Mathusalam trecentis annis
          et genuit filios et filias




(5.24   ambulavitque cum Deo et non apparuit quia tulit eum
              Deus)(cf. V.L.: et [con]placuit Enoch deo et non
              inventus postmodum quia deus illum transtulit)




  5.23   et facti sunt omnes dies Enoch trecenti sexaginta
              quinque anni
[5.25   vixitque quoque Mathusalam centum octoginta septem
              annos et genuit Lamech / 5.26 et vixit Mathusalam
              postquam genuit Lamech septingentos octoginta duos
              annos]
  5.26   . . . et genuit filios et filias
  5.27   et facti sunt omnes dies Mathusalae
              nongenti sexaginta novem anni et mortuus est


  5.28   vixit autem Lamech
              centum octoginta duobus annis
              et genuit filium
```

and syxtig eac.   þa seo sæl gewearð
þæt his wif sunu   on woruld brohte.
se eafora wæs   enoc haten,
freolic frumbearn.   fæder her þa gyt
1190   his cynnes forð   cneorim icte
eafora eahtahund.   ealra hæfde
fif and syxtig   þa he forð gewat
and nigonhund eac   nihtgerimes,
wine frod wintres   þa he þas woruld ofgeaf
1195   Ond geared þa   gleawum læfde
land / and leodweard,   leofum rince.   [P. 60]
enoch siððan   ealdordom ahof,
freoðosped folces wisa,   nalles feallan let
dom and drihtscipe
1200   þenden he hyrde wæs   heafodmaga,
breac blæddaga,   bearna strynde,
þreohund wintra.   him wæs þeoden hold,
rodera waldend.   se rinc heonon
on lichoman   lisse sohte,
1205   drihtnes duguðe,   nales deaðe swealt
middangeardes   swa her men doþ
geonge and ealde   þonne him god heora
æhta and ætwist   eorðan gestreona
on genimeð   and heora aldor nomed.
1210   Ac he cwic gewat   mid cyning engla
of þyssum lænan   life, frean,
on þam gearwum   þe his gast onfeng
ær hine to monnum   modor brohte.
he þam yldestan   eaforan læfde
1215   folc, frumbearne.   *fif* and syxtig   [P. 62]
wintra hæfde   þa he woruld ofgeaf
and eac *preo*hund.   þrage siððan
mathusal heold   maga yrfe.
se on lichoman   lengest þisse
1220   worulddreama breac,   worn gestrynde
ær his swyltdæge   suna and dohtra.
hæfde frod hæle   þa he from sceolde
niþþum hweorfan   nigonhund wintra
and hundseofontig to.   sunu æfter heold,
1225   lamech, leodgeard   lange siððan,
woruld bryttade.   wintra hæfde
twa and hundteontig   þa seo tid gewearð
þæt se eorl ongan   æðele cennan,

1192 fif— v· : MS. **1194** *Point erased after* woruld. **1195** Ond *spelled out.* **1211** *Point after* lænan *added.* **1213** *No point after* monnum. **1215** fif— v · : MS; *no point after* syxtig. **1217** þreo— iii · : MS; *no point after* siððan. **1219** *No points after* lichoman *or* þisse.

5.30 vixitque Lamech postquam (genuit Noe)
         quingentos nonaginta

         quinque annos
      et genuit filios et filias
5.29 vocavitque nomen eius Noe [dicens / iste consolabitur
         nos ab operibus et laboribus manuum nostrarum in
         terra cui maledixit Dominus] / 5.31 [et facti
         sunt omnes dies Lamech septingenti septuaginta
         septem anni] et mortuus est / Noe vero cum quin-
         gentorum esset annorum
         genuit Sem et Ham et Iafeth

6.1   Cumque coepissent homines multiplicari super terram
         et filias procreassent

6.2   videntes filii Dei
         filias eorum quod essent pulchrae
      acceperunt uxores sibi ex omnibus quas elegerant

6.3   dixitque Deus
         (non permanebit spiritus meus in homine in aet-
         ernum quia caro est)

      eruntque dies illius centum viginti annorum

[6.4 gigantes autem erant super terram in diebus illis
      postquam enim ingressi sunt filii Dei ad filias hom-
         inum illaeque genuerunt
      isti sunt potentes a saeculo viri famosi *cf. 1268a*]

        sunu and dohtor.   siððan lifde
1230   fif and hundnigontig   frea, moniges breac
        wintra under wolcnum,   werodes aldor,
        *fif*hund eac heold   þæt folc teala,
        bearna strynde.   him byras wocan
        eafora and idesa.   he þone yldestan
1235   noæ nemde   se niððum ær
        land bryttade   siððan lamech gewat.
        hæfde æðelinga   aldorwisa   [P. 63]
        *fif*hund wintra   þa he furðum ongan
        bearna strynan   þæs þe bec cweðaþ.
1240   Sem wæs haten   sunu noes
        se yldesta,   oðer cham,
        þridda iafeth.   þeoda tymdon
        rume under roderum,   rim miclade
        monna mægðe   geond middangeard
1245   sunum and dohtrum.   Ða giet wæs sethes cynn,
        leofes leodfruman,   on lufan swiðe
        drihtne dyre   and domeadig

               xx .

O Ð ÞÆT bearn godes   bryda ongunnon
     on caines   cynne secan
1250   wergum folce   and him þær wif curon
        ofer metodes est   monna eaforan,
        scyldfulra mægð,   scyne and fægere.
        þa reordade   rodora waldend
        wrað moncynne   and þa worde cwæð:
1255   "Ne syndon me on ferhðe freo   from gewitene
        cneorisn caines   ac me þæt cynn hafað
        sare abolgen.   nu me sethes bearn   [P. 64]
        torn niwiað   and him to nimað
        mægeð to gemæccum   minra feonda
1260   þær wifa wlite   onwod grome,
        idesa ansien   and ece feond,
        folcdriht wera   þa ær on friðe wæron."
        siððan hundtwelftig   geteled rime
        wintra on worulde   wræce bisegodon
1265   fæge þeoda   hwonne frea wolde
        on wærlogan   wite settan

1232 fif— v· : *MS.* **1235** noæ, *written* noẹ. **1238** fif— v· :
MS. **1248** ÞÆT, *spelled out.* **1249** *No point after* caines.
1255 *Very faded point after* ferhðe, *none after* freo. **1264**
wræce, *erasures above and around this word;* bisegodon, e
added above line by scribe, tag added in different ink below
e.

6.5   videns autem Deus
            quod multa malitia hominum esset in terra
       et cuncta cogitatio cordis intenta esset
            ad malum omni tempore

6.6   paenituit eum
            quod hominem fecisset in terra
       [et tactus dolore cordis intrinsecus]
6.7   delebo inquit hominem
            quem creavi a facie terrae
       ab homine usque ad animantia / a reptili usque ad
            volucres caeli /(paenitet enim me fecisse eos)

6.8   Noe vero invenit gratiam coram Domino
6.9   . . . Noe vir iustus atque perfectus fuit (in gener-
            ationibus suis) / cum Deo ambulavit
            (cf. V.L.: et placuit Deo)

(6.11 corrupta est autem terra coram Deo et repleta est
            iniquitate *conflated with 6.12)*
6.12   cumque vidisset Deus terram esse corruptam
       omnis quippe caro corruperat viam suam super terram
6.13   dixit ad Noe *(finis . . . cum terra, omitted)*
6.17   ecce ego adducam diluvii aquas super terram
       ut interficiam omnem carnem
       in qua spiritus vitae est subter caelum
       universa quae in terra sunt consumentur *(cf. 6.7)*
6.18   ponamque foedus meum tecum . . . *(cont. at 1328 ff.)*

6.14   fac tibi arcam [de lignis levigatis]

       mansiunculas in arca facies . . . *(cont. at 1309 f. &
            1322 ff.)* / 6.20 . . . iuxta genus suum . . .
6.16   . . . deorsum / cenacula et tristega facies in ea

  and on deað slean dædum scyldige
  gigantmæcgas, gode unleofe,
  micle mansceaðan, metode laðe.
1270 þa geseah selfa sigoro waldend
  hwæt wæs monna manes on eorðan
  and þæt hie wæron womma ðriste,
  inwitfulle he þæt unfægere
  wera cneorissum gewrecan þohte,
1275 forgripan gumcynne grimme and sare
  heardum mihtum. hreaw hine swiðe
  þæt he folcmægþa fruman aweahte,
  æðelinga ord þa he adam sceop,
  cwæð þæt he wolde for wera synnum
1280 eall aæðan þæt on eorðan wæs,
  forleosan lica gehwilc þara þe lifes gast
  fæðmum þeahte. eall þæt frea wolde
  on ðære toweardan tide acwellan
  þe þa nealæhte niðða bearnum.
1285 Noe wæs god, nergende leof,
  swiðe gesælig, sunu lameches,
  domfæst and gedefe. drihten wiste
  þæt þæs æðelinges ellen dohte
  breostgehygdum. forðon him brego sægde,
1290 halig æt hleoðre, helm allwihta,
  hwæt he fah werum fremman wolde.
  geseah unrihte eorðan fulle,
  side sælwongas synnum gehladene,
  widlum gewemde. þa waldend spræc,
1295 nergend usser and to noe cwæð:
  "Ic wille mid flode folc acwellan
  and cynna gehwilc / cucra wuhta   [P. 65]
  þara þe lyft and flod lædað and fedað,
  feoh and fuglas. þu scealt frið habban
1300 mid sunum þinum ðonne sweart wæter,
  wonne wælstreamas, werodum swelgað
  sceaðum scyldfullum. ongyn þe scip wyrcan,
  merehus micel. on þam þu monegum scealt
  reste geryman and rihte setl
1305 ælcum æfter agenum eorðan tudre.
  gescype scylfan on scipes bosme.

1270 *No point after* selfa. 1272 *No point after* wæron. 1273
No point after -fulle. 1277 *A stain obliterates the point*
after aweahte. 1283 toweardan, *second* a *altered from* e. 1294
gewemde, em *written over an erasure (Holthausen reports se-*
cond e *corrected from* æ). 1306 gescype, *scribe began to*
write gescipe, *but altered the* i *to* y, *erased downstroke of*
the original p *and rewrote* p *further to the right.*

6.15   et sic facies eam trecentorum cubitorum erit longitudo
          arcae / quinquaginta cubitorum latitudo
       et triginta cubitorum altitudo illius

6.19   et ex cunctis animantibus universae carnis
       [bina] induces in arcam ut vivant tecum
       [masculini sexus et feminini]
6.22   Fecit ergo Noe omnia quae praeceperat illi Deus

(6.14 . . . et bitumine linies intrinsecus et extrinsecus)

 7.1   dixitque Dominus ad eum

       ingredere tu et omnis domus tua arcam   *conflated with*
6.18   ponamque foedus meum tecum
       et ingredieris arcam tu
          et filii tui
       uxor tua et uxores filiorum tuorum tecum
 7.2   ex omnibus animantibus mundis tolles septena septena
          [masculum et feminam]

       de animantibus vero non mundis duo duo
          [masculum et feminam]
6.21   tolles igitur tecum ex omnibus escis quae mandi possunt
          et comportabis apud te
       et erunt tam tibi quam illis in cibum

(7.1 . . . te enim vidi iustum coram me in generatione hac)

       þu þær fær gewyrc   fiftiges wid,
       ðrittiges heah,   þreohund lang
       elngemeta   and wið yða gewyrc
1310   gefeg fæste   þær sceal fæsl wesan
       cwiclifigendra   cynna gehwilces
       on þæt wudufæsten,   wocor gelæded
       eorðan tudres.   earc sceal þy mare."
       Noe fremede   swa hine nergend heht,   [P. 66]
1315   hyrde þam halgan   heofoncyninge,
       ongan ofostlice   þæt hof wyrcan,
       micle merecieste.   magum sægde
       þæt wæs þrealic þing   þeodum toweard,
       reðe wite.   hie ne rohton þæs.
1320   geseah þa ymb wintra worn   wærfæst metod
       geofonhusa mæst   gearo hlifigean,
       innan and utan   eorðan lime
       gefæstnod wið flode,   fær noes,
       þy selestan.   þæt is syndrig cynn.
1325   Symle bið þy heardra   þe hit hreoh wæter,
       swearte sæstreamas,   swiðor beatað.

               xxi.

Ð A to noe cwæð   nergend usser: [P. 67]
     "ic þe þæs mine,   monna leofost,
     wære gesylle   þæt þu weg nimest
1330   and feora fæsl   þe þu ferian scealt
       geond deop wæter   dægrimes worn
       on lides bosme.   læd swa ic þe hate
       under earce bord   eaforan þine,
       frumgaran þry   and eower feower wif.
1335   Ond þu seofone genim   on þæt sundreced
       tudra gehwilces   geteled rimes
       þara þe to mete   mannum lifige
       and þara oðera   ælces twa.
       Swilce þu of eallum   eorðan wæstmum
1340   wiste under wægbord   werodum gelæde
       þam þe mid sceolon   mereflod nesan.
       fed freolice   feora wocre
       oð ic þære lafe   lagosiða eft
       reorde under roderum   ryman wille.
1345   Gewit þu nu mid hiwum   on þæt hof gangan
       gasta werode.   Ic þe godne wat,

1308 lang, g *covered by a water-stain, point not visible.* 1314
fremede: *Bouterwek & edd.*— freme: *MS.* 1315 *No point after*
-cyninge. 1316 *Point after* ongan, *none after* ofostlice. 1319
ne, g *erased before* n. 1335 Ond, *spelled out.* 1337 *No point*
after mete. 1338 oðera, *one letter erased between* e *and* r;
no point after oðera. 1340 wiste, t *practically obliterated*
by stain.

7.4   adhuc enim et post dies septem ego pluam super terram

      quadraginta diebus et quadraginta noctibus

      et delebo omnem substantiam quam feci de superficie
         terrae.

7.5   Fecit ergo Noe omnia quae mandaverat ei Dominus
7.7   et ingressus est Noe et filii eius
      uxor eius et uxores filiorum eius cum eo in arcam
         propter aquas diluvii / 7.8 de animantibus quoque
         [mundis . . ./7.9 duo et duo] ingressa sunt ad Noe
         in arcam [masculus et femina]
      sicut praeceperat Deus Noe *conflated with*
7.16 et quae ingressa sunt [masculus et femina] ex omni
         carne introierunt
      sicut praeceperat ei Deus
      et inclusit eum Dominus deforis   *cf. 1390 f.*

7.6   eratque sescentorum annorum quando *conflated with*
7.11 Anno sescentesimo vitae Noe [mense secundo septimo-
         decimo die mensis] . . . / 7.13 in articulo diei
         illius ingressus est Noe et Sem et Ham et Iafeth
         filii eius . . . cum eis in arcam
7.11 . . . rupti sunt omnes fontes abyssi magnae / et catar-
         actae caeli apertae sunt / 7.6 . . . diluvii aquae
         inundaverunt super terram

7.12 et facta est pluvia super terram
         quadraginta diebus et quadraginta noctibus *con-
         flated with* 7.17 factumque est diluvium quadra-
         ginta diebus super terram / et multiplicatae sunt
         aquae . . .
7.19 et aquae praevaluerunt nimis super terram
      opertique sunt omnes montes excelsi sub universo caelo
7.17 . . . et elevaverunt arcam in sublime a terra

               fæsthydigne.   þu eart freoðo wyrðe,
               ara mid eaforum.   ic on andwlitan
               nu ofor seofon niht   sigan læte
1350   wællregn ufan   widre eorðan.
               feowertig daga   fæhðe ic wille
               on weras stælan   and mid wægþreate
               æhta and agend   eall acwellan
               þa beutan beoð   earce bordum
1355   þonne sweart racu   stigan onginneð."
               Him þa noe gewat   swa hine nergend het
               under earce bord   eaforan lædan,
               weras on wægþel   and heora wif somed
               and eall þæt to fæsle   frea ælmihtig
1360   habban wolde,   under hrof gefor
               to heora ætgifan   swa him ælmihtig
               weroda / drihten   þurh his word abead.   [P. 68]
               Him on hoh beleac   heofonrices weard   [P. 69]
               merehuses muð   mundum sinum,
1365   sigora waldend   and segnade
               earce innan   agenum spedum
               nergend usser.   Noe hæfde,
               sunu lameches,   syxhund wintra
               þa he mid bearnum   under bord gestah,
1370   gleaw mid geogoðe,   be godes hæse,
               dugeðum dyrum.   drihten sende
               regn from roderum   and eac rume let
               willeburnan   on woruld þringan
               of ædra gehwære   egorstreamas
1375   swearte swogan.   sæs up stigon
               ofer stæðweallas.   strang wæs and reðe
               se ðe wætrum weold,   wreah and þeahte
               manfæhðu bearn,   middangeardes,
               wonnan wæge,   wera eðelland.
1380   hof hergode,   hygeteonan wræc
               metod on monnum.   mere swiðe grap
               on fæge folc   feowertig daga,
               nihta oðer swilc.   nið wæs reðe,
               wællgrim werum.   wuldorcyninges
1385   yða wræcon   arleasra feorh
               of flæschoman.   flod ealle wreah,
               hreoh under heofonum   hea beorgas
               geond sidne grund   and on sund ahof
               earce from eorðan   and þa æðelo mid
1390   Þa segnade   selfa drihten,

1348 andwlitan, and- *spelled out.* 1358 wægþel, *spaced* þ el,
the loop of an æ erased after þ. 1365 *No point after*
segnade. 1385 *No point after* wræcon. 1388 sidne, d *altered
from* n. 1390 *No point after* segnade.

7.20 quindecim cubitis altior
           fuit aqua super montes quos operuerat

7.23 et delevit omnem substantiam quae erat super terram
           [ab homine usque ad pecus / tam reptile quam volu-
           cres caeli / et deleta sunt de terra]
        remansit autem solus Noe et qui cum eo erant in arca

8.1   Recordatus est autem Deus Noe

           cunctorumque animantium / et omnium iumentorum quae
           erant cum eo in arca
        adduxit
           spiritum super terram et inminutae sunt aquae
8.2   et clausi sunt fontes abyssi et cataractae caeli
        et prohibitae sunt pluviae de caelo
8.3   reversaeque aquae de terra euntes et redeuntes

        (et coeperunt minui post centum quinquaginta dies) *cf.*
           7.24

8.4   requievitque arca [mense septimo vicesima septima die
           mensis] super montes
           Armeniae

8.5   at vero aquae ibant et decrescebant [usque ad decimum
           mensem / decimo enim mense prima die mensis]
           (apparuerunt cacumina montium)

scyppend usser þa he þæt scip beleac.
Siððan wide rad wolcnum under
ofer holmes hrincg hof seleste,
for mid fearme. fære ne moston
1395 wægliðendum wætres brogan
hæste hrinon ac hie halig god
ferede and nerede. fiftena stod
deop ofer dunum sæ drenceflod
monnes elna. þæt is mæro wyrd.
1400 þam æt niehstan wæs nan to gedale
nymþe heo wæs ahafen on þa hean lyft.
þa se egorhere eorðan tuddor
eall acwealde buton / þæt earce bord   [P. 70]
heold heofona frea þa hine halig god,
1405 ece upp forlet ed monne
streamum stigan, stiðferhð cyning.

xxii.

þA Gemunde god mereliðende,   [P. 71]
sigora waldend, sunu lameches
and ealle þa wocre þe he wið wætre beleac,
1410 lifes leohtfruma, on lides bosme.
Gelædde þa wigend weroda drihten
worde ofer widland. willflod ongan
lytligan eft. lago ebbade
sweart under swegle. hæfde soð metod
1415 eaforum egstream eft gecyrred,
torht ryne, regn gestilled.
for famig scip *fiftig* and *hundteontig*
nihta under roderum siððan nægledbord,
fær seleste, flod up ahof
1420 oðþæt rimgetæl reðre þrage
daga forð gewat. ða on dunum gesæt
heah mid hlæste holmærna mæst,
earc noes, þe armenia
hatene syndon. þær se halga bad,
1425 sunu lameches, soðra gehata
lange þrage hwonne him lifes weard,
frea ælmihtig, frecenra siða
reste ageafe þære he rume dreah
þa hine on sunde geond sidne grund
1430 wonne yða wide bæron.
holm wæs heononweard. hæleð langode,
wægliðende, swilce wif heora
hwonne hie of nearwe ofer nægledbord

1400 *Point after* niehstan. 1401 *Point after* wæs, *none after*
ahafen. 1405 *No point after* monne. 1417 fiftig and hundteontig— l · 7 c: *MS.* 1430 *No point after* yða.

8.7   *(V.L.)* et emisit corvum ut videret utrum cessasset aqua
      (et exiens non est reversus donec siccaret aqua)
8.6   cumque transissent quadraginta dies

      (aperiens Noe fenestram arcae quam fecerat) dimisit
              corvum

8.7   [qui egrediebatur et revertebatur donec siccarentur
              aquae super terram]

8.8   emisit quoque columbam post eum ut videret si iam
              cessassent aquae

      super faciem terrae

8.9   (quae cum non invenisset ubi requiesceret pes eius) re-
              versa est ad eum in arcam / *cf*. *V.L.* non inveniens
              columba requiem pedibus suis reversa est ad eum
              in arca(m)
        Vulg.   aquae enim erant super universam terram

      extenditque manum et adpraehensam intulit in arcam
8.10 expectatis autem ultra septem diebus aliis rursum
              dimisit columbam ex arca

8.11 at illa venit ad eum ad vesperam
      portans ramum olivae virentibus foliis in ore suo

      intellexit ergo Noe
              quod cessassent aquae super terram

8.12 expectavitque nihilominus septem alios dies et emisit
              columbam / quae non est reversa ultra ad eum

ofer streamstaðe   stæppan mosten
1435   and of enge ut   æhta lædan.
Þa fandode   forðweard scipes
hwæðer sincende   sæflod þa gyt
wære under wolcnum.   let þa ymb worn daga
þæs þe heah hlioðo   horde onfengon
1440   and æðelum eac   eorðan tudres
sunu lameches   sweartne fleogan
hrefn ofer heahflod   of huse ut.
Noe tealde /   þæt he on neod hine,   [P. 72]
gif he on þære lade   land ne funde,
1445   ofer sidwæter   secan wolde
on wægþele.   eft him seo wen geleah
ac se feond gespearn   fleotende hreaw.
salwigfeðera   secan nolde.
He þa ymb seofon niht   sweartum hrefne
1450   of earce forlet   æfter fleogan
ofer heah wæter   haswe culufran
on fandunga   hwæðer famig sæ
deop þa gyta   dæl ænigne
grenre eorðan   ofgifen hæfde.
1455   heo wide hire   willan sohte
and rume fleah.   no hweðere reste fand
þæt heo for flode   fotum ne meahte
land gespornan   ne on leaf treowes
steppan for streamum   ac wæron steap hleoðo
1460   bewrigen mid wætrum.   Gewat se wilda fugel
on æfenne   earce secan
ofer wonne wæg,   werig sigan
hungri to handa   halgum rince.
Þa wæs culufre eft   of cofan sended
1465   ymb wucan, wilde.   seo wide fleah
oðþæt heo rumgal   reste stowe
fægere funde   and þa fotum stop
on beam hyre.   gefeah bliðemod
þæs þe heo gesittan   swiðe werig
1470   on treowes telgum   torhtum moste.
heo feðera onsceoc,   gewat fleogan eft
mid lacum hire.   liðend brohte
elebeames twig   an to handa,
grene blædæ.   þa ongeat hraðe
1475   flotmonna frea   þæt wæs frofor cumen,
earfoðsiða bot.   Þa gyt se eadega wer
ymb wucan þriddan   wilde culufran
ane sende.   seo eft ne com

1436 *No point after* fandode.   **1445** *No point after* -wæter.
1451 heah, *final* h *added above the line; the caret beneath
in different ink.*   **1461** *No point after* æfenne.   **1469** gesittan:
Etmüller & edd.— gesette: *MS.*   **1476** *Point after* eadega.

8.15   locutus est autem Deus ad Noe dicens

8.16   egredere de arca tu

          et uxor tua / filii tui et uxores filiorum
          tuorum tecum / 8.17 cuncta animantia quae sunt
          apud te (ex omni carne) . . .

8.18   Egressus est ergo Noe

          (et filii eius / uxor illius et uxores filiorum
          eius cum eo)
8.20   aedificavit autem Noe altare Domino
       et tollens de cunctis pecoribus et volucribus mundis
          obtulit holocausta super altare

 9.1   Benedixitque Deus Noe
             et filiis eius . . .
8.21-22   [odoratusque est Dominus odorem suavitatis, *etc.*]

 9.1   . . . et dixit [Deus] ad eos

       crescite et multiplicamini et implete terram *conflated*
             with 8.17? crescite et multiplicamini super terram
 9.2   (et terror vester ac tremor sit super cuncta animalia
             terrae / et super omnes volucres caeli cum uni-
             versis quae moventur in terra / omnes pisces maris
             manui vestrae traditi sunt)

                to lide fleogan   ac heo land begeat,
1480   grene bearwas.   nolde gladu æfre
                under salwedbord   syððan ætywan
                on þellfæstenne   þa hire þearf ne wæs.   [P. 73]

                           xxiii.

        þA TO noe spræc   nergend usser,
          heofonrices weard,   halgan reorde:
1485   "þe is eðelstol   eft gerymed,
                lisse on lande,   lagosiða rest,
                fæger on foldan.   gewit on freðo gangan
                ut of earce   and on eorðan bearm
                of þam hean hofe   hiwan læd þu
1490   and ealle þa wocre   þe ic wægþrea
                on hliðe nerede   þenden lago hæfde,
                þrymme geþeahte,   þriddan eðyl."
                He fremede swa   and frean hyrde,
                stah ofer streamweall   swa him seo stefn bebead
1495   lustum miclum   and alædde þa
                of wægþele   wraðra lafe.
                þa noe ongan   nergende lac,   [P. 74]
                rædfæst, reðran   and recene genam
                on eallum dæl   æhtum sinum
1500   ðam ðe him to dugeðum   drihten sealde,
                gleaw to þam gielde   and þa gode selfum
                torhtmod hæle   tiber onsægde,
                cyninge engla.   huru cuð dyde
                nergend usser   þa he noe
1505   gebletsade   and his bearn somed
                þæt he þæt gyld on þanc   agifen hæfde
                and on geogoðhade   godum dædum
                ær geearnod.   þa him ealra wæs
                ara este   ælmihtig god,
1510   domfæst dugeþa,   þa gyt drihten cwæð,
                wuldres aldor,   word to noe:
                "Tymað nu and tiedrað,   tires brucað,
                mid gefean fryðo,   fyllað eorðan,
                eall geiceað.   eow is eðelstol,
1515   holmes hlæst   and heofonfuglas
                and wildu deor   on geweald geseald,
                eorðe ælgrene   and eacen feoh.

1483 *No point after* usser.   **1485** *No point after* -stol.   **1492**
þriddan: *Grein & edd. (except Wells)—* þridda: *MS.*   **1504** *No*
point after noe.   **1511** wuldres, *the upper halves of* l *and* e
badly rubbed away; Wülker, Holthausen and Krapp report wuldris,
Wells corrects. **1515** heofonfuglas: *Thorpe & edd. (except Bou-*
terwek)— -fugla: *MS.*   **1517** feoh, *what appears to be a black-*
letter r *above* h *(all edd. read* feoh*).*

9.4   excepto quod carnem cum sanguine
           non comedetis

9.6   quicumque effuderit humanum sanguinem fundetur sanguis
           illius . . .

9.5   sanguinem enim animarum vestrarum requiram
           de manu cunctarum bestiarum et de manu hominis
       de manu viri et fratris eius requiram animam hominis

9.6   . . . ad imaginem quippe Dei factus est homo

9.7   vos autem crescite et multiplicamini et ingredimini
           super terram et implete eam.

9.9   ecce ego statuam pactum meum vobiscum [et cum semine
           vestro post vos] / *conflated with* 9.11 statuam
           pactum meum vobiscum / et nequaquam ultra inter-
           ficietur omnis caro aquis diluvii neque erit de-
           inceps diluvium dissipans terram
9.13   arcum meum ponam in nubibus
       et erit signum foederis inter me et inter terram
9.12   *replaced by 9.13 except for* . . . in generationes sem-
           piternas
       1543 ff., cf. 1493 ff. & 8.18
9.18   Erant igitur filii Noe qui egressi sunt de arca

       Sem Ham et Iafeth . . .
9.19   tres isti sunt filii Noe et ab his disseminatum
           est omne hominum genus super universam terram

```
              næfre ge mid blode    beodgereordu
              unarlice    eowre þicgeað,
1520          besmiten mid synne    sawldreore.              [P. 75]
              ælc hine selfa    ærest begrindeð
              gastes dugeðum    þæra þe mid gares orde
              oðrum aldor oðþringeð.    ne ðearf he þy edleane
                                                      [gefeon
              modgeþance    ac ic monnes feorh
1525          to slagan seðe    swiðor micle
              and to broðor banan    þæs þe blodgyte,
              wællfyll weres    wæpnum gespedeð,
              morð mid mundum.    monn wæs to godes
              anlicnesse    ærest gesceapen.
1530          ælc hafað magwlite    metodes and engla
              þara þe healdan wile    halige þeawas.
              weaxað and wridað,    wilna brucað,
              ara on eorðan,    æðelum fyllað
              eowre fromcynne    foldan sceatas,
1535          teamum and tudre.    ic eow treowa þæs
              mine selle    þæt ic on middangeard
              næfre egorhere    eft gelæde,
              wæter ofer widland.    ge on wolcnum þæs
              oft gelome    andgiettacen
1540          magon sceawigan    þonne ic scurbogan
              minne iewe    þæt ic monnum þas
              wære gelæste    þenden woruld standeð."
              Ða wæs se snotra    sunu lamehes
              of fere acumen    flode on laste
1545          mid his eaforum þrim,    yrfes hyrde,
1546          and heora feower wif*    [siððan fæle gestod]
1549          wærfæst metod    wætra lafe.
              hæleð hygerofe    hatenc wæron,
              suna noes,    sem and cham,
              iafeð þridda.    from þam gumrincum
              folc geludon    and gefylled wearð
              eall þes middangeard    monna bearnum.
```

```
         *1547 nemde wæron
          1548 percoba, olla, olliua, olliuani.
```

1521-22a *Pointed* ælc hine selfa ærest · begrindeð gastes dugeðum ·   **1522b** þæra: *Thorpe & edd.*— þære: *MS.*   **1528** *No
point after* godes.   **1546b** *Not in MS; 1546-48 reads* ⁊ heora
feower wif / nemde wæron · pcoba · olla · olliua · olliuani
1551 *Point after* sem.   **1553** *No point after* geludon.

9.20 coepitque Noe vir agricola

    exercere terram
et plantavit vineam

    bibensque vinum inebriatus est
    et nudatus est in tabernaculo suo

9.22 quod cum vidisset Ham pater Chanaan

    verenda scilicet patris sui esse nuda

    nuntiavit duobus fratribus suis foras

9.23 at vero Sem et Iafeth pallium imposuerunt humeris suis
    (et incedentes retrorsum operuerunt verecunda patris
        sui / faciesque eorum aversae erant et patris
        sui virilia non viderunt) / 9.24 evigilans autem
        Noe ex vino / cum didicisset quae fecerat ei
        filius suus minor

xxiiii.

1555   Ð A Noe ongan   niwan stefne
            mid hleomagum   ham staðelian
            and to eorðan him   ætes tilian,
      won and worhte,   wingeard sette,
      seow sæda fela, /   sohte georne   [P. 76]
1560   þa him wlitebeorhte   wæstmas brohte,
      geartorhte gife,   grene folde.
      Ða þæt geeode   þæt se eadega wer
      on his wicum wearð   wine druncen,
      swæf symbelwerig   and him selfa sceaf
1565   reaf of lice   swa gerysne ne wæs,
      læg þa limnacod.   he lyt ongeat
      þæt him on his *inne*   swa earme gelamp
      þa him on hreðre   heafodswima
      on þæs halgan hofe   heortan clypte.
1570   swiðe on slæpe   sefa nearwode
      þæt he ne mihte,   on gemynd drepen,
      hine handum self   mid hrægle wryon
      and sceome þeccan   swa gesceapu wæron
      werum and wifum   siððan wuldres þegn
1575   ussum fæder and meder   fyrene sweorde
      on laste beleac   lifes eðel.
      þa com ærest   cam In siðian,
      eafora noes,   þær his aldor læg,
      ferhðe forstolen.   þær he freondlice
1580   on his agenum fæder   are ne wolde,
      gesceawian   ne þa sceonde huru
      hleomagum helan   ac he hlihende
      broðrum sægde   hu se beorn hine
      reste on recede. /   hie þa raðe stopon,   [P. 77]
1585   heora andwlitan   in bewrigenum
      under loðum listum   þæt hie leofum men
      geoce gefremede. /   gode wæron begen,
      sem and iafeð. /   Ða of slæpe onbrægd   [P. 78]
      sunu lamehes   and þa sona ongeat
1590   þæt him cynegodum   cham ne wolde,
      þa him wæs are þearf,   ænige cyðan
      hyldo and treowa.   þæt þam halgan wæs

1555 ongan niwan, *badly rubbed and blurred; the* a *and the
final* n *of* ongan, *the point and* ni *of* niwan *very indistinct.*
1556 staðelian, -elian *very indistinct.* 1557 *No point after*
him. 1567 inne: *edd.*— innne: *MS.* 1572 *No point after* self;
hrægle, g *over erased* l. 1577 *No point after* ærest, *point
after* cam; siðian, *the scribe wrote* sidian, *the* d *has been
crossed in very faint ink.* 1579 ferhðe, h *added above* r.
1585 *No point after* -wlitan. 1592 þæt, *spelled out.*

9.25 ait
      maledictus Chanaan   *(V.L.* maledictus Cham*)*
      servus servorum erit fratribus suis

9.28 vixit autem Noe

           post diluvium trecentis quinquaginta annis

9.29 [et impleti sunt omnes dies eius nongentorum quinqua-
           ginta annorum] et mortuus est
10.1 (Haec generationes filiorum Noe . . .)
10.2 filii Iafeth

           Gomer . . . / 10.3 porro filii Gomer . . .

10.5 (ab his divisae sunt insulae gentium in regionibus suis
      unusquisque secundum linguam / et familias in nation-
           ibus suis.) / 10.6 Filii autem Ham
           Chus . . . et Chanaan

10.7 filii Chus [Saba et Hevila et Sabatha et Regma, *etc.*]

10.8 (porro Chus genuit Nemrod . . .) *(V.L. & LXX:* Nebroth*)*

10.9 (. . . ob hoc exivit proverbium quasi Nemrod . . .)

10.8 . . . ipse coepit esse potens in terra
10.10 fuit autem principium regni eius Babylon . . . in
           terra Sennaar

```
                  sar on mode.      ongan þa his selfes bearn
                  wordum wyrgean,     cwæð he wesan sceolde
    1595          hean under heofnum     hleomaga þeow,
                  cham on eorþan.      him þa cwyde syððan
                  and his fromcynne     frecne scodon.
                  þa nyttade    noe siððan
                  mid sunum sinum     sidan rices
    1600          ðreohund wintra     þisses lifes
                  freomen æfter flode    and fiftig eac
    1601c         þa he forð gewat.
                  siððan his eaforan     ead bryttedon,
                  bearna stryndon.      him wæs beorht wela.
                  þa wearð iafeðe     geogoð afeded,
    1605          hyhtlic heorðwerod     heafodmaga,
                  sunu and dohtra.      he wæs selfa til.
                  heold a rice,     eðeldreamas,
                  blæd / mid bearnum     oð þæt breosta hord,     [P. 79]
                  gast ellorfus,     gangan sceolde
    1610          to godes dome.      geomor siððan
                  fæder flettgesteald     freondum dælde
                  swæsum and gesibbum,     sunu iafeðes.
                  þæs teames wæs     tuddor gefylled
                  unlytel dæl     eorðan gesceafta.
    1615          swilce chames suno     cende wurdon,
                  eaforan on eðle.      þa yldestan
                  chus and chanan     hatene wæron,
                  fulfreolice feorh,     frumbearn chames.
                  chus wæs æðelum     heafodwisa,
    1620          wilna brytta     and worulddugeða
                  broðrum sinum,     botlgestreona
                  fæder on laste     siððan forð gewat
                  cham of lice     þa him cwealm gesceod.
                  se magoræswa     mægðe sinre
    1625          domas sægde     oð þæt his dogora wæs
                  rim aurnen.      þa se rinc ageaf
                  eorðcunde ead,     sohte oðer lif,
                  fæder nebroðes.      frumbearn siððan,
                  eafora chuses,     yrfestole weold,
    1630          widmære wer.      swa us gewritu secgeað
                  þæt he moncynnes     mæste hæfde
                  on þam mældagum     mægen and strengo.
                  se wæs babylones     bregorices fruma,
                  ærest æðelinga.     eðelðrym onhof,
```

1593 *A comma-shaped point added after* selfes.   1599 *No point
after* sinum.   1601 *Point after* æfter, *none after* flode. 1603
No point after stryndon.   1617 *Fine point after* chus; chanan:
Dietrich (ZfdA *10, 326*) *& edd. (except Wülker & Wells)*— cham:
MS.   1628 nebroðes: *Cosijn/Sievers* (Beiträge *19, 450*) *& edd*—
ne breðer: *MS.*   1630 swa: *edd.*— wwa: *MS.*

11.1   Erat autem terra labii unius et sermonum eorundem

10.20   hii filii Ham in cognationibus et linguis et genera-
        tionibus terrisque et gentibus suis

10.21   De Sem quoque nati sunt patre omnium filiorum Eber . . .
(10.31 isti filii Sem secundum cognationes et linguas et regi-
        ones in gentibus suis)

(10.24 . . . de quo ortus est Eber / 10.25 natique sunt Eber
           filii duo . . .)

 11.2   cumque proficiscerentur de oriente

        invenerunt campum in terra Sennaar et habitaverunt in eo

 11.4   et dixerunt
           venite faciamus nobis civitatem et turrem cuius
           culmen pertingat ad caelum
        et celebremus nomen nostrum
           antequam dividamur in universas terras

        Cf. 1655
[10.9   et (Nemrod) erat robustus venator coram Domino . . .]

 11.5   descendit autem Dominus

1635   rymde and rærde.   reord wæs þa gieta
                eorðbuendum   an gemæne.

xxv.

SVILCE of cames   cneorisse woc
           wermægða fela.   of þam widfolc,
           cneorim micel   cenned wæron.
1640   þa wearð seme   suna and dohtra
                on woruldrice   worn afeded,
                freora bearna,   ær ðon forð cure
                wintrum wælreste   werodes aldor.
                on þære mægðe   wæron men tile.
1645   þara an wæs   eber haten,
                eafora semes.   of þam eorle woc
                unrim þeoda   þa nu æðelingas,
                ealle eorðbuend, /   ebrei hatað.   [P. 80]
                gewiton him þa eastan   æhta lædan,
1650   feoh and feorme.   folc wæs anmod.
                rofe rincas   sohton rumre land
                oð þæt hie becomon   corðrum miclum,
                folc ferende,   þær hie fæstlice
                æðelinga bearn,   eard genamon.
1655   gesetton þa sennar   sidne and widne
                leoda ræswan   leofum mannum
                heora geardagum.   grene wongas
                fægre foldan   him forðwearde
                on ðære dægtide   duguðe wæron,
1660   wilna gehwilces,   weaxende sped.
                Ða þær mon mænig   be his mægwine,
                æðeling anmod,   oðerne bæd
                þæs hie him to mærðe,   ær seo mengeo eft
                geond foldan bearn   tofaran sceolde,
1665   leoda mægðe   on landsocne,
                burh geworhte   and to beacne torr
                up arærde   to rodortunglum.
                þæs þe hie gesohton   sennera feld
                swa þa foremeahtige   folces ræswan,
1670   þa yldestan,   oft and gelome
                liðsum gewunedon.   larum sohton
                weras to weorce   and to wrohtscipe
                oð þæt for wlence   and for wonhygdum
                cyðon cræft heora.   ceastre worhton
1675   and to heofnum up   hlædræ rærdon,
                strengum stepton   stænenne weall
                ofer monna gemet,   mærða georne,
                hæleð mid honda.   þa com halig god

1654 *Point added after* æðelinga.   **1674** ceastre, ea *imperfectly altered from* r *or* m.   **1676** stænenne: *Grein & edd.* — stænnene: *MS.*

(11.5)   ut videret
                civitatem et turrem
                quam aedificabant
                filii Adam

[11.6   et dixit . . .] / (11.7 venite igitur descendamus et
        confundamus ibi linguam eorum / ut non audiat
        unusquisque vocem proximi sui)

11.8   atque ita divisit eos Dominus ex illo loco in univer-
        sas terras . . . / 11.9 . . . et inde dispersit
        eos Dominus super faciem cunctarum regionum.
11.8   . . . et cessaverunt aedificare civitatem / 11.9 [et
        idcirco vocatum est nomen eius Babel / quia ibi
        confusum est labium universae terrae . . .]
(11.10 Hae generationes Sem . . .)

(11.27 Hae sunt autem generationes Thare)
        Thare genuit

        Abram [et Nahor] et Aran

porro Aran genuit Loth

               wera cneorissa   weorc sceawigan,
1680   beorna burhfæsten,   and þæt beacen somed
               þe to roderum up   ræran ongunnon
               adames eaforan   and þæs unrædes
               stiðferhð cyning   steore gefremede.
               þa he reðemod   reorde gesette
1685   eorðbuendum   ungelice
               þæt hie þære spæce   sped ne ahton
               þa hie gemitton,   mihtum spedge,
               teoche æt torre   getalum myclum
               weorces wisan   ne þær wermægða
1690   ænig wiste   hwæt oðer cwæð.
               ne meah/te hie gewurðan   weall stænenne   [P. 81]
               up forð timbran   ac hie earmlice
               heapum tohlodon,   hleoðrum gedælde.
               wæs oðere   æghwilc worden
1695   mægburh fremde   siððan metod tobræd
               þurh his mihta sped   monna spræce.
               toforan þa   on feower wegas   [P. 82]
               æðelinga bearn   ungeþeode
               on landsocne.   him on laste bu
1700   stiðlic stantorr   and seo steape burh
               samod samworht   on sennar stod.
               weox þa under wolcnum   and wriðade
               mægburh semes   oð þæt mon awoc
               on þære cneorisse   cynebearna rim,
1705   þancolmod wer,   þeawum hydig.
               wurdon þam æðelinge   eaforan acende
               in babilone,   bearn afeded,
               freolicu tu   and þa frumgaran,
               hæleð higerofe,   hatene wæron
1710   Abraham and aaron.   þam eorlum wæs
               frea engla bam   freod and aldor.
               Ða wearð aarone   eafora feded,
               leoflic on life.   ðam wæs loth noma.
               ða magorincas   metode geþungon,
1715   abraham and loth,   unforcuðlice
               swa him from yldrum   æðelu wæron
               on woruldrice.   forðon hie wide nu
               dugeðum demað   drihta bearnum.

1692b *Pointed* earm · lice · **1697** *No point after* þa, *point
after* feower. **1702** *Point added after* þa. **1703** þæt, *spelled
out.* **1710** wæs, *imperfectly altered from* wees *by scribe; the
first* e *was a "high"* e *whose top loop was not erased after it
was altered to* a. **1712** *Point added after* wearð. **1716** *No
point after* yldrum.

11.29   duxerunt autem Abram [et Nahor] uxores

nomen autem uxoris Abram Sarai . . .

11.30   erat autem Sarai sterilis
           nec habebat liberos

11.31   tulit itaque Thare Abram
           filium suum et Loth filium Aran filium filii sui
        et Sarai nurum suam uxorem Abram filii sui / et eduxit
           eos de [Ur] Chaldeorum ut irent in terram Chanaan

veneruntque usque Haran et habitaverunt ibi

11.32   et facti sunt dies Thare
           ducentorum quinque annorum
           et mortuus est in Haran.

 12.1   Dixit autem Dominus
           ad Abram
        egredere de terra tua
           et de cognatione tua
           et de domo patris tui

in terram
           quam monstrabo tibi
 12.2   . . . et benedicam tibi et magnificabo nomen tuum
           erisque benedictus
 12.3   benedicam benedicentibus tibi et maledicam maledicen-
           tibus tibi

atque in te benedicentur universae cognationes terrae

[xxvi]   ÞA þæs mæles wæs   mearc agongen   [P. 83]
1720   þæt him abraham   idese brohte,
                wif, to hame   þær he wic ahte,
        fæger and freolic.   seo fæmne wæs
        sarra haten   þæs þe us secgeað bec.
        hie þa wintra fela   woruld bryttedon,
1725   sinc ætsomne   sibbe heoldon
        geara mengeo.   no hwæðre gifeðe wearð
        abrahame þa gyt   þæt him yrfeweard
        wlitebeorht ides   on woruld brohte,
        sarra abrahame,   suna and dohtra.
1730   gewat him þa mid cnosle   ofer caldea folc
        feran mid feorme,   fæder abrahames,
        snotor mid gesibbum.   secean wolde
        cananea land.   hine cneowmægas
        metode gecorene   mid siðedon
1735   of þære eðeltyrf,   abraham and loth.
        him þa cynegode   on carran,
        æðelinga bearn,   eard genamon,
        weras mid wifum.   on þam wicum his
        fæder abrahames   feorh gesealde,
1740   wærfæst hæle.   wintra hæfde
        twa hundteontig   geteled rime
        and fife eac   þa he forð gewat,
        misserum frod,   metodsceaft seon.
        Ða se halga spræc,   heofonrices weard,
1745   to abrahame,   ece drihten:
        "gewit þu nu feran   and þine fare lædan,
        ceapas to cnosle.   carram ofgif,
        fæder eðelstol.   far swa ic þe hate,
        monna leofost,   and þu minum wel
1750   larum hyre   and þæt land gesec
        þe ic þe ælgrene   ywan wille,
        brade foldan.   þu gebletsad scealt
        on mundbyrde   minre lifigan.
        Gif ðe ænig   eorðbuendra
1755   mid wean greteð,   ic hine wergðo on
        mine sette   and modhete,
        longsumne nið.   lisse selle,
        wilna wæstme /   þam ðe wurðiað.   [P. 84]
        þurh þe eorðbuende   ealle onfoð,

1722 wæs, *added by scribe above the line, over the point af-*
ter fæmne. 1723 *Point after* secgeað. 1726 *Point after* hwæðre.
1739 *No point after* abrahames. 1758 wilna, n *written over*
erased l; *no point after* wurðiað. 1759 *Point after* þe.

12.2   faciamque te in gentem magnam . . .

12.4   egressus est itaque Abram . . .
12.5   tulitque . . . universamque substantiam quam posse-
            derant . . .
12.4   . . . sicut praeceperat ei Dominus . . .

12.5   . . . et egressi sunt ut irent in terram Chanaan . . .

12.5   tulitque Sarai uxorem suam
            (et Loth filium fratris sui . . . *cf.* 12.4 et
            ivit cum eo Loth)
12.4   septuaginta quinque annorum erat Abram cum egrederetur
            de Haran
12.6   pertransivit Abram terram

            usque ad locum Sychem (*var.* Sicem) [usque ad con-
            vallem Inlustrem] / Chananeus autem tunc erat in
            terra
12.7   apparuitque Dominus Abram et dixit ei
        semini tuo dabo terram hanc

        qui aedificavit ibi altare Domino qui apparuerat ei

12.8   et inde transgrediens ad montem qui erat contra
            orientem

            Bethel

1760   folcbearn, freoðo   and freondscipe,
           blisse minre   and bletsunge
           on woruldrice.   wriðende sceal
           mægðe þinre   monrim wesan
           swiðe under swegle   sunum and dohtrum
1765   oð þæt fromcyme   folde weorðeð,
           þeodlond monig,   þine gefylled."
           Him þa abraham gewat   æhte lædan   [P. 85]
           of egipta   eðelmearce,
           gumcystum god,   golde and seolfre,
1770   swiðfeorm and gesælig   swa him sigora weard,
           waldend usser   þurh his word abead,
           ceapas from carran.   sohton cananea
           lond and leodgeard.   þa com leof gode
           on þa eðelturf   idesa lædan,
1775   swæse gebeddan   and his suhtrian
           wif on willan.   wintra hæfde
           fif and hundseofontig   ða he faran sceolde,
           carran ofgifan   and cneowmagas.
           Him þa feran gewat,   fæder ælmihtiges
1780   lare gemyndig,   land sceawian
           geond þa folcsceare   be frean hæse,
           abraham wide,   oð þæt ellenrof
           to sicem com,   siðe spedig,
           cynne cananeis.   þa hine cyning engla
1785   abrahame   iewde selfa,
           domfæst wereda   and drihten cwæð:
           "þis is seo eorðe   þe ic ælgrene
           tudre þinum,   torhte, wille,
           wæstmum gewlo,   on geweald don,
1790   rume rice."   þa se rinc gode
           wibed worhte   and þa waldende,
           lifes leohtfruman,   lac onsægde,
           gasta helme. /   Him þa gyt gewat   [P. 86]
           abraham eastan   eagum wlitan
1795   on lande cyst.   lisse gemunde
           heofonweardes gehat   þa him þurh halig word
           sigora self cyning   soð gecyðde
           oð þæt drihtweras   duguþum geforan
           þær is botlwela   bethlem haten.
1800   beorn bliðemod   and his broðor sunu
           forð oferforan   folcmæro land
           eastan mid æhtum,   æfæste men,

1760 freoðo, ð *written over erasure.* **1764** swegle, w *added above the line.* **1768** *No point after* egipta. **1783** sicem: *Dietrich (ZfdA 10, 328) & edd. (except Wülker); Wells reads* Sichem— siem: *MS.*

(12.8)   tetendit ibi tabernaculum suum
          (ab occidente habens Bethel) [et ab oriente Ai]

          aedificavit quoque ibi
               altare Domino
               et invocavit nomen eius

12.10   Facta est autem fames in terra

        descenditque Abram in Aegyptum
             ut peregrinaretur ibi
        praevaluerat enim fames in terra
12.11   cumque prope esset ut ingrederetur Aegyptum

        dixit Sarai uxori suae . . .
12.12   [novi quod] cum viderint te Aegyptii . . .
12.11   . . . [novi quod] pulchra sis mulier

12.12   . . . dicturi sunt uxor ipsius est

        et interficient me (et te reservabunt)

12.13   dic ergo obsecro te quod soror mea sis

        (ut bene sit mihi propter te et vivat anima mea
             ob gratiam tui)

weallsteapan hleoðu   and him þa wic curon
þær him wlitebeorhte   wongas geþuhton.

[xxvii a]
1805   A Braham þa   oðere siðe
wibed worhte.   he þær wordum god
torhtum cigde,   tiber onsægde
his liffrean.   him þæs lean ageaf
nalles hneawlice   þurh his hand metend
1810   on þam gledstyde   gumcystum til.
ðær ræsbora   þrage siððan
wicum wunode   and wilna breac,
beorn mid bryde   oð þæt brohþrea
cananea wearð   cynne getenge,
1815   Hunger se hearda   hamsittendum,
wælgrim werum.   him þa wishydig
abraham gewat   on egypte,
drihtne gecoren,   drohtað secan,
fleah wærfæst wean.   wæs þæt wite to strang.
1820   Abraham maðelode,   geseah egypta
hornsele hwite   and heabyrig
beorhte blican.   ongan þa his bryd frea,
wishydig wer,   wordum læran:
"siððan egypte   eagum moton
1825   on þinne wlite wlitan   wlance monige
þonne æðelinga   eorlas wenað,
mæg ælfscieno,   þæt þu min sie
beorht gebedda,   þe wile beorna sum
him geagnian.   ic me onegan mæg
1830   þæt me wraðra / sum   wæpnes ecge   [P. 89]
for freondmynde   feore beneote.
saga þu, sarra,   þæt þu sie sweostor min,
lices mæge,   þonne þe leodweras
fremde fricgen   hwæt sie freondlufu
1835   ellðeodigra   uncer twega,
feorren cumenra.   þu him fæste hel
soðan spræce   swa þu minum scealt
feore gebeorgan   gif me freoðo drihten
on woruldrice,   waldend usser,
1840   an, ælmihtig,   swa he ær dyde,
lengran lifes.   se us þas lade sceop

1805 *No point after* þa.   1809 hneawlice: *Thorpe & edd.*— hnea
lice: *MS, with a letter, probably w, erased between* a *and* l.
1818 *Point after* drohtað.   1820 *No point after* egypta.   1825
Point after wlance.   1826 *No point after* æðelinga.   1829 onegan: *Thorpe & edd. (Bouterwek,* on ogan*)*— on agen: *MS.* 1832
sweostor, *a small hole in the parchment between* e *and* o, *no
letters missing; point after* sweostor, *none after* min.   1836
feorren, n *altered from* m.

12.14   cum itaque ingressus esset
            Abram Aegyptum

        viderunt Aegyptii mulierem quod esset pulchra nimis

12.15   et nuntiaverunt principes Pharaoni

            et laudaverunt eam apud illum
        et sublata est mulier in domum Pharaonis

12.16   Abram vero bene usi sunt propter illam . . .

12.17   flagellavit autem Dominus Pharaonem plagis maximus et
            domum eius [propter Sarai uxorem Abram]
12.18   vocavitque Pharao Abram . . . / 12.19 . . . nunc igitur
            ecce coniux tua accipe eam et vade

12.20   praecepitque Pharao super Abram viris
        et deduxerunt eum et uxorem illius et omnia quae
            habebat.

 13.1   Ascendit ergo Abram de Aegypto
        ipse et uxor eius et omnia quae habebat . . .
(13.2   erat autem dives valde in possessione argenti et auri)
 13.3   reversusque est per iter quo venerat a meridie in Bethel
        (usque ad locum ubi prius fixerat tabernaculum inter
            Bethel [et Ai])

 13.4   in loco altaris
            quod fecerat prius

þæt we on egiptum   are sceolde
fremena friclan   and us fremu secan."
Þa com ellenrof   eorl siðian,
1845   abraham mid æhtum,   on egypte
þær him folcweras   fremde wæron,
wine uncuðe.   wordum spræcon
ymb þæs wifes wlite   wlonce monige,
dugeðum dealle.   him drihtlicu mæg
1850   on wlite, modgum   mænegum, ðuhte,
cyninges þegnum.   hie þæt cuð dydon
heora folcfrean   and fægerro lyt
for æðelinge   idese sunnon
Ac hie sarran   swiðor micle
1855   wynsumne wlite   wordum heredon
oð þæt he lædan heht   leoflic wif
to his selfes sele,   sinces brytta.
æðelinga helm   heht abrahame
duguðum stepan.   hwæðere drihten wearð,
1860   frea, faraone   fah and yrre
for wifmyne.   þæs wraðe ongeald,
hearde mid hiwum   hægstealdra wyn.
ongæt hwæðere   gumena aldor
hwæt him waldend wræc   witeswingum.
1865   heht him abraham to   egesum geðreadne
brego egipto   and his bryd ageaf,   [P. 90]
wif to gewealde.   heht him wine ceosan
cllor, æðelingas   oðre dugeðe.
Abead þa þeodcyning   þegnum sinum,
1870   ombihtscealcum,   þæt hie hine arlice
ealles onsundne   eft gebrohten
of þære folcsceare   þæt he on friðe wære.
Ða abraham   æhte lædde
of egypta   eðelmearce.
1875   hie ellenrofe   idese feredon,
bryd and begas,   þæt hie to bethlem
on cuðe wic   ceapas læddon,
eadge eorðwelan   oðre siðe,
wif and willan   and heora woruldgestreon.
1880   Ongunnon him þa bytlian   and heora burh ræran
and sele settan,   salo niwian
weras on wonge   wibed setton
neah þam þe abraham   æror rærde
his waldende   þa westan com.
1885   þær se eadga eft   ecan drihtnes

1854 *No point after* sarran.   1865 *Large blurred point after*
heht.   1873 *No point after* abraham.

(13.4) et invocavit ibi nomen Domini

13.5   sed et Loth qui erat cum Abram fuerunt
                greges ovium et armenta et tabernacula
13.6   nec poterat eos capere terra ut habitarent simul

        erat quippe substantia eorum multa
        et non quibant habitare communiter

13.7   unde et facta est rixa
                inter pastores gregum Abram et Loth . . .

13.8   dixit ergo Abram ad Loth

                ne quaeso sit iurgium inter me et te
        (et inter pastores meos et pastores tuos)

        fratres enim sumus

13.9   ecce . . . *cf. 1306b*

(13.7   . . . eo autem tempore Chananeus et Pherezeus habita-
                bant in illa terra)
13.9   . . . universa terra coram te est
        recede a me obsecro
        (si ad sinistram ieris ego ad dexteram tenebo
        si tu dexteram elegeris ego ad sinistram pergam)

13.10   elevatis itaque Loth oculis
        vidit omnem circa regionem Iordanis
                quae universa inrigabatur
        antequam subverteret Dominus Sodomam et Gomorram
        sicut paradisus Domini [et sicut Aegyptus venientibus
                in Segor]

13.11   elegitque sibi Loth regionem circa Iordanem et
                recessit ab oriente . . .

       niwan stefne   noman weorðade,
       tilmodig eorl   tiber onsægde
       þeodne engla,   þancode swiðe
       lifes leohtfruman   lisse and ara.

[xxvii b]
1890   **W** VNedon on þam wicum,   hæfdon wilna geniht
                  abraham and loth,   ead bryttedon
                  oð þæt hie on þam lande   ne meahton leng
                                                     [somed
       blædes brucan   and heora begra þær
       æhte habban   ac sceoldon arfæste
1895   þa rincas þy   rumor secan
       ellor eðelseld.   oft wæron teonan
       wærfæstra wera   weredum gemæne,
       heardum hearmplega.   þa se halga ongan,
       ara gemyndig,   abraham sprecan
1900   fægre to lothe: "Ic eom fædera þin
       sibgebyrdum, /   þu min suhterga.   [P. 91]
       ne sceolon unc betweonan   teonan weaxan,
       wroht wriðian—   ne þæt wille god—
       Ac wit synt gemagas.   unc gemæne ne sceal
1905   elles awiht   nymþe ealltela
       lufu langsumu.   nu þu, loth, geþenc
       þæt unc modige   ymb mearce sittað,
       þeoda þrymfæste   þegnum and gesiððum,
       folc cananea   and feretia,
1910   rofum rincum,   ne willað rumor unc
       landriht heora.   forðon wit lædan sculon
       teonwit of þisse stowe   and unc staðolwangas
       rumor secan.   ic ræd sprece,
       bearn arones,   begra uncer,
1915   soðne secge.   ic þe selfes dom
       life, leofa.   leorna þe seolfa
       and geþancmeta   þine mode
       on hwilce healfe   þu wille hwyrft don,
       cyrran mid ceape,   nu ic þe cyst abead."
1920   him þa loth gewat   land sceawigan
       be iordane,   grene eorðan.
       seo wæs wætrum weaht   and wæstmum þeaht,
       lagostreamum leoht   and gelic godes
       neorxnawange.   on þæt nergend god
1925   for wera synnum   wylme gesealde
       sodoman and gomorran,   sweartan lige.
       Him þa eard geceas   and eðelsetl
       sunu arones   on sodoma byrig,
       æhte sine   [ealle lædde],

1895 *No points after* þy *or* secan.   **1912** *No point after* -wangas.
1924 neorxnawange: *edd.*— neoxna-: *MS.*   **1929b** *Not in MS; sup-*
plied by Grein & Krapp.

13.12 . . . Loth moratus est in oppidis
      quae erant circa Iordanem et habitavit in Sodomis

13.13 homines autem Sodomitae pessimi erant
      et peccatores coram Domino nimis

13.12 Abram habitavit in terra Chanaan . . .

14.1 Factum est autem in illo tempore ut Amrafel rex Sennaar
      [et Arioch rex Ponti]
      et Chodorlahomor rex Elamitarum
      [et Thadal rex (Gentium *cf. 1961a*)]
14.2 inirent bellum
      contra [Bara] regem Sodomorum / et contra [Bersa]
      regem Gomorrae / [et contra Sennaab regem Adamae
      /et contra Semeber regem Seboim / contraque regem
      Balae ipsa est Segor]
[14.3 omnes hii convenerunt in vallem Silvestrem quae nunc
      est mare salis *cf. 1965-66*]

1930 beagas from bethlem and botlgestreon,
    welan, wunden gold. wunode siððan
    be iordane geara mænego.
    þær folcstede fægre wæron,
    men arlease, metode laðe.
1935 wæron sodomisc cynn synnum þriste,
    dædum gedwolene, drugon heora selfra
    ecne unræd. æfre ne wolde
    þam leodþeawum / *loth* onfon   [P. 92]
    Ac he þære mægðe monwisan fleah
1940 þeah þe he on þam lande lifian sceolde
    facen and fyrene and hine fægre heold,
    þeawfæst and geþyldig, on þam þeodscipe,
    emne þon gelicost, lara gemyndig,
    þe he ne cuðe hwæt þa cynn dydon.
1945 Abraham wunode eðeleardum
    cananea forð. hine cyning engla,
    metod moncynnes, mundbyrde heold
    wilna wæstmum and worulddugeðum,
    lufum and lissum. forþon his lof secgað
1950 wide under wolcnum wera cneorisse,
    fullwona bearn. he frean hyrde
    estum on eðle ðenden he eardes breac,
    halig and higefrod. næfre hleowlora
    æt edwihtan æfre weorðeð
1955 feorhberendra forht and acol
    mon for metode þe him æfter a
    þurh gemynda sped mod' and dædum,
    worde and gewitte wise þance
    oð his ealdorgedal oleccan wile.

        .xxviii.
1960 **Ð**A ic aldor gefrægn elamitarna,
    fromne folctogan, fyrd gebeodan,
    orlahomar. him ambrafel
    of sennar side worulde
    for on fultum. gewiton hie feower
1965 þa þeodcyningas þrymme micle
    secan suð ðanon sodoman and gomorran.
    þa wæs guðhergum be iordane
    wera eðelland wide geondsended,
    folde feondum. sceolde forht monig

1938 loth: *Thorpe & edd.* — leoht: *MS.* **1953** hleowlora: *Dietrich (ZfdA, 10, 329) & edd.* — hleor lora: *MS.* **1955** -berendra, a *altered from* n. **1956** *Point after* æfter, *none after* ter a. **1960** *No point after* gefrægn. **1963** *No point after* sennar. **1967** *No point after* -hergum.

(14.8   et egressi sunt rex Sodomorum et rex Gomorrae . . .
        . . . et direxerunt contra eos aciem . . . *cf. 1982-95a*)
(14.9   . . . quattuor reges adversus quinque *cf. 1974, 2074a*)
 14.4   duodecim enim annis

            servierant Chodorlahomor

        et tertiodecimo anno recesserunt ab eo

14.10   . . . itaque rex Sodomorum
            et Gomorrae

            terga verterunt

            cecideruntque ibi

        et qui remanserant
            fugerunt ad montem / 14.11 tulerunt autem omnem
            substantiam
            Sodomorum et Gomorrae / [et universa quae ad cibum
            pertinent]

            et abierunt   *cf. 2086 f.*
 14.12 necnon et Loth et substantiam eius / filium fratris
            Abram (qui habitabat in Sodomis)

<pre>
1970   blachleor ides   bifiende gan
          on fremdes fæðm.   feollon wergend
          bryda and beaga,   bennum seoce.
          Him þa to/geanes   mid guðþræce   [P. 93]
          fife foran   folccyningas
1975   sweotum suðon.   woldon sodome burh
          wraðum werian.   þa wintra *twelf*
          norðmonnum ær   niede sceoldon
          gombon gieldan   and gafol sellan
          oð þæt þa leode   leng ne woldon
1980   elamitarna   aldor swiðan
          folcgestreonum   ac him from swicon.
          foron þa tosomne.   francan wæron hlude,
          wraðe wælherigas.   sang se wanna fugel
          under deoreðsceaftum,   deawigfeðera,
1985   hræs on wenan.   hæleð onetton
          on mægencorðrum,   modum þrydge
          oð þæt folcgetrume   gefaren hæfdon
          sid tosomne   suðan and norðan,
          helmum þeahte.   þær wæs heard plega,
1990   wælgara wrixl,   wigcyrm micel,
          hlud hildesweg.   handum brugdon
          hæleð of scæðum   hringmæled sweord,
          ecgum dihtig.   þær wæs eaðfynde
          eorle orlegceap,   se ðe ær ne wæs
1995   niðes genihtsum.   norðmen wæron
          suðfoloum swice.   wurdon sodomware
          and gomorre,   goldes bryttan,
          æt þæm lindcrodan   leofum bedrorene
          fyrdgesteallum.   gewiton feorh heora
2000   fram þam folcstyde   fleame nergan.
          secgum ofslegene   him on swaðe feollon
          æðelinga bearn,   ecgum ofþegde
          willgesiððas.   Hæfde wigsigor
          elamitarna   ordes wisa,
2005   weold wælstowe.   gewat seo wæpna laf
          fæsten secan.   fynd gold strudon,
          ahudan þa mid herge   hordburh wera,
          sodoman and gomorran,   þa sæl ageald,
          mære ceastra.   mægð / siðedon   [P. 94]
2010   fæmnan and wuduwan,   freondum beslægene,
          from hleowstole.   hettend læddon
          ut mid æhtum   abrahames mæg
          of sodoma byrig.   we þæt soð magon
          secgan furður   hwelc siððan wearð
</pre>

1972 *Point added after* bennum. 1973 *No point after* -þræce.
1974 *Point after* fife, *none after* foran. 1976 twelf— xii:
MS. 2001 ofslegene, s *has an extra stroke on descender, as
if scribe began to write a second* f.

14.13   et ecce unus qui
              evaserat

           nuntiavit Abram Hebreo . . .
14.14   quod cum audisset Abram captum videlicet Loth fratrem
           suum . . .

14.13   (. . . qui habitabat in convalle)
              Mambre Amorrei / fratris Eschol et fratris Aner

           hii enim pepigerant foedus cum Abram

14.14   . . . numeravit expeditos vernaculos suos trecentos
           decem et octo

           (et persecutus est eos usque Dan   = *2045a?; cf. 2074a*)

2015 æfter þæm gehnæste herewulfa sið
     þara þe læddon loth and leoda god,
     suðmonna sinc, sigore gulpon.

xxviiii.

     H im þa secg hraðe gewat siðian,
      an gara laf, se ða guðe genæs
2020   abraham secan. se þæt orlegweorc
     þam ebriscan eorle gecyðde,
     forslegen swiðe sodoma folc,
     leoda duguðe and lothes sið.
     Þa þæt inwitspell abraham sægde
2025 freondum sinum. bæd him fultumes
     wærfæst hæleð willgeðoftan
     aner and manre, escol þriddan.
     cwæð þæt him wære weorce on mode,
     sorga sarost, þæt his suhtriga
2030 þeownyd þolode. bæd him þræcrofe
     þa rincas þæs ræd ahicgan
     þæt his hyldemæg ahred wurde,
     beorn mid bryde. him þa broðor þry
     æt spræce þære spedum miclum
2035 hældon hygesorge heardum wordum,
     ellenrofe, and abrahame
     treowa sealdon þæt hie his torn mid him
     gewræcon on wraðum oððe on wæl feallan.
     Þa se halga heht his heorðwerod
2040 wæpna onfon. he þær wigena fand,
     æscberendra, *eahtatyne*
     and *preohund* eac þe*od*enholdra
     þara þe he wiste þæt meahte wel æghwylc
     on fyrd wegan fealwe linde.
     Him þa /   [P. 95]
2045
       abraham gewat and þa eorlas þry
     þe him ær treowe sealdon mid heora folce getrume.
     wolde his mæg huru,
     loth, alynnan of laðscipe.
     Rincas wæron rofe, randas wægon
2050 forð fromlice on foldwege.
     hildewulfas herewicum neh

2016 *Point after* læddon. **2027** *Point after* aner, *point added
after* escol. **2037** *Point after* torn, *none after* him. **2040**
onfon, *first* n *written above the line.* **2041-42** eahtatyne and
þreohund— xviii · 7 ccc · : MS. **2042b** þeodenholdra: *Grein &
edd.—* þeon den holdra (þeon *at end of MS line*): *MS.* **2045**
Him þa *are last words on P. 94; one leaf has been cut out between P. 94 and P. 95 (the excised leaf was either blank or
illustrated on both sides since no material is missing).* **2049**
wæron: *Grein & edd. (except Wülker)—* waron: *MS;* rofe, *altered from* rore, *by scribe;* wægon, *altered from* wæron.

14.15   et divisis sociis

          inruit super eos nocte

      percussitque eos

          et persecutus est

              usque Hoba   quae est ad laevam Damasci

14.16   reduxitque omnem substantiam et Loth fratrem suum
            cum substantia illius
            mulieres quoque et populum

```
              gefaren hæfdon.      Þa he his frumgaran,
              wishydig wer,     wordum sægde,
              þares afera     —him wæs þearf micel—
2055          þæt hie on twa healfe
              grimme guðgemot    gystum eowdon
              heardne handplegan.    cwæð þæt him se halga,
              ece drihten,    eað mihte
              æt þam spereniðe    spede lænan.
2060          Þa ic neðan gefrægn    under nihtscuwan
              hæleð to hilde.    hlyn wearð on wicum
              scylda and sceafta,    sceotendra fyll,
              guðflana gegrind.    gripon unfægre
              under sceat werum    scearpe garas
2065          and feonda feorh    feollon ðicce.
              þær hlihende    huðe feredon
              secgas and gesiððas.    sigor eft ahwearf
              of norðmonna    niðgeteone,
              æsctir wera.    abraham sealde
2070          wig to wedde    nalles wunden gold
              for his suhtrigan,    sloh and fylde
              feond on fitte.    him on fultum grap
              heofonrices weard.    hergas wurdon
              feower on fleame,    folccyningas,
2075          leode ræswan.    him on laste stod
              hihtlic heorðwerod    and hæleð lagon,
              on swaðe sæton    þa þe sodoma
              and gomorra    golde berofan,
              bestrudon stigwitum.    him þæt stiðe geald
2080          fædera lothes.    fleonde [wæron]
              elamitarna    aldorduguðe
              dome bedrorene    oð þæt hie domasco
              unfeor wæron.    gewat him abraham ða          [P. 96]
              on þa wigrode    wiðertrod seon
2085          laðra monna.    loth wæs ahreded,
              eorl mid æhtum.    idesa hwurfon,
              wif on willan.    wide gesawon
              freora feorhbanan    fuglas slitan
              on ecgwale.    abraham ferede
2090          suðmonna eft    sinc and bryda,
              æðelinga bearn,    oðle nior
              mægeð heora magum.    næfre mon ealra
              lifigendra her    lytle werede
              þon wurðlicor    wigsið ateah
2095          þara þe wið swa miclum    mægne geræsde.
```

2055 hie: *Bouterwek & edd.—* he: *MS.* **2080** wæron, *not in MS;
supplied by Junius & edd. (except Wells); no point after*
fleonde. **2085** *Point after* ahreded *added?*

14.17   Egressus est autem rex Sodomorum in occursum eius . . .

14.18   at vero Melchisedech rex Salem

         proferens panem et vinem / erat enim sacerdos
         Dei altissimi
14.19   benedixit ei et ait

         benedictus Abram Deo excelso (qui creavit caelum et
            terram / 14.20 et benedictus Deus excelsus quo
            protegente hostes in manibus tuis sunt

         et dedit ei decimas ex omnibus
14.21   dixit autem rex
                Sodomorum
                ad Abram
         da mihi (animas)

            cetera tolle tibi

14.22   qui respondit ei

[xxx]   ÞA wæs suð þanon   sodoma folc   [P. 97]
            guðspell wegan   hwelc gromra wearð
            feonda fromlad.   gewat him frea leoda,
       eorlum bedroren,   abraham secan,
2100   freonda feasceaft.   him ferede mid
       solomia   sinces hyrde.
       þæt wæs se mæra   melchisedec,
       leoda bisceop.   se mid lacum com
       fyrdrinca fruman   fægre gretan,
2105   abraham arlice   and him on sette
       godes bletsunge   and swa gyddode:
       "wæs ðu gewurðod   on wera rime
       for þæs eagum   þe ðe æsca tir
       æt guðe forgeaf.   þæt is god selfa
2110   se ðe hettendra   herga þrymmas
       on geweald gebræc   and þe wæpnum læt
       rancstræte forð   rume wyrcan,
       huðe ahreddan   and hæleð fyllan.
       on swaðe sæton.   ne meahton siðwerod
2115   guðe spowan   ac hie god flymde.
       se ðe æt feohtan   mid frumgarum
       wið ofermægnes   egsan sceolde
       handum sinum   and halegu treow
       seo þu wið rodora weard   rihte healdest."
2120   him þa se beorn   bletsunga lean
       þurh hand ageaf   and þæs hereteames
       ealles teoðan sceat   abraham sealde
       godes bisceope.   þa spræc guðcyning,
       sodoma aldor,   secgum befylled,
2125   to abrahame: —him wæs ara þearf—
       "forgif me mennen   minra leoda
       þe þu ahreddest   herges cræftum,
       wera wælclommum.   hafa þe wunden gold
       þæt ær agen wæs   ussum folce,
2130   feoh and frætwa.   læt me freo lædan   [P. 98]
       eft on eðel   æðelinga bearn,
       on weste wic   wif and cnihtas,
       earme wydewan.   eaforan syndon deade,
       folcgesiðas   nymðe fea ane
2135   þe me mid sceoldon   mearce healdan."
       Him þa abraham   andswarode

2096 *No point after* þanon.   2097 wearð, ð *altered from* c.
2101 *No point after* solomia.   2102 *No point after* mæra.
2106 gyddode, *small hole in parchment between* d *and* e, *no
letters missing.*   2107 wæs ðu: *Holthausen & Krapp, from Grein's
suggestion of* wes— wærðu: MS.   2122 *No point after* sealde.
2135-36a mid . . . abraham, *inserted above the line by scribe,
a caret after* me *indicating its place in the text; no point
after* sceoldon *(2135a).*

(14.22)   levo manum meam
             ad Dominum Deum excelsum possessorem caeli
             et terrae

14.23   (quod a filo subteminis usque ad corrigiam caligae)
             non accipiam ex omnibus quae tua sunt

        ne dicas

             ego ditavi Abram

14.24   exceptis his quae comederunt iuvenes
        et partibus virorum qui venerunt mecum Aner Eschol et
        Mambre / isti accipient partes suas.

 15.1   (His itaque transactis)

        factus est sermo Domini ad Abram per visionem

             dicens

        noli timere Abram

        ego protector tuus sum et merces tua magna nimis

```
             ædre for eorlum,    elne gewurðod,
             dome and sigore,    drihtlice spræc:
             "Ic þe gehate,    hæleða waldend,
2140         for þam halgan    þe heofona is
             [and] þisse eorðan    agendfrea
             wordum minum    nis woruldfeoh
             þe ic me agan wille,
             sceat ne scilling    þæs ic on sceotendum,
2145         þeoden mæra,    þines ahredde,
             æðelinga helm,    þy læs þu eft cweðe
             þæt ic wurde    willgesteallum
             eadig on eorðan    ærgestreonum,
             sodoma rice.    ac þu most heonon
2150         huðe lædan    þe ic þe æt hilde gesloh,
             ealle buton dæle    þissa drihtwera,
             aneres and mamres    and escoles.
             nelle ic þa rincas    rihte benæman
             ac hie me fulleodon    æt æscþræce,
2155         fuhton þe æfter frofre.    gewit þu ferian nu
             ham hyrsted gold    and healsmægeð,
             leoda idesa.    þu þe laðra ne þearft
             hæleða hildþræce    hwile onsittan,
             norðmanna wig.    eacne fuglas
2160         under beorhhleoþum    blodig sittað
             þeodherga wæl,    þicce gefylled."
             gewat him þa se healdend    ham siðian
             mid þy hereteame    þe him se halga forgeaf,
             ebrea leod    arna gemyndig.
2165         þa gen abrahame    eowde selfa
             heofona heahcyning    halige spræce,
             trymede tilmodigne    and him to reordode:
       "Meda syndon micla þina.    ne læt þu þe þin mod
                                    [asealcan    [P. 99]
          wærfæst willan mines    ne þearft þu þe wiht ondrædan
2170   þenden þu mine lare læstest    ac ic þe lifigende her
             wið weana gehwam    wreo and scylde
             folmum minum    ne þearft þu forht wesan."
```

2137 gewurðod, ge- *crowded over erasure.* 2141 and, *not in MS; supplied by Grein & edd.* 2147 *No point after* wurde. 2158 hild-, h *altered from partially erased* w *or* þ. 2162 healdend, h *altered from* w. 2164 arna ge-, *followed by a partially erased* m *at end of MS line, rewritten in next line as first letter of* -myndig. 2171 gehwam, w *altered from* r; a *over erasure, altered from another incomplete letter.*

15.2   dixitque Abram

      Domine Deus quid dabis mihi

    ego vadam absque liberis

    (et filius procuratoris domus meae [iste damascus
        Eliezer / 15.3 addiditque Abram / mihi autem
        non dedisti semen]) et ecce vernaculus meus
        heres meus erit

15.4   statimque sermo Domini factus est ad eum dicens
    non erit hic heres tuus
        sed qui egredietur de utero tuo
        ipsum habebis heredem / 15.5 [eduxitque eum foras
        et ait illi] / suspice caelum et numera stellas
        si potes

    [et dixit ei] sic erit semen tuum

15.7   [Dixitque ad eum] ego Dominus qui
        eduxi te de [Ur] Chaldeorum
    ut darem tibi terram istam
        et possideres eam / 15.18 (in die illo pepigit
        Dominus cum Abram foedus dicens)
    semini tuo dabo terram hanc

    a fluvio Aegypti usque ad fluvium magnum flumen
        Eufraten

[xxxi] A Braham þa andswarode,
dædrof, drihtne sinum.   frægn hine dægrime
[frod:
2175   "hwæt gifest þu me,   gasta waldend,
freomanna to frofre   nu ic þus feasceaft eom?
ne þearf ic yrfestol   eaforan bytlian
ænegum minra   ac me æfter sculon
mine woruldmagas   welan bryttian.
2180   Ne sealdest þu me sunu   forðon mec sorg dreceð
on sefan swiðe.   ic sylf ne mæg
ræd ahycgan.   gæð gerefa min   [P. 100]
fægen freobearnum,   fæste mynteð
ingeþancum   þæt me æfter sie
2185   eaforan sine   yrfeweardas.
geseoð þæt me of bryde   bearn ne wocon."
Him þa ædre god   andswarode:
"Næfre gerefan   rædað þine
eaforan yrfe   ac þin agen bearn
2190   frætwa healdeð   þonne þin flæsc ligeð.
sceawa heofon.   hyrste gerim,
rodores tungel   þa nu rume heora
wuldorfæstne wlite   wide dælað
ofer brad brymu   beorhte scinan.
2195   swilc bið mægburh   menigo þinre
folcbearnum frome.   ne læt þu þin ferhð wesan
sorgum æsæled.   gien þe sunu weorðeð,
bearn of bryde   þurh gebyrd cumen
se ðe æfter bið   yrfes hyrde,
2200   gode mære.   ne geomra þu.
Ic eom se waldend   se þe for wintra fela
of caldea   ceastre alædde
feowera sumne,   gehet þe folcstede
wide to gewealde.   ic þe wære nu,
2205   mago ebrea,   mine selle
þæt sceal fromcynne   folde þine,
sidland manig,   geseted wurðan,
eorðan sceatas   oð eufraten
and from egypta   eðelmearce,
2210   swa mid niðas twa   nilus sceadeð,
and eft wendeð sæ,   wide rice.
eall þæt sculon agan   eaforan þine,
þeodlanda gehwilc   swa þa þreo wæter
steape stanbyrig   streamum bewindað,
2215   famige flodas,   folcmægða byht."

2174 *Point after* dædrof; frægn, æg *over erasure.*   2189 eaforan:
Thorpe, Holthausen— eafora: *MS.*   2203 feowera, o *altered from*
w.   2209 *No point after* egypta.

(16.1   Igitur Sarai uxor Abram non genuerat liberos . . .)

16.2   dixit marito suo
       ecce conclusit me Deus ne parerem . . .

(16.1   . . . sed habens ancillam aegyptiam nomine Agar)

16.2   . . . ingredere ad ancillam meam
               si forte saltem
               ex illa suscipiam filios

       cumque ille adquiesceret deprecanti
16.3   tulit Agar Aegyptiam ancillam suam . . .
       et dedit eam viro suo uxorem
16.4   (qui ingressus est ad eam)
       at illa concepisse se videns
       despexit dominam suam

16.5   dixitque Sarai ad Abram

       inique agis contra me
       ego dedi ancillam meam in sinum tuum

       quae videns quod conceperit despectui me habet

Þa wæs sarran   sar on mode
þæt him abrahame   ænig ne wearð
þurh gebedscipe   bearn gemæne,
freolic to frofre. /   ongann þa ferhðcearig[P. 101]
2220 to were sinum   wordum mæðlan:
"Me þæs forwyrnde   waldend heofona
þæt ic mægburge   moste þinre
rim miclian   roderum under
eaforum þinum.   nu ic eom orwena
2225 þæt unc se oeðylstæf   æfre weorðe
gifeðe ætgædere.   ic eom geomorfrod,
drihten min.   do swa ic þe bidde.
Her is fæmne,   freolecu mæg,
ides egyptisc,   an on gewealde.
2230 hat þe þa recene   reste gestigan
and afanda hwæðer   frea wille
ænigne þe   yrfewearda
on woruld lætan   þurh þæt wif cuman."
Þa se eadega wer   idese larum
2235 geðafode.   heht him þeowmennen
on bedd gan   bryde larum.
hire mod astah   þa heo wæs magotimbre
be abrahame   cacen worden.
ongan æfþancum   agendfrean   [P. 102]
2240 halsfæst herian,   higeþryðe wæg,
wæs laðwendo.   lustum ne wolde
þeowdom þolian   ac heo þriste ongan
wið sarran   swiðe winnan.
þa ic þæt wif gefrægn   wordum cyðan
2245 hire mandrihtne   modes sorge,
sarferhð sægde   and swiðe cwæð:
"ne fremest þu gerysnu   and riht wið me.
þafodest þu gena   þæt me þeowmennen
siððan, agar,   ðe idese laste
2250 beddreste gestah   swa ic bena wæs,
drehte dogora gehwam   dædum and wordum
unarlice.   þæt agan sceal
gif ic mot for þe,   mine wealdan,
abraham leofa.   þæs sie ælmihtig

2216 sarran, *one letter erased after* sar- *which is at end of
MS line.* 2221 Me, M *altered from some other capital; no
point after* -wyrnde. 2222 *No point after* -burge. 2225 se
oeðylstæf, seo *written at end of MS line,* eðyl stæf *on next,
no point after* -stæf; æfre, *one or two letters erased after
this word.* 2230 *No point after* recene. 2231 *No point after*
hwæðer, *point after* frea, *none after* wille. 2243 *No point
after* sarran. 2251 drehte: *Thorpe & edd.*— drehta: *MS;* dogora,
a *altered from* e, *point after this word;* gehwam: *Thorpe & edd.*
— geham: *MS.*

(16.5) iudicet Dominus inter me et te
 16.6 cui respondens Abram

       ecce ait ancilla tua

          in manu tua est utere ea ut libet

       adfligente igitur eam Sarai

          fugam iniit

  16.7 cumque invenisset illam
          angelus Domini [iuxta fontem aquae] in solitudine
          [qui est in via Sur] / 16.8 dixit ad eam
       (Agar ancilla Sarai) unde venis et quo vadis

       quae respondit
          a facie Sarai dominae meae ego fugio

  16.9 dixitque ei angelus Domini

       revertere ad dominam tuam et humiliare sub manibus
          ipsius   *cf. 2294b-95 = 16.9*

 16.11 ac deinceps ecce
          concepisti et paries filium

       vocabisque nomen eius Ismahel
       (eo quod audierit Dominus adflictionem tuam)
 16.12 hic erit ferus homo
       manus eius contra omnes et manus omnium contra eum
       [et e regione universorum] (fratrum suorum *cf. 2291a*)
          [figet tabernacula]

2255   [duguða] drihten   dema mid unc twih."
           hire þa ædre   andswarode
           wishidig wer   wordum sinum:
           "ne forlæte ic þe   þen/den wit lifiað bu   [P. 103]
           arna lease   ac þu þin agen most
2260   mennen ateon   swa þin mod freoð."

[xxxii]   ÐA wearð unbliðe   abrahames cwen,
               hire worcþeowe   wrað on mode,
               heard and hreðe.   higeteonan spræc
           fræcne on fæmnan.   heo þa fleon gewat
2265   þrea and þeowdom,   þolian ne wolde
           yfel and ondlean   þæs ðe ær dyde
           to sarran   ac heo on sið gewat
           westen secan.   þær hie wuldres þegn
           engel drihtnes   an gemitte
2270   geomormode.   se hie georne frægn:
           "hwider fundast þu,   feasceaft ides,
           siðas dreogan?   þec sarre ah."
           heo him ædre   andswarode:
           "Ic fleah wean, wana   wilna gehwilces,
2275   hlæfdigan hete,   hean of wicum,
           tregan and teonan.   nu sceal tearig/hleor   [P. 104]
           on westenne   witodes bidan
           hwonne of heortan   hunger oððe wulf
           sawle and sorge   somed abregde."
2280   Hire þa se engel   andswarode:
           "ne ceara þu feor heonon   fleame dælan
           somwist incre   ac þu sece eft,
           earna þe ara.   eaðmod ongin
           dreogan æfter dugeðum.   wes drihtenhold.
2285   þu scealt, agar,   abrahame sunu
           on woruld bringan.   Ic þe wordum nu
           minum secge   þæt se magorinc sceal
           mid yldum wesan   ismahel haten.
           se bið unhyre,   orlæggifre,
2290   wiðerbreca   wera cneorissum,
           magum sinum.   hine monige on
           wraðe winnað   mid wæpenþræce.

2255 duguða, *not in MS; no point after* drihten, *point after* dema; twih, h *written above a* g *with dot underneath to indi-cate deletion of* g. **2256** andswarode, and- *spelled out.* **2259** lease, *a letter erased after this word, no point visible.* **2266** ondlean, ond- *spelled out.* **2271** *No point after* þu. **2273** andswarode, *an unfinished* a *before this word, which is writ-ten, as usual,* ꝺswarode.

16.10   [et rursum] multiplicans [inquit] multiplicabo semen
             tuum et non numerabitur prae multitudine
        2294b ff. cf. 2281 ff.= 16.9

16.15   peperitque Abrae filium qui vocavit nomen eius Ismahel
16.16   octoginta et sex annorum erat quando peperit ei Agar
             Ismahelem.

 17.1   Postquam vero nonaginta et novem annorum esse coeperat
             apparuit ei Dominus dixitque ad eum
             [ego Deus omnipotens] ambula coram me et esto perfectus

 17.2   ponamque foedus meum inter me et te . . .

17.10   . . . circumcidetur ex vobis omne masculinum
17.11   et circumcidetis carnem praeputii vestri / ut sit in
             signum foederis inter me et vos

17.12   infans octo dierum circumcidetur in vobis
             omne masculinum in generationibus vestris
             tam vernaculus quam empticius circumcidetur *(cf. 2312b)*
             (et quicumque non fuerit de stirpe vestra)
17.14   masculus cuius praeputii caro circumcisa non fuerit
             delebitur anima illa de populo suo
             quia pactum meum inritum fecit.
/ 17.16   [et benedicam ei]
             et ex illa dabo tibi filium

        cui benedicturus sum

of þam frumgaran   folc awæcniað,
þeod unmæte.   gewit þu þinne eft
2295   waldend secan.   wuna þæm þe agon."
Heo þa ædre gewat   engles larum
hire hlafordum   swa se halga bebead,
godes ærendgast,   gleawan spræce.
þa wearð abrahame   ismael geboren   [P. 105]
2300   efne þa he on worulde   wintra hæfde
syx and *hundeahtatig.*   sunu weox and ðah
swa se engel ær   þurh his agen word,
fæle freoðoscealc,   fæmnan sægde.
þa se ðeoden ymb   *þreotyne* gear,   [P. 106]
2305   ece drihten,   wið abrahame spræc:
"leofa, swa ic þe lære   læst uncre wel
treowrædenne.   ic þe on tida gehwone
duguðum stepe.   wes þu dædum from
willan mines.   ic þa wære forð
2310   soðe gelæste   þe ic þe sealde geo
frofre to wedde   þæs þin ferhð bemearn.
þu scealt halgian   hired þinne,
sete sigores tacn   soð on gehwilcne
wæpnedcynnes   gif þu wille on me
2315   hlaford habban   oððe holdne freond
þinum fromcynne.   ic þæs folces beo
hyrde and healdend   gif ge hyrað me
breostgehygdum   and bebodu willað
min fullian.   sceal monna gehwilc
2320   þære cneorisse   cildisc wesan
wæpnedcynnes   þæs þe on woruld cymð
ymb seofon niht   sigores tacne
geagnod me   oððe of eorðan
þurh feondscipe   feor adæled,
2325   adrifen from duguðum.   doð swa ic hate.
Ic eow treowige   gif ge þæt tacen gegaþ
soðgeleafan.   þu scealt sunu agan,
bearn be bryde þinre   þone sculon burhsittende
ealle isaac hatan.   ne þearf þe þæs eaforan sceomigan
2330   ac ic þam magorince   mine sylle
godcunde gife   gastes mihtum,
freondsped fremum.   he onfon sceal
blisse minre   and bletsunge,
lufan and lisse.   of þam leodfruman

2293 frumgaran, *Grein* (Germania *10, 418*), *Krapp & Wells*— frumgarum: *MS;* awæcniað, *Krapp reports* apæcniað, *but if* þ *was
written it has been corrected;* c *over erased* n.   **2301** syx and
hundeahtatig— vi · ꝧ lxxx : *MS.*   **2304** þreotyne— xiii · : *MS.*
2306 leofa, *glossed* lyfa *in left margin, by scribe.*   **2313**
gehwilcne, c *altered from another letter, perhaps unfinished*
n.   **2317** hyrað, a *altered from* e.   **2326** gegaþ, þ *altered from*
s.   **2329** *Point after* þæs.

(17.16) eritque in nationes et reges populorum orientur ex eo

17.17   cecidit Abraham
            in faciem et risit
            (dicens) in corde suo

        putasne
            centenario nascetur filius et Sarra nonagenaria
            pariet

17.18   dixitque ad Deum
            utinam Ismahel vivat coram te

17.19   et ait Deus ad Abraham
        Sarra uxor tua pariet tibi filium
            [vocabisque nomen eius Isaac] . . .

17.20   super Ismahel quoque
            exaudivi te
        ecce benedicam ei et augebo et multiplicabo eum valde
        [duodecim duces generabit] et faciam illum in gentem
            magnam
17.21   pactum vero meum statuam ad Isaac
        quem pariet tibi Sarra tempore isto in anno altero *con-*
            flated with
17.19   . . . et constituam pactum meum illi in foedus sempi-
            ternum et semini eius post eum

17.23   tulit autem Abraham Ismahelem filium suum
        et omnes vernaculos domus suae universosque quos emerat
        cunctos mares ex omnibus viris domus suae
        et circumcidit carnem praeputii eorum
        statim in ipsa die sicut praeceperat ei Dominus

2335 brad folc cumað, bregowearda fela
    rofe arisað, rices hyrdas,
    woruldcyningas wide mære."

[xxxiii] A Braham ða ofestum legde [P. 107]
     hleor on eorðan and mid hucse bewand
2340   þa hleoðorcwydas on hige sinum,
    modgeðancel he þæs mældæges
    self ne wende þæt him sarra,
    bryd blondenfeax, bringan meahte
    on woruld sunu. wiste gearwe
2345 þæt þæt wif huru wintra hæfde
    efne *hundteontig* geteled rimes.
    he þa metode oncwæð, missarum frod:
    "lifge ismael larum swilce,
    þeoden, þinum and þe þanc wege,
2350 heardrædne hyge, heortan strange,
    to dreoganne dæges and nihtes
    wordum and dædum willan þinne."
    Him þa fægere frea ælmihtig,
    ece drihten andswarode:
2355 "Þe sceal wintrum frod on woruld bringan
    sarra sunu. soð forð gan
    wyrd æfter þissum wordgemearcum.
    Ic ismael estum wille
    bletsian nu swa þu bena eart
2360 þinum frumbearne þæt feorhdaga
    on woruldrice worn gebide,
    tanum tudre. þu þæs tiða beo.
    Hwæðre ic isace, eaforan þinum,
    geongum bearne, þam þe gen nis
2365 on woruld cumen, willa spedum
    dugeða gehwilcre on dagum wille
    swiðor stepan and him soðe to
    modes wære mine gelætan,
    halige higetreawa and him hold wesan."
2370 Abraham fremede swa him se eca bebead,
    sette friðotacen be frean hæse
    on his selfes sunu. heht þæt segn wegan
    heah gehwilcne þe his hina wæs
    wæpnedcynnes, wære gemyndig,
2375 gleaw on mode Ða him god sealde

2337 *No point after* -cyningas. 2338 *No point after* ða. 2346
hundteontig— · c : *MS.* 2346b-47a rimes · he, *over erasure.*
2347 *Point after* metode. 2353 *No point after* fægere. 2354
No point after drihten. 2358 *No point after* ismael. 2370 *No
point after* fremede. 2372 wegan: *Dietrich (ZfdA 10, 334f.) &
edd.—* wesan: *MS.*

[18.10 . . . quo audito Sarra risit post ostium tabernaculi]
18.12   quae risit occulte [dicens]
        postquam consenui et dominus meus vetulus est voluptati
            operam dabo

18.13   dixit autem Dominus ad Abraham
        (quare risit Sarra dicens num vere paritura sum anus
18.14   numquid Deo est quicquam difficile
        iuxta condictum revertar ad te)
        hoc eodem tempore (vita comite)
            et habebit Sarra filium

18.16   Cum ergo surrexissent inde viri

            direxerunt oculos suos contra Sodomam
        et Abraham simul gradiebatur deducens eos

18.20   dixit itaque Dominus

        clamor Sodomorum et Gomorrae multiplicatus est
        et peccatum earum adgravatum est nimis

18.21   descendam et videbo
            utrum clamorem qui venit ad me
            opere compleverint
        (an non est ita ut sciam)

soðe treowa   and þa / seolf onfeng   [P. 108]
torhtum tacne.   a his tir metod,
domfæst cyning,   dugeðum iecte
on woruldrice.   he him þæs worhte to
2380   siððan he on fære   furðum meahte
his waldendes   willan fremman.

. . . .

Þa þæt wif ahloh   wereda drihtnes   [P. 109]
nalles glædlice   ac heo gearum frod
þone hleoðorcwyde   husce belegde
2385   on sefan swiðe,   soð ne gelyfde
þæt þære spræce   sped folgode.
þa þæt gehyrde   heofona waldend
þæt on bure ahof   bryd abrahames
hihtleasne hleahtor   þa cwæð halig god:
2390   "ne wile sarran   soð gelyfan
wordum minum.   sceal seo wyrd swa þeah
forð steallian   swa ic þe æt frymðe gehet.
soð ic þe secge: on þas sylfan tid
of idese bið   eafora wæcned.
2395   þonne ic þas ilcan   oðre siðe
wic gesece   þe beoð worngehat
min gelæsted.   þu on magan wlitest,
þin agen bearn,   abraham leofa."

xxxiiii.

2400   **G**Ewiton him þa ædre   ellorfuse
æfter þære spræce   spedum feran
of þam hleoðorstede.   halige gastas
lastas legdon.   him wæs leohtes mæg
sylfa on gesiððe   oð þæt hie on sodoman
weallsteape burg   wlitan meahton.
2405   gesawon ofer since   salo hlifian,
reced ofer readum golde.   ongan þa rodera waldend,
arfæst wið abraham sprecan,   sægde him unlytel spell:
"Ic on þisse byrig   bearhtm gehyre,
synnigra cyrm   swiðe hludne,
2410   ealogalra gylp,   yfele spræce
werod under weallum habban.   forþon wærlogona sint
folce firena hefige.   ic wille fandigan nu,
mago ebrea,   hwæt þa men don,
gif hie swa swiðe   synna fremmað
2415   þeawum and geþancum   swa hie on þweorh sprecað
facen and inwit.   þæt sceal wrecan

2381 fremman, *last word on P. 108; one leaf has been cut out
between P. 108 and P. 109, which contained material corresponding to 18.1-11.* 2399 *No point after* ædre. 2409 synnigra,
g *altered from straight stroke, probably of* r.

19.1   Veneruntque duo angeli Sodomam vespere

sedente Loth in foribus civitatis

qui cum vidisset surrexit et ivit obviam eis . . .

19.2   [et dixit] (obsecro domini declinate in domum pueri
        vestri et manete ibi) / [lavate pedes vestros et
        mane proficiscimini in viam vestram] / qui dixerunt

minime sed in platea manebimus

19.1   . . . adoravitque pronus in terra
19.3   conpulit illos oppido ut deverterent ad eum
        ingressisque domum illius fecit convivium
        [coxit azyma et comederunt]

19.4   (prius autem quam irent cubitum)

viri civitatis vallaverunt domum
a puero usque ad senem omnis populus simul

swefyl / and sweart lig,   sare and grimme,[P. 110]
hat and hæste   hæðnum folce."

. . . . . .

.xxx.v.

                              [P. 111]
W Eras basnedon   witeloccas,
2420   wean under weallum   and heora wif soméd.
    duguðum wlance   drihtne guldon
god mid gnyrne   oð þæt gasta helm,
lifes leohtfruma,   leng ne wolde
torn þrowigean   ac him to sende
2425   stiðmod cyning   strange twegen
aras sine.   Þa on æfentid
siðe gesohton   sodoma ceastre.
Hie þa æt burhgeate   beorn gemitton
sylfne sittan   sunu arones
2430   þæt þam gleawan were   geonge þuhton
men for his eagum.   aras þa metodes þeow
gastum togeanes,   gretan eode
cuman cuðlice,   cynna gemunde,
riht and gerisno   and þam rincum bead
2435   nihtfeormunge.   him þa nergendes
æðele ærendran   andswarodon:
"hafa arna þanc   þara þe þu unc bude.
wit be þisse stræte   stille þencað
sæles bidan   siððan sunne eft
2440   forð to morgen   metod up forlæt."
                                [P. 112]
þa to fotum loth
þam giestum hnah   and him georne bead
reste and gereorda   and his recedes hleow
and þegnunge.   hie on þanc curon
2445   æðelinges est.   eodon sona
swa him se ebrisca   eorl wisade
in undor edoras   þær him se æðela geaf,
gleawferhð hæle,   giestliðnysse
fægre on flette   oð þæt forð gewat
2450   æfenscima.   þa com æfter niht
on last dæge,   lagustreamas wreah,
þrym mid þystro   þisses lifes,
sæs and sidland.   comon sodomware
geonge and ealde,   gode unleofe

2418 hat, *one letter erased after this word; Junius prints* hate, *other edd.* hat; folce, *the last word on P. 110; one leaf has been cut out between P. 110 and P. 111, which contained material corresponding to 18.22-33.* **2433** cuman, an *written above the line.* **2439b-40** sunne . . . forlæt, *the last line on P. 111, below which somewhat more than half a line has been erased.* **2447** undor, as *erased after this word, the* e *of* edoras *partially over this erasure.*

19.5   vocaveruntque Loth et dixerunt ei

        (ubi sunt viri qui introierunt ad te nocte / educ illos
            huc ut cognoscamus eos   *cf. V.L.:* educ illos ad
            nos ut coitum faciamus cum eis)
19.6   egressus ad eos Loth [post tergum adcludens ostium]

            ait

19.8   habeo duas filias quae necdum cognoverunt virum
        educam eas ad vos (et abutimini eis sicut placuerit
            vobis / dummodo viris istis nihil faciatis mali
        quia ingressi sunt sub umbraculum tegminis mei
19.7   nolite quaeso fratres mei nolite malum hoc facere)

19.9   at illi dixerunt (recede illuc)
        (et rursus)
            ingressus es (inquiunt)

            ut advena

            numquid ut iudices / (te ergo ipsum magis quam
            hos adfligemus) / vimque faciebant Loth vehemen-
            tissime / (iam prope erat ut refringerent fores)

19.10   et ecce miserunt manum viri et introduxerunt ad se
            Loth clauseruntque ostium

19.11   et eos qui erant foris percusserunt caecitate a min-
            imo usque ad maximum

        ita ut ostium invenire non possent

19.12   dixerunt autem ad Loth

2455   corðrum miclum   cuman acsian
              þæt hie behæfdon   herges mægne
              loth mid giestum.   heton lædan ut
              of þam hean hofe   halige aras,
              weras to gewealde.   wordum cwædon
2460   þæt mid þam hæleðum   hæman wolden
              unscomlice,   arna ne gymden.
              þa aras hraðe   se ðe oft ræd ongeat,   [P. 113]
              loth on recede,   eode lungre ut,
              spræc þa ofer ealle   æðelinga gedriht
2465   sunu arones,   snytra gemyndig:
              "Her syndon inne   unwemme twa
              dohtor mine.   doð swa ic eow bidde
              —ne can þara idesa   owðer gieta
              þurh gebedscipe   beorna neawest—
2470   and geswicað þære synne.   ic eow sylle þa
              ær ge sceonde   wið gesceapu fremmen,
              ungifre yfel   ylda bearnum.
              Onfoð þæm fæmnum.   lætað frið agon
              gistas mine   þa ic for gode wille
2475   gemundbyrdan   gif ic mot for eow."
              Him þa seo mænigeo   þurh gemæne word,   [P. 114]
              arlease cyn,   andswarode:
              "þis þinceð gerisne   and riht micel
              þæt þu ðe aferige   of þisse folcsceare.
2480   þu þas werðeode   wræcoan laste,
              freonda feasceaft,   feorran gesohtest
              þine þearfende.   wilt ðu gif þu most
              wesan usser her   aldordema,
              leodum lareow?"   Þa ic on lothe gefrægn
2485   hæðne heremæcgas   handum gripan
              faum folmum.   him fylston wel
              gystas sine   and hine of gromra þa,
              cuman arfæste,   clommum abrugdon
              in under edoras   and þa ofstlice
2490   anra gehwilcum   ymbstandendra
              folces sodoma   fæste forsæton
              heafodsiena.   wearð eal here sona
              burhwarena / blind.   abrecan ne meahton   [P. 115]
              reðemode   reced æfter gistum
2495   swa hie fundedon   ac þær frome wæron
              godes spellbodan.   hæfde gistmægen
              stiðe strengeo,   styrde swiðe
              werode mid wite.   spræcon wordum þa

2456 þæt, *spelled out.*   **2465** *No point after* arones, *point after* snytra.   **2492** *Point after* here, *none after* sona.   **2493** *Point after* -warena.   **2497** styrde: *Bouterwek, Erläut., 316, suggested* styrede, *Cosijn (Beiträge 19, 455) suggested* styrde *and so Holthausen & Wells—* styrnde: *MS.*

19.12 habes hic tuorum quempiam generum aut filios aut filias

       omnes qui tui sunt educ de urbe hac
(19.17 . . . salva animam tuam . . .)

19.13 delebimus enim locum istum
       [eo quod increverit clamor eorum coram Domino *cf. 18.20*
          = *2408-10*] / qui misit nos ut perdamus illos

19.18 dixitque Loth ad eos [quaeso Domine mi]
19.19 (quia invenit servus tuus gratiam coram te
       et magnificasti misericordiam tuam quam fecisti mecum
       ut salvares animam meam) / nec possum in monte salvari
          ne forte adprehendat me malum et moriar *cf. 2514 f.*

19.20 est civitas haec iuxta

         ad quam possum fugere parva et salvabor in ea
       (numquid non modica est et vivet anima mea)

19.21 dixitque ad eum
       ecce etiam in hoc suscepi preces tuas / ut non subver-
          tam urbem pro qua locutus es / 19.22 festina et
          salvare ibi
       quia non potero facere quicquam donec ingrediaris
          illuc
     [idcirco vocatum est nomen urbis illius] Segor

19.23 . . . Loth ingressus est in Segor

(19.23 sol egressus est super terram . . .)

```
           fæle freoðoscealcas    fægre to lothe:
2500       "Gif þu sunu age    oððe swæsne mæg              [P. 116]
           oððe on þissum folcum    freond ænigne
           eac þissum idesum    þe we her on wlitað,
           alæde of þysse leodbyrig    þa ðe leofe sien
           ofestum miclum    and þin ealdor nere
2505       þy læs þu forweorðe    mid þyssum wærlogan.
           unc hit waldend heht    for wera synnum
           sodoma and gomorra    sweartan lige
           fyre gesyllan    and þas folc slean,
           cynn on ceastrum    mid cwealmþrea
2510       and his torn wrecan.    þære tide is
           neah geþrungen.    gewit þu nergean þin
           feorh foldwege.    þe is frea milde."
[xxxvi]              .    .    .    .    .    .
           Him þa ædre loth    andswarode:                  [P. 117]
           "ne mæg ic mid idesum    aldornere mine
2515       swa feor heonon    feðegange
           siðe gesecan,    git me sibblufan
           and freondscipe    fægre cyðað,
           treowe and hyldo    tiðiað me.
           Ic wat heaburh    her ane neah,
2520       lytle ceastre.    lyfað me þær
           are and reste    þæt we aldornere
           on sigor up    secan moten.
           gif git þæt fæsten    fyre willað
           steape forstandan    on þære stowe
2525       we gesunde magon    sæles bidan,
           feorh generigan."    Him þa freondlice
           englas arfæste    andswaredon:
           "Þu scealt þære bene    nu þu ymb þa burh sprycst
           tiða weorðan.    teng recene to
2530       þam fæstenne.    wit þe friðe healdað
           and mundbyrde    ne moton wyt
           on wærlogum    wrecan torn godes,
           swebban synnig cynn    ær ðon þu on sægor þin
           bearn gelæde    and bryd somed."
2535       Þa onette    abrahames mæg
           to þam fæstenne.    feðe ne sparode
           eorl mid idesum /    ac he ofstum forð        [P. 118]
           lastas legde    oð þæt he gelædde
           bryd mid bearnum    under burhlocan
2540       in sægor his    þa sunne up,
```

2512 milde, *last word on P. 116; between P. 116 and P. 117
one leaf has been cut out which contained material corresponding to 19.14-17.* 2513 *Point after* ædre, *none after* loth.
2514 *No point after* idesum. 2524 *No point after* stowe. 2525
Point after we. 2528 sprycst: *Thorpe & edd. (Sievers,* Beiträge *10, 473 would read* sprycest, *so Holthausen, Krapp &
Wells)*— spryst: *MS.* 2531 *No point after* wyt.

19.24 igitur Dominus pluit super Sodomam et Gomorram *cf. 2560 f.*
   sulphur et ignem a Domino de caelo

19.25 et subvertit civitates has   *cf. 18.20 = 2408 ff.*

  et omnem circa regionem *cf. 2561 f.*
  universos habitatores urbium et cuncta terrae virentia

19.26 respiciensque uxor eius post

   se versa est in statuam salis

19.27 Abraham autem
   consurgens mane ubi steterat prius
   cum Domino
19.28 intuitus est Sodomam et Gomorram . . . / . . . viditque
   ascendentem favillam de terra quasi fornacis
   fumum

folca friðcandel   furðum eode.
Þa ic sendan gefrægn   swegles aldor   [P. 119]
swefl of heofnum   and sweartne lig
werum to wite,   weallende fyr
2545   þæs hie on ærdagum   drihten tyndon
lange þrage.   him þæs lean forgeald
gasta waldend.   grap heahþrea
on hæðencynn.   hlynn wearð on ceastrum,
cirm arleasra,   cwealmes on ore
2550   laðan cynnes.   lig eall fornam
þæt he grenes fond   goldburgum in
swylce þær ymbutan   unlytel dæl
sidre foldan   geondsended wæs
bryne and brogan.   bearwas wurdon
2555   to axan and to yslan,   eorðan wæstma,
efne swa wide   swa ða witelac
reðe geræhton   rum land wera.
strudende fyr   steapes and geapes
swogende for,   swealh eall eador
2560   þæt on sodoma byrig   secgas ahton
and on gomorra.   eall þæt god spilde,
frea mid þy folce.   þa þæt fyrgebræc,
leoda lifgedal,   lothes gehyrde
bryd on burgum,   under bæc beseah
2565   wið þæs wælfylles.   us gewritu secgað
þæt heo on sealtstanes   sona wurde
anlicnesse.   æfre siððan
se monlica,   þæt is mære spell,
stille wunode   þær hie strang begeat
2570   wite þæs heo wordum   wuldres þegna
hyran ne wolde.   Nu sceal heard and steap
on þam wicum   wyrde bidan,
drihtnes domes   hwonne dogora rim,
woruld gewite.   þæt is wundra sum
2575   þara ðe geworhte   wuldres aldor.

.xxxvii.

HIM þa abraham gewat   ana gangan   [P. 121]
mid ærdæge   þæt he eft gestod
þær wordum ær   wið his waldend spræc,
frod frumgara.   he geseah from foldan up
2580   wide fleogan   wælgrimne rec.
hie þæs wlenco onwod   and wingedrync
þæt hie firendæda   to frece wurdon,

2546 *Point after* lean.   **2559** *No point after* for, *point after* swealh.   **2561** *No point after* gomorra; *point added after* eall. **2567** *No point after* -nesse.   **2573** hwonne, *first* n *written a-bove line.*   **2575** *No point after* geworhte.   **2577** he eft: *Thorpe & edd.—* heft: *MS.*   **2579** *Point after* foldan.

19.29   (cum enim subverteret Deus civitates regionis illius)
        recordatus est Abrahae

            et liberavit Loth de subversione urbium
        (in quibus habitaverat.)
19.30   . . . timuerat enim manere in Segor . . .

19.30   Ascenditque Loth de Segor et mansit in monte
        duae quoque filiae eius cum eo . . .

            . . . et mansit in spelunca ipse et duae filiae eius

19.33   dederunt itaque patri suo bibere vinum nocte illa

        et ingressa est maior dormivitque cum patre
        at ille non sensit
            nec quando accubuit filia nec quando surrexit
(19.35 dederunt et illa nocte patri vinum / ingressaque minor
            filia dormivit cum eo / et nec tunc quidem sensit
            quando concubuerit vel quando illa surrexerit)
19.36   conceperunt ergo duae filiae Loth de patre suo
19.37   peperitque maior filium et vocavit nomen eius Moab . . .

19.38   minor quoque peperit filium
            et vocavit nomen eius Ammon . . .

19.37   . . . ipse est pater Moabitarum (usque in praesentem
            diem)
19.38   . . . ipse est pater Ammonitarum (usque hodie).

```
                synna þriste.     soð ofergeaton,
                drihtnes domas    and hwa him dugeða forgeaf,
2585            blæd on burgum.     forþon him brego engla
                wylmhatne lig     to wræce sende.
                waldend usser     gemunde wærfæst þa
                abraham arlice     swa he oft dyde,
                leofne mannan.     loth generede,
2590            mæg þæs oðres,     þa seo mænegeo forwearð.
                Ne dorste þa     dædrof hæle
                for frean egesan     on þam fæstenne
                leng eardigean     Ac him loth gewat
                of byrig gangan /    and his bearn somed      [P. 122]
2595            wælstowe fyrr     wic sceawian
                oð þæt hie be hliðe     heare dune
                eorðscræf fundon.     þær se eadega loth
                wærfæst wunode,     waldende leof
                dægrimes worn     and his dohtor twa.

                   .   .   .   .   .   .   .   .
2600            Hie dydon swa.     druncnum eode      [P. 123]
                seo yldre to     ær on reste
                heora bega fæder     ne wiste blondenfeax
                hwonne him fæmnan to     bryde him bu wæron
                on ferhðcofan     fæste gencarwot
2605            mode and gemynde     þæt he mægðe sið,
                wine druncen     gewitan ne meahte.
                Idesa wurdon eacne.     eaforan brohtan
                willgesweostor     on woruld, sunu,
                heora ealdan fæder.     þara æðelinga
2610            modor oðerne     moab nemde,
                lothes dohter.     seo on life wæs
                wintrum yldre.     us gewritu secgeað,
                godcunde bec,     þæt seo gingre
                hire agen bearn     ammon hete.
2615            Of þam frumgarum     folc' unrim,      [P. 124]
                þrymfæste twa     þeoda awocon.
                Oðre þara mægða     moabitare
                eorðbuende     ealle hataд,
                widmære cynn.     Oðre weras nemnað,
2620            æðelinga bearn,     ammonitare.
```

2586 *Point after* -hatne.   2587 wærfæst, ær *written over erasure.*   2593 eardigean, *written over erasure;* Ac, A *over erased* n.   2599 twa, *the last word on P. 122; one leaf has been cut out between P. 122 and P. 123 which contained material corresponding to 19.31-32.*   2600 *No point after* swa, *point after* druncnum, *none after* eode.   2620 ammonitare, i *added above the line.*

20.1   Profectus inde Abraham [in terram australem / habita-
       vit inter Cades et Sur / et peregrinatus est in
       Geraris] / 20.2 dixitque de Sarra uxore sua
       soror mea est
                                 Cf. 2692 ff. = 20.11

       misit ergo Abimelech rex [Gerarae]

           et tulit eam

20.3   venit autem Deus ad Abimelech per somnium noctis

           et ait ei

       en morieris propter mulierem quam tulisti habet enim
           virum

20.4   Abimelech (vero non tetigerat eam   *cf. 2651b f.*
       et) ait

           Domine num gentem ignorantem et iustam interficies

20.5   nonne ipse dixit mihi

           soror mea est / (et ipsa ait frater meus est)
       [in simplicitate cordis mei et munditia manuum mearum
           feci hoc *cf. 20.4*] / 20.6 dixitque ad eum Deus
       [et ego scio quod simplici corde feceris]. . .
20.7   nunc igitur redde uxorem viro suo

       quia propheta est et orabit pro te et vives
       si autem nolueris reddere scito quod morte morieris tu
           et omnia quae tua sunt

xxxviii.

Ewat him þa mid bryde   broðor arones
Gunder abimelech   æhte lædan
mid his hiwum.   hæleðum sægde
þæt sarra his   sweostor wære.
2625 abraham wordum   bearh his aldre
þy he wiste gearwe   þæt he winemaga
on folce lyt   freonda hæfde.
þa se þeoden his   þegnas sende,
heht bringan   to him selfum
2630 Þa [þe] wæs ellþeodig   oðre siðe,
wif abrames   from were læded
on fremdes fæðm.   him þær fylste þa
ece drihten   swa he oft dyde,
nergend usser,   com nihtes self
2635 þær se waldend læg,   wine druncen.
Ongan þa soðcyning   þurh swefn sprecan   [P. 125]
to þam æðelinge   and him yrre hweop:
"þu abrahames   idese gename,
bryde æt beorne.   þe abregdan sceal
2640 for þære dæde   deað of breostum
sawle þine."   Him symbelwerig
synna brytta   þurh slæp oncwæð:
"Hwæt, þu æfre,   engla þeoden,
þurh þin yrre wilt   aldre lætan,
2645 heah, beheowan   þæne þe her leofað
rihtum þeawum,   bið on ræde fæst
modgeþance   and him miltse
to þe seceð?   me sægde ær
þæt wif hire   wordum selfa
2650 unfricgendum   þæt heo abrahames
sweostor wære.   næbbe ic synne wið hie,
facna ænig   gefremed gena."
Him þa ædre eft   ece drihten,
soðfæst metod   þurh þæt swefn oncwæð:
2655 "Agif abrahame   idese sine,
wif to gewcalde   gif þu on worulde leng,   [P. 126]
æðelinga helm,   aldres recce.
he is god and gleaw,   mæg self sprecan,
geseon sweglcyning.   þu sweltan scealt

2624 his sweostor, *scribe first wrote* hisweostor *and then ad-ded* s *above the line between* is.   2629 *Point after* him.   2630 þe, *not in MS.*   2641 Him, *the ascender of* H *(h-shaped) has a cross stroke added by a later hand.*   2645 beheowan: *suggested by Cosijn* (Beiträge 19, 456), *so Holthausen & edd.* — beheopan: *MS;* þæne : *Grein & edd. (except Wülker)* — þære: *MS.*   2650 *No point after* unfricgendum.

20.8   statimque de nocte consurgens
           Abimelech vocavit omnes servos suos

       et locutus est universa verba haec in auribus eorum
       timueruntque omnes viri valde
20.9   vocavit autem Abimelech
           etiam Abraham
           et dixit ei

       [quid fecisti nobis] quid peccavimus in te

       quia induxisti super me et super regnum meum peccatum
           grande . . .

20.11 respondit Abraham . . .

20.13 postquam autem eduxit me Deus de domo patris mei
           (dixi ad eam / hanc misericordiam facies mecum /in
           omni loco ad quem ingrediemur dices quod frater
           tuus sim)

2660   mid feo and mid feorme   gif ðu þam frumgaran
               bryde wyrnest.   he abiddan mæg
               gif he ofstum me   ærenda wile,
               þeawfæst and geþyldig,   þin abeodan
               þæt ic þe lissa   lifigendum giet
2665   on dagum læte   duguþa brucan,
               sinces gesundne."   Þa slæpe tobrægd
               forht folces weard.   heht him fetigean to
               sprecan sine,   spedum sægde
               eorlum abimeleh,   egesan geðread,
2670   waldendes word.   weras him ondredon
               for þære dæde   drihtnes handa
               sweng æfter swefne. /   Heht sylf cyning   [P. 127]
               him þa abraham to   ofstum miclum.
               Þa reordode   rice þeoden:
2675   "mago ebrea,   þæs þu me wylle
               wordum secgean: hu geworhte ic þæt
               siððan þu usic under,   abraham, þine
               on þas eðelturf   æhta læddest
               þæt þu me þus swiðe   searo renodest?
2680   þu ellþeodig   usic woldest
               on þisse folcsceare   facne besyrwan,
               synnum besmitan,   sægdest wordum
               þæt sarra þin   sweostor wære,
               lices mæge,   woldest laðlice
2685   þurh þæt wif on me   wrohte alecgean,
               ormæte yfel.   we þe arlice
               gefeormedon   and þe freondlice
               on þisse werþeode   wic getæhton,
               land to lissum.   þu us leanast nu
2690   unfreondlice,   fremena þancast."

                 xxxviiii.

      A Braham þa   andswarode: [P. 128]
         "ne dyde ic for facne   ne for feondscipe
         ne for wihte   þæs ic þe wean uðe.
               Ac ic me, gumena baldor,   guðbordes sweng
2695   leodmagum feor   lare gebearh
               siððan me se halga   of hyrde frean,
               mines fæder,   fyrn alæd*de*.
               Ic fela siððan   folca gesohte,
               wina uncuðra   and þis wif mid me,
2700   freonda feasceaft.   ic þæs færes a

2663 *Point after* -fæst   2667 heht, e *altered from* a.   2676 geworhte ic, *crowded, or written over erasure,* h *written over* e-
rased s *or* r.   2683 þæt, *spelled out.*   2685 þurh, h *added above
the line.*   2686 *Point after* yfel *added?*   2691 *No point after*
þa.   2694 *Point after* gumena; *no point after* baldor; *point after* guð.   2697 alædde: *Thorpe & edd.*— alæded: *MS.*

20.11   . . . et interficient me propter uxorem meam

20.11   . . . cogitavi mecum (dicens)
          forsitan non est timor Dei in loco isto

[*cf.* 20.12   alias autem et vere soror mea est / filia patris
          mei et non filia matris meae et duxi eam uxorem]
20.14   tulit igitur Abimelech . . .
          . . . reddiditque illi Sarram uxorem suam . . .

          . . . oves et boves et servos et ancillas et
          dedit Abraham . . .
20.15   et ait
          terra coram vobis est
          ubicumque tibi placuerit habita

20.16   Sarrae autem dixit

                on wenum sæt   hwonne me wraðra sum
                ellþeodigne   aldre beheowe
                se ðe him þas idese eft   agan wolde.
                forðon ic wigsmiðum   wordum sægde
2705   þæt sarra min   sweostor wære
                æghwær eorðan   þær wit earda leas
                mid wealandum   winnan sceoldon.
                Ic þæt ilce dreah   on þisse eðyltyrf   [P. 129]
                siððan ic þina,   þeoden mæra,
2710   mundbyrde geceas   ne wæs me on mode cuð
                hwæðer on þyssum folce   frean ælmihtiges
                egesa wære   þa ic her ærest com.
                forþon ic þegnum   þinum dyrnde
                and sylfum þe   swiðost micle
2715   soðan spræce   þæt me sarran
                bryde laste   beddreste gestah."
                þa ongan abimæleh   abraham swiðan
                woruldgestreonum   and him his wif ageaf.
                Sealde him to bote   þæs þe he his bryd genam
2720   gangende feoh   and glæd seolfor
                and weorcþeos.   spræc / þa wordum eac   [P. 130]
                to abrahame   æðelinga helm:
                "wuna mid usic   and þe wic geceos
                on þissum lande   þær þe leofost sie,
2725   eðelstowe   þe ic agan sceal.
                wes us fæle freond.   we ðe feoh syllað."
                cwæð þa eft raðe   oðre worde
                to sarran   sinces brytta:
                "ne þearf ðe on edwit   abraham settan,
2730   ðin freadrihten,   þæt þu flettpaðas,
                mæg ælfscieno,   mine træde

2702 ellþeodigne, *the second l written above the line.* **2707**
wealandum, *a tag added between* al *by a different hand, to mark
word division?* **2709** *No point after* þina. **2710** geceas, g *over
erasure? or rough place?* **2721** weorcþeos: *Grein & edd. (except
Wülker)*— weorc feos · spræc : *MS;* os · s *is badly rubbed and
over erasures.* Wells, p. xx, *thinks that the scribe inadver-
tently repeated* seolfor *from previous MS line and then altered
it to* feos · spræc. *An examination of the MS supports him.
The lower horizontal stroke of f is of a lighter color, the
up-stroke erased over s could be l, and remains of fo are visible under the point, while s of* spræc *is altered from r;
spræc is written twice, as last word on P. 129 and first on
P. 130, in latter case with capital S.* **2727** þa eft, *written
over erasure; several letters erased before* raðe, *in a space
large enough for 4 or 5 letters.* **2730** flettpaðas: *suggested by
Grimm,* Andreas und Elene, *116, so Bouterwek & edd.*— flett
waðas: *MS.*

(20.16) (ecce mille) argenteos dedi (fratri) tuo
        (hoc erit tibi in velamen oculorum)
        [ad omnes qui tecum sunt et quocumque perrexeris
        mementoque te deprehensam]

20.18   concluserat enim Deus omnem vulvam domus Abimelech
        (propter Sarram uxorem Abraham)

20.17   orante autem Abraham sanavit Deus Abimelech et uxorem
            ancillasque eius et pepererunt

21.1   Visitavit autem Dominus
            Sarram sicut promiserat

            et implevit quae locutus est

21.2   concepitque et peperit filium in senectute sua
        (tempore quo praedixerat ei Deus   *cf. 2776 f.*)
21.3   vocavitque Abraham nomen filii sui quem genuit ei Sarra
            Isaac
21.4   et circumcidit eum octavo die sicut praeceperat ei Deus

<pre>
          ac him hygeteonan   hwitan seolfre
          deope bete.   ne ceara incit duguða
          of ðisse eðyltyrf   ellor secan
2735   winas uncuðe   ac wuniað her."
          Abraham fremede   swa hine his aldor heht,
          onfeng freondscipe   be frean hæse
          lufum and lissum.   he wæs leof gode
          forðon he sibbe   gesælig dreah
2740   and his / scippende   under sceade gefor,   [P. 131]
          hleowfeðrum þeaht   her þenden lifde.
          þa gien wæs yrre   god abimelehe
          for þære synne   þe he wið sarrai
          and wið abrahame   ær gefremede
2745   Þa he gedælde   him deore twa,
          wif and wæpned.   he þæs weorc gehleat,
          frecne wite.   ne meahton freo ne þeowe
          heora bregoweardas   bearnum agan
          monrim mægeð   ac him þæt metod forstod
2750   Oð þæt se halga   his hlaforde,
          abraham, ongan   arra biddan
          ecne drihten.   him engla helm
          getigðode,   tuddorsped onleac
          folccyninge   freora and þeowra,
2755   wera and wifa.   let weaxan eft
          heora rimgetel   rodora waldend,
          ead and æhta.   ælmihtig wearð
          milde on mode,   moncynnes weard,
          abimeleche   swa hine abraham bæd.
2760   Þa com feran   frea ælmihtig   [P. 132]
          to sarrai   swa he self gecwæð.
          waldend usser   hæfde wordbeot
          leofum gelæsted,   lifes aldor,
          eaforan and idese.   abrahame woc
2765   bearn of bryde   þone brego engla
          ær ðy magotudre   modor wære
          eacen be eorle   isaac nemde.
          hine abraham on   his agene hand
          beacen sette   swa him bcbead metod,
2770   wuldortorht, ymb wucan   þæs þe hine on woruld
          to moncynne   modor brohte.
</pre>

2732 him, m *over erasure.*   2757 æhta, æ *over erasure, probably
altered from* h.   2758 weard: *edd.*— wearð: *MS.*   2760 *No point
after* feran.   2768 *No point after* on.   2770 *Point after* -torht.
2771 *No point after* -cynne.

21.8   crevit igitur puer [et ablactatus est] . . .
21.5   cum centum esset annorum / (hac quippe aetate patris
            natus est Isaac) *cf. V.L.:* Abraham autem erat
            annorum centum quando genuit Isaac

21.9   cumque vidisset Sarra
            filium Agar Aegyptiae ludentem

        dixit ad Abraham

21.10   eice ancillam hanc et filium eius

        non enim erit heres filius ancillae cum filio meo
            Isaac

21.11   dure accepit hoc Abraham pro filio suo

21.12   cui dixit Deus

        non tibi videatur asperum super puero et super ancilla
            tua
        omnia quae dixerit tibi Sarra audi vocem eius
        [quia in Isaac vocabitur tibi semen]
21.13   sed et filium ancillae faciam in gentem magnam
        quia semen tuum est

21.14   [surrexit itaque Abraham mane
        et tollens panem et utrem aquae imposuit scapulae eius]
        tradiditque puerum et dimisit eam . . .

21.22   [. . . dixit Abimelech . . .] / Deus tecum est
            in universis quae agis   *cf. 2811b ff.*

.xl.

C NIHT weox and þag   swa him cynde wæron
æðele from yldrum.   abraham hæfde
wintra hunteontig   þa him wif sunu

2775 on þanc gebær.   he þæs ðrage bad
siððan him ærest   þurh his / agen word   [P. 133]
þone dægwillan   drihten bodode.
þa seo wyrd gewearð   þæt þæt wif geseah
for abrahame   ismael plegan

2780 ðær hie æt swæsendum   sæton bu tu,
halig on hige   and heora hiwan eall
druncon and drymdon   þa cwæð drihtlecu mæg,
bryd to beorne: "forgif me, beaga weard,
min swæs frea: hat siððan

2785 agar ellor   and ismael
lædan mid hie   ne beoð we leng somed
willum minum   gif ic wealdan mot.
næfre ismael   wið isace,
wið min agen bearn   yrfe dæleð

2790 on laste þe   þonne þu of lice
aldor asendest." /   Þa wæs abrahame   [P. 134]
weorce on mode   þæt he on wræc drife
his selfes sunu.   Þa com soð metod,
freom on fultum.   wiste ferhð guman

2795 cearum on clommum.   cyning engla spræc
to abrahame,   ece drihten:
"læt þe aslupan   sorge of breostum,
modgewinnan   and mægeð hire,
bryde þinre.   hat bu tu aweg

2800 agar feran   and ismael,
cniht of cyððe.   ic his cynn gedo
brad and bresne   bearna tudre,
wæstmum spedig   swa ic þe wordum gehet."
þa se wer hyrde   his waldende,

2805 draf of wicum   dreorigmod tu,
idese of earde   and his agen bearn.

. . . .

"Sweotol is and gesene   þæt þe soð metod   [P. 135]
on gesiððe is,   swegles aldor,
se ðe sigor seleð   snytrum mihtum

2810 and þin mod trymeð
godcundum gifum.   forðon ðe giena speow

2772 *Point after* weox.   2784 *No point after* siððan. 2785
Point after agar, *none after* ellor.   2790 *No point after* lice.
2793 sunu, *one letter erased before this word.*   2805 draf, r
altered from a.   2806 bearn, *the last word on P. 134; one leaf
has been cut out between P. 134 and P. 135, which contained
material corresponding to 21.15-21.*

21.23 iura ergo per Dominum

        (ne noceas mihi) . . .

     . . . sed iuxta misericordiam quam feci tibi / facies
     mihi
     et terrae in qua versatus es advena   *cf. 2837a*

     . . . . . et posteris meis stirpique meae . . .

21.24 dixitque Abraham
       (ego iurabo)

21.34 et fuit colonus
       terrae Philistinorum
       diebus multis'

(21.31 . . . vocatus est locus ille Bersabee . . .)

21.33 . . . Abraham vero plantavit nemus in Bersabee

     (et invocavit ibi nomen Domini Dei aeterni)

 22.1 (Quae postquam gesta sunt)
     temptavit Deus Abraham
       [et dixit ad eum / Abraham ille respondit adsum]
 22.2 ait ei
       tolle filium tuum (unigenitum quem diligis)
       Isaac / et vade in terram (visionis)

þæs þu wið freond oððe feond   fremman ongunne
wordum oððe dædum.   waldend scufeð,
frea, forðwegas   folmum sinum
2815   willan þinne.   þæt is wide cuð
burhsittendum.   ic þe bidde nu,
wine ebrea,   wordum minum
þæt þu tilmodig   treowa selle,
wæra þina   þæt þu wille me
2820   wesan fæle freond   fremena to leane
þara þe ic to duguðum   ðe gedon hæbbe
siððan þu feasceaft   feorran come
on þas werþeode   wræccan laste.
Gyld me mid hyldo   þæt ic þe hneaw ne wæs   [P. 136]
2825   landes and lissa.   wes þissum leodum nu
and mægburge   minre arfæst
gif þe alwalda,   ure drihten,
scirian wille   se ðe gesceapu healdeð
þæt þu randwigum   rumor mote
2830   on ðisse folcsceare   frætwa dælan,
modigra gestreon,   mearce settan."
Ða abraham   abimelehe
wære sealde   þæt he wolde swa.

.xli.

SIððan wæs se eadega   eafora þares
2835   in filistea   folce eardfæst,
leod ebrea,   lange þrage,
feasceaft mid fremdum.   him frea engla
wic getæhte   þær weras hatað,
burhsittende,   bersabea lond.
2840   Ðær se halga   heah / steapreced,   [P. 137]
burh, timbrede   and bearo setle,
weobedd worhte   and his waldende
on þam glædstede   gild onsægde,
lac geneahe   þam þe lif forgeaf
2845   gesæliglic   swegle under.
Þa þæs rinces   se rica ongan,
cyning, costigan,   cunnode georne
hwilc þæs æðelinges   ellen wære.
stiðum wordum   spræc him stefne to:
2850   "gewit þu ofestlice,   abraham, feran,
lastas lecgan   and þe læde mid
þin agen bearn.   þu scealt isaac me

2816 burh-, *some marks visible under* b *and a stroke over* r
partially erased. 2827 *No point after* alwalda. 2832 *No point after* abraham. 2839 lond: *edd.—* ?lono: *MS (the final letter may be a* d *with ascender rubbed off).* 2846 *No point after* rinces. 2848 *No point after* æðelinges.

(22.2)   atque offer eum ibi holocaustum
        super unum montium
              quem monstravero tibi

22.3 igitur Abraham
              de nocte consurgens

              stravit asinum suum
        ducens secum duos iuvenes
              et Isaac filium suum
        [cumque concidisset ligna in holocaustum]

              abiit ad locum quem praeceperat ei Deus

22.4 die autem tertio

              elevatis oculis vidit locum procul

22.5 dixitque ad pueros suos
        expectate hic cum asino
              ego et puer illuc usque properantes postquam
              adoraverimus revertemur ad vos

22.6 tulit quoque ligna holocausti et imposuit super Isaac
              filium suum / ipse vero portabat in manibus ignem
              et gladium / (cumque duo pergerent simul *cf. 2885 f.*)
22.7 dixit Isaac patri suo pater mi . . .
              . . . ecce inquit ignis et ligna ubi est
              victima holocausti
22.8 dixit Abraham

onsecgan, sunu ðinne,   sylf to tibre
siððan þu gestigest   steape dune,
2855 hrincg þæs hean landes   þe ic þe heonon getæce
up þinum agnum fotum   þær þu scealt / ad gegærwan [P. 138]
bælfyr bearne þinum   and blotan sylf
sunu mid sweordes ecge   and þonne sweartan lige
leofes lic forbærnan   and me lac bebeodan."
2860 Ne forsæt he þy siðe   ac sona ongann
fysan to fore.   him wæs frea engla,
word, ondrysne   and his waldende leof.
Þa se eadga   abraham sine
nihtreste ofgeaf.   nalles nergendes
2865 hæse wiðhogode   ac hine se halga wer
gyrde grægan sweorde,   cyðde þæt him gasta weardes
egesa on breostum wunode.   ongan þa his esolas bætan
gamolferhð goldes brytta.   heht hine geonge twegen
men mid siðian.   mæg wæs his agen þridda
2870 and he feorða sylf.   þa he fus gewat
from his agenum hofe /   isaac lædan,   [P. 139]
bearn unweaxen,   swa him bebead metod.
efste þa swiðe   and onette
forð foldwege   swa him frea tæhte
2875 wegas ofer westen   oð þæt wuldortorht
dæges þriddan   up ofer deop wæter
ord aræmde.   þa se eadega wer
geseah hlifigan   hea dune
swa him sægde ær   swegles aldor.
2880 Ða abraham spræc   to his ombihtum:
"rincas mine   restað incit her
on þissum wicum.   wit eft cumað
siððan wit ærende   uncer twega
gastcyninge   agifen habbað."
2885 Gewat him þa se æðeling   and his agen sunu
to þæs gemearces   þe him metod tæhte
wadan ofer wealdas.   wudu bær sunu,
fæder fyr and sweord.   Ða þæs fricgean ongann
wer wintrum geong   wordum abraham:
2890 "Wit her fyr and sweord,   frea min, habbað. [P. 140]
hwær is þæt tiber   þæt þu torht gode
to þam brynegielde   bringan þencest?"
Abraham maðelode.   hæfde on an gehogod
þæt he gedæde swa   hine drihten het:

2876 deop, o *over erasure, probably of* a.   2890 *No point af-*
ter sweord.   2894 þæt, *spelled out;* gedæde, *scribe wrote* gedæde · H *and then in erasing the* H *erased, and did not restore*
the final -e *and the point (*H *anticipated* Him, *2895a, same MS*
line); traces of the curved descender of the H *show (under* s
of swa) *as does the original* -e *of* gedæde. *A new metrical*
point crowded in between swa *and* hine.

(22.8)   Deus providebit sibi victimam holocausti fili mi

pergebant ergo pariter / 22.9 veneruntque

    ad locum quem
    ostenderat ei Deus

[in quo aedificavit altare et desuper] ligna composuit
cumque conligasset Isaac filium suum / posuit eum in
    altari super struem lignorum
22.10 extenditque manum et arripuit gladium ut immolaret
    filium suum
22.11 et ecce angelus Domini
    de caelo clamavit dicens

Abraham [Abraham / qui respondit adsum] / 22.12 [dix-
    itque ei] non extendas manum tuam super puerum neque
    facias illi quicquam

(nunc cognovi quod timeas Dominum et non peperceris
    filio tuo unigenito propter me)

22.13 levavit Abraham oculos viditque
    post tergum arietem

    inter vepres haerentem cornibus
quem adsumens obtulit holocaustum
    pro filio

2895   "Him þæt soðcyning   sylfa findeð,
          moncynnes weard,   swa him gemet þinceð."
          gestah þa stiðhydig   steape dune
          up mid his eaforan   swa him se eca bebead
          þæt he on hrofe gestod   hean landes
2900   on þære [stowe]   þe him se stranga to,
          wærfæst metod,   wordum tæhte.
          Ongan þa ad hladan,   æled weccan,
          and gefeterode   fet and honda
          bearne sinum   and þa on bæl ahof
2905   isaac geongne   and þa ædre gegrap
          sweord be gehiltum.   wolde his sunu cwellan
          folmum sinum,   fyre sencan
          mæges dreore. /   Þa metodes ðegn   [P. 141]
          ufan, engla sum,   abraham hlude
2910   stefne cygde.   he stille gebad
          ares spræce   and þam engle oncwæð.
          Him þa ofstum to   ufan of roderum
          wuldorgast godes   wordum mælde:
          "Abraham leofa,   ne sleah þin agen bearn
2915   ac þu cwicne abregd   cniht of ade,
          eaforan þinne.   him an wuldres god,
          mago ebrea.   þu medum scealt
          þurh þæs halgan hand   heofoncyninges
          soðum sigorleanum   selfa onfon,
2920   ginfæstum gifum.   þe wile gasta weard
          lissum gyldan   þæt þe wæs leofra his
          sibb and hyldo   þonne þin sylfes bearn."
          Ad stod onæled.   hæfde abrahame
          metod moncynnes,   mæge lothes,
2925   breost geblissad   þa he him his bearn forgeaf,
          isaac, cwicne. /   Ða se eadega bewlat,   [P. 142]
          rinc ofer exle   and him þær rom geseah
          unfeor þanon   ænne standan,
          broðor arones,   brembrum fæstne
2930   þone abraham genam   and hine on ad ahof
          ofestum miclum   for his agen bearn.
          Abrægd þa mid þy bille,   brynegield onhread,
          reccendne weg   rommes blode,
          onbleot þæt lac gode,   sægde leana þanc
2935   and ealra þara   þe he him sið and ær,
          gifena, drihten   forgifen hæfde.

2900 stowe, *not in MS, supplied by Bouterwek, Erläut., 317 &
edd. (except Wülker); no caesural point.* 2909 *Point between*
hlude & stefne *crowded in by scribe.* 2912 *Point after*
ofstum. 2927 *Point after* rom. 2930 *No point after*
genam. 2934 *Point after* lac. 2935 *No point after* ær.

Commentary

NOTE

*Reference to a name alone, is to an edition
by name of the editor (e.g., Grein, Krapp,
etc.), see Bibliography, section C.* Braasch
refers to Braasch's Wörterbuch, *see Bibliography, section F.* Kennedy, Mason *refer to
their translations of GN, see Bibliography,
section E. For other incomplete references,
see Bibliography, section J and Table of
Abbreviations.*

1-111   The opening section of the poem serves as an
"exordium" and may be compared to the opening of BW, an extended thematic introduction to the main narrative (see
Wrenn's note to BW 1-52, p. 182 of his rev. ed.).   It introduces the angelic material traditionally considered an integral part of the literal meaning of Genesis and suggests such
established topics as the nature of the Godhead, time and eternity, sin and free will, etc.   Traditionally, creation was
considered to have taken place in two forms, the prior being
that of the angels and the intelligible heavens (conventionally regarded as first in "time" as well by some commentators)
and the subsequent that of the lower heavens and the earth.
The exordium conforms broadly to the first part of this scheme,
presenting the causes and themes of the narrative to follow.
Bede, explaining the words "heaven and earth" in the first
verse of Genesis, says that the two-fold creation is adum-
brated by Moses, for the upper heavens are comprehended in
"caelum" and the rest of the visible creation, which pertains
most closely to man and his instruction, in "terram" (*In Gen.*,
CCSL 118A, 7).   Augustine refers "caelum" to the superior
creatures, "terram" to the inferior (*De Gen. ad Lit.*, PL. 34,
247, 258, 260).   The "angelic" matter extends to line 81, a
transitional passage deals with the causes of the material
creation and the operation of the Logos, and at line 112 the
paraphrase proper begins, as the treatment of the "visible"
creation is undertaken.   Such a treatment not only accords
with the exegetical tradition, but proves very neat narratively, allowing the poet to dispose of his non-biblical matter in one section at the beginning of the poem.
   1-8   A "hymn" in the Cædmonian manner, contemplating
the power and eternity of the Creator.   It corresponds in
function and statement to lines 1-4 of Cædmon's *Hymn*, outlining the invisible creation, just as GN 112 ff. corresponds to
Hymn 5-9 outlining the corporeal creation.
   1-3a   The poem opens with a reminder that the purpose of
the creation was to establish created things for the praise
of God, in words which reflect the Preface to the Canon of
the Mass: "Vere dignum et justum est . . . nos tibi . . . gra-
tias agere . . ." (the resemblance was first noted by Holthausen in a note to these lines in his ed. and developed by
L. Michel, "*Genesis A* and the Prefatio," *MLN* 62, 545-50).
Huppé, *Doctrine and Poetry*, 109, pointed out the similarity

of the opening of GN to Pseudo-Hilary's *In Genesim ad Leonem
Papem*, lines 7-10 (PL. 50, 1287A): "Dignum opus et justum est
semper tibi dicere grates, / Omnipotens mundi genitor, quo
principe cuncta / Natalem sumpsere diem, atque exorta repente
/ Post tenebras stupido spectarunt lumina coelo." This part
of the mass was associated with the creation and the praise
due the Creator. Failure to praise God was the chief outward
sign of the injustice and pride of the fallen angels. To
praise was to fulfill the purpose of creation (so Eustathius,
In hexaemeron S. Basilii, PL. 53, 879-80), and in such terms
the Prefatio of the Mass was explained, as e.g., in the eighth
century commentary on the Missa Romanae printed in PL. 96, 1488B:
"Condidit autem Deus hominem nulla pravitate perversum, sed
omni bonitate rectum et aequum, ad imaginem scilicet ac similitudinem suam, ut non modo in illa terrena felicitate para-
disi sobrie, juste, et pie viveret, verum etiam in majori
quandoque et spiritali felicitate constitutus, creatorem suum
sine fine laudaret." The poet fuses the traditional topic
"praise of God," the liturgy and the most prominent Cædmonian
formulaic theme to form a fitting, thematically coherent opening for the "Genesis" to follow.

   5b-8   Cf. Ælfric's *Exameron Anglice*, BAP. 10, 62: "Ælc
ðing hæfð anginn and ordfruman ðurh God, buton se ana Scyppend ðe ealle ðing gesceop; se næfð nan anginn ne nænne ordfruman, ac he sylf is angin and soðlice ordfruma ealra ðinga
and æfre ungeendod."

   9-18a   The angels carrying out the function for which
they were created. This passage seems to be describing their
mode of existence in God, in terms similar to those developed
by Augustine, *De ciu. Dei* XI, 24 (CCSL 48, 344): "Inde est
ciuitatis sanctae, quae in sanctis angelis sursum est, et or-
igo et informatio et beatitudo. Nam si quaeratur unde sit:
Deus eam condidit; si unde sit sapiens: a Deo inluminatur; si
unde sit felix: Deo fruitur; subsistens modificatur, contem-
plans inlustratur, inhaerens iucundatur; est, uidet, amat; in
aeternitate Dei uiget, in ueritate Dei lucet, in bonitate Dei
gaudet." The creation of the angels was technically "prior"
to everything except the begetting of the Son and the procession of the Holy Spirit. The poet, following the main line
of thought from Basil to Milton, depicts the angels dwelling
in the "elder state" of intelligible light and bliss before
the Logos undertook the visible creation (see Robbins, *The
Hexaemeral Literature*, 44-45).

   9   *soðfæst and swiðfeorm / sweglbosmas heold*   "Faithful
and self-sufficient, He maintained the heaven-embraces (which
were established)," etc. *swiðfeorm* for MS *swiðferom* follows
1770a. The basic meaning "abundant in food" is used here of
the Creator as a term of self-reliance and hospitality, the
Creator as the unsustained sustainer of the creation (see

E. von Schaubert, *Bedeutung and Herkunft von alteng. 'feormian'
und seiner Sippe* [Göttingen and Baltimore, 1949], 67, 93f.,
97). Probably *sweglbosmas* is meant to show the existence in
God which the angels partake of, rather than the angels themselves.

   12a *gasta weardum*. The guardian angels were a standard
hexameral topic (see Robbins, *The Hexaemeral Literature*, 62).
At 41a *gasta weardas* is used of the angels who fell.

   13a *and heora ordfruman* Here *and* may be taken as a
conjunction, "they possessed jubilation and happiness *and*
their Creator" (zeugma), a development of 9-12a. Or *ordfruman*
may be taken as gen. sing. following *blisse*, "and they possessed the bright bliss of their Creator." Dietrich, *ZfdA* 10,
311, explains *and* as a prep., "before," "in the sight of,"
with the acc. B-T *Supp.*, s.v. *and* II explains as equivalent
to *an* (cf. 1879a, note, and Gradon, *Elene*, 311n.). Holthausen
says he does not believe in *and* as prep. and reads *mid*, as
in line 20.

   16-18a "(thanes) proclaimed praise with joy(s), praised
their life-Lord: they were very blessed among the hosts of the
Lord." Wülker explained *deman* as "celebrare"; see B-T *Supp.*,
s.v. *deman* IV and cf. GU 526: "Forþon is nu arlic / þæt we æ-
fæstra // dæde demen, / secgen dryhtne lof . . . ." Wells
links *deman* here with BW 3174, citing Klaeber's gloss "express
a (favorable) opinion," "appraise," "praise"; he places the
punctuation after *dugupum*, translating "judged well of the
Lord's excellences," but this seems rather impertinent of angels, even those about to fall. Earlier editors produce variations on Thorpe's version: "(they) joyfully praised their
life's Lord, they judged, by the Lord's power, they were most
happy." Grein, *Sprch.* I, 208, proposed emending *drihtenes* to
drihten-nes, "majesty" as obj. of *demdon* with gen. *(Godes)* to
be understood, or alternatively, that *drihtenes æ*, "the law of
the Lord," be read.

   18b-81 The fall of the angels. The narrative material
in this part of GN is drawn from well-established hexameral
topics, nearly every detail being paralleled in Anglo-Saxon
sources alone. But the arrangement and narrative movement are
the poet's. It seems safe to say that this is theologically,
if not dramatically, the most sophisticated and complete re-
alization of the topic in OE. The legend goes back to Jewish
attempts to reconcile various O.T. mentions of angels with
their absence in Genesis 1-3 which had already achieved a high
degree of development before the Christian era. It is therefore not feasible to look for specific sources for a story so
well-known that it was generally assumed to be part of the
literal events of the Creation. It suffices to say that the
main tradition tended to treat the Fall as part of the angelic
creation itself, whether or not specific commentators regarded
it as taking place later in time. The location of the story

in GN derives from this "theological" tradition, but there
was another, more popular, view, which held that the angels
fell on the fifth or sixth days (cf. Ælfric, *Exameron Anglice*,
55): it is the latter which determines the place where GB,
also dealing extensively with the angelic fall, was inserted.
See P. E. Dustoor, "Legends of Lucifer in Early English and in
Milton," *Anglia* 54, 213-68, also *Reallexicon für Antike und
Christentum*, V, 190 ff., s.v. *Engel*.

   18b-20a Cf. Ælfric, "On the Old and New Testament" (EETS
160, 18): "Se ælmihtiga Scippend . . . þa geworhte . . . tyn
engla werod . . . buton eallum synnum on gesælþe libbende, swa
wlitiges gecindes . . . and nan yfel ðing næs on ðam englum þa
git, ne nan yfel ne com ðurh Godes gesceapennisse . . . .

   22-23a *ær ðon engla wearð / for oferhygde // dæl on gedwilde.* ". . . before a part of the angels were in error on
account of their pride." Various suggestions and emendations
for MS *engla weard . . . dæl* have been put forward, Zupitza's
being the simplest and most plausible on paleographical (cf.
2758), syntactical and lexical grounds, as well as making
the text accord with the idea that a tenth part of the angels
fell. Most editors have tried to take *dæl* as a verb: Thorpe
read *dæl on gedwild* "sunk into error." Grein, *Sprch.* I, 187,
proposed a str. vb. *delan* 4, "fall"; Wülker suggested *dælde
gedwilde*; Bouterwek, followed by Krapp, reads *dweal* (Krapp:
dwæl) "err" from *(ge)dwelan*, not well-attested in OE. as a str.
vb. Wells reads *ærðon engla werod . . . dæl on gedwilde, /
noldan . . . ,* "until an army of angels, . . . a portion in
pride, wished . . ." etc.

   28b-31 "Pain came upon them, envy and pride and the special pride (*mod*) of that angel (i.e. Lucifer) (came upon them),
who first began to do evil plan(s), wove (them) and aroused
(them)." An admittedly difficult sentence, which, however, appears to express the idea that the sins of the angels are
"pains" or "torments," *sar* being in apposition with *æfst and
oferhygd*, conjoined with Lucifer's *mod*, which appears equally
to affect them. The poet may be attempting to suggest the
mysterious "efficient cause" of sin. According to Augustine,
who discusses this topic in relation to the reprobate angels,
sin is a defection of will, which becomes its own torment: "Ac
per hoc qui peruerse amat cuiuslibet naturae bonum, etiamsi
adipiscatur, ipse fit in bono malus et miser meliore priuatus"
(*De ciu. Dei* XII, 8 [CCSL 48, 363]). The traditional motives
of the bad angels were held to be envy and pride, prideful
love of self and envy of God and, after the Fall, of Man (Augustine, *De Gen. ad. Lit.*, PL. 34,437). Cf. lines 22b, 25b,
30a, 32a, 47b, 51b, 54a, 66a, 69b, 70a.

   31b-34a Cf. the wording of Ælfric, *Exameron Anglice*, 55-
57: ". . . ac mid dyrstige modignysse cwæð þæt he wolde wyrcan
his cynesetl bufan Godes tunglum ofer ðæra wolcna heannysse on

ðam norðdæle and beon Gode gelic." The placement of Satan's
rebellion in the north goes back to Is. 14.13: "In caelum con-
scendam, super astra Dei exaltabo solium meum; sedebo in monte
testamenti, in lateribus Aquilonis . . . ." Cf. GB 275 and see
P. Salmon, "The Site of Lucifer's Throne," *Anglia* 81, 118-23;
T. D. Hill, "Some Remarks on the Site of Lucifer's Throne,"
Anglia 87, 303-11.

34b-91 The separation of the good and bad angels, corresponding to the separation of light from darkness, another
traditional topic (cf. *De ciu. Dei* XI, 19-20). In the poem
the bad angels are associated with darkness (56b-58a, 71, 72,
76, 86), the good with light (79, 89). The separation in the
proto-creation takes place with the provision of hell as an
abode for the fallen. The ultimate source is II Petr. 2.4:
"Si enim Deus angelis peccantibus non pepercit, sed rudentibus
inferni detractos in tartarum tradidit cruciandos, in judicium
reservari."

44-46 Groups of expanded "hypermetric" lines occur here
and at 155-57, 1015-19, 2168-70, 2328-29, 2406-07, 2411-12,
2855-59, 2866-69. Isolated expanded lines and hemistiches occur throughout the poem, e.g., 128b, 139, 873a, 913, 1172a,
1198a, 1230, 1255a, 1281a, 1320a, 1523a, 1819, 1911b-1912, 2174,
2532b-2533, 2783b. See Schmitz, *Anglia* 33, 1-76, esp. 28-32;
Bliss, *Metre of BW*, 88-97, 167.

50b-51 *honda arærde // hehste wið pam herge*. Most editors, following Grein, take *hehste* as fem. acc. with *honda*,
"raised his most powerful hand," except Holthausen, who reads
hehsta, nom. masc. with *waldend* 49b, "the almighty ruler raised
his hand." The former construction seems preferable, though
Wells suggests that the latter requires no emendation, as
hehste may be taken as a northern form of nom. masc. sing.
(Brunner 304, anm. 5; 276, anm. 6). Kock, *PPP.*, 10, suggests
hæste, "with violence."

60a *strengum stiepe*. Perhaps, "with a violent downward
motion." *Stiep* is taken as an otherwise unattested masc. related to Icel. *steyping* "overthrow," Norw. *stup* "precipice,"
OE. *ástipness* "bereavement," *steop-* (orig. meaning "deprived,"
now preserved only in cpds. such as "stepson") and in the verb
ástýpan "deprive." The root, with related meanings applying
to extremes of height, movement, brightness, etc., is well attested in the later language in adjectival form (cf. *OED.*, s.v.
steep[2]).

60b-61a "It (sc. *torn*?) had enraged the severe mind vio-
lently." *mod* is acc. with impers. or understood subject.

62b *him on fæðm gebræc* It is possible that *him* is either
reflex. sing. (sc. God), or dat. pl. object (sc. the bad angels).

63a *yr' on mode*. Holthausen and Krapp restore *yrre* but
the spelling may represent elision which should be preserved as
evidence of pronunciation; so Wells and cf. Hulbert, *JEGP* 37,
534. See lines 183a, 1957b, 2615b, also 117a *n*.

65a   *Sceop þa and scyrede*   "(our Creator) adjudged then
and separated out (the proud tribe of angels)."   Bouterwek,
followed by Holthausen and Krapp, reads *sceof*, but this is
clearly unwarranted.   *Sceop* in the sense "judge" occurs at
GN 903 and the formula *sceop and scyrede* in *Fortunes of Men*
95a, "the Savior destined and apportioned the talents of men
and brought their fates" *nergend . . . monna cræftas // sceop
and scyrede / and gesceapo ferede*.   Prof. R. Ringler has noted
to me the analogous *skera ok skapa* "divide and appoint" (i.e.,
decide the terms) in *Hrafnkel's Saga*, ed. E. V. Gordon, *Intro.
to ON.* (rev. ed.), 84, 834.   The expression in GN 65 employs
figura etymologica (so too *Fortunes* 95), by which God as both
Creator and   Judge is recalled.

71b-73a "They hovered dark (*or* darkly) in torment afterwards, had no need to laugh aloud on account of that journey."
The journey is the fall from Heaven to hell, cf. 68b.   Wülker
puts a period after *siðe*; Sievers, *Beiträge* 10, 512 and Holthausen put a colon after *swearte*; Cosijn, *Beiträge* 19, 444
finds the passage difficult and would read *heo on wrace seo-
modon // swearte siðe; / siððan ne þorftan*, etc.   Wells punctuates *siðe, ne*   translating, "They lay heavily for a dark
period, nor had cause to laugh aloud."

78-81   The restoration of peace in Heaven and the confir-
mation of the faithful angels.   Cf. *De ciu. Dei*, XII, 9 (CCSL
48, 364): ". . . si utrique boni aequaliter creati sunt, istis
mala uoluntate cadentibus illi amplius adiuti ad eam beatitu-
dinis plenitudinem, unde se nunquam casuros certissimi fierent,
peruenerunt. . . ."

80b-81 *þrymmas weoxon // duguða mid drihtne / dreamhæb-
bendra*.   "The glory of the hosts of the joyous ones increased
in God."   *Mid* may denote either association or instrumentality
(cf. B-T., s.v. *mid*, VI, VIII).

82b *buan*   Taken as equivalent to *buen*, opt., "those who
hope to inhabit."   Holthausen reads *budan = budon* and so Wells.
Krapp reads *buað*.   Hulbert, *JEGP* 37, 536, argues for the retention of *buan*, taking it as indicative because "the uses of
the indicative and optative in OE. are not sharply differentiated."

85a *herewosan*   Usually rendered "warrior(s)."   Holthausen relates the second element to *gewesan*, "strive," *Sol. &
Sat.* 181, itself a word of obscure derivation (cf. *Ae. Etymol.
Wörtb.*, s.v. *wesan²*, *gewesnes*).   Similarly, Marquardt, *Kenningar*, 242-43, links it with *gewesnes*, "discord," hence "rebel," a term which clearly fits Satan.   *Herewosa* occurs also
at DN 628, *herewosa hige*, referring to Nabuchodonosor's state
when "he did eat grass like an ox" (Daniel 4.30): here "rebel"
is strained.   B-T relates the second element to *gewésan* "soak,"
"steep," mod. Engl. *ooze*.   This fits the other *-wósa* cpd.,
ealo-wósa, "boozer," but leaves *herewosa* obscure: perhaps
"steeped in battle," "contentious," "hostile."

86b-91 Empty places are left in heaven by the fall of
the angels and their seats are *buendraleas*. This is the traditional reason given for the creation of man, to replace the
reprobate angels. Cf. Ælfric, *Exameron Anglice*, 57-58: "Ða
wolde God wyrcan ðurh his wundorlican mihte mannan of eorðan,
ðe mid eadmodnisse sceolde geearnian ðone ylcan stede on ðæra
engla geferrædene ðe se deofol forworhte mid his dyrstignysse."
Evans, *Paradise Lost and the Genesis Tradition*, 147-48, cen-
sures the poet's "tendency to reduce supernatural phenomena to
the level of mundane experience . . . [so that] the Church's
doctrine that man was created to replace the fallen angels was
taken . . . to mean that the defection of Satan . . . had literally left unsightly gaps in the heavenly ranks." But that
is just what Augustine says in his simpler exposition of the
faith: "Placuit itaque . . . deo ut . . . creatura rationalis,
quae in hominibus erat . . . ex eius parte reparata quod angelicae societati ruina illa diabolica minuerat suppleretur"
(*Enchiridion* 29 [CCSL 46, 65]).

92-111 The operation of the Logos. Having described the
creation and disposition of the intelligible creation outside
of time, and having concretely established the orthodox reason for the creation of Man, the poet goes on to the next topic of the hexameral tradition—and, following narrative logic,
the next stage of the creative act—the establishment of the
visible world through the operation of the Word. Robbins,
Hexaemeral Literature, 15-16, summarizes Origen's doctrine of
the Logos, which develops earlier thought and represents the
main tradition exclusive of Augustinian peculiarities: "Origen lays even more stress . . . upon the phase of the Word
called . . . *endiáthetos* [i.e., the stage of the divine thought
before utterance, the Logos before the creation]. The Word
or Wisdom contains all the forms (*species*) of things to be
created, whether substantial or accidental, and was itself
created prior to these. God's Wisdom never existed apart from
him. After Origen, the use of the terms Son, Word, and Wisdom,
equivalent to logos, persisted throughout the course of the
tradition." In GN, God *peahtode* (92) in his *modgeponc* (93)
how he would establish the *mæran gesceaft*. In Cædmon's *Hymn*,
modgeponc occurs in exactly the same context, rendered by
Bede *consilium*, the divine ideas which precede their visible
copies (see Bloomfield, "Patristics and Old English Literature," *Brodeur Studies*, 41-43). These ideas were externalized
as "heaven and earth" in the "beginning," "in principio," according to a traditional link-up of Genesis 1.1 and John 8.25
("[Ego sum] Principium qui et loquor vobis"). Creation was
further externalized and differentiated in the separate works
of the Days, although all were ideally contained in the original creative act, commonly held to have been referred to by
the first verse of Genesis (see note 141b-43a, the quotation

from Alcuin). The invisible ideas, patterns for the visible
creation, seem to be suggested by 97b-101, as the Word in-
wardly conceives Genesis 1.1 (cf. GN 112 ff., where 1.1 is
"uttered," *prophorikós*) and 103-06a, paralleling Genesis 1.2
(cf. GN 116b-19a). The ideas exist in the Logos, God contem-
plates the uncreated chaos (106b-111) and then "through the
Word" (111a), the temporal creation begins "in the beginning"
(*ǽrest*, 112a).

    98a *roderas feng* "Orb of the firmament." The expres-
sion merely denotes that the Logos is intending to create a
lower world. Technically, the firmament does not yet exist,
except in the Logos. *roderas* is gen. sing., cf. 148 and GB
485 *dreamas and drihtscipes*, DN 30 *eorðan dreamas*.

    99-100 The inclusion of *sidwǽter* seems a response to the
patristic question of whether the waters antedated the visible
creation, since they are not mentioned as being created in 1.1,
but exist in 1.2. The answer implied by the poet is the orthodox one, that "heaven and earth" includes all the elements
not mentioned separately in Genesis 1.1 and that water at this
point exists only in the Logos (cf. Eustathius, *In Hexaemeron
S. Basilii*, PL. 53,875A). For cpd. *sidwǽter*, see 1445a *n*.

    107a *stiðfrihþ = stiðferhð*; cf. GN 1406, 1683, also GB
241a *stiðferhð cyning*. See Intro., p. 33.

    110b-112 *oð þæt . . . þurh word . . . . her ǽrest ge-
sceop . . .* The poet moves from the operation in the Logos
to the operation through the Logos, as the visible creation
begins. The poet plays on the identity, frequently mentioned
in the commentaries, of the words "in the beginning" and "the
Word" (cf. 92-111 *n*.). By dealing with the traditional Christ-
ological explanation "in principio" in his exordium, at 112
the poet is free to take up the paraphrase in a literal manner, without slighting the traditional meaning or becoming
excessively complex. Cf. Ælfric, *Exameron Anglice*, 37: "On
anginne gesceop se ælmihtiga fæder ðysne middangeard, swa swa
Moyses awrát, and ðæt angin is ðæs ælmihtigan Godes sunu on
gæstlicum andgite, swa swa ðæt godspell us segð . . . *Ego
principium qui et loquor vobis.*" Bede, *In Gen.*, CCSL 118A, 8,
following Augustine *De Gen. contra Manichaeum* I, 9, 15, explains how the same meaning is necessary for a proper understanding of the operations of God: "Quod autem dixisse Deus,
siue ut lux fieret siue ut alia quaeque, perhibetur, non nos-
tro more per sonum uocis corporeum fecisse credendus est, sed
altius intellegendum dixisse Deum ut fieret creatura, quia per
uerbum suum omnia, id est per unigenitum filium fecit." Note
that the Word appears in the works of each day (cf. GN 130,
149, 158).

    114a *rodor* In apposition with *heofon* ("caelum"), this
glosses the idea that it is not the eternal heaven which is
referred to, but the created, visible firmament.

    116b-119a These lines paraphrase 1.2 with elaborate cir-

cumlocution, partly, no doubt, a reflection of the fact that
1.2 has already been rendered more literally by 103-06a. Its
second appearance is an opportunity to suggest more than the
literal meaning. Most commonly, the verse was referred to the
lightless ignorance of those uninstructed in the faith: thus,
"Inanis autem erat terra, quando non fuit qui habitaret, et
incomposita, nondum a mari distincta. Spiritualiter autem
terra, id est caro nostra, erat inanis et vacua, prius quam
doctrinae acciperet formam" (Ps.-Bede, *In Pent. Comm.*, PL. 91,
192-93). Earth alone is mentioned in 1.2, according to Bede,
because "emptiness and void" applies not to heaven (not the
visible heaven but that inaccessible to the sight of mortals)
which is eternally stable and "shaped," but to the as yet form-
less matter called "earth" (*In Gen.*, CCSL 118A, 4). The world,
drihtne fremde (105b), did not gain its form until it was
lighted (*ibid.*, 6). The mention of "grass" or its absence,
is in accord with the commentaries, which frequently mention
at this point that nothing growing was yet apparent (as Bede,
In Gen., CCSL 118A, 4).

     116b-117a *folde wæs pa gyta // græsungrene.* "The earth
was still not grass-green." 117a is a 2A1 type. Cpd. "grass-
green" appears in the *Epinal Gloss* 298, *gresgro(e)ni* "carpas-
sini." The other edd. print *græs ungrene*, but difficulties
are involved. *græs* may be taken as inst. sing. with elision
before the vowel: "The earth was still ungreen with grass."
Hence Bouterwek and Holthausen suggest *græse.* Grein, *Sprch.*
I, 623 suggests *græs* is "instr. acc." Krapp takes *græs* as nom.
sing. parallel to *folde*: "The earth, the grass, was still un-
green." This makes for pale sense as well as pale grass
since the point is that earth has not yet put forth any living thing.

     117b-119a "Black perpetual darkness covered the sea
everywhere [*side and wide*], (covered) the dark waves." At
104b "abyssi" is literally rendered by *grund*, here by *garsecg.*
The identification of "sea" and "abyss" was established: "Abyssi autem qui est intellectus, aqua nimia infinitum habens
profundum" (Eustathius, *In Hexaemeron S. Basilii*, PL. 53,
883C). The formula *wonne wægas* here has full semantic force:
the unformed *hyle*, "sea/earth/abyss" participates in the darkness of chaos. Is *wægas* (MS wegas) intended as a pun here,
suggesting the spiritual interpretation of the verse? Cf.
2933a *n.*

     121b-123a *metod engla heht . . . leoht forð cuman . . .*
This paraphrase of 1.3 recalls the common explanation of the
verse that the creation of light signified the creation of
the angels (cf. Augustine, *De ciu. Dei* XI, 9).

     123b-124a *rape wæs gefylled // heahcininges hæs.* Cf.
Bede (*In Gen.*, CCSL 118A, 3): ". . . tanta celeritate opera-
tionis omnipotentem esse declarat cui uoluisse fecisse est;"
also 121a.

124b *him* Instr., "by him,""by his agency."

128b-131a *sceop pa bam naman . . . . gesceaft.* Though
formulaic (cf. GN 140, BW 78, EX 381, etc.) the expression also suggests the Augustinian doctrine that the thing was created through the Word by the very act of conceiving (naming)
it; cf. *De Gen. ad Lit.* I, 10, 18-20.

131a *gesceaft* Normalized by edd. (except Junius, Kluge,
Wülker) to *gesceaft*, but the MS form may be kept as an example of 11th century pronunciation, looking forward to its
ME. monophthongized form, Brunner, *Outline of ME. Grammar*, par.
10 (B). See Intro., p. 31.

132b *forpbæro tid,* "Time of production," "creative
moment." *forpbæro* may be either an indecl. f. ó-stem or an
adj. Cosijn, *Beiträge* 19, 445, explains as adj. "zum Vor-
schein gekommen," "entstanden," comparing OHG *frambári*, mod.
Dut. *vórbáre.*

134a *swiðrian* Either *swiðrian* ("increase") or *swiðrian*
("decrease") could be understood here, on the grounds that
shadows increase and deepen as light increases, or that shadows disappear as light dispels them. Thorpe, Bouterwek, Greverus choose the former, Grein, Wülker, Holthausen, Braasch,
Wells the latter. The second is probably the more obvious and
idiomatic meaning, light and darkness being regarded as direct
opposites. The orthodox idea, stemming from Basil, was that
before the creation of the sun and moon, the substance of
light was put forth and drawn back by God to make the morning
and evening of each day, this apparently being what is
expressed here (cf. Eustathius, *In Hexaemeron S. Basilii* III,
7; also *Paradise Lost* VI, 4 ff.).

135b *ofer tiber sceacan* Hickes and Lye read *tibersceа-
can*, and so Thorpe. Hickes explained as *"superficies* vel *plan-
ities terrae,"* suggesting that perhaps *tibersceata* ought to be
read. Thorpe expressed doubt about the word. Ettmüller, *Lex.,*
524, construed as "super fructum terrae," Grimm, *Deut. Myth.,*
25, translates "da die zeit fortschritt über die (von Gott
verliehene) gabe die erde." Bouterwek offers "gebäu der mit-
telerde" and suggests emending to *timber*; so Dietrich, *ZfdA* 10,
and all subsequent edd. *sceacan* must be an inf. "hurry off"
with *gewat.* *timber* is a plausible emendation (cf. 146 *heofon-
timber*, "firmamentum"), while *tiber*, "sacrifice," "offering,"
"gift," is obviously strained. But the form has a genuine
ring. The verb *teofrian* (with back-umlaut of the *-i-* of the
root [Campbell, par. 755]) occurs in a similar context in *Paris Psalter* 117.21: "Þone sylfan stan / þe hine swyðe ær //
wyrhtan awurpan, / nu se geworden is // hwommona heagost;/
halig dryhten // to wealles wraðe / wis *teofrade*; / þæt is
urum eagum / eall wundorlic" = *Lapidem quem reprobaverunt æd-
ificantes, hic factus est in caput anguli* ("The same stone
which the builders cast away now has become the highest of cor-
nerstones; the holy Lord, wise, *teofrade* it as the support of

the wall . . . ." B-T defines as "to appoint," "allot," but
perhaps the sense "build," "set up," is better. In *Ruin* 30,
teaforgeap (or *-geapa?*) seems to refer to some part of the
structure, covered with tiles; Mackie (cf. Dobbie's note, ASPR
III) glosses as "arch of red stone." Cf. *tēafor* "red paint,"
ātīefran "to paint," OHG *zoubar* "magic writing," Icel. *taufr*
"sorcery" (runic magic?), dial. English *tiver* "red coloring,"
"tar mixture." The MS *tiber* may represent an otherwise unrecorded *tīfer* "magically erected structure." For the form see
Campbell par. 57 (1) and note 3.

141b-143a *siððan æfre // drugon and dydon / drihtnes
willan* . . . Not a naive comment, but indicating the distinction between the creation of the Six Days, when things were
first set in order, and God's ministry since, when everything
keeps to that order. Cf. 158b-160a and Alcuin, *Interrogationes et responsiones in Genesin*, as translated by Ælfric: "þæt
ðridde [way that God created] wæs þaþa god todælde mislice
gesceafta on þære syx daga gesceapennysse; þæt feorþe is þæt
god gescipð symle edniwan of þa ærran; þæt hi ne steorian
[i.e., so that from that pattern they do not move] (Ælfric's
version edited by G. E. MacLean, *Anglia* 7, 10 = *Int. res. Gen.*,
PL. 100, 519A)

142a *dydon* Sievers, *Beiträge*, 10, 498, would lengthen to
dēdon, regarding the shortness of *dydon* as a sign of revision
of a North. archetype. Holthausen reads *dēdon*. The length-
ened pret. occurs in GN only at 2804a.

146b-153 The creation of the Firmament. The poet follows the text closely and it is difficult to tell what exactly
his conception of the firmament was. It is raised up from the
earth (148b-49a), lifting a portion of the water with it, and
it is a structure. Perhaps the poet conceives it as a roof,
vaulted on the inside and flat on the outside, like Basil's.
roderas fæsten perhaps indicates an icy or crystalline composition, but that idea had passed out of fashion after Basil:
most later comment merely notes that the firmament was "firm"
only relatively, compared to the spiritual world beyond. Augustine says that it formed an impassible barrier between the
world of matter and the world of spirit. His famous comment
tended to quash speculation on the matter: "Quoquo modo autem
et qualeslibet aquae ibi sint, esse eas ibi minime dubitemus;
major est quippe Scripturae hujus auctoritas, quam omnis humani ingenii capacitas" (*De Gen. ad lit.* II 5, 9 [PL. 34, 267]).
See Robbins, *Hexaemeral Literature*, 49-50, 69, 80-81. Ælfric's
idea of the firmament is marked by motion, rather than firm-
ness: "On ðam oðrum dæge ure drihten geworhte ðone firmamentum
ðe men hatað rodor, se belycð on his bosme ealle eorðan brad-
nysse and binnan him is gelogod eal ðes middangeard, and he æ-
fre gæð abutan swa swa yrnende hweowol and he næfre ne stent
stille on anum . . . (*Exameron Anglice*, 45-46).

163b-166a *geseah þa lifes weard // drige stowe . . .eorðan nemde.* The response to 1.9, "et appareat arida," is combined with the Vetus Latina (LXX) reading of 1.2: "terra autem erat invisibilis et incomposita," often explained in connection with 1.9; cf. *Exameron Anglice*, 46: "Seo eorðe wæs æt fruman eall ungesewenlic, for ðam ðe heo eall wæs mid yðum oferðeht." Similarly Eustathius, *In Hexaemeron S. Basilii* II, 4, and Augustine, *De Gen. contra Manichaeum* I, 12, 18.

167a *ónrihtne rýne,* The alliteration is retarded to the second stress. Holthausen reads *ryne onrihtne.*

173b *tiode* From *teon, tion* II, "produce," "create," possibly an Angl. (North.) form (cf. HY 8, *tiadæ*), or poetic, but more likely eWS survival; see Intro., p. 29.

176-191 The creation of Eve, following 2.18-22 and 1.27. This episode is greatly augmented by traditional material of the most eclectic sorts. **176-183a** It was a commonplace question whether Adam had felt any pain when God extracted the rib (cf. Augustine, *De Gen. ad lit.* IX, 15, 26). Jerome had intimated the answer by defining Adam's sleep as no ordinary one, but "grauem et profundem soporem" (*Quaest. heb. in Gen.*, CCSL 72, 4). The specifically "soft" sleep (179a) was well established, as in Hrabanus, *Alleg. in Sac. Scrip.* (PL. 112, 886D): "*caro*, mollities, ut in Genesi: 'Tulit unam de costis ejus, et replevit carnem pro ea,' quod robur Dominus nonnunquam a nobis aufert, et mollitiem in nobis esse permittit." The idea had already been expressed poetically by Cyprianus Gallus: "Metitur solum mordaces uoluere curas, / Ilicet irriguo perfundit lumina somno, / Mollius ut uulsa formetur femina costa" (*Heptateuchos* I, 33-35 [PL. 19, 347A]). **181b** *brego engla* this epithet suggests the common question, whether the angels were agents in the creation of Eve, which arose in Jewish exegesis as an attempt to deal with the plural verb of 2.18. Christian commentators discussed this frequently, usually negatively or allegorically (cf. Ps.-Bede, *De sex dierum creatione*, PL. 93, 227-28), but positively by the Comestor (*Hist. Schol.* I, 17 [PL. 198, 1070B]). Cf. GN 121 *n.* **184b-185a** The creation of Eve verbally parallels the creation of Adam, 2.7, although unfortunately the paraphrase of 2.7 is missing due to the lacuna between P. 8 and P. 9 of the MS. The separate inbreathing of the individual soul of Eve suggests the common hexameral topic of the separate creation of each individual soul often introduced in conjunction with the creation of Eve. Augustine devotes Book Ten of *De Genesi ad litteram* to this topic in relation to Genesis 2: "Si enim propterea putant animam mulieris ex anima viri factam, quia non scriptum est quod in mulieris faciem flaverit Deus; cur credunt ex viro animatam feminam, quando ne id quidem scriptum est?" (X, 1,2 [PL. 34, 408-09]). The poet indicates the proper response and cuts through the doctrinal complexities by simply repeating the inbreathing of the soul in his narrative of the creation of Eve,

as if the processes of 2.7 and 2.22 were identical; cf. 1000b-
1001.   **185b-187a** *heo wæron englum gelice* . . .   Bede stresses
the angelic potential of unfallen man, who would have assumed
"similitudinem angelicae" if he had persevered in virtue (*In
Gen.* CCSL 118A, 30-31) and the Book of the Secrets of Enoch
(ed. Charles, II, 449 ff.) calls Adam "a second angel." That
the poet has some such idea in mind for 1.27 is made probable
by his rendering of 9.6 (cf. 1528b-31).   **187b-189a** The age of
Adam and Eve at the time of their creation was *on geogoðe*: according to Augustine, Adam was created a full-grown man and
in the prime of youth (*De Gen. ad lit.* VI, 13, 23).   The rabbinical tradition, going back to the Babylonian Talmud, stresses the beauty of both Adam and Eve (Ginzberg, I 60 and V, 80,
n. 24), but the poet minimizes this topic as does the Western
exegetical tradition, though it is a favorite subject for elaboration by the neo-classical Christian poets.   Eve is called
freolicu (184a) and *wlitebeorht* (188a) but both of these are
formulaic, carrying a light semantic burden.   Even after the
Fall, Eve is still *freolicu* (895, 998).   The poet is more orthodox in stressing that their beauty is spiritual, the element "in God's image," *gasta gegearwod* (187a) but this phrase
is also formulaic (cf. e.g. EL 888).   **189b-191** The beauty and
moral perfection of Adam and Eve are marred by nothing.   Ælfric's version of Alcuin's *Interrogationes* stresses that the
beauty of the creation, being for the benefit of man, places a
joyful obligation on him, and is a reminder of his duty to
praise God (*Anglia* 7, 20 = *Int. in Gen.* 41).   Augustine greatly
elaborates this idea, making Adam and Eve's love for God the
cause of their perfect joy: their avoidance of sin was tranquil
and so long as it was maintained, no other ill could invade
them and bring sorrow (*De ciu. Dei* XIV, 10; 26).

   183a *wer unwundod.* Wells, following Kock *PPP.* 11, takes
wer as dat. sing. with elision and *unwundod* as uninflec. dat.
adj. This can be accepted, although it may be preferable to
go back to Thorpe's explanation of an absolute (nom. or acc.?)
expression. Grein explains as acc. absol. with uninflec. part.
comparing GU 1040, *sorg geswedrad.*

   185a *saula* This, the form the scribe wrote first, may be
explained as an early Kentish feature (Campbell, par. 587), but
is more likely a reflection of late, uncertain orthography.   In
any case, the form *saulae*, printed by Kluge and Holthausen,
cannot be justified, since the corrector intended to obliterate
the irregular -*a*, by altering to -*e*, not -*ae*.

   185b-186 The faulty scansion of 185b and the isolated
hemistich of 186 suggest corruption. There is no gap in the
sense, however.

   201b-205a "Into your control is the clean beast and the
wild beast given, and the living things which walk the land
(and) the burgeoning species which the water brings forth
throughout the sea." Apparently the poet has anticipated the

distinction of clean and unclean animals from Genesis 7.2-3
(cf. GN 1335-38). B-T *Supp.* s.v. *halig* A, VI gives "tame"
for this occurrence, though "consecrated" is better attested
and gets at a clear sense, animals fit and unfit for sacrifice.
Could it be that the poet, like Milton, is making a distinction between the meanings of words before and after the Fall?

205b For a discussion of the leaves missing after this
line, see Intro., pp. 5-9, *passim*.

209a *god and gastlic,* Most edd. take as *gæstlic* "hos-
pitable" and so Greverus and Holthausen print. But there is
no reason not to take it as *gástlic* "spiritual," especially
when the rest of the sentence is considered: "filled with the
eternal benefits of grace(s)." Cf. the Augustinian formula
"bonus et spiritualus."

210b-217 The description of the plants and waters of
Paradise is rearranged to suggest that the plants, which
sprang up before there was any rain to water them or man to
tend them, depended on the waters of Paradise, verses 2.6,
2.5, 2.10 being dealt with in that order. The poet is here
following the traditional idea of the relation of these verses
to one another. What is implied by selection and reordering
the Jewish tradition made explicit: "But it was only during
the days of the creation that the realm of the plants looked
to the waters of the earth for nourishment. Later on God made
the plants dependent on the rain, the upper waters" (Ginzberg,
I, 70). Augustine reflects a similar idea (*De Gen. ad lit.*
V, 7, 21-22) while Bede is most elaborate and specific in his
rearrangement to make a satisfactory sequence of meaning, suggesting the order 2.6, 2.5, 2.10 (*In Gen.*, CCSL 118A, 42-43).
Later, when dealing with 2.10 in its biblical order according
to the procedure of his commentary, he makes a cross-reference
to his earlier treatment of 2.5-6 (*ibid.*, 48). It should be
noticed that this treatment not only makes the matter clearer,
but allows 2.7, the creation of Man, to stand alone in higher
relief (though in GN the part corresponding to 2.7 is lost in
the lacuna after 168).

210b *leohte* From *leccan* "water," cf. 1923a.

218a *adælte* The scribe appears to have written *adælte*,
though this is not certain, since the space between the *t* and
e is wider than normal and somewhat rubbed. I follow Wells in
admitting *adælte* rather than the corrector's *adælede*, as genuine unvoicing. Cf. *genearwot,* 2604, a corrector's *gesetet*
at 100b, *metot* GB 459. See Brook, "The Relation between the
Textual and the Linguistic Study of OE.," 286.

221-224a A difficult sentence, partly because it tempts
one to see geographical references more precise than are probably intended: e.g., may *sæfoldan dæl* refer to the legendary
salt marshes at the mouth of the Ganges (traditionally identical to Phison). So the earlier edd. (e.g., Thorpe, "the mar-
ine parts"). But the poet is probably following the twists of

the Vulgate as closely as his language will allow. To make
sense of the passage some corruption must be assumed. The
difficult *pære* is most simply resolved as *pæne* (= *pone*), object of *hatað*, antecedent of *sæ* (= *se*) (cf. 2645 *pæne*: MS
pære; 1522 *pæra*: MS *pære*; 1398 *sæ = se*; 986 *pæs = pes*). Dietrich, *ZfdA* 10, 313, Grein, Wülker, Krapp assuming haplography read *pær[a ann]e hatað ylde* to render "nomen uni;" Wells
reads *þ[a] ære[ste]*, but this implies two mistakes. Wells
reads *seo* for *sæ/se* to make Phison the same gender as the
other rivers.

    224b *hebeleat, utan,* The MS *hebeleac utan* disguises the
name *Euilat, Evilath.* Earlier edd. understood *he beleac utan*
("he shut it out," Thorpe). Wülker notes Ælfric's form *Euilað*
but follows the MS, as do Krapp and Wells. Holthausen reads
Hebeleað. Hebeleat is possibly close to the MS form the poet
had before him, assuming a scribe misread *t* as *c.*

    227b *pæs þe us secgað bec.* A series of formulas, based
on the more familiar *ic gefrægn* theme, the poet learning from
oral sources, here presenting the poet as *bocere*, learning
his narrative from books. It is probably designed to give the
poem more authority, and no doubt reflects the poet's consciousness of the poem's "learned" nature, where the traditions
are mostly written. "Book" formulas occur mainly in the first
half of the poem (227, 969, 1239, 1723, 2612f.). The *gefrægn*
formulas begin in the second half (1960, 2060, 2244, 2484,
2542) where the material is less varied in origin; once the
poet betrays more than a formulaic interest in himself as *scop*,
2013b-17.

    231b-232 "It surrounds (*wið . . . belið*) the nation (acc.
or dat.?) (of) Assyria (acc. or gen.?)." The ambiguity of cases does not obscure the meaning.

    232a *ea inflede* An original **inflôdi* (*in-* intensive) is
assumed. The same expression occurs at AN 1504, of a killing
flood. Here it must refer to the fullness of the river. The
condition of the river Tigris is a traditional topic. Its Hebrew name, *Hiddekel*, was interpreted in the Babylonian Talmud
as "sharp" (*had*) and "swift" (*kal*) (cf. Mirsky, *English Studies* 48, 388). A similar interpretation turns up in Strabo
("arrow-swift") (*Geography* II, 14, 8 [Loeb Strabo V, 329]),
in Pliny (*Nat. Hist.* VI, 127-28 [Loeb Pliny II, 434-37]) and
in Isidore, who quaintly finds a parallel between Tigris and
Tiger: "Tigris fluvius Mesopotamiae de Paradiso exoriens et
pergens contra Assyrios, et post multos circuitus in mare Mor-
tuum influens. Vocatus autem hoc nomine propter velocitatem,
instar bestiae tigris nimia pernicitate currentis" (*Etymolo-
gies*, ed. Lindsay, XIII, 21,9; cf. XII 2, 7).

    234-852 After line 234, the last on P. 12, there is a
loss of several leaves. Page 13 begins at the top in mid
sentence *ac niotaþ inc þæs oðres ealles*, etc. This is the
beginning of the interpolated fragment known as *Genesis B*. It

is of distinct origin, being a translation into West-Saxon of
a low-German (Old Saxon) poem on the Fall of the angels and
the Fall of man. It is generally assumed to be of the mid-
ninth century, post-Alfredian in its English form, hence much
later than our poem. For an account of the nature of *Genesis
B* and its discovery, see B. Timmer, *The Later Genesis*, 48-50,
on its MS connections with GN, see Intro. pp. 7, n. 12, and 8-10.
In its own way, *Genesis B* freely covers the material of Genesis 3.1-7. The part of *Genesis A* corresponding to these verses is no longer extant. The insertion of *Genesis B* occurred
in a recension earlier than the Junius MS, as is shown by the
intermittent, but correct, section numbering spanning *Genesis
A* and *Genesis B* (see Intro., p. 12.).

855-856 It is implied that "our savior," the "merciful
father," knew of Adam's sin and anticipated the discovery of
it in his asking. This is an attempt to deal with the difficult question, perennially bothering exegetes, why would
God have to ask Adam what he had done? The standard answer
had been given by Theophilus (*Ad Autolychum* II, 26 [PG. 6,
1094B]), which followed the rabbinical explanation that God
did not ask Adam where he was out of ignorance, but because he
wanted to offer him an opportunity to repent. This is taken
over by the Latin tradition and is explained in terms of God's
mercy: God does not wish those who fall away from faith or
good works into lies to perish in mortal sin, but calls them
back so that they may be changed and live (cf. Isidore, *Quaest.
de vet. et nouo Test.*, I, 5, 3 [PL. 83, 220C]).

856b *hwæt his bearn dyde.* Krapp says *dyde* is for *dyden*,
i.e., subjunctive pl. Holthausen reads *dyden*. For subj. pls.
in -*e*, see 1587a. But it is possible to take *bearn* as sing.,
referring to Adam alone, as in 3.8 itself ("abscondit") and
3.9, where only Adam is addressed. The doctrine on this point
supports the singular, for the Fall of Man took place when
Adam sinned, not because Adam and Eve sinned together. A similar sing. reading occurs at 954b giving rise to the same
problem if the standard emendation is accepted there.

857b *pa he ær wlite sealde.* Bouterwek and Grein suggest
pam for *pa* to provide a dat. object for *sealde*; so Holthausen,
Krapp and Wells. But the clause may be taken absolutely:
"(God) knew those he had given glory had sinned." See BW 1161
for *sellan* without a dat. object, and cf. B-T s.v. *sellan* V
(c) (2).

860-863 The impending judgement of Adam and Eve recalls
the Last Judgement and Creation, the whole scope of divine history. For the diction, cf. CH 918-29, DR 103b-121, and esp.
the opening of *Judgement Day II*: "Ic ana sæt / innan bearwe,
// mid helme bepeht, / holte tomiddes," etc. to line 20.

863a *weard ahsian* Klaeber, Holthausen and Wells take
weard as acc., object of *ongann . . . ahsian*, referring to
Adam, "guard of creation," but Kock, *PPP.* 15, takes *weard* as
nom., appositive to *aldor*. Either is possible, but perhaps
the poet intended both, since God did ask about his creation,

and he did call its guardian to account.

869-871a Adam's reply to God here and in 883-86 is mit-
igated by his immediate admission of guilt. He does not simply attempt to cover himself by pointing to the guilt of the
woman, but confesses immediately. The orthodox position did
not admit such a softening: "Sed est peior damnabiliorque superbia, qua etiam in peccatis manifestis suffugium excusatio-
nis inquiritur . . . . Nam licet isti non sicut Cain quod
commiserunt negent, adhuc tamen superbia in aliud quaerit re-
ferre quod perperam fecit: superbia mulieris in serpentem,
superbia uiri in mulierem. Sed accusatio potius quam excus-
atio uera est, ubi mandati diuini est aperta transgressio....
quasi quicquam Deo, cui uel crederetur uel cederetur, ante
ponendum fuit" (Augustine, *De ciu. Dei* XIV, 14 [CCSL 48, 436]).
Similarly, Eve admits her sin (897-902) and in doing so begins
to repair it. Perhaps the poet merely wishes to make their
guilt more unmistakeably clear than it is in the literal text,
or perhaps he shows a genuine "semi-Pelagian" tendency in his
view of the Fall (see Evans, *Paradise Lost and the Genesis
Tradition*, 166).

869-870a *scyldfull mine, / sceaðen, is me sare // frecne
on ferhðe,* "A guilty, injured conscience is grievously dangerous to me in spirit." This follows Krapp's suggestion that
mine be taken as masc. "mind," but the sentence remains difficult. *sceaðen* is taken as past part. of *sceððan*, modifying
mine, parallel to *scyldfull*. Krapp takes *sceaðen* as a noun,
"A guilty conscience is to me, a sinner (*sceaðen*), grievous,
oppressive in spirit," but this is doubtful, for why is not
sceaðen then inflected and mutated as a dat. fem. ó-stem in
-en, and what case is *sare* as adj.? Rather, *sare* is best
taken as an adv. Klaeber emends *sceaðen* to *sceande* "disgrace,"
taken with *mine* poss. pron., the simplest emendation proposed
if one be called for. Less satisfactory is Ettmüller's insertion of *sceame* after *mine*, though accepted by Grein, Holthausen and Wells. Holthausen, ed. and *Englische Studien* 37, 203,
proposes reading simply *scyldfull sceame*. For the collocation
of this line cf. 1302a.

870b *forðgan* The quasi-advbl. prefix receives the
stress (see Campbell, par. 78). Contrast 2356, where the separation is preferable to make the line metrically heavier.

871b *ic eom eall eall nacod.* All edd. except Junius and
Krapp omit one *eall* (Klaeber only reports one). Probably this
is correct (though dittography is rare with this scribe, occurring only at GN 2721, EX 146, DN 327), but the line is too
effective as it stands to change.

874b-876a All editors, following Dietrich, *ZfdA* 10, 318,
insert *ne* before *anfenge* and place a stop after *eallum*: "You
received moreover no shame from me, but joy in everything."
But *ne* is not necessary if the sentence is allowed to carry
on. Adapting Thorpe, one may translate: "You took shame in

my presence immediately, but amidst every joy why do you know sorrow . . ."

877a *gesyhst sorge* Generally taken as "you see sorrow," but Krapp suggests that it = *gesicst sorge* "you sigh in sorrow."

880b *byrgde* The corrector's *byrgdest* is followed by all edd. exept Junius, Klaeber, Krapp, who take *byrgde* as subj. following "nisi quod . . . comedisti."

885b-886a Pretty clearly a reference to the "new motion of the flesh" which assailed man after his first disobedience, noticed only when man's "eyes were opened" to sin: "Patebant ergo oculi eorum, sed ad hoc non erant aperti, hoc est non adtenti, ut cognoscerent quid eis indumento gratiae praestaretur, quando membra eorum uoluntati repugnare nesciebant. Qua gratia remota, ut poena reciproca inoboedientia plecteretur, extitit in motu corporis, quaedam inpudens nouitas, unde esset indecens nuditas, et fecit adtentos reddiditque confusos" (Augustine, *De ciu. Dei* XVI, 17 [CCSL 48, 439-40]).

888-890a *hwæt druge þu . . . dugeþa genohra . . . gifa* "What did you do, daughter, respecting the sufficient blessings of the new creation of Paradise of growing gifts [or: respecting growing gifts]." The torrent of genitives is remarkable and allows a variety of interpretations, either as parallel or dependent in a stepped-down series. Holthausen reads *Hwæt druge þu, dohtor? / Dugeþa [wæs] genohra,* etc., taking *dugeþa* as a part. gen. (citing Shipley, 94), "There was enough of blessings," etc. Bright takes *dugeþa genohra* as gen. qualifying *þu* (following Shipley, 87): "What didst thou do, daughter, thou of [i.e., endowed with] the abundant blessings." Krapp, following B-T, s.v. *genog*, translates: "What madest thou, daughter, of the abundant blessings . . . when," etc.; but this seems like sleight-of-hand and assumes that *dreogan* may take acc. and gen. objects, a construction for which I can find no parallel (in *hwæt þær man dreoge wordes oððe weorces* [B-T *Supp.*, s.v. *dreogan* I] the gens. are advbl.).

892b *and me on teonan* An a2-type in the off-verse. Edd. emend this and others like it in the off-verse on the grounds that a-types can occur only in the on-verse. But in fact verses of this type occur in the off-verse frequently in GN: cf. 1638b, 1813b, 1876b, 1964b, 2057b, 2149b, 2323b, 2538b, 2613b, 2625b, 2647b, 2790b.

894a *wæstme* Acc. pl., as also at 990a.

898a *scyhte* "Prompted," "instigated;" cf. GU 127 *Oþer hyne scyhte, / þæt he sceaðena gemot // nihtes sohte . . . .* It is not clear whether the pres. stem is **scyccan* (cf. OE. *scucca* "devil," Icel. *skykkjum*, dat. pl., "jerkily") or **scyhtan* (cf. middle Dutch *schüchteren*, "frighten away," Germ. *schüchtern*, "shy") or *scyan* "suggest" (the usual pret. is *scyde*; see Campbell, par. 237. 1 (c) *n.* 3; cf. *scyhend*, "pursuer").

899a *fah wyrm purh fægir word* Klaeber takes *fah wyrm* as
"variegated serpent," citing HL 1877 *the gelouua uurm, / nadra
thiu feha*. The poet is drawing on the tradition of the beautiful serpent, with *fah* and *fægir* concatenating ironically,
for probably a pun on *fah* "accursed" is intended. Cf. Hrabanus, *De universo*, PL. 111, 229C: "Serpentes autem reptilia
sunt, quia pectore et ventre reptant, quorum tot venera quot
genera, tot pernicies quot species, tot dolores quot colores
habentur." By his reference to the "glistening"/"cursed" serpent the poet perhaps recalls, via a formulaic "dragon" nexus
(cf. BW 2576 *gryrefahne*), the enemy, the "old dragon." Krapp
compares the spelling *fægir* to *twegin*, GB 460.

899b-900a *ic fracoðlice // freondræs gefremede*, ". . . I
wickedly furthered the attack of the enemy." Eve is part of
the serpent's plan for accomplishing the Fall, but her act
does not constitute the Fall itself, nor is it identical to
the attack by the devil on Adam. For *feondræs* Bouterwek, Erläut. 304, suggested *feondræd*; Cosijn, *Beiträge* 19, 447,
feondes ræd; Holthausen conjectured that it might stand for
feondræswe (meaning the same thing), presumably on the basis
of AZ 126 *meotudes ræswum* "by the Lord's counsels (?)," B-T and
Clark-Hall inferring a nom. fem. *ræs* "counsel," "deliberation."

903a *sceop* "Adjudged," cf. 65a.

904b-905a *fagum wyrme // wide siðas* "(Our Savior adjudged against the serpent) far journeys for the doomed worm."
Acc. of the thing, dat. of the person judged. The play on *fah*
(see 899a *n.*) has receded, or rather, the emergence of the one
meaning over the other is itself the effect of the curse a-
gainst the serpent, no longer beautiful, only cursed. The
poet phrases the curse quite naturally in formulaic exile terms.

906a *wideferhð* The notion that the serpent is cursed
forever is a natural inference from "cunctis diebus vitae
tuae," but Bede still feels it necessary to explain the verse
as meaning "for all eternity" (*In Gen.*, CCSL 118A, 66), while
Isidore takes it to mean "ante illam ultimam poenam judicii"
(*Quaest. vet. test.*, PL. 83, 221A), which seems to be the idea
suggested by 915b-916a *a penden standeð // woruld under wolcnum*.

906b-907 *werg, pinum breostum, // bearme tredan / brade
eorðan,* "You must forever, accursed, on your breast, on your
belly, tread broad earth." The pointing fails and another
hand has added a point after *pinum*. Many problems arise here:
line division, the length of 906b and 907a, depending on how
they are divided, the grammar of *bearm* and *brade*, both of
which cannot be right as they stand. Klaeber, Holthausen,
Krapp and Wells divide and read: *pu scealt wideferhð, / werig,
pinum // breostum bearm tredan / bradre eorðan* "You must forever, weary, on your breast tread the bosom of broad earth."
There has been some interference with *werg* in the MS, the *g*
standing over an erasure, but it appears that *werg* is the
scribe's final intention, and it makes perfectly good sense

(Klaeber, in the Supp. to his ed., approves *werg*). As the later edd. divide the line, *werg pinum* is too short, hence *werig*
to bring it up to four syllables, but taking *bearm* as acc. requires altering *brade* to fem. gen. sing. By dividing *breostum*
// *bearm*, following the earlier edd. and Kock, *JJJ*. 29, 907a
becomes too short, but an appositive to *breostum* seems required anyhow, and *bearm*e fills the line, with its strong caesura.
Kock points out similar rhythm in 2097a, 2376a, 2652a. Alternatively, a more regular type could be achieved by reading *on
bearm tredan* (2C2) "creeping along on (your) belly [acc.] (you
must) tread," etc.

   908a *faran feðeleas* Apparently a reference to the an-
thropomorphic serpent of Jewish legend, which was supposed to
have been created with feet (and hands) and lost them at the
time it was cursed (cf. Jubilees 3.23 and Ginzberg I, 40, 78;
V, 101, *n*. 84). This natural extrapolation from "super pectus
tuum gradieris" is not prominent in the Latin tradition, though
the Pentateuchal Commentator knew of it, perhaps from a Jewish
source, to judge by his diffident tone: "Serpens enim pedibus
ante hoc ambulare dicitur, quod affirmare non audeo" (PL. 91,
213C). On P. 41 of the Junius MS the illustrator shows the
serpent receiving the curse standing upright and then slinking
away on its belly.

   914b *tuddor* Etmüller would emend to *tuddre*, and so Klaeber and Holthausen print, but the latter in his note explains
tuddor as "probably an old consonantal dative" (i.e., an old
-os stem), referring to *Rune Poem* 52 *butan tudder* and GN 1613
tuddor gefylled. See Brunner, par. 289.2, anm. 6 and Campbell,
par. 636.

   931b-932a Cf. 910b-911a.

   934b-935a *wegan swatighleor* // *þinne hlaf etan* I take
swatighleor as a compound with Dietrich, *ZfdA* 10, 319, Grein,
Wülker, Kock, *JJJ*. 29, responding to "in sudore vultus," cf.
2276b; later edd. uncompound. In either form it is difficult
to translate. Klaeber calls it "a characteristic instance of
parataxis" ("you must carry a sweaty face, [you must] eat your
bread"); Kock would make *hlaf* obj. of both *wegan* and *etan*
("Sweatyface, you must carry your bread, eat it"). Wells'
suggestion is best, that *etan* be taken as inf. of purpose("You
shall bear a sweaty face [in order] to eat your bread").

   948-951 The poet interprets the purpose of the angelic
guard to be the prevention of the reentry into the lost home
of any sinful man, that is, he extends it to include all hu-
manity. The traditional rationale for the guard is given by
Ælfric, *Exameron Anglice*, 69-70: "Hearmlic him wære ðæt he
wurde ða ece and eallum his ofspringe on ðære yrmðe, ðæt we
ealle sceoldon on ecnysse swa lybban on eallum ðam costnungum
ðe us becumað nu, and on eallum ðam earfoðnyssum ðe we on lib-
bað. Ða forwyrnde him God ðæs inganges forðig to ðam lifes
treowe, ðæt we lybban ne sceoldon swylce earmingas on ecum

lichaman, swylc we nu syndon on ðysum sorhfullum life. Wel us
foresceawode se welwillenda God ðæt he on oðre wisan ure yfel
gebette and cydde his mihte and his mildheortnysse . . . ."
Line 951 is ambiguous: how should one translate *dugeðum* and to
what does *deore* refer? Kennedy, *Cædmon Poems*, 38, translates
951a as masc. nom. referring to the angel, "dear unto God in
virtue," Braasch and Wells take *deore* as neut. acc. referring
to *lif*. Isidore, *Quaest. vet. test.*, PL. 83, 223A, suggests
that this passage should apply to those who would come into
Paradise after the Fall: "Nemo enim potest pervenire ad arbo-
rem vitae, nisi per has duas res, tolerantiam scilicet moles-
tiarum et scientiae plenitudinem, id est, per charitatem Dei
et proximi. 'Plenitudo enim legis charitas est' (Rom. 13.10)."
Klaeber takes *lif* as equal to "Paradise," used concretely, as
in such compounds as *munuc- mynster- cot-lif*, but it obviously
refers to the Tree of Life, allowing us at the same time to
see, since "tree" is not mentioned, the usual spiritual interpretation of "viam ligni vitae": "[ðæt] lifes treow, ðæt is
se leofa Hælend ðe ðæt ece lif forgifð ðam ðe hine lufiað and
mid weorcum cyðað ðæt hi wilniað his" (*Exameron Anglice*, 71-
72). Cf. GN 1574b-76.

952-960 God's blessings on the newly fallen human race.
The poet seems to be making the theological point that misery,
in particular the expulsion, stems from sin and its punishment,
while goodness and beauty are inherent in the creation and the
created world's procreative powers will now be the way God will
fulfill the blessing of Genesis 1.28. Creation is still a comfort to man after the Fall, despite his own corruption, yet the
hard realities resulting from that corruption are always apparent. The passage is strategically placed as a transition from
Paradise and the Fall to the Fall of Cain, between, that is,
the two extreme potentialities of the human race. Augustine
elaborately develops this topic in an analogous way in *De
ciu. Dei* XXII, 22-24, and all later commentators follow him
more or less closely.

954b *þeah þe he him from swice* Bouterwek suggests and
later edd. print *hie* for *he*, as referring to Adam *and* Eve. Accordingly, Holthausen reads *hie swicen*. Wells restores *he*,
referring to God (so B-T, s.v. *swican* II.a: "although he had
withdrawn his favour from them"). *he . . . swice* is also perfectly intelligible as referring to Adam: "he (Adam) defected
from him (God)." Eve failed Adam and Adam failed God.

955 *frofre / let* Line-division according to the pointing
of the MS, as Klaeber suggests. Other edd. divide *frofre let /
hwæðere*.

958-960 "He commanded seas and earth to bring forth
fruits of each (of) fertile species [*tuddorteondra*] for the
worldly use of that married couple."

970a *dædfruman* Lit.: "first-doers"; the irony of the
word applied to both Cain and Abel is apparent when its other

occurrences are compared: of King Edward in victory against
the Danes, *dyre dædfruma* (*Five Bouroughs* 3), and of Grendel,
dior dædfruma (BW 2090).

    971b *willgebroðor*. Huppé, *Doctrine and Poetry*, 155,
citing the *Glossa Ordinaria* (PL. 113, 98A), suggests that Cain
and Abel "represent the two directions of man's will on earth."
However we translate, "brothers of the will" (Huppé), "loving brothers," "desiring brothers," etc., we could not capture
concisely the nuance intended by the poet, even if we could be
sure of it. Cf. *willgesweostor* 2608 (Lot's daughters): the
first element seems to be used ironically where the family relationship is somewhat amiss. Similar is *willgesteallum* (the
Sodomites) 2147b*n*., perhaps also *willflod* 1412.

    972 *oðer his to eorðan / elnes tilode*. "One [Cain] tilled
[procured by effort] from the earth his strength [*elnes*, gen.
of the thing procured]." For the construction, compare 1557,
and see B-T s.v. *tilian* III (1) (b). Dietrich, *ZfdA* 10, 319,
suggested *ætes* for *elnes* (as in 1557). But the point is that
Cain is earthy, and looks to the earth for his good: "quod
electus quisque simplices infra se cognitationes nutrit, et
reprobus quilibet, interna sua deferens, terrena diligit"
(Hrabanus, *Alleg. in sac. scrip.*, PL. 112, 856).

    973-975a The central typology of the Cain and Abel epi-
sode as it was generally understood. Cain is "primogenitus"
(Bede, *In Gen.*, CCSL 118A, 81). Abel, whose name means "luc-
tus," sorrow, is nevertheless a comfort to his father for his
loyalty and will come into his possession as the protomartyr
(Isidore, *Etymol.* VII, 6, 8). It is Cain's name which means
"possessio" (Bede, *In Gen.*, 73), but it is he who will lose
the inheritance. Isidore puts the whole thing in simple terms:
"Cain, frater ejus, aetate major, qui eumdem Abel occidit in
campo, priorem significat populum qui interfecit Christum in
Calvariae loco" (*Alleg. quaedam sac. scrip.*, PL. 83, 100A).

    980b *hygewælm asteah* The word division, at the end of
the MS line, *wæl / mos teah*, baffled the earlier edd.: Junius
wælmos teah; Lye-Manning, *hyge wælm ofteah*, and so Thorpe and
Bouterwek, but the latter suggested *hygewælm ofteah*; Grein
hygewælmas teah "es zog Herzwallen aus in der Brust dem Hel-
den." Thus evolved Wülker's *hygewælm asteah* (i.e. *astah*);
cf. *hire mod astah* 2237a.

    982a *yrre for æfstum*. This explains 4.5, "iratusque
est Cain," in terms of envy, the second of the sins traditionally attributed to Cain. See 1023-35 *n*.

    986a *pæs middangeard*, Thorpe changes *pæs* to *pes*, nom.,
and so Bouterwek, Grein and Holthausen. Krapp prints *pæs*,
taking it as *pes*. Wells reads *pæs* as gen. sing. with *cwealmdreore*, parallel to *monnes*: "The earth swallowed gore of that
one, a man's blood." It is syntactically preferable to take
as *pes*, or perhaps better, as advbl., "thereafter"; see Q-W,
par. 102, B-T s.v. *se* V 2 (a). Cf. GB 356, GN 221-224a *n*.

987b-1001   The universal results of Cain's sin. Like the
hearmstafas (939) which immediately result from the Fall, here
the spreading tree of sin, the *hearmtanas*, will plague all
mankind with a spreading moral growth of sin. This growth is
spontaneous, begun even before God interviews Cain, and not
an imposed punishment, for the poet always presents God as a
merciful lord, not a punisher. Beyond this, there is the suggestion of Cain's spreading lineage, more explicitly treated
in the next section (1055 ff.), and the organic image insin-
uates the standard interpretation of the results of Cain's
compound crime, the establishment of the Two Cities, which began visibly on earth when Cain and Abel were morally separated
by their deeds (cf. Augustine, *De civ. Dei* XV, 1). The "civitas" explored a few lines later as a social grouping (1049b
ff.) is here developed as an image of perverted growth, push-
ing itself up from the blood of Abel's murder which wetted
Cain's accursed ground. The natural coherence of the image
is heightened by its reinforcing function, linked to 4.11,
"Nunc igitur maledictus eris super terram," etc. The tree i-
mage recalls also the tree by which Cain's father fell, for
at the end of this passage the poet harkens back to man's original sin with a conventional lamentation for Eve's crime, a
remembrance of the creation and of the spiritual part of man
(997-1001). This may be an implicit development of the idea
that Cain was guiltier than Adam and Eve because his sin was
premeditated and self-seeking and carried out from a position
of experience (cf. Bede, *In Gen.*, CCSL 118A, 78-79). The
growth of evil in the two branches of man's family imaged as
a tree is not without parallel: cf. *Glossa Ordinaria*, PL. 113,
101A, incorporating earlier material, on Cain's lineage, "Non
de omnibus his certa mysteria exsculpuntur, nec invenirentur,
nisi prius quedam radices historiae jacerentur; nec de ramis
arborum fructus legeres, nisi trunces antea plantasses." The
image is very common in Gregory, *Moralia in Job* (e.g. PL. 75,
656C, 858C; 76, 231C, 321D, etc.).

990a   *reðe wæstme*. Nom. pl., cf. 894a *n*.

1003   *hwær abel / eorðan wære*. *eorðan* may be dat., but
more likely is emphatic gen. with *hwær*; see B-T *Supp*., s.v.
hwær II (1) (ca).

1010-1013a   These lines, rendering 4.10, make clear that
God is omniscient, since he knows of the specific crime and
only asks in order to reserve Cain's chance for a truthful response which would mitigate his guilt. The syntax reflects
the standard judgement against Cain in the commentaries: the
wicked man is instrumental (*wraðum*) against the good man (*wærfæsne rinc*). *hwæt* is taken as an interrogative by all edd.
(= "quid fecisti") except Krapp, who punctuates it as an in-
terjection. *befealdest* is from *befyllan* (see Intro., p. 30).
Translate: "Why did you strike down," etc.

1011b   *wærfæsne*   All edd. read *wærfæstne* (Grein so re-

ports the MS) but the loss of *t* between *s* and another consonant is a common lWS feature and should be retained as such:
see Campbell, par. 477 (2).

   1015b-1018a *ne seleð be wæstmas eorðe . . . . grene
folde.* The three elements of the curse of the "terrene" man
are brought together here: the blood which cries "de terra"
(4.10) shall curse Cain "super terram" (4.11) and he shall
wander "super terram" (4.12). In the conceit of the poet, the
blood cries out because it went into the earth, earth with-
holds her fruits because the blood went into it.

   1015a *awyrged to widan aldre.* Like the serpent, Cain is
cursed "forever," a natural inference, but one which apparently has special prominence only in the medieval English tradition of vernacular biblical poetry: see Emerson, "Legends
of Cain," *PMLA* 21, 863.

   1022 *Him pa cain / andswarode:* The a-line is short and
lacks an alliterant. Holthausen and edd. insert *ædre* before
cain (cf. 1003). See R. P. Creed, "Andswarode-system," *Speculum* 32, 523-28.

   1023-1035 Cain's outburst of remorse (4.13-14) is treated along traditional lines, since the elaboration makes clear
that his remorse is in fact hopeless, unavailing despair, one
of his traditional sins. If translated plainly, the words of
Genesis 4.13-14 could be mistaken for an expression of genuine
recognition and acknowledgement of guilt, that is, a redeeming
statement. But the standard interpretation was that the
speech is a typical example of the egotistical self-pity of
the sinful. So Remigius (*Comm. in Gen.*, PL. 131, 70B): "The
sinner, casting about from sin to sin, despairs, not believing
that his salvation is possible or that he might obtain mercy.
And this is a blasphemy against the Holy Spirit . . ." Cain
mourns only because he loses worldly "possession" (cf. 973-75a
n.) and because he fears retribution in the form of bodily
death, not because he has lost "the strength of the ground,"
i.e., the virtue of Christ's crucifixion and resurrection for
saving sinners (Augustine, *Cont. Faust. Manich.* XII, 12 [PL. 42,
260]). In emphasizing murder as Cain's chief sin, the poet is
merely dramatizing and simplifying in poetic style the web of
interconnected sins that were usually assigned to him. Bede
(*In Gen.*, CCSL 118A, 80) comprehensively lists these sins as
bad offering, envy, deceit, murder, lying, self-condemnation
(despair) and refusal to do penance. All of these may be detected in this episode to a greater or smaller degree.

   1027b-1028a *lecgan. // hwonne* Following Wells' punctuation, with a full stop after *lecgan*, paralleling the syntax of
4.14 closely, and focussing both statements clearly. Other edd.
read *lecgan, // hwonne.*

   1038b-1039 *peah pu from . . . fah gewitan.* "Egressusque
. . . profugus," inevitably in OE. poetry, takes on the trap-
pings of the familiar exile theme, but with surprising light-

ness (cf. 1047b-53a). The poet links the poetic theme with
the exegetical theme of the separation of the Two Cities:
Cain's exile is *freomagum feor*, that is, far from the city of
the *freo* line of Abel and Seth.

1040a *gif monna hwelc* Grein, Krapp and Wells insert *þe*
after *gif*, Holthausen *þec*, but this is unnecessary. The poet
is extending the general moralizing of the original, "sed omnis qui occiderit Cain," to a general precept against murder,
"if any man with his hand take life." The use of *beneotan*
without personal obj. occurs in *Fates of the Apostles* 46. To
justify his emendation, Wells calls attention to GN 1830, *þæt
me wraðra sum . . . feore beneote*, but that is translating
"interficient me."

1045a *freoðobeacen* The mark set upon Cain is to identify him so that no one will dare attack him. *freoðo* is "a
formal pledge of protection," "promise to avenge." An outlaw
is one beyond *freoðo*. Cf. *friðotacen* 2371, of circumcision.

1055-1060 The building of the city of "Enoch." The
first communal act of men was the building, literally, of the
City of This World, the "city of blood" (so called by Petrus
Comestor, *Hist. Schol.*, PL. 198, 1078D, citing "Josephus," but
the phrase is not found in the standard text of the *Antiquities*). To the poet, the builders are *sweordberende*, set apart
from the *sædberend*, Seth, the bearer of the true line (cf.
1145 *n*.). This city was "first of all" cities both literally
and spiritually. Its real foundation was when Cain slew Abel.
It is the "old" city; the city of God is "new." Augustine explains the priority of the city of Enoch by recalling I Cor.
15.46, "non prius quod spirituale est; sed quod animale, de-
inde quod spiritale." "Sic ut enim," continues Augustine, "in
uno homine . . . unde unusquisque, quoniam ex damnata propa-
gine exoritur, primo sit necesse est ex Adam malus atque carnalis; quod si in Christum renascendo profecerit, post erit
bonus et spiritualis: sic in uniuerso genere humano, cum pri-
mum duae istae coeperunt nascendo atque moriendo procurrere
ciuitates, prior est natus ciuis huius saeculi, posterius autem isto peregrinus in saeculo et pertinens ad ciuitatem Dei,
gratia praedestinatus gratia electus, gratia peregrinus deorsum gratia ciuis sursum . . . . Scriptum est itaque de Cain,
quod condiderit ciuitatem; Abel autem tamquam peregrinus non
condidit. Superna est enim sanctorum ciuitas. . . . (*De ciu.
Dei* XV, 1 [CCSL 48, 453-54]).

1055b *enos* This substitution for *Enoch* is not an error,
nor does it originate with the poem. It stems from ancient
attempts to make the lineage of Cain and the lineage of Seth
more exactly parallel than they already are (see Bradley, "The
'Caedmonian' Genesis," *Essays and Studies* 6, 15-17, attributing
the changes in the genealogies to the poet). The origins of
heightened paralleling go back to the compilation of Genesis
itself, to the harmonizing of distinct traditions relating to

the kings who lived before the Flood (Cassuto, *Comm. on Gen.*,
I, 266 f.). Both the similarities and divergences can be explained by the normal developmental tendencies towards symmetry and variation inherent in the style of the Pentateuch
and heightened by later ages and traditions, right up to the
Septuagint and on into the Christian era. There is a great
variety of names in Old Latin MSS. Augustine's schematization
of the Two Cities furthered the tendency. The particular versions of the genealogies found in GN bear great similarity to
a fifth century African genealogy which had wide distribution
in Europe in the early middle ages because of its bearing on
chronological disputes. It is printed as "Liber Genealogus"
in *Chronica Minora*, ed. T. Mommsen, Vol. I, MGH., Auct. Ant.
IX, 162-63. The relevant names of the line of Cain are:

Vulgate:	Lib.Gen.:	GN:
Henoch	*Enos*	*Enos*
Irad	*Gedam* (var: *Irat*)	*Iared*
Maviael	*Malaleel*	*Malalehel*
Mathusael	*Matusalam*	*Mathusal*

The names in the line of Seth are *Enos, Iared, Malaleel, Math-
usala* (Vulgate forms). It is interesting to note that *Enoch*,
meaning "dedication," was usually explained in relation to 4.
17 as "dedication to this world," contrasting to that other
Enoch (5.22) who walked with God. The etymology of *Enos* was
explained as "desperatus uel uiolentus," better befitting the
line of Cain than the line of Seth (see Jerome, *Lib. int. heb.
nom.*, CCSL 72, 65).

   1056 *frumbearn caines, / siðð an ongon* Grein inserts
furðum after *siðð an*, improving the rhythm and providing an alliterant, and so Holthausen; Krapp, more pointedly, adds *fæsten* after *siðð an*. The problem goes deeper than a missing word,
however, since *ongon* has no clear subject, and the Vulgate
clearly states that Cain, not Enoch/Enos built the city. It
is likely that a line or more has dropped out. One could make
these lines closer to the Vulgate by punctuating *caines. / sið-
ð an . . . timbran / þæt* but the following lines belie this
arrangement. More likely, the problem is with 1056.

   1061a *his* Refers to Enos.

   1063b *iared* For Vulg. *Irad* (see 1055b *n.*), alliterating
vocalically. Holthausen reads *Iąred*, i.e., *Ired* (and argues
for *Ired* in *Anglia* 46, 60). Perhaps the spelling has been influenced by *Iared* 5.18 (cf. 1174b *n.*).

   1064b-1066a "Afterwards were born those who increased
the descendants of the family, the kindred of Cain." Wells
takes *sunu* 1064a as nom. pl., the subject of *wocan*.

   1070a *bearn æfter bearne* "(One) son [nom.] after (another) son." Technically, *bearn* is appositive to *mathusal* 1069a,
but as Kock, *PPP.*, 15 pointed out, the phrase means practic-

ally "in his turn;" cf. 1129 *eafora æfter yldrum*. Holthausen
takes as *bearn' æfter* (elision before the vowel) and Wells so
reads.

1078a *iabal* For Vulg. *Iubal*; cf. the Old Latin form,
Iobal. But the probability is strong that the poet or a
scribe has merely confused "Iubal" (4.21) with his brother
"Iabel" (4.20), who is not mentioned in the poem.

1090-1103 The Song of Lamech. In 4.23-24 what Lamech's
crime is, what his dealings with Cain are, is not made explicit. In Jewish exegesis, the accidental death of the exiled
Cain at the hand of the blind bowman Lamech came to be elaborately developed (cf. Ginzberg, I, 116-17). Jerome apparently knows something of the story but passes down to the
early middle ages only a hint: ". . . Lamech, qui septimus
ab Adam, non sponte (ut in quodam hebraeo volumine scribitur)
interfecit Cain" (*Epist.* 36, 4 [PL. 22, 455]). GN presents
just enough of the core of Jerome's minimized version to clarify the puzzling text of the Song. Probably the poet knew no
more than Jerome tells, for even Bede merely repeats Jerome.
The full Talmudic versions reappear in the Latin tradition only in Carolingian times and later, fully narrated by Angelomus
(*Comm. in Gen.*, PL. 115, 152A), Remigius (*Comm. in Gen.*, PL.
131, 72A), and Petrus Comestor (*Hist. Schol.*, I, 28 [PL. 198,
1079-80]). For the development of the story in the middle
ages, see Emerson, "Legends of Cain," *PMLA* 21, 874 ff.

1098b *wat geurwe* Probably a defective verse, though
three-syllable verses occur occasionally in GN. Sievers, *Beiträge*, 10, 512 suggested *wat nu gearwe* or *wat peah gearwe*;
Graz, *Festschr. f. Schade*, 70, suggested *wat ic gearwe* and so
Holthausen, Krapp and Wells. The sense is adequate if the subject is carried down from 1093a.

1104-1242a The Sethite Genealogy (4.25, 5.3-31). This
long genealogy is carried out with remarkable fidelity of
structure and nomenclature, yet with considerable variation
and formulaic inventiveness. Most of such elaboration as it
shows stems from the traditional poetic stock rather than from
the exegetical tradition. Earlier critics tended to view the
genealogical passages as the product of later redactors, wel-
ding previously extant Genesis lays into larger and larger
continuous pieces (see e.g., Jovy, *Bonner Beiträge* 5, 5; Sievers, *Britannica*, 60). Common sense and what we can tell of
the poem's usual procedure argue the opposite, that the poet
was working through the text as he found it, representing everything continuously as it occurred, omitting and elaborating
on a strictly *ad hoc* basis. He must have known perfectly well
that the genealogies supply the continuities running from Adam
to Abraham. Klaeber's remark remains the most sensible: "Der
undankbaren aufgabe, die geschlectsregister . . . in ae. verse
umzugiessen, entledigte sich der dichter mit anerkennenswertem
geschick, indem er die dürren angaben der bibel, die sich

nicht über das schema 'er lebte lange, zeugte kinder, und starb' erheben, durch anschauliche unschreibungen zu beleben verstand" ("Die ältere Genesis und der Beowulf," *Englische Studien* 42, 327).

1104-1110a Seth is one of the traditional "figurae Christi" of the Old Testament. The phrases *on abeles gyld, on leofes stæl,* etc., are repeated literal responses to "semen aliud pro Abel," but together with other phrases, *soðfæst sunu, eadig, freolic to frofre, leof* (sc. Abel), they compel our mind to see the intended trope, for "positus est pro Abel non solum ordine nascendi sed et merito uirtutis . . ." (Bede, *In Gen.*, CCSL 118A, 91). "Mystice autem sicut Abel occisus a Cain passum Dominum, ita natus pro eo Seth resuscitatum eum a morte designat" (*Ibid.*). Seth's name means "resurrection," according to the commentators.

1108b-1109a *fæder and meder, // adames and euan,* Wülker and edd. follow the MS *adames,* but Dietrich *ZfdA* 10, 320, suggested *adame,* parallel to dats. *fæder and meder.* Krapp takes *adames* as dependent on *frofre* 1108a, but perhaps *fæder and meder* should be taken as gen. sings. (cf. Campbell, par. 629), dependent on *frofre,* parallel to *adames and euan.*

1111b-1112a *me ece sealde // sunu selfa,* Graz, *Festschn. f. Schade,* 71, suggested transposing *sunu* and *sealde* to take the finite verb out of the stress position: accordingly, Holthausen and Krapp read *me ece sunu // sealde selfa,* the latter commenting that the alteration improves the sense as well as the meter. Wells restores the MS word-order. These lines suggest word-play on the interpretation of Seth's name, "resurrection." Adam says, obviously, "the eternal one himself has given me a son;" he also seems to be saying "The Ruler of victories has himself given me (the) son for all eternity;" *lifes aldor* 1113a can be regarded as parallel to either the subject or the object of the preceding clause (see Huppé, *Doctrine and Poetry,* 164-65).

1118a *eðulstæfe* I.e., *eðylstæfe,* cf. 2225a.

1128b *leof weardode,* Grein queried whether *leod* should be read for *leof,* and so Holthausen, Krapp and Wells read. Reading *leod* supplies an obvious object for *weardode,* and may be correct, but overlooks the suggestiveness of *leof,* the "dear thing" Seth guards, the heritage of Adam (notionally varying *epelstol,* but not grammatically parallel).

1129a *eafora æfter yldrum,* *eafora* is appositive to *seth* (cf. 1070a *n.*).

1131b-1133a *þa heo furðum ongan // his mægburge / men geicean // sunum and dohtrum.* The poet seems to adapt the formula for birth to accomodate the usual interpretation of Enos' name, "homo" (see Jerome, *Lib. int. heb. nom.,* CCSL 72, 65).

1131b *þa heo furðum ongan* Notionally, *heo* must refer to *wif* 1130a. Grein changes *heo* to *he* (sc. Seth), and so

Krapp, Wells. Wülker and Holthausen follow the MS.

1133b-1134 *sedes eafora // se yldesta wæs / enos haten.*
Edd. read *Sethes* (Holthausen: *Seðes*) although the form is acceptable as possibly an early spelling preserved through several copies (Campbell, par. 57 [5], and 1138 *n.*). Wells takes *eafora* as gen. pl., but it is better as nom. sing., "the eldest son of Seth" (cf. 1191a *n.*).

1135-1137 The parallel schemes that are adopted to present the contrasting Cainite and Sethite genealogies are apparent here; as Enos, son of Seth is *ærest ealra* to call upon God, Enos, son of Cain was *ærest ealra* (1059a) to build a city, and as Seth is *sædberend* (1145a), the Cainites are *sweordberende* (1060a). F. C. Robinson, *Archiv* 204, 267 f., relates 1136b-37, "since Adam stepped on green grass, honored by (the) spirit," to the legend that when Adam was expelled from Paradise, his footsteps burned a permanent track in the grass, and it was these that Seth followed when he was sent to recover the oil of life from Paradise (cf. Vita Adae et Evae, 30-44 [Charles, II, 141-45], *Cursor Mundi*, 1252-62 [ed. Morris, EETS 101], *Holy Rood* [ed. Morris, EETS 46, p. 66, 50-52]). Therefore, Robinson interprets GN 1136 ff. to mean "since Adam left Paradise," i.e., Enos is the first to call upon God since the primitive rites of Adam and Eve in Paradise. But in spite of the legendary correlation it seems more within the style of the poem to take the phrase in a simpler sense, not indeed with Holthausen ("since Adam died"), but with Kock, *PPP.* 15, "since Adam trod the earth endowed with a living soul," i.e., since the creation of Man. In other words, Enos is the very first to formally call on God in religious worship, the sense in which 4.26 is taken by the commentators (cf. *Glossa Ordinaria*, PL. 113, 102C; Remigius, *Comm. in Gen.*, PL. 131, 72C).

1142a *pæt he friðgedal* Krapp: "There can be no question that the first element must mean the same as *ferhð*- but the form *frið*- may stand." He compares 107, *stiðfrihð* (see *note* and Intro., p. 33). But "peaceful death" makes sense here.

1143 *him æfter heold / pa he of worulde gewat* The alliteration is defective. Grein prints 1143b *siððan he of eorðan gewat*, Holthausen reads *earde* for *worulde*.

1144b-1145 *siððan eorðe swealh // sædberendes / sethes lice.* Another parallel to the history of Cain. As the blood of Abel was swallowed by the earth (985 f.) watering the tree planted by the sin of Cain, so the second Abel is a seed-bearer, bodily swallowed by the earth after a "peaceful death." The traditional interpretation of Seth's name is "semen" (Jerome, *Lib. int. heb. nom.*, 71), the *sædberend* who, in the conception of the poet, plants the seeds of the tree of the Godly city (see F. C. Robinson, "The Significance of Names in OE. Literature," *Anglia* 86, 29-30). S. Moore, *MLR* 6, 200-01, cited the legend of the Holy Rood, where Seth bears three

seeds from Paradise and plants them in dead Adam's mouth, but
the onomastic explanation is to be preferred (cf. 1135-37 *n.*).

1155b *cainan* As Wells notes, the mistake *caines* 1160
probably accounts for the erasure of *-an* here. The name is
correctly written at 1149.

1161-1162a *siðan eahtahund . . . and feowertigum eac*
"After 800 (years) and (with) forty more, he increased the
count of princes with souls." The dat. *feowertigum* may be
kept as a kind of parenthesis exempt from the temporal acc.
governing *eahtahund*. Holthausen, citing Shipley, *Gen. Case
in AS. Poetry*, 102, reads *feowertig*, and so Krapp and Wells.

1165b-1166 *pa his tiddæge . . . rim* Thorpe reads *tid-
daga* to make a partitive gen. with *rim*, but no later edd. take
up this plausible emendation, since the dat. is intelligible.

1168 *malalehel / siðan missera worn.* The line-division
follows the MS pointing; edd. divide: *Malalehel siðan / missera*, but the scansion is probably *m̄alalehel* 2A1, *siðan mis-
sēra worn* 3B2. Cf. 1962a *n.*

1172a *meowle to monnum brohte* Holthausen omits *meowle*
to relieve the line of the extra stress. Cf. 44-46 *n.*

1174b *iared* Alliterating consonantally, at 1181 and
1195 spelled *geared*, a "Saxonism" phonetically equivalent to
iared. Cf. 1063 *n.* and 1610b *n.*

1180a *land and leodweard.* Identical to GN 1196a and EX
57a. The context can support *leodweard* either as "gubernatio populi" (G-K, Thorpe, B-T), or as "territorium" (G-K, alternate
meaning). Cf. BW 2334 *eorðweard* "stronghold," and the phrases
lond ond leodbyrig BW 2471, *land and leodgeard* GN 229, 1773
(cf. Marquardt, *Kenningar*, 203). Irving, in his edition of
Exodus, emends 57a to *leodgeard.*

1183 *and se frumgar / his freomagum leof.* The line-division follows the MS pointing. Edd. divide: *his / freomagum.
and se frūmgār.* is a light but regular a2-type. 1183b may be
regarded as 3E2 with irregular anacrusis.

1184b *fyore = feore* A survival of eWS *-io-* spelling?
(cf. *wrÿon = wrēon* 1572b). See Intro., p. 29.

1191a *eafora* Bouterwek reads *eaforan*, presumably as an
acc. parallel to *cneorim*, and so Holthausen and Krapp. This
may be preferable to the MS *eafora*, but there is a slight possibility that the form is for gen. pl., parallel to *cynnes.*
Braasch lists it as gen. pl. (but accepting Bouterwek's emendation?) and Wells, citing Brunner, par. 276, anm. 3 and 4,
takes it as gen. pl., though in fact Brunner gives little support for this form as gen. pl. Neither does Campbell, par. 617.
Thorpe emends *eafora* to *wintra*, and Krapp remarks, "supply *wintra* in thought to complete the meaning of *eahtahund . . . .*"
But cf. 1122 *eahtahund / iecte siðan* with no dep. gen. For
forms of *eafora* that present difficulties see 1233b-34a, 2189a,
nn.

1191b-1194 "In all [*ealra*, advbl. gen.] he had when he

went forth [i.e., died] sixty-five and nine-hundred of night
counts [i.e., years reckoned by days: cf. *omnes dies . . .
nongenti sexaginta duo anni*], a friend wintry-wise [i.e., wise
because of long experience, *or* sad (wintry) experience], when
he left the world . . . ." This is the simplest, though not
the only way of arranging and construing the lines. *wintres*
can be taken with *nihtgerimes* (appos. or depnt.). Holthausen
reads *wine wintrum frod*, an improvement, but not necessary.

    1202b-1213 The Translation of Enoch. Genesis 5.22 and
24 are not represented. Instead, the traditional explanation
of "et placuit Enoch deo et non inventus postmodum quia deus
illum transtulit" is substituted. The legends of Enoch concern his literal "translation" to Paradise or Heaven while
still alive and in the body. Such apocryphal stories, as they
appeared in the Books of Enoch, Jubilees, 2 Enoch, Testaments
of the Twelve Patriarchs, leave no trace in authoritative rabbinical writings, but were taken over by Christian writers at
an early date and are commonly mentioned in Latin commentaries.
The tradition of Enoch carried off to the earthly Paradise is
represented in the Comestor's *Historia Scholastica* (PL. 198,
1080D). More commonly, Enoch is said to have been translated
to Heaven while still alive. The details, going back to the
Apocalypse of Paul in the Christian tradition, get treated
more and more generally, while the actual journey is gradually
subordinated to allegorical interpretations which make the literal level increasingly ambiguous (cf. Augustine, *De ciu. Dei*
XV, 19 CCSL 48, 481-82 ; Bede, *In Gen.*, CCSL 118A, 96). Ælfric, in his Treatise on the Old and New Testaments (ed.
Crawford, EETS 160, 23), makes the literal level clearer than
usual: "he worhte Godes willan and God hine ða genam mid
ansundum lichaman of þisum life upp, and he ys cucu git . . . ."
Although bound to a literal presentation, the poem displays
its affinity to the main line of exegesis by spiritualizing the
incident, leaving the literal details unexplained. The illustrator of the Junius MS, on the other hand, is very explicit,
showing on P. 61 angels assisting Enoch into heaven, in a composition which iconographically resembles the Ascension (cf.
Clemoes, "Cynewulf's Image of the Ascension," in *England before the Conquest*, 293-304).

    1208 *æhta and ætwist / eorðan gestreona* "Possessions
and provision of the goods of the earth." Kock, *Anglia* 43,
307, translates: "goods and residence."

    1211b *frean,* Grein and edd. read *feran* (with *gewat*) for
smoother sense, but *frean* may be taken as acc. parallel to
cyning, 1210b.

    1212a *on pam gearwum* "In that clothing," i.e., the body.

    1217a *and eac preohund.* Holthausen reads *ond III hund
eac* in order to bring the alliterating syllable forward.

    1219-1220a *se on lichoman / lengest þisse // worulddreama
breac.* May *þisse* be taken as anomolous dat. with *lichoman*? (So

Wülker and earler edd., except Grein). Grein suggested *pissa*
with *worulddreama*, so Holthausen, Krapp and Wells print. *pisse*
is left as possibly a late spelling of *pissa*.

    1232 *fifhund eac heold / þæt folc teala* 2E2 and 2C2,
following the MS line-division. Other edd., dividing *eac /
heold*, which leaves the a-line a syllable short, must add *and*
before *fif*, as suggested by Graz, *Festschr. f. Schade*, 71. The
translation of 1229b-1232 runs: "The lord lived for ninety-
five (years), the ruler of troops enjoyed many winters under
heaven, for 500 (years) ruled that people well," etc.

    1233b-1234a *him byras wocan // eafora and idesa.* As in
1191a, *eafora* appears to be gen. pl., though the form is
doubtful. Holthausen and Krapp read *eaforan*, nom. pl., appositive to *byras*. Taking the gen., the passage may mean either
"descendants (consisting of) sons and daughters were born to
him," or "descendants were born to him from sons and daughters." In any case, the expression is a loose construction
responding to the Vulg. formula *filios et filias*; cf. 1138,
1153, 1245, etc.

    1240b, 1241b *sunu noes*][*oðer cham* Holthausen, following
Sievers, *Beiträge* 10, 480, prints *Nōēēs*, tri-syllabic, here
and at 1323, 1423, 1551, to gain a syllable. Krapp follows
the MS, but agrees that the word must be trisyllabic. Cosijn,
Beiträge 19, 488-89, notes Otfrid's stress *Noé*, which implies
trisyllabic forms. Holthausen supplies *wæs* before *oðer*, 1241b,
to gain another syllable. Krapp remarks, "If *Noes* can be read
as a trisyllabe, *Cham* can be read as a dissyllable . . . ,"
which is odd logic. Rather, it is more likely that the poet
did not feel constrained to fit foreign names into exactly
regular verse patterns every time they occurred; cf. 1551.

    1245b-1252 *Đa giet wæs sethes cynn . . . on caines cynne
secan . . . scyldfulra mægð, / scyne and fægere.* 6.1-2 is paraphrased so as to make it accord exactly with the main Latin
interpretation of the passage: "In eo autem quod 'videntes filii Dei,' semen Seth significat. Seth quidem semen non incon-
grue Filius Dei dicintur quia pro Abel natus est, ad cujus munera Dominus respexit. Per filias vero hominum filiae seminis
Cain intelliguntur, quarum copulatio cum semine Seth, causa
diluvii super terram . . ." (Ps.-Bede, *In Pent. comm.* PL. 91,
224C). The emphasis of 1245-47 is similar to that of Bede's
commentary: the line of Seth is an example of faithful service to God until it mixes in carnal concupiscence with the
daughters of Cain (*In Gen.*, CCSL 118A, 99). The poet indicates this mixing and its effects by the change from *sethes
cynn* and *bearn godes* to *monna eaforan:* the once favored race
becomes more like the "filiae hominum" it has chosen. The
change in the descendants of Seth is emphasized, whether by
accident or design, by the major sectional division that occurs between 1247 and 1248 in mid-sentence. The traditional
attitude towards the Cainite women in both Jewish and Chris-

tian exegesis is summed up with a nice ironical turn, *scyld-fulra mægð, scyne and fægere*, "wicked women, beautiful and fair." In the Jewish tradition, the beautiful but wicked "daughters of men" lured down the angels of Heaven. The LXX and Old Latin reading, "angeli Dei," influenced the Latin tradition only slightly: Claudius of Turin suggests that "angeli Dei" refers to the Sethites because of their former virtue (*Comm. in Gen.*, PL. 50, 924-25), but the poem shows no trace of it.

1253-1262 God's curse on mankind. Rather than attempting to translate the cryptic and probably corrupt verse 6.3, "non permanebit spiritus meus in homine," the poet freely develops God's speech from the material inherent in the preceding passage. Following Jerome (*Lib. quaest. heb. in Gen.*, CCSL 72, 9), 6.3 was taken by most commentators to refer to God's anger soon to be realized in the Flood; more particularly, "per spiritum in hoc loco spiritus irae intelligitur" (Ps.-Bede, *In Pent. comm.*, PL. 91, 224D). The speech heading at once paraphrases the usual "dixitque Deus" and provides a motivation for the following speech according to the standard explanation of the verse.

1255 *Ne syndon me on ferhðe freo / from gewitene* "(The descendants of Cain) have not departed from my spirit immune (from punishment)." See B-T *Supp.*, s.v. *freo* (9). The poet's interpretation of 6.3 may more freely be understood, "Although my spirit will not remain in man, he will not be separated from my spirit scot-free." Wells emends *freo* to *feor*, translating, "From my mind they are not gone far . . . ."

1256a *cneorisn* Taken as neut. nom. pl., with Holthausen, Krapp, Wells. Grein, *Germania* 10, 417, suggested *cneorim*, as in 1065, 1190; Dietrich, *ZfdA* 10, 322, suggested it was for *cneoriss*, occurring 6x in GN, and so Grein and Wülker print. But Cosijn, *Beiträge* 19, 448, noted *cneorisn* in *Blickling Homilies* (ed. Morris, EETS 73, 7.5; 229.21). It is apparently the same root in both words, one with a neut. suffix in -*(e)n*, the other a fem. in -*ess*.

1260a *pær* "when," cf. BW 286, 420, 508, etc.

1263-1269 The Time of Repentence. The main tradition was that the 120 years that were to be the days of men referred not to a sudden reduction of the life-span, but, following Jewish tradition, that there was to be a time of 120 years between the curse and the punishment in order to allow the human race a chance to repent. So Jerome (*Lib. quaest. heb. in Gen.*, CCSL 72, 9-10), who explains further that when God saw mens' hardness of heart he curtailed the respite to 100 years (inferred from comparing 5.31 and 7.6). The poet keeps the biblical number, but shows God's wrath being fulfilled on *gigantmæcgas* at the end of that time. Thus, the poem combines the traditional understanding of Chapter 6 with the wording of 6.3-4, while avoiding the formidable exegetical tangles that surrounded those verses. It is not said that the

giants are the product of the illicit union of the sons of
God and the daughters of men, although that is the implication of 6.4 and the basis for such a legendary element in the
Christian exegesis of the verse. More important for the poet
is the tradition emphasizing the moral deficiencies of these
"giants:" "et viros potentes genuerunt, immensos scilicet
corporibus, superbos viribus, inconditos moribus, qui gigantes
appellantur" (*Glossa Ordinaria*, PL. 113, 104C). This evocation of giants runs back to Augustine and Ambrose, ultimately
to Baruch 3.26-28: "Ibi fuerunt gigantes nominati illi, qui ab
initio fuerunt statura magna, scientes bellum. Non hos elegit
Dominus, neque viam disciplinae invenerunt, propterea peri-
erunt; et quoniam non habuerunt sapientiam, interierunt propter suam insipientiam." The mention of "giants" compounded
with -*mæcgas* "sons," makes clear the direct familial relationship between the races of men and giants, but the general tone
emphasizes the moral rather than the merely genealogical di-
mension of 6.4: these are wicked men themselves, who perished
in the Flood, true relations of the giants because they are
dædum scyldige . . . gode unleofe // micle mansceaðan.

　　　1264b-1265a *wræce bisegodon // fæge peoda* Krapp takes
bisegodon as intrans., "suffered," not recorded by B-T, and
wræce as instr. : "the doomed peoples suffered by punishment."
Wells takes *bisegodon* in the usual sense, "afflict," construing *wræce* as nom. pl. (citing Campbell, par. 585): "miseries
troubled the fated people." The scribe obviously intended *bisegodon*, since he took the trouble to make the correction: the
regularization to *bisgodon* by a correcting hand has no special
authority, though most edd. follow it; B-T *Supp.* gives several
examples of forms of *bisgian* with intrusive -*e*-, -*i*-.

　　　1270-1276a Closer to the Vulg. as a single sentence (following Wells) than divided into several (edd. put stops after
inwitfulle and *mihtum*). Thus, although the sense of course
anticipates 6.7, the syntax of *pa geseah . . . hwæt . . . and
pæt . . . he . . . gewrecan pohte . . .* corresponds to that of
Videns . . . quod . . . paenituit . . . .

　　　1270b *sigoro* Probably a relatively rare lWS gen. pl. in
-*o* (cf. Campbell, par. 377); cf. *fægerro* 1852b, *egipto* 1866a,
yldo GB 464a.

　　　1280 *eall aædan* "Destroy everything." Early edd. took
the line as *eall a ædan* "forever lay waste," but Dietrich *ZfdA*,
10, 322, recognized the rare *áéðan* (*áípan*), cognate to OHG. *ar-
óden* "destroy," "lay waste."

　　　1285-1554 Noe's Flood. The exegetical tradition held up
Noe as an example of special virtue: a man living in a wicked
time who nevertheless managed to keep his personal integrity
and piety. While the imperfection of Noe's virtue is pointed
out, particularly by Ambrose (*De Noe et arca* 1 [PL. 14, 361A
ff.]), he is treated by most commentators as literally an example of the just man living in a world of sin, and as a type

of Christ, the ark being a type of the Church, the Flood a
type of baptism. Bede states the developed position: "Eadem
laude Noe qua Enoch praedicatur, uidelicet quod diuinae ues-
tigia iussionis rectis operum bonorum gressibus secutus sit,
atque ideo, mundo perituro, ille in paradisum translatus; iste,
mundo pereunte, in arca saluatis est. *Iustus* autem *atque perfectus* fuit Noe, non sicut perficiendi sunt sancti in illa
immortalitate qua aequabuntur angelis Dei, sed sicut esse possunt in hac peregrinatione perfecti" (*In Gen.*, CCSL 118A, 102;
cf. Augustine, *De ciu. Dei* XV, 26). While reading this episode it is necessary to keep in mind the unified interpretation that overlaid the event, an interpretation that appears
to color the diction and organization of this part of GN: "Noe
solus justus, Christus solus sine peccato est. Cui septem animae homines donantur, id est perfecti homines, per septifor-
mem gratiam. Noe per aquam et lignum liberat suos, Christus
per crucem et baptismum liberat Christianos. Arca constru-
itur de lignis non putrescentibus, Ecclesia instruitur hominibus in sempiternum victuris. Arca enim ista Ecclesiam significat, quae natat in fluctibus mundi hujus. Quod autem dicitur esse de lignis quadratis, stabilitatem vitae justorum significat. Intus et foris, id est sive ab his qui intus sunt,
sive ab his qui foris sunt, nunquam dissolvantur. Confertur
sane populus hic qui salvatur in Ecclesia illis hominibus sive
animalibus qui salvati sunt in arca. Quorum quia non unum est
omnium meritum non unam habent in arca mansionem. Licet enim
in Ecclesia omnes intra unam fidem continentur, atque uno bap-
tismate diluantur, non tamen idem omnibus profectus est" (Ps.-
Bede, *In Pent. comm.*, PL. 91, 222).

    1287b-1289a *drihten wiste // þæt þæs æðelinges / ellen
dohte // breostgehygdum.* "God knew that fortitude availed in
the inner heart of the prince [i.e., of Noe]." This emphasizes
fortitude, one of the virtues comprising justice, which Noe is
often said to exemplify (cf. 6.9), and the words also recall
Ambrose's theme of God's ability to know and find out true virtue when it occurs in the secret heart: "Nam cum ipsa prophe-
tia dixerit nihil difficilius quam hominis interiora compre-
hendere, quanto magis difficile viri justi mentem cognoscere?"
(*De Noe et arca*, 1 [PL. 14, 362A]).

    1302b-1303a *ongyn þe scip wyrcan, // merehus micel.* The
ark is called a "ship" several times and Noe is called *forð-
weard scipes* 1436b, "helmsman of the ship." A modern predi-
lection for Anglo-Saxon sea-imagery, plus the spectacular effect of several of the Junius illustrations (PP. 66 and 68),
showing the ark as a tenth-century dragon-ship, have led some
to see in the poem a realistic ship. Utley, "Flood Narrative,"
214, assumes that GN presents us with a stable, conventional
sea-floater, of the Beowulfian kind: "A box-ark merely floating on the waters would need no helmsman." But Noe the steersman is in part a figure of Christ (cf. the OE. "Acts of Mat-

thew," in Cassidy-Ringler, *Bright's OE. Grammar and Reader,
3rd Ed.*, 208, for Christ as actual and symbolic steersman),
as the ark itself is a figure of the Church; the reality is in
the idea behind the thing, and *scip* is merely one of many
words participating in the relatively flat formulaic nexus
inevitably called up by the situation: "floating on the sea/
flood." In fact, there is very little in the poem to sustain
any sea-faring imagery. The ark is a shifting, mysterious object, ship and sacral vessel, a *merehus* (1303a) in which Noe
shall live and life shall be preserved, a *mereciest* (1317a),
i.e., a box, a *hof* (1345b, 1393b, 1489a), Noe's "temple" (cf.
44b, *þæt rædlease hof* = Hell). The pictures of the ark in the
MS also vary—the first artist favors dragon-ships, but the
second depicts an abstract palette-shaped refuge for Noe and
his family (see P. 73). Although the illustrations have nothing to do with the composition of the poem, they do call attention to the fact that the ark as dragon-ship was an icono-
graphical motif for a long time, beginning with the Junius MS
as the earliest extant example: cf. BM. Cotton Claudius B. IV,
ff. 14r,v, 15r,v (facsimile ed. Dodwell and Clemoes, EEMF 18),
and BM. Add. 28162, fol. 7v. (reproduced in D. W. Robertson,
A Preface to Chaucer [Princeton, 1962], pl. 79). Claudius of
Turin (9th century) shows that he did not conceive of the ark
as an ordinary ship by implicitly contrasting it with one
(*Comm. in Gen.* I, 6 [PL. 50, 927C]). See Intro., pp. 85-86.
      1303b-1313 The Construction of the Ark. From the con-
siderable amount of detail about the ark available in 6.14-16,
the poet has drawn enough to suggest the nature of the ark,
and to remain faithful to the spirit of the original, without
bogging down in a mass of details. In fact, remarkably little
is left out (gone is the remark that the ark is made "de lignis levigatis," the window, the top narrowing to one cubit,
the door on the side, but the rest of the specifications are
essentially mentioned). Each of the details had come to represent some point in an elaborate allegory of the Church. No
doubt the mention of any would have suggested the rest, along
with their signification. The tradition of allegorizing the
ark goes back to I Peter 3.20 at least, and a fairly full,
stable codification may be seen in Isidore's *Quaestiones de
Veteri Testamento* (PL. 83, 229-31). The careful preservation
of the numerical proportions of the ark (when most numbers in
the Noe episode are omitted) may perhaps be meant to recall to
the educated aspects of this figure of the Church, perhaps to
convince the audience of the vast size of the ark, adequate
for the numbers of beings assigned to it, but primarily to remind that the God of Noe is the God of proportion, measure and
number who grants wisdom to his faithful craftsmen, poets and
ark-builders alike.
      1303b-1304a *on þam þu monegum scealt // reste geryman*
Rendering "mansiunculas in arca facies," *mansiunculas* appar-

ently being interpreted as sleeping berths for the various
kinds of animals, according to the usual explanation: "Habi-
tationes autem in illa ad hoc factae videntur ut per singulas
mansiones diversa animalium vel bestiarum genera facilius se-
cerni possent" (Ps.-Bede, *In Pent. comm.*, PL. 91, 221-222).
The Old Latin reading, *nidos*, rather than the Vulg. *mansiunculas* may be behind *reste*, a word which deliberately and repeatedly recalls the interpretation of Noe's name (*requies*);
see 1485-87a *n.*

    1307-1310a *þu þær fær gewyrc . . . and wið yða gewyrc //
gefeg fæste* Figura etymologica, the first *gewyrc* being a verb,
the second either noun or verb; *gefeg* is also ambiguous, either neut. acc. sing. "joint " or imperative of *gefegan* "join."
No doubt the syntactical dazzle is evoking some of the magic
of God's command, and hard and fast choices are inappropriate
here, but the possibilities are, "and against the work of the
waves / join (it) firmly;" "and against the waves / firmly
make a joining" (the second elements of both clauses are interchangeable, making four possibilities). Cf. B-T s.v. *wið*,
I [3]. *gewyrc* 1309 may be taken as a form of *geweorc* "work"
(cf. B-T *Supp.*, ad loc. IV: *gewyrces*), or as imperative of *ge-
wyrcan*. The passage is presumably rendering loosely 6.14,
". . . et bitumine linies intrinsecus et extrinsecus," more
elaborately paraphrased at 1322-24. Dietrich, *ZfdA* 10, 322,
queried whether the second *gewyrc* should not be read *gewylc*
"rolling;" Bouterwek suggested *gewyrp*; Holthausen, *note*,
calls attention to AN 306 *ofer waroða geweorp*; Marckwardt-
Rosier suggest *gewealc*, but all edd. follow the MS.

    1307a *þu þær fær gewyrc* Thorpe and all subsequent edd.
except Wells emend *þær* to *þæt*, assuming scribal anticipation
of *fær*, but the MS reading is perfectly intelligible (cf.
Hulbert, *JEGP* 39, 536). As punctuated, *þær* 1307a is coordinate with *þær* 1310b; edd. put a stop after *fæste* 1310a.

    1308b *þreohund lang* Or better as three stressed sylla-
bles? Sievers, *Beiträge* 10, 512, suggests adding *ond* before
þreo to gain a syllable, and so Holthausen, Krapp.

    1309 *elngemeta / and wið yða gewyrc* Holthausen divides
and / wið to eke out the a-line, a very light measure: *éln-
gemèta*. For the use of *eln-*, see 1399a *n.*

    1310b-1313 *þær sceal fæsl wesan . . . gelæded . . . .
earc sceal þy mare.* The Vulgate merely says "lead all living
creatures into the ark in order that they may live." *cwic-
lifigendra* reflects this content but combines "animantibus"
and "ut vivant tecum" into a single generalized concept, *every
kind* of what is essentially one thing must go into a *wudufæsten*—ark, ship and fortress—to find sustenance, protection
and support. So it is with the Ark-Church, subsuming all
forms of life into one organization in order that all may live:
ælcum æfter agenum eorðan tudre (1305, "juxta genus suum" 6.20,

a verse otherwise not represented). This is the theme of Bede:
"Diuersae in arca mansiones ad receptacula sunt diuersorum an-
imantium quae eam erant ingressura dispositae. Et in ecclesia
multi sunt ordines institutionum pro diuersitate eorum qui ad
fidem ueniunt" (*In Gen.*, CCSL 118A, 105). The poet sums up:
earc sceal þy mare, for the ark must be, literally and mysti-
cally, big enough for all its occupants (cf. 1313b *n.*).

    1310b *fæsl* "offspring" (also 1330a, 1359a) and *wocor*
"increase," "offspring" (1312b, 1342b, 1409a, 1490a), both
apparently unique to GN in OE., though both amply documented
by Gmc. cognates, were taken by Menner, *Anglia* 70, 287-88, as
archaic words, evidence of the poem's very early date.

    1312b *wocor* See preceding note.

    1313b *earc sceal þy mare*. "The ark must (be) big e-
nough (for all), lit.: "The ark must (be) all the bigger."
There may be some idea here of an ever-expansible ark so that
it will be adequate for the number of beings assigned to it
(see 1310b-13 *n.*). On a literal level, the verse may reflect
the idea, stemming from Origen, that the ark was big enough
because it was measured in "geometrical cubits" (cf. Augustine,
Quaest. in Hept., IV [CCSL 33, 3]).

    1316 *ongan ofostlice / þæt hof wyrcan*. The alliteration
is defective. Grein and Holthausen emend MS þ [*þæt*] *hof* to
yp-hof. Graphic anticipation of *hof* is possible. But Creed,
MLN 73, 321-25, argues that the lack of alliteration is not
scribal, but a slip by an (oral) poet which has been accurately recorded, who failed to see that *h-* alliteration was
needed when he used the *ofostlice* formula. He therefore suggests that if emendation is to be resorted to it should be of
the a-line, and proposes *ongan hrædlice*.

    1317b-1319a "To his kin [i.e., the descendants of La-
mech? of Seth? or merely 'his sons'?] he [Noe] said that was
a terrible event, a fierce punishment about to befall the people. They took no heed of that." This seems to be a reference to the tradition that Noe preached to the people of the
world during the "time of repentence" (cf. 1263-69 *n.*). Jewish legend has it that for 120 years Noe exhorted the sinners
to change their ways, threatening them with a flood, but they
merely derided him (see Ginzberg, I, 153; V, 174-75, *n.* 19).

    1320-1326 The rendition of "et bitumine linies intrin-
secus et extrinsecus" is remarkably developed, and uncharac-
teristically repeated (cf. 1309b-10a). Utley, "Flood Narrative," 209-10, suggests that the hardening process (1325) may
refer either to the *eorðan lime* with which the ark is caulked,
or to the "gopher wood" of which it is said to be made. But
our poet certainly knew nothing of gopher wood——that is an
A.V. recovery direct from Hebrew and does not appear in any
Latin versions or the LXX. *þæt is syndrig cynn* can refer only
to *eorðan lime*. The expanded comment cannot be explained by
reference to the literal level of the Vulgate, but its promin-

ence is in accord with the traditional explanation of the "bitumen." According to Bede, bitumen is a substance which cannot be dissolved by the boring of worms, or the heat of the
sun, or the blowing of wind, or the continual beating of waves
(cf. 1309 *yða gewyrc*). What is this *bitumen*, then, but faith?
(*In Gen.*, CCSL 118A, 105-06). Isidore gives the form of words
which served most other later commentators: "est enim bitumen
ferventissimum et violentissimum gluten, significans dilec-
tionis ardorem vi magnae fortitudinis ad tenendam societatem
spiritualem omnia tolerantem" (*Quaest. Vet. Test.* VII, 4 [PL.
83, 230A]). The *Pentateuchal Commentary* ventures: "Per bitumen patientia et continentia corporis et animae designatur"
(PL. 91, 225C). However it is phrased, the bitumen of the ark
is always taken as one or more of the virtues, applying to Noe
as the type of the Just Man and *figura Christi*. This section
of the poem ends, then, with an emphatic figure of the ark,
continently embraced by its seal of pitch, keeping out the
killing waters, a figure of love, working by faith for salvation, which is, after all, the emphasis given to the story in
all the commentaries—Christ, within the Church, saving by
love and man being saved by faith.

    1329b-1330 *pæt þu weg nimest // and feora fæsl / þe þu
ferian scealt* Holthausen changes *and* to *mid*. Wells supposes
that there is more wrong here than local emendations can correct because, he thinks, a *pæt*-clause which gave the reason
for or substance of the *wær* has dropped out. Krapp nonsensi-
cally remarks that both *þu* and *feora fæsl* are the subjects of
nimest, and Braasch also lists *fæsl* as nom. But *fæsl* must be
acc., object of *nimest*, which is loosely functioning in two
different constructions. Keeping in mind 7.1, 6.18, 7.2, in
that order, the whole sentence (1328-32a) runs: "Therefore
[*pæs*], I give you my promise [*ponamque foedus meum tecum*],
dearest of men, that you shall take (your) way [*ingredieris*]
and (you shall take) the offspring of the living [*ex omnibus
animantibus mundis tolles*] which you must carry over deep water . . . ," etc.

    1335-1338 *Ond þu seofone genim . . . and þara oðera /
ælces twa* This cuts through the Vulg. "septena (et) septena,"
"duo (et) duo," by rendering as *seofone* (i.e., a total of seven of each species of clean animals, not seven pairs) and *ælces twa* (i.e., two of each species of unclean beasts, one male
and one female). Cf. Alcuin, *Int. & resp. in Gen.*, 110 (PL.
100, 528D), following Augustine (*Quaest. in Hept.* I, 8 [CCSL
33,4]): "*Inter.:* . . .An quatuor ex immundis et quatuordecim ex
mundis animalibus intelligere debemus introducenda esse? *Resp.:*
Non duo et duo propter quatuor, sed propter masculum et feminam. Nam de immundis tantummodo duo, et de mundis solummodo
septem" (cf. Bede, *In Gen.*, CCSL 118A, 113-14). The poet is
careful to explain what "clean" means, 1337a, but does not directly translate "mundis . . . non mundis."

1337 *para þe to mete / mannum lifige* The a-line is of
the doubtful "e1" type (Bliss gives 7 occurrences in BW, *Metre
of BW*, 122). To correct the type Holthausen reads *para þe
mete to* in his ed., and in *Anglia* 46, 61 offers *para þe man-
mum / to mete lifige.* Wells (with others?) construes *lifige*
as subj. pl. (cf. 1587a *n.*), but it can be governed by
gehwilc(es): "take seven of each species . . . of each of
those which lives as food for men."

1338a *oðera* Sievers, *Beiträge* 10, 462 and Wülker report
an *r* erased between *-er-*, Wells says "probably an *a.*" There
is certainly an erased letter in that position, but what it is
is not visible to me in either MS or facsimile. Holthausen,
Krapp, Wells print *oðerra*, but the simplified form is acceptable as the scribe's intention (cf. 1694a *oðere* and Campbell,
par. 457).

1351-1352a *feowertig daga / fæhðe ic wille // on weras
stælan* "For forty days I will avenge (mens') hostility on
men." *stælan* "avenge," "prosecute," takes the object of the
offense; cf. BW 1340, 2485, CS 638f., *Maxims II* 54, and Kock,
Anglia 27, 229-31.

1355a *racu* "Storm," "mist," "driven clouds" is rare, cf.
streamracu AN 1580, PP 71.8. *OED*, s.v. *rack*[2] gives only modern examples. B-T cites *Destr. of Troy* 1984, *A rak and a
royde wyde rose in hor saile.* Cf. collocation in 1375, 1406.

1360b *gefor* Subject is *noe* 1356a.

1363-1367a The Closing of the Ark. Genesis 7.16, ". . .et
inclusit eum Dominus deforis," is considerably elaborated here
and at 1390-91. Traditional comment tends to converge on this
verse. Angelomus, for example, expansively airs a question
about the literal level: "Quomodo enim posteaquam clausam est,
ut nullus hominum extra arcam fuit, imbituminari extrinsecus
ostium potuit? Hoc enim sine dubio divinum opus fuit, ne in-
grederentur aquae per aditum, quem humana non munierat manus"
(*Comm. in Gen.*, PL. 115, 159B). Such a query goes back to
Jewish exegesis. Rabbi Mana (4th cent.) comments: "When all
the creatures entered the ark the Holy One, blessed be He,
closed and sealed with his hand the gate of the ark . . ."
(cited by Mirsky, *ES* 48, 389). Clearly, this parallels the
literal statement of 1363-67. More importantly, in the Christian tradition, the tendency was to interpret the closing of
the Ark on the seventh day as Baptism, which conforms to the
baptismal theme brought out throughout the Flood episode in GN.
So, e.g., 1351b-54, where Vulg. has "I will destroy every substance I have made on the face of the earth," becomes "I will
avenge the hostility of men . . . and kill with water all
those who remain outside the ark," recalling that the waters
of baptism avail for damnation as well as for salvation (see
1376b-81a *n.*). In 1363-67 and 1390-91 the baptismal significance is evoked by *segnade* "made the sign of the cross over,"
while the epithets for God recall the regenerative aspect of

baptism by setting the Flood beside the Creation, for the
Flood is a kind of new creation, a figure of the new creation
of Baptism. In such a vein Augustine addresses the catechumens: "Tunc ergo efficimur uere liberi cum deus nos fingit
id est format et creat, non ut homines, quod iam fecit, sed ut
boni homines simus: quod nunc gratia sua facit, ut simus in
Christo noua creatura, secundum quod dictum est, 'Cor mundum
crea in me Deus' (Ps. 50.12)" (*Enchiridion* IX, 31 [CCSL 46,
66]). The use in passing of the second person (*nergend usser,
scyppend usser*) further establishes an immediate moral tone,
while on the literal level the poem pretty exactly renders
the Vulgate, explains obvious questions that arise from the
literal text and introduces a certain amount of legendary material.

1363a *Him on hoh* "Behind him" (lit.: "on his heel").

1374a *of ædra gehwære* The lWS form *gehwære* is disturbing the meter, and is emended as being a scribal form to *gehwam* by Holthausen (see Sievers, *Beiträge* 10, 485 and Campbell,
par. 716, *n.* 4). Cf. BW 25a *in mægða gehwære*, usually emended
to *in mægða gehwam* by older edd. (but not Dobbie or Klaeber).

1376b-1381a The Destruction of the World. GN is much
more explicit than the Vulgate about the destruction of mankind in the Flood. Many themes of traditional exegesis are
discernible here. The men who are destroyed are "the children of a wicked feud" (taking *manfæhðu* as gen. sing., see Campbell, par. 587), "children of middle-earth," like Cain, born
to the feud which began when men defied God and established
the wicked union which brought forth *gigantmæcgas* (1268a).
God is avenging their *hygeteonan*, "calculated crimes," committed against Him in the old *eðelland*, i.e., *their* proper home,
the City of This World, which is about to be destroyed. Their
world is termed *hof*, in contrast to the other *hof*, the ark
(1345b, 1393b, 1489a). Above all, the recurrent Baptismal motif is evoked as the waters cover the irredeemable part of
mankind: "Quod praeter arcam omnis caro, quam terra sustenta-
bat, diluvio consumpta est: quia praeter Ecclesiae societatem,
aqua Baptismi quamvis eadem sit, non solum non valet ad salutem, sed valet potius ad perniciem" (Augustine, *Contra Faust.
Manich.* XII, 17 [PL. 42, 263]).

1386b-1389 *flod ealle wreah . . . hea beorgas . . . on
sund ahof // earce from eorðan / and pa æðelo mid.* Cf. 7.19,
7.17, 7.20, in that order, and note Bede, *In Gen.*, CCSL 118A,
119: "Quos uidelicet montes aquae operiunt, sed ipsis aquis
arca superfertur, quia temptationum gurges superbos quidem atque impios premit ac demergit, sed ipse a iustis superatur,
qui libero boni operis cursu atque alacri mente ad portum sa-
lutis aeternae tendere non desinunt."

1393a *ofer holmes hrincg* G-K defines *hrincg* here as
"Bezirk," "district"; Marquardt, *Kenningar*, 166, as "horizon."
I take it in the latter sense, perhaps with the force of "or-
bis," and in fact, since the whole earth is covered by water,

the sea has literally become "orbis terrarum." The expression
must be compared to 2855a *hrincg pæs hean landes* = "in terram
Visionis" (see *note*). The usual spelling is *hring*, see Brunner,
par. 215. Rosier, *Anglia* 88, 334-36, following a suggestion
by Bouterwek, argues for reading at 1393 and 2855 *hrycg*, "a
high place on sea or land." He points out that *n* is a frequent scribal intrusion, as in BW 1836 (*hreprinc* for *Hrepric*),
GU 962 (*engle* for *egle*), *Prose Phoenix*, where one version has
hrynge, the other *ricge*; accordingly, Marckwardt-Rosier read
here *hricg*. But the coherence of *hrincg* in both places, and
its appearance twice in similar contexts argue strongly for
the authenticity of the MS forms.

    1394b-1396a *fære ne moston . . . hæste hrinon fære*
may be taken as dat. of *fær* "ship," object of *hrinon* (cf.
1544a, 1307a, 1323b, 1419a) or as instr. of *fǽr* "fear" (cf.
2700b, 2380a) parallel to *hæste*; but *hæste* may be taken as an
adj. "violent," modifying *brogan* or as adv., as well as a noun.

    1398b *sæ drenceflod* Take *sæ* as *se*. The proximity of
sæ to *drence* and *flod* (the latter two words separated by a
space, as is usual in this MS for words considered compounds
by edd.) has naturally caused problems (the same difficulty a-
rises at 221-24a, see *note*). Thorpe printed *sæ-drence flod*
"the sea-drenching flood." Etmüller took *sædrence* "inundatio"
as either nom. or instr. Dietrich, *ZfdA* 10, 323-24, proposed
simplifying to *se drencflod*, Grein restored to *se drenceflod*,
and so all edd. For the form *drenceflod*, cf. B-T *Supp.*, s.v.
drence f., "potion," "drink;" *drencefæt* also occurs. *drenc(e)*
primarily means "drink," secondarily "drowning" (i.e., death
by drinking too much water), and is involved in a conceit
whereby drinking (overdrinking?) and death are conventionally
connected. The examples are too numerous to list, but cf. EX
364b, Noe's flood is *drenc(e)flod* (MS *dren floda*). At *Whale*
29 ff., the idea of drinking with gay companions (an image of
this life) is connected with death by drowning most literally:
". . . garsecges gæst / grund geseceð // ond þonne in deaðsele
/ drence bifæsteð // scipu mid scealcum." At EX 34 a corrector has altered the line (the Junius scribe wrote *deaðe ge...*,
the rest erased) to read *deaðe gedrenced* (of the first-born of
Egypt) where literal drowning is not involved. The correction
shows the widespread familiarity of the conventional concept,
if not the EX-poet's use of it. Cf. also AN 1526b-27a "meodu-
scerwen wearð / æfter symbeldæge" (of a real flood after a
drinking-party) and BW 769 *ealuscerwen* (see Wrenn's gloss,
2d ed., 243-44). The notion occurs again in GN, at 2906b-08a
(see *note*).

    1399a *(fiftena) . . . monnes elna,* Lit.: "fifteen of
forearms of a man," i.e., "fifteen ells" = "quindecim cubitis;"
eln (about 24", the length of a forearm) is the usual OE.
translation of "cubit," but the literalism here is unparalleled.

    1400-1401 *þam æt niehstan wæs / nan to gedale // nympe*

heo wæs ahafen / on þa hean lyft. One of the most difficult
places in GN. No suggestions have been offered which entirely clear up the passage, and as the text is probably corrupt all solutions seem more or less lame. Nothwithstanding
the fact that the MS text can be deciphered as it stands in
several ways, there are disturbing stylistic features indicating deep-seated disruption, probably papered over scribally
on one or more occasions. These are: the awkwardness of *nan*
and *nympe*, the vagueness of *þam* and the ambiguity of *gedal*
and, especially, the extreme weakness of *heo* either as subj.
(if we punctuate with a stop after *lyft*) or as the first element of a broad conceptual variation (*heo, earce bord*, placing a comma after *lyft*). But a comma cannot disguise the fact
that 1400-01 stands independently. The phrase *æt niehstan*
usually means "at last," "soon," "finally," etc. Krapp construes 1400a as *æt þam niehstan* "thereupon" but queries (cf.
Kock, *Anglia* 44, 253). Wells takes *þam* as referring to *dren-*
ceflod 1398b, translating "for that [flood] at last there was
nothing . . ." but *þam*, if demonstrative, is best taken as
referring to mankind in general, "for them." The pointing of
1400 is defective: *niehstan · wæs · nan*; I follow Holthausen's
lineation, metrically superior to Krapp's (*niehstan / wæs*).
1400b *gedal* conveys the idea of "separation," but a confusion
of choices presents itself. Holthausen admits he does not
understand 1400b. Krapp takes *gedal* as "portion" ("there was
nothing . . . for a portion," i.e., nothing else was granted);
Wells translates "divider," i.e., the firmament; Thorpe, taking 1399b as part of the sentence gives, "that was an awful
fate, from which at last was nought exempt [nothing as an
exemption?]." But in GN *gedal* usually means "death": cf. 930b
-931a *þe is gedal witod // lices and sawle* = 3.19, also *frið-*
gedal 114?, *gastgedal* 1127, *lifgedal* 2563, etc. In other texts
gedal in this sense has been highly specialized, e.g., GU 1350
þeodengedal ("separation from a lord by his death"). With
Grein, then, I take *gedal* as "death," "destruction." As it
stands *heo* is fem. nom. sing., referring to *earce* fem., the concept, or to *fær* 1394b, but it is awkwardly isolated. A noun
is wanted, hence Sievers, *Beiträge* 19, 448, suggested *heof,*
"lamentation," taken up by Holthausen, Mason and Krapp, the
latter translating, ". . . nought was their portion (*gedal*)
except lamentation raised . . ."; incidentally, this version
coincides with the Jewish tradition that the sinners, realiz-
ing their plight at the last minute, in anguish pleaded with
Noe and attacked the ark, but were beaten off by the animals
(Ginzberg, I, 148; V 177-78, *n.* 25)—but Sievers offered *heof*
in passing, probably having nothing more in mind than how to
make a noun of *heo.* Wells emends *heo*[*f*] to *heofon* (as if *heof*
had authority), translating impenetrably "For that [flood] at
last there was nothing as a divider except that heaven was
heaved up into the high air." He explains, "the separation of

the waters in the creation is undone in the Flood and only the firmament itself finally divides any water from the mass covering the earth" (xlvii-xlviii, citing Augustine, *De Gen. c. Manich.*, 36). He may be following the equally dark interpretation of Sisam (*Studies*, 42, *n.*), who takes *heo* as referring to *seo dun* (*dunum* 1398a): "Fifteen of our [*monnes*] ells above the mountains stood the whelming flood (that was a great marvel!); and at last there was none to divide the flood unless it rose up to the high firmament." This seems, on the face of it, as absurd as it is obscure, since the firmament is more than 15 ells above the highest mountain. But perhaps Sisam had in mind the common medieval idea (behind Dante's Mount Purgatory, as well as the garbled gloss in MS. Cotton Claudius B. IV, f. 5v [*Hept.*, 419]; cf. PX 28-32) that Eden was located on the top of a mountain that reached to the lunar sphere and therefore escaped inundation. Be all this as it may, *heo* can be construed and justified, however slenderly. I translate 1400-01: "For them [the sinners] there was finally nothing for their death [no means for their death] unless it [the ark, *heo*] was lifted into the high air." In other words, the Flood is the instrument both of the destruction and the salvation of mankind, destroying one part, but not until the other is lifted up. If this interpretation is correct, the sentence is combining, rather unsuccessfully, two distinct ideas, the spiritual idea (already referred to, 1376b-81a *n.*) that the waters of baptism avail both for damnation and salvation, and the literal ideas of 7.17 ". . . et elevaverunt arcam in sublime a terra," 7.19 "sub universo caelo" (cf. 1392), and 7.23 "et delevit omnem substantiam," compacted into a single statement. The poet, characteristically, evokes God's grace even at the most terrible moments. Huppé, following the MS, gives a similar spiritual turn to the sentence, but as is often the case with his translations, the grammatical processes at work are unclear: "there is nothing for man unless she, the ark, is raised up on the waters of baptism" (*Doctrine and Poetry*, 173). Marckwardt-Rosier give an acceptable alternative interpretation, reading on a literal level: "'To them [i.e., *wægliðendum*] finally there was no other allotment [*nan to gedale*] except that the ark [*heo*] was lifted high into the air . . . .' That is, as the flood rose . . . the apportionment to Noah . . . in God's covenant was that he should be lifted above the flood's destruction and thereby saved."

  1404b *hine* The antecedent must be *egorhere* 1402a.
  1405b *ed monne* Retained as manifestly corrupt, but perhaps representing a scribal "emendation," equivalent to *ead monna*, "happiness of men." I take *ed* as parallel to *egorhere* 1402a, the waters of the Flood as the waters of Baptism. More awkwardly, B-T, p. 239, takes the phrase as "the safety of men," the Ark, parallel to *earce bord* 1403b. Both interpretations are based on Thorpe's, "regeneration of men," who,

however, apparently related *ed* to the prefix, as in *edsceaft*
"new creation," DN 112, *edniwan*, "renew," etc. Since *ed* in
this sense as noun is not recorded, it is better taken as a
late spelling of *ead* (cf. Campbell par. 329.2). For the metrical pattern, but not deficient, cf. 1602b, 1891b. Metrically *ed monne* is short a syllable, though three-syllable hemistiches occur elsewhere in GN. The line could be augmented
by reading *ede monne* (dat. sing. + gen. pl.) or *ed monnena*
(gen. pl. of *monna*) but such an obviously defective line does
not call for such tinkering. *monne* may be regarded as a late
reduction of an unstressed syllable, gen. pl. (Campbell, par.
379). Many emendations have naturally been offered, but none
solves the crux. Much the best paleographically is Dietrich's
(*ZfdA* 10, 324-25) *edniowe* "continually renewing itself," implying a previous **edniouue*. Grein, *Germania* 10, 417, elaborated this to *edniowne* (referring to *egorhere*) and Cosijn,
Beiträge 20, 98, mended the meter with *a edniowne*. Holthausen
stretched to *edniowne flod* in his ed., having previously suggested *e[acne an]d wonne* (in *Indog. Forsch.* 4, 380). Wülker
followed the MS but suggested *edmodne* "obedient." Krapp combined Holthausen and Wülker, reading *edmodne flod* (but *edmod-
nesse*, dat., would be better paleographically). Wells strays
furthest afield with *eða wonne = yða wonne*, citing 1430a *wonne
yða*, and DN 57 *eðan* (for *yðan* "lay waste"). Marckwardt and
Rosier follow the MS in their text, but omit 1405b from the
translation of the rest of the sentence.

   1411-1412a *Gelædde þa wigend / weroda drihten // worde
ofer widland*. This development of "adduxit spiritum super
terram" strengthens the creation theme evident throughout the
Noe episode. Most commentators naturally connect the "spirit"
of 8.1 with that of 1.2—Noe and his family are the inheritors
of a new world and are themselves guided by the creative force.
Thorpe would emend 1412a *worde* to *winde* to bring the poem in
line with the text. But Ambrose evokes the Creation in terms
similar to those of this passage, concording the "spirit" to
the Word which effects everything visible: "Non puto hoc ita
dictum, ut spiritus nomine ventum accipiamus . . . . Spiritus
. . . divini virtute invisibili diluvium illud repressum esse
non dubium est, coelesti operatione, non flatu . . . . Est
ergo Spiritus cujus operationi cedere universa videantur, in
quo coeli ipsius virtus sit, sicut scriptum est: 'Verbo Domini
coeli firmati sunt, et Spiritu oris ejus omnis virtus eorum'
(Ps. 32.6): qui Spiritus est creator universorum, sicut etiam
Job dicit: 'Spiritus divinus qui fecit me' (Job 33.4)" (*De Noe
et arca* 16, 58 [PL. 14, 388A-B]).

   1415b-1416a *eft gecyrred, // torht ryne*, "Once again
(the Lord) turned back the shining course (of water)" = "re-
versaquae aquae de terra euntes et redeuntes." *ryne* is parallel to *egstream*, obj. of *gecyrred*. The waters of the earth
have the property of running out ("euntes") and running back

("redeuntes"), hence, *eft gecyrred*. Grein, Braasch take *torht*
as parallel to *metod*. 1416a, *torht ryne*, is metrically defective, with only two (metrical) syllables, and alliterating on
the second stress only; perhaps a word has dropped out. Grein's
rodortorht ryne comes closest to mending the line, but is
still short with two resolved stresses. Krapp's *torhtne ryne*
fails to make up the metrical length or to correct the faulty
alliteration.

    1428 *reste ageafe / pære he rume dreah* Fem. oblique
pære apparently refers to *reste*. Grein and edd. have emended
to *pæra*, gen. pl., agreeing with *siða* 1427b. A similar emendation is traditionally made at 1522. Wells translates 1427b-
29a (reading *pæra*), "when . . . the Lord almighty, from per-
ilous journeys gave him rest, from those that he endured widely
when on water . . . ." Krapp suggests that perhaps *pæra pe*
should be read as in the emended 1522. But *dreogan*, used in-
transitively, means "busy," and *pære* may be taken as fem. dat.
referring to *reste*: "when the Guardian of life, the almighty
Lord, granted him a resting place in which he [Noe] was extensively active while on water . . . ." For the syntax, cf.
1465a *and rume fleah*. The poet is referring to the "rest" on
the ark, corresponding typologically to the seventh day of
creation and anagogically to the spiritual activity of the
blessed before the final Resurrection; see 1431-35 *n*. For the
significance of *reste*, see 1485-87a *n*.

    1431-1435 The Resting of the Ark. The usual interpreta-
tion of the resting of the ark "on the seventh day of the second month" was that it figures the rest of the saints, analogous to the seventh day of Creation, followed by the mystical
"eighth day," i.e., the Resurrection (cf. Augustine, *Contra
Faust. Manich.* XII, 20 [PL. 42, 264-65]). Huppé, *Doctrine and
Poetry*, 174-76, extrapolates from the whole Noe episode in GN
a signification of the saints' yearning for release from the
prison of this life (cf. *of nearwe, of enge*); I do not find
this worked out in any ancient commentary on Genesis 8. Mirsky, *ES* 48, 389-91, has pointed out the correspondence of
these lines to several rabbinical sources, in particular, *Pirke
de Rabbi Eliezer*: "Rabbi Zadok said: 'For twelve months all
the creatures were in the ark; and Noah stood and prayed before
the Holy One, blessed be He, saying before Him: "Sovereign of
all worlds. Bring me forth from this prison, for my soul is
faint, because of the stench of lions . . . ."'" Various O.T.
verses were commonly interpreted as referring to Noe "in prison": e.g., Pss. 141.8, 17.20, 67.7, 145.7; Is. 42.7, 49.9.
Perhaps the poet, by his wording, intends to recall the famous Gregorian allegory of the ark, the highest and fewest
saints figured in the narrow upper story, eager to lead out
the fruits of the Resurrection into Salvation (*Hom. in Evang.*
38, 8 [PL. 76, 1287A]).

1431b *hæleð langode,* impersonal sing.

1438b-1448 The Raven. The elaboration of 8.6-7 is not primarily indebted to the theme-stock of OE. poetry ("the beasts of battle") though obviously it provides the poet with his particular means of expression here, but stems from the Talmudic tradition of the contumelious bird who rather than return to the ark chooses to go to the bodies of those killed in the flood. It passes into Christian tradition and is mentioned by all commentators (as was pointed out long ago by Samuel Moore, *MLR* 6, 201-02, and largely ignored since: Wells [xlviii, & *n.* 60] and Marckwardt-Rosier mention it). Augustine's comment, or some comment directly derived from it, was certainly known to the poet: "Quod scriptum est dimissum esse coruum nec redisse et dimissam post eum columbam et ipsam redisse, quod non inuenisset requiem pedibus suis, quaestio solet oboriri, utrum coruus mortuus sit an aliquo modo uiuere potuerit. . . . Vnde conicitur a multis, quod cadaueri potuit coruus insidére, quod columba naturaliter refugit" (*Quaest. in Hept.*, CCSL 33, 5). The detail that the corpses are *fleotenda* seems to be the poet's addition, a natural inference providing an alliterant. The unique *salwigfeðera* recalls the "beasts of battle" (*salwigpad* occurs 4x in this theme), but is also elaborating *sweartne* 1441b. The black raven, according to Bede, figures those who, having the benefits of the sacraments, go out into the world, preferring "nigredinem terrenae oblectationis" to the security of the Church (*In Gen.*, CCSL 118A, 123; cf. Ambrose, *De Noe et arca* 17, 62 [PL. 14, 390-91]).

1445a *sidwæter* Uncompounded by edd. (2C2). I take it as d3-type, similar in formulation to *widland* 156, 1412, 1538 and *sidland* 2207, 2453. Cf. 100a *and sidwæter.*

1447 *ac se feond gespearn / fleotende hreaw.* ". . . but the enemy perched on floating corpses." Thorpe construed the perfectly straightforward *feond* as present part. "rejoicing," thence Grein suggested *feonde,* supported by Cosijn, *Beiträge* 19, 449, and so Holthausen and Krapp. Hulbert *JEGP* 37, 536, argues for the MS reading and Wells and Marckwardt-Rosier restore *feond.* The poet probably intends *feond* in a multiplicity of ways, for the raven was variously explained as a type of the devil, of sinners, the damned, heretics or the falsely baptized.

1448 *salwigfeðera / secan nolde.* "The dusky-feathered one did not want to return." *secan,* intrans. (cf. 1445, 1559, 2282), is criticized by Sisam, *Studies,* 40: "since *secan* is never left in the air like this in a sound text . . . at least a line is missing . . . which contained the object of *secan.*" But *secan,* intrans. with dat. and prep., is very common (cf. *Finnesburh* 27, PP 121.9, EL 319, AN 911, BW 3001, etc.): here the prep. phrase is elided because it is understood from 1445b-1446a.

1449-1482 The Dove. The consistently bright mood asso-

ciated with the dove, contrasting with *se feond*, follows the
emphasis of the exegetical tradition regarding the two kinds
of birds. The raven figures the "wicked Christians," the dove
"the good" (Remigius, *Comm. in Gen.*, PL. 131, 77C); the dove
represents the spiritual and honest mind of the elect, the raven the "gall of bitterness" (cf. Acts 8.23) of the wicked-
hearted (Bede, *In Gen.*, CCSL 118A, 123 f.). The poet carefully grades the three flights to emphasize the three stages
or states of holiness which they typify: the first signifies—
according to Augustine and most following commentators—the
saints who are not promised rest in this world; the second,
with the olive branch, figures those baptized outside the
Church "quo . . . si eis pingendo non defuerit charitatis,
posteriore tempore quasi vespere, in ore columbae tanquam in
osculo pacis, ad unitatis societatem posse perduci;" the third
which has no return, figures the end of the world when the
saints shall be in eternal safety with the Father (*Contra
Faust. Manich.* XII, 20 [PL. 42, 265]).

  1449b *sweartum hrefne* Governed by *æfter*, 1450b.

  1460b *se wilda fugel* Here and at 1465a, 1477b, *wilde*
(of the dove) must mean "unrestrained," "free to fly wherever
it wills;" cf. 1455.

  1468a *on beam hyre*   *hyre* "sweet one," "gentle one," is
fem. nom. sing. adj., subject of *stop*.

  1471-1474a *heo feðera onsceoc . . . . grene blædæ*. The
rejoicing of the dove is natural, but the diction suggests
also the signification of the second flight, a transitional
baptism where the goal is still far (cf. note to 1449-1482):
hence the dove is *liðend*, "a traveller over water," *bliðemod*
1468b, the olive branch is a *lac*, an offering, but a sign of
hope *grene blædæ*. In the Jewish tradition, the olive branch
signifies the bitter food of the free: better than that it
should be sweet and the dove delivered into the power of men
(cf. Ginzberg, I, 164); perhaps in the same spirit the dove
first returned *hungri to handa* (1463a). Hrabanus, articula-
ting the Christian tradition, sees the olive branch as "affec-
tus bonus . . . quod sancta anima ad quietam mentam affectum
bonum defert in cogitationibus mundis" (*Alleg. in Sac. Scrip.*,
PL. 112, 1037A).

  1475b-1476a . . . *wæs frofor cumen, // earfoðsiða bot*.
The wording (rendering 8.11) suggests the traditional interpretation of Noe's name, "consolatio," derived from 5.29, "vocavitque nomen eius Noe dicens iste consolabitur nos . . ."
(cf. Ps.-Bede, *In Pent. comm.*, PL. 91, 221C). See next note.

  1485-1487a *þe is eðelstol / eft gerymed . . . lagosiða
rest . . . .* "For you a homeland is once again made ready,
happiness in the land, rest for the sea-trip(s), fair on the
earth." *eðelstol* suggests the new Paradise or heaven motif
implicit in this incident. More importantly, the "rest for the
sea-journey" recalls the other interpretation of Noe's name,
a thread running throughout this section of GN (cf. 1303b-05,

1424b-30, 1456b-60a). Bede elaborates the traditional onomastic explanation with the general signification of the Noe
story: "Noe quippe 'requies' interpretatur. In quo iuxta
litteram illud potest intellegi quod temporibus eius omnia retro opera hominum quieuerint per diluuium; iuxta sensum uero
spiritalem, eadem est requies quae et consolatio sanctorum
intueri uidelicet adpropinquante mundi termino et interitum
impiorum et suorum adesse tempus praemiorum. Bene autem Noe,
in cuius meritis Domino deuotis requies et consolatio erat
seculo danda, in decima ab Adam generatione nascitur—quia nimirum per completionem decalogi legis aeterna nobis requies
et uita tribuitur" (*In Gen.*, CCSL 118A, 98). The signification in the poem is drawn on a more functional narrative
plane: while in the commentary Noe's name is symbolic on both
the literal and figural levels (after him all former things
literally cease and figurally his is the rest of the saints),
in GN, "Noe" means *rest* and Noe provides rest for the beings
in his care; see F. C. Robinson, "The Significance of Names
in OE. Literature," *Anglia* 86, 14-58, esp. 33.

   1490-1493 *and ealle þa wocre / þe ic wægprea . . . nerede / þenden lago hæfde . . . þriddan eðyl.* "And all that
offspring which I saved from the wave-punishment on the moun-
tainside when the sea possessed the third home, mightily covered it." With Dietrich, *ZfdA* 10, 325, I take *hæfde* and *gepeahte* as parallel prets., *lago* subj. of both. This is a difficult passage which requires emendation. Krapp's version in-
corporates all the substantial emendations which have been
suggested: *and ealle þa wocre / þe ic wægprea on // liðe nerede / þenden lago hæfde // prymme gepeahtne / priddan eðyl.*
Following Bouterwek, *on* is transposed to 1490b to govern *wægprea*, but this is not grammatically necessary and produces
cross-alliteration. *hliðe* "hillside," is emended to the alliterant *liðe*, "with mercy," following Dietrich (but cf. 1439,
2596: *hliðe* is natural to the context of 8.4). Thorpe took
gepeahte as past. part., modifying *þridda eðyl.* Following
suggestions by Holthausen and Kock, *PPP.*, 15, Krapp reads *gepeahtne* in constr. with *hæfde*, but GN shows only uninflected
parts. in this construction (see Glossary, *habban*). *þridda
eðyl* is the big problem, since what it might be referring to
is unknown. But grammatically, if it is nom., it must be appositive to *lago* and refer to the sea; however, this leaves
no object for *hæfde*, implying the necessity of emending *prymme*
to acc. pl. It is simpler to accept Grein's *priddan*, making
eðyl object of *hæfde*. In this version, the "third home" must
be the earth, which the sea now covers, but why it is the
third home is difficult to tell. Holthausen suggested a series, "heaven, earth and hell," Kock, *PPP.* 15, "heaven (air),
earth and ocean (water)," but these are arbitrary. Marckwardt-Rosier call attention to two quotations in B-T, p. 1069:
"Heofonwaru and eorðwaru, helwaru þridde;" "On nanum heolstrum

heofenan, oþþe eorþan, oþþe sæ þriddan." If the reading
pridda eðyl, "the sea," could be accepted, the problem would
be resolved: the first home was the Paradise of Adam, the second the Earth of Seth, the third the Sea that bore up Noe.
In any case, the poet had something quite specific in mind,
and it is wrong to dismiss *pridda(n)* as "meaningless" (Krapp)
or to attempt to emend it away as Mason and Wells do.

1496b *wraðra lafe.* "The remnants of the wicked ones,"
"the survivors spared from the wicked" (gen. of separation?),
i.e., Noe and his family are not themselves wicked, but are
the surviving members of the race of men who were otherwise
the race of *wraðra.*

1497-1508a Noe's Offering. The episode is spiritualized,
the anthropomorphisms and details of the holocaust being suggested only by the most general indications. By dovetailing
the paraphrases of 8.20 and 9.1, the poet clarifies the two
texts and makes them mean what the commentators traditionally
took 8.21-22 to mean—that Noe offered a good offering with
right worship—but avoids the dangers of too literal a treatment. As Claudius of Turin explains, 8.21 "Odoratusque est
Dominus odorem suavitatis" does not mean that God was pleased
with the odor of the burning flesh of dumb beasts, "sed odor-
atus est, hoc est, delectatus, humani generis ad se conver-
sionem et salutem credentium" (*Comm. in Gen.*, PL. 50, 933A).
The poet reaffirms the theme of Noe's justice (1498a, 1507-10a)
at a place where it was traditionally thought to be signified
(the altar, according to Hrabanus, is "the life of the just"
[*Alleg. in Sac. Scrip.*, PL. 112, 856C]). Bede, *In Gen.*, CCSL
118A, 127, develops 6.9, "Noe vir justus atque perfectus fuit,"
etc., as a meditation on 8.20 and emphasizes Noe's speedy obe-
isance, his piety, his subordination and thankfulness towards
his Creator, his habitual virtue, as does the poem, *on geogoð-
hade . . . ær geearnod* (1507a f.).

1498a *reðran* "To prepare," no other examples occurring,
but Krapp cites *gerépre* "ready," in *Pastoral Care* (ed. Sweet,
EETS 45, 306.15), which implies a verb *réðran.* Other edd. e-
mend to *redian* or *reðian* "furnish," "provide," otherwise attested only in the form *aredian.*

1508 *geearnod. / þa* Grein suggested *þæt* (þ) for MS *þa*,
and Krapp adopts *þæt* in his text as introducing a "necessary"
object-clause after *geearnod.* But B-T *Supp.*, s.v. *geearnian*
I (3) gives several instances of the verb used absolutely.

1513b *fyllað* Braasch and Clark-Hall list this as a masc.
"abundance," presumably following Holthausen, *Etymol. Wörtb.*,
who cites Gmc. cognates. But since the word does not seem
to occur in any other OE. text, it is best to regard it merely
as from *fyllan* "to fill." as in 196, 1533.

1515a *holmes hlæst* "Sea's burden," "fish" = "omnes
pisces maris."

1517b *feoh* Wülker notes that the *r* added above *h* looks "quite modern." Wells remarks: "In fact it [the *r*] is gray, not like ink at all, but more like mold on the M.S.; even in the facsimile its reverse shows on the facing page over *æ* in *ætes*, l. 1557."

1520b *sawldreore*. Scanned ´x :` x 2A1: therefore, Holthausen Reads *sawuldreore*.

1521-1523a "Anyone first destroys his own soul's grace who with a pointed weapon takes another's life." The poet, bound to a paraphrase, allows the form of 9.6, death by slaughter, to take a familiar formulaic expression, *mid gares orde*. He is probably aware of the usual treatment of the superficially ridiculous presciption that blood had to be shed before the murderer was to be punished. What of murder by poison or rope? Bede explains that by "blood" is simply meant the vital principle and "shedding" it is to kill by any means (*In Gen.*, CCSL 118A, 133). The poet, like the commentators, makes it clear that punishment is not merely "blood for blood" but the soul of the murderer against the life of the slain (the murdered victim loses *aldor*, but the murderer loses *gastes duguðe*). "Quod qui effuderit, id est qui aliquo genere mortis hominem occiderit, fundetur sanguis illius quia peccando uitam perdit aeternam, 'Anima enim quae peccauerit, ipsa morietur' (Ezech. 18.20). Cui simile est hoc quod Petro dicitur, 'Omnes enim qui acceperint gladium gladio peribunt' (Matt. 26.52), ac si aperte diceretur, 'Omnes qui iniuste occidunt hominem, et iidem occisione ipsi in anima pereunt'" (*In Gen.*, 33-34).

1522b *pæra* i.e., *para* (for MS *pære*); *ælc* . . . *pæra* = *quicumque* (9.6).

1525a *seðe* The verb *séðan* "to declare true" (cf. *sóð*) is well-attested. Grein takes it to mean "avenge," but it is not clear how he achieves this. Perhaps the idea here is that God will guarantee, or affirm, the spiritual "wergild" or exaction due to the injured against the guilty. If such is the case, 1524b-26 may be translated: ". . . and I will guarantee the life of a man against the slayer much more severely and against the brother of a slayer because he accomplishes bloodshed with weapons, the slaughter of a man . . ." Wells translates: "for the life of a man I charge to the slayer." Cf. Klaeber's note to BW 1106. Dietrich, *ZfdA* 10, 326, after Bouterwek, cuts through the MS reading by suggesting *sece*, "I will seek the life of a man from the slayer" = "de manu viri . . . requiram animam hominis." So Sievers, *Beiträge* 10, 512, Kock, *JJJ.* 31, and Krapp. Wülker and Holthausen read *sette*.

1526a *and to broðor banan* Following Kock, *JJJ.* 31, Krapp and Wells, *broðor* should be construed as dat. (see Brunner, par. 285, anm. 3 [b]) rather than gen., making a much closer rendering of 9.5. Holthausen and earlier edd. read *broðorbanan*.

1528b *monn wæs to godes* 2E1-type with the second stress

resolved. Many will not allow that this type exists (see
Wrenn's note to BW 6, *egsode eorl*). But Kock, *Anglia* 46,
187-88, lists 26 occurrences of this type, including GN 1747b,
1778b, 1805a and 2173a, 1818a, 2099a, 2278b, 2695b. Bliss,
Metre of Beowulf, 126, gives a total of 22 occurrences in BW
alone.

    1539a *oft gelome* "Very often;" Holthausen, citing
1670b, reads *oft ond gelome,* so Krapp and Wells, but the
change is semantically and metrically indifferent.

    1546-1549 Noe's Wife and Daughters-in-Law. Judging by
the rubbed state of PP. 74-75 of the MS, the passage containing the apocryphal names of the ark-wives has been of peculiar
interest since they were written there, and the interest has
not ceased. Many attempts were made by the earlier edd. to
rearrange these lines into meter and sense, but all were rendered otiose by Gollancz' convincing argument (*Caedmon MS*,
lxiii-lxv) that the words *and heora feower wif nemde wæron,
percoba, olla, olliua, olliuani* are a late marginal addition,
not a part of the original poem, not even verse, mistakenly
incorporated into the text by a scribe of a subsequent copy.
Hence, Krapp puts these words (his lines 1546-48) in parentheses without any attempt to make meter of them, while Wells
presents them in a single bracketed line. I have taken the
liberty of restoring the words as a "note," but I take *and
heora feower wif*, a metrically and formulaically normal half-
line (cf. 1334b), to be part of the original text and the occasion for the original gloss. The whole passage, as it appears in the MS, is deficient in sense, and the removal of the
names improves the general drift, but there still seems to be
a verb missing. As it stands, *wærfæst metod* cannot refer to
Noe—either its case must be changed or a verb supplied. Gollancz proposes *wærfæst metodes,* "he [Noe], the faithful servant of the Lord;" Krapp, following Dietrich *ZfdA* 10, 326,
reads *metode*: "he [Noe] faithful to the Lord." How to construe *wætra lafe* in these versions is not transparent: Gollancz
takes as collectively referring to *his eaforum prim*. I prefer
to supply a verb in 1546b, which stands vacant in any case
once the names are removed: this obviates the need for any
change in 1549. Translate: "Then the wise son of Lamech came
from the ship after the flood with his three sons, the guardian of the heritage, together with their four wives [after]
the steadfast Lord [had remained faithful] to the survivor of
the waters."

    The four wives are not mentioned by name anywhere in the
Bible of course, but an ancient tradition of speculating on
the name of Noe's wife had grown up, begetting a wide variety
of forms from many sources (see F. L. Utley, "The 103 Names of
Noah's Wife," *Speculum* 16, 426-52). The particular names in
GN are apparently of Irish origin: the Book of Leinster, f. 136b
shows *Percoba, Olla, Oliuan, Oliuane*, the *Lebor Gabála Erenn*

I, 2 has the verses "Women without evil colour, great excel-
ences, / Above the Flood without extinction, / *Coba,* vigorous
was the white swan, / *Olla, Oliva, Olivana*" (trans. Macalister,
Irish Text Society [1938], 169). The Irish MSS are of the
11th century and later, but the tradition of the names undoub-
tedly is much older (cf. Gollancz, lxiv). In Cotton Claudius
B. IV, f. 14r (the OE. prose Genesis), Noe's wife is glossed
phiarphara, no doubt the same as *Phuarphara* in the near-con-
temporary *Historia Scholastica* of Petrus Comestor (PL. 198,
1084C), and both of these are probably ultimately of the same
tradition that produced *Percoba*. The names of the daughters-
in-law also turn up in the prose *Solomon and Saturn* (ed. Kemble, 184), names ultimately stemming from Ezechiel 23, *Oolla*
and *Ooliva*, traditionally attached to Lot's daughters, with
more obvious appropriateness.

    1555 *ÐA Noe ongan / niwan stefne* This section marks the
beginning of a new stage in Noe's life, his domestic career
as a farmer. It also marks the Second Age of the World, which
was commonly held to have begun with Noe after the Flood (Bede
begins it precisely at the time of Noe's sacrifice [*In Gen.*,
CCSL 118A, 127]). Claudius of Turin begins the second book of
his Genesis commentary at this place because a new world is at
hand (PL. 50, 935A-B). So Bede describes it: "Et egressa post
diluuium animantia de arca ingrediantur in nouam terrae faciem,
nouis uernantem floribus, ibique multiplicentur et crescant"
(*In Gen.,* 126). The expression *niwan stefne* (8x in poetry)
marks the second stage of the dragon's attack in BW (2594) and
seems to mark the second stage of Noe s career here, if not
the Second Age.

    1562-1596a Noe's Drunkenness and the Cursing of Cain.
In origin the story of Noe's drunkenness was probably a primitive Kronos-legend involving the castration or sexual abuse of
the father—so it is understood by some Talmudic commentators.
But by the time of the final Pentateuchal form of Genesis, the
story was taken to refer to Cham's sin of disrespect for his
father (see U. Cassuto, *Comm. on Gen.* II, 150-53). The violence of Noe's reaction to Cham's rather accidental disrespect
was traditionally explained entirely in moral rather than sexual or personal terms. GN follows the Christian tradition as
it had stood from very early times. The shameful gloating of
Cham (1579b ff.), not in the Bible, is derived from the mock-
ing laughter of the Jewish tradition (cf. Josephus, *Antiquities* I, 141 [Loeb Josephus I, 69]), fully articulated in the
Christian attitude to the story: "Cham, qui uerenda sui patris
nudata conspiciens inrisit . . ." (Bede, *In Gen.*, CCSL 118A,
137). On the other hand, the poem suggests no mitigation of
Noe's drunkenness, which the Christian tradition always took
as a figure of Christ's Passion. Indeed, the poem calls to
mind the Fall and the Expulsion (1573-76), suggesting that at

every moment, at every new chance, the elements of the Two
Cities separate themselves, and even Noe, the new man, is subject to sin. His first moments on the new earth see him offending against the injunction against nakedness given by God
to Adam and Eve. The purely narrative phrase *hleomagum helan*
(1582b) suggests the famous Gregorian treatment of the incident, that Japheth and Sem averted their looks as they rev-
erently covered the nakedness of their father because we
should conceal the sins of our superiors from others (*Moralia
in Job* XXV, 16, 37 [PL. 76, 345-46]). The poet, then, seems
to arrange his treatment of the text here so as to suggest,
rather originally, that the very fact that one so great in
virtue as Noe can lapse into sin should be a warning that nothing must be used as a precedent for sin, and that we have no
right to take our virtue for granted or to exult over the sins
of others, least of all, our betters.

    1559b-1560 *sohte . . . pa . . . brohte,* "Sought as to
when he might bring."

    1567a *him on his inne* "To him in his house" (*inne,*
masc. dat. sing.).

    1570b *sefa nearwode* Wells would take *sefa* as acc. sing.
(citing Brunner, par. 276, anm. 6), but it is perfectly acceptable as subject.

    1572b *wryon* = *wreon.* Perhaps the MS form is a late
Kentish form from an exemplar's *wrion* (so Grein prints). Cf.
fyore, 1184b; see Campbell pars. 288, 298 and Intro., p. 29.

    1573b *gesceapu* Neut. pl., nom., "genitals," perhaps
with a play on "fate"?

    1585-1586a *heora andwlitan / in bewrigenum / under lodum
listum* "Their faces being wrapped up under their cloaks with
care." Following Grein, *Sprch* I, 98, and Holthausen, I take
in bewrigenum as dat. absol. Krapp comments: "Perhaps it
would be better to emend to *bewrigene.* The *-um* ending of *bewrigenum* might easily have been anticipated from the dative
endings in the following line."

    1587a *gefremede* Take as subj. pl. Bloomfield, *JEGP* 29,
100-13, establishes the frequent occurrence of subj. pl. in *-e.*
Cf. 1842b, 2184b *nn.,* also 856b, 954b *nn.*

    1587b-1588a *gode wæron begen, / sem and iafed.* Perhaps
a response to 9.26-27 (not otherwise represented): "Benedictus
Dominus Deus Sem . . . . Dilatet Deus Japheth . . .," but the
remark is an outgrowth of the exegetical attitude to the sons
of Noe, emphasizing the two sons against the one. "Proinde in
duobus filiis [i.e., Sem and Japheth], maximo et minimo, duo
populi figurantur, scilicet circumcisio et praeputium . . ."
(Isidore, *Quaest. vet. test.* I, 8, 3 [PL. 83, 235B]). The literal and the figural levels coincide in the treatment of Sem
and Japeth but in Cham the literal and figural levels are od-
dly crosshatched, as if to express the disharmony he evokes:
"Cham, id est, populus impius Judaeorum" (*Ibid.* 235-36). The

poem, following Isidore, adopts the view that Sem is oldest,
Cham the middle and Jafeth the youngest of the sons of Noe
(see 1551-52 and Utley, "Flood Narrative," 211-12, who notes
the alternate tradition that Cham is the youngest).

1594b *cwæð he wesan sceolde* Grein prints *cwæð pæt
he . . . .* The ellipsis is rare, but seems idiomatic. Cf.
GB 344a.

1596a *cham* Substituted for *Chanaan*, 9.25 (perhaps *Cham*
was the word present in the text followed by the poet). Con-
trary to Wells' suggestion, the poet has not made the substitution on his own authority, to get around a difficulty in the
text, but follows the usual understanding of the verse. Cf.
Hrabanus: "Ideo et Cham in filio suo maledictus est, tanquam
in fructo suo, id est, in opere suo. . . . Item quod Cham
peccante posteritas ejus damnatur, significat quod reprobi
hic delinquunt, sed in posterum, id est, in futurum, senten-
tiam damnationis excipiunt" (*Comm. in Gen.*, PL. 107, 526).

1596b *cwyde* "Curses," masc. *ja*-stem, nom. pl. (cf.
Campbell, par. 579 [3]). Older edd. (Thorpe through Grein)
read *cwyðe*.

1601 *freomen æfter flode / and fiftig eac // þa he forð
gewat.* "Then Noe enjoyed . . . 300 (of) years in this life
(assigned to) the noble man after the Flood and fifty more
(years) as well (up to) when he departed" (cf. 9.28-29).
Wülker and Krapp print 1601a,b,c as one line, but obviously it
is three normal half-lines (for b cf. 1126a, 1162a, etc.; for
c cf. 1622b, 2449b). Holthausen shortens *freomen* to *freom*
(i.e., *from* "bold") and attempts to expand 1601c into two half-
lines. Wells supposes that *and fiftig eac* appeared twice,
once for 350 years (9.28) and once for 950 (9.29), a scribe
having omitted one *and fiftig eac* and everything between.
But the passage is perfectly regular and intelligible as it
stands and includes all the essential information of 9.28 and
9.29.

1602-1718 The genealogies of Cain and Seth had developed
important exegetical significance, and the exact numbers,
names, proportions and correspondences of the two families
were thought to have symbolic significance. No such importance was attached to the details of the genealogical portions
of Chapters 10 and 11. So the principle that governs the
treatment of these name-lists is simply to mention the chief
son of each son of Noe and any interesting attendant details.
There is no need to be exhaustive or exact so long as the
bridge from Noe to Abraham is established and the refounding
of the Two Cities is shown.

1606a *sunu* Gen. pl.; an isolated Anglianism, or miswritten for *suna*? cf. Brunner, par. 271, anm. 2; Intro. p. 33.

1607a *heold a rice,* "He always possessed the kingdom
(. . . until)," taking *rice* as noun, cf. Kock, *Anglia* 43,308.
So Holthausen and Krapp. It could also be adv. or adj. (masc.

nom. sing.). For the meaning of *a*, see B-T *Supp.*, ad loc. II, "continuity or continual recurrence in temporary matters."

1610b *geomor = Gomer.* Apparently a "Westsaxonizing," either by purely graphic analogy with such common forms as *geomor* "sad," or by insertion of a palatal glide from front consonant to back vowel (but *Gomer* would not normally be palatalized). Holthausen reads *Gomor*, Wells *Gomer.*

1613-1614 *þæs teames wæs / tuddor gefylled // unlytel dæl / eorðan gesceafta.* Instead of translating 10.5, the poem elaborates the traditional meaning of Japheth's name, derived from 9.27, "Dilatet Deus Japheth," etc. Jerome interprets Japheth as "latitudo" (*Liber int. heb. nom.*, CCSL 72, 67) and Hrabanus explains why *dilatet* is used: "significat gentes ubique diffusas . . ." (*Alleg. in Sac. Scrip.*, PL. 112, 960D); thus, the poet sees the Christian progeny of Japheth filling "not a little portion of the earth's surfaces."

1613b *tuddor gefylled tuddor* must be dat. (*os*-stem); cf. 914b *n.*

1615 *swilce chames suno / cende wurdon,* Bouterwek, Dietrich (*ZfdA* 10, 326), Grein, Holthausen read *Chame*, dat. with *cende*, but Krapp restores *Chames*, Wells pointing out that *cennan* with gen. occurs at 967-68, with dat. at 1149, 1639.

1617a *chus and chanan* Edd. follow Dietrich (*ZfdA* 10, 326), *canan*, for the obviously mistaken MS *chus and cham.* Perhaps the poet misread 10.6, taking *(C)Ham* as part of the series, or perhaps it is the result of scribal carelessness (cf. 1155b *n.*, 1160a). Chus and Chanan are kept at this point (Chanan otherwise receives short shrift) because they conveniently alliterate and enclose the whole series of Cham's sons.

1619 *chus wæs æðelum / heafodwisa,* Holthausen, following Rieger, *Verskunst*, 16, reads *hæleðum* for alliteration, but probably *chus* and *heafod-* are the alliterants; cf. 1617.

1623 *cham of lice / þa him cwealm gesceod.* The pret. of three distinct verbs may be represented by *gesceod.* Most edd. would connect it with *gesceððan* str. vb. 6, "harm" (the usual pret. is *gescod* and so Holthausen reads, but cf. *sceod* 997); earlier edd. emend to *gesceode* from *gesceon* wk. vb., "happen," "come upon," but Sievers, *Beiträge* 10, 485, pointed out that the meter will not support the final *-e. gesceod* is also the normal pret. sing. of *gesceadan* str. vb. 7, "divide," "separate," which gives, "when death divided them," i.e., Cham and his body (cf. GN 2210 *sceaðeð*; BW 2422b-23a *sundur gedælan // lif wið lice*).

1628a *fæder nebroðes.* Early edd. attempted to make sense of MS *fæder ne breðer*, but Cosijn, *Beiträge* 19, 450, noticed Nemrod's name disguised. *Nebroth* is the LXX form, common in Latin MSS.

1628b-1636 The Rule of Nemrod. Nemrod was the first tyrant, the first who ruled by large-scale organized violence, and the priority of his evil reign was commonplace: "Primus

post diluvium inter homines Nemrod filius Chus nova imperii
cupiditate tyrannidem arripuit. . ." (Isidore, *Quaest. de vet.
test.* I, 9, 1 [PL. 83, 237B]). Cain founded the City of This
World but Nemrod institutionalized it: "Progenie Sem et Iafeth
in uitae simplicitatis innocentia permanentibus, nascitur de
stirpe Cham maledicta, qui statum humanae conuersationis nouo
uiuendi genere peruerteret" (Bede, *In Gen.* CCSL 118A, 144).
Such ideas are behind the change of wording when 10.10,"fuit
autem principium regni eius Babylon" becomes "he was the first
king of Babylon" (1633-1634a). The poet is doubtless thinking
of Babylon in its widest allegorical sense. With Augustine,
and any medieval man, the poet probably thought of Nemrod as
a giant (a tradition stemming from the LXX version of 10.8:
"giants upon the earth"). Like a giant, Nemrod has *mægen and
strengo* to a greater degree than any other man *on þam mœldagum,*
in those proverbially wicked days *swa us gewritu secgeað.* See
1649-1701 *n.* and 1263-69 (the giants of the flood).

   The connection between Nemrod, the first ruler, and the
construction of the city with its tower, never explicitly
made in Genesis, but a connection taken for granted by all
commentators, is cleverly suggested in the poem by the inter-
calation of 11.1 between 10.10 and 10.20. By rearranging
these verses, the poet is able to indicate Nemrod's literal
role without interfering with the actual words of the text;
the hint for such a treatment stems ultimately from Augustine:
"Cum ergo in suis linguis istae gentes fuisse referantur, re-
dit tamen narrator ad illud tempus, quando una lingua omnium
fuit, et inde iam exponit, quid acciderit, ut linguarum diuer-
sitas nasceretur. . . . Ista ciuitas, quae appellata est con-
fusio, ipsa est Babylon, cuius mirabilem constructionem etiam
gentium commendat historia. Babylon quippe interpretatur con-
fusio. Vnde colligitur, gigantem illum Nebroth fuisse illius
conditorem, quod superius breuiter fuerat intimatum, ubi, cum
de illo scriptura loqueretur, ait initium regni eius fuisse
Babylonem . . ." (*De ciu. Dei* XVI, 4 [CCSL 48, 504-05]). Bede,
In Gen., CCSL 118A, 145-46, similarly collocates Nemrod and
the beginning of Chapter 11. But the poet is more or less
bound to the order of his original, given the method of paraphrase he has adopted, and he only suggests this collocation,
treating the rest of the Babylonian material in its biblical
order after 10.21 ff., the lineage of Seth.

   1638b-1639 "From those [i.e., *wœrmægða*] great peoples,
mighty families were born."

   1642b-1643 *œr ðon forð cure // wintrum wœlreste / werodes
aldor.* Holthausen and Krapp, following a suggestion by Grein,
Germania 10, 417, change *forð* to *frod* with *wintrum* (cf. 2355
wintrum frod, 1743 *misserum frod*). Wells reads *frod* but construes *wintrum* as "dat. of preference," "the old one chose
deathrest over winters." But *forð* makes perfect sense, "sons
and daughters were born to Sem . . . before he chose for years
henceforth (i.e., forever) a slaughter-bed." Cf. the common

GN expression for dying, *forð gewat*, 1068, 1173, 1192, 1601, 1742.

1645-1648 *para an wæs / eber haten, // eafora semes....
ebrei hatað.* Heber, actually the great-grandson of Sem, is
called his son, following 10.21, a verse which Augustine explains: "Ordo uerborum est: Et Sem natus est Heber, etiam ipsi,
id est ipsi Sem, natus est Heber, qui Sem pater est omnium
filiorum. Sem ergo patriarcham intellegi uoluit omnium, qui
de stirpe eius exorti sunt, quos commemoraturus est, siue sint
filii, siue nepotes et pronepotes et deinceps indidem exorti"
(*De ciu. Dei* XVI, 3 [CCSL 48, 502]). From there it is a short
step to the deduction that Heber gave his name to the Hebrews,
though of course that step had been taken long before Augustine. The poem indicates that the offspring of Sem were especially notable for virtue (*on pære mægðe / wæron men tile*,
1644) and conflates all the details of their lineage into a
single concept, that from this family was born Heber, Abraham
and thence the chosen people. This too was an established topic: "Videtur autem haec sententia [i.e., 10.21] designari
quod cum multi de Sem nati filii multos populos procreauerint,
illa tamen progenies specialius eius sit fidem ac pietatem se-
cuta, quae per Heber ad Habraham ac populum descendit Hebre-
orum" (Bede, *In Gen.*, CCSL 118A, 148). The topic is raised
to a level of universal knowledge and importance in the poem
(*pa nu æðelingas, // ealle eorðbuend, / ebrei hatað*, 1647b-48)
and placed between the two treatments of Babylon (1633-36;
1649 ff.), heightening the contrast between the "famous Hebrews" and the infamous city-dwellers. The confusion of
tongues was the historical event which served to make this
contrast effective and obvious, for the Hebrews were the only
people who at that time kept the original tongue of mankind,
that is, according to Isidore, persevered in the original God-
given order of justice (*Quaest. de vet. test.* I, 9, 4 [PL. 83,
238A]).

1649-1701 The Tower of Babel. The building of the Tower
(11.3-4) is paraphrased fairly closely in 1661-67 and then the
whole episode is virtually repeated in expanded form, with moral commentary woven in (1671b-78a). The gist of the story is
that men abused their power of speech (*larum sohton / weras to
weorce*, etc.), by which they carried out criminal deeds under
the color of collective action in order to gratify their pride.
The theme of Pride is introduced at the beginning of the episode (*folc wæs anmod*, 1650b, perhaps word-play, "the host was
intent on one object" / ". . . was proud;" cf. Abraham at the
time he intends to sacrifice Isaac—*hæfde on an gehogod* 2893)
and relentlessly built up throughout by insinuation and explicit statement. Traditionally it is pride that Nemrod is held
to exemplify: "Faciunt sibi ciuitatem omnes reprobi cum, neg-
lecto praesidio praeceptorum Dei, sensus ac desideria sui cordis in agendis siue loquendis quae ipsos libet sequuntur" (Bede,

In Gen., CCSL 118A, 161). According to Augustine, Nemrod the
giant is a hunter *against* the Lord (so "venator coram Domino,
10.9, is taken) because as a giant of pride, his wickedness is
directly expressed in his work, which is meant as a challenge
to God's work (cf. *De ciu. Dei* XVI, 4) and so the poem implies (1676-77a). Thus Nemrod was naturally seen as a type of
the devil, of heretics, of Jews and persecutors; his city figures the City of This World, of which all earthly cities are
a figure, and his tower is his wickedness as expressed in deed,
standing in the broad plains of Senaar (*sohton rumre land*,
1651b), a figure of incontinence and lack of subordination to
God. GN leaves the city standing like a sign (1699b-1701):
"Mystice turris haec mundi superbiam signat, sive etiam ela-
tionem haereticorum qui turrim pravi dogmatis contra Deum vo-
lunt aedificare" (Remigius, *Comm. in Gen.*, PL. 131, 81C).

    1655-1660 "In their days, the princes of the people set-
tled Sennar far and wide with favorite men. Green places on
the fair earth were a continual blessing to them in the time
of (their) days, growing prosperity in everything they desired
(lit.: in respect of each of their desires)." Some ambiguity
about several constructions does not really blur the meaning
of these sentences. I follow Wells' punctuation and construction of *leofum mannum* with *gesetton* (c. B-T *Supp.*, s.v. *ge-
settan* IV (2) (2a) (2b), cf. GN 94b-95). Wülker takes 1655-60
as one sentence; Holthausen puts colon after *mannum* and in his
note moves it down to follow *foldan*; Krapp takes *leofum mannum*
with *wæron* (parallel to *him*, 1658), taking 1656b-60 as one
complete sentence: "To the dear men in their days, green places
. . . were before them," etc.

    1661-1666a *Ða pær mon mænig / be his mægwine . . . bæd
// pæs hie . . . burh geworhte . . .* Cosijn, *Beiträge* 19, 450,
proposes remodelling the sentence by omitting *be* and altering
pæs to *pæt*; so Holthausen prints, but as Kock, *PPP.* 16, points
out, the idiom is not abnormal; cf. EL 961-62: *Gode pancode...
pæs hire se willa gelamp.* Wells notes that *be* = "with," "in
the company of."

    1664a *geond foldan bearn* "Among the sons of earth," cf.
1682a *adames eaforan* (onomastically = *foldan bearn*) and Caedmon's *Hymn* 5, *eorðan bearnum* (var.: *ylda bearnum*); *foldan
bearn* makes perfect sense in context, linking the tower builders with the "men of earth" who inhabited the city of Enos /
Cain (cf. 972 *n.*). See J. Golden, "An Onomastic Allusion in
Caedmon's *Hymn*?" *NM* 70, 627-29. Grein, *Germania* 10, 417, would
follow Lye-Manning by reading *bearm* for *bearn*, and so Holthausen and Krapp print, losing the sense of the passage for
the sake of a familiar expression (Krapp remarks that *bearn*
makes sense as a kind of pl. amplification of *mengeo* 1663b).
For *geond*, cf. 233b, 991a.

    1666a, 1667a *geworhte]* [*arærde* Subj. pls., cf. 1587a *n.*
    1687a Most edd. begin a new sentence here, or even a new

paragraph, with no stop after *gefremede* 1683b, but 1684-90 run
more smoothly as coordinate *þa*-clauses: "Then He, angry, established for earth-dwellers dissimilar tongues so that they
had no success with (each others') languages when they, successful in might, met in a crowd at the tower, in great numbers, devisers of the work, nor did any of the family of men
understand what another said." A number of translations of
1687a are possible, depending on whether we take *hie* as nom.
or acc., *gemitton* as trans. or intrans. Kock, *PPP.*, 16, takes
hie as reflex., "they gathered together," *spedge*, *teoche* and
wisan being parallel subjects.

    1688a *teoche* = *teohhe*, may be construed as fem. nom.,
acc., or dat. sing., depending on how 1687a is taken. *teoche*
may be a survival of a genuine eWS. spelling (*ch* for earlier
chch, cf. Campbell, par. 63). The regular later spelling occurs at 959, *teohha*.

    1691-1692a *ne meahte hie gewurðan . . . timbran*   "They
could not agree . . . to build." Cf. GB 387 f.

    1693a *heapum tohlodon* "They misbuilt in heaps (i.e.,
amidst masses of rubble?)." The usual meaning of *heapum* is
"in large groups," but such a meaning here causes trouble with
the verb. *heap* "a raised mass of material," is attested in
glosses (see B-T *Supp.*, ad loc. III (2)). In the sense "lay
up," "aggregate," *hladan* occurs at CH 783b (the whole passage
illustrates the meaning, CH 781b-84a): *Is þam dome neah // þæt
we gelice sceolon / leanum hleotan, // swa we widefeorh /
weorcum hlodun // geond sidne grund.* Cf. GN 2902, *hladan*, "to
lay wood on a sacrificial pyre." I take *tohladan* as "misbuild,"
"lay on (bricks) aimlessly." Such an interpretation makes it
clear that the immediate result of the confusion of tongues
was the sudden inability to carry out a coordinated action,
and does away with the need for an emendation. Dietrich, *ZfdA*
10, 327, takes *tohlodon* as "zerstören" but rejects an intrans.
meaning, understanding *hine* (= the Tower). Most edd. take
tohlodon in an unrecorded sense "scattered" (cf. DN 301 *heapum tohworfene*), but as Wells points out, it is too early in
the story for this meaning. Sievers, *Beiträge* 19, 450, suggests *tohlocon*, citing the rare *hlecan* "assemble," from which
he infers a strong verb **tohlacan*, "disperse," and so Holthausen, Krapp print. Hulbert, *JEGP* 37, 536, rejects this hypothetical word. Wells suggests *tohlyddon* "babble," related to
hlúd, hlýdan.

    1694a *wæs oðere* See 1338a *n.*

    1702-1705 *weox þa . . . mægburh semes . . . þeawum hydig.*
We move swiftly from the earthy (*stantorr / and seo steape
burh*) to the consecrated (*mægburh semes*), from the grossly
concrete to the pertinently abstract, omitting 11.10-26, essentially a repetition of the genealogy of Sem given in 10.21
ff.). The commentaries, too, tend to overlook the second,
more detailed genealogy in order to emphasize the procession

directly from Sem, son of Noe to Thare, father of Abraham.
The important function of the genealogies from the heuristic
viewpoint was the establishment of a direct connection between
the righteousness of Noe and Abraham, interrupted by the old
sins of the Babylonian episode. So Bede: "Destructa fabrica
Babyloniae, festinat scriptura, enumeratis generationibus se-
cundae mundi aetatis . . .peruenire ad Abraham patriarcham
tertiae aetatis—immo omnium gentium. Per cuius fidem et ob-
edientiam noua denuo ciuitatis sanctae fundamenta iacerentur,
et in cuius semine dispersio gentium ad unam confessionem ac
fidem diuini cultus rediret" (*In Gen.*, CCSL 118A, 162).

    1704 *on pære cneorisse / cynebearna rim,* With Kock,
PPP. 16, one must explain *rim* as object of the prep., taking
pære cneorisse and *cynebearna* as parallel gens. (so Krapp)
or, better, with Wells, *cynebearna* as dependent on *rim* and
pære cneorisse on *cynebearna*, translating: "until that man was
born among the number of the noble children of that tribe
[viz., *mægburh semes*]."

    1705a *pancolmod wer* I.e., Thare, father of Abraham, who
is not mentioned by name until 2054a, as the patronymic of Abraham. It is tempting to see *wer* as a disguise of the name,
but *pancolmōd pāre* is metrically irregular. Bradley, *MLR* 11,
213, would read Þ*are wæs haten.*

    1706-1711 The Virtue of Thare and his Sons. Tradition-
ally, Thare, the mysterious *pancolmod wer*, is considered blessed as the only true descendant of Heber, all the other seed
of Noe having fallen into false beliefs. "Proinde sicut per
aquarum diluuium una domus Noe remanserat ad reparandum genus
humanum, sic in diluuio multarum superstitionum per uniuersum
mundum una remanserat domus Tharae, in qua custodita est plan-
tatio ciuitatis Dei" (Augustine, *De ciu. Dei*, XVI, 12 [CCSL 48,
516]). This special relationship between the sons of Thare
and God shines out all the more in that they are *in babilone*
(1707a), a phrase rendering the real meaning of "Ur Chaldaeorum" (11.28), that is, "in the fire of the Chaldaeans," the
damnation awaiting those who remain spiritually "in Babylon" (cf.
Jerome, *Liber quaest. heb. in Gen.*, CCSL 72, 15). In the Jewish tradition, the link between Babylon and Thare is even more
literal because Abraham was thought to have been born under
Nemrod's reign and persecuted by him for a long time (Ginzberg
I, 186-217, passim). The pairing of Abraham and Aran, together with the absence of Nachor among the sons of Thare, is
not only alliteratively convenient, but conforms to the usual
reading of Chapter 12. Abraham and Aran are the two pious
sons of Thare: "Tradunt Hebraei quod Abraham et Aran fratres,
cum nollent ignem adorare, in ignem projecti sunt ex quo mis-
erante Deo Abraham illaesus exiuit" (Remigius, *Comm. in Gen.*
[PL. 131, 81D]). The fact that *Nachor* does not alliterate
perhaps suggested to the poet that he did not belong to the
true house, as Augustine had speculated: "forte quod a paterna

et fraterna pietate desciuerat et superstitioni adhaeserat
Chaldaeorum . . ." (*De ciu. Dei*, XVI, 13 [CCSL 48, 517]).

    1710a *Abraham and aaron.* The form *Abram* and the renam-
ing of Abram are ignored in the poem. This is in part a matter of metrical and phonetic convenience, since *Abraham* is
metrically flexible, the uninflected base scannable either
as bi- or tri-syllabic: thus, *pæt him abrahame* (2217, bi-syllabic base, d-type), vs. *abraham pa* (2338, tri-syllabic base,
3E1-type). Once the spelling reflects the bi-syllabic pronunciation, *wif abrames* 2631. But beyond this, it was customary
in commentaries, homilies and even in the biblical text itself, to copy out the more familiar name. As Augustine says,
from a certain time in history, to the present day, they have
been called, not Abram and Sara, but Abraham and Sarra, and
so we all call them now (cf. *De ciu. Dei* XVI, 28). *áaron*
(so it is marked in the MS) is for (H)āran, the accents by another hand being a device for indicating length, but there may
be confusion with the more familiar name.

    1710b-1711 *pam eorlum wæs // frea engla bam // freod and
aldor.* "To those nobles the Lord of angels was both peace and
life." As it stands, the statement is abstract, and perfectly
intelligible. Thorpe and edd. (except Grein and Wülker) want
to make it concrete and familiar, reading *freond and aldor,*
"friend and lord."

    1715b *unforcuðlice* ´x:`xx a type not listed by Bliss.
Fracoð is poetic, *forcuð* prose, but when *un-* precedes, poetry
has *unforcuð-*; see E. G. Stanley, "Studies in the Prosaic Vocabulary of OE. Verse," *NM* 72 (1971), 404. Sievers, *Beiträge*
10, 513 would read *unfracoðlice*, scanned ´:`xx 1D1 and so
Holthausen.

    1718 *dugeðum demað / drihta bearnum.* "Therefore widely
they now judge amidst (heavenly) hosts the sons of multitudes."
Deman "to judge," with dat. is amply documented, see B-T *Supp.*
ad loc. I (2) (a). Earlier edd. wanted an acc. here and emended accordingly: Dietrich *ZfdA* 10, 327, suggested *domiað* and
bearn; Grein read *bearn* as obj. of *demað*; Holthausen read
drihtfolca bearn, acc., "to complete the meter," and so Krapp,
"since *demað* cannot be taken as passive." Wells follows the
MS, taking *demað* as "adjudge," trans. and taking two datives,
"so now they widely adjudge blessings to the children of multitudes." Though the order of words may be construed as they
stand, what is yielded, grammatically and semantically clear
in itself, is obscure in context. The passage seems to be
based on a liturgical form or idea, the poet apparently having
in mind a comparison of the literal *past* (when Abraham and
Loth shared the heritage of righteousness with their forebears
in the time of the old covenant of the flesh) and the mystical
present (when Abraham and Loth are among the blessed saints
sharing the glories of God and judging the children of the new
covenant). Pehaps the familiar concept "Abraham's bosom" as

the dwelling of the saints is behind this, or the poet may have
in mind the usual interpretation of *Abraham*, "pater videns
populum" (cf. Jerome, *Liber int. heb. nom.*, CCSL 72, 61). A
similar type of mystical interpretation of a biblical event
(including the phrase *drihta bearnum*) occurs at 986b-993,
Cain's sin, and another at 1951a *fullwona bearn*[?], the praise
of Abraham by the faithful.

1736b *on carran,* Holthausen, following Rieger, *Verskunst,*
56, reads *on Carrane* to gain the syllable. Krapp suggests
that the word might be tri-syllabic *cárráän*; he stresses 1747b
cárràn ofgíf. Cf. 1240b, 1241b *n.*

1747b *carram* Regularized to *Carran* by Dietrich, *ZfdA* 10,
327, Holthausen and Krapp.

1759-1766 The Blessing of Abraham. Although a general
expression of the blessing is given at 1752b f., the details
have actually been postponed in order that the two main com-
ponents might be brought together: ". . . atque in te benedicentur universae cognationes terrae" (12.3) and "faciamque te
in gentem magnam . . ." (12.2). The commentators stress the
doubleness of God's promise and they also put a higher value on
the promise that through Abraham all the nations of the earth
shall be blessed (cf. Augustine, *De ciu. Dei* XVI, 16). Thus,
the poet rearranges his material in such a way as to bring
the two parts of the blessing together and in the order 12.3,
12.2, thereby retaining the main stress of the traditional
view. "Haec est maior superiore ac longe praestantior promis-
sio benedictionis [i.e., that in 12.3]. Illa enim terrena
haec celestis est, quia nimirum illa propagationem carnalis
Israhel ista spiritalis signiticat—illa populi eius qui de
eo secundum carnem natus est; haec eius qui de uniuersis cognationibus terrae in Christo saluator. In quibus sunt et illi
quicumque ex eo secundum carnem nati, etiam pietatem fidei
eius imitari uoluerunt" (Bede, *In Gen.*, CCSL 118A, 169). In
the same spirit, the important blessing is placed first in the
poem, 1759-62a. The other blessing, the promise to make Abraham a great nation, in a sense only "ad populum Israhel pro-
prie pertinet" (*ibid.*, 168). Increasing the earthly family of
Abraham, the Israelites, not to mention the Ismaelites, Idu-
means and so forth, is of little immediate worth to an audience of Anglo-Saxon Christians, in a word, seems no real blessing at all. But the poet cannot simply omit the lesser blessing either, because he is following an important part of the
text, and the blessing was well-known to be double. The problem is solved by a slight change in the words of the lesser
blessing so that its text accords with the spiritual interpretation given it. Thus 1762a-66, corresponding to 12.2, does
not say "I will make you a great people," but "Your family
will increase until many a land is filled with your descendants." This is thus quite distinct from the promise of 1759-
62a, "through you all the inhabitants of the earth will re-

ceive my blessing," and yet accords with the needs and expectations of the Christian audience. 1766a, *peodlond monig*,
specifically suggests, not Israel, but the gentile nations,
which shall be the ultimate heirs of Abraham. That this blessing will pass through "sons and daughters" (1746b), a common
formula in the poem, should be compared with the further words
of Bede at this point: "in lumbis Abrae erat Maria . . . de
qua nasciturus erat Christus . . ." (*In Gen.*, 169).

    1759a *purh pe eorðbuende* Holthausen, following Graz,
Festschr. f. Schade, 73, regularizes to a d2-type, *eorðbuend*
(cf. *eorðbuend* 1648a, also nom. pl.); perhaps *-buen-* ought to
be considered one syllable here.

    1765a *fromcyme* "Offspring," "race;" Dietrich, *ZfdA* 10,
327-28, would emend this unique word to the relatively common *fromcynne* (4x in GN), meaning about the same thing, and
so Grein, Wülker, Holthausen. Krapp restores the MS reading.

    1767-1768 *Him pa abraham gewat / æhte lædan // of egipta
eðelmearce,* The whole of 1767-76a raises enough doubts to
suggest that the passage is irremediably corrupt. I will dis-
cuss isolable problems in separate notes. 1767-68 corresponds to 12.4, "egressus est itaque Abram [de Haran]" (cf. 12.5
"et egressi sunt ut irent in terram Chanaan"). The fact that
of egipta seems to be functioning as a variation of *from carran* 1772a, makes it appear that *of egipta* is a corruption of
whatever the poet originally wrote, but it is difficult to see
how to mend it, or how to explain how the error came about.
But 1767-68 mirrors almost exactly 1873-74, "*Ða abraham / æhte
lædde // of egypta / eðelmearce*," in fact, 1873-79 should be
compared as a whole, for 1767-68 is a closer translation of
13.1-2 than it is of 12.4. The obvious presumption is that
1874, at least, has somehow intruded here. Wülker tried to
remedy by changing *of egipta* to *on egipta*, but, as Krapp points
out, Abraham goes from Haran to *cananea lond* (1772b-73a) and
thence to Egypt (at 1817 = 12.10). Grein cuts through all
this, but solves nothing, by reading *of Assyria*. Most edd.
retain the MS reading, though as manifestly in error.

    There is a chance that the intrusion, if such it be,
was undertaken deliberately by a revisor interested in making
the journey clearly significant in typological terms by bor-
rowing *of egipta / eðelmearce* from the later line. Both Egypt
and Babylon/Haran are figures of the world, and Abraham leaving Haran was interpreted by some commentators as the Christian leaving the fleshly life of this world behind and entering the Church (see Ambrose, *De Abraham* II, 1, 2 [PL. 14,
456A]). So the *Pentateuchal Commentary*, "Ægyptus significat
mundum, in quem Christus descendit" (PL. 91, 231C).

    1772b-1773a *sohton cananea // lond and leodgeard.* Edd.
consider this a single complete sentence, except Wells, who
thinks it wants a subject and puts a semi-colon after *abead*
1771b, making *ceapas* subj. of *sohton*, "cattle from Haran

headed for the Canaanites land . . .," but this seems odder
than having no subject at all. Wells is probably being over-
rigorous about a passage where a loosely constructed formulaic
"flow" is developing. The general idea: "Abraham (with all
the others)" governs *sohton*, the subject becoming expressed
only in the next sentence.

   1774b-1776 *idesa lædan,* // *swæse gebeddan* / *and his suhtrian* // *wif on willan.* "(The dear one came) . . . leading
the woman, his dear bed-companion and his nephew's wife according to (his) desires [*wif on willan*, perhaps 'with joy'
(Braasch), or merely 'desirable woman']." For 12.5, "tulitque
Sarai uxorem suam et Loth filium fratris sui . . . ." Prof.
L. K. Shook has suggested to me the translation: "God's beloved came to that land bringing of his women that sweet wife
[*swæse gebeddan*], that wife of his choice [*wif on willan*] and
(bringing) his nephew;" this makes sense of the lines but the
phrase-order is perplexing. Almost certainly Loth's name has
been lost and Loth's wife brought forward. If, e.g., *wif on
willan* is read after 1774b, *suhtrian* becomes acc. and Loth's
wife disappears, but the lineation and alliteration get hopelessly disturbed. Perhaps the proper subject of *sohton* is
lost. In any case, it appears that some scribe has tried to
remedy a bad situation as best he could and there is no choice
but to respect the text as it stands.

   1783a *sicem* Wülker retains the MS *siem* as a phonetic
equivalent to *sigem = sichem*.

   1784a *cynne cananeis*. Gen. sing. Cf. "Chananeus autem
tunc erat in terra" (12.6); *-is* for *-es* may be intended to indicate dieresis. Grein suggests *cananea* (but follows the MS
and translates pl.); Holthausen prints *Cananea*.

   1785a *abrahame* Four syllables. Holthausen gains a syllable by transferring *hine* from 1784b, suggesting the alternative of adding *pær* after *abrahame*. 1785a is probably 2A1. At
1805a, 1873a, Holthausen adds *git*, where *abraham* is tri-syllabic.

   1795a *on lande cyst*. The *-e* of *lande* may be taken as a
late reduction of *-a*, gen. pl., but the scribe may have anticipated the dat. after *on*: Grein and edd. read *landa*.

   1795b-1797 *lisse gemunde . . . soð gecyðde* Grein, Wülker, Holthausen and Krapp enclose these lines in parentheses,
with commas after *cyst* 1795a and *gecyðde*.

   1797a *sigora self cyning* 1A2 with the stress on *cyning*
suppressed. Edd. compound *selfcyning*, but lines such as GN
2672b, BW 920b, 1010a, 2702b, CS 661b, etc., where *self* cannot
be compounded suggest the true arrangement for 1797a.

   1799b *bethlem* The Old Latin form for *Bethel*, also at
1876, 1930. Cf. Ambrose, *De Abraham*, PL. 14, 460b, where "Bethel" of the text becomes "Bethlehem" in the commentary.

   1809b *metend* "Measuring one," i.e. God, acc. sing. The
form is recorded as the OE. title of Orosius' *History*: *middan-*

geardes metend = (H)Ormesta Mundi, "the measurer of the world"
(B-T). Cosijn, *Beiträge* 19, 452, suggests *me(o)tud*, Holthausen reads *metud*.

1829b *ic me onegan mæg* "I perforce fear (me) that...,"
ethic dative. An infinitive is required with *mæg*, provided
by Thorpe's transposition of *agen* to *egan*. In any case, *on a-
gane* or *agenum* would have to be read to save the MS expression
and would make slender sense.

1831a *freondmynde* Bouterwek explained as "frauenminne"
(suggesting *freon mynde*), B-T as "an amorous mind," and so edd.
take it. Cosijn, *Beiträge* 19, 451, suggests *freondmyne* "love
of a (woman) friend" on the lines of *wifmyne* 1861, and so
Holthausen prints. Krapp says *-myne* may be an improvement,
and further suggests *freomyne*, doubting *freond* = "lover," but
cf. *Wife's Lament* 25, 33, 47. Its use here is not without
irony.

1836b-1841a "Steadfastly conceal from them the truth
[true saying] because you must protect my life if the Lord,
our Ruler, almighty, is granting [*an*, from *unnan*] me peace,
a longer life, in the world-kingdom as he did previously [i.e.,
when he allowed Abraham to escape from Chaldea?]." For the
logic cf. BW 572b-73, "Wyrd oft nereð // unfægne eorl, / þonne
his ellen deah." Commentators tended to cringe at Abraham's
lie even as they covered him for it; so, seemingly, does the
poet. In Jewish exegesis Sara is identified as Abraham's
niece (Vermès, *Scripture and Tradition in Judaism*, 75); hence,
in the Christian tradition, this is taken to mean that since
she is near in blood she is indeed his "sister" and therefore
he told no lie, and since he held his peace concerning their
marriage, he told no lie on that score either (Augustine, *De
ciu. Dei* XVI, 19 [CCSL 48, 522]). Note Augustine's famous *mot*,
". . . tacuit aliquid veri, non dixit aliquid falsi" (*Contra
Faust. Manich.* XXII, 34 [PL. 42, 422]). If we may take *helan*
as "to remain silent" (cf. the last example in B-T *Supp.*, ad
loc. II), intrans. with instr. (*soðan spræce*), we may translate accordingly, "keep silent about the true matter."

1842b *sceolde* Subj. pl., cf. 1587a *n*.

1843 *fremena . . . fremu* Note the word-play by recurrence. *fremena* is gen. pl., *fremu* probably acc. sing. See
Glossary, *fremu* and *freme*, also Campbell, par. 587.

1849b-1851a *him drihtlicu mæg . . . cyninges þegnum*.
The word-order is unusual, line division uncertain and, in
1850, the alliteration is defective. Various rearrangements
have been suggested, e.g., Kock, *PPP.* 16, and, independently,
Cosijn, *Beiträge* 19, 451, *him drihtlicu / on mægwlite*; Holthausen reads 1850a *modgum wlite on*, but suggests in *Anglia* 46,
61 *on wlite modgum wlancum* (cf. 1825). The meaning is clear
enough, whatever the order: "Noble in countenance [*or*: in her
beauty] the woman seemed to them, to the many proud ones, to
the servants of the king."

1852b-1853 *and fægerro lyt // for æðelinge / idese
sunnon* The chief difficulty is the meaning of the rare str.
vb. *sinnan* 3: Sievers, *Beiträge* 11, 352-53, takes it as "go,"
"walk," "seek for," citing OHG. *sinnan* "gehen;" Jovy, *Bonner
Beiträge* 5, 30, takes it as "desire;" B-T gives "care for,"
"heed," citing Icel. *sinna*, wk. vb., "to care for," "heed."
"Heed" seems the more likely sense when the other OE. occurrences are compared: AN 1277b-78a, of a saint under torture,
Hra weorces ne sann, // wundum werig "(his) body heeded not
the torment, weary with wounds (as it was);" GU 318b-19 *Is
min hyht mid god, // ne ic me eorðwelan / owiht sinne* . . . ."
The other difficulties are ambiguity of construction: is *lyt*
to be taken with *fægerro* or *idese* as gens. or is one or either
or both acc.? I can only list a sample of the interpretations
offered, none of which satisfies completely: Bouterwek, "und
gedachten nicht wenig der schönen frau vor dem edelinge" (suggesting *fæger no lyt*); Dietrich, *ZfdA* 10, 328, "wenig frauen
preisen sie als schöner vor dem könig (*idese* gen. pl. with
lyt); Grein, "wenig gedachten sie vor dem leutefürsten lieb-
licherer frauen" (reading *fægerra* and *idesa*); Mason, following
Wülker, "few women did they repute fairer before the king"
(as if MS had *fægerrō = fægerran*); B-T, "They little heeded fair
women before the prince, (but much more did they praise the
winsome beauty of Sarah);" Jovy, art. cit., "und begehrten wenig eine schönere frau für den fürsten;" Sievers, art. cit.,
"und sie verkündeten ihren herrn, dass [reading *pæt* for *and*]
wenige der frauen, die vor dein edeling wandelten, an schön-
heit sie über träfen;" Krapp, "and few of fairer, of women,
walked before the prince" (reading *idesa*, parallel to *fægerro*);"
Wells, "and cared for little fairer than the woman before the
prince"(taking *idese* as dat.). Amidst such dubious plenty one
more effort would be pernicious were it not that none of these
quite catches what the sentence must be saying: for it is a
rendition of a specific statement: "et nuntiaverunt principes
Pharaoni et laudaverunt eam apud illum." *heredon* 1855b obviously represents *laudaverunt* and *cuð dydon = nuntiaverunt*. Taking *sunnon* as "heed," litotes developing *cuð dydon*, and *fægerro* as gen. pl. with *lyt* (cf. 1270b *n.*), one can translate
1851b-55a: "They made that known [i.e., that the woman seemed
noble in beauty] to their lord and few fairer in comparison to
the woman [*idese*, dat. of comparison] did they heed [i.e.,
take notice of, announce] before the prince, but even more
[*swiðor micle*] in words did they praise her joyful beauty,"etc.

1856b-57a *leoflic wif // to his selfes sele,* Holthausen
and Krapp place *to* in 1856 to gain the syllable, but the MS
pointing, apparently correctly, puts the prep. with its obj.

1865 *heht him abraham to / egesum geðreadne* "He (Pharaoh) commanded Abraham into his presence, (Abraham) transfixed
with terrors . . . ." The acc. *geðreadne* must refer to Abraham, though one would expect it to refer to Pharaoh. Cf. the

similar situation when Abimelech returns Sara, 2669b *egesan gedread*, referring to Abimelech.

1866a *egipto* Gen. pl. (declined masc. pl.); cf 1270b *n.*

1873-1879 See 1767-68 *n.*

1876b *pæt hie to bethlem* Holthausen, following Rieger, *Verskunst*, 56, reads *bethleme* to make a d-type. Cf. 892b *n.* If not scanned as an a-type it must be trisyllabic, *bethlëëm.*

1879a *wif and willan* "Women and (desirable) goods," a phrase of the same type as *bryd and beagas* 1876a, and in fact, a notional variation of it. Thorpe suggests *wif on willan*, as in 1776a (cf. Gradon, *Elene*, note to 311, *7 gedweolan ? = on gedweolan*; also CS 502), and so Bouterwek, Holthausen and Krapp. Both 1776a and 1879a have only the vaguest semantic functions in any case.

1882a *weras on wonge* Functioning as subject of *ongunnon* 1880a and *setton* 1882b, in effect two sentences, which cannot be separated formally.

1884b *pa westan com.* Cf. 13.3, "a meredie," "from the south."

1896b-1898a *oft wæron teonan // wærfæstra wera / weredum gemæne, // heardum hearmplega.* "Again and again, injuries, harmful warfare [*-plega*] were common to the rough ones [*heardum*], to the followers [*weredum*] of the truthfast men." This follows Grein and Krapp, who explain *hearmplega* as apposite to *teonan* and *heardum* to *weredum.*

1905b *ealltela* Compounded on the analogy of *eal(l)wihta* 113, *-mihtig* 1230, *-wealda* 978, *-grene* 193. Grein, *Germania* 10, 417 and Holthausen compound, other edd. do not. Uncompounded, the line is an e-type, compounded d3.

1911b-1913a *forðon wit lædan sculon // teonwit of pisse stowe . . . rumor secan.* "Therefore (since we haven't room enough for our two households, and our neighbors will not leave us in peace) we must remove contention from this place and find for ourselves larger estates." *teonwit* affords an example of how traditional emendations acquire a life of their own. The older edd. through Wülker followed the entirely transparent MS *teonwit* "contention" (a compound on the same pattern as *teonhete* "hostility," *teonræden* "injury," *teonword* "spiteful saying," etc., the second element being the same as in *edwit* "reproach"). *teonwit* is the obj. of *lædan*, trans. 1911b is a faulty type. Holthausen, for reasons unstated, makes the metrically indifferent emendation of *lædan* to *læfan*, intrans. (*landriht* to be supplied in sense) and then finding the obj. redundant, recasts 1912a as the beginning of a new sentence, reading *teon wit*: "let us go from this place," etc. Other commentators, accepting *teon wit*, but not *læfan*, find themselves with an apparently intransitive *lædan*, the possibility of which Cosijn doubts (*Beiträge* 19, 452) and Kock (*PPP.*, 17) defends. Various emendations and explanations of *lædan* follow, until Krapp, rejoining the sentences, construes

teon as inf., intrans., parallel to *lædan*, omitting the
"second" *wit* (i.e., *-wit* 1912a) as redundant. Meanwhile,
Braasch discovers that *teon* is subj. pl., *secan* dependent
on it. The final stage is Wells' non-WS *teonu ut*.

   1915b-1919 *ic þe selfes dom // life, leofa . . . nu ic
þe cyst abead.* The rather cold words of Abram to Loth in 13.9
are deliberately loaded, by use of a "Germanic" formula, to
suggest the Augustinian explanation of the verse: the two depart not in anger, but in charity, Abraham instituting the
custom that in a dispute over property, the greater divides
and the lesser chooses (*De ciu. Dei* XVI, 20 [CCSL 48, 532]).

   1916a *life* From *lyfan* "allow."

   1917a *gepancmeta* Imperative of wk. vb. II, "consider."
Kock, *PPP.*, 18, Cosijn, *Beiträge* 19, 452, question the existence of such a compound verb. Kock proposes *on gepanc meta*,
meta imperative.

   1923a *leoht* From *leccan* "to irrigate," cf. 210b.

   1924b-1926 *on þæt nergend god // for wera synnum / wylme
gesealde // sodoman and gomorran, / sweartan lige.*
þæt is neut. acc. (sc. *land*, understood), *sodoman and gomorran*
fem. dat. sings. For the construction cf. BW 2867-68, *þonne
he on ealubence / oft gesealde // healsittendum / helm ond
byrnan.* Thorpe and subsequent edd. read *oð þæt = antequam* for
on þæt, with period after 1924a, perhaps an improvement, but
not necessary.

   1929 *ealle lædde* A verb must be supplied; cf. 1435,
1649, 1767, etc.

   1931a-1944 The topic of the singular goodness of Loth
among a wicked people goes back to Jewish exegesis, of which
an early reflection is II Peter 2.7-8: ". . . justum Lot opres-
sum a nefandorum injuria ac luxuriosa conversatione eripuit:
aspectu enim et auditu justus erat, habitans apud eos qui de
die in diem animam justam iniquis operibus cruciabant." Augustine sees Loth as a type of the saints serving their time in
this world (*Contra Faust. Manich.* 22, 41 [PL. 42, 425-26]).
Bede literalizes this figure and reapplies it to the biblical
situation, much as the poet does: "Fertilitatem terrae laudat,
simul et incolarum notat impietatem, ut eo maiori damnatione
digni esse intellegantur, quod maxima Dei munera non ad fructum pietatis sed ad incrementum uertere luxuriae. Vbi etiam
tacite laudibus beati Loth additur quia in ipsa terra inter
ipsos degens indigenas, neque ubertate soli diuitis, neque ex-
emplo cohabitantium potuit ullatenus a suae puritatis integri-
tate corrumpi" (*In Gen.*, CCSL 118A, 178-79).

   1938b *loth onfon* The need for an antecedent for *he* 1939a
led Thorpe to surmise that Loth's name was disguised in *leoht*
(*eo* perhaps carried over from *leod-* 1938a). *leoht* might be
saved by putting a full stop after 1938b, but that leaves the
following pronouns awkwardly stranded (cf. 2402b *n.*).

   1951a *fullwona bearn* This has never been satisfactorily

explained or emended. Guesses such as *foldwonga* (Holthausen,
Krapp), *foldwuna* (Bouterwek), *folcworna* (Wells) merely gloss
over the difficulty. *fullwona* appears to be gen. pl.; at least
one is required in the construction. Braasch gives it as
fullwon, fem. ō-stem. The stem may be the same as that in
fullwere, "baptizer," *fullwiht*, "baptism," *fullwian*, "baptize"
(from **full-wīhan*, "to complete the sacrament of baptism," as
distinct from the *prima signatio* of the catechumens). On the
words of this group see H. S. MacGillivray, *The Influence of
Christianity on the Vocabulary of Old English*, Part I, Studien
zur englischen Philologie 7 (Halle, 1902), p. 57. Thus, Thorpe's
guess that *fullwona bearn* = "children of the baptized" is the
one that best grapples with the MS form. Along similar lines,
Bouterwek suggested *fullwodra bearn* (pp. *full(w)ian*) "children
of the baptized." In itself, such a remark is appropriate to
Abraham's Christian descendants, to whom belongs the title
"Father of the Children of God," "Father of the Faithful,"
etc., who is regarded as a type of Christ and St. Peter, and
whose praise occupies Quinquagesima, the pre-Lenten period, after which the catechumens prepared for the long ordeal leading
to baptism (the text for Quinquagesima Sunday is Genesis 12,
the breviary reading for Monday is Genesis 22). Cf. Gueranger,
The Liturgical Year IV, 192-213 and Parsch, *The Breviary Explained*, 290. This passage, and following through to 1959,
should be compared to 1717b-18.

    1953b-59 A loosely written, irregular passage. Krapp
surmises, on the grounds of its "homiletic" content, that it
may be an interpolation. The lines relate the behavior of Abraham to that of good Christians facing judgement (cf. 860-
863), but the remark is detached from the narrative, rather in
the manner of GB. Despite the oddities of style, sense can be
got from the passage, with only one emendation (at 1953b):
"Never will one of living persons, without protection [*hleo(w)-
lora*], in the face of anything, become frightened and terri-
fied before the Judge, who always henceforth will please Him
through prosperity of thoughts, in his spirit and in his deeds,
in his profession [*worde*] and in his intelligence by means of
a wise intention, until death."

    1953b *næfre hleowlora* Dietrich's emendation of *hleor
lora* appears to be the best that can be made. "Without face"
can be teased into some sense, but does it have the meaning
in OE. analogous to our "loss of face?"

    1954a *æt edwihtan* "In the face of anything." The final
element suggests such a meaning, but the compound is unique.
Cf. *æthwæga* "somewhat."

    1954b *(næfre) . . . æfre* Seems unidiomatic, especially
in poetry.

    1956 *mon for metode / þe him æfter a* The alliteration
is defective; edd. repair in various ways, but the text cannot be recovered, if it ever was any different—the shabby

condition of the whole passage suggests that perhaps it was
not.
    1957b *mod' and dædum* With Wells, I regard *mod* as dat.
sing. with -*e* elided before the vowel. Other edd. read *mode*.
See 63a *n.*
    1960-2095 The War of the Kings. The poet selects, clar-
ifies and simplifies the material of 14.1-16 more extensively
than any other part of Genesis. Because this particular section had not acquired any important exegetical tradition un-
avoidably determining its interpretation, as was the case with
almost all else, the poet is freer than usual to elaborate the
literal level of his narrative, according to the resources of
his traditional art. The whole section is marked by an extra-
ordinary amount of expansion of the battle scenes, which are
merely indicated in the original. Isidore allegorized the
four gentile kings coming against the five Canaanite kings as
the vices overcoming the bodily senses (*Quaest. vet. test.*, I,
9, 2 [PL. 83, 239B], repeated by Hrabanus [PL. 107, 539A]),
but such efforts were sporadic and non-influential. Bede is
typically uneasy about the whole episode because it is too "secular" (*In Gen.*, CCSL 118A, 182). The poet certainly treats
it in a secular spirit, after the manner of heroic poetry.
    1962 *orlahomar. / him ambrafel* The poem reduces 14.1-2,
a welter of unfamiliar names, to two foreign kings (but all
four are there, cf. 1964b), and none of the southern kings are
named. The unmetrical *Chodorlahomor* is ingeniously tailored
to *orlahomar*, probably felt as a 2A1-type ($'$ x : $'$ x), alliterating with *ambrafel*. The latter name has picked up an intrusive *b*; cf. such pairs as *simble / simle*, *bræmbel / bremel* and
note, conversely, *mamre* GN 2152, 2027 [MS *manre*] for Vulg.
Mambre. Henceforth the kings are not named, but referred to
by formulaic variation on *elamitarna* (1980, 2004, 2081). But
there may be an allusion to "Thadal rex Gentium," or at least
to his attributive, in *folctogan*. See Pyles, "The Pronunciation of Latin Learned Loan Words and Foreign Words in OE,"
PMLA 58, 891-910.
    1963 *of sennar / side worulde* Probably *sennar = sennäär*
in pronunciation. Thorpe and Wells assume that after *worulde*
some mention of the other kings has dropped out, but see the
preceding note. Bouterwek, Dietrich, *ZfdA* 10, 330, Grein,
Holthausen, Marckwardt-Rosier read *worude* or *weorode*, the last
remarking that the MS reading is "awkward." *side* must be taken
as adv., "(he went) broadly over the world"; cf. 1968b *wide
geondsended*.
    1964b-1965a *gewiton hie feower // þa þeodcyningas* The
line-division follows the pointing, but gives an a-type in the
off-verse. To avoid this, edd. divide *þa / þeod-* ; cf. 1638b
n. Bouterek suggests regularizing *hie* to *him* (with *gewiton*).
    1967b *be iordane* Replaces 14.3, "omnes hii convenerunt
in vallem Silvestrem quae nunc est mare salis." The Vulgate

alludes to the topographical changes consequent on the destruction of Sodom, the poem takes us back to the immediately
preceding description of the fair land of the Sodomites, *be
iordane, / grene eorðan* (1921) which was *gelic godes // neorxnawange* (1923b-24a); the Bible looks forward to God's wrath,
GN back to God's mercy. Bede's comment ironically concords
a Creation / Paradise motif with 14.3: "Pro ualle siluestri
in Hebreo habet in ualle Seddim, quod significat amoena et ne-
morosa loca. Talis enim erat pentapolis quae propter malitiam
inhabitantium non solum ignibus absumi, sed et aquarum abysso
meruit a cunctorum uiuentium intuitu in perpetuum abscondi"
(*In Gen.*, CCSL 118A, 185; cf. Jerome, *Liber quaest. heb. in
Gen.*, CCSL 72, 18).

     1966 *secan suð ðanon / sodoman and gomorran.* A north /
south axis runs throughout the episode of the War. Perhaps
it was formulaically more available than east / west, or perhaps it stems from an independent geographical tradition; cf.
1884b, where the return from Egypt is *westan* rather than "a
meridie." The usual view was that the four kings were easter-
ners, Babylonians (Ps.-Bede, *In Pent. com.*, PL. 91, 233B; Hrabanus, *Comm. in Gen.*, PL. 107, 538A). Angelomus combines the
usual association of Babylon with a moral interpretation of
the four kings as vices (*Comm. in Gen.*, PL. 115, 174D), while
Bede makes Chodorlahomor an historical Persian king (*In Gen.*,
CCSL 118A, 182), following Josephus (who makes him an Assyrian,
Antiquities I, 9 [Loeb Josephus, I, 85]). For the poet, it
appears, "north / south" is more powerful, suggesting the many
prophetical inflictions promised the unfaithful from the north
and above all the north as the habitation of evil, a topic in
the poem already (32 ff.), existing as part of a network of
biblical associations: "*Aquilo*, [id est] populus gentilis, ut
in Isaia: 'Dicam aquiloni: Da; et austro: Noli prohibere,'
(Isa. 43.6) quod inspirabo gentibus ut credant. . . . *Aquilo*
hostis antiqui suggestio, ut Jeremia, facies ollae succensae
'a facie aquilonis,' (Jer. 1.13) id est, regnabo in reprobis.
Aquilo diabolus, ut in Job: 'Qui extendit aquilonem super va-
cuum,' (Job 26.7) quod illorum mentibus, qui gratia sua vacui
sunt, diabolum Deus dominari permittit" (Hrabanus, *Alleg. in
sac. scrip.*, PL. 112, 660A-B; cf. the generally opposite sig-
nifications of *auster, ibid.* 869C). What is meant by "northmen" is thus perfectly clear on both a literal level (men from
a country on the left hand of Egypt, probably Babylon) and on
a moral level (men from the same way as the devil's way). The
poem reinforces this in 1995b-96a (see note). In the discon-
tinuous method of biblical commentary, figures do not consistently retain the same significance at every appearance—at
this point the Sodomites figure weak Christians, not the utterly reprobate and damned that they do in Chapter 19. What
the poet probably could not have had in mind is for the
"northmen" to be identified with Danish or Norse invaders, as

Hofmann, *Anglia* 75, 16-18 implies when arguing for a date
for GN ca. 950 and a provenance in the Danelaw. Cf. the analogous early use of *wicingas* in *Widsith*, 47, 59 (see Chambers'
ed., 205, *n.* 47, 208 *n.* 59).

1973b-2000 The Defeat of the Five Kings. This material
is developed out of the formulaic material from the traditional poetic stock, rather than from the biblical text. Fry,
"Themes and Type-Scenes in EL," *Speculum* 44, 35-45 shows how
all the battle-scenes in OE. poetry are constructed of similar
material and have similar structures, and set up "certain expectations in the reader familiar with formulaic poetry" (40),
or, perhaps we should say, to fulfill certain expectations
which are constants for any audience familiar with formulaic
usages. In the GN battle-scenes there is the added complexity
and interest arising from the fact that the audience has certain well-established expectations regarding the text-based
subject matter, and the pleasure is in seeing the interplay
and resolution of the two contrasting sets of expectations.

1975a *suðon = suðan.* See Brunner, par. 321, anm. 1.

1986b *modum prydge* "Ones strong in heart(s)." *prydge*,
non. pl. masc. of *prydig / pryðig* with syncopation (Wells ex-
lains as instr., "ones brave with might"). That the *d* for *ð*
might be a survival of a very early copy seems the least likely explanation. Cf. BW 2869 *prydlicost* (and Klaeber's note),
prydlice Byrhtferð's *Manual* 46, 5 (ed. Crawford, EETS 177),
also GN 1133b *sedes* for *sethos.* Holthausen and Krapp read
pryðge, the regular form, other edd. connect it to *preodian*
"deliberate," as an adj. having the same meaning as *pryðig.*

1987-1988a *oð pæt folcgetrume / gefaren hæfdon // sid
tosomne* "Until they had reached the broad (place) together
with an army." *gefaren* is perfective; *sid = vallis Silvestris*
understood as the plain of Sennaar, probably by a concordance
with 14.10, "Vallis autem Silvestris habebat puteos multos bi-
tuminis" and 11.2-3 ". . . invenerunt campum in terra Sennaar.
. . . Habueruntque lateres pro saxis, et bitumen pro caemento."
For the formulaic expression, with a different semantic function, cf. 160 ff. *ða stod hraðe // holm under heofonum / swa
se halga bebead, // sid ætsomne*, "then the sea was [*stod*]
quickly all in one place, broad [*sid ætsomne*] under the heavens as the holy One bade."

1993b-1995a *pær wæs eaðfynde // eorle orlegceap, / se ðe
ær ne wæs // niðes genihtsum.* "There was easily found a bat-
tle-bargain for a warrior, one which was not already sated
with war." I.e., splendid weapons could be picked up easily
on the battlefield, practically new ones, because they were
quickly thrown down by their vanquished owners; cf. the "shield"
riddle (No. 5): *Ic eom anhaga / iserne wund, // bille geben-
nad, / beadoweorca sæd, // ecgum werig.* Marckwardt-Rosier
suggest an ironic meaning for *orlegceap* "wealth of violence."
The whole passage, 1985b-2003a, satirizes the Sodomites.

1995b-1996a *norðmen wæron // suðfolcum swice.* "The northern men were a stumbling block to the southern peoples,"
swice (noun); "The northern men were false to the southern
peoples" (i.e., deceived their expectations of victory),
swice (adj.). The word play is particularly rich here, see
B-T, p. 954, for the variety of possibilities.

2007a *ahudan* "Plundered," pret. pl., parallel to *stru-
don,* assuming an otherwise unrecorded str. vb. **ahuðan* 2,
(cf. *huð* "booty," 2x in GN). Grimm, *Andreas und Elene*, 141,
emends to the well-attested wk. *ahyðdon* (same meaning) and so
Dietrich, *ZfdA* 10, 330, Holthausen, Krapp, Wells.

2007b *hordburh wera,* Since two cities are plundered,
Holthausen, *Anglia* 46, 61, and *Englische Studien* 51, 184, suggests *hordbyrh* pl., but follows the MS in his text, while
Grein, *Sprch.* II, 97, suggests that *hordburh* is acc. pl. But
as Krapp points out, such consistency is not to be looked for
where the conventional expression outweighs a detail of the
text; cf. BW 467 *hordburh hælepa.*

2008b *þa sæl ageald,* "When opportunity offered," cf.
2525 and BW 1665; Wells takes *sæl* as subject of *agieldan* with
mære ceastra.

2013b-2017 *we þæt soð mægon // secgan furður . . . sigore gulþon.* An unusual instance of the poet calling attention
to himself as a traditional *scop* rather than as a *bocere*; see
227b *n.*

2025b *bæd him fultumes* "He asked for help for himself;"
cf. B-T *Supp.*, s.v. *biddan* IV (1) (b).

2032b *ahred wurde,* A syncopated form of *ahreded* (cf.
2085 *loth wæs ahreded*), attested in prose and defended by
Hulbert, *JEGP* 37, 536, though rythmically the verse sounds
truncated. Bouterwek, Holthausen, Krapp read *ahreded.*

2037-2038 *treowa sealdon / þæt hie his torn mid him //
gewræcon on wraðum / oððe on wæl feallan.* *feallan* is suspicious. "Obviously preterite," remarks Krapp, emending to *feol-
lan,* parallel to *wræcon,* following Grein and Holthausen. Perhaps the form shows North. confusion of *ea/eo* (see Intro., p.
31, cf.-*treawa* 2369 *n.*,-*heowan* 2645), so if a change is to be
made this is the simplest, but the indicative is difficult.
Both verbs may better be taken as subj. in a clause of purpose
(for the construction cf. 2459b-60): "they gave their pledge
that with him they would avenge his anguish on the foes or
fall in the slaughter." The present follows the preterite to
indicate the contingency of the one pledge on the other (see
Callaway, *Consecutive Subjunctive in AS.*, 18 ff.). For the
confusion of *-en / -an / -on* in lWS see Campbell, par. 735 (f),
(g). Wells takes *gewræcon* as inf. and reads *þæt hie his torn
[woldon] mid him gewræcon.* Cf. GB 686, *bræcon.*

2046-2047 *þe him ær treowe sealdon / mid heora folce getrume. // wolde his mæg huru,* 2046 is defective in alliteration

and 2047 is an isolated hemistich; in spite of many proposed
alterations, the original, if it was different, is not recov-
erable. Possibly some sort of cross-alliteration is in force
in 2046, cf. GN 10 and see Pope, *Rhythm of Beowulf*, 37. Grein
suggests *getrume folce*. Following 1987a, most edd. read
folc(e)getrume. Bouterwek suggests *folces getrume*. The compound may be correct, and the *-e-* a scribal device for separating the palatals, but *folce getrume* makes sense, as Wells
shows: "with their folk in company," or "with their people
in a (single) company," anticipating "et divisis sociis." Cf.
folce firena 2412a *n.*

2049 *Rincas wæron rofe, / randas wægon* Three orthographic slips in this line, two of which the scribe caught and
corrected.

2054b-2057a Grein and Wülker consider all this a parenthesis, taking *cwæð* as a resumption of *sægde*, the rest as in-
terruption, but a comparison with 14.15 shows that Abraham
makes two statements: he said that they would divide into two
groups, and he said that God could easily grant them success.

2055 *þæt hie on twa healfe* An isolated hemistich. The
scribe is still sleepy—he has continued the singular *he* from
2052b, though *eowdon* and the general sense require a pl. subject. Some edd. read *eowde* 2056b and leave *he*.

2058b *eað mihte* "More easily might." Bouterwek suggests, Holthausen, Krapp read *eaðe mihte* because a comparative
is not needed here but another syllable is; cf. 48b, *and swa
eaðe meahtan*. But it is not correct to say that *eað* "makes no
sense," as does Sievers, *Beiträge* 10, 513. It indicates that
God can give them success more easily than they could achieve
it for themselves unaided.

2063b-2064 *gripon unfægre // under sceat werum / scearpe
garas* A brilliant evocation of "inruit super eos nocte;" *under sceat*, "under their clothes," i.e., they are disposed for
sleep, without armor and therefore easy prey.

2072a *on fitte.* "In battle." *Fitt* is unrecorded in this
sense in OE., entering documentary form as "contest" about
1550. See *OED* s.v. *fit*, and cf. OE. *fitung* "fighting."

2077a *on swaðe sæton* "They remained on the path," i.e.,
lay there dead; cf. 2001b *him on swaðe feollon*. *Sittan* in the
sense "to remain," "be located" occurs at 1907b *ymb mearce
sittað*, = "habitabant in illa terra."

2080a *fædera lothes.* "Loth's uncle," i.e., Abraham.

2080b *fleonde [wæron]* Obviously the half-line is deficient, lacking a verb for the clause. Wells objects to this
venerable stopgap on the grounds that it is unidiomatic for
the poem; his *fleon dyde* is more so, although paleographically easier to account for.

2082b *dōmasco* Apparently a Latin ablative in form and
function. The same form (*abute damasco*) occurs in a note on
f. 7v of MS Cotton Claudius B. IV. (*Hept.*, 419). The *ð* from

Lat. *ā* by influence of the following nasal?

2091b *oðle nior* "Nearer home." The division of the
words in the MS is *oð leni / or ·* (*or* on a new MS line),
which caused earlier edd. considerable bafflement. Grein
first perceived the true form and meaning. Apparently here
is one of the rare occasions where the scribe is copying something he does not understand and passes it on as found. It is
therefore possible that *oðle* is an isolated genuine instance
of earlier *oeðle* (cf. 2225a *se oeðylstæf*, MS *seo/ eðylstæf*,
itself suspect). Wells cites Campbell, par. 198: "*œ* remains
in Angl. texts, where occasional *o* . . . spellings can be regarded as errors." Wells also cites Sisam, *Studies*, 105, who
regards *nior* as Kentish. See Intro., pp. 28, 29.

2096-2097a *ÞA wæs suð panon / sodoma folc // guðspell
wegan* "Then a group of Sodomites was (going) south from there
to carry the news about the battle." Wells compares 2096a to
BW 761 *eoten wæs utweard*; closer to home is GN 1431a *holm wæs
heonweard*. Some edd. consider these verses far enough off
from 14.16 to justify a change: hence Kock, *JJJ*. 32, would
read *wegen*, pp., and so Krapp: "then south from there the
battle news was carried to the people of Sodom" implying that
Abraham himself delivered the news. The MS *wegan* may be considered pass. part. (Campbell, par. 735 (*k*), *n*. 1).

2100b-2200 *him ferede mid // solomia / sinces hyrde*.
"He (the king of Sodom) took with him the king of Salem."
2101 = "the guardian of the treasure of Salem," i.e., "Melchisedech rex Salem." The poet pictures both kings going out to
meet Abraham, cf. 14.17-18. *solomia* has the form of a gen.
pl. (cf. *feretia* 1909, "Pherezeus," *filistea* 2835, "Philistinorum," *ethiopia // lond and liodgeard* 228b-29a, "terram Aethi-
opiae," *ebrea* 2164, gens. pl. in -*ia*, -*ea*). For *solom*- Holthausen compares LXX, Old Latin "Hiero-solyma."

2102 *pæt wæs se mæra / melchisedec*, Cf. CH 138 *swa se
mæra iu / Melchisedech*, and a poetic formula which seems to
have crept into the prose Genesis, *Melchisedech, se mæra Godes
man* (*Hept*., 120). The significance of Melchisedech was fixed
by Hebrews 7. Bede (*In Gen.*, CCSL 118A, 192) takes him as a
figure of the "evangelical pontificate" succeeding from the
Apostles to the bishops of the Church, in recognition of which
Abraham gave him a tenth of all. Though *bisceop* is the normal
OE. word for a Jewish high-priest (cf. B-T & *Supp.*, ad loc.
II & III) its use here, and perhaps the progression from *leoda
bisceop* to *godes bisceope*, may suggest Melchisedech's typological role, "sine patre, sine matre, sine genealogia; neque
initium dierum, neque finem vitae habens, assimilatus autem
Filio Dei, manet sacerdos in perpetuum." The poet lightly i-
dentifies Melchisedech's offering of bread and wine, "profer-
ens panem et vinum," with the Eucharist, 2103b, *se mid lacum
com* (cf. Isidore, *Quaest. vet. test.*, PL. 83, 240A).

2107a *wæs ðu gewurðod* I.e., *wes ðu*, for MS *wærðu* =
"benedictus Abram Deo excelso;" Wülker prints *wær ðu*, presumably for *wære ðu* with elision before the appended pronoun.
Wells assumes haplography and reads *weorð ðu*.

2111b-2112 *and þe wæpnum læt // rancstræte forð / rume
wyrcan,* "And [God] allowed you with weapons to clear [*wyrcan*]
a wide warrior-street . . . ." *læt* is for *let*, perhaps influenced by the vowel of *gebræc* 2111a, but cf. 2440b, *forlæt*:
interchange of *a / æ / e* is frequent. *rancstræte* may denote
a path for warriors to pass through (as apparently, in JU 303,
herpað worhton / þurh laðra gemong) or the act of cutting down
the enemies causing the path to appear *on swaðe*. Cosijn, *Beiträge* 18, 453, compares Icel. *rakk-leið* (advbl. only)
"straightway," orig. "a bold path," or "path of bold ones,"
cf. OE. *ranc* "proud," and so Kock, *PPP.*, 19, "a path of bold
ones." Wells emends to *rincstræte*, translating, "manstreet."
I take as does Kock, hence "warriorstreet." Rosier, *Archiv*
202, 269-71, thinks it too odd in meaning and would return
to Dietrich's suggestion (*ZfdA* 10, 331), *randstræte* "shield-
steet." The latter is perhaps morphologically more familiar
than "warriorstreet," but semantically, in the world of com-
monsense, neither more nor less intelligible.

2114a *on swaðe sæton.* Cf. the identical 2077a *n.*; 2077a
is parallel to *him on laste stod* 2075b, which glosses both
occurences. Cosijn, *Beiträge* 19, 453, does not like the
shortness of the sentence and would read *þæt hie on swaðe
sæton*, no stop after *fyllan.* Wells considers 2114a an interpolation imitating 2077a yet suggests reading *Hæleð feollon,
// on swaðe sæton.*

2117b *sceolde* Taken as from *scieldan* "protect" by everybody, hence Dietrich, *ZfdA* 10, 331, suggests altering to
scielde or *scylde.* See Intro., p. 30.

2119a *seo* Read as relative, and taken as nom. head of
clause, "he [God] protected you . . . and the holy covenant
(protected you), which you keep . . . ," but functioning as
acc. Cf. EL 1195b, *se* for *þone* at head of rel. clause.

2120a *him þa se beorn* The *beorn* is Melchisedech, 2120-
21a being a brief reprise of 2105b-19.

2143 *þe ic me agan wille,* An isolated unmetrical hemistich. Grein and Wülker add it on to 2142b. Probably however,
something dropped out, disturbing the meter but not the
sense.

2147b *willgesteallum* "By you pleasant [?] companions,"
taken as instr., with Holthausen. Cf. *willgebroðor* 971b *n.*,
willgesweostor 2608a. In all three places the compound in
will-ge- has sinister and ironic overtones. Probably the poet
makes Abraham reject the king of Sodom's offer in this way because of the traditional distaste for this people, even though
it involves getting ahead of the story. The translator of the
OE. prose Genesis feels so strongly that he replaces 19.4-11

with a little homily: "Se leodscipe wæs swa bysmorful, þæt hi woldon fullice ongean gecynd heora galnyssæ gefyllan, na mid wimmannum, ac swa fullice þæt us sceamað hyt openlice to secgenne, and þæt wæs heora hream, þæt hi openlice heora fylðe gefremedon" (*Hept.*, 132).

2149a *sodoma rice.* Most easily taken as instr., parallel to *willgesteallum.* Thorpe translates as if it were *rices* and so subsequent edd. read, but the whole sentence has more force taken as it stands. The alliteration of 2149 is defective; of the various alterations proposed, that of Grein and Krapp, adding *selfa* after *þu*, 2149b, is simplest.

2159b *eacne fuglas* "Gorged birds (of carrion)." Alliteration is provided and stylistically the line is improved by Grein's clever emendation of 2159b to *ac nefuglas*, "but birds of prey (corpse-birds)," which nearly all edd. accept (in that reading, no period after 2159a). But it makes perfect sense as it stands.

2160b *blodig* Krapp, following Holthausen, *Englische Studien* 51, 184, reads *blodige*, pl., to agree with *fuglas*; such strict concord need not be insisted upon.

2161a *þeodherga wæl*, Grein retains the MS *wæl* as an uninflected instr.; perhaps it is better explained as an endingless locative (see Dahl *Substantival Inflexion in Early OE.*, 48 ff., cited by Campbell, par. 571): "gorged birds . . . sit, bloody, on the slaughter of heathen armies;" other edd. read *wæle.*

2176a *freomanna to frofre* Sisam, *Studies*, 38: "It can hardly be doubted that a scribe has lost the sense by substituting *freomanna*, a legal, not a poetic word, for *fremena*, gen. pl., 'benefits,' depending on *hwæt.*" The legalism is not in itself objectionable, especially in a passage translating "legalisms;" cf. *gerefa* 2182 ("procuratoris"), JL 19, 530 *gerefa* ("procurator domes"), DN 79 ("praepositus eunuchorum"). The sons of Noe are *freomen* 1601a. It is possible that the poet or a later copyist did misunderstand *liberis* 15.2 as "freemen." Cf. 2183a *freobearnum.*

2177b-2178a *eaforan . . . ænegum minra* "For any son of mine . . . ."

2179a *woruldmagas* Apparently for "vernaculus meus," to indicate that the inheritors are related merely by circumstance rather than blood.

2184b *sie* Subj. pl. with *eaforan*, see 1587a *n.* Holthausen reads *sin = sien.*

2189a *eaforan* The emendation seems inescapable, though Wells reads MS *eafora* as gen. pl. (see 1191a *n.*).

2191 *sceawa heofon. / hyrste gerim,* "Look at heaven. Count the ornaments, . . ." etc., for "suspice caelum et numera stellas . . . ." Grein, Wülker and Wells punctuate this way. Since the a-line is light, Holthausen reads *sceawa heofonhyrste / ond hædre gerim*, but that overdoes it. Krapp's

and before *hyrste* repairs the line equally well, and brings
the line closer to the Vulgate and OE. usage.

    2195 *swilc biδ mægburh / menigo pinre* "Such shall be
the multitude of your family . . ." taking *mægburh* as gen.
sing. So Wells, citing Brunner, par. 284, anm. 4, *burug*,
gen. sing. in Lindisfarne Gospels, and Campbell, par. 627,
dat. *burg*, infers "an exactly similar gen. sing." If such
a Northumbrianism cannot be accepted, then we may alternately
read *menigo* as gen. sing., dependent on *mægburh* (Campbell, 589 (7)): "such is the offspring of your multitude,"
regular syntax, but feebler in sense. Comparing 2222 f.
mægburge . . . pinre rim, Grein would, and Krapp does, read
mægburge here, Krapp suggesting that the scribe may have
written a nom. form because it stands next to *biδ*. Holthausen, *Englische Studien* 51, 184, would read *mægbyrh*,
parallel to *folcbearnum frome*.

    2196b-2200 The treatment of 15.4 is elaborated to in-
clude a suggestion of the traditional meaning of the birth of
Isaac, the "son of the promise." This passage has no exact
correspondence in the Latin; rather, the detail is chosen because it prophesies the birth of Isaac in terms of the birth
of Christ; cf. CH 35b-38: "Wæs seo fæmne geong, // mægδ manes
leas, / þe he him to meder geceas; // þæt was geworden / butan weres frigum, // þæt þurh bearnes gebyrd / bryd eacen
wearδ" (see also CH 61-66, 74-77, 297-300, 720-26, PX 355-60).
The birth of Isaac of the sterile woman prefigures the birth
of Christ of the Virgin (Ps.-Bede, *In Pent. comm.*, PL. 91, 244-
45). The injunction not to mourn suggests the etymology of
Isaac's name, "risus," or "gaudium" (Jerome, *Liber int. heb.
nom.*, CCSL 72, 67; *Liber quaest. heb. in gen.*, *ibid.* 22). As
in the poem, two exegetical topics, the prophecy and the name,
are often combined in the commentaries. So Bede: "Specialiter
autem nomen Isaac, id est, 'risus,' qui ex promissione nascitur, congruit mediatori Dei et hominum, et cuius natiuitate
dixit angelus pastoribus, 'Nolito timere, ecce enim euangelizo
uobis gaudium magnum quod erit omni populo' (Luke 2.10)" (*In
Gen.*, CCSL 118A, 208).

    2197a *æsæled = asæled,* which is the form Junius, Wülker
and edd. print.

    2203a *feowera sumne,* Grein alters to *feawera* and Holt-
hausen considers the MS form as equivalent to WS. *feawera*
"with few companions" (this provides a "North." confusion of *ea/eo*), but *four* is obviously the correct meaning—Abraham is one of four, himself, Loth and their two wives.

    2204b-2215 This passage is a response to 15.18, "semini
tuo dabo terram hanc a fluvio Aegypti usque ad fluvium magnum
flumen Eufraten," supplemented by additional geographical lore.
Whereas Genesis mentions only two delimitations of the future
borders of Israel, Euphrates and "the river of Egypt," the
poem names three, Euphrates, Nile and the "sea," presumably
the Mediterranean. This in fact roughly corresponds to the

borders of the territory anciently regarded as the land of
Israel (cf.,e.g., Josue 1.4). Edd. have seemed pretty hazy
about what the passage is saying, and how to construe it, and
it has as a result acquired several unnecessary and confusing
emendations. Dietrich, *ZfdA* 10, 333, blurred matters (already
confused by Junius' misreading *niðas* as *riðas*, which, apparently Thorpe and Dietrich take as the MS reading), by emending
2210 to *swa mid niðas / swa nilus sceadeð* (MS: *swa mid niðas
twa · nilus sceadeð*). Thorpe, grasping the general meaning,
tried to improve it by changing *wendeð sæ* to *Wendel-sæ*, the
Mediterranean, gaining in specificity but losing the verb
which is the key to the passage. Both emendations have been
generally accepted by edd., inducing such a pitch of confusion that Wells, despite some new alterations of his own, dis-
misses most of the passage as a nonsensical interpolation (p.
xlvii). But if one follows the text just as the MS presents
it, including the pointing (except at 2209, where a point has
been omitted), it is not too difficult to arrive at sound
sense: "I to you now, lord of the Hebrews, give my promise
that by your descendants the earth, many a broad land, will
be settled, the surface(s) of the earth up to Euphrates [*oð
eufraten*, "usque ad . . . Eufraten"] and from the borders of
Egypt, just as [*swa* 2210a] Nilus shall divide [*sceadeð*] the
broad dominion [*wide rice*] between two peoples [i.e., Nile
shall mark the future boundary between the Egyptians on one
side and the Hebrews on the other] and the sea shall run back
[*eft gewendeð*, i.e., the Mediterranean coast, running back
northeast shall form the third border of the triangular domin-
ion]. All that will your sons possess, each nation, precisely
as [*swa* 2213b] the three waters [the Euphrates, the Nile, the
sea], foamy floods, enclose [*bewindað*] with their streams the
high stone-cities, the abode of human-tribes." Krapp comes
close to the meaning, but misses the essential point, when he
says "all the passage means to say is that Egypt [sic] is
bounded by *Eufraten*, by *Nilus* and by *Wendelsæ*."

    2210a *niðas twa* Edd. (except Wells), following Dietrich,
ZfdA 10, 333, read *swa* for *twa*, partly on the grounds that
twegen masc. acc. is expected. But *swa* unwarrantedly disturbs
the sense, while *twegen* produces an unmetrical type. Best to
keep the anomalous neut. *twa*; cf. 2603b *n.*

    2210b *nilus* The name of the "river of Egypt" is not
mentioned in Genesis (cf. *Hept.*, 86, translating 2.13, "Gion
. . . is eac gehaten Nilus"). The poet may have used the name,
which he must have known from some precise source, as a general
designation for "fluvius Aegypti," or he may have inferred
a "small Nile" distinct from the "great one" from the standard
commentaries on 15.18. Bede, following Augustine, *De ciu. Dei*,
XVI, 24, says: "Fluuium Egypti, hoc est Nilum, non dicit magnum sed paruum, qui diuidit inter Egyptum et Palestinam, ubi
est ciuitas Rinocorura" (*In Gen.*, CCSL 118A, 199). In another

place Augustine is more explicit about the river which divides
Egypt and Israel: "Flumen quippe Aegypti. . . non est Nilus,
sed alius est non magnus fluuius, qui fluit per Rhinocoruram
ciuitatem . . ." (*Quaest. Iesu Naue*, CCSL 33, 327).

2217 *þæt him abrahame / ænig ne wearð   him* dat. pl.
with *gemæne, abrahame* instr. sing.

2225a *se oeðylstæf   -stæf* requires the masc. article.
Most edd. consider this a genuine eWS or Anglian form, preserved accidentally in the incorrect division: *seo eðyl-*, but
it may be a freak. Cf. 2091b *n.* The edd. report a letter e-
rased after *eðylstæf.* Actually, it is a letter showing
through from P. 102, the *f* of *sarferhð* 2246a. There are several such show-throughs on the page, notably the one in
mæðlan, 2220b.

2236b *bryde larum.* "By the counsel of his wife."

2240a *halsfæst herian,* B-T *Supp.*, s.v. *healsfæst*, gives
"defiant," "proud," "unsubmissive (with unbending neck)."
Cosijn, *Beiträge*, 19, 453, defines as "unfrei" ("shackled by
the neck"?), contrasting with *agendfrean,* "herrin" (usually =
"herr," but here referring to Sarra). *herian* "to scorn" =
"despexit."

2248-2252a "You even allowed that afterwards the serving
woman, Agar, who in the track of a woman [i.e., after Sarra]
ascended into (your) bed just as I had asked, might afflict me
daily by deeds and words in a dishonorable way." Edd. divide
2249 *ðe / idese,* taking *ðe* as dat. of pers. pron., but it
should be taken as pointed, a relative particle.

2251a *drehte dogora gehwam* The emendation to *drehte* is
justified by the presence of two other slips in the same
verse. The scribe obviously is inattentive here, though he
catches one error.

2252b-2253 *þæt agan sceal // gif ic mot for þe, / mine
wealdan,* "That one [sc. *mennen*] I will possess, have power
over my own, if I can with your help [*for þe*]." The precise
meaning of *mine wealdan* is open to question (cf. Kock, *PPP.*
19), but *wealdan* must be construed as parallel to *agan.* Thorpe
needlessly emends *agan* to *Agar*, thus a need arises for a new
inf., if the sentence is not to say the opposite of what it
plainly must say.   Holthausen, reading *Agar*, finds a whole
line missing! Krapp, reading *Agar*, supplies *ongieldan* at end
of 2252b. He also suggests that perhaps *mennen* has dropped
out after *mine*, but if so, *min* is the required reading. Wells
reads *þæt an agan sceal.* The passage may be "careless"(Krapp)
but it is certainly intelligible as it stands.

2254b-2255 *þæs sie ælmihtig // duguða drihten / dema
mid unc twih.* The pointing is incorrect in the MS and when
corrected, *drihten* is isolated. It could be appended to 2245b
if unmetrical scansion were overlooked. But it seems best to
regard *drihten* as the remnant of a partly-lost half-line,
which the erratic pointing is attempting to remedy. Thorpe

reads *drihtna drihten* (cf. JL 594, GB 638), and so edd., but
it seems uncharacteristic of GN. To *duguða drihten*, here supplied, compare 1361b-62a, 2421.

    2264a *frœcne* Perhaps to be regarded as a different
word than *frecne* 1597, cf. Förster, *Englische Studien* 39, 327-
28, who separates *frœclice* "dangerously" and *freclice* "greed-
ily," though scribes often confuse them.

    2293 *of þam frumgaran / folc awœcniað,* "From that pa-
triarch [Ismael], peoples will spring." So Wells construes
the form of Grein's emendation, which Grein interpreted "From
that one, a patriarch [acc.], a people, shall spring . . . ;"
Grein's version seems to add an intermediate patriarch, while
the MS reading *frumgarum* has them fairly multiplying. But
perhaps, if *-um* is what the poet intended, the word is recalling 16.10 or 17.20.

    2296-2297a *Heo þa œdre gewat / engles larum // hire
hlafordum   hire hlafordum* is dat. pl. of destination without
to; cf. 16.9 "revertere ad dominam tuam." In *Sprch.* II, 69,
Grein takes *hire* as adj. "gentle," "submissive to her masters,"
and so Krapp?, Wells, but this strains the context.

    2305b *abrahame* Tri-syllabic, cf. 1710a *n.*

    2306-2307a *leofa, swa ic þe lœre / lœst uncre wel //
treowrœdenne.* "Beloved, as I teach you, keep our covenant
well."

    2312-2314a *þu scealt halgian / hired þinne . . . wœpned-
cynnes* Cf. 17.10, ". . . circumcidetur ex vobis omne masculinum." The poet never translates "circumcisio" any more literally than this. He alludes to the "sign" of circumcision
at 2322b, 2326-27, 2769. "In signum foederis" (17.11) is probably behind such formulas, as is no doubt Romans 4.11, "Et
signum accepit circumcisionis, signaculum justitiae fidei quae
est in praeputio, ut sit pater omnium credentium per praeputium, ut reputetur et illis ad justitiam." The usual exegetical treatment of the topic has probably reinforced this word-
choice. Without explicitly equating circumcision with baptism,
Augustine calls it a "sign of regeneration" (*De ciu. Dei* XVI,
27 [CCSL 48, 532]) and other commentators interpret the injunction to circumcize on the eighth day as a type of the regenerative power of baptism, which like the "eighth day" of Creation
is a type of the Resurrection, as is the day after the resting
of the ark (cf. 1431-35 *n.*): "Quid enim aliud circumcisio significat, nisi renovatam naturam per baptismum post expolia-
tionem veteris hominis? Et quid est octavus dies, nisi Christus, qui hebdomada completa, hoc est, post Sabbatum resur-
rexit?" (Isidore, *Quaest. vet. test.* I, 13, 3 [PL. 83, 242C]).

    2322a *ymb seofon niht* = "octo dierum."

    2323b *oððe of eorðan* Cosijn, *Beiträge*, 19, 454, suggests
adding *beon* after *eorðan*, and so Holthausen, but the inf. required is supplied by *wesan* 2320b. Krapp says that *oððe* is
"emphatic" and therefore receives stress; more likely, the off-

verse is an a-type; see 1638b *n*.

2326b-2327a *gif ge þæt tacen gegaþ // soðgeleafan.*
". . . if you observe that sign with true belief." Cf. B-T,
s.v. *gegan* III. *soðgeleafan* is most naturally construed as
dat., though Wülker takes it as acc., parallel to *tacen*.

2332a *fremum* May be taken as adj., modifying *magorince*
2330a, "I will give my gifts to the prince . . . the good one,"
or as a noun, instr. advbl., "with benefits."

2338-2344a The laughter of Abraham 17.17, and of Sarra
18.12, is treated in both places with similar formulas by the
poet, cf. 2382-86. In both passages God's word is met *(mid)*
hucse—"with mockery." This seems an impossible idea; perhaps *hucse* is meant to convey doubt or confusion. The actual
Christian attitude towards 17.17 was in any case quite different, as authorized by Romans 4.19-21: "Et non infirmatus est
fide, nec consideravit corpus suum emortuum, cum jam fere
centum esset annorum, et emortuam vulvam Sarae. In repromis-
sione etiam Dei non haesitavit diffidentia, sed confortatus
est fide, dans gloriam Deo; plenissime sciens quia quaecumque
promisit, potens est et facere." In this spirit, Augustine
interprets the laughter of Abraham as beneficial: "Risus Ab-
rahae exultatio est gratulantis, non inrisio diffidentis.
Verba quoque eius illa in animo suo . . . non sunt dubitantis,
sed admirantis" (*De ciu. Dei*, XVI, 26 [CCSL 48, 531]). Bede
repeats this (*In Gen.*, CCSL 118A, 207), but when he comes to
Sarra's laughter "post ostium tabernaculi" he stresses the
difference between her reaction and Abraham's: ". . . Abraham
prius riserit admirans in gaudio, et ipsa Sara postmodum dub-
itans in gaudio . . ." (*ibid.*, 217). Sarra's laughter is interpreted by Hrabanus as the prophetic figure of the doubt and
mockery of Christ by the impious, "quod omnes inimicos suos in
judicio suo esset risurus" (*Comm. in Gen.*, II, 21 [PL. 107,
552B]). The poet reflects the plain meaning of the text and
suggests the thrust of these interpretations when he says Abraham *ne wende* (2342a) while Sarra *ne gelyfde* (2385b).

2347b *missãrum* Sisam, *Studies*, 43, regards *missarum*
as scribal corruption of *mioserum*, influenced by Lat. *missa*,
missarum, so Wells reads *misserum*. But cf. Icel. *misseri /
missari* (perhaps from **mis-jãri*, so Holthausen *Etymol. Wörtb.*;
cf. the Gmc. prefix **missa-*, with OHG. alternates *missa- /
missi-*; see Torp-Falk, 321).

2357b *wordgemearcum* An Old Saxonism? Cf. HL 233 *word-
gimerkiun*. The verb *(ge)mearcian* occurs 7x in GB.

2362a *tanum tudre.* "In respect of your offspring (growing) in branches," i.e., your offspring will increase into a
great family (cf. 17.20, "et augebo et multiplicabo eum valde
. . . et faciam illum in gentem magnam"). Cf. the spreading
tree image applied to the family of Cain, 987 ff. Some have
doubted the integrity of the phrase. Cf. AZ 84 *(wudubearwas)
tanum tydrað*, "the wood burgeons with twigs," *tydrian* being

well-attested. Most likely our poet has extended the formula
to the corresponding noun, *tuddor*, but perhaps he has misun-
derstood the formula, though corruption is always possible.
Holthausen, *Anglia* 46, 61, would take *tudre* as verb, equivalent to *tydre*, imperative. Bouterwek explained *tan* as adj.,
"extensus" and so Mason, "with spreading progeny," but the existence of such an adj. is doubtful; see Kock, *JJJ.*, 34.

   2367b-2369a *and him soðe to // modes wære / mine gelætan, // halige higetreawa* "And truly (I will) grant to him my
covenant of the heart, a holy spiritual pact . . . ." The
unique *higetreawa* (= *treowa*), varying *modes wære*, seems to
distinguish Isaac as about to receive a new kind of covenant,
one of the spirit, prophetical of the Christian promise and
of Christ himself, for the previous covenants that Abraham
and Noe received were old, according to the flesh. The flesh
/ spirit dichotomy recalls especially Galatians 5. 6 & 13:
"Nam in Christo Jesu neque circumcisio aliquid valet, neque
praeputium, sed fides quae per charitatem operatur." "Vos enim
in libertatem vocati estis, fratres, tantum ne libertatem in
occasionem detis carnis sed per charitatem spiritus servite
invicem." Most obviously, of course, the poet is referring to
the famous allegory of Galatians 4, Ismael as born of the
flesh, Isaac of the promise: "Nos autem, fratres, secundum
Isaac promissionis filii sumus (4, 28)."

   2368b *gelætan* "Grant," "make over," for 17.19 "constituam," 17.21 "statuam;" cf. *Hept.*, 127 *ic sette min wedd to
[Isaace]*. Thorpe and edd. (except Grein and Wülker) emend to
gelæstan "fulfill," but that is not what God says. Grein and
Wülker take *gelætan* with *wesan*, understood, "bleibe lassen."

   2369a *higetreawa* Pl. form in sing. sense? Dietrich,
ZfdA 10, 334 and edd. (except Wülker) normalize to *-treowa*,
but the form may represent North. confusion of *eo / ea*; cf.
beheowan = beheawan 2645a *n.* and see Intro., p. 31.

   2372b *wegan* The pattern *heht . . . gehwilcne* + inf.
with acc. requires a transitive verb as the inf., "he commanded each to *carry* that sign."

   2380a *on fære* Ambiguous—it could mean either "in fear"
(*fær*, masc.), or "on a journey" (*fær*, neut.), though the former is metrically preferable. Cosijn, *Beiträge* 19, 454, alters to *on feore* "in his life" ("He [God] had done that for
him since he [Abraham] first was able to carry out his Lord's
desires"), and so Holthausen. Wells reads *fære* in his text
but translates "in life." Kock, *JJJ.*, 34, takes *fære* as derived from *feore* through an intermediate **fere*. Cosijn suggests that if "journey" is understood here, then it must be
"the journey of life" that is meant. More precisely perhaps,
the word recalls either the dangers or journeys that Abraham
endured to arrive at his special destiny.

   2382 *Þa þæt wif ahloh / wereda drihtnes* "Then that woman laughed at the Lord of hosts." Cosijn, *Beiträge*, 19, 454,

suggests *be worde drihtnes* to avoid the "unusual" (Krapp) construction *ahloh* + gen. Kock, *PPP.*, 20 defends the gen. here.
Jovy, *Bonner Beiträge* 5, 31, takes *wereda drihtnes* as limiting
wif: "the woman of the lord of hosts," i.e. Abraham's wife.
But B-T and *Supp.* give a total of seven instances of *hliehhan*
with gen., suggesting that that is the regular construction.
Perhaps the edd. recoil from the boldness of the statement.

    2390a   *sarran*   Nominative, cf. 2715b. Krapp leaves this
line alone, but reads *sarra* at 2715. Other edd. variously
emend both lines.

    2396b   *worngehat*   "Promise of multitudes?" or, perhaps
better, "multitude of promises," promises frequently repeated? Certainly the promise of an heir for Abraham has been
made many times up to this point. 2395-2397a may be translated: "When I return to this place another time my frequent
promises (*or*: promises of multitudes) will be fulfilled for
you." Cf. 18.14, "hoc eodem tempore vita comite et habebit
Sarra filium." Bouterwek, Holthausen, Krapp read *wordgehat*.

    2402b   *leohtes mæg*   At 1938b Thorpe's emendation of *leoht*
to *Loth* can hardly be avoided. Later edd. make an identical
change here (Grein, *Germania* 10, 418, first proposing it),
Holthausen, Krapp and Wells reading *Lothes*. But the change
here is both unnecessary and damaging to the sense. There is
a direct contrast between "the kinsman of the light" and the
sinister golden light glittering on the roofs of the Sodomites.

    2403b-2406a   The Jewish tradition concerning the Sodomites
stresses their habitual inhospitality and their richness in
gold. The first theme may be echoed by Alcuin when he says
that the angels test Loth's charity by appearing as guests
(*Int. et Resp. in Gen.* I, 185 [PL. 100, 542A]). But this
theme is not prominent in the Christian tradition nor does it
appear in the poem except in the text-based circumstances of
the Sodomites' bad behavior towards Loth's guests, and in the
word *gistmægen* 2496b. The wealth of the Sodomites was the
cause of their churlishness towards visitors, according to the
rabbis; they were fearful and suspicious (see Ginzberg, I,
248). This element was well enough established in the Christian tradition to appear in Hrabanus' allegorization of *clamor*: "cupiditas reproborum . . . quod . . . importune tumul-
tuatur in auribus Dei" (*Alleg. in sac. scrip.*, PL. 112, 881B).
The topic of its wealth has certainly affected the poetic elaboration of Sodom in GN, where, however, the materials for
elaboration were already inherent in the poetic material:
thus, e.g., Sodom is a *goldburh* 2251b, while its king is a
conventional *goldes brytta* 1997b; cf. 2421-22a.

    2411b-2412a   *forþon wærlogona sint // folce firena hef-
ige.* An intelligible, if inelegant, reading: "Therefore
crimes [*firena*, fem. nom. pl.] of covenant-breakers are heavy
on the people," or "crimes are heavy on the people of the covenant-breakers." The dat. *folce* has proven unacceptable to

edd. (except Wells), who read variously *folcefirena* (Thorpe),
folcfirena (Dietrich), *folca firena* (Grein), *folces firena*
(Holthausen, Krapp). Cf. 2046b *folce getrume (= folc(e)-ge-*
trume?).   Perhaps *folce firena = folcefirena = folcgefirena,*
cf. BW 1792 *unigmetes = *ungemetes* (see Campbell, par. 467).

    2416b *þæt sceal wrecan* Grein, noting shortness of this
verse, supplied *forð* after *sceal*; Cosijn, *Beiträge* 19, 455,
noting 2543-44, supplied *fyr* after *wrecan*, and so Holthausen
and Krapp.

    2417b-2418a *sare and grimme, // hat and hæste* As the
series stands, we have two adverbs, followed by two adjectives:
"painfully and fiercely, hot and vehement." Junius' reading,
hate, assuming the erased letter to be *-e*, yields a smoother
series of four adverbs.

    2419 *WEras basnedon / witeloccas,* "Men awaited the
punishing flames" etc. Edd. have been generally unwilling to
leave *-loccas*. Dietrich, *ZfdA* 10, 335, emends to *witelaces*,
"punishment," gen. sing., dependent on *wean*. So all edd.,
except Wülker, who reads *witeloccan*, "punishment enclosure,"
gen. sing. or acc. pl. But *witelac* is itself unique to GN,
2556b, while *witelocca* is unrecorded. We should compare EX
120-21a, which points to the genuineness of *-loccas: hæfde*
foregenga [the pillar of fire] */ fyrene loccas, // blace*
beamas, where *loccas* "locks (of hair)" designates the flames
of the pillar of fire. It therefore seems best to retain
-loccas, acc. pl., as a similar poetic term for the heavenly
fire sent to punish Sodom.

    2421-2422a *duguðum wlance / drihtne guldon // god mid*
gnyrne "With evil those ones proud in riches paid the Lord
for good." *gyldan* takes the acc. of the thing paid for and
dat. of the person paid.

    2433b *cynna gemunde,* Cf. BW 613 *cynna gemyndig*, "mind-
ful of etiquette."

    2436a *ærendran* "Messengers." All edd. emend to *ærend-*
racan, but the MS form may be genuine. B-T and Wright, *OE.*
Grammar, par. 401, accept it. The agentive affix *-(e)r-* in
a wk. masc. is unusual; perhaps *ærendras* should be read.
According to *OED*, "errander" occurs only in modern instances.

    2439b *sunne* Acc. Edd., exept Holthausen, retain *sunne*
as a unique str. form, but it is elsewhere always weak. Is it
a late form (loss of final *-n*, Campbell, par. 617), or an
otherwise unattested strong form? Wells attributes the form
to syntactic attraction, the scribe taking it as nom.

    2440b *forlæt* Cf. 2111b.

    2450b-2453a "Afterwards night came, behind the day, it
covered the sea-streams, the glory of this life with darkness,
(it covered) the seas and the broad land." *æfter* is advbl.,
lagustreamas, þrym, sæs, sidland parallel objs. of *wreah*. Various constructions and punctuations have been put forward, making little difference for the sense. I follow Wülker. The

only difficulty is *þrym*: it is taken here in the primary
sense, "host of people," referring to the Sodomites—figur-
atively they are like the peoples destroyed by the Flood before and like those facing the Flood of Judgement to come
(cf. CH 806). "Glory" may be the right meaning (so Wells),
though less pointed. B-T, s.v. *þrymm* Ia gives "body of water" (always in a phrase, e.g., *floda þrym*, *yða þrym*) and so
Holthausen construes *lagustreamas . . . þrym*, suggestive of
an anti-creation theme? There may be a play on *þisses lifes*,
dependent on *þrym* or *þystro*: "*þrym* of this life" / "darkness
of this life."

    2472a *ungifre* May represent either *-gīfre* "greedy" or
-gifre "useful"; hence, *ungifre* "unuseful," "unnecessary,"
"gratuitous" (B-T: "harmful," "unfortunate"), or *ungīfre*, prefix best explained as intensive, "very greedy," cf. BW 357
unhar "very old."

    2482a *þine pearfende. / wilt ðu gif þu most* Cosijn,
Beiträge 19, 455, offers the plausible emendation *wine pearf-
ende*, improving alliteration and sense, and all subsequent
edd. adopt it. But the MS reading need not be abandoned.
Dietrich, *ZfdA* 10, 335-36, explained *þine* as for *þigne*, gen.
of *þigen* "food," thus: "being in need of food" (for the absol.
part. cf. 1585b). Alternatively, B-T s.v. *þigen* suggests that
þine is a possessive used substantively, nom. pl. masc., "(you
came here from afar) thy men being in need." If we avoid e-
mendation, it seems necessary to explain the alliteration in
2482 as being dependent on the rhetorical emphasis *wilt* ðu,
gif þu most, x ´ xx ´.

    2487b-2488 *and hine of gromra þa, // cuman arfæste, /
clommum abrugdon* *þa* may be adv., or with Krapp it may be
taken as demonstrative, masc. nom. pl., appositive to *cuman*.

    2496b-2498a *hæfde gistmægen // stiðe strengeo, / styrde
swiðe // werode mid wite*. "The guest-power [i.e., the angels]
had hardy strength, restrained [*styrde*, MS *styrnde*] firmly
the host [of Sodomites] with pain." Wells suggests that *gast-
mægen*, "spirit-power" should be read, considering *gist-* as a
carry-over from 2494b. But the MS reading suggests the traditional topic of the inhospitality of the Sodomites; cf.
2403b-2406a *n.* Most edd. retain MS *styrnde*, unique to this
occurrence, defining as "to be severe" (cf. *stirne* "harsh").
But the dat. obj. *werode* implies *stēoran (stȳran)* "restrain
(from doing harm)," see B-T s.v. *steoran* II, IIa, III, which
better suits the sense of this passage than **styrnan* in any
case. Wells reads *styrde* in his text, but in his note, by
suggesting that the *n* of *styrnde* may have arisen through a
misreading of **styrude*, implies that the verb is *styrian*,
"rouse," "excite," "trouble."

    2505b *mid þyssum wærlogan.* Taken as dat. pl. by Braasch
and others; see Campbell, par. 572.

    2506a *unc hit waldend heht* Cosijn, *Beiträge* 19, 455,

suggests *uncit*, acc. dual, for *unc hit* dat. + acc. *Uncit*
is unknown in poetry (*unket* appears on *Ruthwell Cross* II,3
and in late prose Campbell, par. 703), and is only inferred
from the frequent occurrence of *incit*.

2522a *sigor = Segor* (cf. *sægor* 2533, 2540).

2528b *nu þu ymb þa burh sprycst* For "urbem pro qua locutus est." Thorpe's emendation seems unavoidable, but it is
possible that MS *spryst* conceals a form or corruption of *spy-
rast* from *spyrian* "inquire."

2535-2546a These lines are a greatly elaborated paraphrase of 19.23-24, but the order of the events is changed:
in the Vulgate, the sun rises over the land, Loth escapes to
Segor, and then God rains fire and brimstone on the cities;
in GN, Loth escapes first, followed by the description of the
sun rising, and then the paraphrase of 19.24 is given. The
elaboration of "sol egressus est super terram" and its posi-
tioning serve to separate the events related to the saved and
the damned and to emphasize the contrast. Bede remarks of
this passage (*In Gen.*, CCSL 118A, 226) that by night Loth
faithfully harbored his guests, while the wicked Sodomites
used cover of darkness to rage in sin; at break of day the
rewards of the just and wicked are revealed by the sun of justice. The poet's choice of *friðcandel* is not only ironic, but
refers to God's secure promise of judgement, now being fulfilled. It also is the sign of the *frið* in force for Loth,
who is under God's protection and who himself figures those
secure in the promise of salvation.

2540a *his* With *bryd* 2539a.

2548b-2550a *hlynn wearð on ceastrum . . . laðan cynnes.*
An ironic recollection of the "clamor" which the Sodomites
raised in their sinful days (cf. 18.20, 2408-11a) now turned
to cries of despair; cf. 2562b-65 *n.*

2554b-2555a *bearwas wurdon // to axan and to yslan,* "Or-
chards changed into ashes and cinders." See B-T, s.v. *weorpan*
III (c) (3).

2558b *steapes and geapes* Take as dependent on *eall*
2559b, "(fire . . . swallowed everything together) of the
high and the broad (that men possessed . . .)."

2559 *swogende for, / swealh eall eador* *for*, pret. of
faran. The MS pointing leaves the off-verse deficient: *swogende for swealh · eall eador*. Holthausen reads *leg* after
swogende, citing BW 3145, with *forswealh* in the off-verse, and
so Krapp, also reading *geador* (but *eador* and *geador* are probably phonetically identical, see Campbell, 303, and cf. GB
238, *georne = eorne*). Jovy, *Bonner Beiträge* 5, 31 suggests
the correct line-division: *swogende feor / swealh eall eador,*
and Wells, giving too much credit to Jovy, interprets the
verb correctly. Cf. Dobbie's similar resolution of the lineation, BW 2672b-73, *ligyðum for. // Born bord wið rond*, where
earlier edd. had read *forborn*.

2561b *eall þæt god spilde,* Braasch takes *god* as neut.
acc. sing., "goods," though it is much smoother as masc. nom.
sing.,"God," parallel to *frea.*

2562b-2565a *þa þæt fyrgebræc . . . wið þæs wælfylles.*
fyrgebræc = the crashing noise made by the burning rain. Cf.
the wording of Bede's comment on 19.26: "Et quidem uxor metu
feminae fragilitatis ad clamorem pareuntium repentinum et
fragorem flammarum caelo delapsarum, retro respexit" (*In Gen.,*
CCSL 118A, 227).

2567b-2575 The Pillar of Salt. Josephus remarks that
the pillar stood in his day, and that he had seen it (*Antiquities* I, 203 [Loeb Josephus IV, 101]); his remark was frequently repeated, as e.g., Bede, *In Gen.,* CCSL 118A, 227. The
endurance of the pillar is certified by Sap. 10.7, "incredi-
bilis animae memoria stans figmentum salis." The idea is behind *stille* 2569a, "without changing," rather than "without
moving," but functioning immediately in moral terms—the pillar is an eternal monument to disobedience, a "condiment of
virtue," as the commentators say, forever enduring until all
is changed at the end.

2577b *he eft* This obvious correction of MS *heft* is
thought unnecessary by Hulbert, *JEGP* 37, 534, because he takes
it as evidence of elision of a final vowel before another.
But here a graphic distinction between words seems necessary,
even if one accepts that phonetic elision is operative.

2586a *wylmhatne* The compound is apparently unique,
though B-T s.v. *wilmhat,* notes a ME. *walmhat* (*Jul.* 69, 20).

2600-2601a *Hie dydon swa. / druncnum eode // seo yldre
to* The MS pointing (no point after *eode*) caused the earlier
edd. to assume a loss after *druncnum.* Holthausen's line-division, followed here, clears up the passage; indeed, something is missing, before 2600a where a page has been cut out
so that nothing authoritative can be said about the gaps in
the sense at this point. On the other hand, the capitaliza-
tion of *Hie* suggests that a new paragraph is beginning here,
with only a quick reference to action already treated at more
length.

2603 *hwonne him fæmnan to / bryde him bu wæron* A very
suspect line, since it lacks alliteration, repeats *him* and
does not appear to mention the visit of the younger sister,
though perhaps 2603b was all the poet considered her worth.
As it stands, the line may be translated: "When the women
[*fæmnan*] both [*bu,* nom. pl. fem., but neut. in form, cf.
Campbell, par. 683] were with [*to*] him as a bride." Various
reconstructions have been proposed, but if something has
dropped out it cannot be recovered. Krapp effects a partial
improvement by redividing the line, *hwonne him fæmnan to /
bryde / him bu wæron,* and suggesting the removal of the first
him. Perhaps even more drastic surgery is desirable, such as
reading *hwonne bryde to / him bu wæron.* Most likely, though,

the line is a corrupt conflation of two originally distinct
but similar lines relating to the two similar incidents.

2604b *genearwot* Usually emended to *genearwod*, but Hulbert, *JEGP* 37, 535, argues for the restoration of the MS reading; so too Brook, "Textual and Linguistic Study," 286. For
similar unvoicing, regularly emended, cf. GN 218, 2774a, GB
459, 475, also GN 100. See Campbell, par. 450.

2608a *willgesweostor* "loving sisters?" Cf. *willgebroðor* 971b, *willgesteallum* 2147b and notes to those lines.

2615b *folc' unrim,* The MS reading does not make meter
or conform to the *ja*-stem declension (if *unrim* is an adj.
here). Sievers, *Beiträge* 10, 513, indicates the two possibilities, either *folc unrimu* "peoples uncounted in number," or
folca unrim "a countless number of people." The latter better accounts for the MS forms, if *folc* is taken as elided before the following vowel. Translate 2615-16, "From those patriarchs a countless number of people, two powerful tribes,
were born."

2625-2627 "With words Abraham protected his life, since
[*þy*] he readily knew that he had few of kinsmen, of friends
among (that) people." The older edd. (and Wells) put *þy* at
the end of 2625b to give another stress to that line (avoiding
the a-type), but Krapp rightly restores the MS pointing. Cf.
2695, *lare gebearh.*

2628-2632a *þa se þeoden his / þegnas sende, // heht
bringan / to him selfum // Þa þe wæs ellþeodig . . . on fremdes fæðm.* Edd. put a stop after *selfum,* which leaves *heht*
without an object. Various emendations to supply the obj.
fail to convince, e.g., Bouterwek, *to him selfum / Sarran
sciene,* and in notes, *heht bringan to him selfan bryd(e) Abrahames* (so Grein prints); Holthausen, *beornes wif / bringan
to him selfum*; Wells, *heht bryd bringan / to him selfum* (unidiomatic and the addition to 2629a destroys the alliteration).
What is really required is *heht (him) bringan* + acc. (Krapp
heht hie bringan), and the simplest way to achieve this is to
regard *Þa* 2630a as acc. sing. fem., referring to Sarra, though
this involves ignoring the capital (one can only assert in de-
fence that capitals occur in the middle of sentences frequently
throughout the MS, e.g. 2750) and adding *þe,* the relative particle. I take *ellþeodig* as nom. sing. neut., modifying *wif.*
Translate: "Then the lord sent his officers, commanded to bring
to himself her who was for the second time strange among the
peoples [i.e., a stranger among foreigners], the wife of Abraham, led from her husband into the embrace of a stranger."

2631a *wif abrames* Edd. read *Abrahames,* but since the MS
spelling reflects the pronunciation and rhythm of the line, it
may be left. See 1710a *n.*

2641b-2642 *Him symbelwerig // synna brytta / þurh slæp
oncwæð:* Holthausen, *Anglia* 46, 61, suggests transferring *him*
2641b to before *þurh* 2642b. Thorpe, notes, suggests reading

sinces brytta for *synna brytta* (cf. 2728b [Abimelech],1857b,
[Pharaoh]), followed by Bouterwek, Holthausen, Krapp and Wells
in their texts. Says Sisam, *Studies*, 43,"The error can be attributed to the religious preoccupations of the copyist." Or
the emendation can be attributed to the "heroic" preoccupations of the editors. For the formula, cf. EL 957 *synna bryt-
tan*, JL 362 *synna fruman*, GU 550 *synna hyrdas*. The epithet
is particularly appropriate to Abimelech, the only "heroic"
figure in the poem, type of the worldly lord. Bede explains
him as an apparently righteous man who in fact signifies the
opposite, the good figuring the bad, the bad the good (*In Gen.*,
CCSL 118A, 234-36).
    2645a *beheowan = beheawan* cut off; for the spelling,
cf. 2369a *n.*; for the expression, cf. 2702b *aldre beheowe*.
    2645b *þæne þe her leofað   þæne = þone*, see Campbell,
par. 380, and cf. 1522b, 1428b *nn*.
    2647b-2648a *and him miltse // to þe seceð?* Successive
a1-types, the first in the off-verse, hence frequently emended.
Grein reads *him miltse to þe // sylfum secgað* and so Holthausen, except that he supplies *symle*. Wülker divides as Grein
does, but merely indicates a loss in 2648a. Krapp indicates
an intention to read *and miltse him* but does not transpose in
his text.
    2658-2659a *he is god and gleaw, / mæg self sprecan, //
geseon sweglcyning.* "He himself may speak," i.e., "has authority," is a feeble but intelligible rendition of "propheta est
et orabit pro te," though the parallelism *sprecan / geseon* is
abrupt, and 2658 lacks alliteration. It seems likely that
some corruption is involved. Thorpe omits *self*, substituting
wið god, which smoothes the sense and gives alliteration, and
so Grein, Holthausen and Krapp read. Wells leaves 2658 as it
is and alters *geseon* to *geteon*, translating, "he . . . can
himself speak to move the sky-king."
    2661b-2666a "He, righteous, patient, can pray to me if
he desires to declare [*wile . . . abeodan*] your messages to
me quickly, so that I may still allow you to enjoy mercies,
favors among the living in (your) days, (allow you to enjoy)
treasure with health."
    2662b *ærenda* Neut. (or fem.?) acc. pl. Thorpe, notes,
suggests and Bouterwek, Grein read *ærende*; Grein, *Germania* 10,
418, suggests *ærendu*, and so Holthausen, Krapp, Wells. But
B-T *Supp.*, gives several examples of *ærenda* acc. pl.
    2668a *sprecan sine,* "his counsellors," "omnes servos
suos." *spreca* in this sense is otherwise unattested in OE.,
but cf. OHG. *sprehho*; compounds, OFr. *for-spreka*, OE. *gespreca*,
imply the simplex. Edd. read *gesprecan*.
    2670b-2672a "Men feared the stroke at the hands of the
Lord according to the dream [i.e., the punishment promised in
the dream, cf. 2659b-61a] on account of that deed [viz., the
retention of Sarra]." *him* 2670b, is reflex. (sc. *weres*) with

ondredon.
     2694-2695 *Ac ic me, gumena baldor, / guðbordes sweng //
leodmagum feor / lare gebearh* "But I, O prince of men, being
far from (my own) kin, warded off from myself a clash of the
shield by sleight." *gebeorgan* takes acc. of the thing pre-
vented (*sweng*) and dat. of the person protected (*me*); cf. B-T
Supp., s.v. *gebeorgan* I (1). Kock, *PPP.*, 22, explained *guð-
bordes sweng* as "a blow on the shield," and so Krapp, Wells,
but this does not account for the gen., nor does it express
the thing Abraham really fears, that is, an attack, violence;
"a clash of the shield" does, and is more characteristic of
OE. idiom. *lar* with this shade of meaning, "wisdom which de-
ceives," "deceitful wise speech" may be unique. For the idea
cf. *wordum bearh* 2625.
     2696-2697 *siððan me se halga / of hyrde frean, // mines
fæder, / fyrn alædde.* Translate: " . . .after the holy One
led me far from the household of (my) lord, of my father."
hyrde is generally taken as syncopated dat. sing. of *hyred*
"household," "family;" Bouterwek reads *hyrede*. Holthausen
glosses *hyrde* "Hürde," "Tür," citing Klüge, *Kuhns Zeitschr.*,
26, 100, but *hird* is not attested in the sense "court," "re-
tinue" until early ME.; *frean* is taken as a gen., parallel to
mines fæder (Wells takes it all together, "of my lord father").
Holthausen adds *eðle* after *fæder* to eke out the verse. *alædde*
must be read for MS *alæd* to provide a finite verb.
     2706b-2707 *þær wit earda leas // mid wealandum / winnan
sceoldon.* An early hand has added a mark, apparently to indicate the division *wea-landum.* Lye-Manning remark: "cum pere-
grina terra, vel peregrinae terrae incolis, contendere; malim
tamen legere *wea landum* hostili terra, a *wea* hostilis." Sub-
sequently, Thorpe and Bouterwek take as "hostile nations,"
but the latter in his notes suggests *wællændum wunian* "dwell
among foreign peoples." The difficulty really lies in taking
winnan . . . mid as equivalent to *winnan . . . wið.* Dietrich,
ZfdA 10, 336-37, therefore suggests taking *winnan* as equivalent to *dreogan* "suffer," as in 1014a *wite winnan.* So Krapp,
taking *wealandum* as *wealhlandum* "foreign lands," (which implies a division of the MS form *weal-(l)andum*) though he thinks
taking *-landum* as equivalent to *-lendum* "inhabitants" also
plausible. B-T *Supp.*, s.v. *wealh-land* calls attention to the
OE. prose Genesis, 20.13: *swa oft swa wyt ferdon to fyrlynum
eardum* (*Hept.*, 136), for "in omni loco." In view of the tradition of support for *wealh-landum*, *wealandum* may be so understood, or perhaps an orig. **wealhend*, masc. *nd*-stem "foreig-
ner (the form itself is no trouble, most *wealh-* compounds are
assimilated to *weal-* and a following *-l-* would be simplified
further; cf. B-T entries from *wealh* to *wealhwyrt*). But
frankly I cannot understand why *wea-landum* "(in) evil nations"
is forbidden, except for the usual editorial dislike of abstrac-
tions of any sort. The 11th century notator who divided the

word apparently understood it as *wea-landum.* Take *mid* as
"among" (cf. B-T, s.v. *mid* VI) and translate: ". . . where we
two deprived of homes had to struggle [*winnan sceoldon*] among
foreign nations [*or:* among evil- hostile-nations -peoples]."

    2709-2710a *siððan ic pina . . . mundbyrde geceas* Thorpe
suggests *pine* and so Bouterwek, Grein. Wülker takes *mundbyrde*
as possibly plural and reads *pina* as such, so Holthausen,
Krapp. Wells suggests that *pina* may be a scribal anticipation of *mæra* but cites Brunner, par. 293, showing fem. acc.
sg. in -*a.*

    2713-2716 *forpon ic pegnum . . . beddreste gestah.*
"Therefore I hid the true information [*spræce*] from your officers and above all [*swiðost micle*] from you yourself, that
Sarra came to me into my bed as a bride [*lit.:* following the
path of a bride]."   Cf. the similar formulation of 1836b-41a
and note.

    2720-2721a *gangende feoh / and glæd seolfor // and
weorcpeos.* For ". . . oves et boves et servos et ancillas..."
Grein's *weorcpeos* for MS *weorcfeos* seems inescapable. Junius
reads *weorc feohs* "substance of money," a tempting reading,
accepted by Wülker, but the obvious confusion of the scribe
here, coupled with the plain sense of the Vulgate, overrides
the usual desire to save the MS form. The scribe, having corrected one repetition (see textual note), confusedly made
another, bringing in *feoh* from the previous MS line.

    2725 *eðelstowe / pe ic agan sceal.* "(Choose for your-
self) a dwelling which I do by rights [*sceal*] possess." Most
edd. punctuate 2725b as an independent sentence. Bouterwek
suggests changing *agan* to *ecean*, Holthausen, *Anglia* 46, 61,
suggests *ecan* "endow," "make rich." Mason translates: "I must
have thee," a rendering cryptic even beyond the limits of OE.
poetry. Wells says *agan* here and at 2748b must mean "increase," referring to B-T *Supp.*, 28, which in fact gives him
no support, since it defines *agan* 2725b, 2748b as "endow,"
"make possessor of something" (as an extension of *agun*, "to
do"?), but queried. Krapp improves the meaning by taking *pe*
as relat. part., referring to *wic*, etc. Just as difficult,
really, is the meaning of *sceal*: Krapp takes it as a pure auxiliary, "which I own."

    2732-2733a *ac him hygeteonan . . . deope bete.* Grein
suggests *ic* for *ac* and Wells supplies *ic* between *ac* and *him*;
others take *ic* as implicit in the verb *bete.*

    2733b-2735 *ne ceara incit duguða // of ðisse eðylturf /
ellor secan // winas uncuðe / ac wuniað her.* "Do not you trouble yourselves to seek service, unknown friends, elsewhere
out of this land, but dwell ye here." This attempts to reproduce the grammar of the sentence as Krapp explains it: "The
direct address to Sarah in the preceding passage favors a
singular here [i.e. *ceara*] changing to the plural *wuniað* . . .
because of *incit.*" Grein reads *cearað* to match *wuniað*, but in

Sprch. I, 158, returns to the MS, taking *incit* as acc. with
inf. Holthausen reads *Ne cearað duguða inc . . .*," etc.
    2738b-2739 *he wæs leof gode // forðon he sibbe / gesælig
dreah* Most edd. put a period after *gode:* "He was dear to God.
Therefore he, blessed, enjoyed peace . . . ." Taking it away
makes a difference: "He was dear to God because, blessed, he
worked peaceful deeds. . . ."
    2740-2741 *and his scippende / under sceade gefor, //
hleowfeðrum peaht / her penden lifde.* Is the image of a bird
brooding over her chicks intended to recall Genesis 1.2, the
spirit "brooding" over the waters, and thence the works of
the spirit? cf. Ps. 90.4.
    2747b-2749a *ne meahton freo ne peowe // heora bregowear-
das / bearnum agan // monrim mægeð* The main problem, as in
2725b, is the interpretaion of *agan*, but the solutions are
not necessarily the same, though commentators have naturally
tended to link the two cruces. Bouterwek suggests *ecean*,
Grein, *Germania* 10, 418, *ecan* and so Holthausen, Krapp. Kock,
Anglia 43, 308, takes *agan* as "endow" and construes with
bregoweardas as obj., appositive to *monrim*; Wells takes it in
a similar sense, "endow," but there is not much evidence for
such a meaning. Dietrich, *ZfdA* 10, 337, would understand
a-gān "bring forth," but this seems always to mean "to come
to pass," "to happen (to somebody)." Cosijn, *Beiträge* 19, 457,
takes *bregoweardas* as gen. sing. (cf. Brunner, par. 237, GN
98a *n.*) making *agan* fairly easy in its primary sense, "own,"
"have": "Neither free woman nor bond could have a mancount in
sons for (in respect of) their king." Cf. 20.18, "concluserat
enim Deus omnem vulvam domus Abimelech."
    2747b *ne meahton freo ne peowe* Holthausen, following
Sievers, *Beiträge* 10, 492, reads *pēos* [= *pēowas*?] to remove
the anomalous final syllable. But Campbell, par. 593 (2),
n. 2, considers it to be *peowe*, resolved, hence not unmetrical. Krapp's comparison of 2754b *peowra* is irrelevant since
the syllable there is metrically long whether the vowel be
long or short.
    2751b *arra* The MS reading is probably wrong, equidis-
tant paleographically between the well represented gens. pl.
ara and *arna*: it is possible that the double consonant denotes a long preceding vowel. Edd. since Grein (except Wülker) read *arna*.
    2753a *getigðode* Used absolutely here: "The Protector of
angels gave into him . . ." (i.e., consented); see B-T *Supp.*
s.v. *getipian* I (1).
    2764a *eaforan and idese.* "To the man and the woman,"
i.e., Abraham and Sarra. It appears that the poet has applied
a new meaning to the formulaic collocation usually meaning
"sons and daughters;" cf. 1054, 1076, 2606, etc.
    2768b *his agene hand* Cosijn, *Beiträge* 19, 457, citing
GU 303, *mid gebolgene hand*, supplies *mid* before *his*, and so

Holthausen, Krapp, Wells; Braasch lists *agene* as acc. sing.,
but it may be taken as an instrumental (with Grein and apparently Wells, in his note) without syncopation. On *hand* as
instr., see Wright, *OE. Grammar*, par. 398. Dietrich, *ZfdA*
10, 337, calls it an "instrumental accusative."

2772b-2773a *swa him cynde wæron // æðele from yldrum.*
In his edition, Grein takes *cynde* as adj., "natural," and
æðelo as noun, "pre-eminence": "because pre-eminence (nobility)
was natural to him;" but in *Sprch*. I, 178, he takes *cynde* as
nom. pl. and *æðele* as adj. modifying it; so Krapp, translating, "as his qualities were excellent."

2774 *hunteontig* Thorpe and edd., except Wülker and
Wells, read *hundteontig*, but the MS form is well-attested, cf.
B-T *Supp*. Wells cites Klaeber *MLN* 18, 244 and Campbell, par.
477.

2778-2782a The "heroic" flavor of this passage is odd.
Perhaps the poet is thinking of the great feast "in die ablac-
tationis" (21.8) as a banquet at which the boy enters into
the warrior's life. But the detail may stem from the often-
repeated comment of Jerome on 21.9, that Sarra disapproved of
Ismael playing with Isaac "quod idola ludo fecerit, juxta illud, quod alibi scriptum est 'sedit populus manducare et bibere, et surrexerunt ludere' (Exodus 32.5)" (*Liber quaest. heb.
in Gen.*, CCSL 72, 24). Krapp puts a comma after *eall* 2781b,
which allows the possibility that the boys are the ones drinking and rejoicing. Wells removes the comma—a distinct improvement, lending the passage a certain dignity: "[When] came
the occasion [that] that woman saw Ishmael playing before Abraham where they two [Abraham and Sarra] both sat at a feast,
holy in mind, and all their household drank and rejoiced . . ."
(Wells' translation, modified to fit my punctuation).

2783b-2784a *forgif me, beaga weard, // min swæs frea:*
"Forgive me [viz., for asking what follows], guardian of rings,
my dear lord . . . ." Wells points out the rarity of *for-
gifan* in the sense "forgive," and its absence elsewhere in GN
(it occurs once in GB, 662, taking an acc.). Therefore, he
provides a new object by altering *frea* to *frofre*, taking *me* as
dat. and translating: "My dear guard of rings, give me relief."
Wells' point is a good one, but does not override the intelli-
gibility of the text as it stands.

2784b-2786a *hat siððan // agar ellor / and ismael // lædan mid hie* "Command Agar afterwards (to go) elsewhere and to
lead Ismael with her." Thorpe and edd. read *siðian* for *siððan*
to provide an inf. and eke out the verse. But in itself, the
absence of inf. is not grounds for emendation, cf. 1865, 2672
(*hat . . . to* corresponding to *hat . . . ellor* here). If there
is a fault, the pointing suggests it is that something has
dropped out between *agar* and *ellor*. Cf. 2799b-2800a.

2794b-2795a *wiste ferhð guman / cearum on clommum.* "He
knew (that) the heart of the man (was) in the grips of care

(was depressed by cares)." Cosijn, *Beiträge* 19, 457, suggests
that *cearum = cearigum*, adj. and Braasch gives it as dat. pl.
masc. of *cear*, adj. But the form is best taken as instr. pl.
of *cearu* "care," "sorrow," following Krapp.

2798b   *hire* From *hyran*, cf. 21.12, "audi vocem eius."

2809b   *snytrum mihtum* Probably it is best to regard
snytrum as from an otherwise unrecorded adj., *snytre*, as do
B-T and Braasch. The usual adj. form would be *snottrum*. *snytrum* suggests the noun, of which the correct acc. form would
be *snytru*, to which Cosijn, *Beiträge* 19, 457 suggests emending: "he gives you victory, wisdom with power;" certainly
the emendation of *-um (-ū)* to *-u* is plausible enough on graphic
grounds. Kock, *Anglia* 46, 87, considers *snytrum mihtum* to
be an example of asyndetic parataxis, "with wisdom, with power."

2813b-2815a   *waldend scufeð, // frea, forðwegas / folmum
sinum // willan þinne.* "The Ruler advances, lord, your will
forward [*lit.*: on the way going forward] with his hands." It
is simplest to take *forðwegas* as an advbl. gen., with Grein
in his ed., Wülker and G-K; cf. Q-W, par. 102. Grein, *Sprch.*
I, 320, supplies *on* before *forðwegas* as acc. pl., parallel to
willan þinne. Wells reads *forðwegan* "to bring forth," "the
Ruler strives . . . to bring forth your pleasure . . ." (for
scufan intrans., see B-T, s.v. *scufan* VII). The usual meaning,
or connotation, of *forðweg* is "death," cf. *Menologium* 216-18:
Andreas . . . his gast ageaf . . . fus on forðweg. Here it
must be taken to denote spiritual progress before death is
reached, as in EX, where the word means the Exodus itself: *An
wisode[,] // mægenþrymmum mæst . . . on forðwegas / folc æfter wolcnum . . .* (EX 348b-350). Of course *frea* can be taken
as nom., parallel to *waldend*, as well as voc.

2838-2839   *wic getæhte / þær weras hatað . . . bersabea
lond.* Grein and edd. read *þæt* for *þær*, "God showed him a
place that men call Bersabea," etc. But as Wells points out,
Bersabea is the name of the region, not the name of Abraham's
property in it; thus, translate, following the MS: "To him the
Lord of angels showed a place where men, city-dwellers, call
the land Bersabea" (cf. "vocatus est locus ille Bersabee.. . . .
Abraham vero plantavit nemus in Bersabee)."

2840b   *heah steapreced,* 1D3-type. The MS spaces *heah*
(page) *steap reced.* Edd. read *heahsteap reced*, 2A3b, but
compounding the noun is equally plausible and reduces the redundancy felt in *heahsteap.*

2843   *on þam glædstede / gild onsægde,* Lit.: "at the
happy place," but Grein, noting 1810, reads *gledstede*,"altar,"
and such a meaning is generally accepted. Krapp notes the
frequent exchange of *e* and *æ* in the MS. The scribe, at least,
may have been conscious of a pun. See Intro., p. 28.

2846-2936   The Sacrifice of Isaac. This episode has always been interpreted as a type of the Passion, popularized as
such from the earliest ages of Christianity. Bede tells how

Benedict Biscop returned from his sixth journey to Rome bringing a series of paintings showing the concord of the Old and
New Testaments, among them, "uerbi gratia, Isaac ligna, quibus immolaretur portantem, et Dominum crucem in qua pateretur
aeque portantem . . . . (*Historia Abbatum* I, 9 [Plummer 1,
373])." The *Pentateuchal Commentary* concisely presents the
sum of the correspondences traditionally seen between the Sacrifice of Isaac and the Sacrifice of Christ: "Quando autem
Abraham immolavit filium suum, personam habuit Dei Patris.
Per hoc quod in senectute genuit illum Abraham, figuratur quod
pene in fine mundi Christus esset nasciturus. . . . Quae patri in fine temporum Ecclesia mirabili gratia Dei, non natur-
ali fecunditate procreavit. Sicut autem Abraham unum filium
suum obtulit, et sicut Isaac ipse sibi ligna portavit ita
Christus in humeris portavit lignum crucis. . . . Isaac lig-
atus super struem lignorum ponitur: Christus crucifixis, sus-
pensus in ligno crucifigitur. Quod autem pro Isaac immolatus
est aries, significat quod illaesa divinitate manente, secundum carnem crucifixus est, sive quod idem Christus filius natus est. Aries immolatus cornubus haerebat. Crux enim cornua
habet, unde scriptum est: 'Cornua sunt in manibus illius' (Hab.
3.4). Cornubus enim aries haerens, crucifixum Dominum significat . . ." (PL. 91, 244D-245C).

 2846-2848 *þa þæs rinces / se rica ongan, // cyning, coo-
tigan . . . ellen wære.* 22.1 was a crux. "Temptavit Deus Abraham" was not to be read without considering the problem of
"God tempting" to obedience and faith. As Augustine made quite
explicit in his Second Sermon on the Old Testament (CCSL 41,
9-10), to rightly understand and accept this verse one needed
a sophisticated technique of reading and interpreting, not
only of the extra-literal signification, but of the literal
signification as well. In another place he gives what became
the standard interpretation: "'Et tentauit deus Abraham.' Quaeri
solet quomodo hoc uerum sit, cum dicat in epistula sua Iacobus
quod deus neminem tentat. Nisi quia locutione scripturarum
solet dici 'tentat' pro eo quod est 'probat.' Tentatio uero
illa, de qua Iacobus dicit, non intellegitur nisi qua quisque
peccato inplicatur. Vnde apostolus dicit: 'ne forte tentauerit
uos is qui tentat' (I Thess. 3.5). Nam et alibi scriptum est:
'tentat uos dominus deus uester, ut sciat si diligitis eum'
(Deut. 13.3). Etiam hoc genere locutionis 'ut sciat' dictum
est, ac si diceretur: 'ut scire uos faciat,' quoniam uires di-
lectionis suae hominem latent, nisi experimento etiam eidem
innotescant" (*Quaest. in Hept.* 57 [CCSL 33, 22]). The poet
translates the difficult "temptavit" twice, as if to make sure
that there is no mistake about the meaning. He goes on quickly
to establish the basic lines of the traditional explanation,
that God tested Abraham, not to lead Abraham into sin, or
Isaac into death, but to prove (*cunnian*) "what the fortitude
[*ellen*] of the prince was."

2851b *læde* = "tolle" either as jussive subj., or (with Cassidy-Ringler) as bye-form of the imperative. In either case, it represents "tolle."

2855a *hrincg pæs hean landes* Bouterwek reads *hrycg*, Zupitza *hricg*. See 1393a *n*. The poet may be attempting an interpretation of "terram visionis," i.e., the land of seeing, the high land from which the circle of land (horizon) can be seen. The poet seems to reflect the Old Latin here, which gives prominence to the "high land:" V.L. "terram altam," cf. Vulg., "super unum montium."

2861b-2862 *him wæs frea engla, // word, ondrysne / and his waldende leof.* Edd. (except Bouterwek, Wülker and Cassidy-Ringler) accept Thorpe's readings *frean* and *waldend*, parallel accs. sing.: "To him (Abraham) the word of the Lord of angels was venerable, and his Ruler dear (to him)." This is unnecessary and probably misses the point of the sentence. It clearly means: "To him the Lord of angels, the Word, was venerable and (he) was dear to his Lord." Cf. 2598b, *waldende leof*. The sentence expresses the reciprocity of love between God and Abraham (cf., e.g., 2736-41), offering also the suggestive complication that it is especially the Second Person of the Trinity, the Word in his creative aspect, to whom Abraham, the type of the First Person, responds as he prepares to sacrifice the Son, the Second Person in his sacrificial aspect. Or, from another angle, the man, Abraham, prays to Christ the divine for guidance in his dealing with Christ the man. Cassidy-Ringler maintain the MS reading, taking *word-ondrysne* as a coumpound, "awesome of word," and suggest, in addition to the meaning given above, that 2862b might mean either "and (even when) governing (in such a manner as this), beloved" [taking *waldende* as a pres. part.]; or "and his Lord (was) dear (to him)" [taking *waldende* as a late anomalous nominative].

2887b-2888a *wudu bær sunu, // fæder fyr and sweord.* Creed, "Three OE. Tellings of the Offering of Isaac," 80, suggested that 2887b contains a sort of pun, related to the typology of the scene, since it appears to mean both "son bore wood" and "wood bore son." Cf. 1111b-12a *n*.

2900 *on pære stowe / pe him se stranga to,* Bouterwek supplies *stowe*, giving the needed object of *on*, mending the meter and following 22.9, "ad locum." Cassidy-Ringler note that the OE. prose Genesis 22.9 has the same word: *Hi comon pa to ðære stowe pe him geswutelode God* (*Hept.*, 141).

2906b-2908a *wolde his sunu cwellan // folmum sinum, / fyre sencan // mæges dreore.* For *sencan* here, B-T gives "submerge," "flood," the only available comparative passage being the OE. prose Genesis, 9.11: *ne heononforð ne bið flod tosencende* [= *dissipans*] *ða eorðan* (*Hept.*, 106). Thorpe translates "the fire (dir. obj.) quench with the youth's gore." But the dat. *fyre* as object is difficult (though cf. Icel. *sökkva* "to make to sink" with dat.). Hence, Bouterwek suggests *fyr ge-*

sencan, meaning the same as Thorpe's version. Grein reads
sengan "singe" and *dreor*: "burn, consume the blood of his son
with fire." Kock, *JJJ.*, 34, suggests *sencan = sengan*, "consume with fire his son in his own blood." Jovy, *Bonner Beiträge* 5, 31, suggests *swencan* "afflict," and so Holthausen,
reading *fyre swencan / mæg his deorne* "with fire afflict his
dear son." Bright, *OE. Reader* (1st, 2d eds.), reads *scencan*
"pour out," "give drink to," "to give drink to the fire (by
means of) kin's blood." B-T, s.v. *scencan*, cites Hymn Surt.
31, 15, *deapes scencende drenc* = "mortis propinans poculans,"
perhaps supporting such a metaphorical use of *scencan* here.
Also, at GU 982b-85a a comparable drinking metaphor occurs,
with *scencan* having literal force. See also 1398b *n.* Bright's
scencan has been accepted by Klaeber, *Anglia* 25, 295 (defen-
ding the instr. following *scencan*), Krapp, Wells and Cassidy-
Ringler. Yet it seems rash to accept an emendation introducing such a bold touch when so many simpler alternatives are
available: if a change is to be made, Bouterwek's more modest
fyr gesencan satisfies all requirements (for paleography and/
or phonetics cf. 2412a *folce firena*). After all is said, it
is still perhaps best to keep the MS reading *sencan*, taking as
object not *fyre* but *sunu*, with *dreore* parallel to *fyre*: "he
wished to kill his son with his hands, to immerse (him) in
the fire, in the blood of a kinsman." Or *mæges dreore* can be
construed as parallel to *folmum sinum*: "by means of his hands,
by the blood of his kinsman he immersed his son . . ." [since
he had to kill with the sword in order to be ready to burn the
offering]. Or *mæges dreore* can be taken as dat. of accompani-
ment: "He immersed his son along with the blood of a kinsman . . . ." The sense that this is Christ's blood is no
doubt playing in the background at this high moment, perhaps
causing the seemingly dysfunctional alignments of syntax and
meaning.

    2916b *him an wuldres god,* *an* from *unnan*: "To him God
grants glory." Cassidy-Ringler point out that it may also
mean "The God of glory is pleased with him," see B-T *unnan* IV;
it may also mean, "God wishes him to have glory," ad loc. III.
Probably all these senses are operative, as they all express
the traditional approbation accorded to Abraham, the obedient
servant, at this equivocal moment in his history.

    2921b *leofra = leofre* Fem. nom. sing. comp. Cf. Brun-
ner, par. 304, anm. 5, and par. 276, anm. 6.

    2932b *brynegield onhread,* Lit.: "he adorned the burnt
offering (with the blood of the ram)." The form *onhread* may
be taken as from *onhreodan* "adorn," though apparently only the
past. part. *gehroden* otherwise occurs. Dietrich, *ZfdA* 10, 337-
38 and Cosijn, *Beiträge* 19, 457, suggest reading, or at least
understanding, *onread* "redden," "stain (with blood)," citing
Corpus Gloss 1129 *onread* "imbuit." So Krapp, following the
MS spelling, and Wells, reading *onread.* Cf. the similar prob-

lem at BW 1151b-52a *Ða wæs heal hroden // feonda feorum* "then
was the hall decorated? / reddened ? with the lives (life-
blood?) of enemies." In his Revised Edition, Wrenn reads
hroden "decorated," but in the Supplement he would emend to
roden, following Bugge, *Tidskrift* 8, 64, 295 and Dobbie. Less
ambiguous, seemingly, is EX 411-14 (the narrative situation is
the Sacrifice of Isaac): *Up aræmde / Abraham þa; // se eorl
wolde slean / eaferan sinne // unweaxenne, / ecgum reodan //
magan mid mece, / gif hine metod lete.* "He wished to slay, to
redden by means of edges his kinsman with a sword." Cassidy-
Ringler call attention to *Meters of Boethius* 8.34: *beornes
blode / þe hine bill rude.* As the intrusion of *h* before *r* is
very common in lWS, either understanding is allowable, with
word-play probably operating, as Cassidy-Ringler suggest. Cf.
Dream of the Rood 22b-23: *hwilum hit wæs mid wætan bestemed
. . . hwilum mid since gegyrwed.* Similarly, the blood of the
Christ/ram *onhread brynegield.*

   2933a *reccendne weg* Strictly, "guiding path," "the
strait way;" *reccendne* pres. part., masc. acc. sing. of *reccan.*
Grein and Holthausen read *rēcendne* (= *rēocendne*) "smoking."
Edd. also assume a meaning "altar" for *weg* (= *wig, wih*),
though it always means elsewhere "idol" (the first element of
wig-, weo-bedd "altar"). Probably this is another case of
double meaning, if the "smoking altar" can be accepted at all.
Cassidy-Ringler reject the plain meaning, "the guiding path,"
as "just too bizarre." Taking 2931-32 together, we may understand: "Abraham brandished with the sword, reddened the burnt-
offering, the smoking altar with the blood of the ram;" or
". . . adorned the sacrifice, the guiding way, with the blood
of the ram," and various combinations of these. Considering
that Isaac is Christ in his divine aspect, the ram Christ in
his human aspect as the Crucified One, and that the action
typifies the sacrifice of the Mass, it would be imprudently
limiting to exclude any of these possibilities from the possible range of intended meaning.

   2935 *and ealra þara / þe he him sið and ær* Grein, Krapp
and others supply *sælða* after *þara* to complete the alliteration;
Holthausen mends by reading *ær ond sið.*

   2936 The poem concludes, or breaks off, with the paraphrase of 22.13, not including what might seem the more logical
stopping-place of verse 17. But the omission of the often-re-
peated promise is in line with the usual pattern of omission
of repeated material, and more importantly, perhaps, leaves off
with the icon of the crucified savior triumphing on the altar
as both priest and sacrifice, father and son. The poem thus
finishes at the most effective dramatic moment, concluding, as
Cassidy-Ringler note, with a *figura etymologica* (*gifena/for-
gifen*), so that Christ's merciful grace fills the last lines of
the poem, as the praise of the Creator filled the first. Ælfric indicates that Genesis 22 is a natural stopping place

for a Genesis translation (*Preface to Genesis*, ed. Crawford,
EETS 160, 76, 5); it is a natural stopping place in Genesis
commentaries, and is the last part of Genesis familiar from
the liturgy. In the tradition of Psalter illustrations of
Old Testament history, and in other graphic series, such as
bosses, etc., as well as in the later mystery-cycle tradition,
Genesis 22 frequently concluded the Old Testament episodes
(see Woolf, *The English Mystery Plays*, 63-64).

Glossary

NOTE

This *Glossary is adapted from that of Theodor Braasch,* Vollständiges Wörterbuch zur sog. Caedmonschen Genesis, *Anglistische Forschungen
76 (Heidelberg, 1933). It is intended to account for all words and
forms appearing in the edited text of GN. Each occurrence is listed
and identified, with the exception of a few high-frequency words when
no ambiguity seems likely, and then samples and total frequencies are
given.*

*Words are listed in alphabetical order (æ following -ad-, medial
and final þ/ð following -th-, initial Þ/Ð separately listed after T).
Words with prefixes are listed strictly alphabetically according to
the first letters of the prefix, except that verbs in* ge- *are listed
according to the root. Simplexes that also form the second elements of
compounds have been noted by appending to the simplex-entry a list of
first elements that occur in GN with the simplex as second element.*

The following symbols are used with headwords of entries: ° *(a word
unique to GN, according to Bosworth-Toller, Grein-Köhler and/or Clark-
Hall);* + *(a word unique to GN in poetry, but also occurring in prose
or in glosses);* * *(a hypothetical form, necessary to explain a form
which actually occurs in GN);* [ ] *(a word not in the MS, but supplied
in the edited text);* ( ) *(the regular form of a word, not occurring in
GN with that spelling);* ? *(a word or form whose genuineness has been
doubted by several previous editors on good grounds);* ´ *(marks long
vowels);* ~ *(marks vowels whose quantity is not determined, uncertain
or variable).*

*The part of speech is indicated after each headword. Nouns—stems
are identified after gender. No stem-indication implies a-stem for
masculine (m.) and neuter (n.), ō-stem for feminine (f.). In the entries
s = singular, p = plural; n = nominative, g = genitive, d = dative, a =
accusative, i = instrumental, e.g., np = nominative plural, &c. Adjectives—the stem is only given when not a/ō. In the entries the abbreviations are the same as for nouns, also subs = substantive, comp = comparative, superl = superlative, wk = weak. Verbs—class of weak verbs
is indicated by roman numerals I-III (Ii = weak verbs I without a middle vowel); the class of strong verbs by arabic 1-7; anom. (v.) = anomalous verb. In the entries the order is mood, tense, person, number.
No mood indicated implies indicative (ind; subj = subjunctive; imp =
imperative). Tenses, pr = present, pt = preterit. Persons 1,2,3. Number, s = singular, dl = dual, p = plural: e.g., subj pt3p = subjunctive
preterit third person plural, pr1s = indicative present first person
singular, imps = imperative (2) singular. Participles, prp = present
participal, pp = past participle, followed by case, number, gender, as
adjectives (if pp or prp alone, the use of the participal in a compound
tense is implied).*

*Other abbreviations: absol = absolute; appos = appositive to;
impers = impersonal (construction); sim = similar(ly).*

After a line number, the star * *indicates that a word or construction is discussed in the Commentary at the corresponding number.*

A

á   adv *always, ever* 7 1607*
    2377 2700; á þenden *as
    long as* 915, æfter á...
    oð *always...until* 1956
+á-ǽðan I *destroy* inf 1280*
á-belgan 3 *to anger, cause
    anger* pp ábolgen 1257
á-béodan 2 *announce* inf 2663
    pt3s ábéad 925; *offer*
    pt1s 1919; *command*
    pt3s 1362 1771 1869
+á-biddan 5 *request, pray for*
    inf 2661
á brecan 4 *break into, storm*
    inf 2493
á-bregdan 3 *take away, pull
    out, withdraw* inf 2369
    subj pr3s 2279 pt3p
    ábrugdon 2488 imp s 2915;
    intrans *move quickly*
    pt3s ábrægd 2932
ac conj *but* 1904 2149; *in
    adversative constrs with
    ne* not...but rather,
    ...and yet 7 19 24 875
    1854 2178 &c (41x); *not
    adversative* ne...ac *(does)
    not because* 1016 1459
    1479 1524 2732 2749 nelle
    ...ac 2154; *for, because*
    997 1447
á-cennan I *bring forth, bear
    (young)* pp npm 1706
ácol adj *frightened* nsm 1955
ácsian (áscian) II *to demand*
    inf 2455; *inquire, try to
    discover* inf áhsian 863
+á-cuman 4 *come* pp 1544
á-cwellan Ii *kill* inf 1283

1296 1353 pret3s ácwealde
    1403
á-cweðan 5 *say, speak* pt3s
    ácwæð 1110
ád m. *fire, sacrificial
    fire* ns 2923 ds 2915 as
    2856 2902 2930
á-dǽlan I *to separate* pp nsm
    150 2324 npm ádǽlte 218*
+á-déman I *deprive (as the
    result of a judicial sen-
    tence)* pr2s 1032
ádl f. *sickness* ns 937
á-drífan 1 *drive out* pr2s
    1032 pp nsm ádrifen 2325
    npmf 964
ǽdre adv *quickly, immediately*
    872 1005 2137 2187 2256
    2273 2296 2399 2513 2653
    2905
ǽdr f. *watercourse, spring*
    gp 1374
ǽ-fæst adj *law-abiding, up-
    right, pious* nsm 1182 npm
    1802
æfen n. *evening* ds 1461 as
    138
°æfen-scíma m-an *evening
    light, twilight* ns 2450
æfen-tíd f-i *even-tide, eve-
    ning* as 2426 ("vespere")
ǽfre adv *at any time, ever,
    always* 5 999 1480 1937 2225
    næfre...ǽfre 1954* *inter-
    rog* þu ǽfre...wilt *will
    you at any time?* 2643
æfst (æf-est) m.f-i *envy* ns
    29 dp 982
æfter prep w dat *after, fol-
    lowing (temporal)* 144 961
    964 987 1067 1070* 1074
    1129 1156 1601 2015 2400

329

æfter (*cont.*)
  æfter þon *thereafter*
  1005; æfter ǽ *ever after*
  1956; *according to* 1054
  1305 2284 2357 2672; *conforming to* 1042 1043
  1104; *for, with the aim
  of* 2155 2494 (or *on account of*?); *semi-advbl
  in verbal constrs* æfter
  scéaf 136, æfter héold
  1143, æfter fléogan (*sc*
  sweartum hrefne) 1450,
  me æfter sculon...bryt-
  tian 2178 *sim* 2184, æfter bið 2199
æfter adv. *afterwards*
  1224 2450*
æftra adj *(the) following,
  (the) second* nsf (subs)
  séo æftre 228
°æfter-léan n. *retribution*
  as 76
æf-þanca m-an *spite, hatred*
  dp 2239
æg-hwǽr adv *everywhere* 2706
æg-hwilc pron *each* as subs
  nsm 2043; as adj nsf
  1694
æht f-i *possession(s)* dp
  1499 1802 1845 2012 2086
  ap 973 1208 1353 1435
  1649 1767 1873 1894 1929
  2622 2678 2757
ǽlc pron *each* nsm 1521 1530
  gsn 1338 dsn 1305
ǽled m. *fire* as 2902 (*cf*
  on-ǽlan)
ælf-scíene adj-ja *beautiful like an elf* vsf ælf-
  scíeno 1827 ("pulchra")
  2731
æl- *see also* eal(l)-
æl-gréne adj-ja *all-green,
  completely green* nsf
  1517 asf 197 1787 asn
  1751
æl-mihtig adj *almighty* nsm
  5 116 150 173 852 887
  904 952 1359 1361 1427

  1509 1840 2254 2757 2760
  gsm 1779 2711
ǽnig pron *any* nsm 180 948
  nsn ǽnig...bearn 2217 gsf
  1023 asm 1453 2501 asf
  1591 as (subs *w part gen*)
  nsm 1754 nsf 1690 dsm ǽ-
  negum 2178 asm 2232 asn
  2652
æppel m. *apple* ds æple 937
  as 880
+[ǽr] n. *brass* gs ǽres[t]
  and ísernes ("aeris et
  ferri") 1088
ǽr adv *before, previously*
  35 857 937 1235 1262 1508
  1840 1977 ("already")1994
  2046 2129 2266 2302 2578
  2648 2744 2879; ǽr ðon *before* 1642 2533; swǽ ǽr *as
  before* 78; éode séo yldre
  tó ǽr "the elder went
  first (of the two)" 2601;
  sið and ǽr *lit: later and
  before* 2935*; *comp* ǽror
  before, earlier 1883; *sup-
  erlat* ǽrest *first* 30 112
  129 1061 1149 1521 1529
  1577 2712 2776
ǽr conj *before* (w ind pret)
  ǽr ðon 22; (w subj pr)
  2471; (w subj pret) 1147
  1158 1213 1663 2766
ǽr prep w dat *before (temporal)* 1221
°ǽr-boren part adj [-beran]
  first-born nsm 975
ǽr-dæg m. as sing: *morning*
  ds 2577; as pl: *the old
  days, previous times* dp
  2545
ǽrende n-ja *message, errand,
  business* as 926 2883 ap
  ǽrenda 2662*
°ǽrend-gást m. *message-spirit,
  angel* ns 2298
?ǽrendra m-an *errander, messenger* np 2436*
ǽrest adj *first* nsm 133 1055
  (subs), asn 138; *as subs*

ǽrest (*cont.*)
  w part gen: nsm hérbúen-
  dra...ǽrest 1079, 1085
  1136 1634 nsn 1059
ǽrest adv *see* ǽr adv
ǽr-gestréon n. *ancient treasure* dp 2148
ǽ-sǽlan *see* á-sǽlan
æsc m. *(ashwood) spear* gp
  2108
æsc-berend m-nd *spear bearer, warrior* gp 2041
°æsc-þracu f. *spear-force,
  battle* ds æscþræce 2154
°æsc-tír m. *spear-glory,
  glory in battle* ns 2069
æt prep w dat *local: at,
  near, by, in, upon* 980
  1688 1998 2034 2059 2109
  2116 2150 2154 2428 2780
  æt hléoðre *in a voice*
  1290; *in regard to s.t.*
  æt edwihtan 1954*; *with
  verbs of taking: from*
  874 2639; *temporal: when,
  at, in* æt frymðe *in the
  beginning* 132 954 2392
  æt níehstan *finally, at
  last* 1400*
æt m. *food* gs 1557
æt(e) *see* etan
æt-éowan I *reveal* pp asf
  stówe *(acc)*...ætéowde 165;
  appear, show up inf æt-
  ýwan 1481 (*cf* íewan)
æt-gædere adv *together* 2226
æt-gifa m-an *food-giver,
  provider* ds 1361
æt-somne adv *together* 1725;
  at once 162 (*cf* tó-somne)
æt-wist f-i *sustenance,
  goods* as 1208*
æt-ýwan *see* æt-éowan
æðele adj-ja *noble, excellent* 1182 2447 (subs) ?63
  (subs, sc God, or = éðel,
  q.v.) npm 216 2436 ?npf
  cynde *(np or adj?)* wǽron
  æðele *(or noun?) as his
  qualities were excellent*
  2773* (*see* æðelu, cynd)

dpm 1619 (subs) apmf(subs)
  æðele cennan, sunu and dohtor 1228
æðele 63 = éðele?
æðeling m. *prince, nobleman,
  man* ns 2885 gs 1288 2445
  2848 ds 1706 1853 2637 as
  1662 np 1059 1647 gp 1071
  1161 1237 1278 1634 1654
  1698 1737 1858 2002 2091
  2131 2146 2464 2610 2620
  2657 2722 1826 ap 1868
æðelu n-ja (pl only) *lineage,
  descent* np 1716 ?2772*
  (*see* æðele) dp 1054 1440
  ap æðelo 1389 ip 1533
ǽwisc-mód adj *disgraced in
  mind, ashamed* nsf 896
+á-fandian II *find out, test*
  imps 2231
á-fédan I *bring forth, produce (offspring)* pp nsm
  1641 nsf 1604 npn 1707
ǽ-ferian I *withdraw, remove*
  subj pr2s áferige 2479
afora *see* eafora
ágan pret-pres (1) *own, possess, have* inf 34 48 2143
  2212 2252* 2327 2703 2725*
  2748* ágon 2473 pr3s áh
  2272 pr3p ágon 2295 subj
  pr2s áge 2500 pt3s áhte
  1721 pt3p áhton 1686 2560
á-gangan *see* á-gongan
ágen adj *own, one's own, proper* nsm 2869 2885 nsn þæt
  ǽr ágen wæs ússum folce
  *that had been proper (be-
  longing) to our people*
  2129, 2189 dsm 1580 dsn
  1305 2871 ?isf 2768* asn
  149 2259 2302 2398 2614
  2776 2789 2806 2852 2914
  2931 dpm 2856 dpf 1366
ágend m-nd *possessor, lord* ap
  1353
ágend-fréa m-an *lord* ns 2141
  ("possessorum") as 2239
  ("dominam" sc. Sarra)
á-géotan 2 *pour out, spill*
  pt1s ágéat 1030 pt3s 984

á-gifan 5 *give* pt3s ágeaf
    1428 1808 2121 pp ágifen
    1506 2884; *give back,*
    yield pt3s 1866 2718 imps
    2655; *give up, leave* pt3s
    ágeaf eorðcunde éad *(=he*
    died) 1626
ge-ágnian II *possess, acquire,*
    inf 1829; *dedicate* pp
    2323
á-gongan 7 *go, pass by* pp nsf
    1719
á-gyldan 3 *give over* pt3s
    þá sǽl ágeald *when oppor-*
    tunity offered 2008*
áh, áhte *see* ágan
á-hebban 6 *lift up* pt3s áhóf
    148 1197 ("exalted") 1388
    1419 2388 2904 2930 pp
    nsf áhafen 1401* (*cf* on-
    hebban)
á-hicgan *see* á-hycgan
á-hlihhan 6 *laugh at* (w gen)
    pr3s áhlóh 2382*
á-hóf *see* á-hebban
á-hreddan I *rescue, recover*
    inf 2113 pt1s 2145 pt2s
    2127 pp msn áhreded 2085
    áhred 2032*
áhsian *see* ácsian
*á-húðan 2 [*cf* húð *booty*] *to*
    plunder ?pt3p áhudan
    2007*
á-hweorfan 3 *turn away, turn*
    aside (intrans) pt3s á-
    hwearf 2067 pt3p áhwur-
    fon 25
á-hycgan III *devise (a plan)*
    inf 2182 áhicgan 2031
á-lǽdan I *lead out* pt3s a-
    lǽdde 1495 2222 2697* [MS
    alæded] imps 2503
aldor m. *prince, lord; of*
    God: ns 862 1002 1113
    1511 ?1711* 2575 2763
    2808 2879 as 20 2542; *of*
    a man: ns 1231 1578 1643
    1863 2124 2736 (sc Abi-
    melech) as 1960 1980
aldor n. *life* ns fréod and

aldor 1711* gs 2657 ds
    1041 2625 2644 2702 tó
    widan aldre *forever* 1015
    as 1209 1523 2791 ealdor
    2504
°aldor-bana m-an *life-slayer,*
    murderer ds 1033
°aldor-déma m-an *supreme*
    judge, chief, leader ns
    1156 2483
aldor-dóm m. *authority, po-*
    wer as ealdordóm 1197
aldor-duguð f. *a chief noble,*
    flower of the nobility np
    2081
aldor-gedál n. *parting from*
    life, death as 1071 eald-
    orgedál 1959
aldor-neru f. *a place to save*
    one's life in, refuge as
    2514 ("in monte salvari")
    2521 ("salvabor in ea")
aldor-wísa m-an *a chief ru-*
    ler, leader ns 1237
á-lecg(e)an Ii *lay blame, im-*
    pute inf 2685
á-leoðian II *detach, set free*
    pt3s 177
all-wiht *see* eall-wiht
al-walda m-an *all-ruler, God*
    ns 2827
°á-lynnan 3 *deliver, set free*
    inf 2048
an- prefix *see also* on-
an *see* unnan
án num, adj & subs *one, one*
    of a group, a certain one
    nsm 1645 nsf 1636 dsm 1077
    dsn 219; *one (shading into*
    mod. Engl. 'a,' 'an') nsm
    2019 2269 nsf 2229 asm
    ǽnne 880 2928 asf 1478 2519
    asn 1473; *a single one, a*
    particular one npm 2134 gp
    ánra gehwilcum *in regard*
    to each one (i.e., all)
    2490; advbl asn on án ge-
    hogod *pondered on one thing*
    (i.e. thought of one thing
    to the exclusion of all

án (cont.)
    else) 2893 wk nsm ána a-
    lone 170 2576
and conj and (431x)[always
    abbr 7 in the MS, except
    at 1140, 1195, 1335, when
    it is spelled ond]
and conj? or prep w dat? and
    heora ordfruman 13*
and- prefix [usually spelled
        7- in MS] see also ond-
°and-giet-tácen n. intelli-
    gible sign, sign of a
    plan? sign of counsel ta-
    ken? [cf andgiet n. un-
    derstanding, intellect]
    ns 1539 ("signum foede-
    ris" sc the rainbow of
    Noe) [MS 7giettacen]
and-lifen f. food as 933
and-swarian II to answer
    [written 7swar- except
    at 896, 1005, 2256] pr3s
    882 896 1005 1022 2136
    2172 2187 2256 2273 2280
    2477 2513 2691 andswǽrede
    872 pt3p 2436 andsware-
    don 2527
and-weard adj (physically)
    present asm 871
and-weorc n. material, proto-
    plasm as 176
and-wlita m-an face, count-
    enance dat (absol) heora
    andwlitan [MS 7wlitan]in
    bewrigenum 1585*; face
    (of the earth) as. and-
    wlitan...wídre eorðan
    ("de superficie terrae")
    1348
an-fenge see on-fón
an-lícnes f-jó likeness, i-
    mage ds 1529; image, sta-
    tue ds on sealtstánes...
    wurde anlícnesse she
    turned into a statue of
    salt(stone) 2567
an-mód adj bold, resolute;
    stubborn, proud nsm 1662
    nsn 1650

an-síen f-i (beautiful)
    appearance ns 1261 (cf
    héafod-síen, ge-séne)
ár m. messenger, angel gs
    2911 ap 2426 2458
ár f. honor as 1580 gp ára
    1899 árna 2164 2259 2461;
    help, favor, mercy gs áre
    1023 1591 1842 lisse and
    ára 1889 as 2521 gp ára
    1348 1509 1533 2125 2283*
    árna 953 2437 arra 2751*
    (cf un-ár-líc(e))
á-rǽman I arise, go up pt3s
    2877
á-rǽran I set up, establish
    pt3s 114; raise pt3s 50
    pp nsm 987; raise up,build
    subj pt3p árǽrde 1667*
ár-fæst adj honor-firm, hon-
    orable npm 1894 2488 2527;
    mercy-firm, merciful nsm
    2407 2826
á-rísan 1 arise, get up pt3s
    árás 2431 2462; spring,
    come from (in a line of
    descent) pr3p 2336
ár-léas adj lacking honor,
    dishonorable nsn 2477, npm
    1934 gpm 1385 2549 (subs);
    dishonored, not held in
    honor nsm 1019
ár-líce adv honorably 1870
    2105 2686; mercifully 2588
á-sǽlan I to tie, fetter, im-
    pair pp asn ǽsǽled 2197*
á-scúfan 2 drive away, expel
    pt3s ascéaf 1115
+á-sealcan (á-seolcan) 3 slac-
    ken, flag inf 2168
+á-sendan I send away pr2s
    of líce aldor ásendest
    (when) you die 2791
+á-slúpan 2 slip away inf 2797
á-springan 3 spring out hence
    fall, cease, diminish pp
    nsm ásprungen 83
á-stígan 1 mount up, exult
    pt3s ástáh 2237 ástéah[MS
    mos teah] 980*

á-stríenan I *bear (a child)*
  inf 966 subj pt3s ǽr...
  ástrýnde 1148
á-téon 2 *draw out, extract*
  pt3s átéah 177 182; *set
  out, take the field* pt3s
  2094; *manage, deal with*
  inf 2260 (*cf* of-téon)
á-urnen *see* á-yrnan
á-wæcnan 6 *be born* pr3p 2293
  pt3s áwóc 1703 pt3p á-
  wócon 2616
á-weccan Ii *awaken, animate*
  pt3s áwehte 1080; *create,
  give life to* pt3s áweahte
  174 1277
+á-weg adv *away* 2799
á-wiht pron *anything* nom 1905
á-wóc *see* á-wæcnan
á-wyrged part adj [*cf* á-wyr-
  gian] *accursed* nsm 1015
  1034
axe f-ón *ash(es)* ds 2555
á-yrnan 3 *run, run out* pp nsn
  á-urnen 1626

B

bá *see* bégen
bæc n. *back* as (advbl) under
  bæc beseah *she looked behind* 2564
bǽl n. *funeral pyre, sacrificial fire* as 2904
bælc m. *arrogance* as 54
bǽl-fýr n. *sacrificial fire*
  as 2857 ("holocaustum")
+bǽtan I *to bridle* inf his
  esolas bǽtan ("stravit
  asinum suum") 2867
baldor m. *prince* vs 2694
bám *see* bégen
bán n. *bone, rib* as 182
bana m-an *slayer* gs 1526*
  (*cpd* aldor- feorh- ord-)
básnian II *await* (w acc) pt3p
  básnedon 2419
be prep w dat or instr *local:
  by, near, beside, in, on*

1921 1932 1967 2438 2596;
  local-instr: gegráp sweord
  be gehiltum 2906; *causal-
  instr: by* be fréan hǽse
  947 1781 2371 2737 *sim.*
  965 1370; *of begetting:*
  stríenan bearnes be brýde
  1119 1147 1170 2238 2328
  2767; *with, in the company
  of* be mǽgwine 1661*
béacen n. *sign* ds 1666 as
  1680 2769 (*cpd* freoðo-)
béag m. *ring, bracelet* gp
  1972 2783 ap 1930 bégas
  1876
bealu n-wa *evil, wickedness*
  gp 994
béam m. *tree* as 891 902 1468
  (*cpd* ele- wudu-)
beam-sceadu f-wó *shadow of a
  tree* as 859
bearhtm m. *noise, clamor* as
  2408
bearm m. *bosom, belly* ds
  bearm[e] 907*; *surface (of
  the earth)* as 1488
bearn n. *child, son* vs 1914
  ns 2189 2198 2765 2922 gs
  1119 ds 1070* 2364 2857
  2904 as 1593 2328 2398
  2614 2789 2806 2852 2872
  2914 2925 2931 np 226 856
  1062 1087 1248 1257 1654
  1698 1707 1737 1951 2002
  2186 2218 2620 gp 1135 1171
  1201 1233 1239 1603 1642
  2802 dp 11 993 1284 1369
  1554 1608 1718* 2472 2539
  2748 ap 966 1148 1378 1505
  2091 2131 2534 2594 geond
  foldan bearn *among the sons
  of earth (= the sons of
  Adam)* 1664* (*cpd* cyne-
  folc- fréo- frum-)
bearo m-wa *grove, forest* ds
  902 as 2841 np 2554 ap 1480
béatan 7 *beat* pr3p 1326
be-béodan 2 *command* pt3s be-
  béad 125 161 966 1494 2297
  2370 2769 2872 2898; *offer*

be-béodan (*cont.*)
   (*a sacrifice*) inf 2859
be-bod n. *commandment* ap 2318
be-búgan 2 *surround, encom-*
   pass pr3s 223
be-cuman 4 *arrive, reach* pt
   3p becómon 1652; *befall,*
   come about pt3s becóm 46
bedd n-ja *bed* as 2236 (*cpd*
   wæl- wéo-/wí-; *cf* ge-
   bedda)
bedd-rest f. *bed* as 2248 2716
*be-dréosan 2 [*only* pp bedro-
   ren *occurs*] [*deprive*] *de-*
   prived nsm 2099 npm 1998
   2082
°be-fyllan I *kill, strike*
   down pt2s befealdest 1010;
   deprive pp nsm befylled
   2124
bégen m., bú n. pron, num
   both nom.m bégen 976 1587
   nom.mf bú 187 1699 2258
   bú tú *the two of them*
   both 2780* nom.f bú 2603*
   gen.m bégra 1893 1914 f.
   béga 2602 dat.m bám 128
   1711 mf 191 acc.mf 2799
be-gietan 5 *obtain, get* pt3s
   seth...wíf (*acc*) begeat
   1130; *find* pt3s 1479;
   overtake pt3s híe (*acc*)
   ...begeat wíte (*nom*)2569
be-grindan 3 *deprive* pr3s
   1521
be-habban III *surround* pt3p
   behæfdon 2456
be-healdan 7 *behold, see* pt
   3s behéold 107
be-héawan 7 *cut off, deprive*
   inf behéo[w]an [MS -p-]
   2645* subj pt3s behéowe
   2702
be-lecgan Ii *cover, invest*
   pt3s husce belegde *co-*
   vered (the prophecy) with
   scorn 2384
be-léosan 2 *deprive* pp be-
   lorene 86 (*cf* for-léosan)
ge-belgan 3 *anger, enrage*

pp gebolgen 54 (*cpd* á-)
be-licgan 5 *surround, flow*
   around pr3s beligeð 229
   belíð 232
be-lúcan 2 *lock up, close*
   pt3s beléac 945 1391 1363
   1409 1576 (*cf* on-lúcan)
be-murnan 3 *mourn, be troub-*
   led (intrans) pt3s bemearn 2311
ben(n) f-jó *wound* ds 181 dp
   1972
bén f-i *request* gs 2528
béna m-an *requester, petitioner*
   (*in the exp.* béna wesan,
   to make a request) ns 2250
   2359
be-nǽman I *deprive* inf 2153
   (*cf* be-niman)
be-néotan 2 *deprive* pr3s 1041
   subj pr3s 1831
be-niman 4 *deprive* pt3s be-
   nám 56
béodan 2 *to offer* pt2s bude
   2437 pt3s béad 2434 2442
   (*cpd* á- be- for-)
ge-béodan 2 *to order, command*
   inf 1961
°béod-ge-reordu n-ja (pl)*feast*
   [béod *table* + gereord *food*]
   acc 1518
béon *see* wesan
beorg m. *mountain* ap 1387
beorgan 3 *protect, save* pt3s
   bearh 2625
ge-beorgan 3 *protect, save* inf
   1838; *protect (against)*
   pt3s gebearh 2695*
beorh-hlið n. *mountain-slope*
   dp beorhhleoþum 2160
beorht adj *bright, clear,*
   splendid nsm 1603 nsf 1828
   asf 14 npn 89 dpm 223 (*cpd*
   wlite-)
beorhte adv *brightly, clearly*
   1822 2194
beorn m. *man, warrior* ns 1119
   1583 1800 1813 2033 2120
   ds 981 2639 2783 as 2428
   gp 1680 1828 2469

béot n. *boasting, stubborn-*
ness ns 70 (*cpd* word-)
beran 4 *bear, carry, bring*
pt3s bær 2887 pt3p bǽron
213 1430 pp boren 120
(*cpd* æsc- feorh- sǽd-
sweord-berend, ǽr-boren;
cf rǽs-bora, forð-bǽro)
ge-beran 4 *bear, give birth*
to pt3s gebær 2775 pp nsm
geboren 2299
be-réafian II *deprive* pp
npmf 859
⚥be-rebban 6 *deprive* pt3p
berófan 2078
be-scyrian I *deprive* pt3s 63
°be-sellan Ii *surround* pp
beseald 42
be-séon 5 *look, look at* pt3s
beseah 2564; *look with*
favor pt3s 976 ("respexit")
be-sléan 6 *deprive, take*
away (w dat) pp npf fréond-
um beslægene 2010 pt3s be-
slóh synsceaþan sigore
and gewealde 55 (*or if*
instrs. follow, 'laid low
the sinful enemies by
means of victory and
power')
be-smítan 1 *pollute* inf 2682
pp apn besmiten 1520
+be-strúdan 2 *deprive* pt3s
bestrudon 2079
be-swícan 1 *deceive* pt3s
beswác 897
be-syrwan I *ensnare, trick,*
deceive [*cf* sear(w)o]
inf 2681
bétan I *compensate* pr1s 2733
be-twéonan prep (w dat?) *be-*
tween, amidst 1902 (*postpos*)
be-þeccan Ii *cover* pp npm
beþeahte 76
be-útan prep w dat *outside of*
beútan...earce bordum
1354 (*cf* búton, prep)
be-windan 3 *surround, encir-*
cle, invest pr3p 2214
pt3s bewand 2339

°be-wlítan 1 *look, glance*
pt3s bewlát 2926
be-wréon 1 *cover* pp nsf bewrigen 156 npn 1460 dat
(*absol*) in bewrigenum
1585*
bídan 1 (w gen) *await, stand*
ready inf 39 2277 2572 pt
3s bád 1424 2775 sǽles bídan *await an occasion* 2439
2525; *experience* inf déa-
ðes bídan 922
ge-bídan 1 *wait for, expect*
pt3s gebád...sprǽce (*acc*)
2910; *experience, live to*
see subj pr3s 2361 pp gpm
wintra gebidenra *of years*
lived, years expired 1185
biddan 5 *ask, pray, beseech*
(*freq. w. gen. of thing*)
inf 2751 pr1s 2227 2467
pt3s bæd 2025 2759; *w inf*:
bæd him...þæs rǽd ahicgan
asked them to devise a
plan 2030; *w acc & dep cl*:
pt1s 2816; pt3s bæd þæs
"asked that..." 1662 (*cpd* á-)
bifian II *tremble* prp nsf
1970
bill n. *sword* is 2932
bil-wit adj *merciful, gra-*
cious nsm 856
bisceop m. *bishop, high-priest*
ns 2103 ds 2123
bis(e)gian II *to torment,*
trouble pt3p bisegodon
1264*
blác-hléor adj *pale-cheeked,*
pale (with fear) nsf 1970
blæd n. *leaf* np blado 994
blǽd f. *fruit* ap 883 891 902;
branch, twig as 1474
blǽd m. *glory, blessedness,*
prosperity ns 14 gs 1893
ds 859 as 207 1608 2585
(*cpd* ge-blǽd-fǽst)
blǽd-dagas m. (pl) *prosperous*
or blessed days gp 200 1201
°blátian II (*or* blátan 7? *cf*
blát adj. *livid*) *be pale*

blátian (*cont.*)
  prp nsm blátende níð *pallid hate* 981
blétsian II *bless* inf 2359
ge-blétsian II *bless, consecrate (make the sign of the cross)* pt3s
  192, geblétsade 1505 pp
  nsm 1752
blétsung f. *blessing, (divine) favor* ds 1761 2333
  as 2106 gp 2120
blícan 1 *shine, glitter* inf
  1822
blind adj *blind* nsm 2493
bliss f-jó *bliss, joy* as 14;
  *favor, grace, in the
  phrase:* (ds) onfóð...
  blisse and blétsunge 1761
  2333
ge-blissian II *gladden, make
  joyful* pp 2925
blíðe-mód adj *joyful* nsm
  1800 nsf 1468 (*cf* un-
  blíðe)
blíð-heort adj *kind, gracious* nsm 192
blód n. *blood* ns 181 1012
  ds 1518 2933 as 984 1030
blód-gyte m-i *bloodshed* as
  1526 ("effuderit...san-
  guinem")
blódig adj *bloody* npm 2160
blonden-féax adj *having
  hair flecked with gray,*
  hence, *old (of persons)*
  nsm (subs) 2602 nsf 2343
blótan 7 *sacrifice, kill s.t.
  as a sacrifice* inf 2857
  (*cpd* on-)
bóc f-cons *book, (pl) the
  Bible (or commentaries
  on scripture?)* np béc 227
  969 1239 1723 2613
bodian II *announce* pt3s 2777
  (*cf* be-bod, spell-boda)
bord n. *plank, what is made
  from planks* hence *deck
  of a ship, ship* as 1369
  1433; earce bord *the Ark*

as 1333 1357 1403 dp 1354
  (*cpd* gúð- nægled- salwed-
  wǽg-)
bósm m. *bosom, interior* ds
  1306 1332 1410 (*cpd*swegl-)
bót f. *help* ns 1476; *compensation* ds 2719
°botl-gestréon n. *treasure of
  the household, household
  goods* as 1930 gp 1621 dp
  1075
botl-wela m-an *collection of
  houses, village* ns 1799
brád adj *broad, extensive* asf
  907 1752 npf 994 apn 2194;
  great asn ic his cynn gedó
  brád and bresne ("filium
  ...faciam in gentem magnam") npn 2335
bráde adv *widely* 223
ge-brecan 4 *shatter, destroy*
  pt3s gebræc 62 2111 (*cpd*
  á- *cf* wiðer-breca, fýr-ge-
  bræc)
bregdan 3 *draw (a sword)* pt3s
  brugdon 1991 (*cpd* á- on-
  to-)
brego m-u *prince* ns 1866; *of
  God* ns 181 976 1008 1289
  2585 2765
+brego-ríce n-ja *prince's dominion, kingdom* gs 1633
°brego-weard m. *princely guardian, prince, leader* gs
  bregoweardas 2748* gp 2335
+brember m. *thornbush* dp 2929
bréost n. *breast (as seat of
  emotions), heart, mind,
  thought* as 2925 gp 1608 dp
  191, w sg sense: 981 2640
  2797 2867; *belly, abdomen*
  dp (w sg sense) 906
bréost-ge-hygd f.n-i *inner
  thought, secret heart (as
  opposed to thoughts expressed in words or deeds)* dp
  1289 2318
bresne adj-ja *powerful* asm
  2802
brim n. *sea* ap brymu 2194

°brim-hlæst f. *sea's burden,*
fish gs 200 (*cf* holmes
hlæst 1515)
bringan Ii *bring* inf 2286
2343 2355 2629 2892 pt3s
bróhte 1172 1187 1472
1720 1728 2771 pt3p bróh-
tan 2607 subj pt3s 1213
1560*
ge-bringan Ii *bring* pt3p
1871
brittian *see* bryttian
bróga m-an *terror* ds 2554
as 1037 np 1395 (*cpd* wíte-)
°bróh-þréa f-wó *terrible*
affliction, calamity
ns 1813
bróðor m-r *brother* ns 2621
2929 gs bróðer 1008 bró-
ðor 1800 ds bróður 1526*
as 984 1012 np bróðor
2033 dp 1070 1583 1621
(*cpd* will-ge-)
°bróðor-cwealm m. *fratri-*
cide gs 1030
brúcan 2 (w gen) *have the*
use of, enjoy inf 1893
2665 pt3s bréac 1175 1201
1220 1230 1812 1952 impp
200 1512 1532; *use, em-*
ploy inf 1089
brýd f-i *bride, wife, woman*
ns 186 883 1171 2343 2388
2564 2783 ds 1062 1119
1813 2033 2186 2198 2328
2603 2621 2765 2799 as
bryd 1822 1866 1876 2534
2539 2719 bryde 2639 2661
np 1075 gp 1972 ap 1248
brymu *see* brim
bryne m-i *fire* ds 2554
°bryne-gield n. *burnt offer-*
ing, offering about to
be burnt ds 2892 ("holocausti") as 2932 ("holo-
caustum")
brytta m-an *breaker* [*cf*
bréotan 2 *to break in*
pieces] hence *distribu-*
tor, gift-giver, deter-

miner, ruler (w dep gen,
goldes brytta &c) ns 122
129 1620 1857 2642* 2728
2868 np 1997
bryttian II *distribute* inf
2179 pt3s brittade 1181
pt3p bryttedon 1602; *rule*
pt3s 1226 1236; *enjoy,*
have pt3p 1724 1891; *ex-*
ercise (power) inf mægyn
bryttigan 52
bú *see* bégen
búan 7 *inhabit, dwell in* subj
pr3p búan   *(hope to dwell)*
82*
bude *see* béodan
+búend m-nd *inhabitant* gp 89
(*cpd* eorð- her-)
búr n. *(bower), sleeping-*
quarters, womens' quarters
ds 2388
burh f-cons *settlement, house*
as 2841; *city* ds byrig
1928 2013 2408 2560 2594
as 1666 1700 1880 1975
2528 burg 2404 dp burgum
2564 2585 (*cpd* gold- heah-
hord- léod- mǽg- stán-)
°burh-fæsten n-ja *city-for-*
tress, city as 1680
burh-geat n. *city gate* ds
2428 ("in foribus civita-
tis")
burh-loca m-an *city-enclosure,*
city as 2539 (*cf* hearm-loca)
burh-sittende m-nd (pl) *in-*
habitants of a city, men,
people nom 1089 2328, 2839
dat 2816
burh-stede m-i *city-site, city*
ds 1062
burh-waran m-an (pl) *inhabi-*
tants gp 2493
búton conj (w ind) *except*
that, with the exception
that 1403
búton prep w dat *except* 2151
byht n? *dwelling* ap? 2215
byre m-i *son, (one's) child*
np him byras wócan (ptp),

byre (*cont.*)
  eafora and idesa 1233
byrgan I *eat* subj pt2s 880*
byrig *see* burg
byrnan 3 *burn* prp nsf 191
+bytlian II *build* inf 1880
  2177

C

céap m. *cattle* ap céapas tó
  cnósle *breeding stock*
  1747; *possessions* ds 1919
  ap 1772 1877 (*cpd* orleg-)
cearian II *be concerned, take*
  trouble imps ne ceara þú
  ...fléame dǽlan 2281 impp
  ne ceara incit...sécan
  2733
°cear-sorg f. *care, anxiety*
  as 1114
cearu f. *care, grief* dp 2795*
  (*cpd* líf- *cf* ferhð-cearig)
ceaster f. *city* ds 2202 as
  1057 1674 2427 2520 dp
  2509 2548 ap 2009
cennan I *beget, bring forth*
  (children) inf 923 1228
  pp cenned nsm 1149 npmf
  188 npn 968 1639 npm
  cende 1615 (*cpd* á-)
céosan 2 *choose* inf 1867 subj
  pt3s ǽr ðon...curc...wæl-
  reste *(before he died)*
  1642 pt3p curon 1250 1803;
  accept pt3p 2444
ge-céosan 2 *choose* pt1s ge-
  céas 2710 *(sought)* pt3s
  1051 1927 imps 2723 pp
  gecoren nsm 1818 npm 1734
cígan I *call, call out*(intrans)
  pr3s 1013; *trans: call,*
  warn pt3s cýgde 2910;
  call upon, invoke pt3s
  cígde 1807
°cildisc adj *as a child, while*
  still a child nsm 2320
cirm m-i *clamor, outcry* ns

2549 as cyrm 2409 (*cf*
  wíg-cyrm)
cleopian II *cry, call* pr3s
  1013
clom(m) m. *bond, grasp* dp
  2488 2795 (*cpd* wæl-)
clyppan I *embrace, seize* pt
  3s clypte 1569
cnéo(w)-mágas m (pl) *rela-*
  tions of the same genera-
  tion nom cnéowmágas (sc
  Abraham and Loth) 1733
  cnéowmágas 1778 dp cnéo-
  mágum (sc the family of
  Cain) 1057
°cnéo(w)-rím n. *number of a*
  generation, progeny ns
  cnéorím (appos. wídfolc)
  1639 as cnéowrím 1065
  cnéorím 1190
cnéo-risn n. *family, descen-*
  dants np 1256*
cnéo-ris(s) f-jó *family, race,*
  descendant(s) gs 1155 1704
  2320 ds 1637 np 1950 gp
  1679 dp 1274 2290
cniht m. *boy, (male) child* ns
  2772 as 2801 2915 ap 2132
cnósl n. *race, offspring,*
  family ds 1049 1730 1747
cofa m-an *chamber, the Ark*
  ds 1464 (*cpd* ferhð-)
corðor n. *company, band (of*
  troops), host dp 1652 2455
  (*cpd* mægen-)
costigan II (w gen) *tempt,*
  try inf 2847
cræft m. *strength* dp 2127 as
  1674 (= *skill?*) (*cf* smið-
  cræftega)
cucu *see* cwic
culufre f-ón *dove* ns 1464 as
  1451 1477
cuma m-an *"comer," stranger*
  guest np 2488 ap 2433 2455
cuman 4 *come* inf 122 2233 pr
  1s cymeð 1041 1099 cymþ 6
  2321 pr1dl wit...cumað
  2882 pr3p 2335 pt1s cóm
  2712 pt2s cóme 2822 pt3s

cuman (*cont.*)
  143 180 1783 1884 2450
  2634 pp nsf cumen 1475
  nsn 2198 2365 gpmf feorren cumenra *ones having*
  come from afar 1836; *w*
  predicative inf: pt3s
  cóm...síðian 154 1577
  1844, ...féran 852 2760,
  ...fléogan 1478, ...lǽ-
  dan 1773; *w final inf:*
  pt3s cóm...scéawigan 1678,
  ...grétan 2103 pt3p cómon
  ...ácsian 2453 (*cpd* á-
  be- *cf* from-cyme)
cunnan pret-pres (3) *know,*
  be acquainted with pr1s
  can 1006 pr2s canst 916
  pr3s 2468 subj pt3s cúðe
  1944 pt3p cúðon 74; *know*
  how to, be able (w inf)
  pt3p 18 189 1088
cunnian II *inquire, make*
  proof of pt3s 2847
cúð adj *known, familiar* nsm
  2710 nsn 2815 asn 1503,
  cúð dyde *made (it) known*
  1503 *sim* 1851 apn 1877
  (*cpd* un-, un-for-cúð-líce)
cúð-líce adv *familiarly* 2433
cwealm m. *death, destruction*
  ns 1623 gs 1004 1013,
  cwealmes on óre *at the*
  start of the destruction
  2549 ds 1095 (*cpd* bróðor-
  feorh-)
°cwealm-dréor m. *blood of a*
  slaughtered one (sc of
  Abel) ds 985
°cwealm-þréa f-wó (> indecl
  < earlier -þrawe) *deadly*
  affliction, attack ds
  2509
cweðan 5 *speak, say, talk*
  absol: pr3p 1239 pt3s
  cwæð 31 195 905 1254 1295
  1327 1690 1786 2246 2389
  2727 2782; *w* þæt *follow-*
  ing: subj pr2s 2146 pt3s 1279
  2028 2057 pt3p cwǽdon 47 2459;
  w þæt *elided:* pt3s 1594*;

  w acc: 1510 (*cpd* á- on-)
ge-cweðan 5 *say, speak* pt3s
  gecwæð 2761
cwellan Ii *kill* inf 2906
  (*cpd* á-)
cwén f-i *wife* ns 2261
cwic adj-u (*quick*), *living,*
  alive nsm 1210 asm 2915
  2925 gpn cucra wuhta 1297
°cwic-lifigende part adj [*cf*
  lifian < libban] *living*
  gpn 1311 ("animantibus")
cwíðan I *lament, mourn* inf 996
cwyde m-ja (*judicial*) *sen-*
  tence, curse np 1596* (*cpd*
  hléoðor-)
cýgan *see* cígan
cyn(n) n-ja *race, species* gs
  193 ds 197 as 66 np 204
  gp 1297 1311; *kin, family,*
  tribe ns 1245 1256 2477
  gs 1065 1190 2550 ds 1249
  as 2533 2619 2801; *a peo-*
  ple, nation ds 1784 1814
  ap 2509 np 1935 1944; *kind,*
  sort ns þæt is syndrig
  cynn *that is a special kind*
  (*of pitch*) 1324 (*cpd* from-
  gum- gym- hǽðen- mon-
  wæpned-)
cyn(n) adj-ja *fitting, proper,*
  as subs, *a fitting thing,*
  what is proper, in the
  exp: cynna gemunde *remem-*
  bered fitting things, i.e.,
  was courteous 2433*
cynd f-i *nature, quality* ?np
  2771* (*see* æðele adj)
cyne-bearn n. *noble child* gp
  1704
cyne-gód adj *noble, excellent*
  dsm 1590 npm 1736
cyning m. *king; of a secular*
  king: gs 1851 *otherwise,*
  of God: ns 192 978 1406
  1503 1683 1704 1797 1946
  2378 2425 2672 2795 2847
  cining 107 as mid cyning
  engla 1210 (*cpd* folc- gást-
  gúð- héah- heofon- sóð-

cyning (*cont.*)
   swegl- þéod- woruld-
   wuldor-)
cyrm *see* cirm
cyrran I *betake oneself*
   inf 1919
ge-cyrran I *turn back, re-*
   turn (trans) pp 1415
cyst m.f-i *choice* as 1919;
   what is chosen (above o-
   ther like things) hence
   the best, choicest thing
   (w part. gen.) on lande
   (gp) cyst 1795* (*cpd* gum-)
°cyst-léas adj *worthless,*
   reprobate nsm (subs) 1004
cýðan I *declare, announce*
   inf 2244 pr3p 969; *reveal,*
   make known inf 1591 pr2dl
   2517 pt3s 2866 pt3p 1674
ge-cýðan I *declare, announce*
   pt3s 797 2021
cýðð f. *home* ds 2801

D

dǽd f-i *deed, action* ds 964
   2640 2671 gp 922 dp 2352
   2251 2813 1267 1507 1936
   1957 2308 (*cpd* firen-)
dǽd-fruma m-an *author of*
   deeds, first doer np 970*
   (sc Cain and Abel)
°dǽd-róf adj *strong in deeds,*
   bold, valiant nsm 2174
   2591
dæg m *day* ns 130 133 143 gs
   2351 (advbl), 2876 ds 1031
   1074, on lást dæge *fol-*
   lowing the day 2451 as
   853 gp 1351 1382 1421
   1438 dp 2366 2665 (*cpd*
   líf- mǽl- swylt- ǽr-dæg;
   blǽd- feorh- fyrn- géar-
   dagas)
dæg-rím n. *count of days* gs
   975 ("multos dies"), 1331
   2599 ds 2174
dæg-tíd f-i *era, a certain*

time ds 1659*
°dæg-willa m-an *joy of the*
   (appointed) day, or *day*
   that has been wished for
   as 2777 ("tempore quo præ-
   dixerat ei Deus")
dǽl m-i *part, share, portion*
   ns 23* 1614 2552 ds 2151
   as 180 222 1453 1499 (*cpd*
   norð-, *cf* -gedál)
dǽlan I *divide, break up* inf
   2280 pt3s 146; *share* inf
   26 pr3s 2789; *share out,*
   distribute inf 2830 pr3p
   2193 pt3s 1069 1611 (*cpd* á-)
ge-dǽlan I *separate* pt3s 2745
   pp npm hléoðrum gedǽlde
   separated by (diverse)
   languages 1693
déad adj *dead* npm 2133
deall adj *proud* npm (subs)
   1849
déað m. *death* ns 2640 gs 922
   1037 ds 1205 as 1267
dear *see* durran
déawig-feðere adj *dewy-feath-*
   ered ns (subs) 1984
déma m-jan *judge* ns 2255 (*cpd*
   aldor-)
déman I *to judge* (w dat) pr3p
   1718*; *to praise, worship,*
   celebrate (w acc) pt3p 17*
   (*cpd* á-)
déop adj *deep* nsm 105 1398
   1453 asn 40 1331 2876
déope adv *deeply, entirely*
   2733
déor n. *animal* np 202 1516
deorc adj *dark* asn 108 apn 133
déore *see* dýre
°deoreð-sceaft m. *spear-shaft*
   dp 1984
dihtig adj *strong, doughty*
   apn 1993
dim adj *dark* nsm 105
dógor m.n-a (<-os) *day* gp
   1625 2251 2573
dohte *see* dugan
dohtor f-r *daughter* vs 888 ns
   dohter 2611 np 2467 2599
   ap 924 1229 1729 gp 1139

dohtor (*cont.*)
  1153 1221 1606 1640 dp
  193 1133 1245 1764
dóm m. *judgement* gs 2571;
  decision ap 1625; *choice,*
  option as 1915; *decree,*
  commandment ap 2582;
  glory, honor as 1199 ds
  56 2082 2138; gangan...
  tó godes dóme *die* 1610
  (*cpd* ealdor- þeow-)
dóm-éadig adj *glory-blessed,*
  blessed nsn 1247
dóm-fæst adj *righteous, pow-*
  erful nsm 1287 ("justus,"
  sc Noe), 1510·1786 2378
dón anom. *do, make, cause;*
  absol: pt1s 2692 imps
  2227 impp 2325 2467;
  w acc: inf 190 1918 subj
  pr3p 2413 pt3p 142 1944;
  w acc & prep (tó): pt3s
  2266; *w acc & advbl prep:*
  on geweald dón 1789; *w*
  acc & pred adj: pt3s 1503
  pt3p 1851; *ref to a pre-*
  ceding verb: pr3p 993
  (sc hrínon), 1206 (sc
  "die"), pt3s 1840 (sc
  an), 2588 (sc gemunde),
  2633 (sc fylste); pt3p
  2600 subj pt3p dyde 856*
ge-dón anom. *do, make; absol:*
  pt3s gedǽde 2894; *w acc:*
  pp 2821; *acc w pret adj:*
  pr1s 2801; *acc w advbl*
  prep: pt3s 184
dorste *see* durran
dréam m. *joy, happiness* ds
  56 as 12 gp 40 108 (
  éðel- mon- woruld-)
°dréam-hæbbende adj *posses-*
  sing joy, blissful gpm
  (subs) 81
dreccan Ii *trouble, afflict*
  pr3s 2180 pt3s dreht[e]
  [MS -a] 2251
drence-flód m. *deluge* ns 1398*
dréogan 2 *do, carry out, ac-*
  complish (trans) inf 23

190 2272 pt1s 2708 pt2s
  888 pt3p 142 1936 inflected inf 2351; *enjoy* (trans)
  pt3s 2739; *labor, strive*
  (intrans) inf 2284; *be em-*
  ployed, be busy (intrans)
  pt3s 1428*
dréor m. *blood* ?ds 2908* (*cpd*
  cwealm- sáwl- wæl-)
°dréorig-mód adj *dreary in*
  spirit, dejected asmf 2805
drepan 5 *strike, daze* pp nsm
  1571
drífan 1 *drive* subj pr3s 2792
  pt3s dráf 2805 (*cpd* á-)
dríge adj-ja *dry* asf 164
driht f-i *army, multitude*
  gp drihta bearnum *for the*
  sons of multitudes (= *for*
  mankind) 993 & 1718 (*cpd*
  ge- folc-)
drihten m. *prince, lord* vs
  2227 (sc Abraham); *other-*
  wise used of God: ns 40
  112 1287 1786 2255* &c
  (26x), gs 7 1885 2382*
  drihtenes 17* &c (16x), ds
  26 81 105 951 975 1247
  1818 2174 2421 as 2545
  2752 (*cpd* fréa- man-)
°drihten-hold adj *loyal to*
  (one's) lord nsf 2284
driht-líc adj *noble* nsf 1849
  drihtlecu 2782
driht-líce adv *nobly* 2138
driht-scipe m. *lordship, dig-*
  nity as 1199
°driht-weras m (pl) *chieftains,*
  people nom 1798 gen 2151
drincan 3 *drink; absol:* pt3p
  druncon 2782 pp nsm druncen 1563 2606 2635 dsm
  druncnum...fæder 2600 (*cf*
  wín-ge-drync)
drohtað m. *society, way of*
  living as 1818
drýman I *rejoice, carouse* pt
  3p 2782
dugan pret-pres (2) *avail, be*
  vigorous pt3s dohte 1288

duguð (dugeð) f. [*the various senses seem subject
to word play and in many
instances more than one
sense is appropriate or
seems operative*] *body of
proven men, multitude,
army* gs 1868 as 2023 gp
81 164 [2255] dp 17 1371
1718* 1798 ap 2733;
.*strength, power* ds 56
dp 2821; *prosperity,
good, salvation* ds 1032
sōhte drihtnes duguðe *i.e.,
died* 1205 np 1659 gp 888*
970 2366 2665 dp 930 1500
1849 1859 2308 2325 2378
duguðum wlance *ones proud
in prosperity* 2421 ap
2584*; *gift, favor, grace*
gp 1510 dp 951* 1522*;
what is fit, seemly dp
2284 (*cpd* aldor- woruld-)
dūn f. *hill* gs 2596 as 2854
2878 2897 dp 1398 1421
durran pret-pres (3) *dare*
(w inf) pr1s dear 870
pt3s dorste 2591 subj
pt3s 1046
*ge-dwelan *see* ge-dwolen,adj
dȳre adj-ja *dear, beloved,
precious* nsn 1247 ?nsm
or ?asn dēore 951* dpf
1371 apmf dēore 2745
dyrnan I *hide* pt1s 2713

E

ēa f-cons *river* ns 232
ēac prep w dat *in addition
to, besides* 2502
ēac conj *likewise, also* 925
1372 1440 2721; *with numerals:* 1162 1165 1186
1193 1217 1232 1601 1742
2042
ēacen adj [pp < ēacan 7]
increased, made powerful

nsm 1001 nsn 1517 (*see
next sense*); *pregnant* nsf
2238 2761 npf 2607;
distended (with food) npm
2159* (*cpd* feorh-)
ēad n. *possession(s), riches*
as 1602 1891 2757; *happiness* as ēd 1405* as *or* ap
āgeaf eorðcunde ēad *died*
1627
ēadig adj *blessed, prosperous*
nsm 1107 ēadega 1476 1562
2234 2597 2834 2877 ēadga
2863 ēadig (*"rich"*) 2148
apm 1878 (*cpd* dōm-)
eador (geador) adv *together*
2559*
eafora m-an *son, descendant*
ns 1105 1129 1133 1150
1159 1188 1578 1629 1646
1712 2394 2834 afera 2054
gs 2329 ds 1179 1214 2177*
2363 2764* (*"man"*) as 2916 np
1061 1251 1602 1616 1706
2133 2185 2189* [MS -a]
ādames eaforan (*"mankind"
see 1664a n.*) 1682,aforan
967 ?gp eafora 1191* 1234*
dp 1348 1415 1545 2224 ap
1054 1076 1333 1357 2607
ēage n-an *eye* dp 106 977 1794
1824, *"in their (his) eyes"*
2108 & 2431
eahta-hund num *"800"* acc (*temporal):* 1122 1140 1150 1161
1179 1191*
[eahta-tȳne] num *eighteen* 2041
[MS xviii]
eal(l) adj *all* nsm 199 1554
2492 nsn 205 gsm heretēames
ealles tēoðan sceat *a tenth
part of all the booty* 2122
asf 1409 1490 [1929] 2151
2464 asn 1403 *absol:* 1280
1282 1353 1359 1514 2212
2550 2559 2561 ism ealle 57
npm 219 (sc ēastrēamas)1648
1759 2329 2618 *uninfl* eall
2781 gpm 1124 1140 1163
1191 2092 gpn 1059 1136 2935

eall (*cont.*)
    gpf 4 952 1508 dpm 79 875*
    1339 dpf 1499 apm ealle
    ...héa beorgas 1386;
    advbl: eall 871* ealles
    entirely 1871
eal(l)- *see* al(l)-
eald adj *old, ancient* dsm 2609
    npm 1207 2454 comp nsf
    yldre 2601 2612 superl
    nsm yldesta 1063 1134
    1241 dsm 1214 asm 1234
    npm 1616, *"the most sen-
    ior"* 1670
ealdor *see* aldor n.
ealdor- *see* aldor-
°eall-tela adv *perfectly* 1905*
eall-wiht f-i (pl) *all crea-
    tures, created nature*
    gen 113 978 alwihta 193
    allwihta 1290
°ealo-gál adj *foolish be-
    cause of ale, drunk* gpm
    2410 (*cf* rúm-gál)
earc f. *ark* ns 1313 1423 gs
    1333 1354 1357 1403 ds
    1450 1488 as 1366 1389
    1461
eard m. *abode, dwelling home
    homeland* gs 1952 ds 1019
    1033 2806 as 962 1654
    1737 1927 gp earda léas
    homeless 2706 (*cpd* éðel-)
eard-fæst adj *established in
    a home, settled* nsm 2835
eardigean II *dwell* inf 2593
earfoð n. *trouble, labor* gp
    180
earfoð-síð m. *toilsome jour-
    ney* gp 1476
earm adj *unfortunate, poor*
    apf 2133
+earme adv *miserably, unfor-
    tunately* 1567
earm-líce adv *badly, miser-
    ably* 1692
earnian II *labor for* imps
    2283
ge-earnian II *deserve, have
    merit absol:* pp 1508*

eart *see* wesan
éastan adv *from the east* 1649
    1794 1802
+éast-land n. *eastern land*
    dp 1052 ("in terra ad or-
    ientalem plagam")
éa-stréam m. *river* np 216
éaðe adv *easily* 48 comp éað
    2058*
éað-fynde adj-ja *easily found*
    nsm 1993
éað-mód adj *humble, obedient*
    nsf 2283
°ebbian II *ebb, recede* pt3s
    ebbade 1413
éce adj-ja *eternal* nsm/asm
    1111* nsm éce drihten 112
    925 1745 2058 &c (9x), 1261
    1405 (subs), se éca 2370
    2898 gsm écean 7 écan 1885
    asm 1937 2752; *immortal*
    asf 185
éce adv *always, forever, in
    eternity* 20 143
ecg f-jó *edge (of a weapon)*
    ds 1830 2858 dp 1993;
    sword dp 2002
°ecg-wæl n. *a person slain by
    a sword, a corpse* ds -wale
    2089
éd *see* éad
ed-léan n. *recompense, requi-
    tal* is 1523
edor m. *enclosure, house* ap
    2447 2489
°ed-wihte pron *anything* ds
    1954*
ed-wít n. *reproach, blame* as
    ðé on edwít...settan *"blame
    you"* 2729 (*cf* téon-wít)
efne adv *exactly* 1158 2300
    2346; efne swá *just as* 2556
    emne þon gelícost...þe
    "just as if" 1943
efstan I *hasten, approach*
    pt3s 2873
eft adv *again, anew, a second
    time* 94 1117 1343 1464 1485
    1537 1885 2282 2439 2577
    2755; *in return* 882 1413

eft (*cont.*)
2653 2727; *back* 1415 1471
1478 1871 2067 2090 2131
2294 2882; *in the oppo-
site direction* 2211*; *afterwards* 1446 1663 2146
2703

eg(e)sa m-an *fear, reverence*
ns 2712 2867 ds 920 2592;
fear, terror ds 2669 as
2117 dp 1865

°égor-here m-ja *water-force,
the Deluge* ns 1402 as
1537 ("diluvium")

égor-stréam m. *water-stream,
flood* ap 1374 ("diluvii
aquae")

ég-stréam m. *water, flood*
as 1415 ("cateractae
caeli")

ele-béam m. *olive tree* gs
1473 ("olivae")

ellen m.n *strength* gs 972*;
courage, fortitude ns
1288 2848 ds 2137

ellen-róf adj *bold in strength,
brave, daring* nsm 1119
(subs), 1782 1844 npm
2036 1875 (subs)

elles adv *else, otherwise*
20 1905

ellor adv *elsewhere* 1868
1896 2734 2785

ellor-fús adj *eager to be
elsewhere, ready to go*
nsm 1609 npm (subs) 2399

ell-þéodig adj *foreign, of
a strange people* nsm
2680 nsf (sc þá) 2630
asm (sc mé) 2702 gpmf
1835

eln f. *ell, cubit, yard* gp
fíftena...monnes elna
("quindecim cubitis")
1399*

°eln-gemet n. *ell-measure,
an ell's length, cubit*
gp þréohund lang elnge-
meta ("trecentorum cub-
itorum...longitudo") 1309

emne *see* efne

ende m-ja *end* ns 6

engel m. *angel* ns 946 2269
2280 2302 gs 29 2296 ds
2911 np 2527 gp 13 66 121
157 1530 1711 2837 2861
2909, engla...dǽl 22 &c
(23x) dp 84 185

engu f. *narrowness, confined
place* ds of enge (sc the
Ark) 1435

(ge)éode *see* (ge)gán

eom *see* wesan

eorl m. *noble man, brave man,
warrior, man* ns 1182 1228
1844 1887 2086 2446 2537
ds 1646 1994 2021 2767 np
1826 2045 dp 1710 2099
2137 2669

eorð-búend m-nd *earth-dweller,
human being* np -búend 1648
-búende 221 1000 1759 ("cognationes terrae") 2618 gp
1754 dp 1636 1685

+eorð-cund adj *earthly* apn
ágeaf eorðcunde éad "died"
1627 (*cf* god-cund)

eorðe f-ón *earth (as opposed
to heaven or sea)* ns 99
gs 1208* 1305 1313 1339
1402 1440 1614 2141 2208
2555 on andwlitan...wídre
eorðan 1350 ǽghwǽr eorðan
2706 ds 149 933 1124 1271
1280 1533 1596 2148 2323
gs/ds hwǽr ábel eorðan
wǽre 1003* as 113 143 166
197 219 958 1292 1513;
land, country ns 1787 as
1921; *earth, ground, soil*
ns 1015 1144 1517 gs 1454
1488 eorðan líme ("caulking,"
"pitch")1321; ds 972 1097
1389 1557 as 907*, on eorðan "onto the earth" 1031,
"down into the earth" 2339

eorð-scræf n. *(earth-scraping),
cave* as 2595 ("spelunca")

eorð-wela m-an *earthly weal,
prosperity* ap 1878

éowan *see* íewan
éower posspron *your* isn éowre
   1534 apn béodgereordu...
   éowre 1519
+esol m. *ass, donkey* ap 2867
ést m-i *will, favor, grace*
   as 1251 2445 dp 1952 2358
éste adj-ja *gracious, liberal*
   nsm 1509
etan 5 *eat* inf 909 935* pt1s
   ǽt 902 pt2s ǽte 893
éðel m. *home, dwelling, home-*
   land ds 1076 1105 1150
   1159 1616 1952 ǽðele 63
   óðle 2091* as 83 927 eðyl
   962 1492* éðel 1576 2131
°éðel-dréam m. *joy of a home,*
   domestic pleasure ap 1607
°éðel-eard (*for* éðel-geard?)
   m. *homeland, native coun-*
   try dp 1945
éðel-land n. *homeland* ns 1968
   as 1379
°éðel-mearc f. *boundary of a*
   country ds 1768 1874 2209
°éðel-seld n. *settlement* as
   1896
°éðel-setl n. *settlement* as
   1927
°éðel-stæf m. *foundation of*
   an establishment, family
   ns oéðylstæf 2225* ds
   éðulstæfe [MS edulf stæfe]
   1118*
°éðel-staðol m. *lower cre-*
   ation, a home beneath
   another (sc the world be-
   ing created for mankind)
   ap 94
éðel-stól m. *native seat,*
   country ns 1485 1514 as
   1129 1748
°éðel-stów f. *dwelling place,*
   home as 1052 2725
éðel-turf f-cons *native soil,*
   homeland ds éðyltyrf 224
   1735 2708 2734 as éðel-
   turf 1774 2678
°éðel-ðrym m-ja *strength, dig-*
   nity of a country as 1634

éðul-stæf *see* éðel-stæf
éðyl(-) *see* éðel(-)
exl f. *shoulder* as bewlát
   ofer his exle *"he looked*
   behind" 2927

F

fácen n. *treachery, deceit,*
   evil ds 2681 2692 gp 2651
   as 1941 2416
fæder m-r *father* ns 856 954
   1189 1628 1731 1739 2888
   gs 1074 1611 1748 1779 2697
   ds 974* 1068 1108* (gen?),
   1575 1580 1622 2602 2609
   as 194 1096
+fædera m-an *uncle* ns 1900
   2080
°fæder-geard m. *a father's*
   dwelling, ancestral habi-
   tation dp (w sing sense)
   1053 (sc Eden)
fǽge adj-ja *doomed, given over*
   to death asn 1382 apf (*or*
   npf?) 1265*
fægen adj *rejoicing, happy*
   nsm 2183
fæger adj *beautiful* nsf 1487
   asn 1722 asf 1467 2449 dsf
   1658* npn 79 1933 apf 1252
   apn fægir 899 comp gpf fægerro 1852*
fæg(e)re adv *beautifully, plea-*
   santly 210; *gently, rever-*
   ently, in a friendly way
   1900 2104 2353 2499 2517;
   justly 1941 (*cpd* un-)
fǽhð f. *enmity, hostile deed*
   gs 1029 (*or* acc? *see* ge-
   monian) as 900 1351 (*cpd*
   mán-fǽhðu)
fǽle adj-ja *faithful, dear,*
   good nsm [1546] 2303 2726
   2820 npm 2499
fǽmne f-ón *woman* ns 884 998
   1722 2228 ds 2303 as 184
   2264 np 2010 2603 dp 2473

fær n. *vehicle, ship* ds?1394*
  (see also fǽr*)* fere 1544
  as 1307 1323 1419; *jour-*
  ney ds ?1394* ?2380* *(see*
  also fǽr*)*
fǽr m. *danger* gs 2700 ds
  ?1394* ?2380**(see* fær*)*
°fǽr-cyle m-i *intense cold*
  ds 43
°fǽsl m.n *offspring* ns 1310*
  as 1330* ds 1359
fæst adj *fast, firm, secure*
  nsm 178 2646 nsf 156 *(or*
  adv?) asm 2929 *(cpd* ǽ-
  ǽr- dóm- eard- ge-blǽd-
  gin- háls- rǽd- sóð- tir-
  þéow- þrym- wǽr-)
fǽste adv *fast, firmly, se-*
  curely 156 *(or* adj?) 895
  1310 1836 2183 2491 2604
fǽsten n-ja *firmament* ds fǽs-
  tenne 153 as 148; *strong-*
  hold, city ds 2530 2536
  2592 as 2006 fæsten...
  stéape 2523 *(cpd* burh-
  þell- weall- wudu-)
fǽst-hýdig (-hygdig) adj
  firm-minded, virtuous
  asm 1347 ("justum")
fǽst-líce adv *firmly, securely*
  1653
ge-fǽstnian II *make safe, protect*
  pp asn 1323
fæðm m. *arm(s), embrace,*
  hence *power, control*
  as on fremdes fæðm *"into*
  a stranger's embrace (con-
  trol)" 1971 2632 him on
  fæðm gebræc*"he crushed*
  them in his power"? 62*;
  breast dp 1282
fáh adj *of variegated colors*
  nsm fáh wyrm 899* dsm
  fágum wyrme ?904 *(see*
  next word)
fáh adj *hostile* nsm 1860,
  hwæt hé fáh (nsm *or* asn?)
  werum fremman wolde 1291
  dpf fáum 62 2486; *cursed*
  nsm 1039 dsm ?904* *(see*

  preceding word), asn 913
fámig adj *foamy* nsm 1452 nsn
  1417 npm 2215
fandian II *search out, try to*
  find out, test inf 2412
  pt3s 1436 *(cpd* á-)
+fandung f. *test, trial* as
  1452
faran 6 *go, move, travel* inf
  908 1777 pt3s fór 1394
  1417 1964 2559* pt3p fóron
  1982 fóran 1974 imps 1748
  (cpd ofer- tó-)
ge-faran 6 *go, move, travel*
  pt3s 1360* 2740 pt3p ge-
  fóran 91 1798 pp gefaren
  hæfdon *("had reached")*
  1987, 2052
faru f. *moveables* as 1746
féa adj-wa *few* npm féa áne
  ("a few individuals") 2134
  (cf ge-féa)
feallan 7 *fall* ?subj pr3p
  feallan 2038* pt3p 1971
  2001 2065; *fall* inf 1198
fealu adj-wa *dusky- yellow-*
  colored asf fealwe linde
  2044
fédan I *feed, nourish* imps
  1342; *produce, bring forth*
  inf 960 pr3p 1298 pt3s
  1054 pt3p 1076 pp 1105
  1159 1712 *(cpd* á-)
?ge-fégan I *join, unite* ?imps
  gefég 1310* *(see also* gefég n.)
fela n-u (indecl) *much, many*
  (w gen) nom 1638 2335 dat
  2201 acc 1559 1724 2698
feld m-u *field, plain* as 1668
feng m-i *an enclasping, limit,*
  orb as 98* *(cf* on-fón)
*féogan II *hate* pr3s féoð 911
feoh n. *cattle* ns 201 1517 ds
  feo 2660 as 1299 1650 2720;
  possession(s), money as
  2130 2726 *(cpd* woruld-)
feohtan 3 *fight, serve (by*
  fighting) pt3p fuhton 2155
feohte f-ón *fight, battle* ds 2116

ge-féon 5 *rejoice, be glad*
    inf *(w instr)* 1523 pt3s
    gefeah 1468
féond m-nd *enemy* ns 1261 1447
    as 57 2072 2812 np fýnd
    2006 gp 1045 1259 2065
    2098 dp 1969
°féond-ræs m. *hostile attack*
    as 900*
féond-scipe m-i *hostility*
    ds 2692 2324
feor adv *far, at a distance*
    1029 1039 1053 2281 2324
    2515, *w semi-adj func-*
    tion: ic mé...léodmágum
    feor 2695*; comp fýrr
    2595 *(cpd* un- *cf* feorran)
feorh m.n *life, spirit, soul*
    ns 908 ds feore 1831 1838
    fyore 1184* as 184 1385
    1524 1739 2512 2526 ap
    feorh heora 1999; *a liv-*
    ing being np 1618 2065
    gp feora 1330 1342 dp
    feorum 1162
feorh-bana m-an *life-destro-*
    yer, murderer ds 1020
    ap 2088
feorh-berend m-nd *life-bearer,*
    living person gp 1955
feorh-cwealm m. *mortal pain,*
    death ns 1103 as 1038
°feorh-dagas m. (pl) *days*
    of life gp 2360
°feorh-éacen adj [pp of *éa-
    can 7] *made full of life,*
    living npn feorh-éaceno
    204
feorm f. *food, provision(s),*
    goods ds 1731 2660 as
    1650 *(cpd* swíð- *(adj),*
    cf niht-feormung)
ge-feormian II *serve food*
    (as to a guest), enter-
    tain pt3p 2687
feorran adv *from afar* 225
    1047 2481 2822 feorren
    1836 *(cf* feor)
féorða adj nsm 2870 nsf(subs)
    233

féoð *see* féogan
féower num *four* npm 216 1964
    2074 npn 1546 gpmf 2203*
    apm 1697 apn 1334
féowertig num *forty (subs*
    w gen) apm 1351 apmf 1382
    dpn 1162*
fer *see* fær
féran I *walk, go, make a jour-*
    ney inf 852 1731 1746 1779
    2400 2760 2800 2850 prp
    nsn 1653
ge-féran I *go (in), enter*
    inf 948
ferhð m.n *spirit, soul, mind*
    ns 2311 ds 870 1255* 1579
    as 2196 2794 *(cpd* gamol-
    gléaw- sár- stíð- wíde-)
°ferhð-cearig adj *troubled in*
    spirit nsf (subs) 2219
ferhð-cofa m-an *the place*
    where the mind or spirit
    is situated, heart, breast
    ds 2604
ferian I *bring, carry, con-*
    vey, lead inf 1330, 2155
    pt3s 1397 2089 2100* pt3p
    1875 2066 *(cpd* á-)
ge-feterian II *fetter, con-*
    trol pt3s gefetero[de] 168,
    2903
féðe n-ja *power of walking,*
    pace as 2536
°féðe-gang m. *walking* ds 2513
    (= "on foot")
féðe-léas adj *foot-less, de-*
    prived of feet nsm 908*
feðer f. *feather, plumage* ap
    1471 *(cpd* hléow-feðre *(pl),*
    déawig- salwig-feðera
    (adjs))
fetigean II *fetch, bring* inf
    2667
°fiersn f-jó *heel* gp 913
fíf num *five* npm 1974; *(subs*
    w gen) acc 1131 [1154] 1178
    1184 [1192] [1215] 1230
    1777 fífe 1742
[fíf-hund] num *"500"* acc 1232
    1238 [MS v. hund]

fíf-týne num *fifteen* acc
fíftýno 1151 fífténa
1397
fíftig num *fifty* gen 1307
acc 1601 [1417]
findan 3 *find* pr3p 225 pt3s
fand 1456 2040 fond 2551
subj pt3s 1444 1467 pt
3p 2597; *provide* pr3s
2895 (*cf* éað-fynde)
firen f. *crime, sin* as fléah
...facen and fyrene 1941
np 2412* ap 19
firen-dǽd f-i *evil deed* gp
2582
°fitt ? *fighting (usually =
"section of a poem")* ds
2072*
flǽsc n-i *flesh* ns þonne þín
flǽsc ligeð *"after your
death"* 2190
flǽsc-homa m-an *flesh-cover-
ing, body* ds 1386 (*cf*
líc-homa)
fléah *see* fléogan *and* fléon
fléam m. *flight, escape* ds
2000 2074 2281
fléma m-an *fugitive, exile*
ns 1020
fléogan 2 *fly* inf 1441 1450
1471 1479 2580 pt3s fléah
1456 1465
fléon 2 *flee, run away* inf
2264 prp 2080 pt1s fléah
2274 pt3s 1819 1939
fléotan II *float* prp asn 1447
flet(t) n-ja *floor (of a hall)*
hence *hall* ds 2449
°fle(t)-gesteald n. *household goods* as 1611 dp
1074 (*cf* wuldor-gesteald,
hæg-gesteald)
°[flett-pæð] m. *floor-path,
floor, house* ap flett-
paðas [MS -waðas] 2730
flód m. *flowing water* ns 150
[MS fold] ds 157 167
1457 np 2215; *sea* ns 204
1298 ds 1323; *deluge, the
Flood* ns 1386 1419 ds

1296 1544 1601 (*cpd* drence-
héah- lago- mere- sǽ-
will- *cf* in-fléde)
+flot-mon m-cons *sailor, sea-
farer* gp 1475
flýman I *put to flight* pt3s
2115
folc n. *people, nation* ns
1650 1653 1909 2096 gs
1198 2316 2491 2667 ds
1250 2046* 2129 2412* 2418
2627 2711 2835 is 2562 as
1215 1232 1296 (?pl *"peoples"*) 1382 1730 2022 np
1553 2293 2335 gp 153 1087
2541 folc' unrim 2615*
2698 dp 2501 ap 233 2508;
army gs 1669 (*cpd* súð-
wíd-)
°folc-bearn n. *child of the
nation, (pl) people, man-
kind* np 1760; *descendants,
children* dp 2196
folc-cyning m. *king of a people* ds 2754 np 1974 2074
folc-dryht f-i *multitude of
people* as 1262
°folc-fréa m-an *lord of a
people, king* ds 1852
folc-gesíðas m (pl) *nobles of
a country, nobility* nom
2134
°folc-gestréon n. *treasures
of a people* dp 1981
°folc-getrum n. *army* ds 1987
°folc-mǽgð f. *tribe, nation,
mankind* gp 1277 2215
°folc-mǽre adj-ja *famous among
nations* apn -mǽro 1801
folc-scearu f. *division of
the people, people* as 1781;
land, nation ds 1872 2479
2681 2830
folc-stede m-i *dwelling place*
ds -styde 2000 as 2203 np
1933
folc-toga m. *leader of the
people, king* as 1961
°folc-weras m (pl) *men of the
people, people* np 222 1846

folde f-ón *earth, land* ns
116 157 215 1018 1561
1765 1969 2206 gs 222*
1534 1664* 2553 ds 1487
1658* 2579 as 154 1087
1752
fold-weg m. *earth-way, earth*
ds 2050 2510 2874 ("ad
locum")
folgian II *follow, ensue (w
acc & dat)* subj pt3s 2386
folm f. *hand* dp 62 983 1010
1096 2172 2486 2814 2907
for prep; *w dat.: of local-
ity, before, in front of,
in the presence of* 1853
2137 2140 2253 2474 2779
for þæs éagum *"before
the eyes of that one
(sc God)* 2108 *sim* 2431;
*causal, on account of,
because* 22 1673 (2x) 1831
2592 2692 (2x) 2393, *due
to, because of* 982 1279
1457 1459 1861 1925 2506
2640 2671 2743, *on ac-
count of* 1956 2474, *in
payment for* 2071; *temp-
oral* for wintra fela 2201;
for hwon *why?* 873 876*—
w acc: for þé andweardne
*"before you (being) pre-
sent"* 871, *instead of*
2931
fór f. *journey, a going* ds
2861 as 1006
for-bærnan I *burn up (trans)*
inf 2859
for-béodan 2 *forbid* pt1s for-
béad 881 pp npf forbodene
895
for-berstan 3 *destroy* nsn 70
for-bígan I *to humble, hum-
iliate* pt3s 54 pp nsm 70
fore-meahtig adj *very powerful* npm 1669
for-gifan 5 *give, grant* pt3s
forgeaf 2109 2163 2584
2844 2925 pp 2936 imps
2126; *forgive* imps 2783*

for-gildan 3 *pay (a reward)*
pt3s forgeald 2546
for-grípan 1 *sieze, overwhelm*
inf 1275
for-healdan 7 *to fail in pur-
ity, fall* pp apm 102
forht adj *frightened, terri-
fied* nsm 1955 2172 2667
nsf 1969
for-lætan 7 *allow, let (w acc
& inf)* pt3s forlét 1405
1450, *(w inf understood)*
pt1s 2258 pt3s sunne...up
forlæt 2440
for-léosan 2 *destroy* inf 1281
(*cf* be-léosan)
forma adj *first* asm 998 apmf
194
for-niman 4 *take away, plunder, destroy* pt3s fornám
2550
forod adj *broken* nsm 69
for-sceap n. *(a misshapen
deed) sin* ds 898
for-sittan 5 *delay* pt3s forsæt 2860; *obstruct* pt3p
forsæton 2491
+for-sléan 5 *strike down,
destroy* pp asn -slegen 2022
for-standan 6 *stand in the way
(of an action), prevent*
pt3s forstód 2749; *protect*
inf þæt fæsten fýre...for-
standan *"to protect that
city from fire"* 2524
for-stelan 4 *rob, deprive* pp
nsm ferhðe forstolen *"deprived of consciousness"*
1579
for-swelgan 3 *devour* pt2s ádl
...þe þú on æple...forswulge
938
forð adv *forth, out, hither*
122 2440 2449; *forward, on-
ward* 1801 2050 2112 2537
2874; *forth, away, thither
(in various phrases denot-
ing dying)* 1068 1178 1192
1601c 1642* 1742; *of the
passage of time:* 974 1421

forð (*cont.*)
2356 2392, *henceforth*
1946, *from that time on*
955 1190 1692, *contin-
ually, all the time* 2309
for-þám, for-þon conj *for
that reason, therefore*
97 172 932 938 1017 1020
1026 1289 1717 1911 1949
2180 2411 2585 2704 2713
forðon þe 2811; *?because*
2739*
°forð-bǽro f (indecl) *bringing forth, creation* gp
or adj-ja (forð-bǽre)
creative, productive nsf
forþbǽro tíd 132*
forð-gán anom. *go out* inf 870*
°forð-ryne m-i *course (of a
river) away (from a
source)* as 215 ("egred-
iebatur")
forð-weard adj *continuous,
enduring* npf 1658* dpf
210
°forð-weard m. *leader, pilot,
helmsman* as 1436
forð-weg m. *the way that goes
forward* gs (advbl) forð-
wegas = *forward* 2814*
for-weorðan 3 *perish, be undone* subj pr2s 2505 pt3s
forwearð 2590
for-wyrcan Ii *forfeit* pp forworht 1024; *mis-do, sin*
hence pp (adj) *sinful*
apmf 857
for-wyrnan I *prohibit, deny*
pt3s 2221
fót m-cons *foot* dp 913 1457
1467 2441 2856 ap 2903
°fracoð-líce adv *shamefully,
wickedly* 899
frǽcne *see* frécne adv
(ge)frægn *see* (ge)frignan
frætwa f (pl) *ornaments, treasures* acc 2130 2190 2830
ge-frætwian II *decorate* pp
nsf 215
fram *see* from prep

franca m-an *lance, javelin*
np 1982
fréa m-an *lord* ns 1475 2098
gs 2737 (sc Abimelech);
(father) vs 2890 ns 1230
gs 2696*; *(husband)* vs 2784
ns 1822; *the Lord, God*
5 79 116 150 157 173 852
904 2861* &c (26x) gs 947
1781 2371 2592 2711 ds 132
1493 1951 as mid cyining
...fréan (appos) 1211*
(*cpd* folc- líf- *cf* agend-
fréa)
fréa-drihten m. *lord* vs 884
ns 2730
frec adj *greedy* npm (w gen)
firendǽda tó frece *"(they
were) too greedy for wic-
ked deeds"* 2582 (*cf* scyld-
frecu)
frécne adj-ja *dreadful, terrible* nsm 870* asm 2747;
dangerous gpm 1427
frécne adv *terribly* 1597; *severely* frǽcne 2264*
fremde adj-ja *strange, alien,
foreign* gsm (subs) 1971
2632 npm 1834 1846 dpm
2837; *estranged from, ignorant of (w dat)* nsm 105
nsf óðere...fremde 1695
?freme adj-i *good, vigorous,
bold* ?dsm (subs) þám magorince...fremum *"to the
child...the good one"* (or
is *of* fremu? q.v.) 2332*
fremman I *do, perform, accom-
plish* inf 19 30 1072 1142
1291 2381 2812 pr2s 2247
pr3p 2414 subj pr2p 2471
pt3s freme[de] 1314 1493
2370 2736
ge-fremman I *do, perform, ac-
complish, carry out* pt1s
900* 983 1683 2744 subj
pt3p þe...ǽfre men gefre-
meden *"(original sin)...
which...henceforward men
were always to carry out*

ge-fremman (*cont.*)
  999, híe...gefremede 1587*
  pp 2652
fremu f-i *benefit, advantage*
  as fremu 1843* gp 963 1843*
  2690 2820 dp 210 ?is 2332*
  (*see* freme) (*cpd* un-)
fréo adj *free, free-born,*
  noble npf (subs) fréo ne
  þéowe 2747 gpf (subs)
  fréora and þéowra 2754
  ("uxorem ancillasque") gpm
  fréora 2088 gpn 1642 apn
  2130; *immune (from pun-*
  ishment) nsf 1255* (*cpd*
  ful-fréo-líce)
fréo-bearn n. *free son, no-*
  ble child dp 2183
fréod f. *love, peace* ns 1711*
  as 1026
fréogan 2 *to love, like* pr3s
  fréoð 2260
fréo-líc adj *noble, beauti-*
  ful, good nsm 1108 nsn
  1189 2219 nsf fréolucu
  884 fréolecu 895 998 1053
  2228 asf fréolíce (MS
  -licu) 184 asn 1722 npn
  968 1708
fréo-líce adv *freely, lib-*
  erally 1342
freom *see* from adj
fréo-mǽg m. *relative, kins-*
  man as 983 dp 1039 1183
+fréo-man m-cons *free, noble*
  man np 1601 gp 2176*
fréond m-nd *friend* ns 2726
  2820 as 2315 2501 2812
  gp 2100 2481 2627 2700
  dp 1611 2010 2025
fréond-líce adv *in a friendly*
  way, like a friend 1579
  2526 2687 (*cpd* un-)
°fréond-lufu f. *friendship*
  ns 1834
°fréond-mynd f. *an amorous*
  mind, desire (for a wo-
  man) ds 1831*
fréond-scipe m-i *friendship*
  ds 1760 2737 as 2517

°fréond-spéd f-i *abundance*
  of friends as 2332
freoðo f (indecl) *peace, se-*
  curity, protection gs
  fryðo 1513 freoðo 1838
  ds friðo 57 1151 freðo
  1487 as friðe 2530; *favor,*
  grace gs 1347 ds 1760
°freoðo-béacen n. *protection-*
  mark (the mark placed on
  Cain) as 1045
°freoðo-scealc m. *peace-min-*
  ister, angel ns 2303 np
  2499
freoðo-spéd f-i *protecting*
  power as 1198
°freoðo-tácen n. *mark of*
  peace (circumcision) as
  friðotácen 2371
°freoðo-þéaw m-wa *peaceful*
  behavior np 79
fricgan 5 *ask about* inf þæs
  fricgean ongann...Abraham
  (acc) 2888; *ask* subj pr3p
  fricgen hwæt 1834 (*cpd* un-
  fricgende)
friclan I *desire, seek* inf
  1843
frignan 3 *ask, inquire* pt3s
  frægn 887 1002 2174 2270
ge-frignan 3 *find out by ask-*
  ing, hear pt1s (w acc &
  inf) gefrægn 1960 2060
  2244 2484 2542 (*cf* ge-frǽge)
frið m.n *peace, state of se-*
  curity ds 19 1262 1872
  2530 as 2473; *protection*
  as 1299
°frið-candel f. *peace-candle*
  (i.e., the sun) ns 2541
°frið-gedál n. (? = ferhð-ge-
  dál) *peace-parting, death*
  as 1142*
friðo(-) *see* freoðo(-)
fród adj *wise* hence *old* nsm
  1154 1222 2579; *in the fol-*
  lowing occurences the sense
  is primarily "old" nsm
  1072 1194 1743 2174 2347
  nsf 2355 2383 (*cpd* géomor-

frod (*cont.*)
　hige-)
frófor f. *comfort, help, re-
　lief* ns 1475 gs þé...fró-
　fre tó wedde *"as a pledge
　of comfort to you"* 2311
　ds 2155, tó frófre (w dat
　of pers) 955 1108 2219,
　hwæt gifest þú me...fréo-
　manna tó frófre *"what for
　relief (in the form) of
　noble sons do you give
　me?"* 2176*
from prep w dat *from* 149 919
　943 954 1255* &c (23x)
　fram 1032 2000
from adj *strong, bold* nsm
　2308 freom 2794 nsf 2196
　asm 1961 npm 2495
°from-cyme m. *a thing coming
　forth, progeny, race* is
　1765*
from-cynn n-ja *progeny, des-
　cendant, family* ds 1597
　2316 is 1534 2206
°from-lád f. *a course away
　(from s.t.)* hence *depart-
　ure* ns hwelc gromra wearð
　féonda fromlád *"what kind
　the departure of the fierce
　enemies had been"* 2098
from-líce adv *boldly, strongly*
　2050
fruma m-an *beginning, source*
　ns 5; *inventor, founder*
　ns 1087 1633*; *leading
　person, prince* as 2104
　as folcmægþa fruman (sc
　Adam) 1277 (*cpd* dǽd- léod-
　léoht- ord-)
frum-bearn n. *first-born son,
　oldest son* ns 1028 1056
　1189 ds 1215 2360 np 968
　1618
frum-gár m. *leader, prince*
　[*lit.: "first-spear"*] ns
　1183
°frum-gára m-an *leader,
　prince* ns 1169 2579 ds

2052, frumgaran [MS -um]
　2293* 2660 np 1708 dp
　2116 2615 ap 1334
°frum-hrægl n. *the first
　clothes* ds 943
frum-stól m. *original home
　(sc Eden)* ns 963
frymð f. *beginning* ds 132 954
　2392
fryðo *see* freoðo
fugol m. *bird* ns 1460 1983 np
　2159* ap 1299 2088 (*cpd
　heofon-*)
°ful-fréo-líc adj *very noble*
　npm 1618
ful-gán anom. *serve, help*
　pt3p fulléodon 2154
full adj *full, replete* asf
　unrihte (dat) eorðan fulle
　*"the earth replete with in-
　justice"* 1292 (*cpd* niht-
　in-wit- scyld- sorg-)
full-éodon *see* ful-gán
+fullian II *fulfill, carry
　out (a command)* inf 2319
?fullwon ?f. ?*baptism* ?gp
　fullwona bearn ?*children
　of baptism (i.e., Chris-
　tians)* 1951*
fultum m. *help* gs bæd him
　fultumes *"sought aid from
　them"* 2025 as fultum (*"a
　helper"* = *"adiutorem"*) 173,
　on fultum *"in aid"* 974
　1964 2072 2794
fundian II *strive, attempt,
　aspire* pr2 s 2271 pt3p
　2495
furðum adv *first, for the
　first time* 1131 1238; *even
　as, exactly as* 2380; *just
　as* 2541; *at once, immedi-
　ately* 875*
furður adv *further* 2014
fús adj *quick, speedy, eager*
　nsm fus...mergen 154, 2870
　(*cpd* ellor-)
fyll m-i *fall, death* ns 1103
　2062 (*cpd* wæl-)

fyllan¹ I *to fell, kill* inf
   2113 pt1s 1096 pt3s 2071
   (*cpd* be-)
fyllan² I *to fill* impp fyllað 196 1513* 1533
ge-fyllan I *to fill* pp nsm
   209 1553 1613 nsn 1766
   asm 2161; *to fulfill* pp
   nsf 123 nsn 1166
?fyllað ?m. ?*a filling up,
   abundance* 1513* [*so
   Holthausen and others,
   but probably a shadow-
   word, see* fyllan²]
fylstan I *help (trans, w
   dat)* pt3s 2632 pt3p
   2486
fyore *see* feorh
fýr n. *fire* ns 2558 ds 43
   2508 2523 2907* as 2544
   2888 2890 (*cpd* bǽl-)
fyrd f-i *army* as 1961 2044
fyrd-gestealla m-an *battle-
   companion, retainer* dp
   1999 (*cf* will-gestealla)
fyrd-rinc m. *warrior* gp 2104
fyren *see* firen
fýren adj *fiery* isn 947 1575
°fýr-gebræc n. *crash of fire
   (sc the noise made by the
   fiery rain on Sodom)* as
   2562*
fyrn adv *long ago* 2697
fyrn-dagas m (pl) *days of
   old* dp fród fyrndagum
   "*old by virtue of (many)
   days long-since passed,*"
   "*very old*" 1072
fyrn-wita m-an *ancient (wise)
   counsellor* ns 1154 (*cf*
   stíg-wita)
fyrr *see* feor
fýsan I *impel, incite* inf
   2861

G

ge-gærwan *see* ge-gyrwan
gæst, gasta *see* gist
gǽð *see* gán
gafol n. *tribute* as 1978
°gamol-ferhð adj *of ancient
   life, aged* (hence "*wise*"?)
   nsm 2868
gán anom *go* inf 1970 2236
   2356 pr3s gǽð 2182 pt3s
   éode 2463 2541 2600, w
   inf grétan éode 2432 pt3p
   éodon 2445 (*cpd* forð-
   ful-)
ge-gán anom *observe (a practice), carry out (an action)* inf 2326*; *happen,
   come to pass* pt3s 1562
gangan 7 *go, move, walk* inf
   858 865 1345 1487 1609
   2576 2594 gongan 1050 prp
   asn gangende feoh *living
   cattle* (cf "*on the hoof*")
   2720 (*cpd* á- *cf* féðe-gang)
gár m. *spear* gs 1522 np 2064
   gp 2019 (*cpd* frum- wæl-
   cf frum-gára)
gár-secg m-ja *ocean* as 117
gást m. *spirit, soul* ns 909
   1212 1609 gs 1522 ds 187
   1001 1137 as 1281 gp 12 41
   1793 2175 2422 2547 2866
   2920; *of God,* "*the Holy
   Spirit*" ns 120 1009 gs
   2331; *of angels* np 2401
   dp 2432; *of fallen angels*
   np 90 ap 69 (*cpd* ǽrend-
   wuldor-)
gasta 1346 *see* gist
°gást-cyning m. *spirit-king,
   God* ds 2884
gást-gedál n. *soul parting,
   death* as 1127
gást-líc adj *spiritual* nsm 209*
gé *see* þú
+géan advbl prep *against* him
   ...géan þingade 1009 (*cf*

géan (*cont.*)
  tó-géanes)
géap adj *broad* gsn 2558*
géar n. *year* as 2304 gp 1726
  1932 dp 2383
-geard (*see* fæder- léod-
  middan- wín-)
géar-dagas m (pl) *past time
  of life, former times* dp
  1657*
geare *see* gearwe
°géar-torht adj *(year-bright),
  glorious because of sea-
  sonal fruition* apf wlitebeorhte wæstmas...géar-
  torhte gife 1561
gearo adj-wa *ready, finished*
  asn 1321
gearwe adv *readily, certainly*
  41 1098 2344 2626
gearwe f-wó (pl) *clothes*
  dp 1212
ge-gearwian II *provide with,
  endue* pp nsf gáste ge-
  gearwod 187
ge-bedda m.f-an *bed-companion, spouse, wife* nsf
  gebedda 1828 asf 1775 dpf
  1091
ge-bed-scipe m-i *marriage,
  legitimate intercourse*
  as 1148 2218 2469
°ge-blǽd-fæst adj *prosperous,
  glorious* npn 89
ge-byrd f-i *birth* as 2198
  (*cpd* sib- *cf* mund-byrd)
ge-dál n. *parting, separation* ns 930, hence *death?*
  ds 1400* (*cpd* aldor- frið-
  gást- líf-)
ge-défe adj-ja *just, righteous* nsm 1287
ge-driht f-i *host, company*
  as 2464
ge-dwild n. *error, false
  opinion* ds 23 as 922
ge-dwolen adj [pp of *ge-
  dwelan 4] *led astray, er-
  rant* npn 1936 (*cf* ge-dwild)
ge-féa m-an *joy* ds 57 1513

as 875*
+ge-fég n. *a joining* ?as
  1310* (*see also* ge-fégan)
ge-frǽge n-ja *a questioning,
  knowledge* is míne gefrǽge
  *"according to my knowledge,"
  "as I have heard"* 1173
ge-grind n. *a grinding,
  clashing together* ns 2063
ge-hát n. *promise* gp 1425 ap
  1796 (*cpd* worn-)
°ge-hilte n-ja *hilt (of a
  sword)* dp 2906
+ge-hnǽst n. *conflict, battle* ds 2015
ge-hwá pron *every* dat m. 2171
  dógora geh[w]ám *daily* 2251*
  dat f. gehwǽre 1374* acc f.
  gehwone 2307
ge-hwilc pron *every, absol:*
  acc m. gehwilcne wǽpned-
  cynnes *"everyone of male
  sex"* 2313, heht...gehwilcne
  "commanded everyone who"
  2373; *w gen pl:* nom m.
  2319 gen m. 1660 2274 gen
  n. 994 1311 1336 gen f.
  geh[w]ilcre 959 dat f. 963
  2366 dat n. 2490 acc n.
  1281 1297 2213
ge-líc adj *like, similar (w
  dat)* nsf séo...gelíc...
  neo[r]xnawange 1923 ("sicut paradisus") npmf 185
  (*cpd* un-)
ge-líce adv *as* superl emne
  þon gelícost...þe *"just
  as if"* 1943
ge-lóme adv *often* oft gelóme
  "very often" 1539* oft and
  gelóme 1670
ge-mæcca mf-jan *spouse, mate*
  dp 1259
ge-mǽne adj-ja *common, mutual,
  in common* nsm tuddor (*dat*)
  bið gemǽne incrum orlegnið
  *"there will be conflict
  in common for your off-
  spring* 914* nsf reord...
  án gemǽne *"one common lan-*

ge-mǽne (*cont.*)
  guage" 1636, 1904 nsn 2218
  npm 1897 npn heht...wesan
  wǽter gemǽne 158 ("dixit
  ...congregentur aquae")
  apn þurh gemǽne word *"with
  one voice"* 2476
+ge-mágas m (pl) *relatives*
  np 1904
+ge-mearc n. *region, place*
  gs tó þæs gemearces 2886
  (*cpd* word-)
ge-met adj *fitting, proper*
  nsn 2896
ge-met n. *measure, power (w
  connotation of "what is
  fitting to a thing," rule,
  law, order?)* as ofer monna
  gemet 1677 (*cpd* eln-)
ge-mynd f.n-i *mind, thought,
  memory* ds 2605 as 1085 on
  gemynd drepen *dazed, unconscious"* 1571 gp 1957
ge-myndig adj *mindful (of s.
  t.), having s.t. in the
  memory (w gen)* nsm 1780
  1899 1943 2164 2374 2465
gén *see* gíen
géna adv *yet, up to now* 2652
  gíena 2811; *still* 2248
  (*cf* gíen)
ge-nea adv *enough, suffici-
  ently* 2844
ge-niht n. *sufficiency, abundance* as 1890
ge-nihtsum adj (w gen) *satisfied* nsm níðes genihtsum
  *"satisfied with battle"
  (i.e., of an abandoned
  weapon, worn out in battle)* 1995
ge-nip n. *darkness* ns 139
ge-nóh adj *enough* gpf genóhra
  888*
géo adv *once before* 2310
géoc f. *help* as 1587
°geofon-hús n. *an ocean-house,
  the Ark* gp 1321
geogoð f. *the state of youth,*
  ds 187 1174; *body of young*

persons ns 1604 geogoðe
  strýnde 1152 ds 1370
geogoð-hád m. *the state of
  youth* ds 1507
géomor adj *sad, miserable*
  nsm 1018 apm 69 [Geómor
  1610 *is a proper name,*
  q.v.] (*cpd* hyge-)
°géomor-fród adj *sad and old,
  very old* nsf 2226
géomor-mód adj *sad of heart*
  nsm 1050 asf híe...géo-
  mormóde 2270 npmf géomor-
  móde 858
géomrian II *to lament, be sad*
  imps géomra 2200
geond prep w acc *throughout*
  44 134 1244, *over* 205 1331
  1338 1429; *among* 233 991
  1664* 1781
°geond-féolan[*-felhan] 3 *to
  fill throughout* pp asn
  geondfolen fýre *"filled
  with fire"* 43
°geond-sendan I *spread over,
  cover* pp nsm 2552 nsn 1968
geong adj *young* nsm 2889 dsn
  2364 asm 2905 npm 1207
  2430 2454 apm 2868 comp
  nsf (subs) séo gingre 2613
georn adj *eager, anxious* npm
  mǽrða (*gen*) georne 1677
georne adv *eagerly, dili-
  gently* 1559 2270 2442 2847
ge-réfa m-jan *reeve, steward
  ("procurator")* ns 2182 np
  2188
ge-reorde n-ja (*or* f-ó, *Campbell* §588) *food, (pl) meal*
  ap gereorda 2443
ge-rím *see* ge-ríman
ge-rysne n-ja *what is fitting,
  proper, suitable* ns 169
  1565 gerisne 2478 ap gerysnu 2247 gerisno 2434
ge-saca m-an *adversary* dp 59
ge-sǽlig adj *blessed, happy*
  nsm 1138 1286 2739 npm 18;
  rich nsm 1770
ge-sǽlig-líc adj *blessed,*

ge-sǽlig-líc (*cont.*)
     happy asn líf...gesǽlig-
     líc 2845
ge-sceaft f-i *creation, cre-
     ated thing* ns 199 gescaft
     131* gs 171 as 93 gp 208
     899* 1614 (*cpd* héah-
     woruld- *cf* metod-sceaft)
ge-sceap n. *fate, decree*
     ap gesceapu 2828; *nature*
     ap wið gesceapu "*against
     your natures*" 2471; *gen-
     itals (w play on "fate"?)*
     np 1573
ge-séne (WS -síene) adj-ja
     apparent, easy to see nsn
     2807 (*cf* an- heafod-síen)
ge-sibb adj *peaceful, near,
     related* dpm (subs?) 1612
     1732 (subs)
ge-síð m. *comrade, retainer*
     np gesíððas 2067 dp ge-
     síððum 1908 (*cpd* folc-
     gesíðas, will-gesíð)
°ge-síðð ?n-ja [*cf* Goth.
     ga-sinþja "*companion*"
     OHG gi-sindi "*comitatus*"]
     company of gesíððas,
     comitatus ds on gesíððe
     2403 2808
ge-sóm adj *united, at peace*
     npm 82
ge-stréon n. *treasure, valu-
     ables* as 1071 1208 ap 1831
     (*cpd* ǽr- botl- folc-
     woruld-)
ge-sund adj *safe, prosperous*
     asm þé...gesundne 2666 npm
     2525 (*cf* on-sund)
+ge-sweorc n. *darkness* as 108
ge-syhð *sight, glance* ds of
     gesyhðe þínre 1035 ("a
     facie tua"), gode of ge-
     syhðe 1050 ("a facie Dom-
     ini")
ge-tǽl n. *number* hence *num-
     erous host of people* dp
     híe gemitton...getalum
     myclum 1688 (*cpd* rím-)
ge-tenge adj-ja *close, near*

     to, pressing upon nsf 1814
ge-trum n. *company* ds 2046*
     (*cpd* folc-)
ge-þanc m.n *thought, mind* as
     1078 dp 2415 (*cpd* in- mód-)
ge-þyldig adj *patient* nsm
     1942 2663
ge-weald n.f *power, might* ds
     55 199 920 1867 2204 2229
     2459 2656 as 11 202 1516
     1789 2111
ge-witt n-ja *mind, intellect,
     understanding* ds 1958
°ge-wlóh adj *ornamented* asf
     wæstmum gewló 1789
ge-writ n. *writing, (pl)
     Scriptures* np gewritu
     1121 1630 2565 2612
?ge-wyrc (ge-weorc) n. *a work,
     project* as (*or* imp *of* ge-
     wyrcan?) 1309*
gield n. *substitute, replace-
     ment* ns 1109 as 101, gyld
     1104; *sacrifice, worship*
     ds 1501 as 977, gyld 1506,
     gild 2843 (*cpd* bryne-)
gieldan *see* gyldan
gielp *see* gylp
gielp-sceaþa m-an *a boasting
     adversary* np 96
gíen adv *still, as yet* 2742;
     for yet, moreover 2197; þá
     gén *once again* 2165; þám
     þe gén nis "*for him who
     is not yet*" 2364
gíena *see* géna
giest *see* gist
°giest-líðnys f. *friendliness
     towards a guest, hospital-
     ity* as 2448
gíet *see* gýt
gif conj *if, w ind:* 1040 1754
     1838 2253 2317 2326 2475
     2482 2523 2660 2787; *w
     subj:* 1446 2314 2500 2656
     2662 2827; *whether* 2414
gifan 5 *give* pr2s 2175 pt3s
     geaf 2447 (*cpd* á- for- of-)
gifeðe adj-ja *given, granted
     (by circumstances)* nsn 1726

gifeðe (*cont.*)
2226
gifu f. *gift, grace, favor*
as 2331 gp gifa 890* gi-
fena 209 2936 dp 88 2811
2920 ap 1561 (*cf* ǽt-gifa)
°gīgant-mæcg m-ja *son of a
giant, giant-spawn* ap
1268*
gild *see* gield
ginn adj *broad, ample, huge*
asn (wk) ginne rīce 230
apm 957
gingre *see* geong
gin-fæst adj *ample, vast*
dpf 2920
gist m-i *guest, visitor* np
gystas 2487 gp gasta wer-
ode "*a band of sojourners*"
(*sc the beings in the Ark,
perhaps w a play on* gǻsta
"*spirits*") 1346 dp giestum
2442 2457 gistum 2494 ap
gistas 2474; *stranger,
enemy* dp gystum 2056 (*cf*
giest-liðnys)
°gist-mǽgen n. *a guest-force,
power or army composed of
guests* (*sc the angels who
visited Loth in Sodom*) ns
2496
git *see* þū
gītsian II *covet, desire* prp
nsf 890
glǽd adj *bright, shining* asn
2720; *glad, joyful* nsf
(subs) gladu 1480
+glǽd-līce adv *happily* 2383
°glǽd-stede m. ?*happy place*
ds 2843* (*see* glḗd-styde)
glǽm m-i *brightness* gs 1018
°glḗam n. *joy* as 12
glḗaw adj-wa *wise* nsm 1370
1501 2375 2658 dsm 1195
(subs) 2430 dsf 2298 asm
1078
°glḗaw-ferhð adj *wise-minded*
nsm 1152 2448
°glḗd-styde m-i *place of fire,*

altar ds 1810 (glǽd-stede
2843 *may belong here*, q.v.)
gnyrn f-i *evil, wickedness*
ds 2422
god m. *God* ns 34 97 183 872
887 918 1207 1396 1404
1407 1509 1678 1903 1924
2109 2115 2187 2375 2389
2561* 2742 2916 gs 11 25
88 965 1001 1248 1370 1528
1610 1923 2106 2123 2298
2496 2532 2913 ds 1050
1146 1268 1501 1773 1790 2454
2474 2738 2891 2934 as
46 77 1135 1806
gōd adj *good* nsm 209 1285
1769 2658 asm 779 1346
npm 1587 dpf 1507 (*cpd*
cyne-)
gōd n. *a good deed* as 2422;
property, goods ds 2200
as 2016
god-cund adj *divine* asf 2331
npf 2613 dpf 2811 (*cpd*
eorð-cund)
gōd-spḗdig adj *powerful in
virtue* nsm 1009
gold n. *gold* gs 1997 2868 ds
1769 2078 2406 as 226 1181
1931 2006 2070 2128 2156
gold-burh f-cons *gold-city,
a town rich in gold* (*see
Commentary, 2403b-06a*) dp
gold-burgum (sc Sodom &
Gomorra) 2551
gombe f-ōn *tribute* as gombon
1978
gongan *see* gangan
grǽg adj *gray* dsn 2866
græs n. *grass* as 1137
?græs-un-grḗne adj-ja *un-green,
not yet green, as with
grass* nsf 117*
ge-gremman I *irritate, enrage*
pp 61*
grḗne adj-ja *green* nsf 1018
1561 gsf 1454 gsn 2551 asf
1921 asn 1137 npm 1657 apm
1480 apf 1474 (*cpd* græs-un-)

gréot m. *dust* as 909

grétan I *greet, welcome*
inf 2104 2432; *attack*
inf 1046; *speak to (w evil
intent)* pr3s mid wéan gré-
teð 1755 ("maledicent-
ibus")

grim adj *grim, bitter, cruel*
nsn 46 asn (wk) grimme
(or adv) 2056 ism 1102
(*cpd* wæl-)

grimme adv *fiercely, bitterly*
46 1275 2417 grymme 61

grípan 1 *grip, sieze* inf 2485
pr3s 936 pt2s 890 pt3s
61 1381 2072 2547 pt3p
2063 (*cpd* for-)

ge-grípan 1 *grip* pt3s 2905

grom adj *hostile, angry* gpm
gromra...féonda 2097;
subs: enemy gp 2487

grome adv *troublously* 1260

grówan 7 *grow, increase* prp
npn 88 gpf grówendra gife
890*

grund m. *(surface of) the
earth* ns 104 as 123 134
213 1388 1429

°grund-wela m-an *earthly
wealth* ap 957

grymme *see* grimme

gryre m-i *terror* is 1102

guma m-an *man, warrior* ns
1174 gs 2794 gp gumena
1863 2694 dp 1181

gum-cynn n-ja *mankind* ds 1275

gum-cyst f-i *manly excellence, right, justice*
dp 1769 1810

gum-rinc m. *man* dp 1552

°gum-þeod f. *a nation, people* gp 226

gúð f. *battle, war* ds 2109
2115 as 2019

gúð-bord n. *war-board, shield*
gs 2694*

gúð-cyning m. *war-king, king
who has been fighting* ns
2123 ("rex Sodomorum")

°gúð-flán m. *arrow* gp 2063

gúð-gemót n. *battle assembly,
i.e., battle itself* as 2056

gúð-here m-ja *battle host,
army* dp 1967

°gúð-spell n. *news of battle*
as 2097

°gúð-þracu f. *war-violence*
ds gúðþræce 1046 *("vio-
lence")* 1973 *("warfare")*

gyddian II *speak* pt3s 2106

gyld *see* gield

gyldan 3 *pay, requite, reward* inf 2921 gildan 1978
pt3s geald 2079 pt3p gul-
don 2421 imps 2824 pp nsm
mín...golden...fyll and
feorhcwealm 1102 (*cpd* á-
for- on-)

gylp m.n *boast* ns 69 as gielp
25 gylp 2410 (*cf* gielp-
sceaþa)

gylpan 3 *to boast* pt3p gulpon
2017

gylt m-i *guilt, crime* as 998

gýman I *care for, observe*
árna ne gymden subj pt3p
2461

gym-cynn n-ja *a kind of gem*
ap 226 ("bdellium et
lapis onychinus")

gyrdan I *gird* pt3s 2866

gyrwan I *clothe* pt3s gyrede
941

ge-gyrwan I *prepare, make* inf
gegærwan 2856

gyst *see* gist

gýt(a) adv *still, yet, to this
day* 152 gíet 2664 þá gýt
1189 1437 þá gíet *up to
this point* 1245; *once a-
gain* þá gýt 1476 1510 1793;
w neg: not yet þá gíet 103
212 þá gýt 1727 nú gíet
1038 | gíeta *still, yet*
993 þá gýta 1453 þá gíeta
1635 þá gýt(a) 116; *w neg:*
155 gíeta 2468

H

habban III *have, keep, pos-*
  sess (w acc) inf 1299
  1360 1894 2315 2411 pr3s
  hafað 949 1530 pr1p habbað 2890 pt3s hæfde 60
  1491* 1631 2003 2496 2627
  pt3p hæfdon 12 25 1890
  imps hafa 2128 2437;
  expressing a person's age:
  pt3s 1117 1124 1130 1140
  1153 1157 1164 1170 1177
  1191 1216 1222 1226 1237
  1367 1740 1776 2300 2345
  2773; *w uninfl pp to form
  comp pret:* pr1s ic forworht hæbbe 1024 ic...ge-
  dón hæbbe 2821 pt3s cynn
  hafað...abolgen 1256 pr3p
  wit...agifen habbað 2884
  pt3s hæfde...metod...ge-
  cyrred 1414 sǽ...ofgifen
  hæfde 1454 *sim* 1506 2762
  2893 2923 2936 pt3p hæfdon...gesomnod 45 *sim* 96
  1987 2052; *neg:* pr1s
  næbbe...synne...gefremed
  2651 (*cpd* be- *cf* dréam-
  hæbbende)
hæg-steald adj [*also used as
  adj at BW 1889, usually
  m. "bachelor"*] *young, dependent* gp hægstealdra
  wyn *the flower of the
  young (men)* 1862 (*cf*
  wuldor-ge-steald)
hǽlan I *heal, soothe* pt3p
  2035
hæle(ð) m-cons *hero, man,
  warrior* ns hæle 1222 1502
  1740 2448 2591 hæleð 1152
  1182 2026 np? hæleð langode 1431* np hæleð 1550
  1678 1709 1985 1992 2076
  gp hæleða 2139 2158 dp
  hæleðum 2460 2623 ap hæleð 2061 2113

hǽman I *have sexual intercourse* inf 2460
hǽs f-i *command* ns 124 ds
  947 965 1370 1781 2371
  2737 2865
hǽst f-i *power, violence* ds
  hǽste hrínan 1396* [*may
  be taken as adj w* brogan
  or as adv, see next word]
hǽste ?adj-i *violent* nsm
  2418* *(or adv?)*
hǽðen adj *heathen, godless*
  dsn 2418 apm 2485
°hǽðen-cynn n-ja *heathen-race*
  as 2548
hálgian II *sanctify* inf 2312
hálig adj *holy* nsm 97 946
  1290 1396 1404 1424 1678
  1898 1953 2389 2865, se
  hálga (subs) 161 1744 2039
  2057 2163 2297 2696 2749
  2840 nsf hálegu 2118 nsn
  124 201* gsm 1569 2918 dsm
  1315 1463 1592 2140 ism
  wældréore...hálge 1017 isf
  1484 2166 asn 860 1796
  npm 2401 (uninfl), 2781
  dpn 151 956 apm 1531 2458
  apf? 2369*
°hals-fæst [i.e., heals- q.v.]
  adj *shackled by the neck?
  enslaved* or *stiff-necked?
  arrogant* nsf (subs) 2240
  [*it is not clear whether
  h.-f. is rendering the idea
  "Agar Aegyptiam ancillam"
  or "despexit"*]
hám m. *home, dwelling* ds 1721
  as 33 37 946 1556 advbl acc
  ferian...hám 2156 hám síðian 2162
hám-sittend m-nd *home dwellers,
  ones remaining at home (as
  opposed to Abraham, who
  left)* dp 1815
hand f-u *hand* ds 1463 1473
  1678 as 883 1809 2121 2918
  his ágene hand *with his own
  hand* 2768* gp 2671 dp 1017

hand (*cont.*)
　1080 1572 1991 2118 2485
　ap honda 50 1094 2903
hand-plega m-an *hand-play,
　battle* as 2057
hasu adj-wa *gray, dusky (of
　the color of a dove)* asf
　haswe 1451
hát adj *hot* nsm 2418* (*cpd
　wylm-*)
hátan 7 *command (w acc of
　one commanded and inf)*
　pt3s heht 39 44 121 144
　157 1047 2039 2235 2372
　2506 2668 2868 hét 864
　943 958 imps hát 2230 2784
　2799; *(w inf and ellipse
　of acc)* pt3s heht 1856
　1858 1867 2629 hét 942 pt
　3p héton 1060 2457; *(ab-
　sol)* pr1s háte 1332 1748
　2325 pt3s heht 1314 2736
　hét 1356 2894; *to call,
　call out a command (w el-
　lipse of inf)* pt3s heht
　him...tó *(+ acc)* 1865*,
　2672; *name* inf 2329 pr3p
　221 1648 2617 2838 subj pt
　3s héte 2614 pp nsm 1055
　1063 1082 1134 1160 1174
　1188 1240 1645 1799 2288
　nsf 1723 npm 1550 1617
　1709 npf 1424
ge-hátan 7 *to promise, pledge,
　vow* pr1s 2139 gehét 2203
　2392 2803
hatian II *to hate* pr3s hatað
　912
hé, héo, hit pers pron *he,
　she, it* nsm hé 3 7 31 857
　954* 982 1068 1952 hé eft
　[MS heft] 2577 &c (114x);
　nsf héo 1016 1017 1131*
　1401* 1455 híe 2569 &c
　(21x); nsn hit 901; gsm
　his *of him* 972 ?1567* (*cf
　his poss pron*); dsm him
　5 124* 172 865 882 895 &c
　him on láste *after him*
　1128 1167 &c him æfter

after him 1143 [*at 2072 &
2744* him *may be either s
or p*] (101x); him *reflex:*
　99 1051 1118 1557 1564
　1567 1720 1829 2025 2028
　2030 2057 2603 (twice),
　him miltse...seceð 2647,
　2703 2895 2896 2927, *in
　the expression* heht him *w
　acc:* 864 1865* 1867 2235
　2667 2673; *in the expres-
　sion* gewát him *w inf:* 1049
　1356 1730 &c (17x); dsf
　hire 1482 2256 2280 dsn
　him (sc æfen) 138; asm
　hine 1041 1043 1045 1213
　&c (22x) *reflex:* 1276 1521
　1572 1583 1784 1941 2865
　hine...mid 2868; asf híe
　2268 2270 2651 *reflex:*
　2786; asn hit 41 1325 2506;
　nom p híe 19 24 26 45 1717*
　2055* [MS he] &c héo 47
　71 73 77 185 (47x); gen p
　heora 1893 1936 (*cf* heora
　poss pron); dat p him 28
　46 49 53 62* &c (34x), *re-
　flex:* 861 1250 1258 1663
　1736 1803 1804 1880 2670
　gewiton him 858 1649 2399;
　acc p híe 141 941 943 1396
　2115 2581
héaf m. *lamentation* as 923
　(*cpd* helle-)
héafod n. *head* as 912; *chief,
　leader* ns 4
héafod-mæg m. *chief relative,
　near relative* gp -mága
　1200 1605
héafod-síen f-i *eye* ap 2492
　(*cf* an-síen, ge-séne)
°héafod-swíma m-an *dizziness
　of the head, drunkenness*
　ns 1568
°héafod-wísa m-an *chief* ns
　1619
héah adj *high, elevated, ex-
　alted* vsm þú...engla þéo-
　den...héah 2645 nsf 1422
　gsf héare 2596 gsn héan

héah (*cont.*)
 2855* 2899 dsn héan 1489
 2458 asm 2840* asf héan
 1401 héa 2878 asn 1308
 1451 þæt segn...héah 2373
 npn 1439 dpm héagum 8 apn
 seld...héah on heofenum
 97 superl asf honda...
 héhste 51*
héa(h)-burh f-cons *high city*
 as héaburh (sc Segor, cf.
 19.19) 2519; *chief-city*
 ap héabyrig 1821
héah-cyning m. *high-king,*
 God vs 1025 ns 172 2166
 -cining 50 gs -cininges
 124
+héah-flód m-ja *deep water,*
 the Deluge as 1442
°héah-gesceaft f-i *higher*
 creation, the intelligi-
 ble creation, angels gp 4
°héah-rodor m. *the firmament*
 ds 151
héah-setl n. *high-throne, ex-*
 alted place as 33
héah-stéap see stéap-reced
°héah-þréa (orig f-ó > m-an,
 for earlier -þrawu) *ex-*
 treme affliction ns 2547
healdan 7 *hold, possess have*
 pr3s 2190 pt3s 9 1129 1143
 1167 1218 1224 1607 pt3p
 1725; *guard, defend, keep*
 inf 2135 pr3s 951* pr1p
 2530 pt3s 973 1404 1947;
 keep, observe (laws) inf
 1531 pr2s 2119 pr3p heora
 ryne healdað *"(waters)*
 keep to their proper
 course" 159 *sim* pt3p héoldon forðryne 215; *rule* pr
 3s 2828 pt3s 1232; *behave*
 pt3s hine *(reflex)* fǽgre
 héold 1941 *(cpd* be- for-)
healdend m-nd *keeper, posses-*
 sor, defender ns 172 2162
 2317
healf f. *side, direction* as
 1918 np 2055

heals-mægeð f-cons *woman to*
 be embraced by the neck,
 beloved woman ap 2156
héan adj *low, miserable* nsm
 866 (subs) 879 (subs),
 1595 nsf 921 2275 apm 91
héap m. ?*heap, pile* dp 1693*
heard adj *hard, firm (of ma-*
 terial objects) nsf 2571
 compar nsn 1325; *hard,*
 strenuous, brave nsm 1989
 asm 2057 dpm 1898 dpn
 2035; *hardened, hard-*
 hearted nsf 2263; *hard,*
 painful asm 1815 npm 992
 dpf 1276 apm 38
hearde adv *severely, sorely*
 92 936 997 1862
°heard-rǽd adj *firmly deter-*
 mined, resolute asm 2350
hearm-loca m-an *an enclosure*
 where torture is inflicted,
 Hell as 91 *(cf* burh-loca)
°hearm-plega m-an *dangerous*
 play, battle, strife np
 1898 ("rixa")
hearm-stæf m. *trouble, sorrow*
 np 939
°hearm-tán m. *branches of*
 sorrow (w literal force)
 np 992
hearpe f-ón *harp* gs 1079
hefig adj *heavy, oppressive*
 nsn torn...hefig æt heortan 980 npf 2412*
héhste see héah
helan 4 *conceal, hide* inf
 1582 imps hel 1836*
°helle-héaf m. *lamentation(s)*
 of hell ap 38
°hell-trega m-an *hell-torment*
 dp 73
helm m. *helmet* dp 1989; *in*
 phrases w gen pl = "pro-
 tector of..." vs 2146 2647
 ns 113 1290 1858 2422 2722
 2752 ds 1793
heofon m. *heaven* as 85 113
 2191 gp (w sing sense)
 heofena 33 heofona 50 1025

heofon (*cont.*)
1404 2140 2166 2221 2387
dp (w sing sense) heofe-
num 97 heofnum 66 78 912
1595 1675 2543 heofonum
161 1387
heofon-cyning m. *heaven-king,*
God gs 2918 ds 1315
heofon-fugol m. *bird of hea-*
ven np heofonfugla[s]1515*
("volucres caeli") gp
201 ("volatilibus caeli")
heofon-ríce n-ja *kingdom of*
heaven gs 1363 1484 1744
2073
°heofon-stól m. *throne of*
heaven ap heofenstólas 8
°heofon-timber n. *structure*
of heaven, firmament as 146
°heofon-weard m. *guardian of*
heaven, God gs 120 1796
heolstor n. *darkness, con-*
cealment ds 860
°heolstor-sceado f. *shadow*
of darkness, darkness
ns 103
heonan adv *from here, hence*
1203 2149 2281 2515 2855
+heonon-weard adj *going a-*
way, departing, leaving
nsm holm wæs heononweard
"the deluge was receding"
1431
heorte f-ón *heart, seat of*
life, thought, will ds
980 tó heortan...grípeð
ádl *"sickness siezes at*
the vitals" 936 sim 2278
as héafodswíma...heortan
clypte *"dizziness encom-*
passed his thought" 1569
wege...heortan strange
"have a strong will" 2350
(*cf* blíð-heort adj)
heorð-werod n. *band of peo-*
ple who share a hearth,
live together hence *band*
of retainers, family ns
1605 2076 as 2039 ("ver-
naculos")

hér adv *here* 867 2228 2466
2502 2519 2881 2890; *on*
earth, in this life 103
935 1122 1139 1146 1147
1176 1189 1206 2093 2645
2741; *at this place* 112
2169 2483 2735; *hither,*
to this place 2712
hér-búende m-nd (pl) *those*
living on this earth
gen 1079
here m-ja *army, host* ns 2492
gs herges 2127 2456 ds
herge 51 2007 as 68 np
hergas 2073 gp herga 2110
(*cpd* égor- gúð- þéod- wæl-)
°here-mæcg m-ja *man in a hos-*
tile host ap 2485* *(sc the*
Sodomites)
here-téam m. *spoils of bat-*
tle gp 2121 is mid þý he-
retéame 2163
+here-wíc n. *military camp*
dp 2051
here-wõsa m-an ?*rebel,* ?*war-*
rior np 85*
°here-wulf m. *battle-wolf,*
warrior gp 2015
herges &c *see* here
hergian II *harry, plunder* pt
3s 1380
herian[1] I *praise* subj pr1p
wé...herigen 2, pt3p 15
1855
+herian[2] I (hirwan) *despise,*
scorn inf 2240
hete m-i *hatred* as 2275 (*cpd*
mód-)
hettend m-nd *(hater), enemy*
np 2011 gp 2110
hige(-) *see also* hyge(-)
°hige-fród adj *wise in mind*
nsm 1953
°hige-tréow f-wó *covenant of*
the spirit ap (for sing?)
higetréawa 2369* ("pactum")
°hige-þrýð f-i *pride, arro-*
gance as 2240
hiht-ful adj *pleasant* asm 946
°hiht-léas adj ?*without hope*

hiht-léas *(cont.)*
  *(of a promise being ful-
  filled)* or *?joyless* [con-
  trasting with hleahtor]
  asm 2389
hild f-jó *battle* ds 2061 2150
°hilde-sweg m-i *noise of battle* ns 1991
°hilde-wulf m. *battle-wolf,
  warrior* np 2051
°hild-þracu f. *violence of
  battle* as -þræce 2158
hína *see* híwan
híre 2798 *see* hýran
híred m. *household* as 2310
  ds hýrde 2696*
his, hire, heora poss pron
  *his, her, their (indecl,
  w following noun)* his
  féond 57 *sim* 49 58 64
  80 &c (95x); hire willan
  1455 *sim* 1472 2297* &c
  (8x); heora ordfruman 13
  sim 14 16 20 24 &c (31x)
  (see also hé, gsm & gen
  pl *and* sín poss pron)
híwan m-an (pl) *members of
  a family or household*
  nom 2781 gen hína [*cf* hí-
  gena] 2373 dat 1345 1862
  2633 acc 1489
hladan 6 *pile up, build* inf
  ád hladan *build a pyre*
  2902 *(cpd* tó-)
ge-hladan 6 *load, burden* pp
  apm synnum gehladene *"la-
  den with sins"* 1293
hlæder f-jó *"ladder," rank
  of stories (in a build-
  ing)* ap hlædræ 1675
hlæfdige f-ón *lady* gs 2275
hlæst n. *freight, burden* ns
  holmes hlæst *"sea's burden," i.e., fish* 1515
  ("pisces maris") ds 1422
  (cpd brim-hlæst *"fish")*
hláf m. *bread* as 935
hláford m. *lord* ds hláforde
  *"for his lord" (sc Abime-
  lech)* 2750 as 2315 dp hire

hláfordum *"to her mas-
  ters" (sc Abraham & Sarra)*
  2297*
hleahtor m. *laughter* as 2389
hléo(w) m-wa *protection, cover* as hléow 2443; *heaven* ds hléo 102 *(cf cpds
  in* hléow-)
hléo-mæg m. *near relative
  (i.e., one who offers or
  expects help or protec-
  tion)* gs 1007 gp hléow-
  mága þéow ("servus ser-
  vorum...fratribus") 1595
  dp hléomágum 1556 1582
hléor n. *cheek, face* as 2339
  (cpd blác- swátig- téarig-)
ge-hléotan 2 *get by lot* pt3s
  hé þæs weorc gehléat *"he
  got pain for that"* 2746
hléoðor m.n *(divine) utterance, voice* ds 1290;
  talking dp 1693
hléoðor-cwide m-ja *prophecy*
  as 2384 ap 2340
°hléoðor-stede m-i *place
  where a prophecy is de-
  livered* ds 2401
hléoðrian II *speak* pt3s
  866
hleoðo *see* hlið
hléow *see* hléo
°hléow-feðre f (pl) *protecting wings* dp 2741
°hléow-lora m-an *one lacking
  protection* ns hléo[w]lora
  [MS -r-] ...feorhberendra
  *"a living being lacking
  protection"* 1953*
°hléow-stól m. *shelter-seat,
  home* ds 2011
hlífian II *tower above, stand
  up* inf (w geseah) 2405
  hlífigean 1321 hlífigan 2878
hlihhan 6 *laugh, exult* inf 73
  prp nsm 1582 npm 2067 *(cpd* á-)
hlið n. *slope, hillside* ds
  1491* 2596; np hlioðo 1439
  hleoðo 1459 ap hleoðu 1803
  (cpd beorh-)

hlúd adj *loud* nsm 1991 asm
2409 npm 1982
hlúde adv *loudly* 73, 2909
(or isf?)
hlyn(n) m-ja *loud noise, up-
roar* ns hlyn 2061 hlynn
2548 ("clamor"); *sound,
music* as hearpan...hlyn
1080
+hnéaw adj *stingy* nsm 2824
°hnéaw-lice adv *sparingly*
hnéa[w]líce 1809
hnígan 1 *bow (to s.b.), do
homage* pt3s hnáh 2442
hof n. *temple, house, building* ds 2458 2871 as hof
hergode...metod *"the
Lord harried the struc-
ture (of the world)* 1380*
þæt rædléasne hof *(i.e.,
Hell)* 44; *of the Ark* ns
1393 ds 1489 as 1345; *of
Noe's house* ds 1569
hóh m. *heel* as him on hóh
"behind him" 1363
hold adj *friendly, loyal,
gracious* nsm 1202 2369
asm 2315 *(cpd* drihten-
[þéoden-])
holm m. *sea, water* ns 161
1431 *(the Deluge)* gs holmes hrincg 1393* holmes
hlæst 1515* as 120 ap 146
°holm-ærn *sea-house* gp holmærna mæst *(the Ark)* 1422
hólunge adv *causelessly* nales hólunge *not without
cause* 997
hond *see* hand
hord n. *hoard, treasure* ns
bréosta hord *(the soul)*
1608 ds 1439
hord-burh f-cons *rich city*
?ap 2007*
°horn-sele m-i *gabled hall*
ap 1821
hræ, hréaw n. *corpse* gs hræs
1985 as hréaw 1447
hrægl n. *covering, clothing*
gs 866 879 ds 1572 *(cpd*

frum-)
hraðe adv *quickly, soon, suddenly* 160 1474 2018 2462
[*cf* raðe]
hréaw *see* hræ
hrefn m. *raven* ds 1449 as
1442
hréoh adj *rough, stormy* nsm
1387 npn 1325
hréowan 2 *grieve (trans &
impers)* pt3s hréaw hine
swíðe *"it grieved him
greatly"* 1276
hréðe adj *fierce, cruel* nsf
2263
hreðer m.n *heart, the inner
being* ds 1568
hrínan 1 *touch, reach (w dat)*
inf hrínon 1396* pt3p 992
hrincg m. *ring, circle (the
circle of land or water
visible from a certain
place, the horizon)* as
holmes hrincg 1393* stéæpe
dúne, hrincg þæs héan
landes ("in terram visi-
onis") 2855*
°hring-mæled adj [*cf* hring-
mæl *BW 2037 (adj), 1521
1564 (subs)*] *ornamented
with rings* apn 1992
hróf m. *roof, shelter* as under hróf gefór ("went in-
to the Ark") 1360; *a high
place* ds on hrófe...héan
landes 2899; *the "roof"
of the universe, the vis-
ible heavens* gs under fæs-
tenne folca hrófes *"under
the firmament of the hea-
ven of people (i.e., vis-
ible to people)* 153 as 956
hron-rád f. *whale-road, the
sea* as 205
hróðor m. *joy, pleasure* gp
[eorðe] þe hróðra oftíhð
*"(the earth) withdraws its
pleasures from you"* 1017
hú adv *how; interrog:* 2676;
w ind in depend clause:

hú *(cont.)*
  917 [MS nu] 970 1583; *w*
  subj in depend clause: 93
hucse *see* husc
-hund *(cpd* eahta- [fíf-]
  nigon- syx- þréo-)
hund-eahtatig   num *eighty* acc
  2301 [MS lxxx]
hund-nigontig num *ninety* acc
  1147 1178 1230
hund-seofontig num *seventy*
  acc 1158 1224 1777
hund-téontig num *"100"* acc
  1131 1184 1227 1741 hun-
  téontig 2774* [1417][2346]
  [MS c],[þrittig and hund-
  téontig][MS xxx·wc·]1120*
hund-twelftig num *"120"* nom
  1263
hunger m-u *famine* ns 1815
  2278
hungri(g) adj *hungry* nsm
  hungri 1463
húru adv *indeed, certainly*
  1503 2047 1581; *at least*
  2345
hús n. *house* ds 1442 *(sc
  the Ark) (cpd* geofon-
  mere- wíte-)
+husc (hux) m. *scorn, mockery* ds hucse 2339* husce
  2384
húð f. *booty* as 2066 2113
  2150
hwá m.f, hwæt n. interr pron
  *in direct questions, who,
  what* dsn for hwon *"why,"
  "for what (purpose)"* 873
  876 asn 2175; *in depend
  clauses* nsm 2584 nsn 1271
  1834 asn 856 1291 1690
  1864 1944 2413 *(cpd* ge-)
hwǽr adv *where* 939 1003 2891
  (cpd ǽg-)
hwæt [*nt of* hwá *used as adv
  or interr*] adv *what, why*
  888 1010; interj *lo, lis-
  ten (but often not transl)*
  931 939 2643
hwæðer conj *whether, if (in*

  depend clause) 1437 1452
  2711 2231
hwæðre adv *yet, however, nevertheless* 214 955 1859
  1863 2363; nó hwæðre *not
  yet* 952 1726 nó hweðere
  1456
hwelc *see* hwilc
hweorfan 3 *to go (out or in,
  away or towards)* inf 928
  943 1014 1018 1035 1047
  1223 pt3p hwurfon 2086
  (cpd á-)
hwider interr adv *whither?*
  2271
hwíl f. *a while, a (length
  of) time* as (advbl) hwíle
  "for a moment" 2158
hwilc pron. *(in depend clauses) what kind of* nsm
  hwelc 2014 nsf hwelc 2097;
  which nsm 2848; *as subs:
  any (w gen)* nsm 1045 hwelc
  1040 *(cpd* ǽg- ge-)
hwít adj *white, shining,
  splendid* dsn 2732 apm 1821
hwonne adv *when* 1028 *("at any
  time when"),* 1265 2603
  2701; *until* 1426 1433 2278
  2573
hwópan 7 *threaten* pt3s hwéop
  2637
hwyrft m-i *course, turn* as
  hwyrft dón *"take (one's)
  course"* 1918
ge-hycgan III *think, resolve
  (an issue)* pp hæfde on án
  gehogod *"he had made up
  his mind"* 2893 *(cpd* á- wið-)
hýdan I *hide* pt3p 860
hýdig adj *thoughtful, wise* nsm
  1705 *(cpd* fæst- ofer- stíð-
  wís-)
hyge m-i *mind, spirit* ds hige
  2340 2781 as 2350 *(cf
  bréost-ge-* ofer- won-hygd, *see
  also* hige-)
hyge-géomor adj *sad of mind*
  nsm 879
hyge-léas adj *lacking wisdom,*

hyge-léas (*cont.*)
   foolish npm (subs) 51
hyge-róf adj *strong of mind,*
   brave npm 1550 higeróf
   1709
hyge-sorg f. *sorrow* as 2035
°hyge-téona m-an *intended*
   injury, wilfully inflic-
   ted injury as 1380 2732
   higetéonan 2263
°hyge-wælm m-i *agitation of*
   mind, anger ns hygewælm
   astéah [MS hyge wæl mos
   teah] *"anger mounted"*
   980* ("iratusque est")
hyht-líc adj *happy, joyous*
   nsn 1605 2076; *pleasant*
   asn 146
hylde-mæg m. *near relation*
   ns 2032 gp 1094
hyldo f (ó *or* ín) *favor,*
   kindness ns 2922 gp 2518
   ds 2824 as 1025 1592 (pl?)
hýran I *obey (w dat)* inf
   2571 pr2p 2317 subj pr2s
   1750 híre 2798* pt3s 1315
   1493 1951 2804; *belong to*
   (w play on "obey") pr3p
   Inc hýrað eall *"everything*
   belongs to you (two): e.t.
   will obey you" 205
ge-hýran I *hear (w acc)* pt3s
   2563 pt3p 861; *w depend*
   clause: pr1p 939 pt3s 2387;
   w acc & inf: pr1s ic...
   bearhtm gehýre...werod...
   habban 2408
hyrde 2696 *see* hired
hyrde m-ja *shepherd, guardian,*
   keeper ns 164 172 1007
   1067 1200 1545 2199 2317
   as 2101 np 2336
hýre adj *gentle* nsf (subs)
   1468 *(sc the dove) (cpd* un-)
hyrst f-i *ornament* ap 2191*
hyrstan I *decorate* pp asm
   956 asn 2156

I

ic 1st pers pron ns ic *I*
   867 871 881 885 &c (106x);
   ds mé *me* 869 873 874 &c
   (40x); as mé *me* 867 897
   1028 &c (17x) mec 2180;
   dual: nom wit *we two* 1904
   1911 2438 2530 2706 2882
   2883 2890 wit...bú 2258
   wyt 2531; gen uncer 1835
   1914 2883; dat unc 1902
   1904 1907 1910 1912 2225
   2437; acc unc 2255 2506;
   pl nom wé 939 995 1842
   2013 &c (10x); dat ús 1
   227 939 969 &c (12x), *re-*
   flex 1843; acc ús 997 úsic
   2677 2680 2723 (*see also*
   hé, mín, þín, þú, úre)
ícan I *increase* pt3s ícte
   1190 íecte 1122 2378 pt3p
   1065
ge-ícan I *increase* inf geí-
   cean 1132 pt3s 1162 impp
   geíceað 1514
ídel adj *empty* nsm ídel and
   unnyt 106 ("inanis et vacua")
ides f-i *woman* vs 2271 ns 896
   1054 1728 1970 2229 gs 2234
   2249 ds 1853* 2394 2764
   as 1720 1875 2638 2655 2703
   2806 np 1076 1234 2086 2607
   gp 1261 2468 dp 2502 2514
   2537 ap 1774 2157
(ge-)íecan *see* (ge-)ícan
íewan I *show, reveal* inf ýwan
   1751 pr1s 1541 pt3s 1785,
   éowde 2165 pt3p éowdon 2056
   (*cpd* æt-éowan)
ilca pron *the same* asf 1083
   asn 2708 ap 2395
in prep *in, w dat:* 1707 2551
   2835; *into, w acc:* 2540
in adv *in* in bewrigenum *"wrap-*
   ped up in" 1585*; *in, into*
   184 1577 2447 2489
in(n) n. *dwelling, house* ds

in(n) (*cont.*)
  on his inne [MS innne]
    1567
inc, incit *see* þú
incer poss pron dual *both of*
  yours, belonging to you
  two dsn 915 asf 2282 isn
  incre cynne 197
in-fléde adj-ja *full of wa-*
  ter, overflowing (hence,
  of a river, "*swift*") nsf
  232*
in-geþanc m.n *thought, mind*
  dp 2184
innan adv *on the inside* 1322
  1366; on innan *within* 909
inne adv *inside* 2466
ge-innian II *fill* pp asn 42
in-wit n. *evil* as 2416
in-wit-full adj *sinful, evil*
  nsm 948* npm 1273
°in-wit-spell n. *news of evil*
  as 2024
irnan *see* yrnan
ísern n. *iron* gs 1088

L

lác n. *gift* dp 1472; *sacri-*
  fice as 1497 1792 2844
  2859 2934 ap 975 (*cpd*
  wíte-)
lad f. *path, journey* ds 1444
  as 1841 (*cpd* from-)
lǽdan I *lead, bring* inf 1357
  1435 1649 1746 1767 1774
  1856 1911* 2130 2150 2457
  2622 2786 2871 subj pr2s
  2851* pt2s 2678 pt3s 1873
  [1929] pt3p 1877 2011 2016
  imps 1332 1489 pp nsf 2631;
  bring forth pr3p 1298
  (*cpd* á-)
ge-lǽdan I *lead, bring* pr1s
  1537 subj pr2s 1340 2534
  pt3s 1411 2538 pp nsf wó-
  cor gelǽded 1312

lǽfan I *leave, bequeath* pt3s
  1179 1195 1214
lǽnan I *grant, give* inf 2059
lǽne adj-ja *transitory, tem-*
  porary dsn 1211
lǽran I *teach, instruct, ex-*
  hort inf 1823 pr1s 2306
lǽs adv *less* þý lǽs (*conj w*
  subj) "*lest*" 1045 2146
  2505
lǽstan I *do, carry out, ful-*
  fill (a duty, promise,
  command) pt2s 2170 imps
  2306
ge-lǽstan I *do, carry out,*
  fulfill pr1s 2310 subj pr
  1s 1542 pp 2763 npn 2397
lǽtan 7 *let, allow* inf 2233
  pr1s 1349 subj pr1s 2665
  pt3s lét 955 1198 2755
  imps 2130 2168 2196 2797
  impp 2473; *have, cause (to*
  be) þú...wilt aldre lǽtan
  ...behéowan þæne [MS beheopan þære] "*will you*
  have (him) cut off from
  life?" ("num gentem...in-
  terficies?") 2644 pt3s
  1372, lét...fléogan 1438
  lǽt 2111 (*cpd* for- of-)
ge-lǽtan 7 *make over (to),*
  grant inf 2368*
láf f. *what is left, remnant,*
  survivor ns 2005 2019 ds
  1343 1549* as 1496
lago m-u *water, sea* ns 163 211
  1413 1491*
lago-flód m. *water* ds 127
°lago-síð m. *journey on water*
  gp 1343 1486
lago-stréam m. *stream of wa-*
  ter, river dp 1923; *sea*
  (currents) lagu- 2451*
land n. *land (w various con-*
  notations: earth, country,
  dry land, &c) gs 2825 2855
  2899 ds 163 1486 1892 1940
  2724 as 114 ("terram"), 203
  211 229 961 1167 1180 1196
  1236 1444 1458 1479 1651

land (*cont.*)
  1733 1750 1773 1780 1920
  2557 2689 lond 2839 [MS
  lono?] gp lande 1795* ap
  1801 (*cpd* éast- eðel-
  síd- þéod- wéa- wíd-)
land-riht n. *right to land,*
  possession of land as
  ne willað rúmor unc land-
  riht heora *"(they) do not*
  wish for us a more exten-
  sive possession of their
  land" 1911
°land-sócn f. *search for*
  land as 1665 1699
lang adj *long; of extent:*
  asm 68 asn 1308; *of time:*
  asf 1426 2546 2836 comp
  gsn lengran lífes 1841
lange adv *for a long time*
  1176 1225 longe 1180
  comp leng *any longer* 23
  170 1892 1979 2423 2593
  2656 2786 leng swá swíðor
  "more intensely the longer
  (it went on)" 989 superl
  lengest 1219
langian II *yearn, long for*
  pt3s (impers) hæleð langode...hwonne *"it caused*
  the men desire...when"
  1431
lang-sum adj *long-lasting*
  nsf 1906 asm 1757
lár f. *teaching, doctrine,*
  instruction as 2169 gp
  1943 dp 2348; *suggestion,*
  exhortation, advice gs
  1780 dp 1671 1750 2236
  2296; *skill* hence ?*cun-*
  ning, a trick 2695*
láreow m-w *teacher* ns 2484
lást m. *footstep, track;*ds *in*
  the expression (him) on
  láste = *"behind (him),"*
  "after (him)" 86 945
  1128 1167 1699 2075 *sim*
  1068 1544 1576 1622 2790
  as on lást *"behind"* 138
  1099 2450; *path* ds brýde

láste 2716* idese láste
  2249* wræccan láste *"on*
  the path of an outcast"
  i.e., in exile 2480 2823
  ap lástas...lecgan *"go a-*
  way" 1026 *sim* 2402 2538
  2851 (*cpd* wíd-)
láð adj *evil, displeasing*
  asn 926; *hateful, hostile*
  vsm 917 nsm 1021 gsn 2550
  npm 1934 apm 1269 gpm
  2085 2157
láð-líc adj *hateful, evil*
  asf (or adv?) láðlíce 910,
  931 2684
°láð-scipe m-i *misfortune* ds
  2048
láð-wende adj *evil-minded,*
  hostile nsf 2241 asm 68;
  evil npf 989
léaf n. *leaf* dp 868 878 ap
  1458
léan n. *(s.t. given in re-*
  turn) reward, payment, re-
  tribution ns 46 ds 37 2820
  as 1808 2120 2546 gp 2934
  (*cpd* ed- ond- sigor-)
léanian II *repay, requite* pr
  2s 2689
léas adj *deprived of, lacking*
  (w gen) asm 867 asf 108
  2259 asn 40 np 1706 npn 89
  (*cpd* ár- cyst- féðe- hiht-
  hyge- ræd- wær- wine- wyn-)
leccan Ii *irrigate, water* pt
  3s leohte 210 pp leoht
  1923
lecgan Ii *lay, place, put* pt
  3s legde 2338; *in expres-*
  sion lástas lecgan *"go,"*
  "depart" inf 1027 2851
  pt3s 2538 pt3p 2402 (*cpd*
  á- be-)
lég *see* líg
leng(-) *see* lang(-)
léod m. *man, prince* ns 2164
  2836
léod f. *people, nation, coun-*
  try, race gs 2075 np 1989
  gp 1656 1665 2016 2023 2098

léod *(cont.)*
    2103 2126 2157 2563 dp
    2484 2825
léodan 2 *grow, burgeon* pt3p
    ludon 989 prp líodende 182
ge-léodan 2 *grow, burgeon* pt
    3p geludon 1553
léod-burh f-cons *city, city*
    of a certain people (sc
    Sodom) ds léodbyrig 2503
léod-fruma m-an *founder of a*
    people, patriarch gs 1246
    ds 2334
°léod-geard m. *district,*
    country as 1225 1773 líod-
    geard 229
léod-mæg m. *kin (of the same*
    tribe or country) dp 2695
léod-sceaða m-an *enemy of*
    men vs 917
+léod-þéaw m-wa *practices of*
    a people, local habits
    dp 1938
léod-weard f. *rule over a*
    people, governance as
    1180* 1196
léod-weras m (pl) *men of a*
    country nom 1833
léof adj *dear, beloved* vsm
    2254 2398 2914, *absol*
    1916 2306 gsm 1113 1246
    2859 gsm (subs) 1113 1246
    2859 dsm 175 1196 1586
    asm 2589 asn (subs) 1128*
    dpmf (subs) 2763 dpm 1656
    1998 dpf 1091 superl vsm
    1328 1749; *w dat* nsm 79
    1146 2738, subs: 1183 1285
    1773 2598 2862* npm 2503
    (absol), comp nsf léofra
    2921* superl *(absol)* 2724
    (cpd un-)
léof-líc adj *dear* nsm 1713
    asn 1856
ge-léogan 2 *deceive* pt3s ge-
    léah 49 1446
leoht(e) 210 1923 *see* leccan
léoht n. *light* ns 124 129
    144 gs 2402* ds 86 as 122
    127

léoht-fruma m-an *author of*
    light, God (always in the
    phrase lífes léohtfru-
    ma(n)) ns 175 926 1410
    2423 ds 1792 as 1889
leornian II *study, consider*
    imps leorna þé seolfa
    "look into your heart"
    1916
líc n. *body, corpse, "the*
    flesh" gs 931, líces mæge
    "kinswoman according to
    the flesh" 1833 2684 ds
    177 182 1145 1565 1623
    2790 as 878 2859 gp 1281
    (cpd (adjs) driht- fréo-
    ful-fréo- gast- ge-
    ge-sélig hyht- láð léof-
    stíð- þréa- un-ár- un-ge-
    wræc- *cf* mon-líca, án-
    lícnes)
-líce advbl suffix *(cpd* ár-
    cúð- driht- earm- fæst-
    fracoð- fréo- fréond-
    from- ge- glæd- hnéaw-
    néod- ofest- un-ár-
    un-for-cúð- un-fréond-
    wurð-)
licgan 5 *lie, recline* pt3s
    læg 1566 1578 2635; *be*
    dead pr3s ligeð 2188 pt3p
    lágon 2076 *(cpd* be-)
líc-homa m-an *body, corpse*
    ds 1204 1219 *(cf* flæsc-
    homa)
°líc-hryre m-i *fall of the*
    body, death ds 1099
lícian II *to please* pt3s 131
lid n. *vehicle, ship (the Ark)*
    gs 1332 1410 ds 1479
líf n. *life* gs 122 129 144
    163 175 926 1113 1120 1281
    1410 1426 1576 1600 1792
    1841 1889 2423 2452 2763
    ds 1211 1713 2611 as 944
    950* 1073 2844, sóhte óðer
    líf *"he died"* 1627
líf-cearu f. *care of life,*
    trouble ds 878
líf-dæg m. *day(s) of life* ap

líf-dæg (*cont.*)
  910 ("cunctis diebus vitae tuae")
lífe 1916 *see* lýfan
líf-fréa m-an *lord of life,
  God* vs 868 ds 1808 as 16
líf-gedál n. *parting from
  life, death* as 2563
lifian (libban) III *to live*
  inf 917 1940 lifigan 1753
  pr2s leofast 935 pr3s
  leofað 2645 pr3p lifiað
  2258 subj pr3s lifige 1337
  lifge 2348 pt3s lifde 1146
  1175 1184 1229 2741 pt3p
  lifdon 19 prp asm lifi-
  gende 2170 np (subs) 203
  gpm (subs) 2093 dpm (subs)
  2664* (*cpd* cwic-lifigende
  cf and-lifen)
líg m. *fire, flame* ns 2417
  2550 ds 1926 2507 2858 is
  réade lége 44 as 2543 2586
lím n. *lime, pitch, mortar*
  ds eorðan líme 1322 ("bitumen")
°lim-nacod adj *with naked
  limbs, naked* nsm 1566
ge-limpan 3 *happen, touch,
  affect* pt3s gelamp 28 1567
lind f. *(lindenwood) shield*
  as 2044
°lind-croda m-an *crowding together of shields, press
  of battle* ds 1998
líod- *see* léod-
liss < líðs f-jó *joy, delight,
  serenity, mildness* liss:
  ns 1486 gs 1889 ds 1795
  2334 as 1204 1757 gp 1175
  2664 2825 dp 1949 2689
  2738 2921 | líðs: gp 945
  dp 1671 (*"for pleasure"*)
list m.f-i *art, skill* dp
  (advbl) 177 1586
líðan 1 *go, sail* hence *fly*?
  prp nsf líðend (*sc the
  dove*) 1472 (*cpd* mere-
  wæg-líðend(e))
líðe adj-ja *mild, pleasant*

asn 211 (*cpd* un- *cf* giest-
  líðnys)
líðs *see* liss
lof n. *praise, glory* as 16
  1949
loða m-an *cloak* dp 1586
longe, longsum *see* lang-
(ge)ludon *see* (ge)léodan
lufian II *to love* subj pr1p 3
lufu f-ó, lufe f-ón *love* ns
  lufu 191 1906 ds lufan
  1246 1334 as lufan 1026
  dp 1949 2738 (*cpd* fréond-
  sib-lufu)
lungre adv *quickly* 2463
lust m. *joy* dp 16, (*advbl*)
  "willingly" 1495 2241
lýfan I *allow, grant* pr1s
  lífe 1916 impp 2520
ge-lýfan I *believe* inf 2390
  pt3s 2385*
lyft m-i *air, sky* ns 1298
  as 1401
lýt indecl subs *few* acc (w
  gen) fǣgerro lýt 1852*,
  lýt fréonda 2627; adv *little, hardly* 1566
lýtel adj *little* asf 2520 isn
  lýtle werede 2093 (*cpd* un-)
lýtligan II *diminish, ebb* inf
  1413

M

má comp adv (*cf* micel) *used
  as indecl subs (w gen):
  more* as sorga þý má *"more
  sorrow because of that,"
  "sorrow the more"* 886
mæcg m-ja *man* dp 1123 (*cpd*
  gigant- here-)
mǣg m. *kinsman, blood relative*
  ns 2402 2535 2869 gs 2908
  ds 2924 as 2012 2047 2500
  2590 gp 1218 dp 1048 1069
  1317 2092 2291 (*cpd* fréo-
  héafod- hléo- hylde- léod-

mǽg (cont.)
    wine-mǽg, cneo(w)- woruld-
    ge-mágas)
mǽg f. (kins)woman vs 1827
    2731 ns 895 1053 1849
    2228 2782 (see mǽge)
mǽg-burh f-cons family, lin-
    eage ns 1695 1703 gs-burge
    1132 2222 ?gs -burh 2195*
    ds -burge 2826 as 1066
    1123
mǽge f-ón kinswoman ns 1833
    2683 (see mǽg f.)
mǽg(e)n n. strength, power
    as 1632 mægyn 52 gp 3;
    host, army ds 2095 2456
    (cpd gist- ofer-)
°mǽgen-corðor n. powerful
    army dp 1986
mǽg(e)ð f-cons maiden, woman
    ds 2798 np 2009 2749 gp
    2605 dp 1123 ap 1252 1259
    2092 (cpd heals-)
mǽgð f. a people, tribe, fam-
    ily gs 1244 1624 1763
    1939 ds 1082 1173 1644
    np 1665 gp 2617 (cpd folc-
    wer-)
mǽg-wine m-i friendly rela-
    tive ds 1661 ("proximum")
mǽl n. time, an appointed
    time gs þǽs mǽles wæs
    mearc agongan (pp) "the
    time appointed had come
    and gone" 1719
mǽlan I speak, deliver (a
    speech) pt3s 2913
°mǽl-dæg m. day (in the fu-
    ture), gs 2341; day (of dis-
    tant time) gp 1632
mǽne adj-ja mean, evilly dis-
    posed npm 52
mǽnig see monig
mǽnigo see menigo
mǽre adj-ja illustrious, fa-
    mous, well-known, notor-
    ious vsm 2145 2709 nsm
    53 (subs), 155 853 2102
    2200 nsf 1399 nsn 2568
    asf 93 asn 950* npm 2337

    apf 2009 (cpd folc- wíd-)
mǽrðu f. greatness, honor
    ds him tó mǽrðe "for their
    own honor" 1663 gp 1677
mǽst see micel
mǽðlan I speak inf 2220
mága m-an son ns 1172 as 2397;
    man ns 1082 (see mago)
magan pret-pres (5) to be
    able, have power, can;
    w inf: pr1s mæg 1829 2181
    2514 pr3s 948 2658 2661
    pr1p magon 995 2013 2525
    pr3p 1540 pr1s meahte 1457
    1691 2043 2343 (subj?),
    2380 2606 mihte 1571 pr3p
    meahton 1892 2114 2404
    2493 2747 mihton 51 subj
    pt3s mihte 2058 subj pt3p
    meahton 26 meahtan 48
mago m-u son ns 1160; man vs
    2205 2413 2675 2917
mago-rǽswa m-an leader of
    men, chief ns 1624
mago-rinc m. man, warrior ns
    2287 ds 2330 np 1714
mago-timber n. son, child ds
    2237 is mid þ́s magotimbre
    1115
mago-túdor n-cons offspring,
    child is 2766
mág-wlite (mǽg-) m-i appear-
    ance, form as 1530
man(n) see mon(n)
mán n. evil, sin gs 1271 ds
    1101 as 189
man-drihten m. lord of men,
    lord ds 2245
°mán-fǽhðu f. evil strife,
    wicked feud gs 1378*
manig see monig
manna m-an man as 2589
mán-sceaða m-an evil worker of
    harm ap 1269
°mán-scyldig adj guilty of
    sin asm mé...mánscyldigne
    1028, 1048 (subs)
máre see micel
maðelian II speak pt3s 1820
    2893

mé *see* ic

mearc f. *a limit, point (of time)* ns 1719; *border, limit (of territory)* as ymb mearce 1907 2830; *district, territory* as 2135 (*cpd* éðel- ge-word-ge-)

mec *see* ic

méd f. *reward, payment* np 2168 dp 2917

méder *see* módor

men(i)g(e)o f. *multitude, host, great number of people* ns 1663 2195 mæn-igeo 2476 mænegeo 2590 as géara mengeo 1726, géara mænego 1932 "*for many years*"

+mennen n. *handmaid* as 2260 ap 2126 (*cpd* þéow-)

meotod *see* metod

meowle f-ón *woman* ns 1172

mere m-i *sea* ns 1381

°mere-ciest f. *sea-casket, the Ark* as 1317

mere-flód m. *the waters of the sea* ds on mereflóde middum 145 ("in medio a-quarum") as 1341 (sc the Deluge)

°mere-hús n. *sea-house, the Ark* gs 1364 as 1303

mere-líðend(e) m-nd *sailor, traveller on the sea* ap 1407

mergen m-ja *morning* ns 155 (*see* morgen)

mete m-i *food* ds 1337

+metend m-nd *measuring one, God* ns 1809*

metod m. *the Lord, God* ns 121 136 193 966 1044 1320 1381 1414 1549* 1695 1947 2377 2440 2654 2749 2769 2793 2807 2872 2886 2901 2924 gs 1251 1530 2431 2908 meotodes 189 ds 52 155 1269 1714 1734 1934 1956 2347 as 999

metod-sceaft f-i *destiny, decree of fate* as metod-sceaft séon "*to die*" 1743

micel adj *big, great, much* nsm 14 1990 nsf 1101 2054 nsn 1 1639 2478 dsn 2095 asf 1317 asn 25 924 1303 ism 1965 npf 2168 dpm 1495 dpf 121 2034 2504 2673 2931 dpn 1652 1688 2455 apm 1269; advbl inst, swí-ðor micle "*very much*" 1525 1854 swíðost micle "*the most*" 2714 comp máre nsf 1313* superl mæst nsn 1422 asn 1321 asnf 1631

miclian II *increase, make great(er) (trans)* inf 2223; *grow larger (intrans)* pt3s 1243

mid prep *w dat or instr, with in company with, along with* 214 1057 1300 1046 1513 &c (52x); mid ærdæge "*at early morning*" 2577; *among* 84 2288 2707* 2837; *by means of* 157 878 913 920 &c (26x); *w acc, along with* 1210 2786 hine...mid 1734 2869; *near, among* 20 2210 2723; *between* 2255

mid adv *along with* áhóf earce ...and þá æðelo mid 1389

mid(d) adj *middle* dsm on mere-flóde middum "*in mid-sea*" 145 asm ofer midne dæg 853 ("post meridiem")

middan-geard m. *earth, the world, the place where men dwell* ns 986* 1554 gs 136 1206 1378 as 1244 1536

miht f-i *might, power* as 950 gp 1696 dp *(w sing or advbl force)* 59 98 115 151 189 218 1276 1687 2331 2809 (*cf* fore-meahtig, æl-mih-tig)

milde adj-ja *mild, merciful* nsn 2510 2758

milts f-jó *mercy, favor* as 2647

mín poss pron *my* vs 868 873
    884 2227 2784 2890 nsm
mín...fyll and feorh-
    cwealm 1101, 1901 2182 nsf
    1827 1832 2705 nsn 2397
    gsm 1008 2169 2309 2697
    dsm 1033 dsf 1753 1761
    2333 2826, *(absol)* míne
    ...wealdan 2253* dsn
    1837 asm 1541 asf 1328
    1536 1756 2170 2205 2330
    2368 2514 asn 2789 isn
    1173 vpm 2881 npm 2179
    2467 gpm 1093 1259, *(absol)*
    eaforan...ænegum mínra
    "for any sons of mine"
    2178 gpf 2126 dpm 2787
    dpf 1749 2172 dpn 894
    2142 2286 2391 2817 apm
    2474 2731 apf honda...
    míne 1095 apn 2319
mine (= myne) m-i *mind, con-
    science* ns scyldfull mine
    869* *(cpd* wíf-myne)
missére n-ja *half-year* gp
    1168 dp 1743 missárum
    2347*
ge-mittan I *to meet, come
    across* subj pr3s 1028
    pt3s 2269 pt3p 1687* 2428
mód n. *spirit, mind, heart*
    2260 gp 1085 2245 2368
    ds 63 1115 2028 2262 2375
    2605 2710 2758 2792 mód'
    1957* as 60 2168 is 1917
    dp 3; *courage, mettle* as
    53 2810 dp 1986; *pride,
    arrogance* ns 29 2237 *(cpd
    (adjs)* æwisc- án- blíðe-
    dréorig- éað- géomor-
    réðe- stíð- torht- þancol-)
módor f-r *mother* ns 1213
    2610 2766 2771 ds méder
    1048 1108* (or gen?),
    1575 as móder 194
mód-geþanc m.n *mind, thought,
    divine counsel* ds 1524
    2341 2646 -þonce 93*
°mód-gewinna m-an *conflict in*

the mind, care, anxiety
    as 2798
°mód-hete m-i *hate* as 1756
módig adj *noble-minded, brave
    (subs)* npm 1907 gpm 2831
    dpm 1850 *(cpd* til-)
mon(n), man(n) m-cons *man,
    person* ns 949 1528 1661
    1703 1956 2092 gs 986
    1399 1524 ds men 1586 np
    999 1206 1644 1802 1934
    2413 2431 gp 193 1040
    1085 1244 1251 1271 1328
    1554 1749 1677 1696 2085
    2319 ?monne 1405* dp
    1172 1213 1337 1381 1541
    1656 ap 1132 2869 *(cpd
    flot- fréo- norð- súð-
    wǽpned-)
mon-cyn(n) n-ja *mankind* gs
    1111 1631 1947 2758 2896
    2924 ds 1254 2771
mon-dréam m. *human joy* gp
    1176
ge-monian II *recall, remind*
    subj pr3s fǽhðe gemonige
    bróðorcwealmes 1029 *"who
    will remind me of the
    feud over the slaying of
    a brother?"*
monig adj *many, many a* nsm
    mon mænig *many a man* 1661
    nsn 1766 2207 nsf 1969 gs
    (absol) moniges bréac win-
    tra *"enjoyed many (of) win-
    ters"* (="lived many years")
    1230 npm 1825 1848, *(subs)*
    2291 dpm mænegum 1850, *(absol)*
    monegum 1303 apn 233
mon-líca m-an *human shape,
    statue* ns 2568
mon-rím n. *a (total) number
    of people* ns 1763 as 2749
mon-wíse f-ón *habit of men,
    custom* as 1939
morgen m. *morning* ds (loc)
    tó morgen *"at morning
    tide"* almost = *"tomorrow"*
    2440 *(cf* mergen)

+morð m.n *murder, slaying* as
   1528
morðor m.n *murder, slaying*
   as 1093
*mótan pret-pres (6) *be al-
   lowed, be able, may (w
   inf)* pr1s mót 2253 2787
   pr2s móst 2149 2259 pr1p
   móton 2531 pr3p 1824 subj
   pr2s móte 2829 subj pr3p
   móten 2522 pt3s móste 1470
   pt3p móston...hrínon 1394
   subj pt1s móste 2222
   subj pt3p mósten 1434; *w
   ellipse of inf:* pr1s 2475
   pr2s 2482
ge-munan pret-pres (6) *remem-
   ber, have in mind* pt3s
   1407 1795 2433 2587
mund f. *hand* dp 1040 1364
   1528
mund-byrd f-i *protection* ds
   1753 1947 2531 as 2710*
+ge-mund-byrdan I *protect* inf
   2475
múð m. *mouth* ds 1001; *fig:
   "door"* as merehúses múð
   (the door of the Ark) 1364
-mynd (*cpd* fréond- ge- *cf*
   gemyndig, mine)
myne *see* mine m.
myntan I *think, suppose, intend* pr3s 2183

                    N

nacod adj *naked* nsm 871;
   destitute nsm 929 (*cpd*
   lim-)
næbbe *see* habban
nædre f-ón *adder, serpent*
   ns 897 ds 903
næfre (= ne æfre) adv *never*
   1518 2092 2188 2788 næfre
   ...eft *never again* 1537
   næfre...æfre 1953*
nægled-bord n. *nail-studded*

(deck) as 1433; hence
   *ship with nail studded-
   deck (the Ark)* as 1418
næron, næs *see* wesan
nalles adv *not, not at all*
   212 1198 1809 2070 2383
   2864 nales 997 1205
nama *see* noma
nán (ne án) pron *nothing* nsn
   1400*
ne adv (neg particle) *not* 20
   169 901 &c; *most frequently
   with ac "not (this)...but
   rather..."* 18 51 72 103
   &c (62x) (*see* ac)
ne conj *neither, nor, "neither A was...nor B"* 5-6
   155-56 189-90 1457-58
   1580-81 1902-03 ne...ne...
   ne 2692-93; ór ne fóre
   *"neither (his) starting
   out nor his course"* 1006
   sceat ne scilling 2144 fréo
   ne þéowe 2747; *w positive
   force "therefore not"* 870
   948 1015 1689 1910 2114
   2329 2591 2710 2729 2786
   2860, *w negative force
   "neither"* 1007
néah adv *near* 2519 féor oððe
   néah 1029; prep w dat 1883
   néh 2051 þære tíde is néah
   geþrungen *"it presses near
   the time" (i.e., it is
   nearly time)* 2511 comp óðle
   níor *"nearer home"* 2091*;
   adj superl (advbl) æt níehstan *"at last," "finally"*
   1400*
néa-lǽcan I *draw near* pt3s
   néalǽhte 1284
néan adv *from nearby* 225 1047
nearo adj-wa *narrow, limited,
   oppressive* comp asn nearore
   944
nearo f-wó *narrow place, confinement* ds 1433
nearwian II *to become narrow,
   contract* pt3s 1570
ge-nearwian II *to make narrow,*

ge-nearwian (*cont.*)
  constrain pp nsm genearwot 2604* nsf genearwad
  921
néa-west f.m-i *companionship*
  as 2469
néh *see* néah
nellan *see* willan
nemnan I *to name* pr3p 234
  2619 pt3s 166 1235 2610
  2767 pp nsn genemned 130
  npn nemned 1547; *invoke*
  pt3s 1135 ("invocare")
néod f-i *desire, wish* as
  on néod *"with longing"*
  1443; *w instr force* néode
  sine *"of his own will"*
  854*
néod-líce adv *eagerly* 897
neorxna-wang m. *Paradise* ns
  208 gs 889 929 -wonges
  171 ds 944 neo[r]xna-
  wange 1924 -wonge 217 as
  854
néosian II *find out* inf 855
nergend m-nd (= neriend)
  savior, God, Christ ns
  140 855 903 1295 1314 1327
  1356 1367 1483 1504 1924
  2634 gs 2435 2864 ds 1285
  1497
nerian I *save, protect* inf
  nergan 2000 nergean 2511
  pt1s 1491 pt3s 1397 imps
  2504 (*cf* aldor-neru)
ge-nerian I *save, protect*
  inf generigan 2526 pt1s
  2589
nesan 5 *survive, escape
  (from)* inf 1341
ge-nesan 5 *survive, escape
  (from)* pt3s genæs 2019
néðan I *venture* inf 2060
níed f-i *need, necessity* is
  níede *"out of necessity"*
  1977 (*cpd* þeow-nýd)
°níed-wædla m-an *pauper, destitute wretch* as 929
níehstan *see* néah
nigon-hund num *"900"* acc 1141
  1154 1163 1193 1223 nigen-

hund 1125 (*cf* hund-nigontig)
niht f (cons, infl by ó-stems
  and m-a) *night* ns 2450 gs
  nihte 140 nihtes (advbl)
  2351 2634 gp 1383 1418 ap
  1349 1449 2322
°niht-feormung f. *shelter for
  the night* as 2435
niht-gerím n. *count of nights
  (i.e., years reckoned by
  the number of nights/days)*
  gs 1193* ("anni") (*cf*
  dæg-rím)
°niht-rest f-jó *a place to
  rest at night, a bed* or
  night's rest, sleep as
  sine nihtreste ofgeaf 2864
niht-scuwa m-an *cover, shadow
  of night* ds 2060
niman 4 *take* pr2s þú weg nimest *"you shall take a
  journey"* 1329 pr3p 1258
  pt2s náme 891 (*cpd* be-
  for- *cf* be-næman)
ge-niman 4 *take* pt3s genám
  1498 2930 pt3p eard gená-
  mon *"settled"* 1654 & 1737
  imps 1335; *take away* pr3s
  on genimeð 1209 pt2s ge-
  náme 2638 pt3s 2719
níor *see* néah
nis *see* wesan
níð m. *strife, warfare* gs 32
  1995; *trouble, calamity* ns
  1383 ap 38; *hatred* ns 981
  as 1757 (*cpd* orleg- spere-)
°níð-getéon n. *battle, attack*
  ds 2068
níððas m (pl) *men, human beings* np 225 gp 1135 niðþa
  1284 dp 1223 1235 ap 2210
níwe adj-ja *new* gsf 171 dsm
  217 níwan stefne *"anew,"
  "once again"* 1555 & 1886
  dsf 914 gpf 208 889*
níwian II *renew, rebuild* inf
  1881 (*"rebuild", cf. Gen.
  13.3-4)* pr3s 1258
nó hwæð(e)re *see* hwæðre
nolde *see* willan
noma m-an *name* ns 230 1078

noma *(cont.)*
1106 1713 as 1886 naman
140 ap naman 128
norðan adv *from the north*
1988
norð-dǽl m-i *northern part*
ds 32
norð-man m-cons *man from the
north* (sc the four northern kings, Genesis 14)
ns 1995 gp 2159 norðmonna
2068 dp norðmonnum 1977
nú adv *now, at this moment*
6 196 870 885 &c, nú gíet
"just yet" 1038 (29x); conj
now, since, when 1919
2176 2528
nymþe conj *except for* 21
nymðe 2134; *except* 103
1905; *unless* 880; *except
that* 1401*
nyt(t) adj-ja *useful, advan-
tageous* npmn wídland ne
wégas nytte 156 (cpd un-
woruld-)
nyttian II *make use of, enjoy (w gen)* pt3s nyttade
1598

O

oéðel-stæf *see* éðel-stæf
of prep w dat *from (a source)*
swefl of heofnum 2543, of
...neorxnawonge 217, of
handum þínum 1017 of cá-
mes cnéorisse 1637 &c;
out of (of movement) 176
178 181 182 1992 &c; *ex-
pressing the material
from which s.t. is made*
183 (79x)
ofer prep *over, above; w acc,
of relative position* fléogan...ofer héahflód 1442,
sim 1376 1451 1494 up ofer
déop wæter 2876; *w sense
of movement over or through:*

ofer caldea folc feran 1730
wadan ofer wealdas 2887,
sim 135 1393 1412 1445
1462 2875 bewlát...ofer
exle *"he looked over his
shoulder" (looked behind)*
2927; *expressing extent:*
ofer holm boren 120 ("fer-
ebatur super aquas"),
spræc þá ofer ealle 2464
ofer brád brymu 2194; *w
sense of spreading, cov-
ering, enveloping:* léoht
forð cuman ofer rúmne
grund 123, *sim* 154 213
1538; *"upon"* 143 1087; *expressing power over s.t.:*
hé bið á ríce ofer heofon-
stólas 8; *abstract:* ofer
monna gemet *"exceeding the
power of men"* 1677; *against*
ofer metodes ést 1251;
temporal, "after": 853
ofor 1349 | *w dat: "above"*
125 127 1398 2405 2406; *w
dat and acc in same sen-
tence* hwonne híe of nearwe
ofer nægledbord ofer stréam-
staðe stæppan mósten *"when
they would be able to step
out of confinement cross-
ing over the deck onto the
shore"* 1433-34
ofer-faran 6 *travel over, pass
through* pt3p oferfóran 1801
+ofer-gitan 5 *forget* pt3p
ofergéaton 2583 (*cf* on-gitan)
ofer-hygd n-i *pride, presumption* ns 29* ds 22
ofer-hygdig adj *proud, pre-
sumptuous* asn 66
ofer-mægen n. *superior strength*
gs 2117
ofest f-i *haste* dp (advbl)
ofestum 2338 2504 ofstum
2537 2662 2673 2912 2931
ofest-líce adv *with haste,
speedily, right away* 2850
ofostlíce 1316* ofstlíce
2489

of-gyfan 5 *give up, leave*
inf 1127 ofgifan 1778 pt
3s ofgeaf 1164 1194 1216
2864 pt3p ofgǽfon 85 pp
ofgifen 96 1454 imps of-
gif 1747

of-lǽtan 7 *give up, let go,
relinquish* inf 1073

of-sléan 6 *kill with a blow*
pt1s ofslóh 1093 pt3s 983
1114 pp npm ofslegene
2001 (Campbell, §736.m)

oft adv *often, frequently,
repeatedly* 1896 2462 2588
2633 oft gelóme 1539* *sim*
oft and gelóme 1670

of-téon 2 *withdraw, take a-
way* inf 953; *withhold,
deny* pr3s oftíhð 1017
(*cf* á-téon)

°of-þecgan Ii *destroy* pp npm
ofþegde 2002

of-þyrsted adj (part)*athirst
(for) (w gen)* nsm 32

óht f. *persecution, pursuit*
ns 84

óleccan I *propitiate, work
to gain favor* inf 1959

ombiht (ambiht) m. *servant*
dp 2880

ombiht-scealc m. *serving-man,
servant* dp 1870

on prep *w dat* (192x): *expressing contact with the outer surface, side or part
of a thing*: "on," "at"
tácen wege...on mé selfum
886 *sim* 2313 on lóthe...
handum grípan 2484; *ab-
stract*: on his ágenum fæder 1580 on éðle 1076 1105
1150 &c, on norðdǽle 32 on
(þǽre) stówe 2524 2900 &c,
(ge)wrecan on 59 1381 2038
2532, drihtlicu...on wlite
1850*; "on," "upon" 145
224 1124 1271 1280 &c, on
wolcnum 1538; *advbl*: on
láste "behind," "after"
86 945 1068 &c, *sim* on

swaðe 2077 2114; *expres-
sing contact with the in-
ner surface, side or part
of a thing*, "in," "within"
902 1303 1563 1890 1892
2548 &c, on innan "within"
909 adl...on æple 937 on
fléam "in flight" 2074 on
folce 2627 &c on wénum
"in expectation" 1027 &c;
"from" (w verbs of taking
and receiving): 892 933
1095 1499 2144; *temporal,
"in," "during"* on lífe 1713
&c on tíde 1283 &c on da-
gum 2366 &c on fyore (=
feore) 1184; *postpositive
and stressed*: 1052
1209 1490 2105 | *w acc*
(119x): "on," "upon" 61 62
891 1031 1918 2055 &c on
þæt...god...wylme gesealde
1924* on wæl feallan "fall
in battle" 2038* spræc...
on fǽmnan "spoke to the
woman" 2264; "to," "to-
wards" (some place) gewit
...út of earce and on eorðan bearm 1488 *sim* 1845
1877 2522 &c; "in" 1443
1736; *w verbs of seeing,
"on," "towards," "at"* 106
977 1795 1825 2397; "into"
188 202 220 883 &c, wíf on
willan 1776* 2087 on án
(asn) gehogod "was intent
on one thing" 2893 on sealt-
stánes...wurde anlícnesse
"turned into an image of
salt(stone)" 2566 on slǽpe
"asleep" 1570; *advbl*: on
fultum "as an aid" 974 1964
&c on hóh "behind" 1363*
on þanc "thankfully" 1506
&c on þweorh "perversly"
2415 on téonan "as an in-
sult," "in spite" 888, 892
on déað sléan "slay into
death" (= kill dead) 1267
on morðor ofslóh "slew mur-

on *(cont.)*
    derously" 1093 on fand-
    unga hwæðer *"to find out*
    whether" (lit.: "in a test
    whether") 1452; *temporal:*
    "at" 1083 2307 2393; *post-*
    positive and stressed 1041
    1043 1755 2291 2768 2502
on-ǽlan I *to light (a fire)*
    pp 2923 *(cf* æled)
°on-blótan 7 *to sacrifice* pt
    3s onbléot 2934
on-bregdan 3 *start (from*
    sleep) pt3s 1588
on-cweðan 5 *reply, answer*
    (w dat of pers) pt3s on-
    cwæð 865 1036 2347 2642
    2654 2911
ond *see* and
ond-léan n. *retaliation, re-*
    prisal 2266
on-drǽdan 7 *to fear (w acc*
    obj and relex dat) inf
    1037 2169 pt3p ondrédon
    861, weras him ondrédon
    ...sweng 2670*
on-drysne adj-ja *worthy of*
    reverence, inspiring awe
    nsn 2862*
on-égan I *to fear* inf [MS
    on agen] 1829*
ónettan I *to hasten, move*
    quickly pt3s 2535 2873
    pt3p 1985
on-fón 7 *to take, receive,*
    accept; w acc: pt2s an-
    fénge 875* pt3s onféng
    1212; *w dat:* inf 1938 2332
    ?919 pr3p onfóð 1759 pt3s
    1073 2376 2737 pt3p 1439
    impp onfóð 2473; *w gen:*
    inf wǽpna onfón 2040 *(cf*
    feng)
on-ginnan 3 *begin, set about,*
    do (w inf, often pleonas-
    tic) pr3s 1355 pt2s on-
    gunne 2812 pt3s ongan 30
    1117 1131 1228 1238 1316
    1412 1497 1555 1593 1822
    1898 2239 2242 2406 2635

    2717 2751 2846 2867 2902
    ongann 862 1170 2219 2860
    2888 ongon 1056 pt3p on-
    gunnon 20 77 965 995 1248
    1681 1880 imps ongyn 1302
    ongin 2283
on-gitan 5 *perceive, notice*
    hence perfective *realize,*
    know pt3s ongeat 1474 1566
    1589 2462 ongæt 1863 *(cf*
    ofer-gitan)
on-gyldan 3 *pay (for a crime),*
    be punished pt3s þæs wráðe
    ongeald *"he paid for it*
    bitterly" 1861
+on-hebban 6 *"exalt"* pt3s on-
    hóf 1634 *(cf* á-hebban)
°?on-hréodan 2 *adorn* pt3s on-
    hréad 2932* [?*or for* on-
    (h)réad, on-réodan 2 *red-*
    den with blood]
on-lúcan 2 *unlock, open* pt3s
    onléac 2753 *(cf* be-lúcan)
on-riht adj *proper* asm 167
+on-sc(e)acan 6 *shake out* pt
    3s feðera onscéoc 1471
on-secgan III *offer (a sacri-*
    fice) inf 2853 pt3s 1502
    1712 1807 1887 2843
on-sittan 5 *to fear* inf 2158
on-stellan Ii *to establish,*
    give rise to pt2s onsteal-
    dest 911 932
on-sund adj *unharmed* asm 1871
    (cf ge-sund)
on-wadan 6 *penetrate into,*
    make a way into pt3s wífa
    wlite *(nom)* onwód 1260, híe
    þæs *(advbl)* wlenco onwód
    2581
on-wæcnan 6 *awaken* pt3p on-
    wócan 940
ór n. *beginning* ns 6 ds hlynn
    ...cwealmes on óre *"the*
    outcry of death at its on-
    set" (i.e., as the fiery
    rain began to fall) 2549
    as 1006
ord n. *point* ds mid gáres orde
    1522; hence *first point of*

ord *(cont.)*
  s.t., *a beginning* ns dæges
  ...ord = *"morning"* 2877;
  the first ns ord moncynnes
  (sc Adam) 1111 as æðel-
  inga ord (sc Adam) 1278;
  wedge-shaped military for-
  mation, hence *army* gs 2004
°ord-bana m-an *original mur-*
  derer (sc Cain) or *?one*
  who slays with a point(ed
  weapon) as 1097
ord-fruma m-an *creator* as 13*
°orlæg-gífre adj *battle-*
  greedy nsm sé bið unhýre,
  orlæggífre (sc Ismael)
  2289 ("hic erit ferus
  homo")
°orleg-céap m. *battle-bar-*
  gain (= good weapon
  thrown away in battle?)
  ns 1994*
°orleg-níð m. *battle-hostil-*
  ity, warfare ns 84 915
°orleg-weorc n. *battle-work,*
  military action as 2020
or-mǽte adj-ja *measureless,*
  vast asn 2686 (*cf* un-
  mǽte)
or-wéne *(or* or-wéna *indecl?)*
  adj *without hope* nsf or-
  wéna 2224
oð prep w acc *until* 1959; *up*
  to 2208
oð conj *until* 1343; *combined*
  usually with þæt, conj
  110 899 936 974 &c (31x)
óðel *see* éðel
óðer adj *(frequently as subs)*
  another, (the) other nsm
  1690 gsm 2590 dsf óðere
  1694* asm 1662 asn féowertig daga, nihta óðer swilc
  "forty days and nights"
  (lit., "and a second iden-
  tical number of nights")
  1383 gpn óðera 1338*; óðer
  ...óðer *the one...the*
  other nsm 972/973 asf

2617/2619; *the second (of*
a series) nsm 1241; ism óð-
re síðe *"for a second time,"*
"once again" 1805 1878 2395
2630; *second* nsm 143 isn
2727; *one (of two)* asm
2610; *expressing contrast,*
an other, a different (one)
nsm 1105 gsf 1868 gsn 1118
dsm,1523 asm 927; sóhte
óðer líf *("he died")* 1627
oð þæt *see* oð
oððe conj *or* 1029 1047 2038
  2278 2315 2323 2812 2813;
  combining 3 elements:
  2500/2501
oð-þringan 3 *kill ("force*
  out" life) pr3s 1523
ówðer pron *(w gen) either*
  nsf 2468

                    P

plega m-an *play, exertion (in*
  battle), battle ns 1989
  (*cpd* hand- hearm-)
plegan 5 *to play* inf 2779

                    R

racu f. *storm, cloud* ns 1355*
rǽcan Ii *reach, extend* pt3p
  rǽhton 990
ge-rǽcan Ii *reach, arrive* pt
  3p 2557; *work (for s.t.),*
  obtain by effort inf 934
rǽd m. *counsel, (good) advice*
  as 2031 2182 2462 ds 2646;
  benefit, profit as 24 1913
  (*cpd* heard- un- *cf* tréow-
  un-rǽden)
rǽdan 7 *have disposal of s.t.,*
  possess pr3p rǽdað 2158
rǽd-fæst adj *firm in counsel,*
  wise nsm 1498

ræd-léas adj *without good,
damned* asn 44

ræran I *erect, build* inf
1681 1880 pt3s 1883 éðel-
þrym...rærde *("exalted")*
1634 pt3p 1675; *to raise,
excite, cause* inf 21
(*cpd* á-)

ge-ræsan I *to rush, attack*
pt3s 2095 (*cf* féond-ræs)

ræs-bora m-an *counsellor,
leader* ns 1811

ræswa m-an *leader, prince* np
1656 1669 2075 (*cpd* mago-)

°ranc-stræt f. *path of bold
ones, warrior-street (a
space in battle through
which warriors rush? or
which they make by cut-
ting down enemies?)* as
2112*

rand m. *a part of a shield
(rim or boss)* hence
shield ap 2049

rand-wiga m-an *shield-war-
rior* dp 2829

raðe adv *quickly, at once*
123 1584 2727 (*cf* hraðe)

réad adj *red* dsn 2406 is 44

réaf n. *covering, clothing*
as 1565

réafian II *rob, despoil* pt1s
901 (*cpd* be-)

réc m-i *smoke* as 2580 is 44

?réc(c)an Ii *to smoke, see
next word*

reccan Ii *to direct, guide*
prp asm reccendne weg
"the guiding path" 2933*
[*for* récendne wíg *"smoking altar"* ?]

reced m.n *house, hall* gs 2443
ds 1584 2463 as 2494 ap
2406 (*cpd* stéap- sund-)

recene adv *quickly, immediately* 864 1498 2230 2529

regn m. *rain* as 1372 1416 ap
213 (*cpd* wæl-)

rénian (regnian) II *prepare,
set out* pt3s rénodest 2679

reord[1] f. *voice, speech,
language* ns 1635 as 1684
ds 1484

+reord[2] f. *sustenance, food*
as 1344 (*cf* ge-reorde,
béod-gereordu)

reordian II *to talk, speak*
pt3s 2167 2674 reordade
1253

rest f-jó *rest, peace* gs 1466
ds 178 as 1428 2521; *a
place to rest* ns 1486 as
1456; *bed, nest* as 1304*
("mansiunculas"), 2230
2443 2561 (*cpd* bedd- niht-
wæl-)

restan I *to rest, sleep* pt3s
reste 1584; *to wait* imp dl
2881

réðe adj-ja *severe, angry,
horrible* nsm 1376 1383 nsn
1319 gsf 1420 npf 990 npn
2557

réðe-mód adj *wrathful, enraged*
nsm 1684 npm 47 (subs),2494

°reðran II *prepare* inf 1498*

rib n-ja *rib* as 178

ríce adj-ja *powerful* nsm 7 864
2674 se ríca (God) 148 2846

ríce n-ja *kingdom, dominion*
gs 33 1599 2336 ds 88 2149*
as 230 1607* 1790 2211*;
power, authority as 47 (*cpd*
brego- heofon- woruld-)

rídan 1 *to ride, move, float
along* pt3s rád 1392

riht adj *right, just* nsn 901
dpm 2646

riht n. *right, justice, a law-
ful thing, what is correct*
ns 2478 as 21 2247 2434;
right(s) to property ds
2153 (*cpd* land- un-)

+rihtan I *make straight, erect*
imps 1304

rihte adv *justly, correctly*
2119

rím n. *number, count, total*
ns 1166 1243 1626 2573 gs
geteled rímes *"counted by*

382

rím (*cont.*)
numbers" 1336 2346 ds
2107 geteled ríme 1263
1741 as 1161 on...rím
1704* 2223 (*cpd* cnéo(w)-
dæg- mon- niht-ge- un-)
ge-ríman I *to count* imps 2191
°rím-getæl n. *number* ns
1420 as rímgetel 2756
rinc m. *man* ns 1203 1626 1790
2927 gs 2846 ds 175 1196
1463 as 1011 vp 2881 np
1651 1895 2049 dp 1910
2434 ap 2031 2153 (*cpd*
fyrd- gum- mago-)
rodor m. *heaven, firmament*
gp 2192 rodoras 98* 148
as 114 gp 169 1253 2119
2756 rodera 1 1166 1203
2406 dp roderum 21 109
159 1243 1344 1372 1418
1681 2223 2911 (*cpd* héah-
up-)
°rodor-tungol n. *star(s) of
heaven* dp 1667
róf adj *brave, active,
strong* npm 1651 2049 2336
dpm 1910 (*cpd* dǽd- ellen-
hyge- þræc-)
rom(m) m. *ram* gs 2933 as
2927
rúm adj *broad, spacious* dsm
167 asm 123 213 asf 2112
asn 114 2557, (wk) 1790
comp asn 1651
rúm m. *space* as 1166
rúme adv *widely, extensively,
far (away)* 1428* 1456 2192
comp rúmor *"further,"
"more widely"* 1895 1910
1913; *abundantly* 1243 1372
comp 2829
°rúm-gál adj *happy because
of freedom, rejoicing in
lack of confinement* nsf
1466 (*cf* ealo-gál)
rýman I *extend, enlarge, make
abundant* inf reorde...rý-
man wille *"I will make
food abundant"* 1344 pt3s

1635
ge-rýman *extend, enlarge,
provide* inf 1304 pp nsm
1485
ryne m-i *course (of water)*
as 159 167 1416 (*cpd* forð-)

S

sǽ m-i *sea* ns 1452 2211* np
1375 ap 958 2453 [*at 222*
and 1398* MS* sǽ *is taken
as* se *masc. def. art.*, q.v.]
sǽd n. *seed* gp 1559
°sǽd-berende adj-nd *seed-
bearing* gsm 1145*
sǽ-flód m. *deluge* ns 1437
sæl n. *hall* ap salo 1881 2405
sǽl m.f-i *(a definite) time,
occasion* ns 1186 gs 2439;
good occasion, opportunity
ns 2008* gs 2525
sǽl-wong m. *fertile plain* ap
1293
sǽ-stréam m. *sea-stream, water of the sea* np 1326
sǽtan I *lie in wait for (w
gen)* inf þú scealt fiersna
sǽtan 913 ("insidiaberis
calcaneo eius")
°salwed-bord n. *a wooden deck
caulked with pitch* [*cf*
salwian *to blacken*] as 1481
°salwig-feðera adj (subs)
*dark-feathered one, the
Raven* nsm 1448
°sám-worht part adj *unfinished*
nsmf 1701
sár n. *pain* ns 28 as 75 179
924
sár adj *painful* nsn 1593 2216
superl (absol) nom 2029
sáre adv *painfully, grievously*
869* 992 1257 1275 2417
°sár-ferhð adj *sore at heart*
nsn 2246
sáwan 7 *to sow* pt3s séow 1559
sáwol f. *soul* gs sáwle 931 as

sáwol (*cont.*)
  sáula 185* sáwle 2279
  2641
sáwl-dréor m. *life's blood*
  ds 1520* ("sanguinem...
  animarum")
scǽð f. *sheath* dp 1992
sceacan 6 *hurry off* inf 135
  (*cpd* on-)
scéadan 7 *divide, separate*
  pr3s scéadeð 2210*
scead n. *shade, shadow* ap
  sceado 133; *fig.*: *cover,*
  protection ds 2740
sceadu f-wó *shadow* as sceade
  128, 874 (*w subsidiary*
  sense of "cover," "pro-
  tection") (*cpd* béam-
  heolstor-)
sceaft m. *shaft, spear* gp
  2062 (*cpd* deoreð-)
-scealc (*cpd* freoðo- ombiht-)
-sceap (*cpd* for- ge-)
scearp adj *sharp, pointed*
  npm 2064
scéat m. *region* np 2208 ap
  1534; *clothes* as 2064*
sceat(t) m. *property, goods*
  money ns sceat ne scilling
  2144 as ealles téoðan
  sceat *"the tenth part of*
  everything" 2122
sceaða m-an *evil-doer, sin-*
  ner dp 1302 (*cpd* gielp-
  léod- mán- syn-)
sceaðan *see* sceððan
scéawian II *to look at, see,*
  observe inf ne...scéawian
  979 ("non respexit"),1780
  2595 scéawigan 1540 1679
  1920 imps 2191 pt3s 206
ge-scéawian II *show, accord*
  (*honor*) inf 1581
(ge)scéod *see* (ge)sceððan
sceolde 2117 *see* scyldan
sceomi(g)an II *to be ashamed*
  (*w reflex dat*) inf ne
  þearf þé þæs eaforan
  sceomigan *"you will not*
  need to be ashamed of that

son (*gen*)" 2329 prp nsm
sceomiende (*"acting in*
  shame") 874
sceomu f. *shameful parts,*
  genitals as sceome 876 942
  1573 (*cf* un-scom-líce)
sceond f. *shame, disgrace* as
  874* 1581 2471
(ge)sceop *see* (ge)scippan
scéotend m-nd (*shooter*),
  warrior gp 2062 dp 2144
sceððan 6 *to scathe, harm (w*
  dat) pt3s scéod 997 pt3p
  scódon 1597 ppnsm sceaðen
  869*
ge-sceððan 6 *to harm* pt3s ge-
  scéod 1623*
+scilling m. *shilling, money*
  ns sceat ne scilling 2144
scíma m-an *splendor, light* ds
  128 137 (*cpd* æfen-)
scínan I *to shine* inf wlite
  wídc dǽlað...beorhte scínan 2194
scíon I *to fly, go quickly*
  pr1s þonne ic forð scío
  (*"when I die"*) 1103
scip n. *ship* ns 1417 gs 1306
  1436 as 1302 1391
-scipe (*cpd* driht- féond-
  fréond- ge-bed- láð- þeod-
  wróht-)
scippan 6 *create* pt3s scéop
  1278; *appoint as one's lot*
  (*w acc of thing and dat of*
  pers) pt3s 36 1841; *give a*
  name to (*w acc & dat*) pt
  3s 128 þám...scéop nihte
  (*gen*) naman 140; *adjudge,*
  condemn pt3s scéop...scyp-
  pend úre oferhydig cyn
  engla 65* 903
ge-scippan 6 *create, make* pt
  3s gescéop 112 219 imps
  gescype 1306 ppnsm gescea-
  pen 1529
scippend m-nd *creator, God* ns
  137 scyppend 65 206 942
  1391 ds 2740
scír adj *bright* dsm 137

scirian I *assign, ordain* inf
  2828; *cut off, separate*
  pt3s scyrede 65 (*cpd* be-
  scyrian)
scúfan II *shove, move* pt3s
  scéaf réaf of líce 1564;
  bring into being metod...
  scéaf...æfen ǽrest 136;
  further, advance (cf the
  mod. exp. "to push s.t.")
  pr3s waldend scúfeð...
  willan þínne 2813 (*cpd* á-)
sculan pret-pres (6) *must,*
  ought to, be obliged to
  (occasionally w future
  sense, "will");(w inf):
  pr1s sceal 1026 1034 2276
  2725 pr2s scealt 906 909
  913 917 919 927 932 938
  1013 1018 1020 1299 1303
  1330 1752 1837 2285 2312
  2327 2528 2659 2852 2856
  2917 pr3s sceal 198 1101
  1310 1762 2206 2252 2287
  2319 2332 2355 2391 2416
  2571 2639 pr1p sculon 1911
  pr3p 2178 2212 2327 sceolon 1341 1902 subj pr2s
  scyle 1038 pt3s sceolde
  1072 1127 1142 1222 1609
  1777 1969 pt1p sceoldon
  2707 pt3p sceoldon 1894
  1977 subj pt3s sceolde
  1594 1664 1940 subj pt1p
  sceolde 1842* þe mé mid
  sceoldon mearce healdan
  "who with me will have to
  man this territory" 2135;
  w wesan *understood:* pr1s
  1313* 1904 [*for* sceolde
  2117 see scyldan]
°scúr-boga m-an *rainbow* as
  1540 ("arcam...in nubibus")
*scyh(t)an (*or* *scyccan) I
  instigate, urge pt3s
  scyhte 898*
scyld m. *shield* gp 2062
scyldan I *to shield, protect*
  pr1s 2171 pt3s sceolde
  2117*

°scyld-frecu f. *guilty greed-*
  iness ds 898
scyld-ful(l) adj *guilty, sin-*
  *ful*nsm 869* ap (absol)
  1252 dpm 1302
scyldig adj *guilty* apm 1267
  (*cpd* mán- wom-)
°scylfe f-ón *shelf, gallery,*
  tier, story (of a build-
  ing) ap 1306
scýne adj-ja *beautiful* apf
  1252 (*cpd* ælf-scíene)
ge-scype *see* ge-scippan
scyppend *see* scippend
scyrede *see* scirian
sẽ, séo, þæt dem. pron. *a)*
  dem. adj. & def. art. *the,*
  that; b) subs. *that one,*
  he, she, that, it; b2)
  relat. *that, who, which,*
  what; b3) sẽ *(&c)* þe, relat.
  sẽ nsm (*long when used pro-*
  nominally) a) 53 125 139
  148 1008 &c sǽ 1398* se
  oéðylstæf [MS seo eðyl-]
  2225* (71x) *b1)* 950 973
  1078 1084 &c (14x) *b2)* 1029
  1235 2019 2110 2199 2201
  sǽ 222* *b3)* 1377 1994 2462
  2703 2809 2828
  séo nsf *a)* 49 135 228 233
  1141 &c (20x) *b1)* 231 1465
  1478 1922 2611 *b2)* 2119*
  þæt nsn (*usually spelled* þ
  in MS) a) 911 1256 1819
  2382 2649 2778 2891 *b1)* 979
  1058 1324 1399 1562 1592
  2102 2109 2568 2574 2815
  b2) 2129
  þæs gsm *a)* 29 1013 1288 1569
  1613 &c (15x) *b1)* for þæs
  éagum þe... *"before the eyes*
  of that one who..." 2108
  þǽre gsf *a)* 1155 1686 1704*
  1939 2320 2470 2528 *b2)* 230
  þæs gsn *a)* 1065 1719 1848
  2316 2855 2886 *b1)* semi-
  advbl *"because of that,"*
  "for that" 46 885 887 1116

se, séo, þæt (*cont.*)
    1319 &c (20x); conj *"be-*
    cause," "therefore,"
    "that" 1663* 2144 2311
    2545 2570 2693 þæs þe 77
    1469 1526 1668 2719;
    "since," "after" 1439
    2321 2770; *"as," "just*
    as" 227 1239 1723; adv
    "so much" 2581 *b2)* 2812
    b3) 1114 2266 (*"for what"*)
  þám dsm *a)* 36 51 217 881
    1062 &c þǽm 1998 (28x)
    b1) 1713 *b3)* 2844
  þǽre dsf *a)* 224 1042 1343
    1444 1644 &c (19x) *b2)*
    1428*
  þám dsn *a)* 35 988 1489 1501
    &c (13x) *b1)* 183 1303 1883
    b3) 139 2364
  þone asm *a)* 30 1234 2384
    2777 *b1)* 106 2930 þæne
    [MS þære] 221* *b2)* 2328
    2765 þæne [MS þære] 2645*
  þá asf *a)* 93 107 174 893
    1093 &c (13x) *b1)* 2230 (sc
    ides) *b2)* 165 233 1390
    1796 *b3)* þá [þe] 2630*
  þæt asn *a)* 39 44 176 211
    950 &c (32x)
  þý ism *a)* 2163 2860
  þý isn *a)* 1324 1523 2562
    2766 2932 *b1)* *"because"*
    2626 *"because of that"*
    1895; *w comp, "all the*
    more..." sorga þý má 886
    earc sceal þý máre 1313*
    þý heardra 1325 (*does 1895*
    belong here?); þý lǽs *"lest"*
    1045 2146 2505
  þon isn *b1)* emne þon gelí-
    cost...þe *"just as if"*
    1943; *advbl, w comp* þon
    wurðlícor *"the more wor-*
    thily" 2094 ǽr þon *"after*
    that," "subsequently" 1005
  þá npm *a)* 970 1596 1616
    1669 &c (11x) *b1)* 218 (sc
    éastréamas), 2426 (or adv?)
    b2) 10 1065* 1262 1354

    b3) 82 203 2077
  þá npf *a)* 1979 *b2)* 894
  þá npn *a)* 1944 2211 2556
    b2) 159 2192
  þára gpm *a)* 2609 *b1)* 1077
    þára án 1645 *b3)* 102 1531
    2016 2043 2095 þǽra [MS
    þære] þe 1522*
  þára gpf *a)* 2468 2617 ealra
    þára...gifena 2935 (or gpn
    (*b1)* ?) *b3)* 2437
  þára gpn *a)* 1338 *b3)* 1059
    1281 1298 1337 2575 2821
  þám dpm *a)* 958 1057 1552
    1632 &c (10x) *b1)* 994 1400*
    þǽm 2295 *b)* 1341
  þám dpf *a)* 1212 þǽm 2473
    b3) 1500
  þám dpn *a)* 1738 1890 2570
    b3) 152
  þá apm *a)* 1411 2031 2153
    2340 *b2)* 1647 2474 2503
    apmf *a)* ðá forman twá 194
    b1) 857*
  þá apf *a)* 883 902 *b1)* 2470
  þá apn *a)* 227 1389 *b2)* 96
    b3) 204
sealt adj *salt(y)* nsn 198
+sealt-stán m. *stone made of*
    salt gs 2566 (*"in statuam*
    salis")[*in prose = rock salt*]
searo m-wa *trick, plot* as 2679
secan Ii *to seek, look for* inf
    927 1249 1818 1843 1895
    1913 2522 2734 pr2s 873 pr
    3s miltse...séceð 2648 pt
    3s sóhte 1204 1455 1559
    (intrans), pt3p sóhton 1651
    1671 1772; *to go, return*
    (*intrans*) inf 1445 1448*,
    hortatory subj pr2s 2282;
    (*trans*) inf sécean 1732 pt
    3s sóhte óðer líf (*"he*
    died") 1627; *in the expres-*
    sion gewítan sécan &c (=
    "go" &c) *w imps* 2295, *w*
    pt3s 1461 2006 2020 2099
    2268, *w pt3p* 1966
ge-sécan Ii *to seek* inf 2516;
    to visit pr1s 2396 imps

ge-sécan (*cont.*)
  þæt land geséc 1750 ("e-
  gredere...in terram"),
  pt1s gesóhte 2698 pt2s
  2481 pt3p 1668; *perfective, "reach"* pt3p 2427
secg m-ja *man, warrior* ns
  2018 np 2067 2560 dp 2124
  (*cpd* gár-)
secgan III *say, speak; w acc:*
  inf 2014 pr1s 1915 pr3p
  1949 pt3s sægde...spell
  1090 1625 2024 2407 2668
  2934 pt3p 16 imps saga
  873 *("tell me that"); w*
  þæt-clause as obj: pr1s
  2287 pr2s sagast 878 pr
  3s 1121 2565 secgeað 1630
  2612 pt2s sægdest 2682
  pt3s 1317 2053 2623 2648
  2704 sægde...hwæt 1289
  sægde hú 1583 imps 1832;
  absol: pr3p 227 secgeað
  1723 pt3s 2302 2879; *w*
  direct speech following:
  pr1s 2393 pt3s 2246; *w*
  gen: inf þæs þú mé
  wylle...secgean 2676
  (*cpd* on-)
sefa m-an *mind, understanding* ns 1570 ds 2181 2385
segn m.n *sign, symbol (sc
  circumcision)* as 2372
+segnian II *to sign, bless
  ("to make the sign of
  the cross")* pt3s segnade
  1365 1390
*sél adj *good,* sélra *better*
  dsn 95, sélest *best* nsn
  1393 ism eorðan límes...
  þý sélestan 1324 asm 1419
  apn gold and gymcynn...
  þá sélestan 227
seld n. *house, dwelling* ap
  95 (*cpd* éðel-)
sele m-i *house* ds 1857 ap
  1881 (*cpd* horn-)
self pron *self, the same* nsm
  himself, &c self 139 1572
  1797 2342 2634 2658 2761

sylf 877 2181 2672 2853
  2857 2870 seolf 2376 selfa
  934 938 1036 &c (13x)
  sylfa 865 2403 2895 seolfa
  1091 1916 nsn þæt wíf...
  selfa 2649 gsm selfes
  "own" 59 1593 1857 1915
  2372 2793 sylfes 2922 dsm
  selfum 886 1501 2629 sylfum
  2714 asm sylfne 2429 asf
  sylfan 2393 gpm selfra 24
  1936
sellan Ii *give* inf 1978 pr1s
  1536 1757 2205 sylle 2330
  2470 pr3s seleð 1015 2809
  pr3p syllað 2726 subj pr2s
  selle 2818 pt1s sealde 1097
  pt2s 893 2180 pt3s 174 857
  957 1111 1500 2069 2122
  2310 2375 2719 2833 pt3p
  2037 2046 (*cpd* be-)
ge-sellan Ii *give* inf gesyllan
  2508 pr1s gesylle 1329 pt
  3s 883 his...feorh gesealde
  ("he died") 1739, 1925 pp
  npn on geweald geseald
  "given into (your) power"
  202 *sim* 1516
semian *see* seomian
+sencan I *immerse* inf wolde
  his sunu cwellan...fyre
  (dat) sencan *"he intended
  to kill his son, immerse
  him in the fire"* 2907*
sendan I *send, cause to go* inf
  2542 pt3s sende 67 102 1371
  1478 2424 2586 2628 pp nsf
  sended 1464 npm sende 220
  (*cpd* á- geond-)
séoc adj *sick, hurt* npm wergend...bennum séoce *("mor-
  tally wounded")* 1972
seofon(e) num *seven* acc 1139
  1349 1449 2322, absol seofone 1335
seofon-feald adj *seven-fold*
  ("septuplum") nsf 1042
  1100
seolf *see* self
seolfor n. *silver* ds seolfre

seolfor (cont.)
1769 2732 as 2720

seomian II *to hang, hover*
inf semian 109 pt3p 72

séon 5 *to see* inf gewát...
séon 2084; *to experience*
gewát...metodsceaft séon
("he died") 1743 (*cpd* be-
cf ge-syhð)

ge-séon 5 *to see, perceive,*
look at; w acc: inf 2659
pr2s gesyhst 877* pt3s
geseah 163 1292; *w acc*
& inf: pt3s 108 133 1320
1820 2579 2778 2878 2927
pt3p gesáwon 2087 2405;
w subord clause as obj:
"see," "recognize" pr3p
geséoð 2186 pt3s 1270

?séðan I *to declare true,*
affirm, ?*guarantee* pr1s
séðe 1525*

setl n. *seat, stall* ap 1304
(*cpd* éðel- héah-)

settan I *to set, place* inf
1266 2729 2831 pr1s 1756
pt3s 1044 2105 2371 2769
imps 2313; *erect* inf sele
settan 1881; *set out,*
plant pt3s 1558 2841;
to found, establish inf
1060 pt3p 1882

ge-settan I *to set up, estab-*
lish pt3s 166 1684 pp npm
gesette 10; *create* pp nsn?
gesete[d] 100; *settle,*
colonize pt3p gesetton þá
sennar...ræswan léofum
mannum *"princes settled*
S. with favorite men" 1655*
subj pt2s 94 pp nsfn 2207

sibb f-jó *peace, friendship*
ns 78 2922 ds sinc ætsomne
sibbe héoldon 1725 as 2739
(*cpd* ge-)

°sib-gebyrd f-i *natural*
(blood) relationship dp
1901 *("fratres")*

sib-lufu f (ó & ón) *natural*
love (as between kin) ds

24 as sibblufan 2516

síd adj *wide, broad* nsm 162
gsf 2553 gsn 1599 asm 134
1388 1429 1655 npn folc-
getrume...síd 1988 apm
1293 apn 28

síde adv *broadly, widely,*
extensively 10 118 1963*

síde f-ón *side, flank* ds 178

°síd-land n. *broad land, a*
spacious country ns 2207
ap 2453

°síd-wæter n. *broad water(s),*
the sea ns 100 as 1445*

sie *see* wesan

sígan 1 *to fall (of rain)* inf
1349; *sink, descend, alight*
1462

sigor m. *victory* ns 2067 gs
sigores tácen (*sc circum-*
cision) 2313 & 2322 ds 55
2017 2138 as 2809 gp 126
1036 1112 1365 1408 1770
1797 sigoro 1270* [sigor
2522 = "Segor"] (*cpd* wíg-)

sigor-léan n. *reward of vic-*
tory, prize dp 2919

sín poss pron; *masc s ref "his"*
dsm 2174 2340 dsf 1624 dsn 1049
2904 asm 984 asf 1123 1929 2655
2863, *w instr force:* néode
síne *"of his own will"* 854;
npm 2185 2487 dpm 1599 1621
1869 2025 2291 dpf 1040
1080 1364 1499 2118 2814
2907 dpn 977 2257 apm 2426
2668; *w fem sing reference,*
"her": dsm 2220 dpm 913;
w masc pl reference,
"their": dpm 1070

sinc n. *treasure* gs 1857 2101
2666 2728 ds 2405 as 1725
2017 2090

+sincan 3 *to sink, go down,*
ebb pp nsm 1437

singan 3 *to sing* pt3s sang
1983

sin-híwan m-an (pl) *married*
pair dat 958

sinnan 3 *give heed to, notice*

sinnan (*cont.*)
  pt3p sunnon 1853*
sin-nihte n. *perpetual night*
  ns synnihte 118 ("tene-
  brae") ds 109 synnihte 42
sint *see* wesan
sittan 5 *sit* inf híe...beorn
  gemitton...sittan *"they
  came upon the man (where
  he was) sitting"* 2429 pr
  3p 1907 *("dwell")*, 2160
  pt1s ic...on wénum sæt *"I
  lived in apprehension (that)"*
  2701 pt3p 2780 on swaðe
  sǽton *"remained on the
  path"* (*i.e. were left behind dead*) 2077* 2114*
  (*cpd* for- on- *cf* hám- burh-
  sittend(e))
ge-sittan 5 *sit, rest* pt3s
  gesæt 1421; *take one's
  place* inf gesittan [MS ge-
  sette] 1469*; *possess,
  occupy* pt3p gesǽton 961
síð m. *journey* ds 72* 1783
  2427 2516 is ne forsǽt hé
  þý síðe *"he did not delay
  by making a long journey
  of it"* 2860 asm 68 2267
  gp 1427 ap 905 2272; *undertaking, course of action* as 2605; *how a thing
  goes for s.b., fate* ns
  2015 as 1007 2023; *time,
  occurrence* is óðerne síðe
  1805 1878 2395 2630 (*cpd*
  earfoð- lago- wíg- *cf*
  gesíð gesíðð)
síð comp adv *later, after*
  síð and ǽr *"later and
  before"* ("before and later") 2935*
síðian II *to travel, journey,
  move* inf 154 1577 1844
  2018 2162 2869 pt3p 1734
  2009
siððan (53x) syððan (3x) adv
  *afterwards, from then (now)
  on* 71 141 988 2784* &c
  (18x); *afterwards, there-

upon, then 1056 1064 1069
  &c (15x) | conj *after,
  when* 1144 1235 1418 [1546]
  1824 2854 2883; *since, ever since* 85 90 1000 1136
  1574 &c (11x); *hereafter,
  thus, because, when* 49
  1695 2709; *until* 2439; *so
  that* 2380
°síð-werod n. *a roving army*
  np 2114
sixtig *see* syxtig
slǽp m. *sleep* ds 1570 1588
  2666 as 2642
+slaga m-an *slayer, murderer*
  ds 1525
sléan 6 *slay, kill* inf 1267
  2508 pt3s slóh 2071 imps
  sleah 2914 (*cpd* be- for-
  of-)
ge-sléan 6 *strike repeatedly,
  obtain by fighting* pt1s
  geslóh 2150
slítan 1 *to slit, tear* inf
  2088
°smið-cræftega m-an *one skilled
  in smith-work* ns 1084
  ("malleator et faber")(*cf*
  wíg-smið)
snotor adj *wise* nsm 1543 1732
?snytre adj *wise* dpf 2809*
snytro f (ó < ín) *wisdom* gs
  snytro 1084 gp snytra 2465
sófte adv *softly, deeply (of
  sleep)* 179
ge-somnian II *to assemble,
  collect, heap up* pp 46
somed adv *together, in association, also* 1209 1358 1505
  1680 1892 2279 2420 2534
  2594 2786 samod 1701
som-wist f-i *a living together, life together* as
  2282
sóna adv *at once, immediately*
  2445 2492 2566 2860 þá sóna
  "as soon as" 862, *"at once"*
  1589
sorg f. *sorrow* 2180 as 75 877*
  2245 2279 2797 gp 886 2029

sorg (*cont.*)
  dp 2197 (*cpd* cear- hyge-)
sorg-ful adj *sorrowful* comp
  asn sorgfulre 961
sóð adj *true, correct, cer-*
  tain nsm 1414 1797 (or
  noun acc?), 2793 2807 nsf
  þá wæs sóð swá ǽr sibb
  "then there was true peace
  as before" 78, sóð forð
  gán wyrd *"the event shall*
  turn out true" (i.e. as
  predicted) 2356 asm rǽd...
  sóðne 1915 asf 1837* *sim*
  2715* asn 2313 gpn 1425
  dpn 2919 apf 2376
sóð n. *truth, the truth* as
  1797 (or adj?), 2013 2385
  2390 2393; *justice* as 21
  2583
sóð-cyning m. *true-king, king*
  of righteousness, God
  ns 2636 2895 gs 1100
sóðe adv *truly, indeed* 2310
  2367
sóð-fæst adj *just, upright*
  nsm 9 1106 2654
°sóð-geléafa m-an *true be-*
  lief ds 2327*
°spǽc f-jó [*bye-form of*
  sprǽc f-jó] *speech, po-*
  wer of speech gs 1686
sparian II *spare, not use*
  pt3s féðe ne sparode (=
  "he hurried") 2536
spéd f-i *speed, haste* dp 121
  2034 2400 2668; *success,*
  good outcome ns 2386 ds
  2059 dp 2365; *strength,*
  ability, innate power ns
  3 1660 as 1084 1686 1696
  1957 dp 1366 (*cpd* fréond-
  freoðo- túddor- wuldor-)
+ge-spédan I *to speed, be*
  successful pr3s 1527
spédig adj *happy, successful,*
  powerful nsm 1783 asn 2803
  apm 1687 (*cpd* gód- un-)
spell n. *speech, story, mes-*
  sage ns 2568 as 995 1092

2407 (*cpd* gúð- in-wit-)
spell-boda m-an *messenger,*
  angel np 2496
°spere-nið m. *spear-battle,*
  battle ds 2059
spillan I *destroy* pt3s 2561
ge-spornan 3 *step on, perch*
  (of a bird) inf 1458 pt3s
  gespearn 1447
spówan 7 *to succeed, be suc-*
  cessful inf 2115 pt3s
  spéow 2811
sprǽc f-jó *speech, discourse*
  gs 2911 ds 2298 2386 2400
  as 1696 1837* 2410 2715
  is 2166; *speech together,*
  conference, discussion ds
  2034 (*cf* spǽc)
?spreca [*for* gespreca?] m-an
  counsellor ap 2668*
sprecan 5 *to speak; trans:* pr
  1s 1913 pr3p 2415 pt3s
  sprǽc 2263; *intrans or*
  absol: inf 1899 2407 2636
  2658 pr2s spry[c]st 2528*
  pt3s 918 1294 1483 1744
  2123 2138 2305 2464 2578
  2721 2795 2849 2880 pt3p
  sprǽcon 1847 2498
+sprýtan I *to sprout, spring*
  inf 995
-stæf (*cpd* éðel- hearm-)
stǽl m. *place, stead* as on
  léofes stǽl *"in place of*
  the beloved one" 1113
stǽlan I *lay a charge, prose-*
  cute, avenge inf 1352*
stǽnen adj *(made) of stone*
  asm stǽnenne 1691 *sim* 1676
  [MS stǽnnene]
stǽppan *see* steppan
°stǽð-weall m. *shore-wall,*
  sea-cliff, shore ap 1376
  (*cf* stréam-stæð)
°stán-burh f-cons *stone-city,*
  city ap stánbyrig 2214 (*cf*
  sealt-stán)
standan 6 *stand, remain, exist*
  inf 2928 pr3s 915 1542 pt3s
  stód 105 156 160 208 214

standan (*cont.*)
1397 1701 2075 2923 pt3p
stódan 87 (*cpd* for- ymb-)
ge-standan 6 *stand, remain*
pt3s gestód [1546] 2577
2899
+stán-torr m. *stone-tower*
ns 1700
staðelian (staðolian) II *to
establish, found* inf 1556
ge-staðelian II *to establish,
set up* pt3s gestaþelode
115
staðol-wang m. *a place to
establish in, homeland* ap
1912 (*cf* éðel-staðol)
°steallian II *to take place,
happen* inf forð steallian
"*take place in the future*"
2392
stéap adj *steep, high* nsf
1700 2571 ("*tall*") gsn
2558* asf 2854 2897 asn
þæt fæsten...stéape 2524
npn 1459 apf 2214 (*cpd*
weall-)
°stéap-reced m.n *high-struc-
ture* as 2840*
-stede (*cpd* burh- folc- glæd-
gléd- hléoðor-)
stefn f. *voice* ns 1494 ds
2849 2910
stefn m. *time, occasion* ds
níwan stefne *anew, once
again* 1555 1886
°ge-stefnan I *institute (by
a command)* pp asf 160
stéor f. *check, hinderance*
as 1683
stépan I *erect, build up* pt
3s 1676; *to honor, exalt*
inf 1859 2367 pr1s 2308
steppan 6 *to step, tread,
walk, go* inf 1459 stæppan
1434 pt3s stóp 1136 1467
pt3p stópon 1584
°stíep m ?*overthrow, a throw-
ing down* ds 60*
stígan 1 *to go up, rise (of
water)* pt3s stáh 1494 pt
3p stigon 1375; *rise* ?*ap-*

pear, gather (Uf ? gloud)
inf 1355 (*cpd* á-)
ge-stígan 1 *to go down, descend* pt3s gestáh 1369; *to
go up, mount* inf 2230 pr
2s 2854 pt3s gestáh 2897;
*to go up on, get on to
(a bed) (w dat)* pt3s 2250
2716
stíg-wita m-an *overseer, steward* dp 2079 (*cf* fyrn-wita)
ge-stillan I *to still, make
to cease* pp 1416
stille adv *quietly, unmov-
ingly* 2438 2910 2569*
(or adj nsm?)
stíð adj *firm, hard, strong*
asf 2497 dpn 2849
stíðe adv *severely, bitterly*
2079
stíð-ferhð adj *strong-minded,
wise, resolute, powerful*
nsm 1406 1683 stíðfrihþ
107
stíð-hýdig adj *stern-minded*
nsm (subs) 2897
+stíð-líc adj *strong, firm*
nsm 1700
stíð-mód adj *strong of mind,
wise, resolved* nsm 2425
-stól (*cpd* éðel- frum- heofon-
hléo- yrfe-)
stów f. *place, location* ds
1912 2524 [2900] as 107
160 164 1466
strǽt f. *street* ds 2438 (*cpd*
ranc-)
strang adj *strong, mighty* nsm
1376, (subs) 2900 nsn 1819
strang...wíte 2569 asf 2350
dpf 115 apm 2425
stréam m. *stream, current,
flowing water* dp 223 1406
1459 2214 (*cpd* éa- égor-
lago- sǽ- wæl-)
°stréam-stæð n. *shore* ds 1434
°stréam-weall m. *wall (confin-
ing the) water, shore* as
1494
strenge adj-ja *strong, violent*
dsm 60*

strengðo f (ó < ín) *strength*
   as 950
strúdan 2 *to plunder, ravage*
   pt3p 2006 prp nsn 2558
   (*cpd* be-)
strýnan I (w gen) *to acquire,
   amass* pt3p 970; *beget* inf
   1171 1239 stríenan 1118
   pt3s 1138 1152 1201 1233
   pt3p 1603 (*cpd* a-stríenan)
ge-strýnan I (w gen) *beget*
   pt3s 1220
[stýran] I *restrain* pt3s
   stýrde [MS styrnde] 2497*
styrne adj-ja *stern, severe,
   hard* asn 60
°suhtri(g)a m-an *nephew* ns
   2029 suhterga 1901 gs
   suhtrian 1775 ds 2071
°sulh-geweorc n. *forging of
   plows* gs 1086 ("opera æ-
   ris et ferri")
sum pron *one, a certain one
   (w partitive gen)* nom
   1034 1828 1830 2574 2701
   2909 acc 2203 su[m]ne
   1093
sund m. *sea water* ds 1429 as
   1388
°sund-reced n. *sea-house,
   the Ark* as 1335
+ge-sundrian II *divide, put
   apart, separate* pt3s 126
   141 pp nsn 162
sunne f-ón *sun* ns 2540 as
   (?ó) sunne 2439*
sunnon *see* sinnan
sunu m-u *son* vs 873 ns 1064*
   1081 1086 1106 1158 1163
   1224 1240 1286 1368 1425
   1441 1543 1589 1612 1800
   1928 2197 2301 2465 2885
   2887* as 865 1112 1171
   1187 1408 2180 2285 2327
   2344 2356 2372 2429 2500
   2608 2774 2793 2853 2858
   2906 1551 suno 1615 gp
   1139 1153 1221 1640 sunu
   1606* dp 198 1133 1245
   1300 1599 1764 ap sunu

924 1229 suna 1729
susl n. *torment* ds 42 as 75
súð adv *in a southerly direction, towards the south*
   1966 2096
súðan adv *from the south*
   1988 súðon 1975*
+súð-folc n. *southern people*
   dp 1996
°súð-mon m-cons *man of the
   south, southerner* gp
   2017 2090
svilce *see* swilce
swá *so, as:* adv *absolute:
   so, in this way, in the
   same way* 993 1493 2106
   2600 2833 swa [MS wwa]...
   þæt 1630; *w adj or adv*
   swá éaðe 48, swá ǽr ("just
   as before")* 78, 989 (*see*
   lange), 1567 2095 2414
   2515 2556; swá þéah *"nevertheless"* 2391; conj *as,
   just as* 125 161 966 1206
   1314 1332 &c (44x); *causal:*
   "*ǽs,*" "*because*" 910 1019
   1716 2359; *result:* "*so
   that*" 1669 1837; *concessive:* "*although*" 901
swǽs adj *one's own, dear* vsm
   2784 asm 2500 asf 1775
   dpm 1612
swǽsendu n-ja (pl) *a meal* dat
   æt swǽsendum sǽton "*sat
   feasting*" 2780
swát m. *blood* ds swealh...mid-
   dangeard...swáte 986
°swatig-hléor n. *a sweaty face*
   as 934*
swaðu f. *track, path* ds on
   swaðe (= *left for dead,
   dead*) 2001 2077 2114
sweart adj *black, dark* nsm
   1414 sweart líg ("*dismal
   flame*" ?) 2417 nsf 1355
   nsn 118 dsm 1449 1926 2507
   2858 asm 1441 2543 asn 109
   npm 72 1326 npn 1300 1375
   apn 134
swebban I *put to (sleep of)*

swebban (*cont.*)
  death, kill inf 2533
swefan 5 *to sleep* pt3s swæf
  179 1564
swef(y)l m. *sulpher, brimstone* ns swefyl 2417 as
  swefl 2543
swefn n. *(prophetic) dream*
  ds æfter swefne *"as it
  was foretold in the
  dream"* 2672 as 2636 2654
swég m-i *sound, melody* as
  1081 (*cpd* hilde-)
swegl n. *the sky, the heavens* gs 862 2542 2808
  2879 ds 1414 1764 2845
  as swegl 82
°swegl-bósm m. *heaven-em-
  brace, interior of hea-
  ven, heaven of heavens*
  ap 9*
swegl-cyning m. *heaven-king,
  God* as 2659
swegl-torht adj *heavenly-
  bright* ap 28 95
swelgan 3 *swallow (w dat)*
  pr3p 1301 pt3s swealh
  985 1016 1144 2559* (*cpd
  for-*)
sweltan 3 *to die* inf 938
  2659 pt3s swealt 1153 1205
sweng m-i *clash, a striking
  together* as 2694*; *a punishing stroke* as 2672 (*cpd
  wæl-* cf wíte-swing)
sweord n. *sword* gs 2858 as
  2888 2890 2906 is 947 1575
  2866 ap 1992
°sweord-berend adj-nd *one(s)
  bearing (a) sword(s)* npm
  1060
sweostor f-r *sister* ns 1832
  2624 2651 2683 2705 (*cpd
  will-ge-*)
swéot n. *troop, army* dp 1975
  (*semi-advbl, "in hosts"*)
sweotol adj *open, clear, apparent* asn 886 2807
swícan 1 *withdraw from, rebel against* pt3p swicon

1981 subj pt3s hé him
  from swice 954* (*cpd* be-)
ge-swícan 1 *depart from, give
  up (w gen)* impp 2470
swice +adj-i *false* npm and/or
  + m. *snare* ns 1996*
swilc demon pron *such* nsf
  2195 asn féowertig daga,
  nihta óðer swilc *"40 days
  and another such number
  (40) of nights"* 1383
swilce adv *also, likewise,
  in addition* 233 1339 1432
  1615 SVILCE 1637 swylce
  1082 2552; *in such a manner (as already described)*
  2348
swinsian II *resound, make melody* prp asm (uninfl)
  swinsigende swég 1081
swíðan I *give strength to,
  support (w acc & dat)* inf
  1980 2717
swíðe adv *very, exceedingly;
  w adjs:* 18, on lufan swíðe
  drihtne dýre *"in respect
  of love very dear to the
  Lord"* 1246, 1286 1469 2409;
  *w verbs, "powerfully,"
  "very much" or merely in-
  tensifying their force:*
  59 1276 1381 1570 1764 ↓888
  2022 2181 2243 2246 2385
  2414 2497 2697 2873; comp
  swíðor *"more," "rather,"
  "more strongly"* 1101 1326
  2367, leng swá swíðor 989
  swíðor micle *"much more"*
  1525 & 1854; superl swíðost micle *"even more,"
  "the most"* 2714
swíð-feorm adj *rich, well-
  supplied, self-sufficient
  (of God)* nsm 9* [MS -ferom]
  1770
swiðrian (sweðrian) II *decrease, withdraw* [*or* swíð-
  rian *increase* ?] inf 134*
swógan 7 *to move with noise,
  rush* inf 1375 prp nsn fýr

swógan (*cont.*)
...swógende fór 2559

swylce *see* swilce

swylt-dæg m. *day of death*
ds 1221

sylf *see* self

(ge)syllan *see* (ge)sellan

°symbel-wérig adj *weary from
banqueting, drunk* nsm
1564 2641

symle adv *always, continually* symle bið þý heardra
"it keeps getting harder"
1325

syn(n) f-jó *sin* gs 2470 ds
961 1042 1520 2743 as
2651 gp 2583 2642* dp
1279 1293 1925 1935 2506
2682 ap 18 2414

syndrig adj *special, peculiar* nsn 1324

synnig adj *sinful* asn 2533
gpm (subs) 2409

synnihte *see* sinnihte

syn-sceaða m-an *wicked harm-
doer, malefactor, crim-
inal (of the Fallen An-
gels)* ap 55

[syx] num *six* acc 2301 [MS vi·]

syx-hund num *"600"* acc 1368

syxtig num *sixty* acc 1186
1192 1215 sixtig 1169

T

tácen n. *token, sign, symbol* ds 2322 2326* 2377
as 885 1044 2313 (*cpd*
and-giet- freoðo-)

tǽcan Ii *to show (somebody
something)* pt3s tǽhte
2874 2886 2901

ge-tǽcan Ii *to show* pr1s
2855 pt3s getǽhte 2838;
to assign, grant pt3p
wíc getǽhton 2688

tán m. *twig, branch* dp tánum
túdre *"with offspring

branching off" (lit.:
"growing in branches")*
2362* (*cpd* hearm-)

teala adv *well, properly*
héold þæt folc teala *"well
he kept that people"* 1232
(*cpd* eall-tela)

+téam m. *offspring, family,
line* gs þæs téames...
túddor (*instr*),*"by the
offspring of that line"
(i.e., Japheth's line)*
1613 dp téamum and túdre
1535 (*cpd* here- *cf* wróht-
getéme)

°téarig-hléor adj *with teary
cheeks* nsf (subs) 2276

telga m-an *twig* np 991 dp
892 1470

tellan Ii *count on (s.t.),
believe, suppose* pt3s
tealde 1443

ge-tellan Ii *to count (numbers), to number* pp acc
getelede ríme(s) *"counted
by numbers"* 1263 1336 1741
2346

téman *see* týman

tengan I *to hasten, go with
haste* imps 2529

teoh(h)e f. *band, company* ?as
teoche 1688*; *species* gp
teohha 959

téona m-an *damage, hurt, injury, reproach, insult* as
þé on téonan *"as an insult
to you"* 885, mé on téonan
"as a reproach to me" 892,
2276 np 1896 1902 (*cpd* hyge-)

°téon-wít n. *hostility* 1912*
(*cf* níð-getéon, ed-wít)

téoða ord. num *tenth* asm ealles téoðan sceat *"every
tenth penny"("a tithe")*
2122

tíber n. *sacrifice, offering*
ns 2891 ds 2853 as 979
1502 1807 1887

?tíber m. (? *for* téafor *or* tí-
fer) ?*structure* as 135*

tíd f-i *time, hour, moment*
ns 132* 135 1141 1227 ds
1283 2510 as 1083 2393
gp on tída gehwone *"at
every hour" ("all the time")*
2307 (*cpd* æfen- dæg-)

tíd-dæg m. *time of days, life-
time* ds þá his tíddæge...
rím wæs gefylled (*i.e.,
"he came to the end of
his days," "he died"*) 1165

tíedran I *to multiply, be
prolific   (intrans)*
impp 1512 ("multiplica-
mini")

(tigða) *see* tída

ti(g)ðian II *to grant (w gen
of thing granted)* impp
tréowe and hyldo tíðiað
mé 2518

ge-tigðian II *grant a request*
pt3s getigðode 2753

til adj *good, kind* nsm 1606
asn 1810 npm 1644

tilian II *to gain by labor,
achieve with effort (w
gen of thing)* inf 1557
pt3s 972*

til-módig adj *of good heart,
virtuous* nsm 1887 2818
2167

timber *see* tíber m. 135

timbran I *build, erect* inf
1057 1692 pt3s timbrede
2841 (*cf* heofon- mago-
timber)

tíon (téon) II *produce, create* pt3s tíode 173*

tír m. *glory* gs 1512 as 2108
2377 is 58 (*cpd* æsc-)

tír-fæst adj *secure in glory,
glorious* nsm 1044

tíða adj *in the phrases*
tíða béon, tíða weorðan
"have a request granted"
nsm þú þæs tíða béo *"your
request shall be granted
concerning that"* 2362 *sim*
2529

tíðian *see* ti(g)ðian

tó prep w dat *of motion,
"to," "towards"* 936 1172
1213 1361 &c; *postpositive
and stressed* 864 1258 1865
&c, druncnum éode...tó...
(fæder) 2601 (35x); *of
speaking, "to"* 918 1012
1295 1327 &c, *postpositive
and stressed* 2167 2368 2379
2849 2912 (21x); *of pur-
pose, end "as," "for"* 37
898 955 960 1016 &c (34x);
tó godes anlícnesse *"in
God's likeness"* 1528; *of
becoming or changing (re-
lationship)* tó feorhbanan
1020 *sim* 1033, (*of form*)
tó axan and tó yslan 2555;
"from" 972 1525 1526 1557
2648; *temporal* tó wídan
aldre *"forever"* 1015, tó
dæge þissum *"on this day,"
"today"* 1031 | w gen *"up
to"* tó þæs gemearces 2886|
w acc? tó morgen *"at morn-
ing," "tomorrow"* 2440 | w
inflected inf tó dréoganne
2351

tó adv *too* 1819 2582; *also,
in addition* 1224

tó-bregdan 3 *destroy, dis-
rupt* pt3s tóbræd 1695;
awaken suddenly   (intrans)
pt3s tóbrægd 2666

+to-faran 6 *scatter, go off
in different directions*
inf geond folde bearn to-
faran *"scatter among the
sons of earth" (i.e. among
different nations)* 1664
pt3p toforan 1697

tó-géanes adv *against, in op-
position to* 1973; *towards,
in friendly anticipation of*
2432

°?tó-hládan 6 *pile on, build
aimlessly* pt3p héapum tó-
hlódon 1693*

tohte f-ón *battle* ds 914

torht adj *bright, splendid*

torht (*cont.*)
　dsn 2375 asm 1416* asf
　eorðe...torhte 1788 asn
　2891 ism 58 dpm 1470 dpn
　1807 (*cpd* géar- swegl-
　wuldor-)
torht-mód adj *of illustri-*
　ous mind nsm 1502
torn n. *anger, anguish* ns
　979 as 58 1258 2037 2424
　2510 2532
torr m. *tower* ds 1688 as 1666
　(*cpd* stán-)
tó-somne adv *together* 1982
　1988 (*cf* ǽt-somne)
tó-weard adj *coming, in store,*
　future nsn 1318 dsf 1283
tredan 5 *to tread, spurn* pr
　3s 912; *wander over, walk*
　on inf 907 pr3p 203 pt3s
　trǽde 2731
trega m-an *pain, grief* gp
　988 ap 2276 (*cpd* hell-)
tréow n-wa *tree* gs 892 1458
　1470
tréow f-ó *pact, agreement,*
　covenant: between man and
　man as 2018 ap 2037 2046;
　between man and God ns
　2118 *(w play on "faith,"*
　"loyalty"?) as 1535 ("sta-
　tuam pacutm meum vobis-
　cum") ap 2376 (*sc circum-*
　cision as seal of a cov-
　enant); *favor, grace* gs
　2518 ap 1592 (*cpd* hige-)
tréowigan II *to be true, re-*
　main loyal pr1s 2326
°tréow-rǽden(n) f-jó *agree-*
　ment, covenant as 2307
　("foedus")
trymman I *to strengthen, re-*
　fresh, encourage pr3s
　2810 pt3s 2167
tú *see* twégen
túd(d)or n (a < os) *off-*
　spring, progeny, fruit
　ns 988 gs 1313 1440 ds
　túdre 196 1305 1535 1788

2362* 2802 ds (os-stems)
　túddor...incrum 914* túd-
　dor gefylled 1613 as 1402
　gp 1336 (*cpd* mago-túdor)
°túddor-spéd f-i *abundance of*
　offspring as 2753
túddor-téonde adj-nd *bearing*
　fruit, fruitful gpf 959*
　(*cf* tíon, a- of-téon)
tungol n. *star, heavenly body*
　dp 956 ap tungel 2192 (*cpd*
　rodor-)
twá *see* twégen
ge-twǽfan I *take away* pt3s
　him sé mǽra mód getwǽfde
　"the glorious one (God)
　took bravery from them
　(the rebel angels) 53
twégen (m), twá (f), tú (n)
　num *two; adj preceding noun*
　acc masc twégen 2425 2868
　niðas twá [*for* niðas twé-
　gen ?] 2210*, nom fem twá
　1075 2466 2599 2616 acc
　fem twá 2055 nom neut tú
　1708 twá 968 acc masc &
　fem twá 194 2745 tú 2805
　acc neut twá 1338 gen masc
　twéga 2883 gen masc & fem
　twéga 1835 dat neut twǽm
　1090 acc *in combinations*
　w other numerals twá (and)
　hundtéontig 1227 1741
[twelf] num *twelve* [MS xii]
　1976 1141 (*cpd* hund-twelftig)
twig n. *twig, branch* ds 988
　as 1473
°twíh prep [*cf Goth* tweihnai]
　between mid unc twíh *"be-*
　tween us (two)" 2255 ("in-
　ter me et te")
týman I *to teem, multiply,*
　have offspring pt3p 1242
　impp týmað 1512, témað 196
　("crescite")
týnan I *annoy, provoke* pt3p
　2545
týne num *ten* acc ealra nigon-
　hund...and týne éac 1165

týne (*cont.*)
  (*cpd* fíf- [þréo-])
-týne,-týna,-tíena (suff.)

Þ

þá adv *in principal clauses,*
  "then," "thereupon" 31 34
  54 78 92 1186 1508* 1588
  2052 &c (230x); *coord* adv-
  conj, *"then...when"* 218-19
  1390-91 1402-04 1589-91,
  "when...then" 2387-89
  2778-82; conj *in subord-*
  inate clauses, "when" 41
  96 162 860 1270 1777 2375
  &c (39x), efne þá 2300;
  as causal, "because" 1482,
  sóhte géorne þá *"sought*
  eagerly as to when..."
  1560*, 2237 2925
þǽr dem adv *there* 28 180 948
  1250 &c (27x); relat adv
  where 1053 1721 1804 1846
  2706 2724 2856, *there*
  where 2569 2578 2780 2838*;
  thither, to where, wherein
  1578 1653 1799 2635; *the*
  time where, i.e. "when"
  1260*; *coord "there...*
  where" 1307*-10
þæt conj (*usually spelled* þ)
  when its clause stands as
  subject of preceding clause,
  "that," expressing the sub-
  ject alone 1 170 1228 1277
  1727 2029 2055 2217 2807;
  in a principal clause when
  the subject pron, "þæt,
  þis, hit" is already indi-
  cated 1562 1720 2479; *where*
  the þæt-clause takes the
  place of the obj 26 32 47
  99 879 &c (61x); *heading*
  consecutive clauses, "that,"
  "so that" 1457 1571 1686
  1876 2430 2456 2577 (*"un-*
  til"), 2582 2605 2899; *in*

purpose clauses, "so
that," in order that" 1586
1842 1872 2032 2360 2521;
in causal clauses, "since,"
(that)," "because" 2824
2921; *in temporal clauses*
1142 1187 2778 (*see also*
oð þæt)
þafian II *to consent to, a-*
  gree pt2s 2248
ge-þafian II *to submit to,*
  support, follow (advice)
  pt3s 2235
þanc m. *thought* is 1958; *fa-*
  vor, grace þé þanc wege
  "let him have favor with
  you" 2349; *thanks* ns 1116;
  as 2437 1934 on þanc *"with*
  thanks," "thankfully" 1506
  2444 2775 (*cpd* ge- in-ge-
  ge-þanc *"thought"* cf æf-
  þanca)
þancian II *to give thanks* pt
  3s 1888; *to show thanks,*
  requite pr2s 2690
°ge-þanc-metian II *consider,*
  examine imps 1917*
þancol-mód adj *of thoughtful*
  mind, wise, intelligent
  nsm 1705
þanon dem adv *from there,*
  thence 1966 2096 2928; *tem-*
  poral "from that time" 1061
þe indecl relat particle 30 35
  881 885 2294* [2630] (34x)
  (*see also* sé, séo, þæt, b3
  forms); *as conj* 1325 *"when-*
  ever", emne þon gelícost...
  þe *"even as if"* 1944
þéah conj (*w subj*) *"(al)though"*
  1038 þéah þe 954 1940; swá
  þéah *"nevertheless"* 2391
þeahtian II *to take counsel,*
  ponder pt3s 92*
þearf f. *need (for s.t.), w*
  gen ns 879 1591 2125; *w*
  clause 1482 2054
þearfa m-an *a needy person,*
  beggar ns 866
þearfende adj [*prp of* þearfan I]

þearfende (*cont.*)
  needy, in need of, lack-
  ing nsm 2482*
þearl adj *severe, hard* asn
  76
þéaw m-wa *custom, habit,*
  practice dp 1705 2415
  2646 ap 1531 (*cpd* freoðo-
  léod-)
+þéaw-fæst adj *of a good*
  manner of life, virtuous
  1942 2663
þeccan Ii *cover, protect,*
  hide inf 942 1573 pr1s
  868 pr2s 877 pt3s þeahte
  117 1377 þe lífes gást
  fæðmum þeahte (= "*who are*
  alive") 1282 pp nsm þeaht
  2741 nsf 1922 npm 1989
  (*cpd* be-)
°ge-þeccan Ii *to cover* pt3s
  lago hæfde,...geþeahte,
  þridda[n] éðyl 1492*
þegn m. *man, warrior, servant,*
  royal officer ns 1574 2268
  2908 np 15 1570 dp 80
  1851 1869 1908 2713 ap
  2628
þegnung f. *service* as 2444
°þell-fæsten(n) n-ja *plank-*
  fortress, the Ark ds
  1482 (*cf* wǽg-þel)
þencan Ii *think, intend* pr2s
  2892 pr3p 2438 pt3s þóhte
  1274
ge-þencan Ii *think about,*
  consider imps 1906
þenden conj *while, as long*
  as 908 915 935 1200 1491
  1542 1952 2170 2258 2741
þéod f. *people, nation* ns
  2294 np 1242 1265 1908
  2616 gp 1647 ds 1318 (*cpd*
  gum- wer- *cf* un-ge-þéode
  ell-þéodig)
þéod-cyning m. *a king of a*
  (*gentile*) *nation* ns 1869
  (*sc Pharaoh*) np 1965 (*sc*
  the Northern kings)
þéoden m. *lord, king* vs 2145

2709 ns 2628 2674; *of*
  God vs 1035 2549 2643 ns
  80 92 139 853 864 1116
  1202 2304 ds 1888 as 15
[þéoden-hold] adj (*ones*) *lo-*
  yal to a lord gpm (subs?)
  wigena...æscberendra...
  þéodenholdra [MS þeon den
  holdra] 2042
°þéod-here m-ja *army of a na-*
  tion (= *merely* "*large*
  army" ?) gp þéodherga 2161
þéod-land n. *an inhabited*
  land, country, district
  ns 1766 gp 2213
þéod-scipe m-i *a people, na-*
  tion ds 1942 as (or dat?)
  231*
þéon 1 *to thrive, prosper,*
  grow pt3s ðáh 2301, þág
  2772
ge-þéon 1-2 *thrive, prosper,*
  grow pt3p geþungon 1714
þéostru *see* þ́stru
þéow m-wa *servant* ns 1595
  2431 (*cpd* weorc-)
+þéow adj-wa *servile, in an*
  enslaved condition nsf 2747*
  gpmf 2754
þéow-dóm m *servitude* as 2242
  2265
°þéow-mennen n. *handmaid, fe-*
  male slave ns 2248 as 2235
þéow-nýd f-i *enslavement* as
  2030
þes, þéos, þis dem pron *this,*
  these; as pure demonstra-
  tive nsn þis 1787 2478; *as*
  adj nsm þes 104 1554 þæs
  986* nsf þéos 110 nsn þis
  2699 gsf þisse 2141 gsn
  þisses 1120 1600 2452 dsm
  þissum 1031 dsf þisse 1912
  2408 2438 2479 2681 2688
  2708 ðisse 2734 2830 þysse
  2501 dsn þyssum 1211 2711
  þissum 2724 asf þás 219
  1126 1194 1541 1841 2393
  2480 2678 2703 2823 asn
  þis 114 isn þ́s 1115 gpm

þes, þéos, þis (cont.)
  þissa 2151 þisse 1219*
  dpm þyssum 2505 dpf þissum 2502 2825 dpn 2357
  2501 2882 apn þás 2395
  2508
þicce adv *thickly, frequently*
  féonda feorh féollon ðicce
  "lives of enemies perished
  in great numbers" 2065
  sim þicce gefylled 2161
þicgean 5 *accept (food), eat*
  impp 1519
ge-þicgean 5 *take, accept*
  pt1s geþah 885
(þigen) *see* þín f.
þín poss pron *thy, your* nsm
  1900 ðín 2730 nsf 2683
  nsn 2189 2190 2260 2311
  2922 gsm 2145 gsf 1763
  2195 2222 dsm 1019 2363
  dsf 1035 2328 2799 dsn 1788
  2316 2360 2857 asm 935 1012
  1825 2294 2312 2352 2815
  2917 ðínne 2853 asf 933
  1025 1746 2188 2641 asn 877
  912 2168 2196 2259 2398 2504
  2511 2533 2644 2663 2810
  2852 2914 isn 1766 1917,
  fromcynne...þíne 2206 npm
  2212 npf 2168 gpf 922 dpm
  1300 2224 2713 2856 dpf 1010
  1017 2349 dpn 906 apm 910
  1333, þíne? 2482* (= þigen?
  see next word) apf þíne 2677
  2677 þína 2709 2819
?þín (þigen) f. *food* gs þíne
  (= þigne) þearfende *"being*
  in need of food" (or is
  þíne poss pron? *or to be*
  emended to wine?) 2482*
þincan Ii *to seem, appear*
  (impers, w dat of person)
  pr3s 2896 pt3s þúhte
  169 1850 pt3p þúhton
  2430; *w clause* pr3s 2478
ge-þincan Ii *to seem, appear*
  (impers, w dat of
  person) pt3p him wlite-

beorhte wongas geþuhton
  "the fields seemed beau-
  tiful to him" 1804
þing n. *thing, condition* ns
  þæt wæs þréalíc þing 1318
þingian II *speak, make a*
  speech pt3s 1009
þolian II *to suffer, endure,*
  put up with, experience
  inf 2242 2265 pt3s 2030
þonne adv *then* 1826 2858;
  conj *when* 1103 1207 1355
  1540 1833 2190 2395 2790
  ðonne 1300; *after compar-*
  atives, "than" 963 2922
-þracu (*cpd* æsc- gúð- hyld-
  wǽpen-)
°þræc-róf adj *bold in res-*
  pect of violence, val-
  iant apm 2030
þrág f. *time, period of time,*
  the condition of things
  at a given time gs rímge-
  tǽl reðre þráge 1420; *in*
  advbl expressions: as
  þráge síððan *"after a time"*
  1217 1811, þæs ðráge bád
  "for a time (he) experi-
  enced that" 2775, lange
  þráge 1426 2546 2836
þréa f-wó *punishment, inflic-*
  tion as 2265 (*cpd* bróh-
  cwealm- héah- wǽg-)
ge-þréan III *afflict* pp nsm
  geðréad 2669 asm geðréadne
  1865*
þréa-líc adj *terrible* nsn 1318
þréat m. *host, troop* np 13
  (*cpd* wǽg-)
þréo *see* þrí
þréo-hund num *"300"* gen þréo-
  hund 1308 acc bréac blǽd-
  daga...þréohund wintra *"he*
  enjoyed days of glory for
  300 years" 1202 *sim* 1600,
  [þréo]hund [MS iii·hund]
  1217, 2042 [MS ccc·]
[þréo-týne] num *thirteen* acc
  2304 [MS xiii]

þrí, þréo, þrý num *three* npm
þrý 2033 2045 npn þréo
2213 dpm þrím 1545 apm
þrý 1334

þridda ord num, adj *(the)*
third nsm 155 1242 1552
2869 nsf 231 gsm 2876 asm
þridda[n] 1492* 2027 asf
1477

þringan 3 *to press, force*
(a passage), move hur-
redly inf 1373 pt3s
þrang 139 *(cpd* oð- *)*

ge-þringan 3 *to press, move*
pp (impersonal) þǽre tíde
is néah geþrungen *"it*
has moved near the time"
2511

þríste adj-i *bold, reckless,*
crazy npm 1272 2583 npn
1935

þríste adv *boldly, impudently*
2242

þrittig num *thirty* gen 1308
acc [1120] [1126] [MS xxx]

þrówian II *to suffer* inf þró-
wigean 2424 pt3p 75; *to*
suffer as repayment, a-
tone inf þú scealt...
þrówian þínra dǽda ge-
dwild *"thou shalt expi-*
ate the error of thy
deeds" (B-T) 921

þrý *see* þrí

°þrýdig *(for* þrýðig *?)* adj
powerful npm (subs) módum
þrýdge *"(ones) strong in*
courage" 1986* *(cf* hige-
þrýð)

þrym(m) m-ja [*there is prob-*
ably play between the
various senses in most
instances] *host, army,*
multitude is 1965 dp 8;
strength, power ns 70 ds
27 ap 2110; *glory as* þrym
...þisses lífes 2452* np
80; *advbl* ds 1492* *("migh-*
tily") *(cpd* éðel- *)*

þrym-fæst adj *glorious* npm

15; *powerful, mighty* npf
1908 2616

þrýðig *see* þrýdig

þú pers pron *thou, you* nom
874 916 1010 &c (113x,
incl ðú 6x); dat þé 879
881 885 1015 &c (74x *incl*
ðé 10x); acc þé 911 919
1346 1758 &c (21x *incl*
ðé 4x), þec 2272; nom
dual git 2516 2523; dat
dual inc 198 201 205 894;
acc dual incit 2733 2881;
nom pl gé 1518 1538 2317
2326 2417 gen pl éower
"of you," "belonging to
you" 1334; dat pl éow 1514
1535 2326 2470 2475 acc pl
éow 2467

*þurfan pret-pres (3), w inf,
have need, have good cause,
in neg clauses: pr1s þearf
1023 2177 pr2s þearft 1037
2157 2169 2172 pr3s þearf
2329 2729 ðearf 1523 pt3p
þorfton 72

þurh prep w acc *through; ex-*
pressing state or condi-
tion þurh slǽp oncwǽð 2642
sim 2636 2654, þurh wóp
and héaf on woruld cennan
þurh sár micel 923-24 ("in
dolore paries filios");
expressing means, "by means
of" 11 111 130 149 158 899
998 1362 1696 1759 1771
1796 1809 2121 2198 2233
2302 2324 2476 2685 2776
2918, *shading into expres-*
sion of cause, "through,"
"because of" 1078 1084 1085
1127 1148 [MS þur], 1957
2218 2469 2644

þus adv *thus, so* 2176 2679

+þweorh adj *crooked* asn *(advbl)*
on þweorh *"evilly"* 2415

þý lǽs *see* lǽs

(þyncan) *see* þincan

þýstre adj-ja *dark* nsn 139

þýstro f (ó < ín) *darkness* is

þȳstro (*cont.*)
  2452 dp 76 þéostrum 127
  144

U

+un-árlíc adj *shameful* asn
  1092
°un-árlíce adv *shamefully,
  dishonorably* 1519 2252
un-blíðe adj-ja *unkind, angry* nsf 2261
unc, uncer *see* ic
uncer poss pron, dual *of us
  both, our* asf 2306
un-cúð adj *unknown, strange*
  npm 1847 gpm 2699 ap 2735
under prep *under; w dat (position)* 109 151 161 916
  2060 under deoreðsceaftum
  1984, under weallum (=
  "in one's house" ?) 2411
  & 2420 (28x, *incl* 3x *postpositive*); *w acc (relative
  motion)* 91 1360 1369 2064*
  under burhlocan *"into
  the city"* 2539, in under
  edoras 2489 in undor edoras 2447 *"in (their)
  houses"*, under bæc beseah
  "she looked behind" 2564,
  úsic under *"into our cus-
  tody"* 2677 (16x *incl* 1x
  postpositive); *w acc in
  expressions of extent or
  volume* under roderas feng
  98* under rodera rúm 1166
°un-fǽg(e)re adv *not plea-
  santly, horribly* 1273
  2063
+un-féor adv *not far, near*
  2083 2928
°un-forcúðlíce adv *nobly*
  1715*
+un-fremu f-i *harm, harmful
  thing* as 893 (*sc the forbidden fruit*)
°un-fréondlíce adj *in an un-

friendly manner 2690
°un-fricgende adj [prp of
  fricgan 5] *unquestioning*
  dsm (absol) mé...unfric-
  gendum *"to me who had not
  asked"* 2650
un-gelíc adj *unlike, dissimilar, diverse* asf reorde
  ...ungelíce 1685
°un-geþéode adj *disunited,
  separated from one's own
  people* npm 1698
°un-gífre adj *harmful* [*cf*
  gifre *useful*] or *very
  greedy* [*cf* gífre *greedy*]
  asn 2472*
un-hýre adj-ja *not gentle,
  fierce* nsm 2289 (*"ferus"*)
un-léof adj *not dear, hateful* npm 2454 apm 1268
+un-líðe adj-ja *not gentle,
  harsh, severe* nsf 937
un-lýtel adj *not little,
  great, long* nsm 1614 2552
  asn 2407
un-mǽte adj-ja *immense* nsf
  2294 (*cf* or-mǽte)
unnan pret-pres (3) *grant (w
  gen)* pr3s an 1840 2915*;
  *wish (w gen of thing &
  dat of person)* pt3s úðe
  2693
un-nýt adj *unused, idle* nsm
  grund stód...ídel and un-
  nýt 106 (*cf.* Gen. 1.2,
  *"terra autem erat inanis
  et vacua"*)
un-rǽd m. *evil counsel, wicked plan* gs 1682 as 30;
  harm, disadvantage as 1937
°un-rǽden f-jó *evil action*
  as 982
un-riht n. *injustice, evil* ds
  geseah unrihte eorðan fulle
  *"he saw the earth (to be)
  filled with injustice"* 1292
un-rím n. *a countless number*
  ns 1647 folc' unrím 2615*
°un-scomlíce adv *shamelessly*
  2461

+un-spédig adj *poor, barren*
asm comp 962

un-weaxen adj [pp of weaxan
7] *not fully grown, young*
asn 2872

un-wemme adj-ja *spotless,
pure, unviolated, vir-
gin* npf 2466

°un-wundod adj [pp of wun-
dian II] *unwounded* nsm
(or acc?) 183*

úp, upp adv *up, upwards* 149
1375 1419 1667 1675 1681
1692 2440 2540 2579 2856
2876 2898, upp 1405; on
sigor up 2522 *(cf héa-
burh 2519)*

úp-rodor m. *the heaven above,
the firmament* ns 99

úre poss pron *our* nsm 40 65
92 137 140 147 206 2827

ús, úsic *see* ic

ússer poss pron *our* nsm 855
903 942 1116 1295 1327
1367 1391 1483 1504 1771
1839 2483 2587 2634 2762
dsmf ússum fæder and mé-
der 1575 dsn 2129

út adv *out* 1435 1442 1488
2012 2457 2463

útan adv *from (with)out, on
the outside* 1322 úton 229
(cf be-útan prep, ymb-
útan adv)

W

wadan 6 *walk, go* inf 2887
(cpd on-)

wæcnan 6 *(wake), be born*
pt3s wóc 1637 1646 2764
subj pt3s wóce 1158 pt3p
wócon 2186 wócan 1061
1064 1233 pp nsm wæcned
2394 *(cpd* á- on-)

wæd f. *clothing* gp 867 dp
941

wæg m. *wave, sea* as 1462 is

1379 np wǽgas [MS wę̄gas]
119

°wǽg-bord n. *wave-board,
ship, the Ark* as 1340

wǽg-líðend m-nd *wave-travel-
ler, sea-farer* np 1432 dp
ne móston wǽglíðendum...
hrínon (inf) 1395*

wǽg-þel n. *wave-plank, a ship,
the Ark* ds 1446 1496 as
1358 *(cf* þell-fæsten)

°wǽg-þréa f-wó (indecl) *wat-
er-punishment, the Deluge*
ds wǽgþréa *"from the De-
luge"* 1490*

°wǽg-þréat m. *wave army, the
Deluge* ds 1352

wæl n. *a fallen warrior (collectively, "the slain")* ds
(? uninfl locative) wæl
2161* as on wæl *"in the
slaughter"* 2038* *(cpd* ecg-)

wæl-bedd n-ja *bed of a murdered person (= condition
of being dead ?) or simply
= "grave"* ? as 1011

°wæl-clomm m. *lit.: grip of
slaughter, = "fatal bond-
age" i.e., servitude, in
which one is liable to be
slain* dp 2128

wæl-dréor m. *blood of a murdered person* ds 1016 ("sanguinem"), as 1098

wæl-fyll m-i *a slaying* as
1527*; *destruction* gs
2565

wæl-gár m. *deadly spear* gp
1990

wæl-grim(m) adj *slaughter-
cruel, cruel, destructive*
nsm 1384 1816 asm 2580 asf
996

°wæl-here m-ja *destructive
army* np wráðe (wǽron) wæl-
herigas 1983

°wæl-regn m. *destroying rain
(sc at the Deluge)* as
wællregn 1350 ("pluam")

wæl-rest f-jó *resting place*

wæl-rest (*cont.*)
    for one slain, grave as
    ǽrðon forð cure...wælreste
    "ere he did choose a grave,"
    (= *before he died*) 1643
wæl-stów f. *place of slaugh-
    ter* ds 2595 (sc Sodom af-
    ter its destruction);
    battle-field as 2005
°wæl-stréamas m (pl) *deadly
    streams (the Deluge)* nom
    1301
°wæl-sweng m-i *deadly blow*
    ds 987
wǽpen n. *weapon* gs 1830 gp
    2005 2040 dp 1527 2111
wǽpen-þracu f. *force of arms*
    ds wǽpenþræce 2292
°wǽpned part. adj *male* as
    (subs) wíf and wǽpned 195
    sim 2746
wǽpned-cynn n-ja *male sex*
    gs 2314 2321 2374
wǽpned-mann m-cons *man, the
    male* 919 ("viri")
wǽr f. *covenant, pledge,
    promise* gs 2374 as 1329
    1542 2204 2309 2368 2833
    ap 2819 *("assurances")*
wǽr-fæst adj *true to a pro-
    mise, faithful, trust-
    worthy* nsm 1320 1549 1740
    2026 2587 2598 2901 1819
    (subs), asm wǽrfæsne 1011*
    asn mód...wǽrfæst 2169 gpm
    1897
wǽr-léas adj *faithless* asn 67
wǽr-loga m-an *faith-breaker,
    one who is false to a pro-
    mise* gp wǽrlogona 2411 dp
    2532 wǽrlogan 2503 wǽr-
    logan 36 ap 1266
wæstm m.f *growth, produce,
    fruit of the earth* np
    wæstma 2555 ds 214 1339
    1789 1922 ap wæstmas 1015
    1560; *a fruit, fruit* ludon
    ...réðe wæstme 990 ap
    wæstme 894; *progeny, off-
    spring* dp 2803 ap wæstmas

960; *abundance, prosper-
    ity* as wæstme 1758 ap
    wæstma 207 dp 1948
wæter n. *water* ns 100 152 198
    gs 1395 ds ánum...wætre
    wlitebeorhtum 220 1409
    as 1331 1445 1451 1538
    2876 np 158 1300 1325 2213
    gp 1549 dp 152 1377 1460
    1922 (*cpd* síd-)
waldend m-nd *wielder, ruler
    king (of God)* vs 2175 ns
    49 147 1043 1112 2201 2578
    &c (26x), gs 2381 2670 ds
    1791 1884 2598 2804 2842
    2862*; *of persons* vs hæl-
    eða waldend (sc rex Sodo-
    morum) 2139 ns 2635 (sc
    Abimelech) as 2295 þinne
    ...waldend (sc Sarra, "dom-
    inam tuam") (*cf* al-walda)
wan(n) *see* won(n)
wana adj (indecl) *wanting,
    lacking, destitute* nsf
    wana wilna gehwilces 2274
wé *see* ic
wéa m-an *woe, sorrow, unhap-
    piness* ns 987 gs 1027
    2693 ds 1755 as 74 876
    1819 2274 gp 2170 ap 2420
°?wéa-land (*or* wea(l)-land)
    n. *foreign land* (= weal(l)-
    land)? hence *hostile land*,
    or wéa-land ?*evil nation*
    [*or does MS* wea land *imply*
    *wealhend m-nd "foreign-
    er"* ?] dp 2707*
weald m. *wooded country* ap
    wádan ofer wealdas 2887
wealdan 7 *rule, have control
    over, possess (w gen or
    instr)* inf 2253* 2787 pt3s
    wéold 1377 1629 2005 (*cf*
    ge-weald n.)
weall m. *wall, walled structure*
    as 1676 1691 dp under weal-
    lum *"in their houses"* 2411
    2420 (*cpd* stæð- stréam-)
weallan 7 *to well, flow, surge*
    prp asn 2544

weall-fæsten(n) n-ja *fortress, city* gp 1058
°weall-stéap adj *high as regards walls, having high
walls* asf 2404 apn 1803
weard m. *guard, watcher,
protector, lord* vs 2783
(sc Abraham) ns 1157 (sc
Cainan) ns or as 863* (sc
God or Adam?); *of angels*
ns 949 dp 12 ap 41; *of
God* ns 144 163 941 1426
1484 1744 1770 2073 2667
2758 [MS wearð] 2896 2920
gs 2866 ds 169 as 1 2119
(*cpd* brego- forð- heofon-
léod- yrfe-)
-weard adj (*cpd* and- forð-
heonon- tó-)
weardian II *to guard, watch*
pt3s 1128
weaxan 7 *grow, grow up, increase, be produced* inf
45 1902 2755 pt3s wéox
1702 2301 2772 pt3p wéoxon
80 impp wexað 196 weaxað
1532 prp nsf 1660 (*cf*
un-weaxen)
wecc(e)an Ii *arouse, excite,
instigate* inf weccean 31;
animate, give life to pr
3s 204 pp nsf séo wæs wæ-
trum weaht *("refreshed"
cf* "inrigabatur") 1922;
kindle (a fire) inf 2902
(*cpd* á-)
wed(d) n-ja *ransom, tribute,*
ds 2070; *promise, guarantee* ds 2311
wefan 5 *weave, arrange, put
together* inf anræd...
wefan 31
weg m. *way, road, direction*
as weg nimest *(= "go")*
1329 np wídlond ne wegas
(i.e. dry land) 156 ap
1697 2875 ?as reccendne
weg *"guiding path"* [*but
MS form may stand for
next word*] (*cpd* fold-

forð- á-weg *(adv)*)
?wég (= wíg, wéoh?) m. *(idol)*
? *altar* as réccendne wég
smoking altar 2933* (*see
preceding word*)
wegan 5 *carry, bear, have*
inf 934 2044 2372* [MS
wesan], 2097* (or pp?),
pr1s 885 subj pr3s 2349
pt3s higeþrýðe wæg *"be-
haved with arrogance"* 2240
pt3p wægon 2049
wél adv *(always stressed)
well* 131 1749 2043 2306
2486
wela m-an *wealth, goods, a-
bundance* ns 1603 gs 971
as 1931 2179 (*cpd* botl-
eorð- grund-)
welig adj *rich (in s.t.)* npn
setl wuldorspédum welig 87
ge-wemman I *to spot, spoil,
defile* pt1s 1094 pp nsm
gewemmed 71 apm gewemde
1294 (*cf* un-wemme)
wén f-i *hope, expectation* ns
49 1446 dp 1027 2701 (*cf*
or-wéne)
wéna m-an *anticipation* ds 1985
wénan I *to look for, expect,
hope* inf 1023; *to suppose,
think* pr3p 1826 pt3s 2342*
wendan I *to turn, go, go a-
way* pr3s eft wendeð sǽ
*"the sea shall run along
in a returning direction
(i.e. as a boundary)* 2211*
imps 919 (*cf* láð-wende)
wéo-bedd *see* wí-bedd
weorc n. *work, project, labor,
deed* gs 1689 (sc the tower
of Babel) ds 37 1043 1672
as 1679 gp 207; *pain, torment* as 2746; weorce adv
(instr. s.) *in the expression* weorc wesan: *painful*
weorce on móde 2028 2792
(*cpd* and- suhl-ge-weorc,
ge-wyrc)
weorc-þéow m-wa *or* f-ó *worker,*

(male) slave masc: ap
weorc[þ]éos [MS -feos]
2721* ("servos"); fem:
handmaid, (female) slave
ds worcþéowe 2262 ("an-
cilla")
weorðan 3 *come to be, arise,
happen; absolute:* inf 145
pt3s wearð 2061 2548;
w prep: become, turn into
tó aldorbanan weorðeð 1034
sim pt2s wurde tó feorh-
bana 1019, pt2s wearð
[MS weard]...on gedwilde
22*, pt3p wurdon...on
fléame 2073 2554 subj pt
3s wurde 2566; *w pred subs
or adj: come about, happen
(shading into "be")* inf
2529 pr3s 1954 subj pr3s
weorðe 2225 pt3s 34 1000
1563 1726 1814 1859 2014
2097 2217 2261 2492 2757
pt3p 2582 2607 subj pt1s
wurde 2147 subj pt3s wor-
den 2238 pp worden 1694;
*as auxiliary w pp (ex-
pressing the passive):*
inf wurðan 1102 2207 pr3s
1765 2197 pt3s 54 1104
1149 1159 1553 1604 1640
1712 2299 pt3p 964 1615
1706 1996 subj pt3s 100
2032 *(cpd* for-)
ge-weorðan 3 *to agree* inf
ne meahte híe gewurðan...
timbran 1691; *come about,
come to pass* pt3s 111
1141 1186 1227 2778 pp
wæs geworden *(cf "factum
est")* 6 104
weorðian II *to honor, hold
in honor, respect* pr3p
þám þe wurðiað *"to those
who honor you"* 1758; *hold
up to honor, praise* pt3s
weorðade 1886; *show honor
to, glorify, reward* pt3s 35
ge-weorðian II *to honor, reward, embellish* pp nsm

geweorðad 1137 gewurðod
2107 2137
wer m. *man* ns 183* (or acc?),
1476 1562 1630 1705 1823
2053 2234 2257 2804 2865
2877 2889 gs 920 1098 1527
ds 979 2430 np 234 1672
1738 1882 2419 2459 2619
2670 2838 gp 1262 1274 1279
1379 1679 1897 1925 1950
1968 2007 2069 2107 2128
2290 2506 2557 2755 dp
1291 1384 1574 1816 2064
2544 ap 1352, Noe gewát...
eaforan lǽdan, weras...
1358; *husband* ds 2220 ("marito suo"), 2631 *(cpd* driht-
folc- léod-weras)
wergend m-nd [*cf* werian] *defender* np 1971
werg (wearg) adj *accursed* nsm
906* dsn 1250
wergðo f. *a curse* as 1755
werian I *defend* inf 1976
wérig adj *tired, exhausted*
nsm 1462 nsf 1469; *miserable* npm 74 90 *(cpd* symbel-)
wér-loga *see* wǽr-loga
wer-mǽgð f. *tribe, people* gp
1638 ("cognationibus"),
1689
werod n. *army, host, people*
gs 27 1231 1643 ds 35 95
1346 2498 as 67 2411 is
werede 2093 gp 1362 1411
wereda 2 1786 2382 dp 1301
1340 weredum 1897 *(cpd*
heorð- síð-)
wer-þéod f. *tribe, people;* pl
humans, nations as 2688
2823 werðéode 1480 ap 991
wesan, béon, eom anom. *to
be (sometimes used as auxiliary w trans or intrans
verbs)* pr1s eom (anom. v.)
871 1900 2176 2201 2224
2226, pr2s eart 1347 2359,
pr3s is 1 3 201 230 869 &c
(26x); negat. nis 2142 2364,
pr1dl wit synt 1904, pr3p

wesan, béon, eom (*cont.*)
    syndon 1255 2133 2168
    2466, sint 2411; *w pp:*
    hátene syndon 1424, subj
    pr2s síe 1827 1832 subj
    pr3 síe 879 1116 1834 2254
    2724 subj pr3p síe 2184*
    síen 2503 | wesan (5) inf
    158 920 955 1310 1594 1763
    2172 2196 2288 2320 2369
    2483 2820 pt1s wæs 1007
    2824 pt3s wæs 14 69 78 901
    963 &c (105x); negat pt3s
    næs 5, pt3p wǽron 10 17
    82 1262 1617, 2049 [MS wa-
    ron] &c (32x); negat nǽ-
    ron 155; subj pt3s wǽre
    170 1438 1872 2028 2624
    2651 2683 2705 2712 2766
    2848, imps wes 2284 2308
    2726 2825 wæs [MS wær]
    2107* | béon anom.v.
    (*frequently w general,
    abstract or future sense*)
    pr3s bið 2195 pr3p béoð
    1354 2786; *w predicate*
    pr1s béo 2316 pr3s bið
    7 914 1325 2199 2289 2646
    imps béo 2362; *w pp:* pr3s
    bið eafora wæcned 2394
    pr3p béoð...gelǽsted 2396
westan adv *from the west* 1884*
wéste adj-ja *useless, empty*
    asn wonn and wéste 110
    ("inanis et vacua" *cf*
    106a); *deserted, uninhab-
    ited* apn 2132
wésten(n) n-ja *desert land,
    an empty place, nothing-
    ness* ds 125 2277 as 2268
    2875
wí-bed(d) n-ja *altar* as 1791
    1806 1882, wéobedd 2842
wíc n. *place, dwelling place,
    town, camp (pl often w
    sing meaning)* as 928 1051
    1721 1803 2595 2688 2723
    2838 dp on his wícum 1738
    ("in tabernaculo suo"),
    1812 1890 2061 2275 2572

2805 2882 ap wuldorfæstan
    wíc (sc Heaven) 27, 1877
    2132 2396
wíd adj *wide, broad, exten-
    sive, huge* nsm 104 gsf
    1350 dsn tó wídan aldre
    (*"forever"*) 1015 asm 1655
    asn 1307 2209 apm 905*
wíde adv *widely, far* 10 87
    118 165 234 990 1027 1089
    1392 1430 1455 1465 1717
    1782 1950 1968 2087 2193
    2204 2337 2556 2580 2815
wíde-ferhð m.n (*occurs only
    as advbl acc*) *forever* 906
°wíd-folc n. *a large tribe,
    a great people* np 1638*
wídl m.n *pollution, corrup-
    tion* dp 1294
wíd-land n. *a broad land* as
    1412 1538 np wídlond 156
wíd-lást m. *a track stretch-
    ing far (sc Cain's career
    after the curse, hence
    "the career of an exile"*)
    as 1021
wíd-mǽre adj-ja *very famous,
    known far and wide* nsm
    1630 asn 2619
wíf n. *woman, wife* ns 911
    1187 2345 2382 2631 2649
    2699 2774 2778 gs 1848
    ds 1147 1170 as 174 195
    1130 1721 1776 1855 1867
    2233 2244 2656 2685 2718
    2746 np 1432 1546 2087
    2420 gp 1260 2755 dp 1090
    1574 1738 ap 1250 1334
    1358 1879 2132
°wíf-myne m-i *love for a wo-
    man, desire, lust* ds 1861
wíg m.n *warfare* as 2070 2159
wiga m-an *warrior* gp 2040
    (*cpd* rand-)
°wíg-cyrm m-i *noise of battle*
    ns 1990
wígend m-nd *warrior, fighter,
    hero* ap 1411 (sc Noe and
    his family)
°?wíg-ród f. (= wíg-rád? or

wíg-ród (*cont.*)
   for wíg-trod n. ? *cf EX
   492) war-road, the path
   an army takes* as 2084
   (*cf* wiðer-trod)
wíg-sigor m. *victory in battle* as 2003
°wíg-síð m. *expedition for
   battle* as 2094
wíg-smið m. *war-smith, warrior* dp 2704
wiht f.n-i *creature, being*
   gp cucra wuhta 1297; *something, anything (in negat.
   clauses)* ns 104 ds 2693
   as 2169 (*cpd* eall-   *cf*
   á-wiht, ed-wihte *prons*)
wilde adj-ja *wild, free, unrestrained* nsm 1460* nsf
   1465 asf 1477 npn 202
   1516
willa m-an *will, desire, purpose* gs 2169 2309 as 142
   1776* 2352 2381 2815 dp
   2787; *pleasure, joy* as
   2087 (cf 1776) gp wilna
   1890; *something wished
   for, a desired thing, a
   pleasurable thing* as 1455
   1879 gp wilna 1532 1812
   1620 1660 1758 1948 2274
   willa 2365 (*cpd* dæg-)
willan anom. v. *to want,
   wish, desire; w inf:* pr1s
   wille 1296 1344 1351 1788
   2143 2358 2366 2412 2474,
   negat nelle 2153; pr2s
   wilt 2482 2644 pr3s wille
   1751 wile 1531 1959 2390
   2920 pr2p willað 2318
   2523 subj pr2s wille 1918
   2314 2819 þæs þú mé wylle
   wordum secgean *"you perhaps may wish to tell me"*
   2674, subj pr3s wille 2234
   2828 wile 1828 2662, pt2s
   woldest 2680 2684 pt3s
   wolde 855 952 978 1265
   1282 1291 1360 1580 1590

1732 2047 2265 2571 2906
leng ne wolde *"no longer
wanted"* 2423, æfre ne
wolde *"never wanted"* 1937,
negat nolde 1448 1480, pt3p
woldon 1975 1979, *negat*
noldan 23, subj pt3p wol-
de 34 1279 1445 2703 subj pt
3p wolden 2460 woldan 48; *w
inf elided:* pt3s þæt hé
wolde swá (sc dón) 2833;
w dep þæt-*clause:* pt3s 99;
w acc: pr3p 1910 subj pr3s 1903
°wille-burne f-ón *well-spring,
gushing spring* ns wylle-
burne 212 ("fons...e ter-
ra"), ap willeburnan
("fontes abyssi") 1373
°will-flód m. *welling-flood
(or "the flood purposed by
God")* ns 1412 ("aquae")
°will-gebróðor m-r ?*dear brother* np 971* (sc Cain &
Abel)
will-gesíð(ð) m. *dear comrade*
np 2003
°will-gestealla m. ?*pleasant
companion* dp 2147*
°will-gesweostor f-r ?*dear
sister* np 2608* (sc Loth's
daughters)
°will-geðofta m-an ?*dear comrade,* ?*willing comrade,
ally acting voluntarily*
ap 2026
wín n. *wine* ds 1563 2606 2635
wind m. *wind* ds 214
windan 3 *to twist* pp asn 1931
2070 2128 (*cpd* be-)
wine m-i *friend* ns 1194 np
1847 gp 2699 ap wine 1867
winas 2735; *powerful friend,
lord* vs 2817 (*cpd* mǽg-)
wine-léas adj *friendless* nsm
1051
wine-mǽg m. *a dear kinsman,
friendly kinsman* gp 2626
dp 1021 (*cf* mǽg-wine)
wín-geard m. *vineyard* as 1558

win-gedrync n. *wine-drinking
(= drunkenness)* ns hie
(acc)...wlenco onwód and
wingedrync 2581
winnan 3 *to fight, struggle,
do battle (intrans)* inf
77 2243 pr3p 2292; *to
toil, labor* inf 932 pt3s
won 1558; *to suffer* inf
1014 2707* *(cf* mód-ge-
winna)
winter m.n *winter, year* gs
1194* gp 1121 1125 1130
1147 1157 1164 1170 1177
1185 1202 1216 1223 1226
1231 1238 1264 1320 1368
1600 1724 1740 1776 1976
2201 2300 2345 2774 dp
forð cure wintrum 1643*
2355 2612 2889 ap winter
1139
wis adj *wise* ism 1958
wisa m-an *guide, leader,
chief* ns 1157 1198 2004
ap 1689 (*cpd* aldor-
héafod- mon-)
°wis-hýdig adj *wise in thought,
wise* nsm 1816 1823 2053
wishidig 2357
wisian II *guide, lead the
way* pt3s 2446
wist f-i *food, provisions*
gs stryndon...wiste *"they
laid up provisions"* 971
as 1340
wit *see* ic
-wit (*cpd* bil- in- in-wit-
full in-wit-spell *cf* gewitt)
witan pret-pres (1) *know; w
acc:* pr1s wát 886 1346
2519 pr2s wást 876 pt3s
wiste 41 79 857 2794; *w
a clause as obj:* pr1s
1098 pt3s 1287 2043 2344
2626 pr2s wást...hú 916
pt3s wiste...hwæt 1690
wiste...hwonne 2602
ge-witan pret-pres (1) *know
(w acc)* inf 2606
ge-witan 1 *go, depart; w inf
of* vb *of motion and reflex
dat:* pt3s gewát 1049 1730
1779 2018 2162 2576 2593
2885 pt3p gewiton 2399
gewitan 858; *sim but w/o
reflex dat:* pt3s 135 1210
1471 imps gewit 1345 1487
1746 2850; *w inf of a vb
implying purpose or need
of departure, and w reflex
dat:* pt3s 1356 1767 1793
1817 1920 2045 2083 2098
2621 2870 pt3p 1649; *sim
but w/o reflex dat:* pt3s
1460 1742 2005 2264 2267
pt3p 1964 1999 imps 2155
2294 2511; *w/o inf, but
w prep or adv:* inf from
...gewitan 1039 pt3s forð
gewát *("went")* 974 1421 2449, of
woruld gewát *("died")* 1143
forð gewát *("died")* 1068
1178 1192 1601 1622, ædre
gewát 2296, pp nsm 1255*;
absol: subj pr3s gewite
2574 pt3s 1236 *("died")*
wite n-ja *punishment, torment,
pain* ns 1043 1319 1819 ds
2498 2544 as 1014 1266
2570 2747
wite-bróga m-an *fear of torment, fearful punishment*
ap 45
wite-hús n. *house of punishment, Hell* as 39
°wite-lác n. *punishment* np
2556 *(see next word)*
°?wite-locc m. *flame of punishment* ap 2419*
°wite-swing m. *punishment-
stroke* dp 1864 ("flagellavit autem Dominus...plagis
maximis")
wið prep; *w gen: "towards,"
"at"* beseah wið þæs wæl-
fylles 2565 | *w dat: of
speaking, "to," "with"* wið
abrahame spræc 2305; *of
hostile action, "against"*
51 52 77 2095 2743-44; *of*

wið *(cont.)*
   protective action, "a-
   gainst," "from" 1323
   1409 2171; *of separation,*
   "from" 26 127-28 163 | *w*
   acc: of speaking, "to"
   2407 2578; *of hostile ac-*
   tion, "against" 46 999
   2243 2471 næbbe ic synne
   wið híe...gefremed *(or =*
   "with" ?) 2651; *of asso-*
   ciation, "with" 2119, wið
   fréond oððe féond 2812;
   of protective action, "a-
   gainst," "from" 1309 | *acc*
   & dat alternating 2788-89;
   where case is ambiguous
   ne fremest þú...riht wið
   mé 2247, ðé...wið ofer-
   mǽgnes egsan sceolde *"pro-*
   tected you from fear of
   superior force" 2117; séo
   wið þéodscipe...belíð *"it*
   surrounds the nation" 231
wiðer-breca m-an *adversary,*
   enemy ns 2290 ap 64
wiðer-trod n. *retreat* as 2084
   (cf wíg-ród = wíg-trod?)
wið-hycgan III *oppose, be*
   set against pt3s wiðhogode 2865
witod adj [pp of *witian]
   appointed, fated nsn 930
   gsn (subs) witodes bídan
   "await (one's) fate" 2277
wlanc adj *powerful, proud,*
   brave npm 1825 (subs),
   2421, wlonce 1848 (subs)
wlenco f (ó < ín) *pride* ns
   2581 ds 1673
wlítan 1 *to look, gaze* inf
   1794 1825 2404 pr2s 2397
   pr3p 2502 pt3s wlát 106
   (cpd be-)
wlite m-i *countenance, (per-*
   sonal) beauty ns 1260 ds
   1850* as 1825 1848 1855;
   beauty (of a thing) as
   207 857; *brightness,*
   splendor ns 71 ds 36 as

   2193 *(cpd* mág- *cf* and-wlita)
wlite-beorht adj *bright in*
   beauty, beautiful nsf 131
   1728 dsn 220 npm 1804 npmf
   188 apm 1560
wlitig adj *beautiful* apm
   wæstmas...wlitige 1016
wlonc *see* wlanc
wóc, wócon *see* wæcnan
°wocor f. *increase, progeny*
   ns 1312 as wocre 1342 1409
   1490
wolcen m.n *a cloud; (pl) the*
   sky, heaven np wolcnu 212
   dp 1538; *in the expression*
   under wolcnum *"under the*
   heavens," i.e. on earth,
   earthly 916 1058 1231 1392
   1438 1702 1950
womm m.n *disgrace, sin* gp 1272
°wom-scyldig adj *guilty of*
   sin, shameful nsm 949*
won(n) adj *dark, black (fre-*
   quently of water) nsm se
   wanna fugel 1983 dsm 1379
   asm 1462 asn 110 npm 119
   1301 npf 1430 npn wolcnu
   ...wann 214
wong m. *field, plain* ds 1882
   np 1657 1804 *(cpd* neorxna-
   sǽl- staðol-)
won-hygd f-i *or* n-ja *lack of*
   mind, folly dp 1673
wóp m. *weeping, cry of grief,*
   lamentation ds 996 as 923
worc-þéow *see* weorc-þéow
word n. *word, utterance* ns
   2862* ds 31 195 905 1002
   1254 1412 1958 2727 as
   (some instances prob pl)
   111 130 149 158 860 899
   1110 1362 1511 1771 1796
   2302 2670 2776 dp 2 881
   894 1090 &c (36x) ap þurh
   gemǽne word *"with joined*
   voices" (i.e. as with one
   voice) 2476
word-béot n. *promise* as 2762
°word-gemearc n. *[cf Heliand*
   233 uuordgimerkion] *the*

word-gemearc (*cont.*)
  exact terms or conditions
  of an utterance, a pro-
  mise dp 2357*
worn m. *a multitude, host,*
  a great many (of), w part
  gen ns 975 1641 as 1168
  1220 1320 1331 1438 2599
  feorhdaga...worn 2361
°worn-gehát n. ?*multitude of*
  promises, promises fre-
  quently repeated or
  ? *promise of multitudes*
  (sc the promise of des-
  cendants often made to
  Abraham) ns 2396*
woruld f. *world* ns 916 1542
  2574 gs 199 ds 1121 1143
  1264 1963* 2300 2656 as
  188 220 923 1226 1373
  1724 2233 2321 2365 woruld ofgyfan &c *("to die")*
  1126 1164 1194 1216 on
  woruld bringan &c *("to*
  give birth") 1187 1728
  2286 2344 2355 2608 2770
woruld-cyning m. *earthly*
  king, king of a nation
  np 2337 ("reges populo-
  rum")
woruld-dréam m. *earthly joy*
  gp þisse worulddréama
  1220*
°woruld-dugeð f (orig. i)
  worldly goods 1620 dp
  1948
°woruld-feoh n. *worldly*
  wealth ns 2143
woruld-gesceaft f-i *creation,*
  created world ns 110 np
  101 gp 863
woruld-gestréon n. *worldly*
  treasure gp 1177 dp 2718
  ap 1879
°woruld-mágas m (pl) *worldly*
  relatives, kinsmen ac-
  cording to the world nom
  2179*
°woruld-nýtt f-jó *worldly*
  need, worldly use ds 960*

1016
woruld-ríce n-ja *kingdom*
  of the world, world ds
  1024 1110 1185 1641 1717
  1839 2361 2379 1762
+woruld-yrmðo f. *worldly mis-*
  ery ns 940
wracu f. *punishment, ven-*
  geance ns 1042 1100 ds
  wræce 2586; *pain, suffer-*
  ing ds wrace 71 np? wræce
  1264*
wræc n. *exile* as 928 1014
  2792
wræcca *see* wrecca
wræc-líc adj *miserable* asm 37
+wræc-stów f. *place of exile*
  or place of misery, Hell
  as 90
wráð adj *wroth, angry, evil*
  nsm 35 1254 nsf 2262 npm
  940 ("evil"), 1983 dpf
  (advbl?) folmum þínum wráðum *"with your angry hand"*
  1011; *as subs, "angry one,"*
  "enemy," "devil" gp 101
  1034 1496* 1830 2701 dp
  wráðum werian *"protect*
  from foes" 1976, 2038 ap 61
wráðe adv *bitterly, fiercely*
  1861 2292
wraðu f. *support, help(mate)*
  as 174
wrecan 5 *to drive out* pt3p
  wræcon 1385; *punish* inf
  2416 pt3s wræc 1864; *avenge*
  inf 2510 2532 pt3s 1380;
  to travel, follow (trans)
  inf 1021
ge-wrecan 5 *avenge (w dat of*
  pers & acc of thing) inf
  1274 pt3s gewræc 58 pt3p
  gewræcon 2038
wrecca m-jan *an exile, ban-*
  ished person, wretch ns
  1051 gs wræccan láste *"on*
  the track of an exile (=
  "in exile") 2480 2823 gp
  wræcna 39
wréon 1 *cover, hide, protect*

wréon (*cont.*)
   inf wrýon 1572* pr1s 867
   2171 pr2s wríhst 876 pt3s
   wréah 1377 1386 2451 (*cpd*
   be-)
+wrídan, wríðan 1 *to put out
   shoots, grow* impp wrídað
   1532 prp nsn wríðende 1762
wríðian II *to grow, increase*
   inf 1903 pt3s wríðade
   1702
wrixl f. *exchange, interchange* ns wælgára wrixl
   *"exchange of spears," i.e.
   battle* 1990
wróht m.f *crime, wrong* as
   911 932; *strife, enmity*
   ns 83 1903; *injury, harm*
   gs 991 as 2685
°wróht-getéme n-ja *a series
   of crimes, mass of wrongs*
   as 45
°wróht-scipe m-i *crime* ds
   1672
wrýon *see* wréon
wuce f-ón *week* as ymb wucan
   after a week 1465 2770
   sim 1477
wudu m-u *wood* as 2886* (*w
   play on nom sing*)
wudu-béam m. *tree* ds 881
   ("ligno")
+wudu-fæsten m-ja *wooden-
   fortress, the Ark* as 1312
wuduwe *see* wydewe
wuht *see* wiht
wuldor n. *glory* gs 11 83 941
   1002 1511 1574 2268 2570
   2575 an wuldres *"granted glory"* 2916* ds 36
wuldor-cyning m. *glory-king,
   God* ns 165 gs 111 wuldor-
   cyninges ýða (nom) 1384
   as wuldorcining 2
wuldor-fæst adj *glory-firm,
   glorious* asm 2193 apn 27
°wuldor-gást m. *glory-spirit,
   an angel* ns 2913
wuldor-gesteald n. *glorious
   dwelling* or *glorious pos-*

session dp 64 (*cf* flett-
   gesteald, hæg-steald)
°wuldor-spéd f-i *abundance
   of glory* dp 87
wuldor-torht adj *bright with
   glory, splendid, radiant*
   nsm 119 nsn 2875 asn 2770
wulf m. *wolf* ns 2278 (*cpd*
   here- hilde-)
wundor n. *a wonder, an aston-
   ishing thing* gp 2574
wunian II *to dwell, remain,
   exist* inf inc...wunian on
   gewealde *"remain in your
   power"* 199 pr3s 908 pr3p
   152 pt3s 1812 1945 1931
   2569 2598 egesa...wunode
   "terror existed" 2867, pt
   3p 74 WVNedon 1890 imps
   wuna þǽm þe ágon *"stay with
   those who own you"* 2295
   2723 impp 2735
ge-wunian II *be accustomed, be
   used (to doing s.t.)* pt3p
   1671
(ge)wurðan *see* (ge)weorðan
(ge)wurðian *see* (ge)weorðian
wurð-líce adv *worthily, honorably* comp wurðlícor 2094
wydewe f-ón *widow* np wuduwan
   2010 ap wydewan 2133
wylle-burne *see* wille-burne
wylm m-i *a surging* or *boiling
   (of fire)* ds wylme gesealde...sweartan líge *"gave
   black flames with a surging (motion)* 1925
°wylm-hát adj *surging with
   heat* asm 2586
wyn(n) f-jó *joy, delight,
   pleasure* ns 1862 ds 919
   gp 945
wyn-léas adj *deprived of joy*
   comp apm 928
wyn-sum adj *pleasant, lovely*
   asm 1855
wyrcan Ii *to work, make, do,
   build (trans)* inf 1302
   1316 2112 pt3s worhte 1791
   1806 2842 pt3p 1674; *w gen*

wyrcan (*cont.*)
pt3s hḗ him þæs worhte tṓ
"he carried it out (i.e.,
circumcision) on them"
2379, *absol* won and worhte
1558 (*cpd* for- *cf* sam-
worht adj)
ge-wyrcan Ii *to work, make,*
create, build pt3s ge-
worhte 147 subj pt3p
burh geworhte and...torr
...ārǣrde *"they hoped to*
build a city and erect a
tower" 1666, ?imps (or
nom?) gewyrc 1307*; *carry*
out, perform pt1s 900 pt
3s 2575, hū geworhte ic
þæt...þæt... *"what did I*
do (to deserve)...that...?"
2676

wyrd f-i *fate, destiny, one's*
lot gs 2572; *an event,*
what has happened, is
happening or will happen
ns 1399 2357 2391 2778
as 996

wyrgean I *to curse* inf ongā́n
þā his selfes bearn (acc)
...wyrgean *"he began to*
curse his own son" 1594
(*cf* ā-wyrged)

wyrhta m-jan *a doer, perpe-*
trator ns 1004; *creator*
ns 125

wyrm m-i *(worm), serpent* ns
899 ds 904

wyrnan I *to hold back, keep*
s.t. from s.b. pr2s 2661
(*cpd* for-)

wyrðe adj-ja *worthy, deser-*
ving nsm 1347

Y

yfel n. *evil* as 2266 2472
2686
ylde m-i (pl) *people, men,*
human beings nom 221 gen

2472 dat 2288
yldra, yldest *see* eald
yldra m-an (pl) *elders, su-*
periors, leaders dat 1107
1129 1716 2773
ymb prep w acc *around* 1907;
about, concerning 1848
2528; *temporal, after*
1320 1438 1449 1465 1477
2304 2322 2770
ymb-standende part adj (subs)
(people) who are standing
around, surrounding others
gp 2490
ymb-ūtan adv *around about*
ymbūtan...geondsended wæs
2552
yrfe n. *inheritance, property*
gs 1067 1545 2199 ds 2189
as 1144 1167 1218 2789
yrfe-stṓl m. *seat from which*
property is distributed;
hereditary seat'(B-T) ds
1629 as 2177
yrfe-weard m. *guardian of an*
inheritance, an heir, in-
heritor as 1727 ("liberos")
np 2185 ("heres") gp 2232
("filios")
yrnan 3 *run, flow, hasten* pt
3s arn 138 prp nsm 211
(*cpd* ā-)
yrre n-ja *anger* ns 982 as
2644
yrre adj-ja *angry* nsm 34 1860
2637 (adv?), 2742 yr on'
mṓde 63*
yrringa adv *angrily* 918
ysle f-ōn *ash(es)* ds 2555
ȳð f-jṓ *wave, water* np 1385
1430 dp 166 ap 1309
ȳwan *see* īewan

*   *   *   *

Proper Names

The predominant form(s) in the text are given, then the Vulgate form(s) in quotation marks and, if different from the Vulgate form, the RSV form(s) follow, in Italics. For the scansion of these names see Campbell §§ 549-558

Aaron, Áron m. ("Aran" *Haran*)
  nom aaron 1710* gen árones
  (sunu árones = *Loth*) 1914
  1928 2429 2465 (bróðor á-
  rones = *Abraham*) 2621 2929
  dat aarone 1712
Abel m. ("Abel") nom 969
  1003 gen ábeles 977 985
  1006 1097 1104 1109 dat
  ábele 1019
Abimélech m. ("Abimelech")
  nom abiméleh 2669 abimǽ-
  leh 2715 dat abimélehe
  2742 2832 abiméleche 2759
  acc 2622
Abraham m. ("Abram," "Abraham")
  [*see Commentary 1710a*]
  voc 2254 2398 2677 2850
  2914 nom 1710 1715 1720
  1735 1767 1782 1794 1805
  1817 1820 1845 1873 1883
  1891 1899 1945 2024 2045
  2069 2083 2089 2122 2136
  2173 2338 2370 2576 2625
  2691 2729 2736 2751 2759
  2768 2773 2832 2863 2880 2893
  2930 gen 1731 1739 (fæder abrahames = Thare), abrahames mǽg
  (= *Loth*) 2012 2535, abrahames cwén (= *Sarra*)
  2261, bryd abrahames (=
  Sarra) 2388, abrahames
  idese (= *Sarra*) 2638,
  2650, wíf abrahames (=
  Sarra) 2631* dat abrahame 1727 1729 1745 1785
  1858 2036 2125 2165 2217
  2238 2285 2299 2305 2655
  2722 2744 2764 2779 2791

  2796 2923 acc 1865 2020
  2099 2105 2407 2588 2673
  2717 2889 2909
Ada f.("Ada" *Adah*) nom 1077
  dat ádan ("Adae") 1092
Adam m. ("Adam") nom 170 882
  1000 1117 1124 1136 gen
  ádames 176 186 967 1109*
  ádames eaforan (= *"men,"
  "mankind"*) 1682 dat ádame
  893 925 953 1104 acc 1278
Agar f. ("Agar" *Hagar*) voc
  2285 nom 2249 acc 2785
  2800
Ambrafel m. ("Amrafel" *Amraphel*) nom 1962*
Ammon m. ("Ammon" *Ben-ammi*)
  acc 2614
Ammonítare m (pl) (*of* "pater
  Ammonitarum" *Ammonites*)
  acc 2620
Áner m. ("Aner") gen áneres
  2152 acc 2027
Arménia f. (*cf* "montes Armenia" *Ararat*) nom on dú-
  num...þe arménia hátene
  syndon 1423
Áron *see* Aaron
Assiria f. (*cf* "Assyrios"
  Assyria) acc (or gen?)
  assirie [*corrected to* -æ]
  232

Babylon n. ("Babylon" *Babel*)
  gen babylones 1633 dat
  babilone 1707
Bersabéas m (pl) (*cf* "Bersabee *Beersheba*) gen bersa-
  béa lond 2839

413

Béthlem f. ("Bethel") nom
   1799* dat bethlem 1876*
   1930

Cáin, Cáīn m. ("Cain") nom
   969 985 1022* 1049 1114
   gen cainès 978 1056 1066
   1256 cáīnès 1095 1249
   acc 1004
Cainan m. ("Cainan" *Kenan*)
   nom 1149 cain[an] 1155*
   gen cain[an]es 1160
Caldeas m (pl) ("Ur Chaldeorum") gen caldea folc
   1730 caldea ceastre 2202
Cám *see* Chám
Cananéas m (pl) ("terra
   Chanaan" *Canaan*) gen 1814
   1946 cananéa land 1733
   1772 folc cananéa 1909
Cananéus m. ("Chananeus"
   Canaanite) gs cananéis
   1784*
Carran ("Haran") dat 1736*
   1772 acc carram 1747
   carran 1778
Chám, Cám m. ("Cham," "Ham"
   Ham) nom 1241 1551 1590
   1596 1623 cám 1577 gen
   chámes 1615* 1618 cámes
   1637
[Chánan] m. ("Chanaan" *Canaan*) nom 1617* [MS cham]
Chús m. ("Chus" *Cush*) nom
   1617* 1619* gen chúses
   1629

Dámascus f. ("ad laevam
   Damasci") dat dómasco
   2082*

Éber m. ("Eber") nsm 1645
Ebreas, Ebrei m (pl) (*Hebrews*) gen (as attributive
   of Abraham) ebréä léod
   &c 2164 2205 2413 2675
   2817 2836 2917 acc ebréï
   1648
ebrisc adj (*"hebrew"*) nsm

2446 dsm 2021 ("Abram
   ᵕ Hebreo")
Égipte m (pl) ("Aegyptii"
   Egyptians) nom égypte *(the
   Egyptian men)*...móton...
   wlítan 1824 gen égipta
   1768* égypta 1820 1874
   2209 égipto 1866* dat on
   égiptum *"among the Egyptians"* 1842 acc 1817 1845
égyptisc adj nsf 2229
Elamítare m (pl) ("rex Ela-
   mitarum" *king of Elam*)
   as an attributive of Chodorlahomor gen elamítarna
   1960 1980 2004; of the
   ᵕ Elamites 2081
Énoch m. ("Enoch" *son of
   ᵕ Iared*) nom 1197 énoc 1188
Énos¹ m. (= "Enoch" *son of
   Cain*) nom 1055* gen énoses
   ᵕ 1064 1096
Énos² m. ("Enos" *Enosh, son
   of Seth*) nom 1134 1144 gen
   énoses 1163 dat énose 1156
Escol m. ("Eschol" *Eshcol*)
   ᵕ gen escoles 2152 acc 2027
Éthiopias m (pl) ("terra Ae-
   thiopiae" *land of Cush*)
   gen éthiopia land *"land
   of the Ethiopians"* 228
Éue f. ("Heva," "Eva" *Eve*)
   gen éuan 967 1109* dat
   éuan 918 953 acc éuan 887
Eufrates f. ("Eufrates" *Euphrates*) acc eufraten 234
   2208

Farao(n) m. ("Pharao(nis)"
   Pharaoh) dat faraone 1860
Feretias m (pl) ("Pherezeus"
   Perizzites) gen feretia
   1909
Filisteas m (pl) ("terra
   Philistinorum" *Philistines*)
   gen filistea 2835
Físon m. ("Phison" *Pishon*)
   acc 222

Geáred *see* Iáred
Geómor m. ("Gomer") nom 1610*
Geön f. ("Geon" *Gihon*) nom
    230
Gomorra f. ("Gomorra" *Gomor-
    rah*) acc gomorran 1926
    1966 2008
Gómorre m (pl) ("Gomorrae"
    *(gen.) the people of Go-
    morrah*) nom sódomware and
    gómorre 1997 dat gómorra
    2561 acc 2078, unc...
    heht for wera synnum só-
    doma and gómorra swear-
    tan líge fýre gesyllan
    *"commanded us for the
    sins of men to give over
    to fire by means of black
    flame the Sodomites and
    the Gomorrans"* 2507

[Hebeleat] ?m. ("terram Evi-
    lath" *var.* "Evilat," "E-
    philat" *Havilah*) acc 224*
    [MS hebeleac]

Iared[1] m. ("Irad" *son of the
    Cainite Enoch*) nom 1063*
    dat íarede 1067
Isaac m. ("Isaac") dat ísace
    2363 2788 acc ísaac 2329
    2767 2852 2871 2905 2926
Isma(h)el m. ("Ismahel" *Ish-
    mael*) nom ismahel 2288
    ismael 2299 2348 2788 acc
    ismael 2358 2779 2785
    2800

Iabal m (*for* "Iubal...pater
    canentium cithara et or-
    gano") nom 1078*
Iáfeð m. ("Iafeth" *Japeth*)
    nom 1552 1588 iáfeth 1242
    gen iáfeðes 1612 dat iá-
    feðe 1604
Iáred[2] m. ("Iared" *the Seth-
    ite*) nom 1174* geáred 1181
    1195
Iordan ?f. ("regio Iordanis,"
    "circa Iordanem" *Jordan*)

dat iordane 1921 1932
    1967

Lámech[1] m. ("Lamech" *the
    Cainite*) nom lámeh 1073
    1091 gen lámehes 1081 1086
Lámech[2] m. ("Lamech" *the fa-
    ther of Noah*) nom 1225
    1236 gen lámehes (sunu
    lámehes = *Noe*) 1543 1589
    lámeches 1286 1368 1408
    1425 1441
Lóth m. ("Loth" *Lot*) voc 1906
    nom 1713 1715 1735 1891
    1920 [1938*] [MS leoht],
    2085 2441 2463 2513 2593
    2597 gen lóthes 2023 2080
    2563 2611 mǽge lóthes (=
    Abraham) 2924 dat lóthe
    1900 2484 2499 acc 2016
    2048 2457 2589

Malaléhel[1] m. ("Maviahel"
    son of Ircd [Iáred[1]], *Me-
    hujael*) nom 1066
Malaléhel[2] m. ("Malalehel"
    *son of Cainan the Sethite,
    Mahalalel*) nom 1160 1168*
    1176
Mamre m. ("Mambre" *Mamre*) gen
    mamres 2152 acc manre 2027
Máthusal[1] m. ("Mathusahel"
    son of Maviahel [Malalé-
    hel[1]], *Mathushael*) nom
    1069
Máthusal[2] m. ("Mathusalam -ae"
    *son of the Sethite Enoch,
    Methuselah*) nom 1218
Melchísedec m. ("Melchisedech"
    Melchizedek) nom 2102
Móäb m. ("Moab") acc 2610
Móäbítare m (pl) ("pater Mo-
    abitarum" *Moabites*) acc
    2617

[Nebroð] m. ("Nemrod" LXX "Ne-
    broth" *Nimrod*) gen nebr[o]-
    ðe[s] [MS ne breðer] 1628*
Nílus m. ("fluvius Aegypti")
    nom 2210*

Nōë m. ("Noe" *Noah*) nōǣ [MS
  noe] 1235 nőë 1285 1314
  1356 1367 1443 1497 1555
  1598 gen nőés (= nőéës)
  1240* 1323 1423 1551 1573
  dat nőë 1295 1327 1483
  1511 acc nőë (= nőéë?)
  1504

Olla f. ⎫ *Daughters-in-*
Ollíua f. ⎬ *law of Noe*
Olliuáni f. ⎭ nom 1548
Orlahőmor m. ("Chodorlaho-
  mor" *Chedorlaomer*) acc
  1962*

P[er]coba f. *Noe's wife*
  nom 1548 [MS pcoba]

Sǣgor ("Segor" *Zoar*) dat
  sígor (*for* ségor?) 2522
  acc sǣgor 2533 2544
Sarra f. ("Sarai," "Sarra"
  Sarai, Sarah) voc 1832
  nom 1723 1729 2342 2356
  2624 2683 2705, sarre
  2272, sarran 2390* 2715
  gen sarran 1854 dat sarran 2216 2267 2728, sar-
  rǽï 2743 2761 acc (dat?)
  sarran 2243
Sella f. ("Sella" *Zillah*)
  nom 1077 dat sellan 1092
Sém m. ("Sem" *Shem*) nom 1240
  1551 1588 gen sémes 1646
  1703 dat séme 1640
Sennar m. ("Sennaar" *Shinar*)

dat sennar 1701 1963*
  sennar acc 1655
Sennere m (pl) *"Shinarites"*
  gp sennera feld (*cf 11.2*
  "invenerunt campum in
  terra Sennaar") 1668
Séth m. ("Seth") nom 1106
  1128 1138 gen sédes 1133*
  séthes 1145 1245 1257
Sí[c]em ("Sychem" *var.*
  "Sichem" *Schechem*) dat
  sí[c]em [MS siem] 1783
Sígor *see* Sǣgor
Sōdom(e) f. ("Sodom -is")
  gen sodome burh 1975 acc
  sōdoman 1926 1966 2008
  2403
Sōdoma m (pl) ("Sodomorum"
  the people of Sodom) gen
  sōdoma 1928 2013 2022
  2096 2124 2149 2427 2491
  2560 acc 2077 2507
sodomisc adj ("homines...
  Sodomitae") npn sodomisc
  cynn 1935
Sōdomware m (pl) *"inhabitants*
  of Sodom" nom 1996 2453
Sōlómia m (pl) (*cf* "Salem"
  people of Salem) gen 2101*

Tígris f. ("Tigris") nom 231*
Túbal-Caïn m. ("Tubalcain")
  nom 1083

Þáre m. ("Thare" *Terah*) [*see*
  Commentary 1705a] gen
  eafora þáres (= *Abraham*)
  2834 *sim* 2054

MANUFACTURED BY CUSHING MALLOY, INC.
ANN ARBOR, MICHIGAN

Library of Congress Cataloging in Publication Data
Genesis (Anglo-Saxon poem)
Genesis A : a new edition.
Bibliography: p.
1. Bible. O.T. Genesis--Poetry. I. Doane, Alger
Nicolaus, 1938-   II. Title.
PR1611.A3D6   829'.1   77-77437
ISBN 0-299-07430-7